How Asia Found Herself

HOW ASIA FOUND HERSELF

A STORY OF INTERCULTURAL UNDERSTANDING

Nile Green

Yale UNIVERSITY PRESS   NEW HAVEN AND LONDON

Published with assistance from the Mary Cady Tew
Memorial Fund.

Yale University Press books may be purchased in quantity
for educational, business, or promotional use. For
information, please e-mail sales.press@yale.edu (U.S. office)
or sales@yaleup.co.uk (U.K. office).

Set in Scala type by Newgen North America.
Printed in the United States of America.

Library of Congress Control Number: 2021953518
ISBN 978-0-300-25704-5 (hardcover : alk. paper)

A catalogue record for this book is available
from the British Library.

This paper meets the requirements of
ANSI/NISO Z39.48-1992 (Permanence of Paper).

10 9 8 7 6 5 4 3 2 1

To the unsung interpreters

Seek knowledge even unto China.

—Hadith of the Prophet Muhammad

By the rivers of Yangtze and Han, a stranger who thinks of home.

—Poem by Du Fu

Contents

PREFACE AND ACKNOWLEDGMENTS

At the age of forty, I made my first journey to Japan. After more than twenty years spent wandering around the Middle East, Pakistan, and India, I found myself in what the Bengali critic Rustom Bharucha has called "another Asia." My bafflement at Japan's written language and wider cultural codes made me rethink everything I thought I knew about the continent. Treating myself to a night in the old Nara Hotel, which still serves the curry sauce introduced through Japan's nineteenth-century links with India, I wondered what the people I studied from the Asia I did know made of Japan. A few emails to librarians furnished me with a scan of an Urdu book by Ross Masood, a Muslim educationist and close friend of E. M. Forster (*A Passage to India* was dedicated to him), who stayed at the same hotel while likewise marveling at Nara's Buddhist temples a century before me. Reading Masood's response to Japan marked my first step along the tortuous paths of Asia's self-discovery.

Later, as I turned to other Urdu and then Persian and Arabic accounts of Japan, I began to ask how Asians themselves negotiated the differences with other parts of the continent that had so struck me. I pondered whether there was some common insider understanding that I, as a European outsider, was missing. This in turn made me curious about more such books in languages I could read about other parts of Asia, prompting further journeys, both bibliographical and literal, to Myanmar and China. But as I delved deeper into many a forgotten text I located from libraries and booksellers across three continents, I found that the intercultural knowledge they contained was neither wholly separate nor wholly derived from its colonial European counterparts. The book that resulted is the story of how one half of Asia—India-Pakistan and the Middle East—attempted to comprehend the societies and cultures of the other half, from Sri Lanka and Myanmar to China and Japan. In other words, how modern people from South and West Asia made sense of Southeast and East Asia. As such, it is a history of human attempts at understanding others—the many different peoples whom ancient European geographers had grouped together as "Asians."

It is also a story of human fallibility, because not to understand a place or people is not necessarily to be parochial or prejudiced. Shaped by the uneven relationship between connection and comprehension, and by the perpetual interplay of self and other, intercultural understanding is never the automatic and inevitable outcome of history, even at maximal moments of globalization.

Besides the happenstance of my own experience in Nara, I was also driven by discussions among historians over the past few decades trying to push back against "Orientalism" and "Eurocentrism" by following "inter-Asian" interactions that might allow us to understand Asia on its own terms. Rather than retell the more familiar story of Orientalism, I set out hoping to find its finer alternative, even remedy. But the more books I read in Asian languages, the more my search for an Asia-without-Europe slipped over the horizon, as my sources revealed a more entangled and surprising story than I had expected. Having searched for Asian ways of understanding "untainted" by Western provenance, the findings of a decade finally put an end to any such illusions. For ultimately, there is no Asia without Europe, just as there is no Europe without Asia. For world historians, the only meaningful large continental space is that of Eurasia. In the modern era especially, the notion of a self-contained Asia is ideology, not history.

And world history is not defined by easy patterns of cultural cohesion, or ready-made units—whether Europe or Asia, the East or the West—whose populations automatically comprehend and cohere with each other. Knowledge does not obey national, ethnic, or even continental boundaries. It follows less neat routes, finding its own trickling rivulets and dead ends, as well as artificial channels and wide, flowing deltas. Ultimately, people learn however, wherever, and from whomever they can.

During the years in which this book took shape, I have acquired numerous debts to institutions and colleagues who assisted me in my travels, travails, and inquiries. For funding a series of R&R—research and rethinking—visits to Afghanistan, China, Myanmar, and Japan, along with visits to libraries in Europe, which built on my many previous journeys through West and South Asia, I am grateful to the American Institute of Afghanistan Studies, the UCLA Terasaki Center for Japanese Studies, the UCLA Department of History, and more recently the magnanimous patron of the Ibn Khaldun Endowed Chair in World History. I was also supported by a Guggenheim Fellowship in writing the first draft of the manuscript during a sabbatical. For finding a home for the eventual book, I owe especial thanks to Don Fehr, my agent at Trident Media, and to Jaya Aninda Chatterjee, my editor at Yale, who have supported the project through its several incarnations. At the final stages, my trusty undergraduate assistants, Arman Abrishamchian, Sara Eckmann, and Ani Ghazarian, typed my endless revisions, Ann Twombly acted as a meticulous copyeditor, and the Yale production team turned my manuscript into a handsome book.

For helpful suggestions and conversations over the course of a decade of research, I would also like to thank the following colleagues: Sunil Amrith, Moinuddin Aqeel, Cemil Aydin, Sohaib Baig, Nandini Bhattacharya, Ulrich Brandenburg, Erik Braun, Sonja Brentjes, Robert Buswell, Michael Charney, Houchang Chehabi, John Chen, Sebastian Conrad, Michael Dodson, Selçuk Esenbel, Ather Farouqui, William Figueroa, Chiaki Fujii, Brian A. Hatcher, Suzuki Hideaki, Richard Jaffe, Hirano Katsuya, Morimoto Kazuo, Arash Khazeni, Ilham Khuri-Makdisi, Mana Kia, Charles Kurzman, David Lelyveld, Su Lin Lewis, Jonathan Lipman, Claude Markovits, Afshin Marashi, Matsumoto Masumi, Llewelyn Morgan, Ali Mousavi, Misawa Nobuo, Michael O'Sullivan, Alexandre Papas, Spencer Pennington, Bojan Petrovic, Patrick Pranke, Teren Sevea, Konishi Sho, Yamane So, Sanjay Subrahmanyam, Oishi Takashi, Rian Thum, Eric Tojimbara, Torsten Tschacher, Farzin Vejdani, Marjan Wardaki, Jeffrey Wasserstrom, Thomas Wide, Bin Wong, Renée Worringer, Yang Xi, Luke Yarbrough, Tonaga Yasushi, Ishteyaq Ahmad Zilli, and the two anonymous reviewers of the manuscript. I have been further aided by the countless previous researchers whose work is acknowledged in the notes.

I owe a bibliomane's gratitude to Khalkedon Books of Istanbul, who during the height of the Covid crisis kept me contentedly supplied with textual rarities. And I am especially indebted to Sohaib Baig (UCLA Middle East & South Asia Librarian), Nandini Bhattacharya, Michael O'Sullivan, and Eric Tojimbara for sharing with me information and translations from several works in Bengali, Burmese, Gujarati, Ottoman, and Japanese, each of which I have acknowledged in corresponding notes. Unless indicated otherwise in specific notes, other digests, summaries, and translations are my own. My final and fullest thanks are due to my wife, Nushin, and our companion, Pasha, for their patient encouragement as I collected the many scattered threads I have tried to weave together here.

Parts of chapters 2 and 3 include heavily revised and expanded sections from my articles "Buddhism, Islam and the Religious Economy of Colonial Burma," *Journal of Southeast Asian Studies* 46, 2 (2015), and "Shared Infrastructures, Informational Asymmetries: Persians and Indians in Japan, *c.* 1890–1930," *Journal of Global History* 8, 3 (2013), which are published with permission of the original copyright holder, Cambridge University Press. Parts of chapter 4, similarly, are heavily revised and expanded sections of my "Anti-Colonial Japanophilia and the Constraints of an Islamic Japanology: Information and Affect in the Indian Encounter with Japan," *South Asian History and Culture* 4, 3 (2013), which are published by permission of the publisher, Taylor & Francis Ltd. (http://www.tandfonline.com).

A Note on Names and Spellings

Dealing with so large a geographical space presents dilemmas of many kinds, including those of naming and spelling. None of these dilemmas looms larger than the label of "Asia" itself. As we will see in the introduction, the term has a history in its own right and so cannot be taken at face value. For reasons that will become clear, the following chapters use the term "Asia" in two ways. The first usage is the obvious one: Asia refers to the concrete continental space marked on standard modern maps. The second usage—signaled by quotation marks—is less obvious: "Asia" refers to the *idea* of a single continental space that was invented by European geographers and then gradually adopted in the region itself as one of several competing conceptions of space.

When used in this book in its primary concrete sense, Asia therefore refers to the entirety of the continent marked on modern maps (including the map printed in this book), hence reaching from Istanbul in the west to Yokohama in the east. Despite the cartographic efforts of geographers, even this obvious Asia—the continent rather than the concept—can present confusion because of the widespread convention of referring to West Asia as the Middle East. Though I have on occasion used the term "West Asia" to emphasize a particular point, I have more often referred to that tranche of the continent by its more familiar moniker, the Middle East. For the same reason of familiarity, I have used "South Asia" only sparingly, giving preference to the more familiar "India," albeit referring in this period to the larger colonial entity of British India, which included what is now Pakistan and Bangladesh as well as the present Republic of India.

Writing about the colonial era raises other issues of naming, particularly for cities and states whose names were changed during the postcolonial period. Some of the key cities discussed in the book (such as Lahore) are now in a country—Pakistan—whose name had not even been invented before the 1930s, let alone come into existence during the century this book surveys. Despite reservations, I have ultimately opted to use period names for Ceylon and Burma (in lieu of Sri Lanka and Myanmar). My reasoning is partly that versions of these names are those that occur most frequently in the Asian-language sources on which I have drawn, and partly that their later renaming reflects the complex postcolonial politics of majority nationalisms. Historical names also provide a useful degree of distance that prevents the immediate slippage of associating the developments described in these pages with contemporary events in, say, Myanmar and Sri Lanka. I have used the same logic to refer to key cities, referring to Kolkata as Calcutta, Mumbai as Bombay, and Yangon as Rangoon. Fortunately, the names of Chinese and Japanese cities present fewer problems. Except when specific period alternatives are used in a primary source (such as Peking and Canton), I have used standard romanization of the Chinese character names for cities, such as Beijing and Guangzhou. While this does create a certain unevenness of treatment between South and East Asia, I have ultimately come down on the side of using names that are most widely recognizable to a broad readership.

There is also the issue of rendering in Latin script names and words from so many Asian languages and writing systems, each of which has its own (in some cases several) conventions for romanization. I have opted to provide romanizations in their simplest form, without macrons, underdots, or other diacritical marks. While this breaks certain scholarly conventions (not least with Japanese long vowels and Sanskritic consonants), when so many languages are being discussed, it is the cost of seeking compromise for the sake of readability. Nonetheless, I have tried to provide consistent romanizations by using Hanyu Pinyin for Chinese and a simplified version of the *International Journal of Middle East Studies* system for Arabic-based scripts. Chinese and Japanese personal names are given in their traditional order, that is, family name followed by given name.

Finally, to mark a break before each chapter's conclusions, I have adopted the sign ۞, known as *rub' al-hizb*. Used in traditional Arabic manuscripts to mark the end of a chapter, its combination of circle and square also carries echoes of Buddhist and Hindu mandalas. This is my small typographic homage to Asia's older modes of learning.

How Asia Found Herself

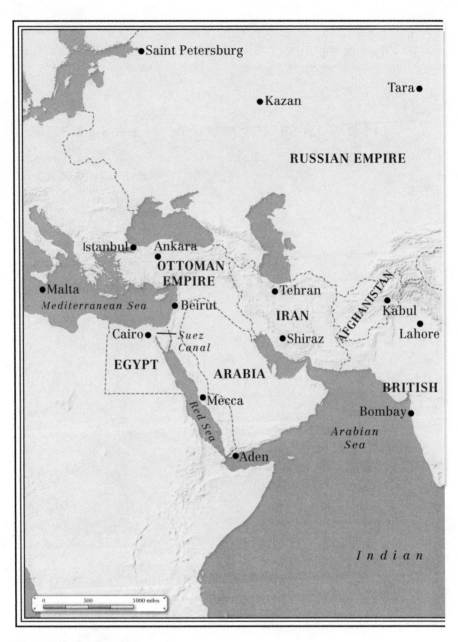

Cartography by Gerry Krieg

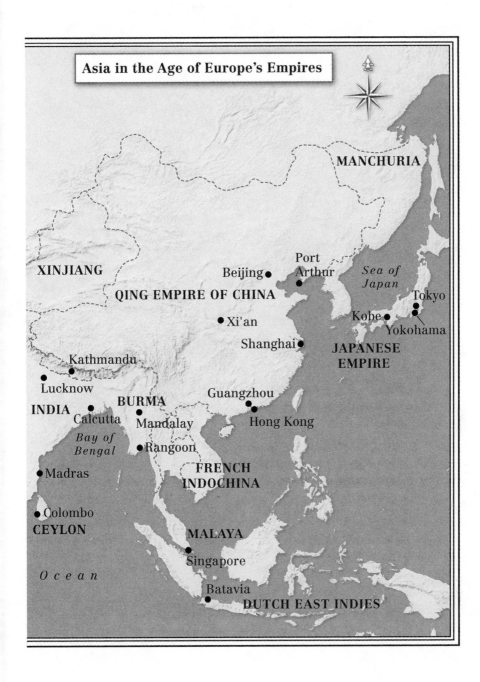

Asia in the Age of Europe's Empires

MANCHURIA

XINJIANG

QING EMPIRE OF CHINA

Beijing

Port Arthur

Sea of Japan

Tokyo

Kobe

Yokohama

Xi'an

Shanghai

JAPANESE EMPIRE

Kathmandu

Lucknow

INDIA

BURMA

Guangzhou

Calcutta

Mandalay

Hong Kong

Bay of Bengal

Rangoon

Madras

FRENCH INDOCHINA

Colombo

CEYLON

MALAYA

Ocean

Singapore

Batavia

DUTCH EAST INDIES

Introduction

An Encounter in Calcutta

In 1901, the roving Japanese art historian Okakura Kakuzo penned the memorable opening line of his latest book, declaring "Asia is one."[1] A few months later, Okakura boarded a steamship in Yokohama to see something of the continent whose unity he'd casually declared at a distance.[2] After a short stopover in Colombo, he disembarked in Calcutta, the port city capital of colonial India, which over the previous half century had become the informational hub for new understandings of Asia. During the following months, he met the Bengali philosopher-poet Rabindranath Tagore, who later became the first non-European Nobel laureate for literature. Amid the intellectual ferment of the nascent Indian nationalist movement, Tagore in turn took an increasing interest in Japan, and subsequently China, traveling to both countries on lecture tours and learning what he could of their cultural heritage. At a casual glance, Okakura's claim of Asian unity seemed to be borne out by such connections.

Yet whether by way of Tagore's conversations with Okakura in Calcutta, or his later lectures in Shanghai and Tokyo, these inter-Asian interactions were all based on common knowledge of English rather than any shared Asian language. When Tagore's poetry was translated into Japanese and Chinese, it was likewise from English rather than directly from Bengali. Having learned the language at a Christian missionary school, Okakura even wrote his own book in English and published it in London, far from the intellectual centers of Asia, basing it on lectures he had given to British and American visitors to Tokyo.[3] When several decades later his *Ideals of the East* eventually appeared in Japanese (it would take a century to be translated into other Asian languages), its famous opening phrase had to rely on an English loanword to communicate its key geographical claim. And so "Asia is one" was rendered "*hitotsu no Ajia.*"[4]

Over two thousand years earlier, the word—and idea of—"Asia" had been invented by ancient Greek geographers.[5] It was not until the seventeenth century, in the nascent age of European expansion, that the term was exported across the regions to which it lent a simple, and single, name. After being slowly taken up by local thinkers, in around 1900 "Asia" took on new meaning as the likes of Okakura and Tagore used the idea of a single continent, separate and distinct from Europe, to defend what they presented as a common "Asian" heritage from the cultural and political pressures of colonization. This was, in essence, the new paradigm of Asianism (sometimes called Pan-Asianism), which has been defined as "discourses and ideologies claiming that Asia can be defined and understood as a homogenous space with shared and clearly defined characteristics."[6] But then, as now, making declarations of unity was easy compared to the far more challenging enterprise of fostering mutual comprehension between the different cultures and languages of so vast a proportion of humanity.

In fact, when Okakura made his bold claim, there were not even dictionaries between Japanese and the many languages spoken in India (that is, South Asia), let alone between the other languages of East Asia and the Middle East (which technically constitutes West Asia). Correspondingly, in Arabic and Persian even Japan's name was spelled inconsistently (and taken indirectly from English or French), while major religions like Buddhism, Shinto, Daoism, and Confucianism lacked proper names, let alone translations of their key texts into the languages of the western and southern sections of this notionally unified continent.

Though Okakura and Tagore became icons of Asian solidarity, the grittier groundwork of inter-Asian understanding was left to a series of lesser-known and often entirely forgotten figures from India, China, Iran, Afghanistan, Japan, Burma, and the Ottoman Empire who traveled and translated, interpreted and misinterpreted, in their attempts to decipher the different societies and cultures of other regions of Asia.[7] This book tells their story as they confronted a sequence of obstacles—whether linguistic or moral, philosophical or practical—in their attempts to render other regions of Asia intelligible to ordinary readers in their own languages rather than to the privileged few who knew English or French.

This is, then, the story of how Asia was seen from the inside, through works written in the languages of West and South Asia about the societies and cultures of Southeast and East Asia; or, put differently, how the majority Muslim and Hindu regions of Asia in the Middle East and India made sense of the Buddhist, Shinto, Daoist, and Confucianist cultures of Burma (now Myanmar), Japan, and China. By not taking the unity of Asia for granted, and looking instead at how people from its different regions tried to understand one another, here we embark on an altogether more revealing journey. And our travel companions will be not only lofty idealists like Okakura and Tagore, but also a lesser-known crew of intercultural explorers. It was these largely forgotten figures who tried to comprehend the peoples, places, and cultures with which they were brought into contact by the empire-driven globalization of the nineteenth through mid-twentieth centuries.

Just as Okakura adopted the idea of "Asia" from Europe, by carefully examining the multilingual results of these inter-Asian explorations, we will see that while some authors drew on sources and concepts from within their own traditions, others derived their information and interpretive categories from European writings. It would be easy to present this as yet another case of despotic Orientalism: of the "discursive power" of colonialism over the minds of people who implicitly could not think for themselves. But as we will see, at both the individual and the collective levels, Asia's intellectual history is more complex than this, with much room for chance and deliberation, for "agency" and "contingency," and not merely colonial hegemony. For whether by way of printing in vernacular languages, linking Asia together by steam travel, or disseminating information about other Asian cultures, the empires of Europe inadvertently triggered a continent-wide communications revolution that did as much to enable inter-Asian understanding as to dominate it.

Asia's self-discovery unfolded through the same communication technologies that assisted colonization, but to present these developments in the polarized terms of Asia versus Europe would not only obscure the complexities of how intercultural understanding emerged across this vastly diverse continent. It would also hide the inherent contradictions in the claim of Asian unity: Okakura's declaration that "Asia is one" raised an unstated question in turn, namely, unity on whose terms?

As it turned out, none of the implicit answers to this pressing question proposed over the following decades proved satisfactory for different people from all regions of Asia alike. The reason was that, all too often, "Asia" constituted an imaginative space for projecting the self rather than a living environment for encountering the other.

And so, while the promoters of Asian unity shared a common outward-looking agenda of anticolonial politics, they disagreed on the internal criteria,

Icons of Asianism: Rabindranath Tagore and Okakura Kakuzo. Wikimedia Commons.

whether cultural or political, of *what* it was that tied Asia together, and thereby on the question of *who*—which specific people from which region or community—should define the terms of unity.[8] During the decades after Okakura's declaration, various competing criteria were presented, whether of Asia as a "Greater India" or a "Greater Japan"; as a catchment area of potential converts to Baha'ism or to Islam; or as a Buddhist federation that Japanese and Indians competed to direct at the very moment when Chinese modernists were rejecting the religion as the cause of their country's decline. Even Tagore's ecumenical model of a "spiritual East," which sought a cannily vague concord between quite different religious traditions, collapsed when he was confronted by militant Japanese nationalists and scientizing Chinese secularists.[9]

And so, in the first half of the twentieth century, the competing and sometimes cooperating proponents of Asianism struggled to reconcile their rhetoric of continental unity with the facts of cultural diversity.[10] In this respect, the dream of Asian unity was undermined by the continent's sheer cultural wealth, by its unrivaled range of literary traditions in different written languages and scripts, by its sophisticated spectrum of legal codes and ethics, and by its abundance of philosophical and religious systems. Even when two areas of Asia seemed to share the "same" religion—such as Islam or Buddhism—

closer inspection revealed how widely these traditions had diverged since first putting down roots in the rich cultural soil of different regions.

Two leading experts on Asianism have pointed out how "such calls for Asian solidarity, integration, and unity were accompanied by endeavors to create an Asian identity by postulating commonalities and identifying traditions of interaction and interrelationship."[11] This is quite correct. But it is only half of the story: in the century on either side of 1900, while Asia's heightened interactions sometimes constituted a cosmopolitan encounter with other Asian cultures, such connections also led to the promotion of one region or religion across other parts of the continent. Whether by Muslim, Baha'i, and Buddhist missionaries who learned the methods of their Christian counterparts, by merchant capitalists seeking to enrich their own communities, or by Indian and Japanese nationalists who regarded themselves as the continent's rightful leaders, we will see how knowledge about other regions of Asia was gathered for a range of distinct purposes.[12]

For this reason, the notion of Asia's self-discovery carries a deliberately dual meaning, suggesting that at the same time that heightened inter-Asian interactions enabled deeper appreciations of the other, they also led to more strident projections of the self.

Clearing an Interpretive Pathway

Since the publication of Edward Said's *Orientalism* over forty years ago, a vast number of studies have examined how Europeans conceived and depicted the various peoples they colonized across Asia. But the more complex question of how those peoples understood and represented each another in their own writings has been relatively overlooked.[13] Drawing from the multilingual library of Asian-language publications, and looking at regions that were formally colonized (such as India, Burma, Ceylon), regions that were not (such as Iran and Afghanistan), and regions that ceded control of key ports (such as Japan and China), the following chapters provide an answer to this long-neglected question of how different regions of modern Asia came to learn about each other's histories and cultures.

Like their many ideological heirs, Asianists such as Okakura and Tagore were ultimately aspirational figures. They were trying to conjure with words a unified continent not merely in the absence of tangible unity, but in the absence of detailed knowledge of the languages and cultures, peoples and places, whose vivid diversity belied the singular label of "Asia." As the Dutch historian

Carolien Stolte has written of the competing conceptions of what Asian unity comprised, "Asia was indeed a terra incognita onto which multiple regionalist ideas and visions could plant their flag."[14] More than a century later, it is hard now to imagine the degree to which, for Asians who were unable to read European languages, other regions of the continent were indeed terrae incognitae at the time Okakura met Tagore. Though by 1900 large numbers of Asians had direct experience of various corners of the continent—as laborers and soldiers, pilgrims and traders—very few of them had published articles or books about their experiences to pass on what they had learned to the far larger number of their compatriots who never left home. And among those who did write such accounts, even fewer could read the languages of those other regions of Asia, which with their wholly different writing systems presented major barriers to intercultural understanding. Even when books were translated between different Asian languages, their translators had to find ways to bridge what professional interpreter Anna Aslanyan has called "gaps between languages: gaps created by conceptual differences and cultural assumptions."[15]

And so, as we will see by perusing many works of cultural interpretation published across Asia in the century of heightened interactions between around 1850 and 1950, much of the continent remained a mystery unto itself well into the modern era.

The Illusion of "Asia"

So why is this not already well known? There are several reasons, to which we must first turn to make sense of Asia's apparently belated self-discovery.

The first reason is the concept—one might almost say the illusion—of Asia itself.[16] Far from emerging from the region it labels, the word "Asia" was coined by ancient Greek geographers as a convenient moniker for the lands that lay east of their Mediterranean-based world. Yet even in antiquity, as the armies of Alexander and then the emissaries of imperial Rome gained more direct experience of the vast terrestrial expanse beyond Persia, "Asia" was not used as the catch-all category that it later became by subsuming China, India, and Japan, along with the lands that twentieth-century geographers would alternatively dub the "Middle East" or "West Asia."[17] It was only in the early modern period, after Vasco da Gama reached India, that European geographers adopted a four-part continental model of the planet that was expanding before them, prompting cartographers to divide their maps into four neat spaces: Europe, Africa, America, and Asia.[18]

But how did this European idea of "Asia" come to be adopted so widely by cultures that had for centuries cultivated their own conceptions of geography? The initial transfer took place through the translation of European maps and geographical works, beginning in the seventeenth century. Then, in the eighteenth and especially nineteenth centuries, the idea was distributed farther across the continent through the spread of print technology. In most cases, as an etymological record of its European origins, the originally Greek word "Asia"—or some version of it—was retained through these translations, whether as *Asiya* in Arabic, Ottoman Turkish, Urdu, and Persian, *Eśiya* in Bengali and Gujarati, *Yaxiya* in Chinese, or *Ajia* in Japanese.

The initial transfer took place from the two opposite ends of the Asian continent at around the same time. Adapted to Chinese phonology as *Yaxiya*, "Asia" was introduced to China in 1602 through the world map the Jesuit missionary Matteo Ricci (1552–1610) translated with the help of local scholars. Twenty years later, other local literati helped Ricci's successor, Giulio Aleni (1582–1649), complete the translation of *Zhifang Waiji* (*Record of Foreign Lands*), a compilation of European atlases that was in turn transmitted to Korea and Japan.[19] It was not until the mid-nineteenth century, however, that more intense interactions with Europe spread the concept further, partly through the effect of a new generation of (by now Protestant) missionaries.[20] This time an alternative Chinese term was created as part of the adoption of a wider package of geographical knowledge. "Asia" now became *Yazhou*, a term that implied its place in a larger schema of continents (*zhou*) and its relational opposition to Europe, or *Ouzhou*.[21]

Although the earlier Jesuit-inspired Chinese maps had made their way to Japan, where they were supplemented by the input of Dutch merchants, it was not until the second half of the nineteenth century that the idea of "Asia" gained traction in Japanese. As Japan opened to the world in the Meiji era (1868–1912), modernizers such as the journalist and teacher Fukuzawa Yukichi (1835–1901) disseminated the European loanword *Ajia* as a contrast to the older, Chinese-derived geographical concepts of *Toyo* ("Lands of the Eastern Ocean") and *Seiyo* ("Lands of the Western Ocean"). Even so, "Asia" was initially seen in negative terms—even as a region from which Japan should detach itself—so much so that it was not until the early 1900s that Japanese Asianists lent it more positive connotations.[22]

Since the seventeenth century, a similar process had been under way on the western frontiers of the continent through Ottoman interactions with Europe. A particularly important figure was the Ottoman polymath Katib Çelebi

(1609–1657), whose 1648 *Cihan-nüma* (*Mirror of the World*) drew heavily on the famous *Atlas Minor* of the Flemish geographer Gerardus Mercator (1512–1594).[23] Simultaneously introducing America to the Ottomans, Çelebi's work spread the notion of a continent called *Asiya* that included Anatolia (*Anatuli*), Iran (*'Ajam*), India (*Hind*), China (*Chin*), and some mysterious islands called Japan (*Yabuniya*); the last's Turkish spelling was probably taken from Mercator's Latin *Iaponia*.[24] The arrival of printing in the Middle East spread the idea of *Asiya* farther when in 1732 the pioneer Ottoman printer Ibrahim Müteferrika published an edition of Çelebi's Turkish *Cihan-nüma*. Then, a century later, the rise of Arabic printing saw the concept of an Asian continent spread farther around the Middle East. After Rifa'a al-Tahtawi (1801–1873) returned to Cairo from Paris, where he had served as imam to the first Arab Muslims to study in Europe, he was appointed head of a translation office dedicated to introducing modern knowledge to readers of Arabic. Geography formed part of this, and Tahtawi translated and published the *Précis de géographie universelle* by the Danish Parisian Conrad Malte-Brun (1775–1826).[25]

In the meantime, the British Church Missionary Society had established an Arabic press on the island of Malta, whence printed books were distributed to the Middle East.[26] Among its earliest publications was an Arabic geography primer based on the *Rudiments of Geography* by William Channing Woodbridge (1794–1845), an American evangelical who taught at Yale.[27] In 1834 it was revised and republished by Tahtawi.[28] A year later, the missionaries on Malta issued an Arabic atlas. Its brightly colored maps by Charles Frederick de Brocktorff (1775–1850) brought the new space of *Asiya* vividly to life.[29] Thenceforth the concept of an Asian continent—which included the Ottoman, Arab, and Iranian lands—spread through the Middle East, which Arabic maps and geographies now designated as the western part of *Asiya*.

Parallel developments were under way in Persian. From Calcutta in 1802, Iranian émigré 'Abd al-Latif Shushtari reported how Europeans divided the planet into four continents, one of which they called *Asiya*. The return of the first Iranian students from Europe around 1820 coincided with the adoption of printing.[30] The reformist minister Amir Kabir (1807–1852) introduced textbooks from Europe: in 1849 alone some 293 books and 323 world maps were imported from France.[31] Rafael Yunani, a Greek printer based in Tabriz, translated an English geography and maps of Asia by the Scottish explorer Sir Alexander Burnes (1805–1841).[32] Over the following decades, a series of geography textbooks was printed in Iran, beginning with a state-sponsored translation of *A Comprehensive System of Modern Geography and History* by an eccentric English schoolmaster called William Pinnock.[33] (In later chapters we will see just how unreliable a guide Pinnock proved to be.) By the early 1900s, the founding of the first modern school in Kabul saw the idea of "Asia" reach Afghanistan, albeit now as *A'ishiya* in a spelling that echoed the English pronunciation of the Indian teachers who imported it.[34]

This Indian role was no coincidence; by this time the educational policies of British colonial officials, and especially Christian missionaries, had been promoting European geographical knowledge in India for the best part of a century. The idea of "Asia" had probably first reached the Indian subcontinent in the sixteenth or seventeenth century by way of the Portuguese Empire and the Jesuit missions to the Mughal court that paralleled the Jesuit presence at the Ming court in China. But in 1784 the term was institutionally amplified by the founding of the Asiatic Society of Bengal by British Orientalists for whom "Asia" served as a unifying category for comparative inquiries across their widening imperial horizons.[35] Yet it was not until the spread of printing in Indian languages after 1800 that the concept began to proliferate, particularly through translations sponsored by missionaries in Calcutta, which we will see featuring as a major colonial bridgehead for European ideas. From the 1830s, several such textbooks, such as Horace Clift's *First Geography,* began to appear in Bengali and Urdu.[36] Three decades later, the Hindu print impresario Nawwal Kishore was issuing multiple Urdu editions of another English geography with short chapters on each of the many lands contained in that novel loanword *A'ishya.*[37] As the missionaries introduced printing to other languages such as Tamil and Telugu, the idea spread still further: by 1861 Henry Morris's *Geography* became one of the first books ever printed in Sindhi, and it featured an entire section on "Asia."[38] Farther south, through Sinhala translations, such as *Asiya-vistaraya* (*Geography of Asia*), missionaries promoted the concept among Buddhists in Ceylon (now Sri Lanka).[39] Still, the concept was not so easily domesticated, and by the late 1870s South Indian translations of English geographies used variant spellings of *A'ishya,* even in the same book.[40]

So it was that the idea of "Asia" spread unsteadily across the continent it designated through translations of European maps and textbooks, and missionaries played an important part in the process. Having been adopted to varying degrees into the continent's own languages, by 1900 this led to unintended consequences when "Asia" became a conceptual tool for anticolonial activism that aptly reached all the way from Tokyo to Istanbul. But ironically such declarations of unity were the least challenging part of Asia's self-discovery. In the chapters that follow, we will see just how difficult it was to fill that vast singular space on the map with accurate cultural knowledge, whether with or without European input.

In each of the varied contexts of its use, the term "Asia" invoked an arbitrary unity that bore little relation to the political, social, or cultural facts on the ground. As the Chinese scholar Wang Hui has explained, "The category of an Asian totality was established in contradistinction to Europe, and it encompasses heterogeneous cultures, religions, and other social elements. . . . Buddhism, Judaism, Christianity, Hinduism, Islam, Sikhism, Zoroastrianism, Daoism, and Confucianism all originated on this continent we call Asia, which represents three-fifths of the world's landmass and contains more than half of the world's population; thus, any attempt to characterize Asia as a unitary culture is not plausible."[41] In recent years there have been increasing calls to write world histories that go beyond Eurocentrism. Paradoxically, to do so will therefore mean reducing our reliance on the framing concept of "Asia," which merely disguises the problem.

Periodic Connections, Presumed Continuities

Moving from cultural to more concrete factors, the fact that these different regions had at times enjoyed (or endured) various degrees of economic or military connection was insufficient to produce meaningful continental unity: even the short-lived Eurasian empire of the Mongols was repulsed in West, South, and (far) East Asia. As the Indian historian Sanjay Subrahmanyam has written, despite "the existence of many complex networks both within Asia and involving Asia, which were created by the imperatives of trade, conquest, or pilgrimage, . . . none of these was historically capable over the medieval and early modern centuries of creating anything that resembled a coherent Asian whole."[42] This had crucial implications for the intercultural comprehension that this book explores. Referring to India and China by way of example, Subrahmanyam goes on to note "how tenuous the relations between the two regions remained, and how great the potential for misunderstandings was."[43] We will see how this potential for misunderstandings continued well into the twentieth century by moving from the early modern to the modern era and toward the larger question of how people from India and the Middle East tried to interpret the languages and cultures of Burma and Japan, as well as China.

When we recognize the extraordinary human diversity of Asia, whose cultural traditions are embedded in many unrelated languages with distinctive writing systems, the fact that people from different regions of what European geographers had decided was a single continent could not easily comprehend one another's cultures becomes less surprising than commonsensical. Intercultural understanding is never a natural or inevitable process, particularly between highly developed literate cultures that have evolved over many centuries with limited or sporadic contact with each other.

Close and sustained interactions between different communities had certainly produced intercultural knowledge *within* particular Asian regions and states. One example is the Mughal Empire in India, where the shared use of Persian between Hindus and Muslims fostered translations of such key texts as the *Bhagavad Gita* (though these were manuscript translations of limited circulation).[44] Another example is the Qing Empire, where shared access to the Chinese educational system saw Muslims write accounts of Islam that were comprehensible, and palatable, to ruling Confucianists.[45] But such forms of shared knowledge *within* the geographical confines of particular empires (and their courts) are harder to identify among the more sporadic interreligious interactions *across* Asia as a whole. Moreover, as historians of the Indian Ocean have shown, the western and southern regions of Asia have long had closer and more continuous interactions with Europe and Africa than with East Asia, despite the short-lived Chinese maritime outreach of the early Ming period.[46] Paradoxical as it may sound, the best way for us to begin our investigation of how people from different parts of Asia came to understand each other's cultures is therefore by downplaying the category of "Asia" itself. In this way, we will not be misled by a single word—hoodwinked through lexical legerdemain—into expecting that either cultural unity or intercultural intelligibility was somehow a default historical setting. On the contrary, ventures in inter-Asian understanding were extraordinary rather than routine achievements. Moreover, they were breakthroughs in which Europeans also participated.

One reason that the late development of inter-Asian understanding is so little known is the result of a kind of modern myth, one more historiographical than geographical: that of the Silk Road. In recent years, its lingering romance and subtle ideology has bewitched many a gifted historian. Yet, like the idea of "Asia," the notion of a "Silk Road" is also a European invention, albeit a more recent one. The term "Silk Road" was coined in 1877 as *die Seidenstrasse* by the Prussian geologist Ferdinand von Richthofen (1833–1905). Far from trading textiles on the ancient camel routes he so memorably branded, Richthofen was employed by the ailing Qing imperial government to explore potential coal supplies for a railway intended to unite the Chinese capital with its provinces. But his redolent neologism would wind its way only very gradually into other languages, not reaching English in any significant degree until the 1938 translation of *Sidenvägen* (*Silk Road*), the influential book by his Swedish protégé, Sven Hedin. Though Japanese imperial interests saw Hedin's book translated into Japanese the following year, it would take several more decades for the term to be adopted by authors writing in other Asian languages.[47] The term "Silk Road" truly proliferated only in the globalizing decades after 1990 through book titles, museum exhibitions, and cultural diplomacy projects that drew on the open-border ethos of recent times.[48] In many ways, the term tells us more about our own times than earlier eras.

For all its fashionable appeal, the scale, longevity, and degree of connectivity of the historical Silk Road are still debated by historians.[49] But the larger problem with the idea is the illusion of continuity that so often distorts our understanding of the past. Though in the early medieval period Buddhism and even Manichaeism spread east and north along trade routes into Central and East Asia, and Islam followed later, the scale and scope of such trade-enabled interactions fluctuated greatly over time. It is always worth remembering that world history has been characterized not only by connection, but also by long periods of disconnection.[50] Outside specific regions such as the oasis towns of Turkistan and the Tang imperial capital of Chang'an, inter-Asian interactions were more typically episodic and sporadic. Even then they involved quite limited social groups, such as merchants and monks, who did not necessarily share what they learned of the different cultures they moved between, insofar as they were able to comprehend them for themselves.

While a tiny cadre of Buddhist monks moved between early medieval India and China, translating Sanskrit texts into Chinese, such Silk Road exchanges marked an extraordinary episode of cultural transfer rather than a perpetual long-term pattern. Explaining the religious or cultural system of one region of Asia in the language and categories of another region was an extremely challenging—and rare—venture. Certainly, there was the occasional medieval travelogue by Asian Marco Polos who went on trading or diplomatic missions. But these solo ventures rarely went beyond visual descriptions and did not include investigations of the local written languages in which the detailed meanings of culture were embedded. By the time Okakura met Tagore at the turn of the twentieth century, there had still been no reciprocal translations of the most canonical Confucian or Daoist texts into the languages of India, still less of works in Japanese, or even on the Buddhism that Bengali intellectuals like Tagore had recently rediscovered and then reclaimed as part of their "own"

Indian heritage. Nor for that matter had the Quran, or *Bhagavad Gita*, been translated into Japanese or Chinese, let alone texts of lesser significance.

The illusion of long-term continuity implied by celebrated Silk Road inter-actions is misleading, then. So is the assumption that manuscript travelogues on other regions of Asia written in the medieval and early modern period continued to be known and accessible to later Asian travelers of the nineteenth century.[51] As we will see, the half century on either side of 1900 represented an era of far more intense connection between different regions of Asia that was not only distinctive in being wrought by the political-economic infrastructures of European empires, but also unprecedented in its intellectual scope. For this was a period that saw the birth of printing in the many languages of the Middle East and India (as well as the adoption of European printing techniques in China and Japan), which fostered a new public sphere with far more participants than the earlier age of manuscript communication. This public sphere of print became the means by which new—if not always reliable—information about other cultures spread between different parts of the continent.

The fact that this new corpus of knowledge was not the cumulative outcome of long centuries of continued connections and investigations helps explain what we will see was the introductory (and sometimes plainly erroneous) character of inter-Asian understanding, as well as the widespread resort to European knowledge (neutrally termed "Orientalism" here), which, for reasons that many other researchers have explained, had developed in a more formal, sustained, and collective fashion than its Asian siblings.[52] If the model of a Silk Road that ran from Rome to Chang'an has anything useful to tell us about the period we are investigating here, then it is to remind us that the dichotomy of Asia and Europe is a false one: in antiquity as in more modern times, ideas circulated and mingled across Eurasia as a whole, albeit at very different paces. Just as the notion of a unitary Asia that is opposite to and apart from Europe is an illusion, so is the search for a discrete inter-Asian understanding that is wholly separate from European knowledge.

Rather than resulting from the continuity of ancient overland connections, this new body of inter-Asian (or simply Eurasian) knowledge emerged from a maritime geography of port cities that had nothing to do with the Silk Road. Like the Calcutta where Okakura encountered Tagore, many of these port cities—whether Bombay or Rangoon, Yokohama or Shanghai—were minor settlements before European expansion. In the modern era at least, the geographical reality of an interlinked continent was the result of political and economic infrastructures that consolidated colonial conquests. But as the nineteenth century continued, these infrastructures inadvertently fostered an Asian communications revolution through the spread of steam travel and print technologies.[53] As Prasenjit Duara, an Indian historian of China, has noted, "Colonial empires, most notably the British Empire, created significant regional interdependencies in Asia. This had the effect of intensifying some of the old relationships and generating new linkages between the cities (and hinterlands) of Aden, Bombay, Calcutta, Singapore, Hong Kong, and Shanghai as entrepôts and financial centers for Asian trade."[54] But these ports were far more than commercial centers. Through their combined roles as transport hubs and printing emporia, port cities enabled a two-tier spread of information about different parts of Asia: directly through contact with other regions of the continent and indirectly through newspapers and books in European languages. With the opening of the Suez Canal in 1869, this chain of steam ports reached from Istanbul to Yokohama at the two far ends of Asia.

Ironically, perhaps, the Suez Canal also linked the new Asian public sphere to the Arabic print centers of Alexandria and Cairo, despite both ports being technically part of Africa.[55] As we will see by perusing the books and journals that emerged from these maritime connections, despite being constructed to serve British, Dutch, and French colonial interests, this port city infrastructure enabled an unprecedented degree of inter-Asian understanding. But far from flowing smoothly and by default, such intercultural knowledge faced obstacles of many kinds, not least those of language.

This brings us to the next reason the interpretive obstacles to inter-Asian understanding have not been recognized. This is the assumption, encouraged by the neoliberal globalization of the late twentieth century, that intercultural trade automatically gives rise to intercultural knowledge.[56] Yet though material goods move easily between different societies, knowledge is not so simply transferred. This is particularly the case for knowledge of the sophisticated religious, political, and cultural repertoires of Asia's various written traditions. Trade has always enabled simplified forms of oral communication. (This is best exemplified by the term "pidgin," which aptly derives from the local pronunciation of "business" in the ports of China during the 1850s.) But the transfer of complex cultural understanding demands the rarer skills of deciphering books and manuscripts in literary languages using a medley of different scripts. Commercial exchanges across Asia have long fostered oral forms of communication, and sometimes the use of written contracts drawn up by literate middlemen. But understanding different cultural, religious, and ethical systems requires much more demanding skills of interpretation that are based on the mastery of literary languages, scripts, and concepts that do not necessarily have counterparts in the interpreter's own language. The transfer of knowledge therefore cannot be equated with commercial cargo because it is always linguistically—and often textually—embedded, which renders accurate cultural knowledge far less transferable than trade goods.[57]

Even when commercial exchanges led to a degree of "multiliteracy" in different languages (as distinct from literacy in a shared commercial lingua franca), neither the requirements of trade nor the interests of traders routinely led to the production of books about the little-known regions where merchants operated. There were good reasons why not. Whatever intercultural knowledge that merchants did develop was a valuable commercial asset. As such, they were unlikely to make it available to their competitors by placing it in the public domain, particularly through printed books that anyone could potentially access. Consequently, commercial connections did not typically disseminate intercultural knowledge beyond the often-closed circles of merchant families or communities. Asian traders have rarely written detailed accounts of the cultures they encountered, still less been involved in translating written works from the different traditions of the people they traded with. As a paradigm of the merchant–turned–public informant, Marco Polo is as false a friend as the Silk Road, setting up expectations that are rarely borne out by the historical record.

So, while the following chapters will lead us along what were some of the busiest trade routes on the planet from the nineteenth to mid-twentieth century, we will see that the spread of intercultural understanding cannot be collapsed into the story of capitalism, whether we cast the latter as hero or villain. Knowledge follows more tortuous and challenging pathways than commodities. On the balance sheet of history, neither the volume of trade nor the movement of traders has automatically generated corresponding intellectual profits; commercial connection does not automatically lead to cultural comprehension.

By contrast, the producers of inter-Asian understanding were more often missionaries than merchants. But here there was, as it were, a trade-off. For whether they were Muslims, Baha'is, or Buddhists, the Asian evangelists who adopted the methods of Christian missionaries to promote their own traditions across other regions of the continent did not produce an objectively disinterested corpus of knowledge. On the contrary, like their Christian competitors, they often took an interest in other cultures to learn how best to convert them to their own religion. This meant in turn that knowledge sometimes emerged from polemics and disputes that nonetheless constituted forms of dialogue with other religions. Over time, this generated understanding and sometimes even sympathy for religions the missionaries sought initially to undermine.[58] Here, too, Asia's self-discovery took place through a complex interplay of promoting the self and appreciating the other.

The final reason that the history of inter-Asian understanding has remained so little known is perhaps the simplest of all: very few of the Asian-language texts that document its development have been brought to light and examined. For this reason, the following chapters tell the story of the forgotten books and journals in which people from different corners of the continent struggled to make sense of each other's cultures.

As we will see, these interpretive challenges were particularly the case for initial translations of key texts, which between various parts of Asia occurred as late as the 1920s and 1930s, when Confucius's *Analects* first appeared in Arabic and Urdu, and the Quran in Japanese and Chinese. The problems facing initial familiarization are far from unique. It is easy to forget that in English, a now-commonplace word like "nirvana" would have meant nothing to even the most learned English speakers a century or so ago. Moreover, the ontological doctrines associated with nirvana—that the highest human endeavor is to "snuff out" our individual existence—was initially shocking to European and American Christians reared on the notion of an individual afterlife.[59] It is therefore only by looking at the sequence of specific texts through which inter-Asian understanding gradually took shape that we can recognize the challenges involved. For all that, the story of the various, and sometimes vicarious, ventures in pursuit of such understanding is a fascinating one.

Inter-Asia beyond Asianism

To focus on books in Asian languages is not to say that such works emerged in a pure inter-Asian vacuum, untainted by European ideas. To expect that would be to fall prey to the lingering illusion of a discretely self-contained Asia, to the seductive appeal of Asianism. Instead, by looking carefully at particular texts, we will see a variety of positions along a spectrum of informational and discursive independence. Some authors used only data and concepts derived from previous works in their own or other Asian languages (or, more often, their direct observations). And other authors drew many of their explanatory concepts, or data sets, from previous European studies, or else produced partial or wholesale translations of Orientalist texts. This entanglement reflected both the origins of the idea of "Asia" itself and the material interconnection of the continent through the infrastructures of empire. This entanglement with (and sometimes outright reliance on) European sources also points to the informational asymmetry between the detailed, language-based European investigations of Asian cultures and what we will see as the more indirect and sometimes vicarious studies produced in Asian languages themselves.

Undoubtedly, this was partly a product of colonialism, as countless studies of Orientalism have shown. But there was more to the matter than this. By taking seriously the books that Asian authors wrote in their own languages, we will see that they were far more than the discursive prisoners of empire. Looking not only at India but also at regions such as Iran, Afghanistan, and the Ottoman Empire, as well as at the fading empire of Qing China and the rising empire of Japan, will help us reckon with more complex ratios and relations of power. Moreover, as has been shown by subtle recent investigations of the sharing of ideas between European Orientalists and Asian intellectuals writing in their own languages, informational asymmetry is not necessarily the same as informational dependence.[60] Just as many Orientalists wrote their books with the help of Asian scholars, so for their own varied purposes did other Asian scholars draw on European works. While the European idea of "Asia" became a conceptual aid for anticolonial Asianists, European knowledge of Asia became a resource for a far larger number of Asian authors whose agendas ranged from innate curiosity about other cultures to commercial gain on the booming vernacular book market.

The mechanisms through which Europeans acquired knowledge about Asian societies and cultures have been explored through a vast body of scholarship. With its origins in literary studies, one branch of this scholarship has emphasized the "discursive" and "representational" dimensions of such Orientalism by highlighting the importance of tropes, stereotypes, and larger schemas for depicting and even exacerbating otherness.[61] Another branch of inquiry has looked at the "informational" basis of the knowledge aiding European expansion by focusing on the methods of data collection and the use of local informants employed to ascertain facts on the ground—with varying degrees of accuracy.[62] Over the course of the following chapters, insights from both of these branches of research into how knowledge is formed—the textual-representational and the informational-institutional—will help us chart the ambit and limits of the intercultural knowledge produced by Asia's own investigators as they contemplated the vast continent connected by European empires.

In reconstructing this process of discovery, we will not only trace the *scope* of comprehension by way of what was (and was not) understood about different regions; we will also bring to light the underlying *mechanisms* of understanding by way of the steam routes, publishing houses, lexicographical tools, translations, organizations, and institutions (or lack thereof) that helped (or hindered) the different writers who tried to learn about other regions and then place their findings before the reading public. The people we will see involved comprise a wide cast of characters—missionaries, students, soldiers, journalists, traders, and teachers—who wrote books, translations, or articles to widen public awareness of previously obscure regions and religions.

Ultimately, the focus will be on these individuals, the forgotten "discoverers," and the books they published across the Middle East and especially the great informational entrepôt of India. By looking at printed books and magazines in Urdu, Persian, Arabic, Gujarati, Ottoman, and occasionally Bengali, Japanese, Burmese, and other languages, we will try to reconstruct what the broader reading public knew—or at least potentially knew—about other parts of Asia. This will allow us to look beyond what was known to the narrower Anglophone, Russophone, and Francophone elites of colonial India, the independent Ottoman Empire, Iran, and Afghanistan, who whether for better or worse had easier access to European knowledge of Asia.

Since the scope and reliability of any field of knowledge depend on its ability to progressively integrate the findings of multiple investigators who are separated across time or space, we will look too at the mechanisms for disseminating the findings of individual Asian investigators to other interested parties who could then assess—accept, reject, or modify—such separate discoveries and thereby build on them. It is easy to see that literacy in a shared and preferably printed language is a basic prerequisite for such collective and cumulative developments. But complex bodies of knowledge require more than these communicational basics. They also require some form of collective organization, even institutionalization, whether by way of learned societies, reliable funding sources, shared journals, educational skill-building systems, or common access to investigative tools such as dictionaries and grammars. As we follow our Indian and Middle Eastern investigators on their direct or armchair journeys across the Bay of Bengal and beyond to Japan and China, we must keep these larger issues in mind. For as we will see, the fact that many individuals wrote books about other regions of Asia did not automatically snowball into the founding of learned societies or other institutions, particularly when prestigious colonial institutions like the Asiatic Society in Calcutta (and the Tokyo School of Foreign Languages) drew some of the most gifted Asian scholars into their own institutional orbit.

Despite the relative lack of organizations and institutions for fostering inter-Asian intercultural investigations, there was one major mechanism that all the authors we will examine did have available to them. This was the printed public sphere that emerged during the nineteenth century as print technology was taken up for the first time by locals across the Middle East, Southeast Asia, and India, allowing them to distribute their findings to far wider audiences.[63] A "public sphere" can be defined as "the social space in which different opinions are expressed."[64] This helps us recognize how the massive expansion of printing in Asian languages we will see spreading through the ports of maritime Asia produced an arena of competing normative claims.[65] From Calcutta to Rangoon, Singapore, and ultimately as far as Shanghai and Yokohama, ports served as printing and distribution hubs for books, magazines, and newspapers in an increasing variety of vernacular languages. Whether in Urdu, Bengali, Gujarati, Chinese, Japanese, Burmese, Malay, or even Thai, new printed genres and corresponding forms of simplified "vernacular" prose radically widened both the social and geographical reach of written information about—and representations of—other Asian regions, religions, and cultures. But as a space of competing norms, the maritime public sphere also enabled disagreements and disputes to be printed and circulated, texts that we will see challenging casual claims of Asian unity.

Though China and Japan had developed block-printing techniques many centuries earlier, with the exception of Jewish and Christian communities and a pioneering Muslim printer in the Ottoman Empire, precolonial printing had never developed in the languages of Western, Central, or South Asia. But from approximately 1830, and through the influence of Christian missionaries especially, printing spread widely across Asia, even to the point of replacing the indigenous block-printing methods of China and Japan. As the ports of Yokohama, Shanghai, and Istanbul became major printing centers, along with inland cities such as Tehran and Kabul, it was the ports of colonial India—Calcutta and Bombay especially—that became the largest multilingual entrepôts of Asia's new print-based public sphere.

Crucial to these developments was the spread of a new technology known as lithography. Invented in the 1790s by Alois Senefelder, a failed comic actor aptly from Bohemia, lithography was originally intended to simplify the printing of music scores. Its ingenious method—using a wax crayon to write or draw on a limestone slab, which was slotted into an iron press to run off reproductions (lithography literally means "stone printing")—proved remarkably versatile. After the East India Company introduced it to Calcutta in 1822 for the purpose of printing maps, its alternative potential was quickly recognized: lithography could easily be used to reproduce Asia's many different writing systems.[66] From Calcutta to Tehran, Singapore, and ultimately Shanghai, Senefelder's invention inadvertently enabled an Asian printing revolution as one local entrepreneur after another invested in lithographic presses of his own.[67] When coupled with the new transport technologies of steamships and trains, the result was an inter-Asian communications revolution more broadly.

The spread of printing—particularly cheap commercial printing—was therefore of immeasurable importance not only to Asia's intellectual life in general but also to the spread of inter-Asian understanding in particular: the printed public sphere allowed far larger numbers of people to learn about the places, peoples, and cultures of other Asian regions. And so Asia's self-discovery was inseparable from this new intellectual infrastructure that made it possible. But by the same token, it was also inseparable from the European empires that had laid the foundations of that inter-Asian communications infrastructure, which in turn linked Asia with European ideas.

Nonetheless, the knowledge that passed through the public sphere was not simplistically subject to colonial control. Though the publications of political activists (including anticolonial Asianists) were sometimes censored by the British, for example, comparatively liberal publishing laws ensured that printing in colonial India, Burma, and Ceylon was far freer than in the Ottoman Empire, Iran, and Afghanistan, including material regarding the transfer of cultural and religious knowledge about other regions of Asia.[68] Moreover, despite the attention they have subsequently received, anticolonial Asianists were not necessarily major contributors to vernacular knowledge of the regions they sought to unify. As we will see, many of the printing enterprises that spread inter-Asian knowledge were market-oriented commercial concerns. Others were directed by independent governments beyond European control that had a variety of different agendas. Still other texts were promoted by the various new missionary groups, whether Muslim, Baha'i, or Buddhist, that made extensive use of printing to project their own teachings among other Asian peoples. In short, the public sphere—and the knowledge that passed through it—was far more than a discursive mirror of European power.

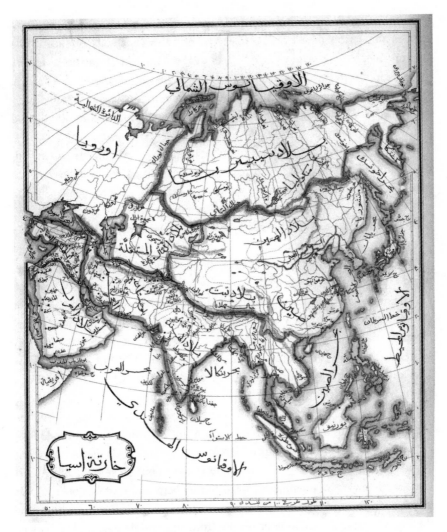

"Asia" travels east: map from an 1835 Arabic missionary atlas. Charles Frederick de Brocktorff, *Atlas, ay Majmuʻa Kharitat Rasm al-Ard* (Malta: Church Missionary Society, 1835).

Wide as it was, Asia's new maritime public sphere still had many fractures and blind spots. This was partly a question of the relative degrees of informational institutionalization discussed earlier that rendered intercultural knowledge a more ad hoc enterprise in Asian than in European languages, at least till around 1920, when more Asia-based organizations and universities became involved. But these fractures and blind spots also reflected the sociolinguistic profile of the public sphere, which had limited mechanisms for translation and other transfers of information between the different languages and scripts used by particular communities. As a consequence, while the public sphere of print was an Asia-wide development, it was not a unitary sphere of communication through either a single language or lingua franca. Instead, Asia's public sphere developed multiple linguistic and thereby informational "channels," a term that we will use to capture both their media and maritime dimensions.

From this grainy ground-level analysis of specific texts of inter-Asian understanding and the infrastructures that enabled them, we will see a broad pattern emerge: the farther an author's home region was from the place being described, the greater the reliance on European sources of information. By contrast, the cultures (and in some cases the languages) of the Middle East and India (that is, West and South Asia) were already relatively familiar to each other through long centuries of sustained contact that included the widespread use of shared languages, such as Persian, and the shared political and administrative traditions of Muslim-ruled empires.[69] The same can be said for China, Japan, Korea, and Vietnam (that is, East and parts of Southeast Asia) through the long-standing shared use of literary Chinese that has recently been described as constituting a regional "Sinosphere."[70] But for the Middle East and India at least, in the early nineteenth century China and especially Japan were effectively unknown, as were the Buddhist cultures of Southeast Asia in any degree of doctrinal detail. Aside from a handful of largely forgotten manuscripts from earlier centuries—only a few of which were subsequently rediscovered, translated, and printed in modern Asian vernaculars—there was a much smaller legacy of precolonial knowledge about these regions.[71] Again, we should be wary of the illusion of continuity between what was once known to the ancient Sogdian merchants who followed the Silk Road to China, and the knowledge available to later people from the Middle East and India who made their own journeys in modern times.

To disaggregate Asia in this manner into regions of greater and lesser comprehensibility—a western and an eastern half, as it were—is not to reinstate a fixed model of timeless "civilizations" that remained as cognitively incommensurable as they were morally irreconcilable. On the contrary, Asia's two "hemicontinents" were not perpetually impenetrable. So, while our investigations will not lead us to conclude that, by the time of Asian independence in the 1950s, people all across that great continent enjoyed perfect comprehension of each other's cultures, we will see that far more was understood at empire's end than had been understood a century—or even a millennium—earlier.

The Lingering Question of Language

Although we will grapple with the challenges of explaining the teachings of Buddha and Confucius for the first time in the modern languages of the Middle East and India, we will see the larger obstacles were those of language and script. Again, this is not because of their radical incommensurability: there is no inherent reason Middle Eastern and South Asian scholars could not learn to read Chinese and Japanese, as various distinguished scholars from the region have over the past half century. But as we will see, in the absence of dictionaries, teaching institutions, and governmental sponsors, Asia's sheer variety of written languages formed the most enduring barrier to the spread of detailed and accurate intercultural comprehension. Asia was not the mirror of Europe, with its mere two major alphabetical zones, Latin and Greco-Cyrillic, and its far smaller geography of intertwined intellectual centers. In this respect, inter-Asian understanding was undermined by the sheer written wealth of its intellectual and literary heritage.

This brings us to the question of which languages will be used here to trace the spread of intercultural comprehension between one half of Asia and the other by way of Middle Eastern and Indian attempts to understand the societies and cultures of Burma, Japan, and China. The issue of language is central to any attempt to understand how different cultures and communities understand one another. Since knowledge is always linguistically embedded—especially complex forms of cultural knowledge—the challenges of transferring understanding between the different literate cultures of Asia were more extreme than for any other region of the world. Asia is not only home to an extraordinary number of language groups (Sino-Tibetan and Turkic, Indo-European and Semitic, Dravidian and Japonic, Austroasiatic, and others). It is also home to a far wider variety of writing systems than Europe, Africa, and the Americas combined. The implications become clear when we begin to consider the process of translation (a term that etymologically means "to move from one place to another") in so linguistically and orthographically diverse a section of the planet. As we will see, in terms of dictionaries, grammars, and even basic word lists, the lexicographical mechanisms for translation between different Asian languages remained startlingly underdeveloped as late as the 1900s (indeed, even today). It comes as little surprise, then, that when we look at how the Middle East and India understood Japan and China, we will see that texts were more often translated through English or French rather than between different Asian languages directly.

Moreover, this is only to approach translation in its most basic sense as a process of word-for-word substitution. But as anyone knows who has attempted to translate between languages from markedly different cultural environments, there is no guarantee that an equivalent word exists in the target language for the concept, emotion, doctrine, or even object described in the language being translated. Moreover, just because a particular text is translated accurately into another language, it does not inevitably follow that its meaning and implications will be clear to a reader from a different culture. As any adolescent who picks up the *Tibetan Book of the Dead* quickly realizes, texts make sense only in relation to a larger body of tacit knowledge that the native reader acquires casually and unconsciously over the course of a lifetime. As anthropologists have demonstrated through their long debates over "cultural incommensurability," the degree to which one culture can be explained both accurately *and* intelligibly in the language and concepts of another culture is no straightforward matter.[72] Even though this book rejects the radical position in the incommensurability debate—that different cultures can never accurately comprehend one another—just because something is possible does not necessarily imply that it actually developed during a given period. So, as we will see, while in principle the cultural systems of Asia's different regions are mutually comprehensible, in practice these possibilities of intercultural understanding were only partially realized during the century of increased interactions between the 1840s and 1940s. At least this is the case in terms of knowledge that was made available in books and articles printed in the languages that were most widely understood in West and South Asia.

To provide both a broad and comparative picture, the following chapters draw on sources in the South Asian languages of Urdu, Gujarati, and to a lesser extent Bengali and the West and Central Asian languages of Persian, Arabic, and Ottoman Turkish, with occasional comparisons to reciprocal or related works in the South, Southeast, and East Asian languages of Marathi, Punjabi, Telugu, Sinhala, Burmese, Thai, Malay, Japanese, and Chinese. In each case, the sources comprise printed books and journals from the new public sphere that emerged during the century of Asia's empire-based interconnection between around 1840 and 1940.

One language is used more than any other, however—a language whose importance is less recognized than it should be. That language is Urdu. As the spoken and written language of the Indian subcontinent's most densely populated regions in the Ganges plain and Punjab, Urdu was South Asia's most important vernacular language, read by many North Indian Sikhs and Hindus, as well as Muslims from every corner of the subcontinent. As the main lingua franca of British India, it was also extensively used by the Christian missionaries and colonial officials whose early investments in Urdu printing made it the only truly all-Indian language, used by publishers and readers spread from Peshawar to Madras, and Calcutta to Bombay.[73] As a result, not only was Urdu, together with Persian, Arabic, and Bengali, the earliest vernacular language to be printed in the Asian informational hub that was Calcutta, it was also the most widespread; books and journals were subsequently published in Lahore, Bombay, and Rangoon for readerships that ultimately reached across the Bay of Bengal and eastward as far as the Indian merchant diaspora in Japan. Some Urdu texts were translated into other South Asian languages, such as Gujarati, whereas others were read or translated in Afghanistan, where they shaped local perceptions of the other regions of Asia, which Afghan traders and diplomats were reaching by the early twentieth century.[74] Like the Persian books we will see printed in India for export to Afghanistan and Iran, such Urdu texts allow us to trace the effect India had on other regions as the combined result of its more developed publishing industry and its greater access to multiple sources of information.

This was because Urdu became integrated into more linguistic and thereby informational networks than any other language of West or South Asia. With their links to colonial British institutions, numerous writers of Urdu could read English with perfect fluency. And through their affiliations with Muslim institutions, many Urdu writers could also or alternatively read Arabic, Persian, and occasionally Ottoman Turkish. And as Indians reared in different regions, other Urdu authors could read or at least speak various other South Asian vernaculars and, in the case of learned Urdu-writing Hindus, occasionally Sanskrit. The subcontinent's other vernaculars were more confined to specific regions and communities; only Urdu was linked to so wide a range of potential informational sources.

Although Urdu is far less famous than Arabic and Persian, or even Bengali and Hindi, no other language in West or South Asia combined a comparable number of speakers, readers, publishers, journals, books, and writers with so widespread an informational network that reached westward to the Middle East and Europe and eastward as far as the Indian trading diasporas in China and Japan. By comparison, even the Gujarati that was the first language of so many Indian merchants remained a regional community language that perpetually maintained an informational deficit compared to Urdu. Even Arabic, Persian, and imperially sponsored Ottoman Turkish seem to have produced fewer direct book-length accounts of Southeast and East Asia and studies of their religions and cultures. As the preeminent printed vernacular in the geographical center of the maritime public sphere that stretched from Istanbul to Yokohama, Urdu became the flagship language of Asia's self-discovery—albeit one that was still accessible only to a minority of India's population, let alone to a readership across Asia at large. By comparing what was published in Urdu about different regions of Asia to texts written in various other languages, we will see that inter-Asian understanding was very unevenly spread.

Nonetheless, even Urdu, let alone the other Asian languages we will examine, remained at a disadvantage to imperially sponsored English and French. Drawing on a geographically wider and more effectively institutionalized "information order," English especially combined the advantages of colonial intelligence gathering with the far-reaching cultural investigations of the Christian missionary societies and the commercial data-gathering organizations exemplified by London-based Reuters, which opened its Bombay office as early as 1851, followed by Hong Kong in 1871, and then Tokyo and Shanghai two years later.[75] In a reflection of what the Indian economic historian Bishnupriya Gupta has described as the "informational asymmetry" between the knowledge available to Indian and British companies about market conditions around Asia, we will see a similarly asymmetrical pattern characterizing the gathering and communicating of data about cultural conditions in different corners of the continent.[76]

Nonetheless, by selectively transferring English materials into Urdu and other languages, Indian authors remained better positioned to make vicarious use of this colonial informational order than many of their counterparts in the Middle East or other regions of Asia. Various Middle Eastern authors and printers even moved to Calcutta and Bombay to take advantage of both the greater access to information and the lesser constraints of censorship (not to mention the opportunities of trade). From around 1900, a rival to this information order emerged as the rise of the Japanese Empire led to sustained attempts to gather and institutionalize knowledge in Japanese about other regions of Asia. But as we will see, as an imperial latecomer, Japan turned to a series of Indian and European informants, by way of both teachers and textbooks.

It was India, then, that became the key—if by no means the sole—informational hub for Asia's self-discovery. It was no coincidence that it was to Calcutta that Okakura sailed to deepen his previously theoretical appreciation of the continent's other cultures (though his writing maintained its Japanocentrism). Colonial Calcutta and Bombay served as Eurasia's foremost communication hubs, which we will see used by intercultural investigators from the Middle East, China, and Japan no less than from Europe. More than a plainly political matter, the prominence of these two great ports resulted from their sheer volume of human traffic, their polyglot publishing industries, their access to European information, and their position in the middle of the sea routes that tied Asia—and Europe—together.

In comparison to this maritime informational geography, the so-called Silk Road was largely irrelevant in this age of imperial steam and print, whether in providing input to the public sphere or even as an inspirational idea. Having been invented by the Prussian Baron von Richthofen, the term "Silk Road" was not translated into Asian languages till the very end of the period we are examining, which renders it irrelevant even as a conceptual charter for Asian unity. It would have to wait until the dawn of the twenty-first century for its season in the sun of Chinese soft-power diplomacy.[77]

Across Asia in Six Chapters

In the nineteenth century, as the infrastructures of European empire brought the peoples of Asia into closer interaction than ever before, the spread of printing therefore enabled Indian, Iranian, Arab, Turkish, Burmese, Afghan, Japanese, and Chinese writers to disseminate reports about previously poorly understood cultures across the continent they were now calling "Asia" by adopting an ancient Greek label in their own languages. But the bundled arrival of the communicational package of steam and print not only widened intellectual horizons but also disseminated misunderstandings, disputes, and polemics that rippled through what became a querulous public sphere. The Asian printing revolution did not herald a utopia of ecumenical understanding any more than its latter-day online heir did. Consequently, to trace the intercultural knowledge that spread through steam and print communications, we must disentangle the mechanical process of *connection* from the semantic process of *comprehension*. However coeval, these two processes were by no means proportionate.

Covering the breadth of Asia during its period of maximal integration in the Age of European Empires, the following chapters reveal the opportunities and constraints that rendered intercultural understanding less the inevitable byproduct of political or economic integration than the variable outcome of subtler moral and hermeneutic processes. Over and again, we will see how the communications infrastructures of European empires laid the basic structural parameters of interaction. But beyond these mechanics of connection, when we turn to the semantic evidence of specific texts, we will see there was no single ideology leading the improvement of inter-Asian understanding. For all their latter-day celebrity in histories written since the end of empire till today, anticolonial Asianists voiced only one set of motivations, which in terms of knowledge of the varied cultures they sought to unite were by no means the most productive. Instead, we will see how perceptions of Asia's different regions were shaped by more varied factors of interaction and fickle fluctuations of interest, as well as the persistent challenge of the continent's many writing systems. The obstacles, contingencies, and idiosyncrasies that shaped understanding between the different peoples of Asia show that there is no natural or inevitable course for the development of knowledge of other cultures. This is the primary lesson of global intellectual history.

As we follow Asia's own interpreters across that great continent, we will come to recognize what we might call the dialectic of discovery, by which different places served as venues for the projection of the self as much as the appreciation of the other, which generated new understandings of self and other in turn. Keeping this dialectic in mind, the following chapters constitute the first sustained attempt to trace how people from one side of Asia across the Middle East and India tried to comprehend the cultures of Burma, Japan, and China on the other side of the continent they were just learning to call "Asia." Over the course of our journey, we will meet scores of writers in West and South Asian languages who sought to present Buddhism, Shinto, Confucianism, and Daoism in terms that were linguistically comprehensible and philosophically commensurable to their Muslim, Hindu, and Baha'i readers, albeit often by drawing on prior investigations by Christian missionaries. But we will also see the prominent roles of non-Christian religious actors in the spread of inter-Asian understanding, particularly Muslims. Ironically, these were the very people who, in the paragraphs that followed his declaration that "Asia is one," Okakura dismissed and denigrated for having blocked the Buddhist-led path to Asian unity.[78] He was far from alone in such attitudes.

Knowledge of Asia's other cultures did not develop in pace with economic and political integration any more than it did with Asianist calls to unite against this Europe-dominated imperial system. Nor for that matter did colonization tear apart a continental cultural unity that had previously flourished unimpeded but could be easily reinstated if everyone followed the true path of Buddha, Muhammad, or, later, Mao. Even the Asian communications revolution that fostered a new public sphere did not always spread accurate information or universal sympathy, for the era of print was no more an age of innocence than that of the internet. For whether through finding catchment areas to win converts, seeking comparative lessons on self-empowerment, or building a continental circle of religious solidarity, Asia's self-discovery was shaped by the tangled motivations of projecting the self and appreciating the other.

And so, as we commence our journey in the Calcutta where Okakura met Tagore, we will follow a vacillating course marked by false trails and breakthroughs, positive encounters and heated polemics, remarkable discoveries and interpretive misadventures. Like all meaningful journeys, the transfer of knowledge across cultures involves many obstacles and challenges. It should never be taken for granted.

1 • Learning through Polemics in the Bay of Bengal

At once separating and connecting the Muslim, Hindu, and Buddhist populations of India, Burma, and Ceylon, the Bay of Bengal forms the maritime meeting place of several of Asia's major cultures.[1] During the early modern period, its hinterlands alternated between periods of cooperative commerce and times of competing sovereignty among the rival Mughal, Arakanese, and Konbaung states and their Muslim or Buddhist rulers. These centuries of slowly evolving contact cultivated various mechanisms of cultural accommodation, whether in composite rituals of kingship or hybrid literary genres in regional languages like Bengali. But literary fashions at court and commercial or diplomatic contacts did not necessarily lead to detailed inter-Asian understanding by way of Indian-language accounts of Buddhism, reciprocal translations of scriptures, or even dictionaries to enable such intercultural transfers. Like any other aspect of inter-Asian understanding, these deeper intellectual developments took fuller if nonetheless fraught form during the nineteenth century in the wake of the gradual British conquest of the region. The ensuing integration of the Bay of Bengal into the political structures and commercial networks of the British Empire enabled far more people to travel between the key ports of Calcutta, Rangoon, and Colombo. These heightened interactions—both between Asians and Europeans and between different Asians—also found expression in the maritime public sphere that emerged from the colonial introduction of printing to the region's various languages.

Despite what we have seen of attempts by Anglophone intellectuals like Okakura and Tagore to promote an "Asian" identity in Calcutta around 1900 through appropriating the European concept of "Asia," such claims of unity did not widely register in the local language publications of this new public sphere. For intercultural comprehension, let alone conceptions of cultural unity, did not emerge easily from the political and economic connections wrought by European empire. Even in as closely connected a region of Asia as the Bay of Bengal, inter-Asian understanding faced a great many barriers, even knowledge of as major a religion as Buddhism, which had disappeared from India in the medieval era and remained all but unknown in the Middle East. As a public sphere of print expanded through the ports of India, Burma, and Ceylon, information about the religion of the other was shaped by rival missionary projections of the religion of the self.

By following the evolution of the maritime public sphere through which responses to other religions reached broad audiences, we will see how polemical texts played important roles as biased brokers of inter-Asian knowledge. Whether written by Christians, Muslims, Buddhists, or even Baha'is, such critical engagements with religious difference comprised many of the most detailed interactions with the unfamiliar cultures encountered around the Bay of Bengal in the nineteenth and early twentieth centuries. By looking at the written evidence, we will see how comprehension emerged from conflictual as much as from amicable encounters. For such religious debates were also forms of dialogue that contributed to the deepening of knowledge. We will also see the role of European empire not only in providing the mechanisms of heightened inter-Asian communication, but also in introducing the Christian missionaries who served as models for the Muslim, Baha'i, and Buddhist proselytizers who turned the infrastructures of empire to their own conversionist purposes. Following these disputatious interactions between different religious actors reveals how the dialectic between projection of the self and recognition of the other shaped the jagged contours of intercultural cognition.

The Maritime Expansion of a Polemical Public Sphere

After the Battle of Plassey in 1757, the administrative demands that accompanied the rapid expansion of the British East India Company's territory in Bengal fueled demand for teaching materials, law manuals, and other texts in Persian and Bengali, the chief languages of regional bureaucracy. This in turn created incentives for the considerable investments of man hours and money required to develop the fonts, punches, and machines for printing the distinct scripts of Persian and Bengali. During the two decades between the East India Company's founding of schools for secretaries by way of the Calcutta Madrasa in 1781 and the establishment of the Fort William College in 1800, a series of technical innovations among British Orientalists, Indian secretaries, and émigré typesetters brought about the beginning of printing in the numerous scripts of India.

The early focus of these efforts was on Bengali as the chief regional language and on Persian as the administrative language of the company's territories till 1837.[2] This led in turn to the development of Urdu printing, which had a far larger influence in being understood much more widely across India than both the learned language of Persian and the regional vernacular of Bengali.[3] Although small numbers of Christian texts had previously been published in local languages in the Portuguese colony of Goa, printing in Calcutta was distinguished by the invention of fonts for printing languages in their own scripts.[4] Consequently, the readership of Calcutta's printed books rapidly widened.

It was not only East India Company officials who were pioneering printing in Indian languages. It was also the Christian missionaries whom the company had long tried to ban from its territories for fear of provoking opposition to its profit-driven rule. Amid Britain's evangelical awakening of the early 1800s, Protestant activists regarded the company as addicted to the godless profits of commercial exploitation. In many a damning tract and parliamentary debate, the evangelicals condemned the company for leaving the people of India to roam freely down the road to damnation lest intervention in religious matters upset their plans for economic exploitation. Despite the company's objections, in 1801 a handful of British missionaries set up the Baptist Mission Press in Serampore, a Danish trading post a few miles upriver from the company's Calcutta headquarters. There they set about printing tracts and Bible translations in local languages. Soon their numbers overtook the secular book production of the company's own printers. By 1813, when parliamentary negotiations in London for the renewal of the East India Company's charter allowed missionaries to directly operate in its territories, an influx of other missionary organizations descended on Calcutta. Among them were the Prayer-Book and Homily Society and the Christian Tract and Book Society, which by the 1820s were issuing pamphlets in Urdu and Bengali that critiqued Islam and Hinduism alike. Far from limiting themselves to local Indian languages, Calcutta's missionaries set about translating the Gospel into every language of Asia. The Baptist Mission Press alone issued works in nearly fifty languages— many never previously printed—that ranged from Sinhala, Burmese, and Pashto to Malay, Chinese, and Arabic. Through Calcutta's foundational role in printing these languages, the colonial port became the epicenter of an Asian communications revolution. As print technology was increasingly adopted by the speakers of these languages themselves—even China and Japan would replace their traditional woodblock printing with European typography and lithography—there emerged a truly continental public sphere that reached from the Bosphorus in the west to the Sea of Japan in the east.[5]

During the first half of the nineteenth century, Calcutta's Christian missionaries mounted a printed assault on what they saw as the false beliefs that denied Indians and other non-Christian Asians the possibility of eternal life. Their fierce objections to "heathen" religions constituted what can be called the polemical paradox: attacking Asian cultural and religious practices was the collateral damage wrought by the higher cause of saving Asian souls. Then, during the second half of the nineteenth century, the same techniques were adopted by a sequence of new Asian missionaries, whether Muslims, Buddhists, Baha'is, or, in the case of the Gaudiya Math and Arya Samaj, even Hindus, who had not traditionally accepted converts.

The policies of religious freedom that helped justify the rule of the East India Company (and from 1858 direct British rule) protected the rights of both Christians and non-Christians to promote their own religions. This also meant the right to promote their religions as superior to others. As a result, interreligious polemics were rendered as the social cost of press and religious freedoms. These freedoms were never absolute. Throughout the colonial era, their scope remained in a flux of negotiation, not least through changing legal categorizations of what constituted religion and thereby gained the right to free expression.[6] Nonetheless, as printing spread through the colonial ports of the Bay of Bengal, the outcome was a public sphere in which religious disputations were not merely prominent but in some sense in-built. When printing spread in turn to independent Asian states, such as Iran, Afghanistan, and the Ottoman Empire, their governments imposed much stricter rules of censorship, particularly with regard to matters of religion. This made India's printing emporia all the more important by attracting from elsewhere a range of religious activists to issue their works in Calcutta and Bombay, not least because publishing was better developed and cheaper in these port-city print hubs.

Print, Polemic, and the Key Position of Calcutta

Throughout the nineteenth century and well into the twentieth, India would remain the leading multilingual producer of printed books—and interreligious polemics—throughout maritime Asia as the printing emporia of first Calcutta, then Bombay, Lucknow, Lahore, and Madras issued books in languages that ranged from Bengali, Urdu, Gujarati, and Tamil to Arabic, Persian, Malay, and even Chinese that were shipped out to the far ends of Asia. Even after printing spread to other imperial ports such as Singapore, India's publishing centers retained their combined advantages of early adoption, a skilled workforce, and the economies of scale enabled by the combination of massive domestic and overseas markets. The outcome was the creation of a maritime public sphere in which India—and especially Calcutta—played a key role as a polemical no less than informational hub of inter-Asian interaction.

By 1900 Asia's bustling port cities were awash with multilingual waves of books, tracts, and journals. But few people possessed the skills to read several of these different languages, particularly those written in the varied scripts associated with different religious communities and their distinct traditions of learning. Consequently, the transfer of intercultural knowledge among these many languages continued to face enduring obstacles that the rise of printing in itself could not overcome. While learned religious figures were often the most qualified to navigate these linguistic impediments, most were concerned with promoting or defending their own belief systems, particularly after the rise of new Asian missionary organizations.

In some cases at least, however, the ensuing interreligious disputes that spread through print did paradoxically contribute to intercultural understanding. For such critiques of other religions were part of a dialogical process that involved the collection and dissemination of more detailed information about the religion being rejected.

By perusing a sequence of polemical texts and countertexts that were published around the Bay of Bengal in the nineteenth and early twentieth centuries, we will see how the participants in these disputatious dialogues gradually widened to include Muslims, Hindus, Buddhists, and Baha'is no less than the Christians who first introduced printing to the region. As a result, how interreligious comprehension was forged partly in the crucible of conflict will become clear.

Many of these disputes were serious and sustained engagements with the languages, scriptures, and belief systems of other people that led to reflections on their theological and moral implications. Rather than conceiving the history of Asian interactions through the narrow prism of Asianist ideology, or the anachronous projection of either modernist secularism or postmodernist cultural relativism, the printed texts that constituted publicly available knowledge about other Asian cultures allow us to document more complex engage-ments with religious difference.

In his typology of religious polemics, the Brazilian-Israeli philosopher and linguist Marcelo Dascal identifies three basic types: the discussion, the dispute, and the controversy.[7] As Dascal explains, "Discussions are basically concerned with establishing *the truth*, disputes with *winning*, and controver-sies with *persuading* the adversary and/or a competent audience to accept one's position."[8] These subcategories of polemic—especially the dispute and the controversy—quickly emerged as prominent features of the maritime public sphere around the Bay of Bengal. By pointing to the communicational character of "polemical exchanges," Dascal helps us recognize from the out-set that disputes and controversies are by definition "dialogical events involv-ing at least two contenders defending opposite views and arguing against each other."[9] Despite their critical content, religious polemics represent an engagement with difference. As different communities came into closer con-tact around the Bay of Bengal, such disputatious dialogues became impor-tant media of interaction through which intercultural knowledge was at once conveyed and contested.

Polemical conversations that were carried out in print therefore cannot be easily dismissed as outcomes of mere ignorance or narrow prejudice. On the contrary, whether written by Christians or Muslims, Baha'is or Buddhists, many such works emerged from the careful scrutiny and ethical assessment of competing religious doctrines. And so it was that, as the wheel of knowl-edge gradually turned, disagreement could generate deeper understanding and not only discord.

Widening Ripples of Disputatious Dialogue

From the early nineteenth century, the doctrine of sincere conversion held by Calcutta's Protestant missionaries promoted proselytizing policies that were based on the ideal of rational individual persuasion. According to this doctrine, all humans were endowed with God-given reason, however mis-led they might be by false beliefs. This in turn required the missionaries to undertake a rational engagement with the very belief systems they sought to undermine, which in turn necessitated the investigation of such doc-trines, whether Hindu, Muslim, or Buddhist. In this way, the evangelical push into Asia involved a serious intellectual encounter with non-Christian religions.[10]

This approach to reasoned, argumentative, and knowledge-based conversion was not unique to Christianity. Muslims, Hindus, and Buddhists had their own traditions of persuasive debate. But it was the Christian version that first found printed expression through the dialogue format of textual disputation that the Calcutta missionaries issued by the thousands. One of the earliest such polemics was *Dharma Pustakera Duta* (*Messenger of the Book of Religion*), a short, versified chapbook composed by the missionaries' assistant Ram Ram Basu (1757–1813), which contrasted Hindu beliefs with the message of the Bible.[11] Such was the unfamiliarity of the Bible that it had to be referred to in Indic terms as the "Book of Dharma." It was followed by a series of other Bengali tracts, such as *Bhedabheda* (*Difference*), which critically compared Krishna with Christ.[12] Written with the help of learned locals by Joshua Marshman (1768–1837), the son of a poor weaver who became a prominent Baptist missionary, it used the sophisticated terminology of Vedanta philosophy to make its comparisons more compelling. Such critiques prompted Hindus to defend—then reform—their religion against charges of idolatry.[13]

Since the missionaries were as critical of Islam as they were of Hinduism, some such works appeared in both Urdu and Bengali editions, such as *Sacha 'Isa'i: Ramhari aur ek Shakhs Sadhu Apas mein in Baton ki Guftagu Karti Hain* (*The Christian Indeed: A Dialogue between Ramhurree and a Sadhu*), issued in 1829.[14] To better enable its distribution by up-country and port-based preachers, the Christian Tract and Book Society sold it in bundles of a hundred copies priced at a mere three rupees.[15] Other texts published in the 1830s by the Christian Tract and Book Society included pamphlets aimed at Muslims such as *Muhammadi u 'Isawi Din ka Muqabala* (*Comparison between Christianity and Islam*), which developed the model of critical comparison on which many later works were modeled, and *Tahqiq al-Iman* (*Verification of Faith*), which moved beyond abstract dogma to criticize various kinds of Muslim rituals.[16] Similarly printed in an edition of two thousand and sold in three-rupee bundles of one hundred copies, *Tahqiq al-Iman* deployed a scrupulously critical reading of the Quran that drew on the philological expertise of evangelical Orientalists.[17] For example, to demonstrate the inconsistency of Muhammad's message, it cited verse 142 of Surah al-Baqarah ("Chapter of the Cow"), which refers to the changing of the Muslim direction of worship from Jerusalem to Mecca.[18] Over and again, repeated recourse was made to the words of the Quran itself as "proof" (*sabit*) against the teachings of Islam.[19] Critique, then, required closer knowledge of the Muslim scripture.

Other works issued by the Christian Tract and Book Society used the same methods of detailed scriptural comparison. For example, *Is Mursala mein Nabi*

Allah Hone ki Dalilen Hain (*Distinguishing Marks Whereby a True Prophet May Be Known*) refuted the prophetic status of Muhammad by citing specific verses of the Quran in the original Arabic.[20] These were then systematically refuted to prove the status of Jesus as the sole savior of humankind. Issued with a first edition of two thousand copies, the forty-four-page pamphlet *Musalmani Mazhab ko Chor Dene ka Sabab* (*Reasons for Not Being a Muslim*) similarly cited select Quranic verses before making a studious "refutation" (*radd*) of them.[21] As a work of scriptural comparison, *Musalmani Mazhab* repeatedly quoted the Quran and then countered its teachings with verses from the Old and New Testaments. The pamphlet focused in particular on Quranic references to the Bible, such as verse 37 of Sura Yunus (Chapter of Jonah), which in confirming that the Quran was itself a continuum of the revelations previously sent to the Jews and Christians opened the possibility that the Bible rather than the Quran contained the true revelation.[22]

Through such texts, in the 1830s the Christian Tract and Book Society was issuing what were effectively some of the very earliest works ever printed in Urdu.[23] The same was true for Bengali. By 1834 the Baptist press at Serampore had issued Bible translations in nearly fifty languages, the overwhelming majority of which had never previously been printed.[24] Unlike the East India Company's expensive publications, these texts were intended not for a small readership of British officials and Orientalists, but for the Indian public at large, to whom they were distributed either at nominal cost or, more often, for free. Moreover, such was the godly ambition of the missionaries, and such was the proximity of Serampore to Calcutta, that their translations were shipped not only upriver across India, but overseas across Asia at large.

Yet over time, these evangelical printing endeavors had the unintended consequence of encouraging members of the Muslim, Hindu, Zoroastrian, and Buddhist communities who were the target of these textual assaults to take up printing for their own parallel purposes.[25] In a pattern that unfolded first in Calcutta, then subsequently across the widening public sphere in Bombay, Burma, Ceylon, Singapore, and Iran, these missionary polemics provoked members of other confessional communities to publish works defending their own religions, propounding their own tenets, and launching countercritiques in turn. Over time, these responsive polemics expanded in ripples from initial exchanges with Christians to disputatious engagements with other religious groups.[26]

Calcutta is usually associated with the Bengali language, but Urdu was also a major language of the city, as nineteenth-century migration from other regions of North India made Urdu speakers the majority of Calcutta's Muslims.[27] It

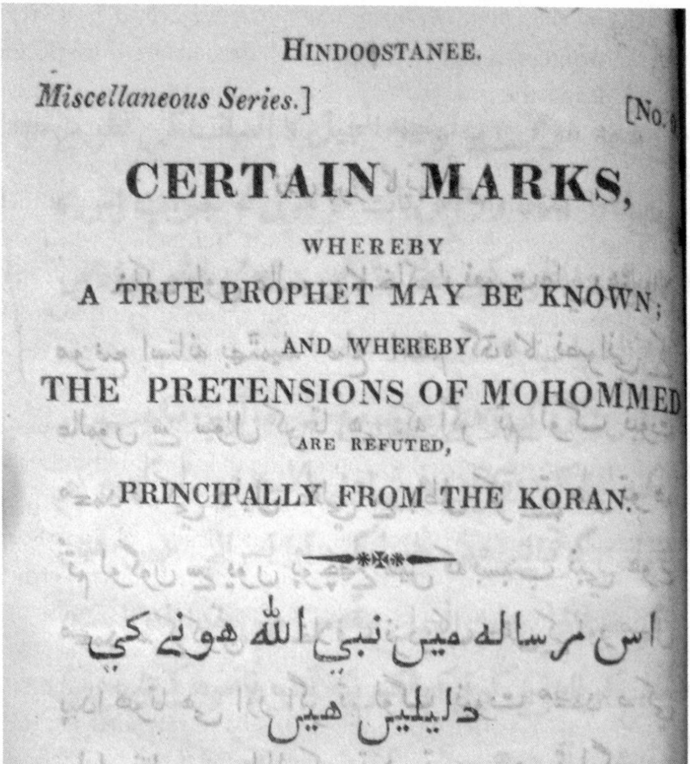

Miscellaneous Series.]

[No.

CERTAIN MARKS,

WHEREBY

A TRUE PROPHET MAY BE KNOWN;

AND WHEREBY

THE PRETENSIONS OF MOHOMMED

ARE REFUTED,

PRINCIPALLY FROM THE KORAN.

اس مرسالہ میں نبی اللہ ہونے کی
دلیلیں ہیں

اتفاقاً عیسائی مذہب کے کسی خادم دین اور
اہل اسلام کے کسی عالم سے بنارس میں ملاقات
ہوئی اور محمد کی نبوت پر بات چلی تو اُسنے
اسے کہا کہ عیسائی اہل اسلام سے محمد کی نبوت کی
صداقت اور دلیل چاہتے ہیں اس بات کے جواب
میں مولوی صاحب نے دوسرے روز یہ پرزہ بھیجا
اور اُس کا جواب عیسائیوں سے چاہا ۰

Christian catalysts: Calcutta missionaries' critique of Islam. *Is Mursala mein Nabi Allah Hone ki Dalilen Hain* (Calcutta: Calcutta Christian Tract and Book Society, n.d. [c. 1835]). Photograph by Nile Green.

was only natural, then, that Urdu became the language of choice for Calcutta's early Muslim printers, proselytizers, and polemicists. The first Indian-owned presses in Calcutta thus began issuing pamphlets modeled on the vernacular tracts of the missionaries not only in Bengali, but also in Urdu as well as the traditional learned languages of Arabic and Persian. Such religious works formed among the earliest sets of texts printed by non-Europeans anywhere in the Middle East and India, laying the polemical foundations of the new public sphere. As early as 1814, the Iraqi émigré Jawad ibn Sabat printed in Calcutta his *al-Barahin al-Sabatiyya fi ma Tastaqimu bihi du'a'm al-Millat al-Muhammadiyya wa Tatahaddamu bihi Asatin al-Shari'at al-Mansukhat al-'Isawiyya* (*The Sabatean Proofs Which Support the Pillars of the Community of Muhammad and Subvert the Columns of the Abrogated Christian Faith*).[28] Having briefly converted to Christianity, Sabat had first been employed as a language assistant by the Serampore missionaries before returning to the fold of Islam and using the printing skills he had learned from the Christians to produce an extremely detailed refutation of their doctrines, which was nearly 250 pages long.

Soon printing was taken up for inter-Muslim disputes. By 1822 the controversialist Muslim reformer Sayyid Isma'il Dihlawi (1779–1831) was printing in Calcutta his Persian *Sirat al-Mustaqim* (*The Straight Path*), followed two years later by the adoption of Urdu to issue his *Taqwiyyat al-Iman* (*Strengthening of Faith*).[29] By 1832 his followers had issued seven books from the Muslim-owned presses that were beginning to appear in Calcutta.[30] Other Muslim religious activists followed Sayyid Isma'il's example by printing their own texts in Calcutta. Among the earliest was *Haqiqat al-Salat* (*The Truth of Worship*), a treatise on the importance of the Muslim prayers that was printed in 1837.[31] Yet Sayyid Isma'il also inadvertently set in motion the use of print for the inter-Muslim polemics that would spread widely across maritime Asia, an early example of which was Mawlwi 'Abd al-Jabbar of Calcutta's 1843 Urdu counterblast to Sayyid Isma'il's *Taqwiyyat al-Iman*.[32]

These disputes were not merely a mimetic response to Christian missionaries.[33] They comprised the expansion into print of contentious debates that had previously circulated through the more restrictive medium of manuscripts. Legal "disagreements" (*ikhtilaf*) and theological "polemics" (*jadal*) had been a feature of inter-Muslim interactions for so long that a substantial learned literature—a "science of disagreement" (*'ilm al-khilaf*)—had developed around such disputes to minimize their divisive social effect.[34] But this had not always been possible, even in the centuries of more limited circulation of Arabic and Persian manuscripts, let alone with the rise of the public sphere of vernacular print.

A similar pattern unfolded around the southern reaches of the Bay of Bengal, where, after the East India Company introduced print to the port of Madras in 1761, missionary printing also took root. By the early nineteenth century, a whole range of evangelical organizations, such as the Madras Tract Society, the Christian Vernacular Education Society, and Tamil Christian Book Society, were printing in Tamil.[35] As in Calcutta, aside from Bible translations, the early output of the Madras-based missionaries comprised critiques of Hinduism and Islam, which were closely compared to the teachings of Christianity. Like Calcutta, Madras was also home to many Urdu speakers, who in 1840 used Urdu to issue the city's first Muslim newspaper. For their part, Christian evangelicals made use of the language for distributing Urdu refutations of Islam they had printed in Calcutta.[36] Other Christian missionaries in Madras produced new disputatious works. Among them was Edward Sell (1839–1932), whose output included *Aqa'id-i Islamiyya* (*Creeds of Islam*), translated by his Indian convert-assistant, Muhammad Shafqatullah, and *Kashf al-Qur'an* (*The Quran Unveiled*), which pointed out inconsistencies intended to "shake the confidence of the Muslim reader in the inspired character of the Quran."[37]

As in Calcutta, these polemics catalyzed the onset of South Indian Muslim printing in Urdu and Tamil. Issued in Arabic-script Tamil (known as Arwi), these pamphlets included countercritiques of Christianity, which were among the earliest Tamil Muslim printed books.[38] As the ripples of polemic widened around the Bay of Bengal, by the early twentieth century the focus of these printed Tamil disputes included rival new Muslim and Hindu missionary groups, such as the Ahmadiyya and Arya Samaj.[39]

Even as far away as Iran, the state-led decision to found the country's first printing press in 1817 was a more or less direct response to the influence of the Persian New Testament translated by Henry Martyn in Calcutta, printed in Saint Petersburg in 1815, and then distributed across Russia's border with Iran.[40] Completing the circle between India and Iran, the person responsible for printing the Persian New Testament in the Russian imperial capital was the erstwhile British ambassador to Iran, Sir Gore Ouseley (1770–1844), who had spent his earlier career in Bengal.

As the likes of Martyn and Ouseley expanded the reach of their Christian publications from Calcutta to Shiraz, Iranian Shi'i scholars responded by developing a new theological genre. In a borrowing of the Anglo-Italian loanword for a Christian priest, they termed the genre *radd-i padri* (refutation of the padre).[41] Such works had an older pedigree in the age of manuscripts, but the closer connections of the nineteenth century saw them expand across maritime Asia in printed, mass-produced form. Yet again, such texts were far from being expressions of blind ignorance. The Shi'i works written in response to Martyn's disputations involved serious engagements with Christian doctrines, deploying theological reason to point to the logical or ethical flaws in the Christian message, which was itself more fully understood as a result of missionary translations into Arabic and Persian.[42] Predicated on the deep investigation of difference, whether Muslim or Christian, these disputatious works became a major vehicle for intercultural knowledge: in promoting the religion of the self, such textual dialogues served as informational building blocks that made possible, if not inevitable, a richer understanding of the religion of the other.

Even farther from Calcutta, the printed output of Christian missionaries provoked similar responses in Istanbul. There in 1867 the Indian Muslim scholar Rahmatullah Kairanawi (1818–1891) published his Arabic *Izhar al-Haqq* (*Revealing of the Truth*) in response to the earlier *Mizan al-Haqq* (*Balance of Truth*) of the German missionary Karl Gottlieb Pfander (1803–1865), which had been issued in India in various languages.[43] But whereas Pfander's book had weighed the balance of comparative scriptural evidence in favor of the Bible, Kairanawi's response used the same investigative techniques to prove the superior truth of the Quran. Circulating widely through the Asian public sphere, *Izhar al-Haqq* was subsequently translated into Turkish, Gujarati, and Urdu.[44]

Yet despite his careful investigations, not all Kairanawi's sources were reliable. Among the various sources he used to critique Christianity was the so-called Gospel of Barnabas, which presented Jesus predicting the coming of Muhammad.[45] Over the following years, as Muslim-Christian polemics spread through the widening public sphere, other Muslim authors took a closer interest in this mysterious Gospel, particularly after a published English translation of one of its two surviving manuscripts made it more readily available in 1907.[46] Its extraordinary contents presented Jesus very much in Muslim form: passionately denying he was the Son of God; extolling the asceticism he was famed for in Islamic tradition; and repeatedly foretelling the advent of Muhammad. A year after the English version appeared, it was used as the basis for an Arabic translation, which was in turn translated into Urdu, thus completing the polemical circle by taking the text in full to Kairanawi's homeland, where it fed back into debates with Christian missionaries.[47] The result was a highly learned intercultural engagement with the Christian other through debates based on evidence that wholly eschewed violence. But it was also based on a falsified document that was taken to be a trustworthy source: the Gospel of Barnabas was a late medieval forgery, probably composed by a Moorish forced convert to Christianity in the Andalusia of the Spanish *Reconquista*.[48] We will see this problem of unreliable sources recurring again, with attempts not only to understand Christianity but also to make sense of less familiar Asian religions.

Debating with Buddhists in Burma and Ceylon

Besides moving westward from Calcutta toward Istanbul, Christian missionary disputes expanded eastward and southward into Buddhist-majority regions beyond India itself, where Buddhism had effectively disappeared in the medieval period. The two main fields of this outreach were Burma and Ceylon, which were both conquered by the British in the course of the nineteenth century.

Laying the linguistic foundations for these evangelical endeavors were newly compiled lexicons and dictionaries, such as the comparative vocabulary of Burmese, Malay, and Thai compiled by John Leyden (1775–1811), a Scottish Orientalist at Calcutta's Fort William College, which was published by the Serampore missionaries as early as 1810.[49] Seven years later in Ceylon, the combined efforts of the Bible Society and Baptist missionaries in the British port city capital of Colombo saw the Bible printed in the Sinhala language of the island's Buddhist majority.[50] Two years later, Siam (now Thailand) fell within the ambit of evangelical print when the American Adoniram Judson (1788–1850) worked with the Baptists of Calcutta to print a Protestant catechism in Thai. Echoing older fractures within Christianity itself, this was a sectarian response to the earlier enterprises of Arnaud-Antoine Garnault (1745–1811), who in 1788 had invented Thai printing in the French-controlled port of Pondicherry, where he had issued a Catholic catechism in romanized Thai.[51]

Burma was also becoming part of the widening public sphere fostered by evangelical print. Christian missionaries had begun printing in the ports of Moulmein and Rangoon as early as 1817, when Judson issued eight hundred copies of his Burmese translation of the Gospel of Matthew. A major contribution to the Asian communications revolution, this was the first book in Burmese ever printed in Burma.[52] Judson followed it by gradually publishing the entire Bible in Burmese, a massive undertaking in logistical no less than linguistic terms. Importing the comparative critiques of his fellow Baptists in Bengal, in 1829 Judson printed the first of many editions of his Burmese tract, *The Golden Balance,* which weighed up the logical and moral merits of Christian and Buddhist teachings. (In the same year, he also spread further the idea of "Asia" by issuing a Burmese textbook on geography.) Meanwhile, after the First Anglo-Burmese War of 1824–1826, the piecemeal annexation of Burma was accompanied by an influx of Christian missionary organizations. Enabling their activities were dictionaries—Judson also compiled the first ever Burmese-English dictionary—that enabled dedicated missionaries not only to translate Christian texts into Burmese, but also to read Burmese Buddhist texts. By 1852 Judson's Baptist successor, Jonathan Wade (1798–1872), had printed in Moulmein a bilingual dictionary of Burmese Buddhist terms, laying further linguistic foundations for the study of the region's own religious traditions.[53]

After the Society for the Propagation of the Gospel established itself in Rangoon in 1862, many other Christian organizations followed, whether funded by American Methodists, French Catholics, or Calcutta-based Armenians, further expanding the reach of print in Burmese and the other languages of Burma.[54] The bibliographical scale of these endeavors was astonishing and wholly unprecedented in a region where printing had not previously existed. To take just the example of the Baptist mission at Moulmein, between April 1830 and December 1832 it issued a quarter of a million Christian tracts amounting to over four million pages of Burmese text.[55] Catholic missions tried to compete with this massive Protestant outreach.[56] In 1884 even the Mormons sent a pair of preachers from distant Utah to distribute their tracts in Rangoon.[57]

The Burmese port was also soon playing host to the new Hindu missionary organizations that emerged in response to the Christian missionaries. In 1889 Swami Atma Ananda Saraswati of the Bombay-based Arya Samaj disembarked in Rangoon, and the Ramakrishna Mission also dispatched representatives to Burma from its headquarters outside Calcutta.[58] Later, the Gaudiya Math—the Vaishnava Hindu forerunner to the Hare Krishna movement founded in Calcutta in 1920 by Bhaktisiddhanta Sarasvati (1874–1937)—established a base in Rangoon. Since all these organizations were keen users of print, their expansion across the Bay of Bengal further signaled that the maritime public sphere was washing over Burma.

Yet as we will see, initially at least, competing ventures of projecting the self—first by Christian missionaries, then by their non-Christian imitators—played a larger part in this public sphere than dispassionate investigations of religious difference. As we have seen happening first in Calcutta, the unintended consequence of these Christian investments in Burmese printing was

THE

NEW TESTAMENT

OF OUR

LORD AND SAVIOUR

JESUS CHRIST.

ကယ် တင် တော် မူ သော အ ရှင်

သ ခင် ယေ ရှု ခ ရ စ် ၏

 နှစ်ဆယ်ခုနှစ်ကျမ်ကိုဟောလသပါ ဦ့တော်မှမြမ္မာဘာသာ အားဖြင့်
အနက်ပြန်ချို၍ရိုက်သောစာစောင်။

2D BURMESE EDITION.—10,000.

MAULMEIN:

AMERICAN BAPTIST MISSION PRESS.

1837.

Christian missionary role models were offered in Baptist Bibles in
Burmese. *The New Testament*, 2nd Burmese ed. (Moulmein: American
Baptist Mission Press, 1837). Photograph by Nile Green.

the creation of not only Muslim but also Buddhist counter-missions, which developed their own printing operations.

Members of Burma's Buddhist-majority community did not sit by and idly watch while other religions were being promoted. Even before the last Buddhist capital of Mandalay fell to the British in 1885, print technology reached it by way of the French Catholic bishop Paul-Ambroise Bigandet (1813–1894), who imported a press for King Mindon (r. 1853–1878). Responding to what was by then half a century of Christian Bible printing in Burma, in 1864 this Mandalay royal press undertook the first printing of the Pali Buddhist scriptures, the *Tipitaka* (*Triple Basket*), just as thirty years earlier an imported Russian press had enabled the initial printing of the Quran in Tehran by an Iranian who had learned to print by helping the Bible Society.[59] By 1870 Burmese-owned presses had spread to Rangoon, and by the 1900s Burmese religious activists such as Taw Sein Ko (1864–1930) were adopting print to promote other Buddhist religious texts.[60]

As Rangoon played host to an increasing multiplicity of missionaries, the port also fostered a new generation of Buddhist proselytizers who sought to respond to what they regarded as the combined threats of British colonialists, Indian merchants, and missionaries of various persuasions. And so by 1900 this led to the emergence of new Buddhist missionary organizations that similarly invested in multilingual print as a medium of self-projection across maritime Asia. Chief among the new Buddhist missionaries was the Ceylonese Anagarika Dharmapala (1864–1933). He visited Rangoon as early as 1891 to meet Buddhist leaders there before returning to Colombo to found his Maha-Bodhi Society, which soon shifted its headquarters to Calcutta, where it set up its own printing operation.[61] On the Protestant Christian model, Dharmapala effectively invented a new kind of Buddhist missionary whom he dubbed *dhammadutta* (messengers of *dhamma* [Buddhist doctrine]). Burma served as one of the key areas of interest for his Maha-Bodhi Society, and by 1901 its *Maha-Bodhi News* was being published in Burmese in Rangoon, projecting Dharmapala's reformed, Protestant-influenced Buddhism as a counter to the Christian missionaries who preceded him.

In 1892 Calcutta also became the headquarters of the newly founded *Bauddha Dharmankura Sabha* (Bengal Buddhist Association), whose own founder, Kripasaran Mahathera (1865–1926), would aid the further propagation of Buddhism around the Bay of Bengal.[62] Among the new Burmese missionary organizations, the most active were the *Thathana Hita Athin* (Foreign Mission Society, founded 1905) and the Young Men's Buddhist Association (founded

1906), both based in Rangoon. Other societies soon followed in the Burmese port, such as the Buddhist Propaganda Society, which established its own Buddhist Mission Press there, while the *Sasana Noggaha Athin* (Mission Association, founded 1897) was established inland in response to Christian—and, as we will see, Baha'i—proselytizing in Mandalay.[63] As their names suggest, these Buddhist missions were hybrid organizations, in many cases formed through associations with Europeans that allowed Ceylonese and Burmese Buddhist leaders to adapt Christian concepts and technologies for their own purposes.[64]

By the end the end of the century, Christian polemical investigations had paved the way for more sympathetic engagements with Asian religions, including outright conversion. In 1891 Dharmapala's American mentor, the Theosophist-turned-Buddhist (and fierce anti-Christian) Henry Steel Olcott (1832–1907), had his *Buddhist Catechism* translated into Burmese (it had already appeared in Japanese).[65] Subsequently, British converts, such as Charles Bennett (known as Ananda Metteyya, 1872–1923), joined this Buddhist revival through missionary print. In 1903 he established the *Buddhasasana Samagama* (International Buddhist Society) in Rangoon, from where he set out on a maritime circuit of missionary tours.[66] Bennett was followed to Burma by other Europeans attracted to Buddhism, such as the German Anton Gueth (known as Nyanatiloka Mahathera, 1878–1957), who converted in Rangoon in 1903.[67] Burma's new entrepôt of proselytizing Buddhism also attracted other European converts, such as Laurence O'Rourke (known as U Dhammaloka), an Irish sailor who, like a Hibernian Dharmapala, promoted Buddhism along the steam routes that linked Burma with Bengal, Ceylon, and ultimately Japan.[68] A century after Christian missionaries began printing in Burmese, their ventures had been matched by a countereffort intended not only to win back Burmese support for Buddhism but also to convert other Europeans.[69] As a result, new English-language propagational publications were launched, such as the journal *Buddhism*, printed by Rangoon's Hanthawaddy Press from 1903 to 1908.[70]

These complex dynamics of projecting the self and appreciating the other meant that by now Christian missionaries might well be Indians, like the Tamil Lutherans who preached across Burma, whereas the promoters of not only Buddhism but also Islam might be British or American.[71] The latter included Muhammad Alexander Russell Webb (1846–1916), who in 1893 delivered lectures in Bombay and Rangoon on the reasons behind his conversion.[72] He made full use of the public sphere, having the text of his Rangoon lecture translated into Urdu and printed as *Isha'at-i Islam (The Propagation of Islam)*.[73]

For added effect, the Bombay publisher Badr al-Din 'Abdullah Kur published several of Webb's letters in his newspaper. Another such missionary convert was the Scotsman John Parkinson (known as Yehya-en-Nasr, 1874–1918), who between 1908 and 1910 used his two-year tenure as deputy editor of a Rangoon newspaper to publish several books in Burma aimed at promoting Islam.[74] Several years later the disputational dialogues begun by Christian missionaries came full circle when a Burmese Muslim published a tract in Rangoon that used the Bible to prove Muhammad was a true Prophet of God.[75]

Parallel developments were also under way in the southern sector of the Bay of Bengal among the Buddhists of Ceylon.[76] After taking up printing in Sinhala in 1818, seven years later British missionaries introduced the disputatious genre of the dialogue to the Buddhist-majority island when the Colombo Auxiliary to the Religious Tract Society issued its translation of *A Dialogue between a Buddhist and His Christian Friend*.[77] The missionaries' output subsequently expanded to such a degree that in little more than a decade, between 1849 and 1861, more than 1.5 million Christian missionary tracts and pamphlets circulated around Ceylon.[78]

In Ceylon, as in Calcutta, however, this prompted local responses, in this case from Buddhists who adopted Sinhala-language printing to proselytize their own teachings and refute those of their Christian critics, before later turning on Ceylon's Muslim communities. In 1862 the purchase of a second-hand mission press previously owned by the Church Missionary Society enabled the first of these new Buddhist proselytizers, Mohotivatte Gunananda (1823–1890), to start publishing large numbers of pamphlets and chapbooks from Colombo. He began his disputational activities by responding in print to *Kristiyani Prajñapti* (*Evidences and Doctrines of Christianity*), an 1848 tract by the Wesleyan missionary Daniel Gogerly (1792–1862).[79] In his rejoinder, Gunananda claimed that Moses was little more than a murderer and that the birth of Jesus was accompanied by the mass execution of children, all of which proved Christianity to be a vicious and bloodthirsty creed.[80] His polemics went further than those of his Muslim counterparts in Calcutta, for whom Moses was as revered a prophet as Muhammad.

By the 1870s the Buddhist Tract Society was issuing numerous Sinhala works in response to the Christian critique of Buddhism. These strident Buddhist propagational tracts were printed in editions of up to eight thousand copies.[81] Yet in some cases at least, these polemics produced more accurate understanding of the other religion: Gogerly's *Kristiyani Prajñapti* was probably the first accurate European presentation of the Buddha's teachings that was based on sources in the ancient Pali language, and even Gunananda meticulously cited the Bible to support his case.[82] This is not to say that more accurate understanding necessarily led to agreement, because as each partly realized, the tenets of the other were contradictory or irreconcilable with their own. Such exchanges were therefore not prejudicial polemics so much as responses to the considered conclusion that different moral and theological systems were not all commensurable. Examples included *Sadakalika-mevum-kara-devi-kenek Neti Bava* (*On the Nonexistence of an Eternal Creator*) and *Yehovah-visin Satdavase Kala-ki-de* (*What Jehovah Has Said and Done in Seven Days*), published in 1892 and 1894, respectively, which rejected the Christian Creation story as incompatible with Buddhist cosmological doctrines.[83] Such findings were enabled by the comparisons made possible by scripture translations; critical comparison was promoted further through the format of the printed dialogue. Among the many examples of such printed disputational dialogues were the 1889 *Gautama-Budun-kavuda* (*Who Is Gautama Buddha?*), a Catholic tract against the Buddha, and *Mithya-vada-khandana* (*False Condemnation*), its Buddhist response from later the same year.[84]

Yet other responses to this polemical exchange of information tried to find common ground between Christianity and Buddhism. As early as the 1830s, the monk Bovala Dhammananda presented Jesus as having been sent, like Buddha, to the material world out of compassion for humankind, whereas the knowledge of Buddhism that missionaries transmitted to Europe and America eventually led to the emergence of a "Protestant Buddhism."[85] In 1880 the arrival in Colombo of Henry Steel Olcott, the American founder of the Theosophical Society, helped promote this new, "Protestantized" Buddhism through his erstwhile disciple, the aforementioned pioneer Buddhist missionary Dharmapala. Olcott's arrival led to the creation of the Buddhist Theosophical Society, which founded its own press in Colombo in 1883. In less than a decade, it issued over 80,000 books promoting its quasi-Christian version of Buddhism, not least through the Sinhala translation of Olcott's Christian-style *Buddhist Catechism*, which ironically drew on Orientalist studies.[86] Its Sinhala version, *Bauddha-kathopakathana*, went through several printings of 27,000 copies each.[87] Anglophone periodicals such as the *Buddhist* and the *Maha-Bodhi Journal* allowed a new generation of bilingual Buddhist readers to share their ideas, which they in turn passed on to publications in their own languages. This led to the founding of Sinhala journals such as *Bauddha-gedara* (*The Buddhist Home*) and *Kalyana-mitraya* (*The True Friend*), which copied the names of rival Christian journals.[88]

Along with the translation of Olcott's *Buddhist Catechism* into Sinhala and Japanese, his and Dharmapala's proselytizing travels encouraged other new Ceylonese missionaries to engage with other Buddhist regions of Asia. By 1895 Singapore had also become an outpost for their Christian-influenced Buddhism through the arrival of the Buddhist Theosophical Society and Dharmapala's offshoot Maha-Bodhi Society. The new Protestant Buddhism that spread through the ports of maritime Asia enabled Colombo to become the hub for new forms of Buddhist education predicated on close attention to the Pali canon, attracting students from Burma, Siam, and even Japan.[89] This was not, then, the discrete solidarity of an "Asia without Europe" that Asianist ideologues were just beginning to envisage: in theological no less than infrastructural terms, Europeans played key roles in these inter-Asian Buddhist exchanges.

Yet what is striking about the spread of the maritime public sphere to Ceylon is the limited effect it had on understanding other non-Buddhist cultures of Asia. Though close engagement with Christianity spurred the production of many self-projecting Sinhala works on Buddhism, as well as renewed connections with coreligionists in Burma, Siam, Singapore, and Japan, before 1900 at least very few works were printed in Sinhala that dealt with the religious traditions of other Asian peoples.[90] The main exception were a number of Hindu texts, which Buddhist scholars were able to translate through their knowledge of Sanskrit.

In terms of literary translations into Sinhala from other Asian traditions, the main example comprised the several editions of the *Arabian Nights*, though these were translated from the English versions of Edward Lane and James Mason rather than directly from Arabic.[91] There appears to have been no Sinhala version of the Quran available to Buddhist readers on Ceylon, whether for sympathetic study or disputatious rebuttal.[92] Although the trilingual Galle stone inscription in Chinese, Persian, and Tamil testified to Ceylon's brief medieval links with China, even foundational works on China's Daoist and Confucianist traditions remained similarly inaccessible in Sinhala.[93]

Calcutta as a Buddhological Crossroads

The polemical exchanges provoked by the first generations of Christian missionaries in Ceylon and Bengal, however, formed only part of the picture of intercultural exchange around the Bay of Bengal. Calcutta especially, and also Colombo, became the focus for the more secular investigations of Buddhism by the Orientalists and their Indian interlocutors. Meanwhile, as the nineteenth century wore on, a number of missionaries and other Christian writers developed more appreciative approaches to the Buddhist religion they better understood through the linguistic researches of their forebears. Through these twofold approaches, toward the end of the century Calcutta emerged as the key site in Asia for sifting and sharing information on Buddhism between European and Asian intellectuals. For all parties involved, however, their inquiries still faced numerous obstacles and followed many a false trail.

Through such shared but tortuous routes, modern Indian conceptions of Buddhism were forged through the creative dialectic of projecting the self and appreciating the other in which Europeans also played an important part. After the disappearance of the Buddhist religion from its original Indian homeland during the medieval period, it was only in the mid-nineteenth century that Indian scholars began to research the history of Buddhism, particularly as presented in the lost texts of ancient Buddhists themselves rather than in the antagonistic accounts of medieval Hindu Brahmins for whom the Buddha had become the acme of the arch-heretic.

A major impetus came from the textual and then archaeological investigations of the Orientalists associated with the Asiatic Society of Bengal (founded in 1784), which had issued some of the very first European accounts of Buddhism in the pages of its Calcutta-based journal, *Asiatick Researches*. Even so, by the 1820s not only were European researchers still debating whether "Buddoo" was a historical figure or a mythological god; they were also still unclear whether his religion had originated in Persia, Mongolia, or even Africa.[94] But by the 1850s the argument was firmly won in favor of the Indian origins of Buddhism, not least through deciphering the linguistic evidence of lost Sanskrit scriptures recovered from Kathmandu by Orientalists and their Indian and Nepalese colleagues.[95] Gradually, the Buddha was returned from mythology to history and, by the same token, reclaimed for India.

As the Orientalists' Buddhological subfield expanded over the following decades, it came to encompass lexicographical aids like grammars and dictionaries, translations of Buddhist scriptures, and historical reconstructions of the doctrinal development of the religion's varied forms. By the 1870s, through further probing of ancient Sanskrit and Pali sources by local Buddhist scholars in Ceylon, the erstwhile colonial official Thomas Rhys Davids (1843–1922) established a biographical outline for the career and teachings of the historical Buddha Gautama as they unfolded across northern India around the fifth or sixth century "before Christ."[96] The Christian dating system provided a chronological rubric for ancient history that would in turn be borrowed for books in Asian languages. Meanwhile, the founding of the Archaeological Survey of India in 1861 saw its longtime director Sir Alexander Cunningham (1814–1893) make the discovery of material remains of the religion his chief mission so as to fill out the sparse textual evidence of early Buddhism.[97]

Christian missionaries also played a role in distributing this newfound information. In the introduction, we saw how such missionaries affected intercultural engagements around the Bay of Bengal through their many polemical texts that kickstarted the public sphere. But this was only one aspect of the European contribution to inter-Asian understanding. There was also a more secular, empirical, and in some cases ecumenical pattern of engaging with non-Christian religions. This would incrementally produce a large body of knowledge about Buddhism in the major European—and Asian—languages. Even as early as 1850, the missionaries' educational role in translating the geographical books we saw spreading the idea of "Asia" also saw the same textbooks informing Indian readers in neutral terms that the people of Burma, Siam, Japan, and China mostly followed the religion of Bodh.[98]

As the century progressed, a new generation of Christian activists renounced the polemical mode of interreligious engagement their predecessors had favored. Taking up the cause of education for the masses, numerous missionaries became involved in the distribution (if less often the actual investigation) of the more positive picture of Buddhism taking shape through the Orientalists' research. A case in point is John Clark Marshman (1794–1877), whose father we have seen penning Bengali critiques of Hindu beliefs as one of the polemical pioneers of printing in Calcutta. As numerous other missionaries established Bengali and Urdu schools for Hindu and Muslim children across northern India, Marshman junior turned to writing educational textbooks, most influentially his *History of India from Remote Antiquity to the Accession of the Mogul Dynasty*, which was first published in Calcutta in 1836.[99] Over the subsequent decades, Marshman's history not only went through numerous revised editions to keep pace with the Orientalists' latest discoveries; it also went through numerous translations into such major Indian languages as Bengali, Hindi, and Urdu.[100] Marshman was hardly a promoter of Buddhism—he remained a committed Christian who carefully inserted the birth of Jesus into his depiction of the Indian past—but he did disseminate basic historical knowledge of the religion to the many Indians who attended missionary schools. In recounting the life of "Goutumu the Boodh" as having taken place in India, he also presented Buddhism as an Indian religion.

At the same time that Marshman was active, the cause of Indian education was also taken up by the Reverend Alexander Duff (1806–1878), albeit in his case by promoting Anglophone education for Indians.[101] In addition to founding many schools across Bengal (and helping establish the University of Calcutta), in 1844 Duff cofounded the *Calcutta Review,* which sought "to bring together such useful information, and propagate such sound opinions, relating to Indian affairs" that might contribute "to the amelioration of the condition of the people."[102] Among the varieties of "useful information" included in its pages over the following decades were dozens of articles on Buddhism, some written by such leading Orientalists as the Oxford-based Sanskritist Sir Monier Monier-Williams (1819–1899) and the aforementioned Pali specialist Thomas Rhys Davids.[103] Other articles had a more Christian flavor, albeit finding ecumenical common ground with the teachings of a compassionate Gautama who gradually took on the guise of an Indian Jesus.[104] Though these articles were published in English, the *Calcutta Review* was targeted at Bengal's growing Anglophone middle class, who, through conversations or publications of their own, filtered these ideas into Bengali. Yet even when such bilingual Bengalis bridged the barrier of language, the *Calcutta Review* still presented conceptual obstacles to inter-Asian understanding. In line with the journal's aim of disseminating "useful information . . . relating to Indian affairs," its articles on Buddhism overwhelmingly focused on India. Aside from the occasional foray into Tibet and Nepal, Buddhism was presented primarily as an ancient Indian religion rather than a living tradition of other Asian regions.[105]

Fortunately, missionary ventures like Marshman's *History* and the *Calcutta Review* were by no means the only mechanisms for distributing findings on Buddhism through Calcutta's informational bridgehead; a series of pioneering Bengali scholars contributed more directly to the rediscovery of Buddhism. Since European researchers almost always relied on the (sometimes very substantial) assistance of Indian (and, farther south, Ceylonese) scholars, this gradually led to the formation of a circle of Indian Buddhologists, based mainly in Calcutta. Yet these Bengali investigators of Buddhism did not merely echo the Indian orientation of the *Calcutta Review.* By focusing on Sanskrit texts that were more linguistically familiar through their own Hindu backgrounds, they in many cases amplified this Indocentric interpretation as

Buddhism eventually became a cultural asset of the nascent Indian nationalist movement.

Rather than coming from living Buddhist societies across the Bay of Bengal in Burma, Siam, or Ceylon, much of their informational input came from the Royal Durbar Library of Nepal (itself regarded as a repository of lost Indian manuscripts). Since the 1830s, knowledge of its holdings had been transmitted to Calcutta by Brian Houghton Hodgson (1801?–1894), the lone East India Company representative in Kathmandu. By collecting Buddhist texts in Sanskrit, Pali, and Tibetan with the help of his Nepalese associate, Pandit Amritananda, and sending copies to the library of the Asiatic Society in Calcutta, Hodgson gradually transformed both the European and Indian scholarly understanding of Buddhism.[106] As the codicological findings of Amritananda and Hodgson were gradually followed up in Calcutta, they shaped the interpretive trajectory of a small circle of Hindu scholars, many of whom had studied at the city's elite Presidency College.

The earliest significant figure was Raja Rajendralal Mitra (1822–1891), whose early writings expressed the sort of wild speculations that characterized initial European theories about the origins of Buddhism. In 1858 Mitra's first book compared Buddhist doctrines with those of the Norse cult of Odin, taking the Buddha about as far as possible from the living societies of maritime Asia and instead plunging him into the cold ancient waters of the North Sea.[107] But over the following decades, Mitra—who held the position of librarian at the Asiatic Society—began to draw on the manuscripts being sent to the society's library by Amritananda and Hodgson. By making use of the Sanskrit texts from Kathmandu, Mitra and his younger contemporaries began the process of reclaiming Buddhism as part of their own Indian heritage.

By working with the colonial Calcutta School-Book Society, and founding his own journal, *Bibhidartha Sangraha*, Mitra began transferring these new ideas into Bengali. His most influential contribution to Buddhist studies, however, was his English work, *The Sanskrit Buddhist Literature of Nepal*, published in Calcutta in 1882.[108] It would later provide the celebrated poet Tagore with much of his information on Buddhism, leading him and other Anglophone Indian intellectuals in turn to form an Indocentric conception of a religion that, ironically, had been kept alive for most of the previous millennium by other Asian peoples.[109]

Over the following decades, Himalayan pandits, colonial Orientalists, and Anglophone Indians continued this Buddhological supply line to Calcutta.

When in 1895 another learned Bengali Hindu, Nobin Chandra Das, published his English rendition of the Sanskrit *Sakya Sinha* under the title *Legends and Miracles of Buddha*, the manuscript on which he based his translation had been brought to Calcutta from Tibet.[110] Like Mitra, who translated European maps and geographies into Bengali, Nobin was involved in disseminating— and pushing back in time—the European idea of Asia.[111]

Further breakthroughs were made by Hariprasad Sastri (1853–1931), who took his BA in Sanskrit from Presidency College before heading overland to the Nepalese sources of Amritananda and Hodgson's discoveries. In 1898 he joined the British Museum's Sanskritist, Cecil Bendall (1856–1906), in Kathmandu to further investigate the Durbar Library.[112] The landmark English catalogue he produced of its Buddhist manuscripts was published in Calcutta by the Baptist Mission Press, which by then had long moved on from diatribes against non-Christian religions. In the meantime, the daring Bengali explorer-turned-scholar Sarat Chandra Das (1849–1917) drew on his imperial intelligence missions to Tibet to produce an important body of work (albeit mainly in English) on Tibetan Buddhism, the sources of which were traced to the final, Tantric phase of Buddhism in India (and more specifically Bengal).[113] Sarat subsequently served as secretary to the Buddhist Text Society of India, which was founded in Calcutta in 1893.

In such ways, Calcutta played the key role of informational crossroads for the Indian rediscovery of Buddhism. In varying degrees of collaboration with their Orientalist counterparts, it was from the intellectual emporium of the British imperial capital that learned Bengali Hindus such as Mitra, Sastri, Sarat, and Nobin presented their investigations to the English and to a lesser extent the Bengali-reading public. Yet despite Mitra's and Sastri's port city location, their focus was principally on the early Indian Sanskrit canon of Buddhism, rather than on the ancient Pali texts kept alive elsewhere in Burma, Ceylon, and Thailand. Not only were their main sources of information both ancient and Indian, but, with the exception of Chandra Das, who had resided in a Tibetan monastery, they were also removed from the living Buddhist religiosity of Asia. And so Buddhist literatures in Burmese, Thai, and Sinhala were wholly overlooked in favor of either ancient Sanskrit texts or medieval Bengali ones that could be claimed, like the Buddha himself, for India.

Nonetheless, by around 1890 a learned Indian intellectual engagement with Buddhism had reemerged after a silence of many centuries. It soon led to publications in Bengali, such as Sarat Chandra Das's translation from Sanskrit of legends of the Buddha.[114] In a few cases, these Bengali works were translated into other Indian languages, as was the 1883 *Buddhadeva-charita* (*Life of Buddha*) by Krishnakumar Mitra (1852–1936), which six years later was reissued in Gujarati from Bombay, and the 1892 *Asoka-charita* (*Life of Ashoka*) by Krishna Bihari Sen, the Anglophone rector of Calcutta's Albert College.[115] But these too were based on the Sanskrit sources uncovered by Mitra's circle, as well as English studies in the case of Sen's book, bearing little if any relation to the living Buddhism practiced in other regions of Asia.[116] Moreover, while Bengali journals such as *Prabasi* and *Vasumati* began to include articles on Buddhism, most of the erudite works written by Mitra, Sastri, and the Bombay-based Parsi scholar Gushtaspshah Nariman (1873–1933) were still published in English as part of the combined investigations of Indian and British scholars, not least those of a markedly Christian inclination. Even Girishchandra Ghosh's Bengali play, *Buddhadev-charit,* first performed in 1885, was based on the appealing depiction of the Buddha in Sir Edwin Arnold's book-length poem, *The Light of Asia,* which had appeared in 1879.[117]

A hugely popular biography of the Buddha, *The Light of Asia* built on the positive Christological depiction of Buddha that had gradually emerged among the second and third generation of missionaries in Ceylon and Bengal and found further expression in the *Calcutta Review.* Pointing to the dialogical character—the multilingual conversation—that produced both European and Asian intercultural knowledge, Arnold also drew on his studies of Sanskrit with Krishna Shastri Chiplunkar (1824–1878), who for his part had previously learned English and translated Samuel Johnson's *Rasselas* into Marathi.[118] Arnold's paean to the gentle Buddha exerted a considerable influence not only on the Calcutta intelligentsia after *The Light of Asia* appeared in Bengali in 1885, but on countless other Indians who read it in a series of other translations, including Marathi (1894), Tamil (1898), and Telugu (1902).[119] By the end of the century, Arnold's book had been through over a hundred editions, not only in Indian languages, but also in Japanese and later in Thai.[120] While it is difficult to statistically verify, Arnold's *Light of Asia* was probably the most widely translated work on Buddhism into Asian languages during the entire period covered in this book. This points again to the complex role played by Christian scholars in the newfound Indian—and even Japanese—understanding of Buddhism.

By the fin de siècle, Arnold was not the only European mediating knowledge of the Buddha back to India in Jesus-like form. In 1894 the German theologian Paul Carus (1852–1919) published a pair of Buddhaphilic books. One was *Buddhism and Its Christian Critics,* a defense of the religion that drew on Carus's deep awareness of earlier missionary polemics. The other was the cross-Atlantic best seller *The Gospel of Buddha*. It was soon being translated into Asian languages too: after a young graduate from Tokyo called Suzuki Daisetsu Teitaro (1870–1966) went to study with Carus in Illinois, he was soon put to work on a Japanese version. The book proved similarly successful in Indian translation, though the resulting Urdu text was a strange fruit indeed.[121] Carus had tried to present a plain Protestant Buddhism, shorn of rituals and statues and centered on the moral message of a scriptural "gospel." In a corresponding Indian domestication of Buddhist teachings, the Hindu translator instead made use of the religious vocabulary of Hinduism and Islam.[122] Still, the translated *Gospel of Buddha* effectively repackaged the lost religion for Indian readers. In place of the countless complex sutras preserved in Pali and Sanskrit manuscript scrolls, the pared-down teachings of the Buddha were now readily available in a single and simple vernacular volume. The translation of Carus's book was also issued before the *Dhammapada*—probably the closest record of the Buddha's actual teachings—was translated into Bengali, Urdu, or any other major modern Indian language.

Half a century later, *The Gospel of Buddha* would also become one of the earliest book-length accounts of the religion in Arabic.[123] Meanwhile, by 1916 the works of Carus and Arnold had jointly inspired Ananda Kentish Coomaraswamy (1877–1947), an influential Ceylonese Hindu art historian and metaphysician, to write his *Buddha and the Gospel of Buddhism*.[124] Though Coomaraswamy was also influenced by Okakura, the Japanese art historian and impresario of Asianism, whose work he read in English, he drew most of his information on Buddhism from European sources.[125] And so, less than a century after Christian missionaries began their research on Buddhism to better refute it, Europeans were effectively promoting the religion they had come to appreciate through their investigations. Through the likes of Coomaraswamy and the Buddhist reformist missionary Dharmapala, this was even the case in Buddhist-majority Ceylon.

Meanwhile, back in Calcutta, the Bengali researcher Hariprasad Sastri continued to work closely with British scholars as the next librarian of the Asiatic Society in Calcutta. Further cementing Buddhism's newfound ties to India, he turned to the study of what he called "living Buddhism in Bengal."[126] Published in 1897, his pamphlet traced the survival of a form of vernacular Buddhism in Bengal after what he characterized as the medieval "invasion of the Mussulmans [Muslims], who massacred a very large number of Buddhist priests," with the result that Buddhism was "suppressed by fire and sword

... and the wholesale massacre by Mussulmans."[127] This idea of a widespread Muslim "massacre" of medieval Buddhists—itself previously promoted by British historians—was further publicized by such influential figures as the Bengali newspaper impresario Narendranath Sen (1843–1911), whose *Indian Mirror* shaped the image many Anglophone Indians acquired of Buddhism's demise in its original homeland.[128] This narrative was also picked up by Okakura, who included a version in the very paragraphs that followed his declaration of Asian unity in *The Ideals of the East,* which he completed in 1902 during his stay in Calcutta.[129]

Sastri's research involved little direct contact with "living Buddhists" outside his Indian homeland, however. His investigative scope remained not merely India, but his home region and, through the verses he cited in his *Discovery of Living Buddhism,* his own Bengali mother tongue. Here was the encounter with the religious other as a form of self-discovery. Indeed, Sastri found this folk Buddhism right on his doorstep in the temple to Dharma on Calcutta's Jaun Bazaar Street. Despite Calcutta's close connections with Rangoon, he compared these Bengali rituals with those of ancient Nepal rather than with living Buddhists across the sea-lanes in Burma.[130] After all, it had been in Kathmandu that he had discovered the palm-leaf manuscripts of the early Buddhist mystical songs known as *Charyapada (Songs of Realization),* which in 1916 he would publish in Bengali (with Sanskrit commentary) as a part of his *Hajar Bacharer Purano Bangala Bhasaya Bauddhagan-o-Doha (Thousand Years of Buddhist Songs and Couplets in the Bengali Language).*[131]

This textual rather than ethnographic orientation continued through the archaeological excavation of Buddhist sites not only in India, but in the Chinese Central Asian province of Xinjiang, whence many ancient manuscripts (not least in Indian languages) were carried back to the museum and libraries of Calcutta.[132] These excavations of lost Buddhist temples and monasteries were based largely on the travelogue of the Chinese pilgrim Xuanzang (c. 602–664), which had been translated into French, English, and Urdu. Xuanzang also pointed to India's Buddhist-mediated connections with China, which we will later see being taken up by several of India's pioneering Sinologists as evidence of India's shaping influence on East Asian civilization.[133] It is likely that the Urdu version of Xuanzang (which stated on the cover that it was "translated from English") was based on the translation made in 1884 by the Reverend Samuel Beal, sometime naval chaplain and professor of Chinese at University College London.[134] But when Xuanzang's travels appeared in Urdu in 1921, the continued unfamiliarity of Indian readers with basic Buddhist

terminology meant that his translator chose to deploy a Muslim (and particularly Sufi) vocabulary, with which his readers were far more familiar.

By this time, the manuscript discoveries made along Xuanzang's ancient
itinerary across Central Asia were also shaping the *Literary History of Sanskrit
Buddhism*, written (albeit in English) by Gushtaspshah Nariman.[135] In 1927
Nariman built on the Central Asian excavations of the Hungarian Aurel Stein
(1862–1943) and the Nepalese investigations of Britons and Bengalis by heading to Afghanistan, where he inspected the Indic inscriptions recently found
in the Buddhist monasteries of Bamiyan.[136] As we will see when we turn to the
parallel Muslim engagement with Buddhism during the same decade, Nariman's visit coincided with a new generation of Afghan intellectuals' discovery
of "their" Buddhist past by way of the translation into Dari-Persian of French
archaeological reports on Afghanistan's ancient sites.[137]

Although in his *Literary History of Sanskrit Buddhism* Nariman did make
various references to Burma and Ceylon, the chief purpose of his book was
to promote the status of Sanskrit texts (presented as the "ancient Indian national literature") over the Pali canon of Burma and Ceylon, which he claimed
European scholars had unduly emphasized.[138] Effectively, in a series of investigations oriented more toward the Indian self than the Asian other, Nariman
and his Bengali colleagues focused on the Sanskrit-based Mahayana school,
and to a lesser degree Bengal-disseminated Tantric Buddhism, rather than the
Pali-based Theravada traditions that had spread around the Bay of Bengal. As
we will see, even when Bengali scholars turned to the study of Chinese Buddhism, this Indian and Sanskritic orientation would remain in place, seeing
China serve as a site of self-projection for a "Greater India" whose cultural
influence reached right across Asia.[139]

Nonetheless, three important informational currents from maritime Asia
did contribute to the Indian engagement with Buddhism, and Calcutta played
a key role in channeling each of them.

The first current came from the Maha-Bodhi Society, which the Ceylonese
missionary Anagarika Dharmapala founded in Colombo in 1891 before shifting its base to Calcutta the following year.[140] Dharmapala launched the society
with the express goal of reclaiming from Hindu control the eponymous Maha-
Bodhi (Great Awakening) temple, some three hundred miles inland from Calcutta, which marked the spot where the Buddha had achieved enlightenment.
Yet the Ceylonese (and later Japanese) Buddhist rediscovery of their Indian
past was inseparable from European interest in recovering the history of a reli-

gion that had disappeared from India in the medieval period. Thereafter, the ruined Maha-Bodhi temple came under the control of a neighboring Hindu monastery, whose Buddhist past was not widely known till the 1880s, when the archaeologist Alexander Cunningham began his attempts to restore it, and Edwin Arnold, the Buddhaphile author of *The Light of Asia*, published a series of articles that drew the plight of this holiest of sites to the attention of Buddhists in Ceylon, including Dharmapala. Dharmapala's consequent attempt not only to reclaim the temple but also to project Buddhism back into India at large built on the Bay of Bengal's missionary exchanges as well, not least through his own tutelage with the American cofounder of the Theosophical Society (and later Buddhist convert), Henry Steel Olcott. Subsequently, Dharmapala's Maha-Bodhi Society had a tense relationship with India's non-Buddhist communities, whether the Hindus, from whom he sought to reclaim the temple as his society's founding goal, or the Muslims, whose medieval forebears he held responsible for the destruction of Indian Buddhism.[141]

Perhaps unsurprisingly, Dharmapala's Bengali contemporary—and Hindu missionary rival—Swami Vivekananda (1863–1902) showed a marked ambivalence toward Buddhism. Probably the most influential figure in modern Hinduism, Vivekananda admired the Buddha as an Indian sage while blaming his religion for India's martial decline.[142] Insofar as he presented the Buddha positively, it was in "Hinduized" form, as a paragon of ancient India's high morality.[143] His views hardened after an 1889 visit from Calcutta to Ceylon (which, he declared, "entirely disillusioned me"), prompting him to critique living Buddhism as a degraded religion by comparison with his revivified brand of muscular Hinduism.[144] As Vivekananda viewed matters, having received the sweet spiritual fruits of India by way of the Buddha's teachings, the Ceylonese had not only corrupted them; they were now daring to reexport these degraded doctrines back to India through the missionizing activities of Dharmapala.[145] Meanwhile, as debates about control of the Maha-Bodhi temple continued, Bengali newspapers such as *Bangavasi* protested at what they saw as the colonial government's preferential treatment of Buddhist rather than Hindu monuments.

The second informational channel was the Calcutta-based Buddhist Text Society of India, which Dharmapala helped establish and which held its first meeting in Calcutta's Albert Hall in 1892. The expertise and interests of its largely Bengali Hindu membership saw its early journal articles retain the focus on Indian and Himalayan forms of Buddhism rather than their counterparts across the Bay of Bengal, particularly in their living forms and "nonclassical" expressions through Burmese or Sinhala texts.[146] The editions of Sanskrit Mahayana texts from Japan and China prepared by the Oxford-based German scholar Max Müller (1823–1900) helped a small number of Indian scholars gain access to such lost works. But for the most part, the Buddhist Text Society was anything but a popular enterprise, producing learned articles in English and costly edited texts in Sanskrit that bypassed the affordable side of the public sphere, as did the Devanagari-script edition of the Pali *Sutta Nipata,* published in 1924 by P. V. Bapat (1894–1991).[147]

The third informational channel was Calcutta University, which around 1900 expanded its Buddhological training beyond Sanskrit by starting an MA degree in Pali that used textbooks drawing on earlier missionary investigations.[148] In 1901 the first person to graduate with this degree was the Bengali scholar Satish Chandra Vidyabhusan (1870–1920). Eight years later he sailed to Ceylon to deepen his knowledge of Pali, before returning to Calcutta to take up a teaching position at Presidency College and serve as assistant editor for the Buddhist Text Society. After Calcutta University founded a proper Department of Pali in 1907, it attracted another Bengali scholar, Benimadhab Barua (1888–1948), who made major contributions to the history of Indian philosophy. Barua, however, had a doctoral degree from London, so most of his highly erudite monographs were written in English; even his 1921 edition of an early Prakrit version of the *Dhammapada* (*Footsteps of the Law*) was issued in romanized script intended for an Anglophone readership.[149] Moreover, far more Indian graduates of Calcutta University took positions in the colonial bureaucracy in Burma than devoted themselves to the study of books in Burma's languages.

Yet even if the study of Buddhist languages—especially living ones like Burmese—remained the rare and recondite pursuit of a tiny cadre of Bengali scholars, their investigations marked an informational sea change in the Indian understanding of a religion that had all but disappeared from the subcontinent in the medieval era. But this recovery of the Buddhist past was not just a matter of assembling reliable and neutral data, as the proselytizing efforts of the Ceylonese missionary Dharmapala ran into the competing religious mission of the reformist Hindu Vivekananda. Nor were these two campaigners, Ceylonese and Indian, the only Asians using Calcutta as a base for promoting or critiquing Buddhism. For the great colonial port also became a site for émigré Iranians to engage with the unfamiliar Buddhist culture across the Bay of Bengal in Burma.

A Persian Channel in the Polemical Public Sphere

Just as the infrastructures of empire enabled Dharmapala to project his Protestant-influenced Buddhism through his printing activities in Calcutta, so they enabled many Iranians to make ample use of printing in the closely connected ports of Calcutta and Rangoon. Whether by participating in the polemical public sphere to promote their own religions, or by grappling with the sheer unfamiliarity of the Buddhist religion, for which there was not even a proper name in Persian, inter-Asian interactions between the Bay of Bengal and Iran formed another case of projecting the self and appreciating the other.

As far back as 1805, the increasing involvement of Iranian merchants in the Bay of Bengal had led Iran's Qajar government to dispatch embassies there.[150] These diplomatic missions continued sporadically over the next half century, leading to the 1858 journey of the Iranian official Fazlullah Husayni, which would produce a combined account of both India and Burma. Husayni's Persian travelogue was based on a fact-finding journey via Calcutta to Rangoon and thence upriver to what was then still the Kombaung dynastic capital at Mandalay.[151] Upon arriving in Calcutta, his party stayed as guests of the Iranian merchant Mirza ʿAbd al-Karim Shirazi.[152] Through him and the British officials they met, the Iranian visitors primarily gathered information on the region's trade while also attempting to make sense of its unfamiliar peoples.

Husayni's Persian report gives us a sense of the kind of intercultural knowledge that such a commercially oriented fact-finding mission might collect. He took extensive notes about the British system of administration, including the army composed of European and Indian troops.[153] He recorded his impressions of Calcutta, describing its British section, where its grand buildings were set in wide and clean streets, and its "native" section, where "Indians, Bengalis, and Hindus" resided in small houses on streets that he described as narrow and very dirty.[154] Nonetheless, he pointed out positively, there was a great deal of trade and many large shops. While there were unsurprisingly many wealthy British merchants, there were also prosperous Armenian traders from Isfahan who dealt in opium and indigo.[155] Like other traveler-investigators we will encounter, Husayni was hosted by either fellow expatriates or followers of the same religion, which limited the intercultural scope of the information he could gather. As for non-Shiʿis, Husayni's brief depiction of Calcutta's other inhabitants was effectively limited to their physical appearance.[156] The superficiality of this description suggests that his interaction with these other peoples was minimal; the only specific cultural group he mentioned was the Zoroastrians, who were already familiar from his homeland.

When his party moved on to Burma and the Buddhist-ruled city of Mandalay, however, Husayni tried to go beyond the surface-level observation of physical appearance and outward behavior to understand more of the history and belief systems of its inhabitants.[157] Yet there were clear constraints on his investigations, both linguistic and conceptual. Like many of the other Middle Eastern and Indian authors to whose books we will turn, Husayni arrived in Mandalay with no preconception of, or even name for, the Buddhist religion. As a result, he used only the general term "religion of Burma's people" (*mazhab-i qawm-i Barma*) and the generic notion of the idol (*but*). Ironically, the term *but* had been adopted into Persian over a thousand years earlier from the Sanskrit term for the Buddha through early Muslim encounters with Buddhist temples in Central Asia. Following what subsequently became standard usage in Urdu as well as Persian, Husayni used the term *but* to refer to an idol in the most general sense. For he had no specific notion of the Buddha, still less of the many other celestial beings in the Burmese Buddhist pantheon.

Even so, Husayni attempted to grapple with the cultural differences he observed between the regions he visited, recognizing that Burmese "idol-worship" (*but-parasti*) differed from that of India, not least through the rules followed by the reclusive monks whom he correctly called *pongyis* (*pangi*), by borrowing the Burmese word into Persian.[158] Although his report was limited in its grasp of what it clearly presented as a markedly mysterious country—indeed, a land where trees turned into snakes—it was nonetheless sympathetic in its depiction of difference. Nonetheless, this was neither a deep nor an accurate depiction of Buddhism. Nor was it published, meaning that, such as it was, the information it contained was available only to government officials in Iran and not to the wider public.

As we will see, it would be another half century before even basic accounts of Buddhism began to be published in Iran. In the meantime, however, exiled Iranian printers who were active in India's ports provided their compatriots with glimpses across the Bay of Bengal. In 1847 the Bombay-based printer Zayn al-'Abidin Kirmani published the Persian travelogue *Tuhfat al-'Alam* (*Rarity of the World*), written half a century earlier by Mir 'Abd al-Latif Khan (1757–1806).[159] An Iranian émigré to Calcutta, 'Abd al-Latif included in his book a description of the geography and exports of Burma, along with a portrayal of the customs of the Burmese court, which, like Husayni's work, presented Burma's political culture in the commensurable terms of Persianate kingship. Hinting at informational collusions that we will see shaping Indian and Middle Eastern knowledge of other regions of Asia, 'Abd al-Latif also partly drew on a colonial study of Burma by way of Michael Symes's *Account of an Embassy to the Kingdom of Ava*.[160]

By the 1900s other Iranian émigrés had founded several newspapers in both Bombay and Calcutta, which were exported to readers back in Iran. Reflecting Calcutta's formative role in the maritime public sphere, the first newspapers ever published in Persian had in fact appeared there rather than in Iran itself.[161] The most influential of the exile papers was *Habl al-Matin* (*The Strong Cord*), established in Calcutta in 1893 by Sayyid Jalal al-Din Kashani (1863–1930).[162] Calcutta's far-reaching communications infrastructure allowed *Habl al-Matin* to gather information from the Bay of Bengal to the Sea of Japan, so that its weekly Persian edition effectively served as Iran's main window onto the wide vistas of maritime Asia. Nonetheless, it drew much if not most of its information on these other regions from the English newspapers that were readily available in Calcutta through the network of Anglophone newspapers that reached from Calcutta to Singapore, Yokohama, and Guangzhou.

But when Kashani turned to printing books as well as newspapers, he waded into the public sphere's polemical currents. One of the books he published was *Mukalima-yi Sayyah-i Irani ba Shakhs-i Hindi* (*Conversations of an Iranian Traveler with an Indian Person*), an imaginary dialogue written by his brother, Sayyid Hasan Kashani.[163] As the format of the text shows, the genre of the debate used in Christian and Muslim missionary publications could also serve as a vehicle for political no less than religious discussions. Here, though, the Indian was a friend who gave liberal advice to the fictional Iranian traveler, presenting colonial Calcutta as a role model for Iran, with its press, religious, and other freedoms presented positively in comparison to what Iranian exiles like the Kashani brothers increasingly regarded as the corrupt and backward condition of their own homeland.

It was not only imaginary debates but also invented travel books that served this polemical purpose of self-critique. In 1906 the Habl al-Matin Press in Calcutta also published the *Siyahatnama-yi Ibrahim Beg* (*Travelogue of Ibrahim Beg*), an account of an invented journey from Egypt to Iran.[164] Written by the merchant-turned-journalist Zayn al-'Abidin Maragha'i (1840–1910), the fictional travelogue used positive accounts of other cultures to critique Iranian social customs and politics, which Maragha'i hoped to reform. Yet the *Siyahatnama-yi Ibrahim Beg* was not so much a work of intercultural engagement as an ethnographical fantasy in which the knowledge of the other lent reforming lessons for empowering the self. The Habl al-Matin Press rapidly ran off an Urdu version, but it was not translated into other Asian languages, which for better or worse limited the distribution of its depiction of the Middle East.

By the end of the nineteenth century, echoing what we have seen among the Bay of Bengal's Buddhists, new kinds of Iranian religious organization were founded in the ports of India and Burma. Iranian missionaries, both Muslim and Baha'i, similarly adapted the techniques of the Christian missionaries whose publications we have already seen spreading from Calcutta to Iran. As a result, the Persian channel in the maritime public sphere became increasingly characterized by political and religious controversies that ranged from critiques of the Qajar Dynasty's despotism, such as those of Maragha'i and Kashani, to vehement responses to the combined missionary threats of Christianity and Iran's home-grown Baha'ism.

In 1903 ongoing Christian proselytizing in Isfahan prompted the founding of a counter-organization called the *Anjuman-i Safakhana* (Society of the House of Peace) in response, where Muslim scholars hosted debates with local Christian converts. The society then launched a journal called *al-Islam* that published these discussions, emphasizing the rational basis of interreligious debate.[165] As the journal circulated through the ports linking Iran with both British India and the Ottoman Empire, it added further to the public sphere in which the genre of the theological debate played so central a role. In 1906 the key figure behind *al-Islam*, Sayyid Muhammad 'Ali (1878–1951), settled in Bombay. His proselytizing activities had already won him the sobriquet Da'i al-Islam (Missionary of Islam) after his earlier encounters with missionaries had led him to learn English and Hebrew so he could better refute—and understand—Christian doctrines.

Amid Bombay's manifold publishing opportunities, he founded a journal called *Da'wat-i Islam* (*Propagation of Islam*) that specialized in polemics against the various other religions being propagated from India's port, the effect of which had been felt in Iran for decades.[166] Published bilingually in Persian and Urdu, *Da'wat-i Islam* saw the anti-Islamic polemics that Christian missionaries had printed in Calcutta and Bombay in those same languages almost a century earlier come full circle as their Muslim missionary mirror made its return journey from Iran to India. Da'i al-Islam made full use of Bombay's mail steamers; the cover of his journal listed subscription rates for India, Iran, the Ottoman Empire, and even China.[167] Through the communication infrastructures of empire, Iranian missionaries were then able to project their own religion far across Asia.

This was the case not only for Muslims like Da'i al-Islam. In the meantime, wealthy members of Bombay's and Calcutta's substantial Parsi communities were funding the publication and export of numerous Zoroastrian texts in a manner that their impoverished coreligionists in Iran could ill afford.[168] Following the Bible-printing model of the missionaries, these printed books included ancient Avestan and Pahlavi liturgical texts conceived as Protestant-style "scriptures," such as Mubad Tirandaz Irani's translation of the *Khorda Avesta* (*Concise Avesta*) from Avestan to modern Persian, published in Bombay in 1882, and the various translations of the *Gathas* and *Yashts* subsequently made by Ibrahim Pourdavoud (1886–1968) and similarly issued in Bombay with the financial support of the merchant Peshotan Marker (1871–1965).[169]

Yet around the Bay of Bengal at least, the trajectory of this projection of Zoroastrianism diverged from that of Iranian Muslim (and, as we will see, Baha'i) missionaries through the decision by Parsi religious leaders not only to eschew the proselytizing path to winning converts, but ultimately to restrict the possibility of conversion entirely by promoting ideas of Persian ethnic purity.[170] By the late nineteenth century, the Parsis' commercial preeminence in Bombay, Calcutta, and Rangoon combined with the famed generosity of their community charities to make conversion to Zoroastrianism an attractive prospect for many underprivileged inhabitants of those cities.[171] But amid the expanding populations of the three great ports, fears that the number of potential converts could rapidly drain community resources led Parsi priests and lawyers to close the conversional gates to the community for Indian, Burmese, and even European outsiders. This process culminated in a series of trials that began in Rangoon in 1914 and finally reached the Privy Council in London, addressing the question of which community was responsible for the welfare of a girl called Bella, who was born in Burma in 1899. The focus of immense controversy, the trial became a test case for whether it was possible to convert to Zoroastrianism and thereby become a Parsi.[172] The Parsis were cultured urban citizens who deservedly won fame for their charitable contributions to many public causes that benefited various other communities. But the complexities of the inter-Asian encounter ultimately led them to prevent rather than promote conversion so as to protect the coffers of the communal self from the endless demands of impoverished others.

Though Parsi priests opted to prevent conversion to Zoroastrianism, the leaders of Iran's newest religion—Baha'ism—began an Asian-wide missionary venture in which the ports of the Bay of Bengal played a key self-projecting role. From its origins in the 1840s to its formal founding in 1863, Baha'ism had adopted the Protestant model of a printed vernacular scripture. Known as the *Bab* (Gateway), Sayyid 'Ali Muhammad Shirazi (1819–1850) served as the forerunner of Baha'ism. Yet in his earlier career, he had been a merchant in the

Persian Gulf, where many Indian (and British) traders were present. Having been exposed there to Christian missionary texts shipped out from Calcutta, he devised his *Kitab al-Bayan* (*Book of Explanation*) in corresponding mode, making many references to both the missionaries and their use of printing. This in turn influenced the decision of the founder proper of Baha'ism, Mirza Husayn-'Ali Nuri Baha'ullah (1817–1892), to likewise publish his revelations. He and his followers opted to do so in the ports of India, since by the 1880s religious censorship in Iran rendered Bombay the main early Baha'i publishing center.[173] Hence it was in Bombay that Baha'ullah's Persian scriptural revelations, *Kitab-i Yaqin* (*Book of Certainty*) and *Kitab-i Mubin* (*Book of Revelation*), and his Arabic text *Kitab al-Aqdas* (*Most Holy of Books*) were first printed by the Hasani Ziwar Press and Nasiri Press, which were operated by Iranian exiles.[174] Despite being fiercely criticized—indeed, violently persecuted—in Iran itself, Baha'ullah found supporters among the Iranian trading diaspora, particularly the Afnan family of Shirazi merchants, who underwrote the cost of this publishing and proselytizing effort through their trading network, which reached from Iran through the British imperial ports of Bombay and Calcutta and as far as Hong Kong.[175] Through the printing of proselytizing pamphlets and their own latter-day scriptures, Baha'is found themselves drawn into the polemical public sphere.

As Baha'ism became a missionary religion for which printing was of crucial importance, Bombay and Calcutta emerged as the centers of a small but expanding community of Indian converts. The next stage of this self-projecting encounter with other regions of Asia would see the dispatch of Baha'i missionaries to the bustling ports of Colombo and Rangoon (as well as Japan). Consequently, the intense controversies that surrounded the new religion found their way to Burma as Baha'is sought new converts there among its Christian, Buddhist, and Muslim communities alike. Yet as we will now examine, the ensuing exchange of rival tracts led to increased understanding of the doctrines of this unfamiliar new religion and of their potential implications for those who converted. Once again, inter-Asian understanding emerged through complex and contested channels rather than simple slogans of solidarity.

Debating Baha'ism between Bombay and Burma

The Baha'i outreach to the Bay of Bengal began in 1876, when the charismatic Iranian preacher Jamal Effendi (d. 1898) sailed from Bombay to Colombo, where he was met with such opposition from local Buddhist leaders that he was soon forced to retreat to Madras.[176] It was there that he converted a young Iranian Muslim textile trader called Sayyid Mustafa Rumi (d. 1942 or 1945), with whom by way of Calcutta he subsequently set off for Burma. Arriving in Rangoon in May 1878, the two men were helped by another Iranian merchant, Hajji Sayyid Mahdi Shirazi, who after converting to the new religion helped them rent a house near the magnificent Iranian Shi'i mosque in the heart of Rangoon. It was there, amid the shops and trading offices on Mogul Street, that they set about preaching Baha'ullah's message. Their proselytizing immediately caused controversy. When Shirazi dared make a pronouncement about Baha'ism during Friday prayers at the mosque, he was reportedly lucky to escape alive.[177] Nonetheless, amid the theological debates and denunciations, he and Rumi did win followers. Among their early converts were not only Iranian merchants, but also a number of Indian Sunni traders and a Khoja Isma'ili Muslim called 'Ali Bhuga.[178] Buddhists would soon follow.

In early 1879, Effendi and Rumi moved on to Mandalay, at this point still the capital of the Buddhist Konbaung Dynasty. Although the protests of local Buddhists and Muslims forced them to move, they continued both to preach and to publish; Effendi paid one of Rangoon's Indian publishing houses to issue several pamphlets in the widely read language of Urdu, as well as an Urdu book entitled *Ma'yar al-Haqiqat* (*Touchstone of Truth*).[179] As a result, they gradually won followers among the Indian Muslim trading groups that had followed the railroad up from the coast, as well as local Burmese Muslims, including the silk merchant 'Abd al-Sattar (who bore the Burmese name U Koo).[180] At this point, the two Baha'i missionaries returned to Rangoon, where Rumi would spend the rest of his life propagating the new religion among Buddhists and Muslims alike. Yet while these were indubitably inter-Asian encounters, the flow of intercultural knowledge was overwhelmingly one-way: Effendi and Rumi taught Burmese Buddhists about Baha'ism rather than vice versa.

When in 1905 the American Baha'i convert Sydney Sprague reached Rangoon with his Iranian coreligionist Adib Talaqani (1848–1919), he found a flourishing Baha'i mission there; public meetings convened weekly at the large house of the merchant Shirazi and his son, Sayyid Isma'il.[181] Even so, Sprague reported, there was much opposition: he recorded a long sequence of denunciations as "the Roman Catholic priests forbade their flocks to come to the meetings, the Protestant ministers spoke against us. A Mohammedan Mulla preached openly in a city square, warning the Mohammedans to keep away from the Bahá'ís, who possessed a power able to turn them away from the true faith. One ardent Buddhist used to come to the meetings with the sole purpose of drawing away the Buddhists, a Hindu came regularly to interrupt and argue against us."[182] Nonetheless, Baha'i missionaries continued to cross the Bay of Bengal, among them Fazil Mazandarani (1881–1957), who sailed to India then Burma in 1911 after being expelled from the Shi'i holy city of Najaf, where he had tried to present senior Shi'i clerics with Baha'i missionary publications. He would later briefly describe his travels in his triumphant nine-volume history of the Babi and Baha'i religions, *Tarikh-i Zuhur al-Haqq* (*History of the Manifestation of Truth*).[183] Here, the different regions of Asia merely formed a narrative backdrop for the triumphant tale of the spread of of Baha'i truths.

It was Mustafa Rumi, however, who made the most enduring efforts to promote the new faith from Rangoon, albeit by making full use of the greater capacity of the Indian publishing houses across the Bay of Bengal. In 1908 he completed *Bab al-Hayat* (*The Gateway of Life*), his Urdu translation of the Persian biographies of the Bab and Baha'ullah, the two founders of Baha'ism. He sent the translation to Lucknow to be printed by the great Hindu commercial publisher Munshi Nawwal Kishore for the *Anjuman-i Baha'iyan-i Rangun* (Baha'i Association of Rangoon).[184]

Although on its cover the book was presented in objective terms as "an account of the lives of the Bab and Baha'ullah, the Baha'i sect [*firqa*], and its teachings by an [anonymous] Iranian traveler [*sayyah-i Irani*]," its original author was 'Abd al-Baha 'Abbas Effendi (1844–1921), the eldest son of Baha'ullah who from 1892 until 1921 served as head of the Baha'i faith. The book was, then, an official hagiography of Baha'ism's two founding figures. Published by Nawwal Kishore as high-quality lithography with a print run of a thousand copies, it was intended for distribution to the wide Urdu readership stretching from Rangoon to Calcutta and Madras, where Mustafa Rumi himself had converted. Pointing further to the early reliance of the new religion on the maritime public sphere, the original Persian edition of the book had been issued in Bombay in 1890.[185] By taking a closer look at the text, we will see the ways in which Baha'i missionaries sought to win converts from other religions not only by promoting their own religion, but also by engaging closely with the teachings of other religions (or at least, engaging with the familiar teachings of Islam, more so than with Buddhism, whose doctrines remained considerably more obscure).

Signaling his self-projecting intentions, Mustafa Rumi used his preface to make the case for the reliability of the book he had translated for the readers

who lay far beyond the Iranian homeland of Baha'ism. He began by acknowl-
edging that "countless books" had already been published on Baha'ism (albeit
refraining from mentioning how many of these books comprised denunciations of the new faith).[186] What made this book different, he explained, was
that it was based on "research" (tahqiq) and "facts" (waqa'at).[187] In a disingenu-
ously anonymizing disguise of 'Abbas Effendi's identity, he claimed that its
original author was simply "a great Iranian scholar" rather than the son and
heir of the religion's founder.[188] Using terms that recurred in many other intercultural investigations of the period, Rumi further claimed that the book was
based entirely on what the anonymous author "had seen with his own eyes"
(chishm-did).[189] As such, it was more reliable than the various accounts of the
Bab and Baha'ullah written by Europeans and other authors who had not been
present in Iran at the time.

Turning to the main text itself, the first quarter of Bab al-Hayat focused
on the life of Baha'ullah's forerunner, the Bab, which was presented through
the classic tropes of the Islamic hagiographical tradition intended to persuade
Muslims of the veracity of his divinely ordained mission.[190] Thus, the Bab had
fulfilled all the formal requirements of Islam, including performing the hajj
to Mecca, while his teachings had won many followers who included the rhetorical likes of "a famous Muslim scholar" (mashur 'alim).[191] Foreshadowing
the multireligious public of Rangoon that included many Parsi Zoroastrians
to whom Mustafa Rumi was also now promoting the new religion, other early
followers of the Bab included a "fire-worshipper [atash-parast] who found
faith."[192] But in a presentation more in line with the classic tropes of Shi'i
martyrology, the text explained that as the Bab's following had grown larger,
he had been persecuted and finally executed.

After recounting the martyrdom of the Bab, Rumi's book turned to the life
and teachings of Baha'ullah, which Rumi translated over the course of 150
pages.[193] The result was not merely a hagiographical text so much as a disputational text in line with the other proselytizing works we have seen emerging
through competing forms of missionary printing. Like earlier Christian tracts
issued from Calcutta and Madras that cited the Quran only to either refute it
or turn its words toward proving the doctrines of Christianity, Bab al-Hayat
repeatedly cited the Quran and the Hadith, only to use the Muslim scriptures
as proofs that Baha'ullah was a true messenger of God and, moreover, the
rightful successor to the Prophet Muhammad. Since the very ability to present these scripture-citing arguments in an Urdu text relied on rendering the

relevant quotations from Arabic into Urdu, Rumi's promotion of Baha'ism also relied on vernacular Quran translations that had emerged in response to Christian Bible translations.

It was not long before these Baha'i publications prompted a Muslim response, which in turn required Muslim respondents to investigate Baha'i teachings. The considered rejoinder came from an associate of Rangoon's Anjuman-i Islam (also known as the Burma Moslem Society). Just as the Maha-Bodhi Society was set up in Calcutta to promote the claims of Ceylonese and Burmese Buddhists over the holy site of Bodhgaya, which Hindus had controlled for centuries, organizations such as Rangoon's Anjuman-i Islam were founded to defend Burmese Muslims from this newly assertive Buddhism— and now also from Baha'ism. Indeed, the Anjuman was established a year after the publication of the Baha'i *Bab al-Hayat*. Its stated objectives were to "promote debates on useful and important subjects" while also raising "the moral and intellectual tone of its members."[194] Toward these ends it issued free primers of religious instruction in Burmese and Arabic through its Burma Muslim Press, such as *'Aqd al-Fara'id* (*Necklace of Pearls*), a versified catechism written in 1910 by Mawlwi 'Abd al-Hayy, who was the preacher, or *khatib*, of Rangoon's main Sunni Friday Mosque.[195] By this time, however, 'Abd al-Hayy was also busy defending Islam from the critiques of the Baha'i missionaries.

For as Jamal Effendi and Mustafa Rumi continued their projection of Baha'ism through preaching and publishing in Rangoon, their activities generated printed rejoinders from Mawlwi 'Abd al-Hayy and others.[196] Published in 1910, his *al-Mudafa' al-Illahiyya fi al-Radd 'ila al-Babiyya* (*Defender of the Divine by Refutation of the Babis*) appeared two years after the Urdu translation of the Baha'i missionary text, *Bab al-Hayat*. As 'Abd al-Hayy expressly stated, his own book was written in direct response to Rumi's proselytizing.[197] Like his Baha'i antagonist, 'Abd al-Hayy had his book printed by one of the more efficient and inexpensive publishers in India rather than in Rangoon, in his case Delhi's Matba'-i Ansari, which was known for issuing many Muslim religious texts. While Rumi made his translation of the Bab and Baha'ullah biographies available for the price of ten annas, however, 'Abd al-Hayy was able to distribute his *al-Mudafa' al-Illahiyya* for free, probably through subsidies raised through his position at Rangoon's main Sunni mosque.[198]

A century after the Christian missionaries of Calcutta began subsidizing their own publications for free distribution, to which Muslim leaders responded with printed *radd* (refutations) of the Christians' teachings, the likes of 'Abd al-Hayy were using the same techniques of propagation and the same *radd* genre to debate newer religious groups from other regions of Asia. Yet again, such disputes were nonetheless a form of dialogue that created greater understanding—albeit not acceptance—of the religion of the other. This was true at least between Baha'is and Muslims, who shared the same written languages. The irony was that despite taking place in Rangoon, these interreligious exchanges fostered little by way of formal printed knowledge of the Buddhist religion of Burma's majority community. For Baha'is, Muslims, and Hindus alike, overcoming the linguistic, conceptual, and social obstacles to reading books in Burmese or Pali was far more difficult than reading works in languages and scripts they already knew. As a result, whether from Sanskrit, Pali, or Burmese, there were no printed translations of core Buddhist texts into Arabic and Persian, the most widespread languages of Muslim learning. Neither the new Buddhist missionaries nor the curious scholarly Muslims appear to have been inclined—or even able—to make such direct translations, since there were no printed and therefore accessible dictionaries of Pali to Arabic or Sanskrit to Persian that could help them do so. And so, as we will see, when books, articles, and poems about Buddhism began to appear in the modern languages of India and the Middle East around 1900, they were largely translations or digests of European studies built on the fuller bibliographical apparatus of Orientalism.

In Rangoon, by 1910, the Baha'i works being issued there comprised not only *Bab al-Hayat,* but also several other works that the Muslim respondent 'Abd al-Hayy also had in his possession. They included such works as *'Uruj u Nuzul* (*Ascent and Descent*), *The Revelation of Baha'ullah* (in English), and the dialogical *Jawab-i Likchar-i Qadiyani* (*Response to a Qadiani Lecture*).[199] As the last work showed, by this time the Baha'is were having not only to preach to the Shi'i and Sunni Muslims of the Bay of Bengal, but also to respond to the public preaching of "Qadiani" Ahmadiyya missionaries, whose own latter-day messiah, Mirza Ghulam Ahmad, presented formidable competition to their own messiah, Baha'ullah, not least in continuing to print his own voluminous teachings till his death in 1908.

Turning more closely to *al-Mudafa' al-Illahiyya,* 'Abd al-Hayy's refutation of Baha'ism, far from being an expression of ignorant prejudice, it contains a closely argued response to the scriptural and theological arguments made by the Baha'i propagandists. 'Abd al-Hayy explained that he had felt it his duty to write his denunciation of Baha'i teachings because their books were claiming that the Shari'a had now been "abrogated" or "canceled."[200] The Baha'is claimed that after 1,260 years since the Prophet Muhammad's revelation, a new age had been initiated by the appearance of the Bab as the *mahdi* (guided one) and then Baha'ullah as the *masih* (messiah), both having been after all "predicted" in Islam's own eschatology.[201] Since in their publications Rumi and his fellow Baha'i propagationists were using quotations from the Quran, Hadith, and Bible to support their false claims, 'Abd al-Hayy continued, the "common people of Burma were being led astray [*gumrah*]."[202] As a preacher and teacher, he keenly felt the responsibility to respond by writing his own tract, not in learned Arabic but in Urdu aimed at the same "common" readers, albeit only those who could read Urdu, which effectively meant Burma's North Indian migrant community.[203] Even the partial understanding passed on through polemics was constrained by linguistic boundaries.

With this higher purpose in mind, 'Abd al-Hayy gave his own brief counter-biography of the Bab and Baha'ullah, refuting the hagiographical rhetoric of Rumi's recent translation of *Bab al-Hayat* with a more down-to-earth depiction of the origins and spread of the new religion.[204] Far from being a *mahdi* to be mentioned by the use of respectful titles, the Bab was simply "an Iranian called 'Ali Muhammad Bab" who one day outrageously declared, "Islam has been canceled."[205] Several years later, Baha'ullah had begun his own "messianic propagation" (*da'wa-i masihat*) by declaring himself the *masih* to the wealthy merchants of Shiraz.[206] Then, after Baha'ullah died in 1896, "various companies" began to propagate his new religion.[207] By categorizing Baha'ism as a religion (*mazhab*) rather than a mere sect (*firqa*), as it had been termed on the title page of the Urdu *Bab al-Hayat*, 'Abd al-Hayy was making it clear that to follow Baha'i teachings was not merely to adopt another theological school.[208] It was to apostatize from Islam, with all the social and soteriological risks involved. Though this was not the happy picture of Asian spiritual unity that Rabindranath Tagore was painting in the poems he was printing at this same time in Calcutta, the detailed printed information about the new Iranian faith that 'Abd al-Hayy had at his disposal was indubitably a form of inter-Asian understanding.

Having presented his counternarrative of the rise of Baha'ism through the wealthy Iranian merchants whom Rangoon's ordinary Muslims knew all too well, 'Abd al-Hayy devoted the second half of his tract to an examination of the quotations from the Quran and Hadith that Baha'i propagationists used to support their claims. As he plainly put the matter, the Baha'i readings of Muslim scripture were based on a "completely mistaken understanding."[209] This was true especially of their citations of Hadith regarding Muhammad's status as the last prophet and of their related claims of the finite, replaceable status of Shari'a. In response, 'Abd al-Hayy cited another Hadith of Muhammad that put the matter in as terse and simple an Arabic phrase as possible: "*La nabi ba'di*" ("No Prophet after me").[210] Outlining these theological debates as plainly as he could for his broad readership, in the final section of his tract 'Abd al-Hayy turned to the Shi'i traditions that the Baha'is also used to support their doctrines, showing that these too had been misunderstood.[211] He closed his *al-Mudafa' al-Illahiyya* with a repudiation of the claim that Baha'ullah was the incarnate spirit of Allah.[212] In measured and precise prose, he used his considerable learning to refute the very foundations of Baha'ism by undermining the prophetic status claimed for its founders. 'Abd al-Hayy could not accept that all religions were of equal value. As he saw the matter, to do so would mean accepting the Baha'i premise that Shari'a had been abrogated, rendered redundant—and the result would be moral chaos in this life and damnation in the afterlife. And so, as he explained, in refuting the teachings of the Baha'i missionaries, he was fulfilling his duty as a preacher by trying to protect ordinary people who were being destructively "led astray."

'Abd al-Hayy was far from the only Muslim publicly objecting in print to Baha'i attempts to proselytize among the Muslim communities of Asia. The pioneer Salafi and self-appointed defender of Islam, Rashid Rida (1865–1935), repeatedly criticized the Baha'is in his Arabic journal *al-Manar* (*The Lighthouse*), which was read by an Asia-wide subscriber base that stretched from Beirut and Aden to Calcutta, Rangoon, Singapore, and Guangzhou.[213] Spreading through print the negative intercultural knowledge of the interreligious polemic, *al-Manar* also included printed debates (called *munazarat*) that served Rida's dual goals of refuting both Baha'i and Christian missionary claims.[214] In the next chapter, we will see such staged debates extending deeper into Burma and involving not only Christians, Muslims, and Baha'is but also Buddhists. In doing so, they would again spread knowledge of another religion that was morally partial but informationally accurate—or at least more accurate than previous conceptions of Buddhism.

Nevertheless, the Baha'is remained undeterred. In 1923 Rumi founded a trilingual Persian-Burmese-English journal, which he edited under the title *al-Ishraq* (*The Dawn*).[215] Making use of the Gujerat Electric Press in Rangoon, owned by the Gujarati businessman M. S. Desai, he planned to distribute *al-Ishraq* far and wide by mail steamer, listing subscription rates on its cover that ranged from five rupees for India to two tumans for Iran and two dollars for the United States.[216] In elegant lithographic calligraphy, the Persian front cover of its first issue declared that "the aim of *al-Ashraq* is the unity

လူသတ္တဝါတို့မှာ အနှစ်နဲ့ ဂုဏ်တန်ခိုးဖြစ်မြောက်ခြင်းမှကား၊ မိမိချက်မြှုပ်ရာအ
ရပ်ဒေသကိုချစ်ခင်ခြင်းကြောင့်အလျှင်မဖြစ်နိုင်။တလောကလုံးကို
ချစ်ခင်ခြင်းကြောင့်သာဖြစ်နိုင်၏။

BAHA'U'LLAH.

ဤမဂ္ဂဇင်းသတင်း
စာကို။ မြန်မာနိုင်ငံ
နေ။ဘဟာ၁အဇီ။သဘ
သနာတော်၊ မဟာ
ဝွေလေ-ရှုဟာ၁ရန်အ
သင်း ကား။ ပု နွ့ရိ
ထုတ်ဝေကြသည်။

အယ်ဒီတာ၁
ဆိုက်ယာဒန့်, မွတ်စ
တဖ္ဖာရူမီ။
ရန်ကုန်မြို့။
စာတိုက်သေတ္တာ၁
နံပါတ် ၂၉၉။

P. Box No. 299.
Rangoon.

အာနန္ဒီမျာ၁
မြန်မာပြည်နှင့်
အိန္ဒိယပြည်များ။
၁ ၊ဟ ၅။
အိဒီရာနီ ၁ ၂ ၊ဟ။
၂-လှုမ်း
အဖေရိက၁။
၁ ၂ -ဟ။ ၂-စေါလ၁။
အင်္ဂလန်ပြည်။
၁ ၂ဟ။ ၇၇ ရှီလင်္ဂ
အချစ်နှင့် ပါလတ်
စတိုင်ပြည်များ၊
ကိုရွတ်ရှ။ ၅၀ဂ
တစေဒင်လျှင် ၅ပဲ။
စာတိုက်စ အခြင်း။

ADDRESS.
S. M. ROEMI.
No. 2-B. 41st Street
RANGOON.

ဒီခိုလောက်သူလောကီသား၁ လူအ
ခပါင်းတို့။သင်တို့သည်။ သစ်ပင်တပင်
တည်းမှ သီးပွင့်သေဝသစ်သီးများနှင့်။
အကိုင်းတကိုင်းတည်းမှ ပေါက်ရောက်
လေသော အရွက်များပင် ဖြစ်ကြကုန်
သည်ဟု။ဘဟာ၁ဒ္ဒလ္လာ၁ဟ်၊အရှင်မြတ်
မိန့်တော်မူ၏။

| ပဌမတွဲ။ | ၁၉၂၃-ခု၊ နိုဝင်ဘာ၁လနှင့်ဒီဇင်ဘာ၁။ | နံပါတ် ၃-နှင့်-၄။ |

ရော်ပြည်၁ဘာ၁.၅ဇင်၌ရှိလိုရင်းတည်း။ဟူ၁သသ၀တ်တရားအကြောင်းမှ၁တက၁မှ၁လူ၌ရှိ နကြသေသ၁နသ၁လူ၁သတ္တ ပါ၁အပေါင်းတို့ကို၊ ညီအစ်ကိုရင်း။ဟူ၍၊ ချစ်ခင်မြတ်နိုးခြင်းအ၁းဖြင့် တလုံးတဝတည်း။နှင့် ၁း စိုတ်တသဘော၁တည်းဖြစ် အောင်ပြုလုပ်ခြင်း။ မျက်မှာ၁က်တွင်အသင်၍ရှိကြသည်၁အလုံးစုံသော၁သနုတော၁ဖြတ်ကိုမ၍ မုလအခြေ၁အမြစ်ဓရင်းတရ ကညီ၁နှဉ်၁ကမျိုးမည်၁ဖြစ်ကြောင်း။ကိုလည်းကောင်း။ ညွှန်ပြခြင်းမျ၁းဖြစ်၏။ယင်းသို့ဆောင်ရွက်အပ်လ၁ဝင်ရတ်တရ၁းမျ၁း
နှင့်သက်ဆိုင်သော၁ အကြောင်းမျ၁းကိုရေး၁သ၁း၍ ပုံမ၍ထုတ်ဝေရ၏။ရင်း၁ဝတ်တရ၁းမျ၁းနှင့်စင်လျဉ်း။မျှ၁ချ၁ရ၁ရေး၁သ၁း
၁၁သ၁ဆ၁ခ်၁များ။ကိုး၊ ညည်သည့်ဆ၁ရင်နှင့်ပည္လ၁သူ၁ထ၁ကဖြစ်စေ၁၊အကြောင်း။ရောက်လ၁သေ၁ အ၁ခါ၊ ၎င်၊တွက်ခြင်း၊ မြှ၁ဲဂံ၍စ
ထုတ်ဝရုဖိ၁မည်၁ပေ၁ည်၁တော်ဝတ်တရ၁းမျ၁း၁သက်သက်ဆ၁ဒ၁င်ရွက်ပါ၁သည်။ ရင်းမှ၁တပါ၁။အရ၁ရ၁း၁၁ရ၁ပြည်၁ရ၁ပြ၁း၊
ဖြင့်၁ဆိုင်ရ၁။ မြေ၁ရ၁ရ၁ပူ၁မျ၁းတွင်၁ပ၁ဝင်၁ အသိ၁အ၁၁တ၁ါသ၁ားက၁ ကိုယ်၁အရင်၁ချင်၁စ်နတ်ဆ၁ထိ၁ုက်၁ ဆ၁ဒ၁င်ငြ၁
သော၁ရှိ၁၁သ၁အ၁ချ၁က်များ၁ကို၁ အလေ၁လ၁ဂ၁ရှမ၍ပြ၁ဆ၁လျ၁၁ ရ၁ၒနေ၁ရ၁ပါ၁သည်။

The Baha'i message in Burmese: Mustafa Rumi's Rangoon journal, *al-Ashraq/The Dawn* 1 (1923). Photograph by Nile Green.

[*wahdat*], brotherhood [*ukhuwwat*], and oneness [*yiganigi*] of the whole world of humankind."[217] While this was undoubtedly a cosmopolitan sentiment of not merely Asian but of global unity, it again raises the question of unity on whose terms?

Two years after Rumi founded *al-Ishraq,* and a decade after 'Abd al-Hayy refuted his teachings in *al-Mudafa' al-Illahiyya,* it was the turn of the Ahmadiyya Muslims to rebut their Baha'i missionary rivals. The respondent was Fazl al-Din, a law court pleader from the Ahmadi missionary center at Qadian. In 1925 he published his *Baha'i Mazhab ki Haqiqat (The Truth about the Baha'i Religion)* in an edition of one thousand copies.[218] It began with a brief history of the origins of the Baha'i faith before turning over the next 125 pages to a detailed scrutiny—and step-by-step, attorney-style rejection—of the religion's various teachings.[219] Fazl al-Din devoted around two-thirds of his book to the supposed "new law" (*na'i shari'at*) with which Baha'ullah claimed to have replaced Shari'a. Particularly vivid in the Baha'i publications in Arabic, Persian, and Urdu to which Fazl al-Din was responding was a linguistic and cultural continuum between Baha'ism and Islam that helped Baha'i missionaries win Muslim followers. So, to put an end to any perceptions of such apparent continuity of revelation, Fazl al-Din stated from the outset that Baha'i law had absolutely no relation with Islam.[220] Far from seeking interfaith unity, he considered drawing a clear distinction between the two religions as a matter of crucial salvational importance.

To make his reasons plain, Fazl al-Din went through a sequence of issues on which Baha'i teachings were irreconcilably in conflict with the laws of Islam. His chosen examples focused on both the religious and social dimensions of Shari'a. He criticized the Baha'i practice of worshipping at the tomb and house of Baha'ullah, and the undertaking of pilgrimages to Acre in Palestine (where Baha'ullah was buried); to Shiraz (where his forerunner the Bab had resided); and to Baghdad (where Baha'ullah had lived). But as it happened, Baha'ullah's house in Baghdad had already been seized by Iraqi Shi'i leaders three years before Fazl al-Din published his book.[221] As for prayers, he emphasized what he claimed was the Baha'i ban on the collective worship that was incumbent on all Muslims on Fridays, as well as Baha'ullah's abrogation of the Quranic rules regarding ablutions of hands, head, and feet before worship.[222] Another major issue was the differences in various aspects of marital law, whether dowry or divorce.[223] Then, in the second section of his book, Fazl al-Din went in systematically legal thoroughness through the seventeen commandments (*hukm*) of the Bab to make his crowning argument that the Babi-Baha'i religion was a "peace-destroying" (aman-shikan) project that stood in determined opposition (mukhalif) to Islam.[224] As for 'Abd al-Hayy, what was especially alarming for Fazl al-Din was the Baha'i claim that Islamic law had been abrogated, which presented the dire prospect of moral and social collapse.[225]

Having presented all his evidence, the colonial lawyer Fazl al-Din finally passed his judgment by issuing a ruling on the incompatibility with Islam of the teachings of the Babi and Baha'i "deniers of God."[226] Yet it is important to recognize that, for all its rejection of Baha'ism, Fazl al-Din's book was not motivated by ignorant prejudice. Far from emerging from an absence of knowledge, and from judgment before understanding, it was based on remarkably detailed and precise information about Baha'i doctrines. Here again was the polemic as a negative form of inter-Asian understanding.

Adopting the earlier techniques of learned Christian missionaries, over and again Fazl al-Din quoted directly in Arabic from the Baha'i scriptures, such as the Kitab al-Aqdas, which, we saw, was printed in Bombay. For each point of doctrinal difference, he provided the page numbers and precise references (hawala) that constituted the critical apparatus of what was a serious intellectual—indeed, ethical—engagement with Baha'i teachings and their implications for Muslims. Cosmopolitan sympathy and the collapsing of boundaries were not, then, the only possible outcomes of intercultural knowledge between followers of Asia's different religions. For various moral actors around the Bay of Bengal, not all revelations were equal and not all doctrines compatible.

Yet while the likes of Fazl al-Din were making such distinctions clear, they were not calling for violence. Indeed, the Ahmadiyya branch of Islam to which Fazl al-Din belonged reformulated the doctrine of jihad to expressly reject the use of violence to promote Islam. Instead, its adherents followed the doctrine of a peacefully persuasive "jihad by the pen" (jihad bi'l-qalam), which in practice involved the printing press more than the pen.[227] By such means, Ahmadiyya and other missionaries used the new public sphere to highlight what they saw as crucial ethical and theological distinctions between different religions that, if concealed, put people's very souls at peril.

Nonetheless, when Ahmadiyya missionaries tried to promote their own teachings in Rangoon, they too faced rejection from the city's Sunni Muslims. Ahmadiyya doctrines had already triggered a massive polemical response across India, including journals in Arabic-script Tamil read by the Tamil Muslim diaspora in Burma and Ceylon. So when the famous Ahmadiyya preacher Kamal al-Din (1870–1932) lectured in Rangoon in 1920, he found himself challenged to a public debate.[228] His disputant was another émigré Indian preacher, 'Abd al-Shakur Lakhnawi (d. 1962), who was already known for anti-Shi'i agitation in his home city of Lucknow. Their contentious public disagreements were subsequently published in a book with the apt title of *Ma'raka-i Rangun* (*Battlefield of Rangoon*).[229] Despite his public showdown, Kamal al-Din remained undeterred, and from Rangoon he boarded a ship for Surabaya and Batavia in the Dutch East Indies, where he continued his preaching tour of the colonial ports of maritime Asia.[230] Partly in response to his proselytizing there, new Javanese religious organizations were established. One was the Persatuan Islam (Islamic Union), founded in 1923, which arranged public debates with Ahmadiyya missionaries that drew more than two thousand listeners.[231] By then, the polemical public sphere had reached far beyond the Bay of Bengal.

In the course of this chapter, we have seen how in the ports of Calcutta, Colombo, and Rangoon, Christian missionaries became unwitting models for a wide range of Indian, Iranian, Ceylonese, and Burmese religious organizations, which adapted the communicative and investigative methods of the Christians for their own purposes of self-projection. As the expansion of European empire integrated different regions of Asia, it led to competing efforts to project the religion of the self over the belief systems of various other communities. As we have seen, polemical and disputatious works occupied a prominent position in the maritime public sphere that expanded out from Calcutta.

By the 1930s, the social effects of such printed disputes led to increasing censorship across British India and Burma as the colonial government diluted its long-standing policies supporting freedom of religious expression. Surviving records of censored books show that by this time dozens of polemical works in Indian languages were being banned each year, followed by attempts to withdraw them from distribution.[232] As the ripple effects of religious polemics had widened in line with the spread of print, these prohibited books ranged from Sunni denigrations of Shi'is and anti-Islamic diatribes by the Hindu Arya Samaj to rival denunciations between Sanatani and reformist Hindus, strident expressions of Buddhist nationalism, repudiations of Christian converts, and a flurry of disputes about the messianic Muslim Ahmadiyya.

Though disputational works did not promote the equal validity of Asia's different religions and cultures, most did not promote violence against the religious others whose doctrines they sought to disprove through debate. For whether penned by Muslims or Christians, Baha'is or Buddhists, such texts were intended to reveal truths that would save the souls of those who accepted them. In trying to draw together the different peoples of Asia into the recognition of the one true religion that could save them, whether that religion was Islam, Buddhism, Hinduism, Christianity, or Baha'ism, some at least were expressions of a paradoxically compassionate polemicism. Rather than the cold, abstract, and external idea of "Asia" that had been introduced from Europe, it was these religious systems, at once comforting and complex, that were seen as the stronger moral and intellectual cords for joining different people together around the Bay of Bengal.

Yet in what we will see as an enduring feature of the development of intercultural knowledge across the continent, these competing projections of the self also generated increased understanding (if not always appreciation) of the other. Such polemical and proselytizing texts did not by any means monopolize the public sphere, as we have seen with the emergence of positive accounts of Buddhism that the heirs of the Christian missionaries were among the most influential disseminators through translations of such works as Edwin Arnold's *Light of Asia*. All around the Bay of Bengal, commercial printers also issued more secular expressions of cultural exchange through literary translations such as Muhammad Shams al-Din's Burmese translation from Urdu of the tales of Hatim Ta'i that were popular throughout North India among both Muslim and Hindu readers.[233] Around the same time that Muslims and Baha'is were publishing their debates in Rangoon, up-country in Mandalay, learned local Muslims like Maung Myit and Maung Mya translated into Burmese a history of the Ottomans and other Muslim rulers from a selection of sources in Urdu, Persian, Arabic, and English.[234]

As we will now see, attempts to project Islam deep into Burma also enabled new levels of knowledge about Buddhism, whose history and teachings remained little known in even its original homeland of India in the late nineteenth century, let alone across the western regions of Asia in the Middle East.

2 • The Muslim Discovery of Buddhism

Through its gradual annexation in the nineteenth century, Burma became one of the British Empire's two Buddhist-majority colonies. Like Ceylon, conquered first along its littoral before the fall of the highland kingdom of Kandy in 1818, Burma was absorbed in several stages beginning in 1824 and culminating in 1885, when the inland capital at Mandalay was finally captured. So ended centuries of Buddhist rule over Burma, where the Konbaung Dynasty had continued to offer state support to Buddhism right up to its demise. For the patronage of countless monasteries connected to an Ecclesiastical Council coordinated by the key figure of the thathanabaing, or chief prelate, was woven within the fabric of this Buddhist state.[1] The penultimate ruler of Mandalay, King Mindon, had supported some 217 monasteries with over 15,000 monks.[2] With the destruction of Burmese statehood through the Third Anglo-Burmese War, this old pattern of state and monastic interdependence was abruptly ended. Thereafter, the British Empire instituted policies of religious noninterference previously applied on the other side of the Bay of Bengal in India. Five years earlier, the same developments had taken place in Ceylon, when in 1880 British policies of religious equality disestablished Protestant Christianity and placed all Ceylon's religions on an equal footing before the colonial state. Although this notionally demoted Christianity, it also left Buddhism with no more privileges than Hinduism or Islam. The 1880s thus marked the onset of a religious crisis for both Ceylonese and Burmese Buddhists. As an increasing variety of missionaries expanded across Burma from Rangoon on the coast, the thathanabaing and his Theravada Buddhist followers were left to religiously fend for themselves.[3]

The combined shock of state disenfranchisement and intensified competition from non-Buddhist religious organizations would lead not only to the assertive missionary Buddhism we saw emerging in the previous chapter. Crisis also led to the development of new inter-Asian knowledge through the collaborating intercultural investigations, and competing self-projections, of European Christians and Indian Hindus and Muslims alike. One such missionary was a North Indian Muslim called 'Abd al-Khaliq Muwahid. Arriving around the time of the fall of Mandalay, he went on to publish a book in Urdu describing not only the history and beliefs of the Burmese people, but also his disputations with the disenfranchised followers of the Buddha.[4] Through a case study of this remarkable text, we will not only see how intercultural knowledge could emerge from such disputative encounters. We will also identify the various barriers, both informational and linguistic, that constrained 'Abd al-Khaliq's understanding of Buddhism, as well as that of other Indians and Muslims from the Middle East who tried to understand a religion that had disappeared from India in the Middle Ages and had never spread to the Arab and Iranian regions of West Asia.

What is most striking about 'Abd al-Khaliq's book is that it reveals how, at the end of the nineteenth century, even a highly educated Indian raised only 150 miles from the Buddha's birthplace could possess no knowledge of Buddhism, forcing him to investigate its teachings ex nihilo. For as we will see when we turn to the writings of various other participants in the Indian rediscovery of Buddhism, as late as the 1890s, when colonial Orientalists had been digging Buddhist sites and deciphering Buddhist texts for over half a century, such knowledge had not widely filtered into books in major Indian languages such as Urdu. This left Indian intercultural investigators like 'Abd al-Khaliq to make their own separate discoveries of Buddhism using the investigative tools and interpretive concepts their own intellectual heritage made available to them.[5] For this reason, 'Abd al-Khaliq's book, Sayr-i Barhma (Journey to Burma), forms an illuminating example of how knowledge about unfamiliar peoples encountered around an increasingly interconnected Asia was privately conceived and then publicly communicated through cheap printed books in Indian languages.

Following the widening polemical ripples of the maritime public sphere upriver and inland from Rangoon to Mandalay, we will see more fully that Asia's interreligious disputes were not necessarily based on ignorance. 'Abd al-Khaliq was a scrupulous investigator of what, for want of a more precise label for Buddhism, he called simply the "religion of Burma" (mazhab-i Barhma).

The port city as gateway to Buddhism: the sacred portal to Rangoon's Shwedagon
Pagoda. Postcard, c. 1910. Collection of Nile Green.

Yet he was also unwilling to grant that mysterious belief system a moral or
soteriological equivalence with his own religion of Islam; such a casually cosmopolitan gesture would condemn to eternal damnation the followers of the
false prophet he called Shingutama, better known as Gautama the Buddha.

Before turning to 'Abd al-Khaliq's encounters across the Bay of Bengal, we
must bear in mind that the wider Indian rediscovery of Buddhism we have
seen unfolding in Calcutta in the decades before he published his book in 1893
was expressed mainly in languages he was unable to read, whether Bengali,
Sanskrit, or English. Pointing to the fractured linguistic profile of inter-Asian
understanding as it took shape in separate languages, the new understanding
of Buddhism developing in Calcutta did not automatically filter into India's
many other written languages, particularly before 1900. This background picture of patchy transmission helps us understand how, as late as the 1890s,
even an educated North Indian like 'Abd al-Khaliq could publish a book on the
"religion of Burma" without any knowledge of the Buddhist religion that had
once flourished in his own homeland.

Being unable to read the languages in which we have seen most Indian accounts of Buddhism being published, 'Abd al-Khaliq was forced to make his
own investigations in Burma from scratch.

Yet even as his inquiries were disputatious, they came through direct engagements with living Buddhists. This was in itself a contrast with many of his learned Hindu counterparts in Bengal, for whom ancient Indian texts (primarily in Sanskrit) and Indian archaeological sites formed the data set for a distinctive rediscovery of Buddhism that subsequently encouraged nationalist scholars to conceive the religion as primordially "belonging" to India. As we will see in chapter 6, even when Bengali scholars developed an interest in Chinese Buddhism in the 1920s, they did so in terms that accentuated China's civilizational debt to India.

And so, whether with regard to China or Burma, the modern Indian encounter with Buddhism became as much a project of projecting the self as appreciating the other. This was no less the case with the Muslim missionary 'Abd al-Khaliq, in whose investigations we will see the complex interplay of learning, discernment, and disagreement that, as it did for his Christian counterparts, paved the way for more positive evaluations of Buddhism by a later cohort of learned fellow Muslims.

The Making of a Muslim Missionary

From his North Indian childhood to his adult years in Burma, Christian missionaries were an important feature of 'Abd al-Khaliq's life. In the preface to his book, *Sayr-i Barhma*, he explained that he was raised in the town of Rae Bareli, near Lucknow. It was an appropriate hometown for a future Muslim missionary to grow up in, for shortly after Rae Bareli's annexation by the British, in 1864, it became host to a busy branch of the American Methodist Mission.[6] By 1878 the affiliated Methodist Press in nearby Lucknow was reportedly printing "millions of pages annually in English, Urdu and Hindi," which were distributed through its branches in Rae Bareli and elsewhere.[7] The mission was still active fifteen years later, when 'Abd al-Khaliq wrote his book on Burma's religion.[8]

As he went on to explain in his preface, by the time he sat down to write the book, he had resided for a long time in Rangoon and Mandalay, as well as in the town of Minbu, which lay around 250 miles north of Rangoon along the river Irrawaddy.[9] During these years in an unfamiliar land, he had decided to learn the Burmese language in order to discover the truth about what he called the "religion of Burma." Emphasizing his higher motivations, he repeated that he had done so from a "desire for the truth" (*shawq al-haqq*).[10] Finally, having returned to his hometown in India in 1891, he had been encouraged by a close friend to write about the religion and culture of Burma "because no such book existed in Urdu." So 'Abd al-Khaliq agreed, writing *Sayr-i Barhma* for his "compatriot brothers" who were unacquainted with the country to which so many of them were emigrating in pursuit of the economic opportunities of empire. In the Islamic *hijri* calendar, he gave the date of its completion as August 9, 1892. The conquest of Mandalay, and with it the opening of the Burmese interior to Indian, Iranian, and British missionaries no less than merchants, had taken place less than seven years earlier. This was precisely the period when 'Abd al-Khaliq described himself heading to Mandalay.[11]

The two decades leading up to 1900 were also a time when Indian Muslim migration to Burma led to the founding of a string of mosques from Rangoon to the towns of the interior like Minbu, all of which required imams to oversee them. As immigrants laid down roots, madrasa schools were also founded, generating further demand for educated religious teachers, or *mawlwis*, like 'Abd al-Khaliq. In the previous chapter, we saw another such figure, Mawlwi 'Abd al-Hayy, publishing a religious primer for Rangoon's Muslims, along with a confutation of the Baha'i missionaries who were trying to convert them. Such was the expansion of these madrasa schools that 'Abd al-Hayy later wrote an Urdu history of Muslim education in Rangoon.[12] That 'Abd al-Khaliq was employed in one of these mosques or schools seems to be confirmed by the linguistic evidence of his book, which had many Arabicisms and other learned phrases, along with references to his theological research (*tahqiq*) and other religious activities.

As for his intended readership, the only explicit evidence is the statement in the preface to *Sayr-i Barhma* that it was written "for fellow countrymen who were unacquainted with Burma."[13] Given the traffic in both people and books across the Bay of Bengal, it is quite possible that he found readers in Burma as well as India. By the time he was writing, Urdu was Rangoon's lingua franca, used in its written form between Muslims and some North Indian Hindus and in its simplified "Hindustani" spoken form among colonial officials, Parsi and Hindu migrants, Bohra, Khoja, and Iranian merchants, and the local Burmese with whom they interacted. As early as 1836, a Tamil-Urdu vocabulary book was printed in Rangoon to help Tamil Cholia migrants master the city's Urdu vernacular.[14] Such was Urdu's status in Rangoon that, in *Burmese Days*, George Orwell's fictional Mrs. Lackersteen explains how "only missionary-women spoke Burmese; nice women found kitchen Urdu quite as much as they needed."[15] The city had its own Urdu newspaper, *Akhbar-i Barma,* and even the Iranian Baha'i missionary, Mustafa Rumi, learned the language there, composing poetry in Urdu and penning a proselytizing treatise called *al-Ma'yar al-Sahih (The Correct Criterion).*[16] Numerous other Urdu poets emerged in Burma, such as Sayyid Husayn Sayyid (born in 1870 in the Indian town of Panipat) and Ahmar Ranguni (born around 1900 in Rangoon), whose work was published in an anthology called *Gulshan-i Sukhan (The Garden of Eloquence).*[17]

Rangoon's cosmopolitan poetic output coincided with more contentious developments, however, even among fellow Muslims. For as Islamic education expanded through such schools as the Madrasa Shirkat al-Islam in Rangoon, as well as others in Bago and Mandalay, the primacy of Urdu or Burmese as a language of instruction became a major issue of contention, leading some Indian religious teachers to declare that those who discussed Islamic topics in Burmese were "Muslim bodies with Buddhist souls."[18] Responding to such concerns, the Urdu-promoting All-India Muhammadan Educational Conference held its large annual convention in Rangoon, promoting Urdu as Rangoon's primary language of public discourse and bringing many religious figures from across India, such as Sayyid Shah Sulayman Chishti, who preached to the delegates in Urdu.[19]

Echoing what we will see of 'Abd al-Khaliq's engagement with the Burmese language, Muslim instructional publications had already begun to appear in Burmese by the time he arrived (though, in a reflection of the dominant position of India's print emporia, some of the earliest were issued in Bombay). A case in point was Muhammad Ibrahim's *Hukm al-Salat (Rules of Worship),* a compendium of the obligatory Muslim prayers in Arabic with rubrics in Burmese, published in 1890.[20] As printing capacity developed in Burma itself, other Islamic texts, including translations into Burmese, began to be issued from the ports of Moulmein and Rangoon. Echoing the earlier Christian missionary catechisms, those printed in the 1890s comprised works of basic religious instruction, including a Burmese hagiography of the Prophet Muhammad translated from Urdu; a celebration of Muslim generosity attributed to the Prophet's son-in-law Imam 'Ali; and two books on the correct observance of Muslim prayers, fasts, and festivals issued in Arabic and Burmese script.[21] Others, including two Burmese pamphlets by Muhammad Ibrahim of Rangoon, echoed the comparative religious investigations of Christian missionaries by comparing the merits and demerits of Islam, Christianity, and

Buddhism; the first emerged as superior.[22] In the Muslim as in the Christian and Baha'i cases, such religious motivations led to a deeper linguistic engagement with written Burmese than the better-known political projects of Asianist ideologues. Even someone as sensitive to language as Tagore could address local audiences only in English and Bengali when he made his three brief steamship visits to Rangoon.[23]

Such was the context—of more intense inter-Asian connections but constrained intercultural comprehension—in which 'Abd al-Khaliq wrote his *Sayr-i Barhma* as a pioneering Muslim investigation of Buddhism. At the time, even the spelling of the place name—as *Barma* or *Barhma*—was inconsistent in Urdu. But as we will now see, understanding its language, culture, and religion presented even bigger investigative challenges.

Islam's Buddhological Lacunae

What is most striking about 'Abd al-Khaliq's categorization of the religion he set out to investigate is his constant reference to it as the "religion of Burma" (*mazhab-i Barhma*), which is to say that he had no conception of a more general categorical entity of "Buddhism" with followers in other parts of Asia. His misapprehensions were far from unique. We have seen that by the time he was writing in the 1890s, British and Indian scholars in Calcutta had published important findings in English, Bengali, and to some extent other Indian languages that provided a more detailed and accurate picture of Buddhism, albeit largely pertaining to its history in India rather than Burma or elsewhere in Asia. Yet as *Sayr-i Barhma* makes clear, 'Abd al-Khaliq was unfamiliar with even the basic findings of what was by then an extensive body of Anglophone and to some extent Bengali books on Buddhism, still less with the archaeological investigations by then taking place across his home province and neighboring Bihar. When combined with his links to the epicenter of Urdu publishing in Lucknow, where his own book was published a short distance from his hometown of Rae Bareli, this raises the question of how unusual it was for such a well-educated Indian Muslim, who had even resided in Burma, to have neither a conception of the Buddhist religion nor an awareness of its connections to India? To answer this question, we will have to determine what books on Buddhism were potentially available at the end of the nineteenth century to him and to Indian Muslims unable to read either English or Bengali. Addressing this question will help us better understand

the informational constraints under which ʿAbd al-Khaliq operated and to better appreciate the scale of his achievements.

During previous centuries, in India as in the Middle East, the long history
of Muslim coexistence with Hindus, Christians, and Jews had produced an
extensive (if sometimes polemical) literature in Arabic and Persian that described their beliefs and histories. But the same was not true of Buddhism.[24]
This seems in part to have reflected the more limited and peripheral geography of Muslim-Buddhist cohabitation in parts of China, Tibet, Champa,
Pattani, Ceylon, and Burma. Whatever local and oral knowledge of Buddhist
beliefs Muslims may have developed in such regions, it was apparently not
transmitted in manuscript or especially print to Muslims living elsewhere.

There were a few exceptions to this chasm of inter-Asian understanding.
Under the medieval Mongol Empire, the brief moment of political union between Persia and China saw an invaluable ration of information on Buddhism
sent west into the Middle East. It found its principal expression in the *Jami'
al-Tawarikh* (*Compendium of Histories*) written by Rashid al-Din (1247–1318), a
learned Jewish convert-cum-vizier to the Mongols.[25] But after almost two thousand years of religious transformations among Buddhists in various regions,
Rashid al-Din's Kashmiri (and possibly Chinese) informant had little firm
knowledge of the historical Buddha, Gautama. Nor did the Kashmiri monk
inform him about the development of the Theravada (meaning "Way of the
Elders" in Pali), which was the distinct form of Buddhism that spread through
Ceylon, Burma, and Southeast Asia more generally.

So, while a certain amount of information (as well as rather more speculation) about Buddhism was recorded by medieval authors such as Rashid
al-Din, it was scattered in poetry anthologies and histories that remained in
manuscript and had not entered the public sphere of print.[26] This reflected
the lack of informational continuity that shaped the contours of intercultural
investigation across Asia at large, particularly in the Middle East, South Asia,
and Southeast Asia, where printing did not develop before the nineteenth century, leaving the overwhelming majority of earlier manuscript works unpub-
lished.[27] *Jami' al-Tawarikh* does not appear to have been one of the various
Persian histories that were printed in India before 1900.[28] As a consequence,
ʿAbd al-Khaliq had no access to the very limited—and as yet unprinted—body
of precolonial Muslim accounts of Buddhism, mistaken as they in any case
were on various points of fact, for he showed no awareness of these earlier
researches. And even if he had managed to access a manuscript copy of *Jami'
al-Tawarikh*, its contents would not have helped him recognize the religion

he was investigating in Burma as contiguous with the Kashmiri and Chinese religion that Rashid al-Din had described.

An alternative—and potentially more useful—source of information were the Persian translations and descriptions of Buddhism in the Bengal-Burmese borderlands of Arakan that Calcutta-based Orientalists had commissioned from local scholars in the late eighteenth and early nineteenth centuries.[29] These included several Pali-to-Persian translations sponsored by the Asiatic Society scholar John Murray MacGregor (1745–1822).[30] But apparently 'Abd al-Khaliq was unaware of them, since their tiny number of manuscripts seems only to have circulated among Orientalists and their direct Indian interlocutors associated with the Asiatic Society in Calcutta. In any case, these early researches were misleading in their findings, as the subsequent generation of colonial scholars of Buddhism, such as Rhys Davids, established in the second half of the nineteenth century.

Yet since 'Abd al-Khaliq lived amid the Asian communications revolution that was brought on by print, his inability to access unique copies of manuscripts kept in colonial libraries in Calcutta should not, at least in principle, have presented an overwhelming informational obstacle. For there were three other avenues of information open to him by way of printed accounts of Buddhism in the main languages he could read—namely Arabic, Persian, and Urdu.

Turning first to Persian printed books, the translation of European texts in Iran, and their printing for the new educational system heralded by the founding of Tehran's Dar al-Funun polytechnic in 1851, had already disseminated information on unfamiliar regions of Asia among the Persian-reading public. The most influential such work was probably *Kitab-i Jam-i Jam* (*Book of the World-Revealing Goblet*), published in 1855 in Tehran as a geography textbook for the Dar al-Funun.[31] The following year, an Indian edition was published in Bombay, rendering it potentially available to 'Abd al-Khaliq, not least since it included a section on Burma. Despite the indigenous idiom of its title, *Kitab-i Jam-i Jam* was a translation of a primer of world geography by an English schoolmaster, William Pinnock.[32] The Iranian translator, Prince Farhad Mirza, tried to reconcile Pinnock's European model of space with the traditional Greco-Arabic model of seven "climes" (*iqlim*), while also incorporating the new notion of a continent called *Asiya*. These conceptual compromises led to such formulations as "The empire of China is in the central clime of the earth, which is situated in the southeast of Asia (*Asiya*)."[33] But as for information about the religion of such regions, in the absence of a specific Persian term for what in English Pinnock had vaguely called "the sect of Boodh," Farhad simply stated that "their religion is idol worship" (*but-parasti*).[34] Even had he read it, this would have been of little help to 'Abd al-Khaliq.

Three decades later, Persian accounts of Buddhism had not developed much further, even with regard to regions neighboring Iran, let alone distant Burma. An example is seen in an article about the giant Buddhist statues of Bamiyan in central Afghanistan that appeared in 1885 in the influential Tehran journal *Sharaf*.[35] By this time, accounts of Bamiyan had been penned in Persian for the best part of a millennium, though in each case the statues had been simply presented as idols (*but*), with no specific names other than those of pagan deities mentioned in the Quran.[36] In the continued absence of a Persian term for Buddhism, let alone wider information about the religion, the statues were described in the journal *Sharaf* merely as "two enormous idols [*but-ha*] made of stone, which are interesting to see, even though it is not known in what era they were made."[37] Insofar as the article did offer specific data, it came by way of a series of measurements and short descriptions of surrounding cells and wall-paintings. As was true of *Kitab-i Jam-i Jam,* rather than being a direct result of inter-Asian informational exchange, the source was a travelogue by the Russian diplomat Ivan Lavrovich Yavorski, who accompanied the 1879 Russian mission to Kabul.[38] The editors of *Sharaf* may well have accessed Yavorski's report through the English translation published earlier the same year in Calcutta, whose Iranian community, as we saw, was developing a substantial publishing industry that exported many books and journals to Iran.[39]

Be that as it may, the lithographic technology used to print *Sharaf* was certainly imported from Russia, which enabled the editor to reproduce a dramatic full-page illustration of the statues. This was likewise based on Yavorski's account, though in a further signal of the Eurasian transmission routes of inter-Asian knowledge, the Russian had himself copied the illustration (and some of his information) from *Travels into Bokhara* by the Scottish spy and diplomat Sir Alexander Burnes.[40] Not that in the 1830s Burnes himself had a much clearer idea about these "gigantic idols," other than to state that "conjecture attributes these images to the Boodhists."[41] But by the time Burnes's data and drawing were reproduced in Tehran, it was fifty years since their original publication, a half century in which both European and Indian understandings of Buddhism had moved on markedly. And so, all told, by the time 'Abd al-Khaliq was writing in the early 1890s, there were few if any reliable published Persian accounts of Buddhism to which he might have resorted for information on the "religion of Burma."[42]

A vicarious view of Buddhist idols: Alexander Burnes's sketch of Bamiyan in Tehran's *Sharaf* (September 1885). Photograph by Nile Green.

As for Arabic, an awareness of Buddhism was only just seeping into the Arabic channel of the public sphere. As late as 1879, an Indo-Arabic survey of the world's religions presented detailed depictions of ancient Greek, Egyptian, and Hindu religiosity, while providing effectively no coverage of Buddhism.[43] In the 1880s the Beirut-published pioneering encyclopedia, *Da'irat al-Ma'arif* (*Circle of Knowledge*), included several entries on Buddhism, drawing on European research to present Gautama as a historical figure who had lived in ancient India.[44] These entries included an Arabic translation of an American article on Buddhism. Echoing the Christological conception of "the gentle Buddha" we have seen in India, the article was probably drawn from New England Transcendentalist circles, which were linked to Beirut via the Lebanese Christian diaspora in New York and the Syrian Protestant College (now the American University of Beirut), which opened in 1866.[45]

Regardless of this Protestant spin, the fact that the multivolume *Da'irat* was issued on the other side of Asia, in Beirut, rendered it a tremendously expensive work that was scarcely available to ordinary readers, whether in India or in the Middle East. Although in the early 1890s the royally endowed Asafiyya Library in the Indian princely state of Hyderabad did subscribe to the *Da'irat*, it was not readily available to Muslims elsewhere in India, particularly scholars affiliated with the hundreds of small madrasas in towns like Rae Bareli that reared the likes of 'Abd al-Khaliq. Evidently, its contents did not reach him. By around 1900, a few short articles on Buddhism began appearing in several Arabic journals, such as *al-Hilal* (*The Crescent*).[46] But though such cheaper print media circulated more widely around Asia, this was marginally too late to be of use to 'Abd al-Khaliq. His case therefore reminds us that inter-Asian understanding was not some mystical state of intuitive awareness. On the contrary, it comprised information contained in particular texts that were more or less accessible in different languages and regions of that diverse great continent.

In principle at least, this still left 'Abd al-Khaliq with the final possibility that the abundant sphere of Urdu print provided knowledge of the religion of Burma (or Buddha). India's central position as Asia's informational hub made this the more promising of the informational avenues that were linguistically open to him, albeit to a lesser degree than might be expected. For even in this most widespread of Indian printed languages, entire books devoted to Buddhism appeared only toward the end of the nineteenth century.

Nonetheless, short accounts of Burmese religiosity did appear in Urdu translations of geography books. In the years on either side of 1860, India's first publishing magnate, Nawwal Kishore, published several editions of an English geography of Asia that hinted helpfully that the people of Burma "follow the religion of Bodh . . . and believe in reincarnation [*tanasukh*]."[47] The book even provided the proper name of the historical Buddha when it recounted how "in the Burmese city of Ava there is a beautiful temple of the Bodh religion, inside which stands a statue [*murt*], some eight yards high, of Gautam."[48]

As we saw earlier, shorter accounts of the Buddha had already appeared in some of the histories of India translated from English by the likes of the missionary John Clark Marshman for the vernacular schools that expanded over the second half of the century. But the distribution of such textbooks through specific schools limited their social reach: they apparently did not reach 'Abd al-Khaliq, who probably studied at a local madrasa rather than at a government (still less a missionary) school. Even in the case of Muhammad Kazim Barlas, a prolific North Indian author who in 1898 published a detailed Urdu travel account of the Buddhist-majority island of Ceylon, information was hard to come by.[49] Despite coming from the region of India where the Buddha spent most of his life, Barlas declared that Bodh had been born in China.[50] With no access to the Bengali or English texts we have seen published in Calcutta, Barlas based his depiction of what he called the religion of Bodh on his own ad hoc observations; the results were considerably less accurate than those of the more doctrinally curious 'Abd al-Khaliq. Unlike his missionary coreligionist, Barlas was a merchant who didn't go to the trouble of learning the written Pali and Sinhala in which Ceylon's Buddhist texts were written. Instead, he based his account of the religion on the shallower evidence of watching street processions and peeping inside temples.

Nonetheless, from the 1880s, Urdu books dealing specifically with Buddhism did begin to make their appearance in the open book market as bilingual Indians began translating or summarizing the contents of what was by then an abundant body of not only Orientalist scholarship but also popular English books on the Buddha. One of the earliest appeared in 1889 by way of an Urdu rendition of one of Rhys Davids's many books, apparently his *Buddhism: Being a Sketch of the Life and Teachings of Gautama, the Buddha.*[51] Reflecting the attraction many liberal Victorian Christians now felt for the "gentle Buddha," it was originally commissioned by the Society for Promoting Christian Knowledge and translated by a Hindu pundit called Lala Śrirama. The latter summarized Rhys Davids's biographical reconstruction of the historical Buddha "Gutam" in the lowlands between Nepal and Bihar.[52] Moreover, the book was published in Moradabad, a few hundred miles west of 'Abd al-Khaliq's hometown, making it a far closer and cheaper source of information than the Arabic encyclopedia from Beirut. Nonetheless, he seems not to have known of it; or, at least, he had not linked it to the religion he had studied. As 'Abd al-Khaliq stated plainly in his preface, there existed no books in Urdu about the "religion of Burma."

Then, in 1892, the same year that he finished his *Sayr-i Barhma,* a shorter Urdu life of the Buddha was published in Lahore by another Hindu scholar, Pandit Ramnath Kushal.[53] Like Śrirama's translation of Rhys Davids, Kushal's book had the potential to transform 'Abd al-Khaliq's understanding of Shingutama and the religion he founded. After rendering sections of Edwin Arnold's versified *Light of Asia* into a *masnawi* poem, Kushal laid out the bare historical facts about the origins of the religion as established by the Orientalists during the previous half century.[54] By drawing on several other English works, Kushal identified the Buddha with "Gutam" and precisely plotted his life as it unfolded on the soil of India "six hundred years before Jesus."[55] He then summarized the Buddha's teaching in the form of ten rules (a curious departure from the Orientalist emphasis on the Noble Eightfold Path) and provided the key dates of the Buddha's biography in tabulated form, using the Christian "Before Christ" (*qabl-i masih*) calendrical system for want of a standard Indian equivalent for the dating of antiquity.[56]

Of even greater potential use to 'Abd al-Khaliq was Kushal's second table of dates because this outlined the spread of the "religion of Buddha" (*Bodh mazhab*) from its Indian homeland to Burma (including the date of AD 450) as well as China and Japan.[57] Yet even though Kushal had written his book precisely to make the life of the historical Buddha available in the "commonly understood" (*'am fahm*) Urdu, and had it published in an edition of 1,500 copies to reach the print-based public (*pablik*), it had clearly not reached 'Abd al-Khaliq.[58] As a result, he still regarded Shingutama as a uniquely Burmese figure with no relationship with either India or the wider religion of Buddhism being practiced around Asia and revived in his North Indian home region by the new missionaries sailing from Ceylon and, increasingly, Burma itself.[59]

As for the Buddhist scriptures that 'Abd al-Khaliq worked so hard to directly access through studying the Burmese language, it would not be till some years after the appearance of his own book that such scriptures began to be translated into modern Indian languages, albeit largely by way of previous English translations. Aside from the Bengali Hindu scholars discussed earlier, who published in either Bengali or English, there were some Muslim scholars learning Sanskrit. One was the Sayyid 'Ali Bilgrami (1851–1911), an official in the employ of the Nizam's state of Hyderabad in southern India who from 1890 to 1892, while 'Abd al-Khaliq was struggling to learn Burmese, also served as a Sanskrit examiner for the University of Madras. Unfortunately, Bilgrami's only book in Sanskrit was an edition of a poem by Ramadasa Chabildasa on the famous legend of the Rajput princess Padmini, which he published in Bombay in 1888.[60] Far from being a study of Buddhism, Burmese or otherwise, it was a romance about a Hindu princess. Printed translations of the Sanskrit, Pali, or Burmese Buddhist canon into languages that 'Abd al-Khaliq and other ordinary North Indians could read were quite another matter. None appears to have existed by the time he set off for Burma.

And so, for want of resources in languages he could read, our Muslim investigator was forced to fall back on his own efforts and intelligence. Though these were considerable indeed, such a solitary enterprise inevitably had its limits.

Investigating the "Religion of Burma"

By the time 'Abd al-Khaliq arrived in Mandalay, the former Buddhist capital was not only teeming with the British officers and Indian soldiers who had recently conquered it; it was also brimming with both Christian and Baha'i missionaries. When the American Baha'i convert Sydney Sprague turned up, he found "the Bahá'ís number several hundreds in Mandalay and are nearly all native Burmans."[61] Partaking in the same self-projecting endeavors, 'Abd al-Khaliq set about investigating what these "native Burmans" believed so he could better engage them—and their leader the thathanabaing—in what he conceived as a rational doctrinal debate.

Though 'Abd al-Khaliq repeatedly described as research (*tahqiq*—literally, "finding truth") his investigations into the religion, language, history, and ethnography of Burma, he was absolutely clear about the superiority of Islam and his hope that the Burmese would be converted. Yet he was by the same token sincerely interested in what the indigenous population of Burma believed, taking seriously not only their doctrines but also their capacity to reason, "reason" (*'aql*) being one of the key terms of his subsequent debate with the thathanabaing. Nor did he regard the Burmese as inherently immoral, despite their indecent clothes and customs. Consequently, as he saw matters, when he explained to them the logical inconsistencies and ethical contradictions of such chief doctrines as reincarnation (*tanasukh*), the Burmese would be able to see the reason and morality of his arguments and in turn accept the more logical and moral teachings of Islam, pointing again to the crucial role of reason in his critique of Buddhism.

'Abd al-Khaliq had both the intellectual acuity and motivation to move beyond older generalizations that the "religion of Burma" was mere idolatry. He eschewed the term *but-parasti* (idol worship) that was long familiar in Persian and Urdu depictions of Hindu and, a thousand years earlier, Buddhist religiosity. (Ironically, *but* originally derived from the early medieval Indian Prakrit name for Buddha that Muslim settlers encountered in Central Asia and then adopted in Persian and Urdu as the generic word for an idol.)[62] As we saw in the previous chapter, even the open-minded Iranian commercial official Fazlullah Husayni still wrote about Burmese *but-parasti* in his report on his journey to Mandalay in 1858. The British-sponsored manuscript translations of Buddhist texts from Pali into Persian made by Kyaw Jain and 'Azizullah Bukhari had likewise opted (presumably at the latter's discretion) to present Burmese practices in the same terms of *but-parasti*, though 'Abd al-Khaliq had in any case apparently not read them.[63] By contrast, 'Abd al-Khaliq began his first chapter by explaining that the Burmese in fact worship one God (*khuda*) and follow one scripture (*kitab*).[64] Far from idol-worshipping polytheists, they were therefore monotheists like Jews and Christians, albeit similarly misled ones. Drawing on similarly commensurate Islamic terms, he wrote approvingly of Burmese monks (to whom he correctly referred as *pongyis*), explaining how "the monks are considered the learned clerics [*'ulama*] and dervishes [*darwish*] of this religion, renouncing the world and refusing to accept gold, silver, rupees, or pennies."[65] In such ways, 'Abd al-Khaliq depicted the Burmese as full and equal human beings: they were fellow monotheists who possessed a civilization, a history, and a literate high culture. But that very humanity meant that they deserved to be guided away from their false religion to the light and salvation of Islam.

In line with these primary concerns, 'Abd al-Khaliq devoted around three quarters of *Sayr-i Barhma* to the discussion of religion. He felt it necessary to provide the most basic information, such as the fact that their statues were in human form and hence dissimilar to those of Hindu gods. At a time before photography and religious commodification had spread the "Buddha image" worldwide, the iconography of Buddhism remained remarkably unfamiliar even in the country—India—where the religion originated. Filling this informational void, 'Abd al-Khaliq covered almost every aspect of Burmese belief and practice, from the creation of the world and its place in their cosmology to the history of what in Islamic terms he called Burma's prophets, the teachings of their scriptures, their rules of monastic life, and the rituals and festivals of the common people.

While we have already seen a separate rediscovery of Buddhism taking place in Calcutta through conversations between Anglophone Bengali scholars and British Orientalists, 'Abd al-Khaliq did not draw on Orientalist studies to paint his picture of Burmese religion. He was also evidently unfamiliar with the translations from Pali to Persian that John Murray MacGregor, a prominent member of Calcutta's Asiatic Society, had commissioned from the aforementioned Buddhist monk Kyaw Jain and the Muslim secretary Shah 'Azizullah Bukhari during a journey they made together through the Arakan region that bordered Bengal.[66] Despite the fact that these "Anglo-Persian" collaborations translated into Persian a great deal of information on Buddhism, the texts remained in rare, even unique manuscripts that were apparently never published.

Instead of drawing on such earlier investigations, 'Abd al-Khaliq drew directly from his own discussions with Burmese monks and studies of Burmese texts, activities made possible by his study of the Burmese language. As he explained, his time in Burma comprised many years of intense (albeit presumably part-time) study of the Burmese language, which opened up for him the mental and philosophical world of his learned counterparts. These were the Buddhist monks and, ultimately, the man he described in commensurable Muslim terms as the "head of the clerics" (*malik al-'ulama*), or *thathanabaing*, the Burmese word being carefully transliterated into Arabic script.[67] This was not the first time this had happened, any more than the translations that Shah 'Azizullah Bukhari had made with the Buddhist monk Kyaw Jain: local Muslims and Buddhists in Burma had explored one another's belief systems before, just as learned Hindu and Muslim neighbors had in India. What was new was the ability to make the findings of such an investigation available to a larger reading public by means of the public sphere of print.

Given that 'Abd al-Khaliq set out with no inherited knowledge base about Buddhism—not even a category or name for it—much of what he discovered was impressively accurate. While he did not realize that the person he called Shingutama (i.e., Gautama) was more widely known as the Buddha (or Bodh), he correctly understood that Shingutama had left no book of his own; rather, he had passed on his teachings orally to disciples who had subsequently compiled his teachings in textual form, among which was a canon of the ten most respected books.[68] He also gave a detailed and accurate account of the monastic rules of the *pongyis*, including dress, dietary rules, and vows of poverty and chastity; of the education of boys by local monasteries; of the forms of lay worship, including the popular celebration of holy days; of the learned conception of the universe, from its multiple heavens to the relation between the sun, moon, and earth; and thence of the lunar calendar, which, unlike the Islamic calendar, began with the setting rather than new moon.[69]

As to how he learned all this, on several occasions he claimed not only to have mastered the language of Burma, but to have studied the key texts of its religion, phonetically naming several Burmese texts that he had inspected, including the *Pahasya,* his term for the Burmese Buddhist scriptures.[70] Here 'Abd al-Khaliq was probably referring to the *Tipitaka* (that is, the Theravada Buddhist canon), as transmitted through commentaries either in Burmese or in the Pali he also learned. He may have taken his term *Pahasya* from local pronunciation of the Sanskrit *bhasya* (words, speech), which was often used in the compound form *Buddhabhasya* ("words of the Buddha"), which, through the Pali *Buddha-bhasa,* provides the common Burmese word for Buddhism, *boda-batha.*[71] Alternatively, *Pahasya* may have merely been his Urdu rendering of the Burmese word *peza* for a palm-leaf manuscript. In either case, the other Burmese loanwords he transcribed into his book point to the genuine linguistic basis of his investigations.

Yet as 'Abd al-Khaliq tried to make philosophical sense of these *Pahasya* texts, and to explain them to his Indian Muslim readers, he needed to find the nearest equivalents in his own conceptual system. Following Islamic

theological conceptions of the primacy of prophethood, he therefore summarized what he took to be a faint Burmese echo of the Muslim model of
prophethood by way of a system in which God manifested himself in various
incarnations. Pointing to his accurate grasp of Burma's religious lexicon, the
term he used here for incarnation—*pahya*—is a common Burmese epithet for
the Buddha, literally meaning "Lord."[72]

During this discussion he cited a Burmese text, for which he gave the phonetic title *Zi-Na-Tha-Paka-Tani*. The text in question was clearly the *Zinatthapakathani* (from the Pali *Jinatthapakasani*), the major Burmese-language
biography of the Buddha written by Kyi-thay Le-htat Sayadaw during the reign
of King Mindon just a few decades earlier. According to 'Abd al-Khaliq's reading of the *Zinatthapakathani*, there were thousands of these divine incarnations, though only five major ones who revealed scriptures. He transcribed
their names as Gugatagu, Gunagun, Gataba, Shingutama, and A'yi Madi.[73] He
was referring, respectively, to Gaguthan (Pali: Kakusandha); Gonagon (Pali:
Konagamana); Kathapa (Pali: Kassapa); Shin Godama (Pali: Gotama, i.e., the
historical Buddha); and Ayi Medaya (Pali: Ariya Metteyya). The last was the
fifth, final—and future—Buddha of the current cosmic aeon. Given the challenges of rendering into Arabic script names he had read in Burmese, the recognizable congruity and accuracy of his recording of these names are further
testament to the high philological standard of his research.

The era of Shingutama, he went on to explain, was said to be still ongoing,
after which the coming of A'yi Madi would herald the end of the world. (Here
he used the Muslim term *qiyamat*, or Day of Judgment.) While the name A'yi
Madi may have been a reference to the future Maitreya (Pali: Metteyya) of Buddhist eschatology, for 'Abd al-Khaliq the sound of his name prompted what
was effectively an Islamic exegesis of the *Zinatthapakathani*, which he interpreted by finding points of congruence rather than contradiction with Islam.
Given the emphasis of the Buddhist text on a sequence of teachers bringing
teachings before a final cosmic reckoning, this suggested to 'Abd al-Khaliq
that the "religion of Burma" sounded somewhat similar to Islam—or, rather,
like Christianity and Judaism, a partially true corruption of the pristine teachings of Islam.

In the following sections, 'Abd al-Khaliq made these comparisons explicit,
providing more detail on several of the other *pahya* incarnations. Among the
thousands of these he said the Burmese believed had existed, he singled out
Sulamani, Dajalla, Ma Daniga, and A'yi Madi, since their names or biographies voiced what seemed to be clear echoes of Muslim tradition. Though he

gave no further detail on Dajalla, the name itself was presumably suggestive enough for his readers to realize it closely resembled the Urdu and Arabic name Dajjal for the false messiah or Antichrist at the end of time. In the case of Sulamani, he made his comparison more explicit, pointing out that, since Sulamani was said to have been either a great king who ruled the whole world or another divine incarnation, Muslims in Burma believed he was none other than the Quranic Sulayman (that is, the biblical Solomon), who in Islamic tradition was both a great king and a prophet.[74]

In fact, the Burmese term *Sulamani* (from the Pali *Culamani*), meaning "crest jewel," is not usually associated with a particular Buddha incarnation but is instead the name of an important pagoda in the medieval capital Pagan. While this seems to be echoed in 'Abd al-Khaliq's own uncertainty about whether Sulamani was a king or an incarnation, his interpretive framing of Sulamani as the Quranic Sulayman points again to his larger interpretive attempt to reconcile the Burmese scriptures with his own. As he testified in his preface, he was motivated by the search for truth; the word he used for his research (*tahqiq*) literally meant to "find truth" or "verify." Since he was a committed Muslim (indeed, a religious teacher), such truth necessarily had to be in harmony with the Quran, and he faced two options when confronted with the very different teachings he found in the Burmese texts. One option, which he rejected, was to declare them entirely erroneous and false. The other, which he adopted, was to reconcile their contents with the Quran and, in doing so, bestow on them the partial accolade of being a truthful but distorted revelation. Paradoxically, and yet with perfect theological logic, converting the Burmese to Islam was, therefore, to return them to the misinterpreted universal truths that still dimly glimmered in their own scriptures. For 'Abd al-Khaliq was no cosmopolitan sceptic, happy to regard all religions as equally valid (or invalid). Rather, his investigations of the "religion of Burma" were motivated by his humanitarian desire to save Burmese souls, albeit at the cost of extinguishing their religion—or, as he saw matters, by restoring to the Burmese the original truths that were concealed by their corrupted beliefs.

He continued his investigations in this salvational mode. Turning to the subsequent incarnation—Ma Daniga—he explained that the author of the *Zinatthapakathani* wrote that Ma Daniga had been born in the "navel of the world." 'Abd al-Khaliq then referred to a Burmese history book, which he phonetically transliterated as *Niya Ta Dana Chhun*—this appears to have been the mixed Pali-Burmese text *Niyatadana Kyam* (*Book of Perpetual Donation*). This work, he continued, detailed how Ma Daniga had revealed a "truthful book";

had once ascended into the heavens; had subsequently returned to earth and killed a great many of his enemies; and had then cut the moon asunder.[75] For his explanation, 'Abd al-Khaliq resorted to what "the [local] Muslims say." This was that Ma Daniga was actually another name for the Prophet Muhammad because he too had been born in the navel of the world (Mecca); had brought a book (the Quran); had made an ascent to heaven (the celestial ascent or *mi'raj* of the Quran); had returned to earth to wage war (the jihads against the pagan Arabs); and had also cut the moon in two (the celebrated miracle of the *shaqq al-qamar* or "splitting of the moon"). Turning to the next figure in the list, 'Abd al-Khaliq likewise explained that "the People of Islam" claim that the *pahya* A'yi Madi is none other than the figure Muslims know as the Mahdi, who will usher in the end of time.[76]

If this interpretive method was plainly Islamocentric, then it was not a uniquely Muslim approach. A decade later, similar attitudes shaped a Bengali account of Burma by the highly educated Indumadhab Mallick (1869–1917), who held two master's degrees, in philosophy and physics. But Mallick interpreted Burmese culture through a correspondingly Hinducentric lens, which led him even to claim the name Burma was derived from the moniker of the Hindu creation god, Brahma, whom he declared the Burmese acknowledged as the creator of humankind.[77] This was no more linguistically accurate than 'Abd al-Khaliq's attempt at Arabic-based etymology. It was a parallel part of a wider pattern of projecting the self while engaging the other.

'Abd al-Khaliq's comparative method also allows us to make sense of the factual mistakes he made through the lack of a reliable corpus of existing research in Urdu on Buddhist history or doctrine. On several occasions, he claimed that Shingutama (that is, Gautama, the historical Buddha) was born *after* the Prophet Muhammad.[78] Indeed, relying on the ingenious (if ultimately erroneous) calculations that 'Abd al-Khaliq based on dates given by his sources in the Burmese calendar, he declared that Shingutama—the Buddha—was born on 12 Shawwal 123 Hijri (August 30, 741) and died some time during the year 203 Hijri (818).[79] He also seemingly suggested that Shingutama died in the Burmese city of Moulmein.[80] Yet as British scholars and their Bengali and Ceylonese colleagues had by this time established, Gautama the Buddha had not only lived over a thousand years earlier, but had in fact died in the Indian town of Kushinagar. Far from being in distant Moulmein, this was a mere 180 miles from 'Abd al-Khaliq's hometown.

Yet if 'Abd al-Khaliq's calculations were another of the many errors of empirical fact made by European and even Asian investigators of Buddhist history during the nineteenth century, then this was not a meaningless mistake. For the time line he provided was logically consistent with the larger theological schema into which he placed the "religion of Burma." His late date for the Buddha's death fitted coherently with the truth claims of Islam: if Shingutama was born *after* Muhammad, who was by long-standing dogma considered the "last Prophet," then he could not be the final and definitive messenger of God. So, rather than undermine 'Abd al-Khaliq's achievements, the factual discrepancies in *Sayr-i Barhma* draw our attention to his theological purposes and their own cultural logic.

Improvised Methods of Intercultural Learning

To accomplish his goal of understanding (albeit then refuting) the "religion of Burma," 'Abd al-Khaliq would have been greatly helped by Muslim counterparts to the dictionaries and grammars that were among the earliest works published by the European missionaries in Calcutta and without which the Christian understanding-cum-critique of Asia's religions would have been impossible. But at the time he was writing, there was very little available by way of a comparable printed corpus of inter-Asian dictionaries in languages he could read—which, judging by the evidence of his writing, comprised Urdu, Hindi, Persian, Arabic, eventually Burmese, and to some degree Pali. Such is its significance that this relative underdevelopment of inter-Asian dictionaries needs explaining.

Of course, merchants and other people moving across Asia had always found ways to communicate, principally through the spoken word. Members of Asia's various trading communities probably learned to speak several languages—or, at least, mercantile pidgins—as part of their on-the-job apprenticeships and without the need for written textbooks, just as those born in multilingual cities learned to converse with varying proficiency in several languages. Written lingua francas like Persian—or farther east, classical Chinese—also spread as an aid to communication among bureaucrats, diplomats, and cultural elites. But the range of multilingual—and, moreover, multiliterate—skills required to read the literature or scripture of another religious community required more specialized linguistic tools than either spoken pidgins or written lingua francas.

During the early modern period, Indian Muslims had certainly been major compilers of Arabic and Persian dictionaries, as well as occasionally of ones in Chaghatai Turkish and even Sanskrit. These works and their updated successors had been among the earliest Asian-language books published in Calcutta, whether in the case of the medieval Arabic-Persian lexicon known as the *Kitab al-Surah* or Joseph Baretto's trilingual Arabic-Persian-Turkic dictionary, *Kitab-i Shams al-Lughat*. Such printed dictionaries reached their apogee in 1886 under the patronage of Shahjahan Bigam, the female ruler of Bhopal, with the publication of *Khazanat al-Lughat* (*The Treasury of Words*), an Urdu-based hexaglot that provided word equivalents in Arabic, Persian, Ottoman Turkish, Sanskrit, and English.[81] But even as late as the 1890s, when 'Abd al-Khaliq was writing—and indeed, much later—very few word books were designed for communication between the languages of Asia's different religious traditions. This was especially true of formal dictionaries that incorporated not merely transliterated word lists for simple spoken usage, but also the alphabets used by languages as orthographically varied as Arabic, Hindi, Tamil, Burmese, Sinhala, Malay, Javanese, and Thai, let alone Chinese and Japanese.

Insofar as they existed, dictionaries and grammars between Asian languages were directed toward enabling specific types of linguistic—and cultural—interaction, overwhelmingly *within* rather than *between* the religious traditions of Asia.[82] Building on centuries-old precedents with regional equivalents from Anatolia to Japan, there were many dictionaries that enabled the speaker of Turkish to study Persian; the speaker of Malay to master Arabic; the speaker of Japanese to study classical Chinese; or the speaker of Thai to learn Pali. But such works were intended to deepen students' understanding of their *own* religious or cultural heritage, so that a Malay Muslim might read the Quran, or a Thai Buddhist read the *Tipitaka*. This was quite a different enterprise from learning to read the literature or scripture of an entirely different religion or culture, whether for purposes of pleasure or of polemic.

In India, centuries of close contact between Hindu and Muslim savants at the Mughal court had created a corpus of philological literature that allowed the small numbers of readers who had access to such manuscripts (and sufficient talent and commitment to study them) to translate between Persian and Sanskrit.[83] Under the Qing Empire in China, similar learned interactions between Confucianist and Muslim literati had created a comparable linguistic apparatus. But beyond these "intra-religious" or "intra-imperial" interactions, there developed no comparable body of lexicographical works between the languages of Asia at large, even between such major languages as Chinese and Hindi or Japanese and Arabic. Well into the twentieth century, and even today in many cases, there are simply no inter-Asian equivalents to the vast range of grammars and dictionaries created by Europe's missionaries and Orientalists.

As a consequence, the translation of texts between Asia's different languages often had to rely on either the mediation of English-based dictionaries or previous translations into European languages that were rendered into different Asian languages in turn. We will see many such cases later.

Yet this was not the whole story. For by the late nineteenth century, printed language guides were beginning to appear, albeit slowly, at least around the Bay of Bengal. 'Abd al-Khaliq was one of the first to make cultural rather than commercial use of them. For as his *Sayr-i Barhma* makes clear, he began his research by first purchasing dictionaries, then employing a local language teacher, and finally reading core texts under his guidance. This pedagogical route would allow him to enter religious debates with local scholars, just as the same methods enabled Christian missionary disputations. His was no minor achievement: very few British officials learned to read Burmese and, unlike the missionaries, relied instead on either English or the spoken "Hindustani" Urdu that had effectively become Rangoon's oral lingua franca.[84] Yet for 'Abd al-Khaliq, reliance on Urdu was simply insufficient because most ordinary Burmese could not speak it, particularly in inland regions. "Yes," he conceded, "in Rangoon some of the important local traders do speak Urdu, but they speak it with many mistakes, so one cannot have a proper conversation."[85] This throwaway remark is direct testimony to the linguistic challenges that surrounded even everyday inter-Asian interactions, let alone the sustained exchange of complex ideas about one another's beliefs and cultures.

'Abd al-Khaliq also explained that he initially tried to learn Burmese with what he referred to as "the dictionary of W. H. Sloane."[86] This was an updated edition of the pioneering Burmese dictionary of the Baptist missionary Adoniram Judson, which was published in 1877 by W. H. Sloane for Rangoon's American Baptist Mission Press.[87] What is revealing about this method of learning is that it shows that 'Abd al-Khaliq turned first to a dictionary prepared by a Christian missionary, presumably choosing Judson's because, having already gone through a series of editions, it was simply the most widely available. The problem was, he went on, that this was too technical for the beginner, because the dictionary required the reader to already know the Burmese script (in which all the Burmese words were printed) as well as both the English language and script (in which all the definitions were given). Fortunately, though, 'Abd al-Khaliq had arrived in Burma at a time when vernacular lexicography was also making advances. As a result, he was able to find a more useful language book compiled by a learned Indian bureaucrat called Munshi Hanuman Parshad, in which Burmese words were given in the Devanagari

script used for Hindi, followed by Hindustani translations given in both Devanagari and Arabic script.[88]

By the time of his residence in Burma in the 1880s and early 1890s, there
were also several other dictionaries that brought Urdu together with Burmese.
Aside from Parshad's, there was William Henry Begbie and Abraham Joseph's
Vocabulary: English, Burmese, Hindustani & Tamil, issued in 1877 in Rangoon,
though like Judson's, this also used "English characters with the Burmese also
in native letters."[89] In 1892 a fifty-page Gujarati-Burmese lexicon was issued
in the port of Surat as an aid for Gujarati traders.[90] There was also its Tamil-
based equivalent, compiled by Muhammad Ghous, in which Urdu, Burmese,
and Tamil vocabulary was given in the Tamil script. Filling a gap in the market,
in the mid-1880s it rapidly went through two editions from Rangoon.[91] Other
cheap published works of inter-Asian lexicography included *Lisan al-Jaza'ir*
(*Language of the Islands*), a short lexicon of Urdu, Sinhala, Malay, and Tamil
compiled by Muhammad Kazim Barlas, who, we saw earlier, also wrote a detailed Urdu account of Ceylon.[92]

So why, then, could 'Abd al-Khaliq or other intercultural investigators not
rely on these new linguistic tools? The problem was that almost all such works
included only the script of their intended Indian users, be it Tamil, Devanagari, or Urdu's modified Arabic letters. For anyone picking up a local book in
Burma—whether the Pali *Tipitaka* or an anthology of Burmese poetry—they
were effectively useless, because they did not include the Burmese alphabet
(or in most cases even the basic elements of grammar). This rendered them
useful as phrase books for the simple, spoken conversations of merchants and
migrants, but far less helpful for the kind of learned cultural investigations
that 'Abd al-Khaliq had in mind.

Several other language guides approached these interlinguistic exchanges
from the Burmese side, such as San Hia Hbaw's 1882 manual of Hindi and
Burmese conversation, and Hba Kyu's later handbook of useful phrases in
Urdu, English, Tamil, Chinese, and Burmese.[93] But the problem here was the
same in reverse. Since the books were intended for Burmese readers, all the
other languages were transliterated into Burmese script, so the user had to be
able to read Burmese to begin with. Similarly unhelpful for 'Abd al-Khaliq's
purposes was the Tamil-to-Burmese-to-Gujarati-to-English reference work
compiled by Yussuf Rautar, a Tamil merchant from Nagapattinam who had
settled at 16 Moghul Road at the heart of Rangoon's business district.[94] Far
from being intended to help Indians read books in Burmese, it comprised a
set of conversion tables for weights and measurements meant to ease transac-

tions in the marketplace. As Rautar explained in his preface, his pamphlet was aimed at "the commercial public." More useful for Indians hoping to learn to read Burmese texts was the *English, Hindustani and Burmese Manual*, published by a Burmese Muslim with the bilingual names U Aung Hmat and Ahmad 'Ali in 1905, since the manual also included the Burmese script.[95] But it had not yet been published at the time of 'Abd al-Khaliq's investigations.

So, for Indians hoping to read the Buddhist scriptures in Burmese or Pali, there was quite simply no equivalent to such Christian works as *Taqdis al-Lughat (The Sanctifier of Language)*, an Urdu dictionary and concordance of the Bible printed in Lucknow twenty years before 'Abd al-Khaliq's own book made its appearance there.[96] Moreover, *Taqdis al-Lughat* was only one of many such Indian-language guides to the Christian scriptures, many of them published by the Methodist Mission that had an outpost in 'Abd al-Khaliq's hometown. In short, it was far easier for Indians to learn about Christianity—indeed, to read its entire voluminous scriptures—than it was to parse even a single sentence of a Buddhist text in Burmese, let alone Pali, Chinese, or Thai.

Consequently, as his studies advanced, 'Abd al-Khaliq found Parshad's Urdu-Burmese lexicon of limited help: its lack of Burmese letters limited its use for reading the Burmese texts that were his primary interest. Since aside from Judson's dictionary, he knew of no other language aid (he explicitly stated as much), he decided to learn to read Burmese directly from a local teacher.[97] As his competence increased, he found fault with Parshad's dictionary, pointing to mistakes in its translations, whether by missing the Burmese tone of politeness, ignoring the decorous periphrasis used when speaking of royal or religious figures, or failing to recognize the dual meanings of various homonyms.[98] Cognizant of the pioneering character of his investigations—he proudly declared as much in his preface—he included in *Sayr-i Barhma* a transliteration table that placed the Burmese alphabet alongside its phonetic and written equivalent in Arabic script.[99]

Such was the importance he gave to transmitting to other Indians the ability to acquire literacy in Burmese that his sections on the language, its written forms, and key texts amounted to almost a quarter of his book.[100] He produced eight different tables, not only detailing the alphabet, but covering the numbers, days, months, years, weights, and reckoning systems used in Burma.[101] Although he warned that learning Burmese was "extremely difficult"—it was after all a tonal language with no lowland South Asian equivalent—he raised the linguistic bar still higher by outlining the difference between Burmese and Pali, noting how the latter was not understood by ordinary Burmese.[102]

جدول حروف برھما

اُردو	تلفظ	صورت حروف	اُردو	تلفظ	صورت حروف
ط	ڈاؤُ		ا	گاجی	
ظ	ڈااوجھی		ب	گھانگوبی	
ع	نا گنی		پ	گانگنی	
غ	یانزاکُو		ت	گاجی	
ف	چھنا اوکتو		ث	ٹوؤُ	
ق	نا گۀ جنی		ج	ساکون	
ک	نا گُوڈ		چ	سائین	
گ	ٹا		ح	ڈاگُوڈ	
ل	یا		خ	ڈامین نزوے	
م	یاگُوڈ		د	ہناؤُ	
ن	لا		ڈ	ٹھائین جنی	
و	گوا		ذ	ٹھاؤُن بی	
ہ	ٹا		ر	ڈامین گاؤُ	
ء	کا		ڑ	ڈامین ٹو	
ی	لاجنی		ز	ناجنی	
ے	آ		س	ٹاؤُن لاؤُ	
			ش	ٹھاٹھین ڈو	

Learning to read Burmese: 'Abd al-Khaliq's alphabetic conversion table. 'Abd al-Khaliq Khan Muwahid, *Sayr-i Barhma* (Lucknow: Matba' Mina Lakhnaw, 1893). Photograph by Nile Green.

In view of his missionary concerns, 'Abd al-Khaliq pointed out that there were only a few books in Burmese on Muslim prayers and fasting and that, so far, only a few short sections of the Quran had been translated.[103] Nonetheless, he added, the Burmese seemed to be very interested in "printed books."[104] Insofar as Muslim printed books in Burmese were only just appearing when he was writing in the early 1890s, he was largely correct. For in trying to promote Islam in Burma, 'Abd al-Khaliq's was not a lone voice. In the years directly on either side of the publication of his *Sayr-i Barhma* in 1893, a number of religious books were translated into Burmese from Arabic or Urdu. Some were printed in Bombay, others by the new presses of Moulmein and Rangoon, including texts comparing the teachings of Islam with those of Buddhism.[105] In the years after 'Abd al-Khaliq published his book, still more translations from Urdu began to be published in Mandalay, including a life of the Prophet Muhammad and his wife Khadija and a translated catechism of Muslim beliefs that contained a defense of Islam, presumably in response to critiques from the more assertive new Buddhist organizations.[106] By 1909 two Burmese versions of the Quran were published, one translated in Rangoon by a Burmese Muslim called U Kran and another by an Indian Muslim who was born and raised in Burma.[107] Like the many translations of the Quran made in colonial India, this was a response to the Christian translations that had flooded the streets of Burma with vernacular Bibles before locals had learned to print a single book of their own.

Even as 'Abd al-Khaliq made advances in intercultural understanding, he also therefore participated in the polemical public sphere that surrounded and shaped him. For by making sense of the "religion of Burma" in Muslim terms, he hoped to direct those whom it misled toward the saving light of Islam. And what better way to do this than to hold a public debate, or *munazara*, with their leader?

Debating the Thathanabaing

The debate that 'Abd al-Khaliq described purportedly took place in Mandalay, the capital of Burma's last Buddhist kingdom, which fell to British and Indian troops in November 1885, seven years before 'Abd al-Khaliq completed his book.[108] The end of royal patronage of monasteries deprived many thousands of monks of their livelihoods, and between 1885 and 1892, a series of fires destroyed many of the city's monasteries.[109] During the 1890s, Indians played a key part in installing the new colonial order, as some 4,000 Indian troops and over 10,000 mostly Indian military police were stationed in the defeated provinces of Upper Burma, which centered on Mandalay.[110] Since Mandalay Hill and all the Buddhist shrines near the old city were included in the new military cantonment, "many of them were used to house Indian troops, most of whom were Muslim or Sikh."[111] And as in Rangoon beforehand, annexation was followed by economic migration: by 1901 Indians predominated among Mandalay's 21,000 foreign-born residents.[112] Enabling this was the railway—staffed largely by hardworking Indians—that from 1889 connected Rangoon with Mandalay. Since 'Abd al-Khaliq recorded the date of his debate with the thathanabaing as taking place in 1307 Hijri (that is, 1889–1890), there is every reason to suppose that he was one of the thousands of Indians who used the new train service during its first year.[113]

He was following the evangelical trail opened up by Christian missionaries. American Baptists were the missionary pioneers in Upper Burma, followed by the Society for the Propagation of the Gospel, which arrived under Burmese royal protection fifteen years before Mandalay's conquest, by which time the Methodists had also arrived. In 1887 the British authorities provided the Methodist preacher Joseph Bateson with one of the many abandoned monasteries in which to establish his mission.[114] By the 1890s, as we saw in the previous chapter, the emissaries of such new religions as Baha'ism and the conversionist Hinduism of the Arya Samaj also arrived, seeing at least a dozen Baha'i texts published in Mandalay in Burmese translation.[115] It was amid this wider self-projecting pattern of intercultural interaction that 'Abd al-Khaliq claimed to have debated the thathanabaing.

An office given shape by King Bodawpaya in 1788, the thathanabaing (or "controller of the religion") was the royally installed primate of the Thudhamma monastic lineage of Burmese Buddhism. His task was to ensure the orthodoxy of monks and manage the king's donations, along with the generations of inherited monastic and temple properties, duties undertaken with the *mahadan-wun* ("minister of great donations," which was actually a council).[116] As 'Abd al-Khaliq explained matters: "In the whole of the country of Burma, there is one very great monk (*ponji*) who is like the emperor of all the other monks. All the other monks bow down before him. They call him Tada Bin [i.e., thathanabaing]; that is, the King of Clerics (*malik al-'ulama*) or Chief Interpreter (*mujtahid*)."[117] This rendering in Islamic terms was certainly a simplification of the complex structures of Buddhist religious authority. The thathanabaing was not the sole leader of all of Burma's Buddhists in the way that

'Abd al-Khaliq understood. But he was still a highly prominent opponent in a public debate. To try to defeat and, moreover, convert the thathanabaing was therefore a bold stratagem indeed. It was nonetheless a peaceful one, based, as 'Abd al-Khaliq emphasized, on rational persuasion.

In the lead-up to the debate section of his book, 'Abd al-Khaliq explained that an influential monk who had taught him Burmese had eventually become a Muslim and renounced his monastic vows to take a wife after the example of the Prophet Muhammad. This convert then led fourteen of his disciples to similarly break their vows of celibacy and embrace Islam.[118] The defeat of the thathanabaing offered the possibility of saving even more Burmese souls because, as 'Abd al-Khaliq explained, "all the ordinary Burmese monks respect [Tada Bin] so much that they ask him to adjudicate any disagreements or agreements in the scriptures. They completely follow his command and do not interpret or investigate religious matters for themselves."[119] Setting the competitive scene in his text, he noted that Christian missionaries had already been quite successful in converting the Burmese by giving them money, legal aid, or employment.[120] By contrast, 'Abd al-Khaliq pledged to rely on reason alone.

On the day of the debate, in which he claimed the thathanabaing was keen to participate, 'Abd al-Khaliq was accompanied by a Hindu, who opened the dramatic scene by declaring: "We will see whether the thathanabaing will convert to your religion [mazhab] or not."[121]

In what followed, 'Abd al-Khaliq presented the debate in the form of a dialogue that highlighted his exposition of the logical inconsistencies of Buddhist doctrine.[122] The debate itself focused on the doctrine of reincarnation (tanasukh), a belief that was also being subjected to critique in another Urdu book published in the same year as Sayr-i Barhma.[123] For his part, 'Abd al-Khaliq viewed reincarnation through its relationship to the moral problems of sin and punishment. As he argued back and forth with the thathanabaing, 'Abd al-Khaliq tried to demonstrate the illogical character of such a doctrine. For example, if one was born again in a new body, and was then punished for a sin one committed in a previous life, one would not be able to understand what it was one was being punished for.[124] By comparison, the Islamic belief was preferable, because Muslim teachings held that the same body—and hence the same consciousness and conscience—that committed the sin would be punished for it.[125] After 'Abd al-Khaliq pushed this point through several iterations, the thathanabaing was forced to admit that reincarnation was indeed contrary to reason, and that there could logically be no such thing as rebirth.

'Abd al-Khaliq capped his conceding point: "Aye, our Islam is, as you say, both rational and natural. One needs nothing more than reason to understand this pure religion."[126]

Warming to his theme, 'Abd al-Khaliq moved on to what he regarded as the morally repugnant implications of Buddhist teachings, teasing responses from the thathanabaing that demonstrated his point for him. Thus, the tha-thanabaing admitted that, if a soul was reincarnated, it was possible that in his next life the same man could unknowingly marry his own mother or sister. Claiming to cite the Buddhist scriptures, 'Abd al-Khaliq added that "according to this belief, there are thousands of people alive who are of forbidden [i.e., incestuous] birth and who in turn innocently commit incest by marrying their mother or daughter or sister, or even their father, son, or grandfather!"[127] For 'Abd al-Khaliq, all this proved that the "religion of Burma" promoted a per-verse theology in which humans were cosmically compelled to commit what were the most heinous of sins. Moreover, the religion also logically implied the existence of a deceitful and "blameworthy" deity. For "why would God not explain to someone in their second birth that 'such-and-such is your mother or daughter, so don't marry her!'"[128]

By combining theological reason with what he had learned through his studies to cite proofs of his argument from the Buddhist scriptures them-selves, according to his own account at least, 'Abd al-Khaliq forced the tha-thanabaing to admit the superiority of Islam. In the end, the Buddhist prelate conceded, "Your explanations have proved to me that your religion, Islam, is a true religion [apka mazhab islam ek sacha mazhab ha'i] that pleases myself and every rational person alike."[129] Closing the debate section of his book, 'Abd al-Khaliq added that he had met many ordinary monks who similarly knew in their hearts that Islam was true.[130]

Unfortunately, the available evidence affords no certainty about whether the debate ever actually took place. In this respect, Sayr-i Barhma may belong to the genre of "fictive polemical exchanges," which, as the expert on reli-gious polemics Marcelo Dascal has explained, "to be effective, must mimic as much as possible a real polemic."[131] Even if it were a fiction of 'Abd al-Khaliq's invention, by printing it he rendered it a public disputation. Yet, given the cir-cumstances in Mandalay and the importance of the public debate, or "staged polemic," to the Indian missionaries of the time, there is reason to accept that some form of debate may well have taken place.[132] If it indeed did, then the thathanabaing involved would have been Taungdaw Sayadaw, who had been appointed by King Thibaw in 1883 and died in 1895, some six years after the purported debate. Taungdaw Sayadaw certainly became embroiled in colonial attempts to alter the status of Buddhism in Burma, in the early 1890s blocking British attempts to use monasteries as bridgeheads for a secular educational curriculum.[133] But there is no evidence that he ever abandoned his religion.

Even if we must therefore doubt the dramatized version of the dialogue as 'Abd al-Khaliq recounted it, his book was nonetheless part of the polemical public sphere we have seen expanding across the Bay of Bengal. For as 'Abd al-Khaliq followed sundry Christian, Baha'i, and Hindu missionaries to Mandalay, they provoked Buddhist printed responses in turn. One of the new Buddhist missionary societies was the *Sasana Nuggaha Athin* (Mission Association), founded in Mandalay 1897, six years after the purported debate.[134] New Buddhist propagationists also appeared, such as Ledi Sayadaw (1846–1923), who through printing simple works in vernacular Burmese brought to the masses mystical teachings and meditation techniques that were previously the preserve of ordained monks who read Pali.[135] Among the many works that Sayadaw printed was a polemical study of the "four great religions" (*Batha-kyi le-ba*), in which he compared his own reformist version of Theravada Buddhism with Hinduism, Christianity, and Islam.[136] Naturally, all three fell short, Islam being the target of particular hostility. According to Sayadaw, Muslims worshipped a powerful god who demanded sacrifices of human and animal blood, and whose legion of evil spirits spread epidemics and chaos. Tellingly, in his Burmese book the name that Sayadaw used for the Muslim God was not the Arabic word *Allah,* but the Urdu (and Persian) word *Khuda.* Here the polemicist inadvertently pointed back across the Bay of Bengal to the Indian sources of the religion to whose proselytization he responded with the same disputational methods. It was part of a polemical push-back as Buddhists undertook their own ventures in assertive self-projection that saw missionaries embark for Calcutta to revive their religion in its original homeland.

Yet, as was true of the Christian missionaries, such disputatious ventures could also pave the way for more positive engagements with the religion under scrutiny. Such was the case with a subsequent Indian Muslim religious teacher in Burma, Mawlwi Muhammad Husayn, who founded an Urdu journal in Rangoon entitled *Ittihad-i Mazahib-i 'Alam* (*The Unity of the World's Religions*).[137] Launched in 1907, the journal continued its ecumenical outreach during the years that saw Ledi Sayadaw's rise to polemical prominence. Even so, like 'Abd al-Khaliq before him, Husayn faced the same linguistic barriers, so that the reference points of his journal remained primarily on Islam and the Urdu and Arabic texts he was able to read. But the Christian translations of the Gospels (which he referred to repeatedly) and the larger shelf of Urdu books on Buddhism available to him, compared with 'Abd al-Khaliq more than a decade earlier, enabled Husayn to develop a universalist approach to religious pluralism that was nonetheless rooted in Islam. For as he explained, Allah sent many different prophets to guide his creation, each of them matched to the milieu, disposition, and language of the people they were intended to guide, conditions that inevitably changed over time and place.[138]

Drawing on the Quranic concept of *fitra*—the primordial state of human nature that inclines toward pure worship—Husayn outlined a comparative theology that drew together the Islamic tradition that Allah had sent numerous prophets to humankind with the more recent Muslim recognition of the full range of Asian religions. By way of examples, he turned first to the gods of the Hindu scriptural Vedas, such as Agni, though such deities were long familiar to Indian Muslims from centuries of coexistence. But he then brought up a more recent Muslim discovery: "Gautam Bodh," who, he explained, was venerated "in Burma, Nepal, Tatari [Mongolia?], Siam, Tibet, Cambodia, Ceylon, over half of China, and almost all of Japan."[139] (Drawing on demographic overestimates that circulated widely from European sources, he added that this meant that the followers of Buddha constituted the world's largest religious community.) He then brought up the founding figures of Asia's other religious traditions: Krishna, Zoroaster, Confucius, Tao, and Shinto. Evidently, he had little data on some of these figures: he apparently took "Tao" and "Shinto" to be the names of prophets. Nonetheless, he bestowed on each of them the honorific *Hazrat,* a title usually reserved for Muslim holy figures, and presented them as the counterparts of Biblical-Quranic prophets like Moses-Musa and Jesus-'Isa.[140]

As to the tricky theological question of why Gautam Bodh wasn't mentioned in the Quran if he was a genuine prophet, Husayn explained that this was because in the original time and place of the Quranic revelation, the Arabs had never heard of the Buddha, so the mention of his name would have been meaningless. And so, as religious competition was transformed into ecumenical congruence in the pages of his journal, the absence of intercultural information became a theological device that could be projected back in time to harmonize the Quran with the recent Muslim discovery of Buddha.

India's Buddha between Frauds, Patriots, and Poets

In the decades after 1900—and in the nationalizing 1920s especially—more and more books on Buddhism began to appear in Indian languages. Yet despite what was by then the presence of literally millions of Indian settlers

in Burma and Ceylon, relatively few detailed studies emerged from direct contact with Buddhists. Many continued to draw on Orientalist—or even pseudo-
Orientalist and Theosophical—sources, while others continued the process
of reclaiming the Buddha for India as part of the ongoing interplay between
projecting the self and appreciating the other.

Some of these European sources pointed to deliberately false trails. In 1902
a Hindu author in Punjab by the name of Sena Nayaka issued his translation of an English text that claimed the teachings of the Buddha formed the
source of Christianity.[141] Nayaka's source was an English version of *La vie inconnue de Jésus-Christ* (*The Unknown Life of Jesus*). Its author, the influential
Crimean Jewish adventurer—and fraud—Nikolai Notovich (1858–after 1916),
claimed to have found a Tibetan manuscript in a Buddhist monastery in Ladakh that proved that Jesus had studied among the spiritual masters of India before returning to teach in Judea.[142] Since its first publication in Paris in
1894, Notovich's book had been translated into English and gained massive
media attention around the world, including India, where his purported findings were taken up for a variety of causes. For Nayaka, the idea of a Jesus
who had sat at the feet of Indian sages proved the clear superiority of India's
religions over Christianity, reversing a century of missionary claims to the
contrary. Other Indians saw the matter somewhat differently, however, including Mirza Ghulam Ahmad, the messianic founder of the Muslim Ahmadiyya
movement. Under the title *Masih Hindustan Mein* (*Jesus the Messiah in India*),
Ahmad published an alternative take on Notovich's claims, which he issued
from his own Mission Press in Punjab.[143] Ahmad drew on Notovich and his
supposed Tibetan source text to support his main allegation that Jesus had
indeed traveled to India and was even buried in Kashmir rather than Jerusalem, as the corrupted Christian Gospels maintained. (Ahmad also drew on the
forged Gospel of Barnabas.)[144] But in refutation of the Russian's larger theory,
Ahmad argued that rather than Buddhism shaping Christianity, it was the ex-
emplary life of Jesus—albeit this time the *Muslim* Jesus—that had influenced
the legendary biographies of Buddha.[145]

The next contributor to these self-projecting interpretations of a fraudulent
Buddhist manuscript was the Reverend Ahmad Shah, an Indian Muslim convert to Christianity. Determined to scrutinize the source of Notovich's claims,
he hardily made his way to the Himalayan region of Ladakh (known as Little
Tibet), traversing icy ravines and bridges made of rope. As meticulous as he
was courageous, like a theological detective he systematically inspected every
stage of Notovich's alleged itinerary, conducting interviews in translation with

the aid of a Ladakhi official and trader who spoke Tibetan and Urdu.[146] At the Mulba monastery, where Notovich reported first learning that Jesus was venerated by Buddhists, Shah craftily questioned the senior lama:

> "I admire your Buddha who is called 'Isa [Jesus]; read me something from his life and teachings."
> "Our Buddha, 'Isa," [the lama] said.
> "Yes," said [Rev. Ahmad], "Your Buddha 'Isa, nineteen centuries ago was born in Judea, travelled through India, passed through Nepal into Tibet."
> "Quite strange and unknown to me, he is none of our Buddhas," said [the lama].[147]

Encouraged by this negation of Notovich's heresy, the Christian detective trekked to the monastery at Hemis, where the Russian said he had seen the Tibetan manuscript of the "hidden life" of Jesus. There, too, Ahmad found that "the Tibetan Buddhists have never dreamt of any such thing."[148] In 1906, in an Indian Christian refutation of a European Buddhist fraud, he published his findings in Benares. Putting the results of his fact-finding mission before the reading public, he declared Notovich's book to be "the boldest attempt . . . to impose upon the public that always expect from a nineteenth century traveler correct and matter of fact information."[149] Three years later Ahmad's book was translated into Urdu under the title *Sayr-i Tibbat* (*Journey to Tibet*).[150] Its contents offered a very different dialogue with Buddhists from that in 'Abd al-Khaliq's *Sayr-i Barhma* (*Journey to Burma*). Yet both journeys were undertaken to protect or project the religion of the self through investigations that sought to reconcile evidence of Buddhist beliefs with matters of Muslim or Christian faith.

Around 1905, another firsthand Urdu account of Tibet was written by Khwaja Ghulam Muhammad (1857–1928), a Kashmiri merchant who had traveled to Lhasa some twenty years earlier.[151] Written by a trader rather than a missionary, his account offers a useful counterpoint to those of Ahmad and 'Abd al-Khaliq, not to mention the fantasies of Notovich. After describing the practical matters of routes, villages, and dangers (both climatic and human), he turned to the social and cultural practices he had observed during his residence in Lhasa. On the one hand, Muhammad was an effective ethnographer, describing fortified monasteries (which he called by the Tibetan term *gonpa*), the different materials used to make idols (*but*), and more significantly the actual beliefs of local people. Here he outlined the Tibetan version of the doctrine of the Three Jewels, which he tried to transcribe from Tibetan as *kanjusum* and then translated as meaning "three gods" (*tin khuda*), a trinity which he claimed actually consisted of their holy books, community of monks, and idols.[152] Usually the Three Jewels are listed as the Buddha, the teachings or *dharma,* and the monastic order or *sangha,* so Muhammad was not too far off. He also explained the status of the Dalai Lama, who "as well as being recognized as their head priest (*muqtada*), is regarded—may Allah protect me—as the god of the Buddhists." He then sketched the divinatory procedures for finding the next reincarnation of the Dalai Lama on each incarnation's decease.[153]

Describing all these teachings of an unknown tradition presented terminological problems that Muhammad shared with 'Abd al-Khaliq in his attempt to describe what he saw in Burma. Both of them tried the method of borrowing local words but, realizing that readers would not understand them, had to gloss or translate them into Urdu terms that were not merely dissimilar but disapproving, or at least theologically dubious. Thus, for the Three Jewels, Muhammad used the Arabic term for the Christian Trinity (*taslis*); for incarnations the heretical term *hulul;* and for the specialists who located reborn lamas the pejorative Quranic noun *kahin* for a pagan soothsayer. Rather than reflecting ideas through a neutral linguistic mirror, translation was fraught with terminological challenges. Language—religious language especially—was quite simply loaded. But at least Muhammad found a way to avoid referring to the Tibetans as idol worshippers (*but-parast*): he adopted into Urdu the English word "Buddhist."[154]

Fortunately, by the early 1900s primary sources on Buddhist beliefs also began to be translated that took Indian readers beyond the descriptions of varyingly sympathetic or perceptive travelers, let alone outright frauds like Notovich. While the search for neutral terminology remained a challenge (albeit less so for Hindus who already accepted reincarnations and statues), the intertwined Indian and European discovery of the *Dhammapada* presented a textual picture of a Buddhism that was more concerned with ethics than metaphysics, still less with problematic idols. The key moment came in 1904, when Charuchandra Basu—who was closely associated in Calcutta with the Maha-Bodhi Society and *Bauddha Dharmankura Sabha* (Bengal Buddhist Association)—published his Bengali translation of the *Dhammapada.*[155] In another signal of Calcutta's role as informational entrepôt, this was probably the earliest published translation of a substantial Pali text into a modern Indian language. Arguably the most important text for the Theravada tradition of Burma and Ceylon, the *Dhammapada* had already been identified by Orientalists as the closest record of "what the Buddha truly taught." Along with

Basu's links to Dharmapala's Maha-Bodhi Society, this Protestant-shaped notion of the *Dhammapada* as the Buddha's own "testament" prompted its appearance in Bengali.

Five years later an Urdu version of the *Dhammapada* appeared.[156] Reflecting the circuitous routes of India's rediscovery of Buddha, it was made by Bishan Nara'in, a Kashmiri Hindu member of the Theosophical Society, whose cofounder Colonel Olcott had mentored Dharmapala's missionary projection of Buddhism from Ceylon. Nara'in based his Urdu version on the English translation by German linguist Friedrich Max Müller (1823–1900), which was first published in 1870. Rendered into Urdu from English, the Buddha's many cosmic forms were stripped away by high Victorian historicism to leave only the sermons of the mortal Gautama, who, in an introduction drawing on Müller's research, Nara'in placed in his temporal *Sitz im Leben:* a life setting now firmly fixed on planet earth, at Kapalivastu, "a hundred miles north of Benares."[157] The Orientalist determination to remove the Buddha from the fog of myth had brought him back to India, and to Indians.

By the 1920s, the Indian rediscovery, and reclaiming, of Buddha was in full swing: within the space of twelve months, another Urdu version of the *Dhammapada* appeared, along with a reprint of Basu's Bengali version and a new translation into Sindhi.[158] That same year, the ashram that published the Sindhi version issued a book on reincarnation by Annie Besant (1847–1933), by then the most prominent (and anticolonial) member of the Theosophical Society.[159] Works on Buddhism were also appearing in Hindi, especially through the dedicated efforts of Rahul Sankrityayan (1893–1963), a North Indian Hindu Brahmin who converted to Buddhism in the early 1920s during a visit to Ceylon, where he studied Pali after learning Sanskrit, and hearing about Buddhism, in Calcutta.[160] By 1929 he was in Tibet, the lack of relevant dictionaries forcing him to master Tibetan by comparing Sanskrit grammatical works with their Tibetan translations so as to gradually compile his own grammar and wordlists.[161] After fourteen months, he left the Himalayas for Europe, where he met leading scholars such as the Jewish linguist Sylvain Lévi (1863–1935), who taught Sanskrit and Tibetan in Paris (and briefly in Bengal).[162] Then, in 1931, Sankrityayan published his *Buddhacharya* (*Life of Buddha*), a groundbreaking Hindi biography that largely comprised translations from Pali. Four years later, he completed *Tibbat me Baudhh Dharm* (*Buddhism in Tibet*) in which he drew together his manuscript studies with the historicizing approach that (like his later Marxism) he adopted through reading European writers.

If the subsequent output of Sankrityayan increasingly cast the Buddha as the forebear of Marx, the prior Christian recasting of Buddha maintained its place in the Indian imagination, not least in South Indian languages, such as Marathi. The key figure here was another pioneering Indian scholar of Pali, Dharmanand Kosambi (1876–1947).[163] As with Sankrityayan, Kosambi's initial studies were of Sanskrit, echoing their common background as Hindu Brahmins. Then he had his first positive exposure to Buddhism through reading Narayan Kane's Marathi translation of Edwin Arnold's *Light of Asia*. As Kosambi later recalled in his own Marathi autobiography, "Kane's translation is not as good as the [English] original, but I liked it so much at the time that I read some portions over and again. It became for me an original religious text at the time."[164]

Inspired by Arnold's Christianized Buddha to read the original Buddhist scriptures, in 1902 Kosambi sailed from Calcutta to Ceylon, where he began learning Pali with local monks. After several years, he embarked on a journey to Burma, where in a courageous renunciation of his ancestral Hindu self, he made his own monastic vows and converted to Buddhism in the ultimate act of appreciating the other. Over the following decades, Kosambi drew on his deepening knowledge of the Pali canon to produce several popular works in Marathi that could be read by ordinary people in his home region. His printed output began with his 1910 work, *Buddha, Dharma ani Sangha* (*The Buddha, the Law, and the Monastic Community*), which, like his subsequent works, was also translated into Gujarati.[165] Making the Buddhist scriptures more accessible, he also issued several editions of Pali texts, starting with the *Laghu-patha*, which in 1917 he published from Bombay, together with a Marathi translation, like the Christian missionaries before him.[166]

In the South Indian languages of Malayalam and Telugu, rather than such Buddhist texts from other regions of Asia, it was again Edwin Arnold who lent the initial informational and representational wherewithal.[167] In 1902 *The Light of Asia* was rendered into artful Telugu verse by a pair of celebrated poets, Venkata Sastri (1870–1950) and Tirupati Sastri (1872–1920), at the request of a local landowner.[168] For two strict Brahmins, the commission was not without its dilemmas. But Venkata and Tirupati managed to maintain their scruples by giving the historically dubious impression that the Buddha's teachings were a version of the *jñana-marga* ("path of knowledge") of Brahminic Hinduism.[169] Five years later, another Telugu translation of Arnold appeared.[170] In 1927 a Telugu verse translation of the *Dhammapada* was made (it is unclear whether this was a direct or indirect translation from Pali).[171] It was followed by a direct translation of a Sanskrit text, Aśvaghosa's *Saundarananda* (*Poem of Sundari and Nanda*), though the Telugu version was not entirely faithful, for it downplayed Buddhist doctrine in favor of a Gandhi- and Christian-influenced image of the Buddha as primarily a servant of the poor and needy.[172] As nationalist ideas spread farther through southern India, other Telugu writers began to celebrate a Buddhism that did not belong to Burma, still less to Japan or China, but was part of their own Indian heritage on their own soil, albeit as first recovered through colonial excavations of the beautifully sculpted stupas at nearby Amaravati and Nagarjunakonda. Farther south in India, four Malayalam translations of Arnold appeared between 1912 and 1917, including a version by the Hindu social reformer and poet Kumaran Asan (1873–1924), who drew on Arnold's liberal egalitarian Buddha to present the latter as an anticaste reformer like himself.[173]

In northern India, too, learned Sikhs took a new interest in Buddhism, inspired equally by the archaeological excavations at Taxila in Punjab, overseen by John Marshall from 1913, and by Arnold's ever-present poem. By the 1930s, *The Light of Asia* was rendered into poetic Punjabi.[174] The translator was the Sikh novelist Gurbakhsh Singh Preetlari (1895–1977), who as editor of the journal *Preet-Lari* (*Linked through Love*) was deeply drawn to Arnold's ecumenical depiction of a Buddha for all peoples. Meanwhile, further translations of Arnold's epic poem appeared in Hindi, Gujarati, and Sindhi by local poets and scholars who were likewise bilingual in English.[175]

This was no less the case amid the growing nationalism of the 1920s that cultivated a blossoming of books on Buddhism in other Indian languages. Among them were digests of colonial histories of ancient India; translations of Orientalist biographies of the Buddha; and depictions of the Buddha as an Indian sage by such nationalist poets as Brij Narayan Chakbast and Sir Muhammad Iqbal.[176] Ironically, these works were written far from the living Buddhist societies of Asia. For in inland Indian cities like Lucknow and Lahore, Buddhism could be comfortably claimed as an Indian tradition with ancient and enduring roots in the sacred soil of the nation. Perhaps the most influential of these champions of the Indian Buddha was Mahatma Gandhi, who in his Gujarati autobiography, published in his newspaper *Navjivan* (*New Life*) from 1925 to 1929, recalled how he too first learned about the Buddha's teachings by reading Arnold's *Light of Asia*.[177]

Yet as Gandhi's large-hearted comparison of the Buddha's teachings to the Sermon on the Mount suggests, this nationalist mode of self-discovery never

fully eclipsed the earlier engagement with Buddhism in which Christian missionaries played an enabling role. Nor did Indian nationalists uniformly ap-
prove of the Buddha: for V. D. Savarkar (1883–1966), the leading theorist of
Hindu nationalism, centuries of Buddhism had robbed Indians of their martial virility by spreading "mealy-mouthed formulas of *ahimsa* [nonviolence]."[178]
Such false morality had paved the way for the Muslim invasions of the Middle
Ages, he claimed, and then the marauding British in turn. As far as Savarkar
was concerned, it was to India's continued detriment that such Buddhist
pacifism was being revived by Gandhi—whose assassin would be inspired by
Savarkar's ideas.[179]

Widening Islamic Appreciations

Meanwhile, more accurate and appreciative Muslim accounts of Buddhism, and Burma, had become available in Urdu. In 1901, some eight years
after 'Abd al-Khaliq's book first appeared, an Urdu history of Burma, and of
the Anglo-Burmese Wars in particular, was published under the title *Waqa'at-i
Barhma (Events in Burma)*.[180] The main body of the text recounted the political
history of the various Burmese kingdoms and their relations with neighboring polities, and eventually with British India, building up to its central focus
on the campaigns that brought about the gradual conquest of Burma. Showing how intercultural knowledge could also pass through the prism of military encounters, however, the early sections of the book also gave an overview
of Burmese life and customs. Although the Muslim author devoted fewer
than seven pages to religion in Burma (three of which focused on Islam),
his discussion of Buddhism was quite sympathetic.[181] Using the same Burmese terms that 'Abd al-Khaliq had, he noted that the "followers of Bodh" held
in great respect the celibate holy men called *pongis* (monks), the most high-
status of whom were called *pahyas*, "which in our language means 'God's
blessing.'"[182] Though the author cited an English text here, his account seems
to have drawn largely on his own observations of monasteries and temples,
which he presented in neutral terms that eschewed the old language of idol
worship.[183]

It was not that 'Abd al-Khaliq's earlier account disappeared from collective
memory: the commercial forces in the public sphere combined with growing
interest to ensure that in 1917 his book was reissued by India's most popular publisher.[184] But by then, other relevant Urdu works were also appearing,
and while primarily oriented toward India, as part of India's Buddhological

self-discovery, they had implications for understanding other Buddhist regions of Asia, including Burma. For example, in his *Mukhtasar Tarikh-i Dakan* (*Concise History of the Deccan*), Muhammad Sultan, a historian based in the princely state of Hyderabad, devoted a section to Buddhism in which he made clear that the Buddha had been born in India, providing a precise birthdate of 596 "Before Christ" (*qabl-i masih*) that drew on the revised European scholarly consensus.[185] But he also detailed how, soon after the Buddha's death, his teachings had spread "to Lanka in the south and to Tibet and China in the north," clarifying that "the Buddha, whose name means 'the enlightened one,' was also the same person known as Gautama."[186] The rediscovery of Buddhism now linked India to other regions of Asia, as we will see again in later chapters with regard to China, but it did so by placing India in the self-projecting role of dominant cultural exporter.

In 1893, however, 'Abd al-Khaliq had no idea that the Burmese prophet he called Shingutama was the same person as this ancient Indian compatriot Gautama. But by the time another Muslim religious scholar, Sayyid Abu Zafar Nadwi, published his travelogue to Burma in 1921, the spread of this improved understanding allowed Nadwi to declare with casual certainty that "the cradle of the Buddhist religion is northern India."[187] Washing away 'Abd al-Khaliq's confusion, Nadwi named the religion's Indian founder as "Gautam Bodh," who had lived around 500 BC rather than after the time of the Prophet Muhammad over a millennium later, as 'Abd al-Khaliq had miscalculated. Nadwi even spent several pages examining the historical evidence for how the religion first reached Burma.[188] Yet despite Nadwi's travels, it was not through learning Burmese or engaging with living Buddhists that he corrected these earlier misunderstandings. Although he cited 'Abd al-Khaliq, his knowledge of Buddhism came from another work he referenced, which had been written by "the Frenchman, doctor monsieur Liban."[189]

The source in question was *Les civilisations de l'Inde* by the influential French polymath and amateur Orientalist Gustave Le Bon (1841–1931). Originally published in Paris in 1887, it was translated into Urdu in 1913 by Sayyid 'Ali Bilgrami, scion of one of colonial India's most intellectually distinguished families.[190] Le Bon's appraisal of Buddhism was highly positive, like his account of Indo-Islamic civilization later in the same book, rendering it highly appealing to Bilgrami, Nadwi, and many subsequent Muslim readers.[191] Even so, Le Bon was very far from being an expert on Buddhism, having spent only a few months touring India in general, and having no direct experience of Burma. In fact, his firsthand experience of the religion came from a short visit to Nepal in 1885, on which he wrote a travelogue, augmenting his observations with reference to Raja Rajendralal Mitra's *Sanskrit Buddhist Literature of Nepal*.[192] Aptly, this investigative mode—of a European traveler leveraging his direct observations by reading the studies of an Indian scholar—was the counterpart to what we will see later by way of Indian travelers to China and Japan. As a result, Le Bon's conception of Buddhism was based on the Sanskrit Mahayana tradition we have seen Mitra and his British colleagues recovering from Kathmandu's libraries. This Mahayana version of the religion was quite distinct from the living Pali-based Theravada tradition of Burma and Ceylon. Nonetheless, by way of the influential intermediaries Bilgrami and Nadwi, the Frenchman Le Bon—and the Bengali Mitra—would become additional sources through which Indian Muslims began to learn more about the Buddhist religion.

In addition to translating *Les civilisations de l'Inde* (and its counterpart, *La civilisation des Arabes*), Bilgrami wrote a short English guidebook to India's Buddhist cave temples at Ellora. Here he included a brief biography of the Buddha, describing how, from his Indian homeland, his religion had spread "fast into the outlying countries of Ceylon, Burmah and Tibet and had found its way even to China and Japan."[193] Though Bilgrami had learned this through English and French books rather than by direct encounters with living Buddhists, his more informed—and sympathetic—appreciation of Buddhist culture signaled a major shift in inter-Asian understanding. Earlier Indo-Persian accounts of the Ellora caves, such as that in the royal history of Rafi' al-Din Shirazi from 1612, showed no such knowledge of Buddhist history, presenting the sculptures either as marvelous relics of unknown ancient emperors or as the dubious decoration of generic "idol temples."[194]

Broadening awareness of this new cultural as distinct from theological approach, Bilgrami's account influenced other publications in turn, such as the article-length guide to the Ellora caves that later appeared in the influential Urdu journal *Ma'arif* (*Spreading Knowledge*).[195] Here the Hyderabadi scholar Tamkin Kazimi presented a highly sympathetic appreciation of the caves that began with a historical outline of the emergence of Buddhism. Turning to the individual caves themselves, Kazimi drew on the earlier survey report by James Burgess (1832–1916), the pioneer of cave temple archaeology, to identify different sculptures and provide the precise measurements of each cave in feet.[196] But as a resident of the region, he also drew on his own direct response to the caves, describing their dramatic rock-carved interiors. Moreover, rather than using the old vocabulary of "idols" (*but*), he deliberately deployed the more positive (albeit Hindu) term "embodiment" (*murt*) and the neutral term "sculpture" (*mujasima*). By the time Kazimi was writing in 1926, he could also draw on the recent Urdu translation of Rhys Davids's detailed history of Buddhist India that had recently been issued as a textbook for Hyderabad's first university.[197] Following Rhys Davids, Kazimi gave the Buddha's date as 481 BC, and he repeatedly situated developments so many "centuries before the Messiah [*qabl-i masih*]."[198] Like many other authors across India and the Middle East, he had adopted a Christian time line to chart the antiquity of a continent whose name had itself been borrowed from Europe.

By 1932 the journal *Ma'arif* would feature a similarly positive account of the Gandhara Buddhist sculptures unearthed around Peshawar near the Indo-Afghan border, a large stash of which had been transported to the Indian Museum in Calcutta.[199] More than merely passing on the new understanding of the Buddhist past, the anonymous contributor to *Ma'arif* explained how this rediscovery of Buddhist monuments had come about. The key breakthroughs, he explained, came by way of the English translation of the travelogue of the Chinese pilgrim Xuanzang made by the Reverend Samuel Beal, followed by the efforts of various Indian scholars to correlate the place names recorded in Xuanzang's text with their surviving Sanskrit counterparts.[200] Through this joint effort, the glorious artistic achievements of Gandhara were uncovered and appreciated for what they were.

Whatever its origins, the rise of a Muslim aesthetic appreciation of Buddhist "idols" as "art"—a loanword that itself now appeared in the pages of *Ma'arif*—was a valuable new mode of cross-cultural understanding. What is perhaps most noteworthy about the article on Gandhara is that it appeared in a journal associated with a major Muslim seminary, the Nadwat al-'Ulama. Forty years after 'Abd al-Khaliq wrote his account of the religion of Burma, fellow Muslim clerics in his home region around Lucknow had adopted a very different approach to Buddhism, not least through reclassifying it as art.

Yet in an era of ascendant nationalism, even art could become a venue for self-projection, particularly among Hindu scholars associated with the University of Calcutta. Among them was Niharranjan Ray (1903–1981), whose 1932 *Brahmanical Gods in Burma* used the new art-historical methods to argue for the profound influence of Hinduism on Burma.[201] A few years later, his *Sanskrit Buddhism in Burma* similarly deployed archaeological discoveries to present a "survey of Indian projection into the countries of Indo-China."[202]

Fortunately, not all Bengali accounts of India's Buddhist artistic past were concerned with appropriating it for the greater glory of Hinduism. A few years

Recognizing the religion of Bodh: Ramnath Kushal's Urdu iconography of Buddhism. Ramnath Kushal, *Mahatma Bodh ke Mukhtasar Sawanih 'Umri* (Lahore: Khadim al-Taʿlim, 1892). Photograph by Nile Green.

before the Ellora Caves were featured in *Ma'arif,* the Bengali painter Mukul
Chandra Dey (1895–1989) made an artistic pilgrimage to the Buddhist caves at
Ajanta in a remote, forested corner of the Nizam's state of Hyderabad.[203] There
he set about making copies of the gorgeous frescoes depicting the previous
lives of the Buddha. Having studied painting and printmaking in Yokohama,
Chicago, and London, Dey had a strong sense of the universalism of art, seeing his mission as promoting India's place in that universal art history. Echoing the humanism of his chief mentor, Tagore, he concluded his book on the
cave paintings with the hope of "making available to mankind the record of a
perfect expression of human life."[204] As a participant in the visual no less than
textual dimension of the public sphere, Dey intended to make the paintings
available by means of "a great album of coloured collotype reproductions."[205]
He would not have to wait long: two years after he voiced this hope, an illustrated guide to the Ajanta frescoes was issued in Hyderabad, followed in 1935
by a volume in Urdu with color reproductions, published by a specialist German art press.[206] The compiler was Ghulam Yazdani (1885–1962), a highly cultured North Indian Muslim and prizewinning graduate of the Muhammedan
Anglo-Oriental College at Aligarh and director of the Hyderabad Archaeological Department.

By this time, Yazdani was by no means the only Muslim taking an interest
in the art and archaeology of Buddhism. The late 1920s and 1930s also saw new
appreciations—and appropriations—of Buddhism unfold in Iran and particularly Afghanistan as access to publications from India and Europe gradually
fed into new publications on other religions of "Asia." Here, too, Orientalist translations, archaeological excavations, and the language of art history all
made contributions. By the time Yazdani published his first tomes of photographic plates, Afghanistan was also beginning to use such new methods and
technologies to make its own claims over the legacy of early Buddhism.

Though both Iranians and Afghans gained access to more detailed information on Buddhism, it came more often from European sources than from
direct engagements with Buddhist texts or practitioners. In 1927, for example,
the modernist Iranian journal *Taqaddum* (*Progress*) featured a summary of a European travel report that provided more specific information about Buddhism
than we have seen available in generic nineteenth-century Persian accounts of
Chinese or Burmese "idol worship" (*but-parasti*).[207] A crucial conceptual step
was the recognition of what was now called the "religion of Buddha" (*mazhab-i
Buda*). Describing a Chinese monastery in Yunnan that was famous for its five
hundred statues (presumably the famous Yuantong Temple in Kunming), the

article in *Taqaddum* explained key Buddhist terms (such as the term *arhat* for someone who has achieved enlightenment) through reference to the *Samañ-ñaphala Sutta* (*Fruit of Contemplative Life*), a key text of the Pali canon.[208] There was, however, little possibility of a direct translation of such *Suttas* because there existed no dictionary of Pali into Persian any more than between Pali and other languages of the Middle East. But even though accessed indirectly, Buddhist doctrines could be made meaningful to Iranian readers. Far from regarding such teachings with suspicion, the article concluded that "although the world today is always on the move, the religion of Buddha offers perpetual stillness and eternal peace."[209] Given that in the 1920s, as motor roads rap-idly spread across the Middle East, many Persian and Arabic journals were complaining about this new "age of speed" (*'asr al-sur'ah*), this was a timely message.[210] It expressed also a markedly different sentiment from that of the Iranian attempts we have seen to convert Buddhists to Baha'ism.

Two years later, a similar article appeared in another Iranian journal, *Far-hang* (*Culture*), as part of a series titled *Great Men of the World* (not, it might be noted, *of Asia*).[211] Like its predecessor in *Taqaddum*, it signaled the new informational specificity made possible by recourse to European—most likely French—sources.[212] It presented a historical biography of the Buddha that gave his various names, Siddhartha and Sakyamuni, along with the specific places where he lived out his life, such as his home city of Kapilavastu and the *Bodhi-manda* ("site of awakening") at Bodhgaya. In describing Bodhgaya, which had been firmly identified through Indian and European scholarly collaboration, the *Farhang* article drew on the account of "a Chinese traveler called Xuan-zang, who arrived there in 632, that is, twelve hundred years after the Bud-dha's death."[213] As we have already seen, Xuanzang's travelogue had guided the archaeological recovery of India's (and Central Asia's) Buddhist past. By the 1920s it had also been translated into Urdu from Beal's earlier English translation, which was itself preceded by a French translation by Stanislas Julien (1797–1873) of the Collège de France—perhaps the version used by the Iranian contributor to *Farhang*.[214]

There seems to have been no Persian translation of Xuanzang, but the ar-ticle's author could still draw on French sources to sketch a far more precise picture of the Buddhist past than had previously been available in Iran, albeit a picture that replicated the historicizing approach of the Orientalists rather than the more complex metaphysical identities of the Buddha upheld by his living followers in various parts of Asia. Though these cosmic Buddhas were notably absent from the Persian text, there was nonetheless a sense of the

Buddha as a moral figure, if one entirely assimilated to the Perso-Islamic tradition of the Sufi *faqir*, or mendicant. Aside from the Buddha's names, the article used no ethical or doctrinal terms from Sanskrit or Pali, however vicariously sourced. Instead, in a series of dramatized dialogues between the young Buddha Siddhartha and his father, the king of Kapilavastu, the Buddha was presented in terms that were drawn entirely from the classical Persian tales of Sa'di about the admonishing encounters between a *faqir* and a *shah*. Forty years earlier, Edwin Arnold and then Paul Carus had promoted a Christianized image of a meek and gentle Buddha. Now he was correspondingly—if no less sympathetically—being Islamized. And so, for Iranian readers in the secularizing 1920s, the fables of the Buddha became a means of rediscovering their own moral compass.

New approaches to Buddhism were also slowly beginning to emerge in Afghanistan. In 1903 King Habibullah Khan (r. 1901–1919) had founded his country's first modern educational institution, the Maktab-i Habibiyya (Habibia High School). Its teaching staff largely comprised Indian Muslim alumni of the modernizing colleges of colonial India. Within a couple of years, curricular needs led to Afghanistan's first printed textbooks. Among them was *Mir'at al-Arz: ya'ni Mukhtasar Jughrafiya-yi 'Alam* (*Mirror of the Earth: Being a Short Geography of the World*), which carried the concept of "Asia" from across the border in British India, its Anglophone origins indicated clearly in a spelling—*A'ishiya*—that reproduced the English pronunciation used by similarly imported Indian teachers.[215] (Decades later, the Afghan Dari-Persian spelling was "corrected" to *Asiya* to more accurately transcribe the English and ultimately Greek term.) But conceptions of the cultures of Asia were not so easily transformed. In a section devoted to religion, the textbook declared: "In the whole world, there are only four historical religions: the Christians [*Nusara*], who comprise 375,000,000 people; the Jews [*Yahud*], who are 600,000; the people of Islam, who comprise 160,000,000; and the idol worshippers [*but-parast*], of whom there are 70,000,000."[216] Even in official schoolbooks from the early twentieth century, the vast but vague category of "idolatry" persisted. But it was already giving way; in a subsequent short section of the textbook on Burma, there appeared the more differentiated statement that "most of the population follow the religion of Buddha [*Bodh mazhab*]."[217]

Like those in Iran, Afghan publications from the late 1920s saw the old generic category of idol worship increasingly replaced by a more detailed understanding of Buddhism that developed through contact with the French researchers who expanded the archaeological recovery of the Buddhist past that began across the border in India. In 1922 the Délégation Archéologique Française en Afghanistan arrived in Kabul under the leadership of Alfred Foucher (1865–1952), an expert on Gandhara Buddhist statuary who had spent the previous three years in India.[218] Over the next decade, studious Afghan modernists who worked alongside the French initiated a root-and-branch re-assessment of a past that had long been described in the idolatrous terms we saw used in the Persian article on Bamiyan from 1885.[219]

With the founding of the journal *Kabol*—the country's first cultural pe-riodical—in 1931, articles presented ancient Buddhist ruins and excavated sculptures (*mujasima*) in the new terms of art history and "national heritage" (*asar-i watan*).[220] By 1936 a young Francophone historian called Ahmad 'Ali Kuhzad (1907–1983) embarked on a brilliant career as a historian of antiquity by translating a two-volume study of the Buddhas of Bamiyan by the Déléga-tion's leading scholars.[221] Its detailed synopsis of over a century of European research on early Buddhist history presented Afghan readers with an entirely new picture—and time line—of their pre-Islamic past. In 1939, eight years before the Wheel of Chakra graced the flag of independent India, the rival Af-ghan nationalist appropriation of Buddhism saw the giant statues of Bamiyan appear on Afghan banknotes.[222] Once again, as much as the rediscovery of Buddhism involved an appreciation of the other, it formed a patriotic means of promoting the self.

In Afghanistan and Iran, the new appreciation of Buddhism that emerged in the 1920s and 1930s was not the informational legacy of the Afghan mer-chants and Iranian missionaries who over the previous century had roamed widely round the Bay of Bengal. Far from emerging from direct inter-Asian encounters, this new intercultural knowledge came via more vicarious routes involving Europe that we have also seen shaping the Indian rediscovery of Buddhism that began decades earlier through closer access to the informa-tional hub of Calcutta. Not that European sources were necessarily accurate, as we have seen with Pinnock's schoolmasterly amateurism, Notovich's fake Tibetan manuscript, and Arnold's Christological distortions. When what ap-pears to have been the first Turkish book on the Buddha was published in 1933, it was a translation of a biography written fifty years earlier by the French occultist Édouard Schuré (1841–1929), who was first drawn to Buddhism by reading Arnold's *Light of Asia* and then joined the Theosophical Society.[223] The point of all these comparisons among Middle Eastern, Indian, and European

understandings of Buddhism is therefore not to engage in a positivist competition over who was better informed, more factually accurate, or ideologically
correct. Rather, it is to show just how difficult it was for even highly educated
and motivated investigators, such as 'Abd al-Khaliq, to access reliable information about the very different societies they encountered across Asia.

Of course, books were not the only form of knowledge. Long-term settlers
acquired a direct day-to-day familiarity with the cultural others with whom they
resided in the same cities, if not neighborhoods, in the ports of maritime Asia.
But such as it was, such informal knowledge was not easily transferred to the
public sphere of print so that it was available to other people elsewhere. Nor
was geographical proximity any guarantee of knowledge production, since before the 1920s at least, there do not appear to have been any books about Buddhism published in Malay, despite the fact that the Buddhist-majority parts of
Southeast Asia bordered the Muslim Malay-speaking regions that were themselves previously home to several major Buddhist kingdoms.[224] This further
suggests that intercultural knowledge cannot be taken for granted as an inevitable given. Whether in the Indian, Iranian, Arab, or Afghan case, firsthand
encounters around the Bay of Bengal did not produce an abundant published
corpus of cross-cultural knowledge that was available to their compatriots back
home. As a consequence, by the 1920s, the booming Indian (and then Middle
Eastern) interest in Buddhism looked to the more cumulative and thence robust research of European Orientalists and missionaries, which were published in colonial languages—notably English and French—that were more
widely understood than their regional Asian counterparts, whether Burmese
or Bengali.

Against this background, 'Abd al-Khaliq's *Sayr-i Barhma* stands out as a rare
outcome of direct engagement with a living Buddhist society. If his investigations were intended as aids to the disputational defeat of Buddhism, then they
were at least the result of personally communicating with the followers of
Shingutama, for whom he showed considerable compassion as misguided fellow humans. As a product of a polemical public sphere that reached across the
Bay of Bengal, *Sayr-i Barhma* adapted techniques pioneered by the Christian
missionaries of Calcutta in the early nineteenth century. Those techniques of
disputatious investigation spread to Burma, where they became favored tools
for Muslim, Baha'i, Hindu, and finally Buddhist missionaries alike. Yet, in
some cases at least, such disputatious dialogues served to generate and distribute information about the culture, religion, or scriptures under critique.

This was certainly the case with 'Abd al-Khaliq's book, which for all its mis-understandings and misgivings was nonetheless a milestone for Indian Muslims' awareness of "the religion of Burma." And so, despite 'Abd al-Khaliq's intention of projecting his own religion into distant Mandalay, he contributed considerably to the widening of intercultural understanding.

Just as Christian missionary encounters with the religions of Asia gradually paved the way for not merely critical but also ecumenical approaches, as expressed in Carus's *Gospel of Buddha,* comparable developments occurred among Muslims. We have already seen an Urdu journal titled *Unity of the World's Religions,* founded in Rangoon in 1907. Similar approaches to Buddhism were under way in the Middle East, where the Syrian reformist Jamal al-Din al-Qasimi (1866–1914) was writing an influential commentary on the Quran. Drawing on the new information on Buddhism becoming available in Arabic through the printing presses of Beirut, al-Qasimi presented a radical new reading of a part in the Quran that had puzzled exegetes for centuries. These were the verses in which Allah declares: "I swear by the fig and the olive,/And Mount Sinai,/And this city made secure."[225] Al-Qasimi agreed with his forebears that the olive tree was a symbol of Jerusalem, and hence of Jesus; Mount Sinai was an allusion to Moses; and the "city made secure" was a reference to the Medina of Muhammad. But for the long-mysterious fig (*al-tin*), he offered the interpretation that it symbolized India, and hence the Buddha, who had famously reached enlightenment beneath a fig tree. This in turn implied that the Buddha belonged to the line of true prophets sent to guide humankind by Allah. It was a remarkable shift from long-standing Muslim perceptions of Buddhist idolatry. But in claiming the Buddha for the prophets of Islam while eliding basic differences of Buddhist doctrine, al-Qasimi's accommodating move was part of the larger dialectic of self-discovery. Once again, the recognition of the Buddhist other involved the promotion, or at least the preservation, of the Muslim self.

Like the formidable interpretive barriers we have seen 'Abd al-Khaliq trying to surmount, all this points to both the reach and limits of the intercultural knowledge that emerged from the more intense inter-Asian connections that were paradoxically made possible by the infrastructures of Europe's empires. Yet despite the achievements of the many (especially Indian) investigators of Buddhism whose bold efforts we have necessarily condensed, the constraints of inter-Asian understanding did not disappear in the 1930s amid either the high tide of colonial connection or the ascent of ideological Asianism. Aside from *intra*-religious lexicons, there were few if any published dictionaries be-tween the languages of Asia's different regions that went beyond basic phrases and compendia of trading terms.

Despite 'Abd al-Khaliq's exceptional study of Burmese texts, the Indian rediscovery of Buddhism was made far from the meeting places with living Buddhists in Rangoon and Mandalay. Much more common was the resort to Sanskrit manuscripts that could be regarded as luminous remnants of an ancient Indian heritage, albeit one better preserved in libraries in Nepal (itself, it should be noted, an overwhelmingly Hindu country). By the time public intellectuals such as Mahatma Gandhi and Jawaharlal Nehru began invoking the Buddha, he was no longer a foreign figure, a Shingutama who led the pan-theon of another people. For such nationalists, the Buddha had become—or been claimed as—a fellow Indian (or Afghan). So it was that in the decades after 'Abd al-Khaliq wrote his book, the larger Indian rediscovery of Buddhism assumed a markedly Indocentric trajectory, in which the religion was con-ceived as part of a proprietary Indian heritage that was benevolently bestowed on Asia at large.

Yet direct inter-Asian connections had played little part in providing the new understanding that raised the formerly foreign Buddha to the status of revered national sage. Such introspective engagements with a determinedly *Indian* Buddhist past belonged to a nationalist conception of the Buddha that ultimately found expression on the flag of independent India, with its Wheel of Chakra copied from columns carved for an ancient Indian Buddhist em-peror.[226] Meanwhile, the Muslim exegetical heirs to al-Qasimi tried to find a place for the Buddha in the Quran and so formulate meanings for religious difference that were larger than the narratives of nations.[227] Here they turned to the words of their own scripture: "O mankind, indeed We have created you from a male and female and made you peoples and tribes that you may know one another."[228]

3 • Lessons from Japan between India and Iran

In the last decades of the nineteenth century, after almost two and a half centuries of isolation through the *sakoku* or "closed country" policy of the Tokugawa shogunate, the ports of Japan were opened to foreign trade. Though the catalyst had come across the Pacific in 1854 with the arrival of a U.S. naval expedition led by Commodore Matthew Perry, new links with Asia were not long in coming. Describing the British P&O steamer he took to Yokohama just a decade later, in 1864, the German archaeologist Heinrich Schliemann (1822–1890) noted in his diary, "The crew of our paddle steamer comprised Chinese, Malays, lascar sailors (being Hindus from the Bombay region), indigenous peoples of Manila, Englishmen, Arabs from Mokha, and black Africans from Zanzibar."[1] His words capture the human dimensions of the imperial infrastructures that quickly connected the Japanese treaty ports with their colonial counterparts in Southeast Asia, the Middle East, and especially India. By the end of the century, Japan had joined the maritime trade networks of Asia at large. Not only were European companies from British India, French Indochina, imperial Russia, and the Dutch East Indies involved. So were their Asian competitors: among the many Indian merchants that established themselves in Japan were wealthy Hindu companies from Sind, as well as Memon and Khoja Muslim firms from Gujarat that already dominated trade with Burma and Ceylon.[2] Even Iraqi Jewish trading houses became major players, particularly Sassoon & Company, which had previously relocated from Basra to Bombay. A number of prosperous Iranian merchants followed in turn.

The "opening" of Japan has often been seen as a trans-Pacific process in which America played the leading role, but the older and larger Asian markets that were now tied by empire to Europe held a stronger gravitational pull.

After all, Japan is effectively equidistant from India and North America.[3] And while, aside from Hawaii, the trans-Pacific route from Yokohama to San Francisco crossed commercially worthless empty waters, the sea-lanes to Bombay passed through some of the most profitable ports on the planet—Hong Kong, Manila, Singapore, and Colombo. As Japan's own industrialization caught up with America's and Europe's, India played a central role, initially by providing a vast market for the matches that represented one of Japan's main exports and subsequently as Bombay merchants supplied Indian raw cotton to Osaka's massive textile mills.[4]

As a result, Indian merchants became well established in the key commercial ports of Yokohama and Kobe.[5] Indians were among the earliest outsiders to arrive after Yokohama became a treaty port in 1859, seeing famous Bombay companies such as the Parsi-owned Tata & Company opening branches there.[6] Correspondingly, the Yokohama Specie Bank opened its principal overseas office in Bombay.[7] After British steamships linked Yokohama with Calcutta in the 1860s, Japanese shipping companies followed suit: the Nippon Yusen Kaisha launched its service to Bombay in 1885, later followed by the Osaka Shosen Kaisha service between Bombay and Kobe. In many respects, Yokohama and Kobe developed into the sibling cities of Calcutta and Bombay, acting as their country's earliest railheads and leading steamship ports, their main trading emporia, and industrial centers. Both pairs of ports also played parallel informational roles through the rise of the multilingual printing in Asian and European languages that linked them to the larger Asian public sphere, albeit often with European languages serving as intermediaries between their East, West, and South Asian counterparts.

Yet for all the booming traffic between Bombay and Kobe, the accurate understanding of Japanese culture presented many more obstacles than the trade in cotton. The flow of trade did not easily translate into knowledge any more than it had around the Bay of Bengal. As we will see, even the most well-educated Indian and Middle Eastern travelers struggled with the informational barriers to understanding Japan's distinctive society and culture. Intercultural understanding was dependent on many different factors from commerce, ranging from the individual interests of specific investigators to the interpretive resources available in their languages. This was all the more so for Japan, which, in being closed to Indian and Middle Eastern merchants for centuries, was not even known through the residual knowledge of medieval travelogues and early modern traders. It would have to be discovered anew.

Even the one notable account of Japan to emerge from such earlier connections—the seventeenth-century Persian *Safina-yi Sulaymani* (*Ship of Solomon*)—was based on secondhand news gathered far away in what is today
Thailand.[8] Moreover, because it was not printed, the manuscript languished
forgotten and uncited by the Iranian, Indian, and Arab writers on Japan who
emerged after 1900. Such was the degree of uncertainty with which Japan
was seen that this indeterminacy reached even to its name, which authors
in the same language spelled differently, as in Arabic, Persian, and Urdu it
was alternatively rendered with *y* (*ya*), *j* (*jim*) or *zh* (*zhe*), as well as vowels
long or short. Not only do these spellings point to the unsettled newness of
Japan on the horizons of inter-Asian knowledge, but they also hint at the
European information on East Asia that slipped through print into the languages of South and West Asia. As these orthographic clues clearly show,
neither the Indian nor Middle Eastern names of the country were derived
from the Japanese language itself: Arabs, Turks, Iranians, and Indians did
not write about a place they called Nippon or Nihon. Instead, they borrowed
the English, French, or Russian versions of the name by transliterating "Japan," "Japon," or "Yaponiyya" into their own languages as part of a larger
informational bundle. It was part of the intellectual traffic with Europe that
we saw in the introduction, which began with the translation of Mercator's
maps that rendered the Latin name *Iaponia* into Turkish along with the en-
compassing label "Asia."'

When Indian and Middle Eastern authors began writing about Japan in the
early 1900s, they were drawing no more on the commercial inter-Asian connections of the previous decades than on rare Persian manuscript reports of
former centuries. Despite the increasing presence of Indian and Middle Eastern merchants in Japan, they produced few if any book-length accounts of the
country. Instead, the sudden burst of books on Japan had a specific trigger that
was more political and military than market-orientated: the defeat of imperial
Russia in the Russo-Japanese War of 1904–1905.[9]

A news sensation reported across Asia's new public sphere—often via more
direct reports in the European press—Japan's extraordinary victory awoke
widespread curiosity about the secret behind its rapid modernization and
military empowerment.[10] The result was a multilingual corpus of pioneering
texts about Japan, from panegyric poems to heroic plays, history books, and
first-person travelogues published in languages ranging from Arabic, Persian,
and Turkish to Malay, Gujarati, Bengali, and Urdu.[11] In some cases, reports
even moved between the different languages and port city hubs of the public

sphere, as when Mustafa Kamil Pasha's Arabic account of Japan's war with Russia was translated into Malay and published in Singapore in 1906.[12]

During the three decades that followed the Russian defeat, Japan attracted more detailed interest, which led to further studies of the country and its culture. The nascent ideology of Asianism played a role here, shaping motivations and interpretations that were framed primarily in terms of either allying with or learning from Japan.[13] In the decades after 1905, Japan's transformation into a modern industrial nation that at the same time maintained its cultural traditions through a policy called *wakon yosai* ("Japanese spirit, Western technology") made it a role model for modernist and nationalist intellectuals across the Middle East and India alike. As a Hindi article in the journal *Sarasvati* viewed the matter, Japan had "put Western civilization [*sabhyata*] on a Japanese template."[14] And so, by turning with admiration to the Japanese other, intellectuals across India and the Middle East looked for lessons in empowering the self.

Nonetheless, this potent dialectic generated new levels of knowledge about a country that, in textual terms at least, was otherwise known mainly through translated European textbooks on world geography and history. But at the same time, such Asianist motivations produced a distorted discursive mirror in which the reflection of the self morphed into the image of the other. The newfound Japanophilia born from the defeat of imperial Russia quickly grew into attempts to claim Japan as part of a Hindu-based "Greater India" or to convert its people to Islam or Baha'ism. Appreciating the subtleties of Zen Buddhist poetry, or the autochthonous powers of Shinto *kami* spirits, was an altogether more challenging enterprise. For as we will see, Japanophilia was not necessarily the same as Japanology, which is to say that positive attitudes were not necessarily the outcome or guarantee of direct, accurate, and linguistically informed knowledge. The relationship between affection and understanding could even be an inverse one—a lesson learned by the Bengali poet Tagore, who renounced his early Japanophilia as increasing knowledge of the country confronted him with the darker reality of its colonial ambitions and nationalist politics.[15]

The case of Japan therefore offers both contrasts and continuities with the patterns we have seen emerging from the interconnection of other regions of Asia. None of these contrasts was more important than Japan's shifting—and inspiring—status from a semicolonized country to an imperial power in its own right. This economic and especially military ascent drew a far wider range of authors to write about Japan than we have seen writing about Burma.

Though Japan also attracted Muslim, Baha'i, Hindu, and even Theosophical Buddhist missionaries, many of the Indian and Middle Eastern authors who wrote books about its rapid ascent were state officials and educationalists who tried to decipher the relationship between specific cultural traditions and economic development that was capable of being imitated. But like inter-Asian understanding around the Bay of Bengal, their writings were no less shaped by circumstances and contingencies, shared ideologies and individual idiosyncrasies. And so, in a subtly altered eastern echo of what we heard around the Bay of Bengal, these broader ventures in inter-Asian understanding were motivated by desires for self-empowerment that gradually generated a deeper, if partial and indirect, appreciation of the Japanese other.

Unreliable Intermediaries between *Perushia* and *Zhapun*

Turning first to perceptions of Japan in the Middle East, the patchy development of publicly available information in Persian points to the wider difficulties of developing a robust and reliable corpus of knowledge in the nineteenth century effectively ex nihilo. Although Japan had been indirectly described in the seventeenth-century *Safina-yi Sulaymani* (*Ship of Solomon*), written as part of a Safavid embassy to Siam, the manuscript seems to have languished lost and forgotten in Iran thereafter. As a result, knowledge about Japan had to be sourced and transmitted anew through printed books, particularly those associated with Iran's first modern educational institutions. An influential example was the two-page description of Japan in the *Kitab-i Jam-i Jam* (*Book of the World-Revealing Goblet*), which we have seen spreading the concept of a single continent called *Asiya* after it was published in Tehran in 1855 for Iran's French-inspired polytechnic, the Dar al-Funun.[16] Despite the indigenous idiom of its title, *Kitab-i Jam-i Jam* was a translation by the statesman Farhad Mirza of an amateur geographical textbook by an overly prolific English schoolmaster by the name of William Pinnock.[17] Far from constituting a reliable source, Pinnock's short account of Japan was both indirect and incorrect. Having originally been published in 1834, more than twenty years before Japan opened its ports to European travelers, it was also woefully outdated by the time it first found readers in Tehran, a year after Commodore Perry's gunboats had put an end to Japan's isolation.

Pinnock's understanding of what was during his own lifetime still the closed country of the Tokugawa shoguns was minimal. He gave the name of its capital as "Jeddo" (a corruption of Edo that Farhad Mirza in turn passed into

Persian as *Jidu*) and provided a few bits of concrete data.[18] As for religious matters, he vaguely declared that "their religion is Paganism," albeit adding the qualification that "they are moral and recommend a virtuous life."[19] Residing in the Iranian city of Tabriz, Pinnock's translator, Farhad Mirza, had no means of knowing that the book he was translating—probably passed on to him by one of the British military officers or missionaries serving nearby—was full of incorrect and out-of-date information.

A year after the translation was published in Tehran, an Iranian publisher in Bombay issued a reprint, presumably for the use of Bombay's Iranian merchants. Yet not only was the book read in Iran and India, it was also influential in neighboring Afghanistan, which had even more limited access to reliable information. Consequently, in Kabul, *Kitab-i Jam-i Jam* was still being read and cited by state officials as an authoritative source until at least 1895, almost thirty years after "Jeddo" had changed its name to Tokyo.[20]

After the early vicarious informational access afforded by the likes of Pinnock, direct connections between Iran and Japan commenced in 1880 with the diplomatic mission of Yoshida Masaharu (1852–1921). But as was so often the case, whether between Asia and Europe or across Asia itself, the exchange of information was not equally distributed on both sides. While on the Japanese side of the balance sheet Yoshida's mission led to two books by his companions—Furukawa Nobuyoshi's *Perushia kiko* (*Travels in Iran*) in 1890 and Yoshida Masaharu's *Kaikyo tanken Perushia no tabi* (*Adventures in Muslim Persia*) four years later—these contacts produced no equivalent book in Persian, not least because the Qajar government sent no reciprocal mission to Tokyo.[21] The outcome was more Japanese public awareness of Iran than vice versa, a pattern of informational asymmetry that over the following decades would gradually develop into a cumulative corpus of Japanese "Iranology."[22] Nonetheless, Yoshida's and Furukawa's pioneering texts were based on the limited observations of two travelers unable to speak the local language. For want of a shared Asian language, Yoshida and his companions had to converse with their hosts in English, which Mirza 'Ali Khan Atabak of the Qajar foreign ministry then translated into Persian.[23] Aside from observations gathered on the spot, further information on Iran had to be sourced from the vast library of European texts on the country. And so, just as Iranians adopted the French name *Japon* as *Zhapun*, so did such early Japanese investigators adopt the English name Persia as *Perushia*, even though, like *Japon* and *Zhapun*, this was a name that wasn't used in the Persian language itself.[24]

From the 1880s, more information about Japan began to trickle into Iran through its growing links to Asia's maritime public sphere. More accurate accounts of Japan began to appear as articles in the Istanbul-based Persian newspaper *Akhtar* (*Star*).[25] Just as Calcutta and Bombay served as informational hubs in the maritime heart of Asia, so on the western edge of the continent did Istanbul, with its even closer ties to Europe that funneled information into Persian, Turkish, Ladino, Arabic, and Armenian newspapers alike.

Then, in 1893, Bombay's Dutt Prasad Press issued another of the rare Persian accounts of Japan to be published before the Russo-Japanese War. Compiled from much earlier accounts by the Iranian émigré publisher Mirza Muhammad Shirazi, the book bore the attention-grabbing title *Mirat al-Zaman dar Tarikh-i Chin u Machin u Japan* (*The Mirror of the Times through the History of China, Greater China, and Japan*).[26] Unfortunately, it dealt with Japan only in the last—and by far the shortest—of its twelve chapters. In fewer than three pages, this brief epilogue outlined basic geography, explaining that the country was made up of several islands, which were extensively settled and built up, and that the locals called their country *Nipun* or *Nifun*.[27] In dealing much more fully with China, *Mirat al-Zaman* marked a moment of transition between an older Iranian recognition of the imperial might of China and a glimmering realization that an unknown power was rising in the still lesser-known lands farther east. Yet for all that, despite being published in 1893, *Mirat al-Zaman* was even more woefully outdated than Pinnock's geographical book: it drew on a translation of Jesuit reports written almost three centuries earlier.[28]

Four years after these vicarious and dated accounts appeared, however, the Iranian merchant Ibrahim Sahhafbashi wrote a pioneering firsthand Persian account of a trade mission he made to Yokohama by steamship. Written around 1896, Sahhafbashi's travelogue is particularly useful for portraying Iranian attitudes *before* the defeat of Russia, in 1905, inspired a public chorus of Persian Japanophilia. For what is most striking about his description is its relative negativity in comparison to the subsequent Persian panegyrics published in response to the Russo-Japanese War. While recording such elements of modernity as the many Japanese warships at anchor in Yokohama, where the port's telegraph system could alert newspapers worldwide about the safe arrival of ships and their cargoes within six hours, Sahhafbashi framed them in terms of the old literary trope of the "weird and wonderful" (*'aja'ib u ghara'ib*).[29] Turning to the inhabitants of this unfamiliar land, he was nevertheless a careful describer of Japanese customs and lifestyles, whether in terms of food habits, patterns of socializing, or glimpses of domestic life. Like other indigenous ethnographers who ventured along Asia's connecting infrastructures, he paid particular attention to culinary alterity, recording the custom of dining on "raw fish . . . with two delicate wooden sticks," and drinking "alcohol made from rice."[30] He described a party in which a young woman (a geisha?) played a stringed instrument he called a *tar-i zhapuni* (Japanese lute), presumably a *biwa*, for male guests amid much bowing and mannerisms.[31] He found other customs more familiar, some of which he compared to Iranian practices, such as removing shoes before entering a house.[32] He also remarked approvingly on the fact that there were very few beggars on the street, and that all Japanese children began work or study from the age of four or five.[33]

Sahhafbashi was also curious about Japanese religiosity, penning a brief account of the altars placed in every shop and home, as well as the priests who, despite police bans, continued to be called on to provide the sick with "prayer water" (*ab-i du'a*).[34] He scribbled a brief pen portrait of the visibly observable practices of Buddhism. But like 'Abd al-Khaliq in Burma a couple of years earlier, he had no concept or name for such a religion, which forced him to deploy Muslim religious terms to make sense of what he saw. But whereas the missionary 'Abd al-Khaliq devoted years to studying the Burmese language, in a further hint at the informational constraints of commercial compared to missionary encounters, Sahhafbashi's six-week business trip lent him little incentive or opportunity to understand the religion or culture in its own terms through learning the Japanese language. As a result, his description of Buddhism was framed through the older Perso-Arabic lexicon of idolatry that in previous centuries had been deployed for broad-brush portrayals of ritual practices from India to China.

Recording his visit to a Buddhist pilgrimage site, he thus recounted: "One day I went to see the spectacle of the idolatrous statues [*mujasimaha-yi buti*], of which there are several made of iron that are so large that a man can fit through their nostrils. Together they look like an iron mountain made into the shape of an idol [*sanami*]. And this is a place of worship [*sata'ishgah*]!"[35] In addition to the Persian word *but*, he made use here of *sanam*, the uncompromising Quranic Arabic term for an idolatrous image. Nonetheless, the statues held a certain infernal appeal, for Sahhafbashi expressly described his visits to the Buddhist statues and similar ethnographic sites as a *tamasha* (spectacle), using a traditional term for gazing at fascinating things.

In its investigative methods, Sahhafbashi's pioneering firsthand Persian depiction of Japan had much in common with other Middle Eastern and Indian travel accounts of other regions of Asia. Lacking the ability to communicate with locals, he was forced to rely on the simple empiricism of watching people in public places and then making what interpretations he could through the semantic toolkit he carried from home. No Japanese-Persian dictionary for Iranians would exist for over another fifty years, three and a half centuries after the publication of the Japanese-to-Portuguese *Vocabulario da lingoa de Iapam* (*Vocabulary of the Japanese Language*) by Jesuit missionaries in 1603.[36]

Sahhafbashi's timing was unfortunate in that the year after he returned home to Tehran, a multilingual commercial lexicon was compiled that included Persian and Japanese terms. Reflecting the more formal development of intercultural knowledge in modernizing Meiji Japan, its author was Gozaemon Gi, a Japanese official from a family of government translators based at Dejima Island, which during the previous centuries had served as Japan's only open window to the world.[37] As an East Asian counterpart to the lexicons published around the Bay of Bengal, it included a list of Persian words relating to trade goods and their Japanese equivalents. In principle, this might have aided Sahhafbashi's commercial exchanges, but its context was too limited for comprehension of complex cultural practices. And in practice it would have been useless to him: in being designed to aid Japanese speakers, Gozaemon's book was printed entirely in Japanese characters.

In the complete absence of such interpretive resources, Sahhafbashi turned to his own powers of observation and moral sensibility. Making sense of what he saw through the lens of his own values, Sahhafbashi voiced criticism for various customs in a way that would become far less common a decade later in works of Persian Japanophilia. He was particularly upset by what he regarded as immodest female behavior: one of his earliest sights in Yokohama was of a woman rising naked from the sea and casually strolling up to a group of men to dress herself.[38] He later described in disapproving detail how in Japanese bathhouses it was the custom for men and women to bathe together naked, even mixing fathers with their wives, daughters, and sons-in-law.[39] He also wrote with stern concern about Japan's flourishing "business of harlotry" (*asbab-i harzigi*).[40] Nor did he acquire a taste for Japanese food: raw fish appeared oddly primitive, and he found sake particularly unpleasant.[41] Here he echoed 'Abd al-Khaliq's disapprobation of the Burmese taste for stinking pickled fish.[42]

Amid this vivid sense of difference, in contrast to later Iranian and Indian (as well as Arab and Ottoman) accounts of Japan, Sahhafbashi made no recourse to the emerging vocabulary of "progress" (*taraqqi*). Nor was there any sense of being part of a common "Eastern civilization" (*mashriqi tamaddun*) that would soon become a byword for the new ideology of Asianism. Nor, with his lack of a lexicographical aids, did he use any Japanese loanwords. Lacking even vicarious access to information about the country's past, he did not write even the most cursory summary of its history, and he showed no awareness of the cultural achievements of Japan, or of the meanings of its religions or arts. And so, when he did venture into intercultural interpretation, he had no option but to depict Japanese cultural practices in the familiar terms of Iranian customs and Persian vocabulary. Ultimately, his was a Japan of *hammams* (bathhouses) and *mahfils* (music gatherings), *mullas* (mullahs) and *akhunds* (Muslim clerics)—as well, of course, as idolatrous *buts.*

In the unsentimental prose of this Tehrani merchant, there was no room for Japanophilic fascination. He had traveled too early: before the defeat of Iran's imperial Russian foes rendered Japan a model of self-empowerment for the reformists and nationalists of the early 1900s. Perhaps this explains why his diary was never published at the time. In and of itself, Japan was as yet of too little interest.

Nonetheless, when a Japanese army intelligence officer called Fukushima Yasumasa (1852–1919) reached Tehran after a journey by steamer via Burma and India, Sahhafbashi himself proved of interest.[43] Since the Iranian had only recently returned from his travels, Fukushima was told about him and the two men met. But even in Tehran, such inter-Asian encounters were not entirely unmediated. A fluent German speaker, Fukushima spent most of his time in Tehran with Wagner Khan, an Austrian military adviser to the Qajar court and teacher at the Dar al-Funun polytechnic who accompanied his Japanese fellow officer to most of his meetings.[44] When he returned to Tokyo, Fukushima published a travelogue. The borrowed words of its title—*Chuo Ajia yori Arabia e* (*Traveling from Central Asia to Arabia*)—bore subtle testimony to Europe's mediating role.

More Positive Persian Impressions

Seven years after Sahhafbashi met Fukushima, his compatriot Mahdi Quli Hidayat (1864–1955) disembarked in Nagasaki. In contrast to his merchant predecessor, Hidayat was a government official who had studied in Berlin and worked in the Telegraph Office, and then later at the Dar al-Funun polytechnic. Reflecting the official positions held by other subsequent authors on Japan, he also served at the court of Nasir al-Din Shah (r. 1848–1896), translating German books for educating civil servants.[45] It was through these state connections that he traveled as part of the small party that accompanied the former prime minister Mirza 'Ali Asghar Khan (1858–1907) on a world tour that included Japan. Since Hidayat did not publish his travelogue—a blend of diary and commentary—till later in life, the attitudes recorded in it were probably shaped by the defeat of Russia that followed soon after his return. For an official tasked with empowering Iran to withstand its imperious northern neighbor, the lessons offered by the Japanese victory would have been particularly meaningful. Following Sahhafbashi's account from a few years before the war, Hidayat's travelogue captures a transitional moment in the development of a Persian Japanophilia.

Upon sailing into Nagasaki from Shanghai, Hidayat noted the presence of a German warship in the harbor bearing a Japanese prince. Before he even disembarked, his narrative signaled Japan's newfound international status after the recent Anglo-Japanese Alliance of 1902.[46] From here on in, Hidayat displayed a much fuller awareness of Japan's modern history and recent achievements than Sahhafbashi. Drawing on German books, he provided a brief history of the opening of Japan's ports to global trade since the first treaty with the Portuguese in 1571.[47] From his years in Berlin, Hidayat was well aware of the political importance of Japan as a potential ally against Russia. As a result, he and his senior companion, Mirza 'Ali Asghar Khan, held many meetings with Japanese military officials and politicians, several of which he detailed. Recognizing Japan's importance in a way Sahhafbashi had not, the Iranian party discussed such topics as the German input into the new Japanese legal system.[48] Hidayat also inspected several Japanese schools, including, in a suitably progressive mode, a tour of a girls' school.[49]

Hidayat also collected detailed information on all manner of practical issues: the number of newspapers in Nagasaki, the routes of railways, the specialties of factories (several of which he inspected), the topography of the European quarters in different ports, the standard of hotels in Tokyo, the well-stocked emporia of Yokohama.[50] By the time he had set off from Tehran in 1903, Japanese goods had already penetrated Iran's markets: it is in fact Hidayat rather than Sahhafbashi who tells us the latter brought back so many goods that every house in Tehran contained something made in Japan.[51]

This trade in knickknacks connects the emergence of Iranian Japanophilia with its French aesthetic forebear, *Japonisme*. The fascination with Japan that spread rapidly through Parisian artistic circles in the second half of the nineteenth century was based on the export of material culture by such merchants as Philippe Sichel (1839–1899) that resulted from the opening of Japan's ports to global trade. In 1897 alone—the same year as Sahhafbashi's trade visit—Sichel shipped from Yokohama some forty-five crates packed with five thousand objects to sell in his Parisian emporium.[52] Like Sahhafbashi, Sichel also wrote an account of his commercial journeys under the title *Notes d'un bibeloteur au Japon* (*Notes of a Knickknack Collector in Japan*).[53] Although French *Japonisme* was an artistic and aesthetic appreciation, and its Iranian counterpart was motivated primarily by political and military admiration, these motivations became the means for a heightened if nonetheless constrained comprehension of Japanese culture. As for Hidayat, he recorded how his party arrived just in time for the famous cherry blossom festival, and his appreciation of Japanese culture and religiosity was both more respectful and better informed than Sahhafbashi's. The day after his arrival, he was already visiting a Japanese shrine, recording both the correct name of the religion (Shinto) and the shrine (*jingo*), as well as buying souvenir photographs of its picturesque views.[54] He later penned an appreciative account of the Buddhist heritage of Kyoto and the various Shinto shrines around the pilgrimage town of Nikko.[55] A newfound appreciation of Japan's cultural heritage thus began to emerge from the positive attitude toward its economic and political importance.

Hidayat's book included long sections devoted to history, religiosity, geography, and cultural etiquette that went far beyond Sahhafbashi's more meager, albeit wholly firsthand, reports.[56] Here was the richly detailed prose of a nascent Persian Japanophilia, accompanied, however, by clear political lessons, at least for his senior companion, the former prime minister Mirza 'Ali Asghar Khan. At the moment when Iran was about to launch a constitutional revolution to restrict the powers of the shah, 'Ali Asghar returned from Japan with the opposite conviction, that a strong, centralized government was a necessity for progress.[57]

These concerns were far from unique to Iran. On the contrary, they closely reflected the interest that Indian and Southeast Asian anticolonial intellectuals took in Japan as a potential ally against either Britain or Holland. Pointing directly to these parallels, several Indians appear in Hidayat's travelogue. In Tokyo, for example, the Iranian party was visited by a group of twelve Indian students, who presented them with a copy of the Persian newspaper *Habl al-Matin,* published in Calcutta.[58] As a legacy of the enduring and much older ties between India and Iran, the students could apparently all speak Persian and begged the influential Iranians for help in India's nascent freedom struggle. A few weeks later, Hidayat's party was invited to dinner in their Kyoto hotel by an Indian prince, whom Hidayat recalled as being named Raja Kapur Talo.[59] The prince in question was Jagatjit Singh (1872–1949), maharaja of the princely state of Kapurthala in Punjab, who in 1906 published his own memoir (in Urdu and English) of the journey that took him to Japan as well as China and Java.[60] Trivial as the incident was, the meeting in Kyoto forms a rare case of an encounter recorded from both sides. According to Singh's travelogue, his "Indian cook prepared a number of savory dishes, which met with high approval from my guests, who declared that they had enjoyed nothing so much in the way of food since their departure from Persia."[61] But this would appear to have been polite Persian *ta'aruf* (etiquette). According to Hidayat's recollection of the dinner, while the rice was excellent, the "pepper and spices burned the tongue and mouth."[62] However discreetly, Hidayat was echoing various other ethnographers of the inter-Asian encounter for whom descriptions of food served as vivid markers of cultural difference.

A Military Informational Turning Point

If Hidayat shows the complex interplay between concerns for the self and admiration of the other, then the Japanese defeat of Russia prompted more detailed accounts in Persian by way of the first book-length accounts of Japan. By the time Hidayat returned home, the Japanese victory was being reported in the Iranian newspapers of the freer public sphere that briefly flourished in the constitutional era of 1905 to 1911.[63] Even so, these were mainly derived from more established European newspapers that dispatched correspondents to observe the war directly. Nor did everyone like the ensuing Japanophilia: a poet in *Nasim-i Shamal (Northern Breeze)* declared, "Russia and Japan are nothing to us! . . . This Quran is sufficient for us."[64]

From similarly indirect sources, the onset of the war instigated the compilation of what appears to have been the first complete book about Japan to be published in Iran. This was *Mamlikat-i Shams-i Tali'* (*The Land of the Rising Sun*), compiled in 1904 by an Iranian called Mata'us Khan Malikiyans, an otherwise obscure figure who was apparently an Armenian Christian in government service.[65] Such an identity would make sense: as a result of the schools European and American missionaries founded for them, Armenian Christians had greater access to European languages, books, and information than many of their Muslim compatriots. For as the cover of the *Mamlikat* made clear, the book was not a work of direct observation but was instead "compiled and translated" by Malikiyans. For want of earlier sources in Persian—

he showed no awareness of the as-yet-unpublished reports of Sahhafbashi or Hidayat, or of the Bombay-printed *Mirat al-Zaman*, still less the seventeenth-century *Safina-yi Sulaymani*—the Iranian-Armenian compiled the text from several unnamed European works.

Despite his derivative sources, Malikiyans drew together their data into a purposeful message for his countrymen. As he explained in his introduction, the rise of Japan and its war with Russia formed an example that Iran should follow as a fellow "Eastern" (*sharqi*) nation.[66] This marked a major conceptual shift from the vivid sense of otherness writ large in Sahhafbashi's travelogue of just seven years earlier, a shift that was perhaps easier for Malikiyans in merely having to imagine Japan rather than confront its alterity firsthand. Yet there was nonetheless an informational trade-off between sitting in Tehran and translating secondhand sources. For at nearly 150 pages, his *Mamlikat* was far longer than Sahhafbashi's and Hidayat's direct accounts combined. Drawing on the fuller Japanological developments in Europe, its wide-ranging contents covered history, ethnography, religion, climate, education, arts and industries, travel infrastructure, printers and publishers, religion, urban and rural geography, flora and fauna, and, finally, the recent military ascent that enabled Japan's ongoing war with Russia.

Rather than directly translating his French sources, Malikiyans made a selective adaptation, which he semantically modified for his Iranian audience and ideological purpose. Nowhere was this more apparent than in his attention to the new nationalist virtue of "love for one's country" (*hubb-i watan*). This formed the central feature of a section nominally devoted to the traditional Persian concept of ethics (*akhlaq*).[67] As he explained, what not only gave Japan the epithet of the "Valley of Happy Faces," but also made its people more attractive than Westerners, was the unwavering love for their country that characterized every stratum of society.[68] Whether describing educational, military, or economic progress, he consistently returned to his central political theme: all this had been made possible through the people's loyalty to their wise emperor, the mikado. Japan's progress had come about through the mikado's leadership. Such was the unswerving loyalty his people showed that anyone who mourned or wept over the death of his loved ones in fighting for their emperor was scorned by his neighbors.[69]

As much as the *Mamlikat* was a work of Japanophilia, it was also therefore a treatise on the virtues of autocracy and nationalism. These were certainly the lessons that some other Iranian thinkers took away from new Japanophilic works like the *Mamlikat*, not least the influential Mirza 'Abd al-Rahim Talibuf

(1834–1911), who in his 1906 *Masa'il al-Hayat* (*Matters of Life*), proposed that Iran adopt the Japanese model of "enlightenment from above."[70] From a version in Russian, Talibuf also published a translation of the Meiji Constitution that lent a central role to the emperor as enlightened despot.

Since Malikiyans's *Mamlikat* served primarily as a Franco-Japanese lesson for Iran, its sole section on Japanese language comprised a few short lines stating that the language was a mixture of Chinese with the "original dialect" of Japan.[71] Yet the *Mamlikat* was nonetheless groundbreaking when it came to presenting Japanese religiosity in Persian. It provided one of the earliest accounts of Buddhism, and almost certainly the first of Shinto, ever published in Iran. As we saw in the previous chapter, in 1885 a report about the great Buddha statues of Bamiyan in the prestigious Tehran journal *Sharaf* had classified them merely as idols, making no reference to any specific religion and even omitting the reference to "Boodhism" in its English source text. Less than two decades later, and prompted by the war with Russia, Malikiyans's book was another small milestone in inter-Asian understanding. A chapter titled "Religion and Traditions" (*Din u A'yin*) began by explaining that there were three religions (*din*), or sects (*mazhab*), in Japan, namely, those of Shinto (*Shintu'i*), Buddhism (*Buda'i*), and Christianity (*din-i 'Isawi*).[72] Turning first to Shinto, Malikiyans described it as "the way and path of the ancient gods and laws," albeit a religion that had no "heavenly book."[73] Drawing clearly from his French sources, which carried a Persian echo of Rousseau's noble savage, he conceptualized Shinto as an expression of natural law (*a'yin-i tabi'i*).[74] This kind of religiosity could be found among many "savage tribes" (*tawa'if-i wahshi*), having no ethical or moral teachings as such; hence the Shinto principle that everyone had access to reason (*'aql*) allowed its followers to decide for themselves how best to behave.[75] Connecting this reliance on reason to his book's larger political message, Malikiyans added that Shintoists called their highest god Lord Sun, whose living "representative" is the emperor.[76]

Turning next to Buddhism, Malikiyans provided a historicist account that explained how the Buddha had lived in India around sixteen centuries before Christ. Although this very early date derived from European debates on the historical Buddha, by the 1900s Orientalists had settled on around 600 BC. Like other translators who had to rely on whatever materials were available to them, Malikiyans was drawing on outdated scholarship.

Being considerably less positive than his depiction of Shinto, his presentation of Buddhism also diverged from what by the late nineteenth century had become a highly positive image in the majority of European studies, as well as in the Indian works that were appearing by the 1900s in the wake of Arnold's *Light of Asia*.[77] Thus, in the *Mamlikat*, the Buddha was described as a "pretender to occult knowledge" (*mudda'i-yi 'ilm-i ghayb*) whose "business took off" (*kar-i u bala girift*) and then spread from India to China, Korea, and Japan.[78] Reflecting European demographic misperceptions at the time, Malikiyans also reported an overestimate that the worldwide Buddhist population stood at some 400 million. He then moved on to a summary of doctrine. Whereas 'Abd al-Khaliq in Burma had dwelt on the moral problems posed by reincarnation (*tanasukh*), Malikiyans focused on the doctrine that the world was an illusion with no real existence. While the Iranian took this idea from his European sources, like 'Abd al-Khaliq responding to his Burmese readings, he was wary of the theological implications of such teachings. As he explained, the Buddha's doctrines meant that God's creation did not have to obey Him.[79] To Iranian Muslim and Christian readers alike, the implication was clear: Buddhism undermined the moral order of collective human life.

Malikiyans wrapped up his account of religion with a short history of the rise of Christianity, which had spread fast "since the gates of Japan were opened," that is, since the founding of the treaty ports in the 1860s.[80]

Aptly, the next major Persian account of Japan appeared from the port of Calcutta, from which British missionaries began their maritime printed outreach across Asia. The *Mikadunama* (*Book of the Mikado*) was written by Husayn 'Ali Shirazi, another obscure figure. He was described on the cover of his book as a merchant, which suggests he was one of the many Iranian traders based in Calcutta.[81] Published in July 1907—almost two years after the Treaty of Portsmouth formalized the Japanese victory—the *Mikadunama* celebrated the events of the war in epic verse modeled on the medieval Persian *Shahnama* (*Book of Kings*). It comprised just over one hundred pages of heroic couplets telling of glorious battles in the region glossed as the "Far East" (*Aqsa-yi Sharq*). Printed by Calcutta's expatriate Iranian publishing industry—specifically on the press belonging to the newspaper *Habl al-Matin*—the *Mikadunama* was intended for both an Iranian and an Indian readership (prices in two currencies appeared on the cover: one tuman or three rupees). Although the book-length poem was *about* Japan, its communicational ambit—whether in price, post, language, or genre—encompassed only India and Iran. Not only was Japan not part of the conversation; it was apparently not the source of the information either; its most likely source was the *Habl al-Matin* newspaper itself, which had previously issued a special issue on the war based on English newspaper reports.[82] As we will see below, the European press also provided the dramatic pictures used to bring the verses of the *Mikadunama* vividly to life.

Yet despite—or even because of—its indirect sources, it promised readers that its information was trustworthy. Since there is no evidence that Shirazi ever went to Japan, his verses appear to have been based on the news reports that flowed daily into Calcutta, which allowed his publisher, the editor of the newspaper *Habl al-Matin,* to write a preface in which he assured readers the *Mikadunama* was based on "reliable sources" (*makhiz-i sahih*).[83]

The epic poem recounted not only the war itself, but also its historical background, both of which were framed in terms that were meaningful to the modernizing nationalist intellectuals for whom Japan offered lessons in self-empowerment. As the ideology of Asianism took shape in the same Calcutta where Okakura had met Tagore and dreamed up his famous declaration of unity a few years before the *Mikadunama* was published there, these lessons now began to shift their geographical focus away from Europe. And so, while a background section was devoted to Russia's "progress" as a result of the reforms made by Peter the Great—a figure who had long fascinated Iranian political thinkers—it was followed by a stirring rhythmic summary of the rise of Japan as a superior military power. First came victory in the First Sino-Japanese War of 1894–1895, then the more recent defeat of Russia.[84] After narrating in valiant terms the various land and sea campaigns, the *Mikadunama* culminated in the great sea battle in the Tsushima Straits where the Russian fleet was all but annihilated. A final section turned to the peace treaty.[85] All throughout, Shirazi's verses were illustrated with what in his preface his publisher described as "fifty-eight pictures of true photographs."[86] By this somewhat convoluted phrase, he was referring to hand-drawn copies of the photographs that reached the Calcutta office of the publisher's newspaper by way of the British papers from which his *Habl al-Matin* drew much of its international coverage.

Comprising mainly battle scenes, the *Mikadunama*'s illustrations bear the signatures "HW Koekkoek" and "Bose," showing that, before they were reissued in the Persian text, they were copied by a Bengali artist named Bose from originals drawn by the Dutch news illustrator and painter of militaria Hermanus Willem Koekkoek (1867–1929).[87] Before being adapted for the *Mikadunama,* Koekkoek's illustrations—including the same portrait of Admiral Kamimura—had appeared in the *Illustrated London News,* which was mailed to Calcutta, then copied by Bose for reexport to Iran.[88] Just as Calcutta had pioneered the printing of Persian words over a century earlier, followed by the lithographic images to illustrate them, now the Indian port was exporting a new mode of representation that promised visual, if nonetheless vicarious, information about faraway regions of Asia. The historical irony is that the ideology of Asianism that such words and images helped inspire demanded the removal of Europe's enabling role from the story of inter-Asian connections.

During the next decade, the war with Russia continued to dominate Persian accounts of Japan, while also featuring in Turkish poems published in newspapers in Istanbul.[89] Back in Tehran, in 1913 Baqir Khan Tabrizi published his *Tarikh-i Aqsa-yi Sharq ya Muharaba-yi Rus u Zhapan* (*History of the Far East or the Russo-Japanese War*), which at two volumes totaling 720 pages dwarfed all previous Persian studies of Japan.[90] Like Malikiyans's *Mamlikat* nine years earlier, on its title page the *Tarikh-i Aqsa-yi Sharq* was described as having been "compiled and translated" rather than directly written by its Iranian author, who mentioned two of his sources directly.[91] The first was by a *"misyu Galli"* (perhaps a Monsieur Gallée?).[92] The second is clearer: the Ottoman Turkish *Rus-Zhapun Seferi* (*Russo-Japanese Journey*) by Major Osman Sena'i and Captain 'Ali Fu'ad, which had been published in five volumes by the Ottoman military press in Istanbul in 1905.[93] At that point, the Ottoman imperial outreach to Japan was already well-developed, not least through the goodwill voyage to Yokohama of the naval frigate *Ertuğrul* in 1890. When the latter was accidentally sunk off the coast of Kii Oshima, the assistance of local fishermen in rescuing survivors helped consolidate relations between the two Asian empires, one rising, one falling, through widespread coverage in both the Ottoman and the Japanese press. Yet, as in neighboring Iran, the sudden interest in Japan that followed the *Ertuğrul* disaster saw Ottoman Turkish knowledge about Japan similarly draw on European accounts. As in the Iranian case again, the books available were not always by reliable informants, which led in the Turkish case to the translation of a travelogue on Japan by the French romantic novelist Pierre Loti (1850–1923).[94]

With the outbreak of the Russo-Japanese War, however, a party of Ottoman military officials was sent to Japan as observers, producing several direct accounts of the conflict and the reasons behind Japan's victory. Such was the scale of Ottoman interest in the conflict that, of around fifty books and pamphlets about Japan that were published in Turkish between 1891 and 1928, almost half focused on the war with Russia.[95] Among the smaller number of firsthand Turkish accounts was a book by the German-educated Colonel Pertev Demırhan (1871–1964), as well as the five aforementioned volumes by Sena'i and Fu'ad used in Tabrizi's subsequent Persian account.[96] Strategically valuable as their findings were, their focus was primarily military rather than cultural, shaping Tabrizi's depiction of Japan in turn.

As for Tabrizi's *Tarikh-i Aqsa-yi Sharq* itself, its Iranian compiler explained that the length of his French and particularly Turkish sources had required him to "summarize" them into his own two volumes. For military affairs at least, there was an informational overload. Nonetheless, this was at least hard empirical data, Tabrizi claimed, which led him to emphasize that his book was not an *afsana* (fairytale), like the Persian literary texts of previous centuries.[97] (This may also have been a swipe at the *Mikadunama*.) Instead, he declared that his study was based on eyewitness reports (albeit by French and Ottoman observers). There was therefore more than a touch of irony that its lithographic illustrations of battle scenes—probably commissioned by the publisher and possibly to Tabrizi's annoyance—were in the style of traditional epics, showing medieval paladins that Iranian artists were more used to drawing.

Samurai as pictured in Persia: a lithographic illustration of Japanese warriors. Baqir Khan Tabrizi, *Tarikh-i Aqsa-yi Sharq*, 2 vols. (Tehran: Hajji Shaykh Ahmad Kitabfurush-i Shirazi, 1913). Photograph by Nile Green.

Like his compatriot Malikiyans, Tabrizi directed the lessons of Japanese empowerment toward his own countrymen, explaining that "nations cannot improve without understanding what makes other countries fail or succeed."[98] His focus was overwhelmingly on military expansion, beginning with a long account of the Sino-Japanese War before moving to the main theme of defeating the Russians. Insofar as Japanese cultural traditions were discussed, they were those that befitted the role of martial exemplars, such as the practice of "self-sacrifice" through cutting open one's belly.[99] Japan may have acquired the admiration of Iran. But whether in martial prose, epic verse, or dramatic illustration, it was based on an appreciation of military prowess that patriotic Iranians hoped to acquire for themselves. By the same token, as the political potential of Russia's defeat faded in significance, the Iranian interest in Japan dwindled to near silence. Despite the rapid output of thousands of printed Persian pages on Japan in the years following the war, after the publication of Tabrizi's *Tarikh* in 1913, it would apparently be another quarter century before the next Iranian book on Japan was published.[100] By then, Japan had transformed even further and lost its fascination: that next Persian book was a study of Japanese imperialism.[101]

An Offshoot Afghan Japanophilia

Over the course of the nineteenth century, Afghan merchants also made extensive connections with maritime Asia, establishing themselves in Calcutta and Bombay, then venturing farther to Burma, Ceylon, then farther still. But such traders did not transfer cultural knowledge into the emerging public sphere in Afghanistan, where state-controlled printing began in the late nineteenth century with printers and presses imported from India. Once again, it was politics, war, and the more circuitous data route of Turkish translations that provided Afghans with their first printed accounts—and pictures—of Japan. As in neighboring Iran, the earliest Afghan account had the same focus on the defeat of Russia by way of a long section of Muhammad Yusuf Riyazi's 'Ayn al-Waqayi' (*The Wellspring of Events*).[102] In 1906 this illustrated book was published by its Afghan Shi'i author in the Iranian border city of Mashhad, where he had fled to escape the anti-Shi'i policies of the ruler 'Abd al-Rahman Khan. Amid a recounting of the same battles reported again later by Tabrizi, the most striking feature of 'Ayn al-Waqayi' was its extraordinary lithographic images, especially that of the decisive Russian defeat in the Sea of Tsushima (*Bahr-i Sushima*), a maritime space previously unknown to Afghan readers.[103]

Unlike Calcutta, where the *Mikadunama* had been printed with glossy illustrations drawn from the *Illustrated London News,* Iran's less well-developed lithographic printing industry became a spur to artistic invention: the fantastical drawings of warships in *'Ayn al-Waqayi'* look like they sprang from the imagination of a Persianate Leonardo.

Over the following years, other Afghans developed a closer—and more accurate—interest in the defeat of Russia. In a speech at Kabul's recently established military college in 1911, the heir-apparent, Prince 'Inayatullah, praised "the sobriety and patriotism and discipline of the Japanese soldier, and the ardor of the Japanese officer," which he contrasted with "the drunkenness of the Russian soldier, and the foppishness of the Russian officer."[104] A year later, the leading nationalist (and later foreign minister) Mahmud Tarzi (1865–1933) drew the lessons of the war directly to the service of the Afghan state. In his Kabul newspaper *Siraj al-Akhbar* (*Lantern of News*), he published various translated reports on Japan, including a travel account.[105] Then, in 1915, Tarzi used the semiofficial 'Inayat Press, one of only two publishers in Afghanistan, to issue *Tarikh-i Muharaba-yi Rus u Zhapun* (*The History of the Russo-Japanese War*).[106] Having been exiled to the Ottoman Empire for seventeen years, Tarzi not only knew Turkish but was also aware of the larger amount of information on Japan available in that language. Consequently, like Tabrizi's Iranian book, Tarzi's was also a translation—albeit in this case a complete one—of the Turkish *Rus-Zhapun Seferi* by Major Osman Sena'i and Captain 'Ali Fu'ad. Given that printing had been introduced to Afghanistan only a few decades earlier by importing a press from Punjab with Indian workers to operate it, the Afghan edition was a huge undertaking. Such was the importance of the self-empowering lessons Japan had to offer that Tarzi's five thick volumes amounted to nearly 1,500 pages. This was by far the longest text by then published in Afghanistan.

Unlike Tabrizi's more selective translation, Tarzi's fuller rendition of the Ottoman survey included various historical and cultural sections. While the focus remained on military matters, the translation served to transmit to Afghanistan a pioneering account of Buddhism and Shinto, the latter being formulated as a national religion (*mazhab-i milli*), in line with Tarzi's own favored ideology.[107] Yet while Tarzi recognized the importance of Buddhism for China and Japan, he made no mention, even in a translator's footnote, of Buddhism's historical connections with his own homeland. Faced with the dilemma Tarzi and his Turkish informants shared with many Muslim reformers of how to model their own country on a Japan whose Shinto-Buddhist traditions were entirely foreign, Tarzi included a short section on the spread of Islam among the Japanese.[108]

This was a topic of great concern among many other Muslims of the period, not least the small cadre of Islamic missionaries who sailed to Japan's newly opened ports. Having been introduced to China just fifty-six years after the death of Muhammad, Tarzi's translation explained, Islam had subsequently spread to Japan through the efforts of Chinese merchants. But more recently, thousands of Chinese Muslims had come to study in Japan's military and trade schools.[109] For Tarzi, as for his late Ottoman informants, China's Muslims served as legitimizing role models for how their own Muslim countrymen might learn lessons from a country of erstwhile idolaters that, before the defeat of Russia, few if any of them had ever visited, or in the Afghan case, even read about.

From Admiring Japan to Converting the Mikado

There was another way of dealing with the problem of imitating a country whose Shinto-Buddhist culture was just emerging from centuries in the conceptual penumbra of "idol worship." Reflecting what we saw around the Bay of Bengal, the solution was to convert the Japanese to Islam. Partly this was sheer wishful thinking. After the defeat of Russia, from Iran and the Ottoman Empire to Central Asia and India, rumors spread widely that the mikado was on the verge of converting to Islam; some even declared it had become Japan's new state religion.[110] Such rumors may have been behind the attention given to the success of Christian missionaries there, and to the country's policies of religious freedom in the Ottoman, Iranian, and Afghan books we have seen published around this time. The war had also been widely reported in the Arabic press, and soon after the conflict ended, the journal *al-Manar* (*The Lighthouse*), widely distributed around maritime Asia, published two articles about converting Japan to Islam and calling on its pious readers to travel there to do so.[111] A month earlier *al-Hilal*, another Arabic journal read by Muslims across Asia, had reported on the influence of Buddhist missionaries in Britain, so perhaps anything seemed possible amid such unlikely Eurasian exchanges.[112] These rival missionary ventures led several Muslim evangelists to respond to *al-Manar*'s call. One of them was Hajji Muhammad 'Ali, a Georgian from the fringe of Russia's empire whose long steamship itinerary took him from the Black Sea port of Batumi via Istanbul, Aden, Colombo, and Port Louis on Mauritius and saw him preach in the mosques that graced each of these ports, before he finally reached Yokohama.[113] Though as yet there were no mosques in Japan, through such missionary ventures the Muslim encounter with East Asia became a means of self-projection as well as self-empowerment.

An Indian who took up this cause was 'Azmi Dihlawi (1867–1934), who in the last months of 1905 set sail from Calcutta. Having practiced his preaching techniques in India and Burma, in Japan he delivered several lectures on Islam (perforce in English), along with a sermon in a Buddhist temple in Nagasaki, which he later claimed led to numerous conversions.[114] One of his lectures was translated by his Buddhist contemporary Nukariya Kaiten (also 1867–1934), who the previous year had published a biography of Muhammad. Ironically, the translation appeared in a Japanese Christian journal called Rikugo Zasshi (Cosmos), one of the counterparts to the proselytizing journals spreading from Calcutta to Rangoon and Singapore. By 1906 even the Ismaili religious leader Aga Khan sailed to Yokohama from Bombay in a widening of the visits he previously made to his Gujarati followers in Rangoon, though he was more concerned with attending to his existing followers than with finding new ones.[115]

Two years later, an editorial in the Rangoon-based Muslim journal Ittihad-i Mazahib-i 'Alam queried the widespread rumor that the mikado had embraced Islam, before going on to praise Japan in a mode of self-reflecting appreciation.[116] Despite such rumors in Ittihad-i Mazahib and Dihlawi's later claims of winning many converts, both the Japanese and Anglo-Japanese press reported that Dihlawi won no converts at all.[117] That did not stop other Muslim missionaries from setting out from even the most remote regions of a continent now connected through the infrastructures of empire. Among them was the Siberian Tatar 'Abd al-Rashid Ibrahim (1857–1944), who traveled on the Trans-Siberian Railway. Somewhat more successful than Dihlawi, on leaving Japan in 1910, Ibrahim escorted Kotaro Omar Yamaoka (1880–1959) to Mecca, making him the first Japanese to perform the hajj.[118] Twenty years earlier, portraits of Noda Shotaro, the first Japanese Muslim convert rather than pilgrim, had appeared on the front pages of several Ottoman Turkish newspapers, celebrating his conversion.[119] Now Ibrahim published in Istanbul a two-volume Turkish account of his attempts to promote Islam in Japan.[120] It included a brief aperçu of the Japanese writing system, explaining that the Japanese had borrowed ancient Chinese characters to develop their own writing system.[121] In an approach that hints at the interplay of interpretive categories, to categorize the yamatogana, hiragana, and katakana syllabaries, Ibrahim borrowed the European term "hieroglyphics."

Ibrahim's proselytizing pursuits overlapped those of his Indian counterpart, Muhammad Barakatullah (1854–1927), who from 1909 to 1914 worked as a language teacher in Tokyo.[122] During those years, he published a journal titled *Islamic Fraternity*, which contained articles with titles such as "Christian Combination against Islam."[123] Aware of the advances Christian missionaries had already made in Japan by their printing and translation activities, Barakatullah tried to adopt those same methods for his own journal. But unlike the well-funded and linguistically capable enterprises of the British and Foreign Bible Society, active in Tokyo since 1875 (and in Calcutta since 1811), Barakatullah's journal appeared only in English.

Nonetheless, he certainly tried to launch a Japanese edition of *Islamic Fraternity*, explaining in its 1912 issue that he was planning this through "cooperation on the part of our two Japanese friends, Prof. Fujita and Mr. Hatano. The former one is a wonderful polyglot who knows almost all European languages and has a fair acquaintance with Arabic, Persian, Turkish and Hindustanee. Mr. Hatano is a bright young author. He possesses a facile pen and produces brilliant prose."[124] Barakatullah went on to explain that, through these local language helpers, it would prove "possible to bring principles of Islam home to Japanese people, who have so far got no conception of Islam whatsoever."[125] His younger associate, Hasan Hatano Uho (1882–1936), would indeed convert to Islam: he later edited a Japanese journal of his own called *El-Islam*. Japan's Christian missionaries soon took note, as did British officials, wary of Barakatullah's anticolonial politics.[126] In 1913 both journals were closed by the local authorities, who acted on advice from their British diplomatic allies. By then, despite almost four years in Tokyo, Barakatullah had made little contribution to the Indian or wider Muslim understanding of Japan. He had ultimately been less interested in learning from its Shinto-Buddhist culture than in teaching its people about his own religion.

Such South Asian projections of the self were by no means solely Muslim concerns. While the Pan-Islamist Barakatullah was trying to promote his own religion, the Ceylonese missionary Dharmapala was trying to build parallel "Pan-Buddhist" solidarities through his four visits to Japan between 1889 and 1913.[127] On the last of these visits, he met Barakatullah. Learning with consternation of his opposing missionary plans, Dharmapala penned an article for his own outlet, the *Journal of the Maha-Bodhi Society*, alerting fellow Buddhists to the dangers of promoting among the Japanese a religion he declared "unsuited to civilized people."[128] Yet even as he tried to build intra-Buddhist solidarities, seeking donations for his Maha-Bodhi Society from wealthy Japanese businessmen, Dharmapala found Japan's form of Mahayana Buddhism perplexing in its difference from his own Ceylonese Theravada tradition.[129] The more time Dharmapala spent in Japan, the more he realized how far its various Buddhist sects had diverged from what he regarded as the Buddha's true teachings—namely, the substantially reformed version of the religion that Dharmapala developed in collaboration with the American Theosophist Henry Steel Olcott.[130] We have already seen Olcott's Christian-style *Buddhist Catechism* being translated into Sinhala and Japanese. The ensuing intra-Buddhist encounter—with an American as the mediating doctrinal partner—led to debates that found their way into print. One example came when Dharmapala failed to convince the nationalist Nichiren missionary Tanaka Chigaku (1861–1939) to adopt his and Olcott's doctrines during a debate in Kamakura.[131] A skilled disputant who had previously defended Buddhism against Christian missionaries, Tanaka triumphantly concluded the debate by declaring his own Nichiren tradition the true fulfillment of Buddha's teachings.

Sailing in the direction opposite Dharmapala's, from the 1880s a series of Japanese Buddhist monks boarded steamships for Calcutta and Colombo. The earliest to arrive were Shaku Kozen (1849–1924), who disembarked in Colombo in 1886 and stayed for seven years, and Shaku Soen (1860–1919), who arrived in 1887 and stayed for two years.[132] These Japanese monks took home warnings from their Ceylonese encounter with religions other than their own. Soen wrote two books about Ceylon, *Saiyu Nikki* (*Diary of a Western Journey*) and *Seinan no Bukkyo* (*The Buddhism of the Southwest*).[133] Exporting the lessons he had learned from his travels, in *Seinan no Bukkyo* he gave a stark warning of the perilous plight of Buddhism across Asia at large: "At the front door the wolf of Christianity opens its jaws; at the back door the tiger of Islam sharpens its claws."[134] As though to reiterate these lessons, just a month after the book was published, Dharmapala and Olcott arrived in Japan on their mission to persuade Japanese Buddhists to unite in common cause with their Ceylonese and Burmese coreligionists.[135] If this appears a quite different proposition from that of Okakura, with his claim of a few years later that "Asia is one," then it is worth noting the similar suspicions toward Islam that were voiced in the following paragraphs of his book.

For his part, the Japanese pilgrim Kozen similarly joined his fellow Ceylonese Buddhists in their opposition to the Christian missionaries, working closely with Dharmapala and Olcott.[136] Widening the self-projecting pattern of Muslim proselytizers in Japan, on his return home in 1893 Kozen founded his own missionary organization, the Shakuson Shofu Kai (Society for the True

Way of Shakyamuni), near the port of Yokohama.[137] Sailing between Colombo, Calcutta, and Yokohama, over the next four decades many other Japanese followed him and Soen to both Ceylon and India. As Japanese and Ceylonese Buddhists converged on the site of the Buddha's enlightenment at Bodhgaya in the North Indian province of Bihar, they joined Dharmapala's energetic campaign to restore Bodhgaya to Buddhist control after centuries as a place of Hindu worship.[138]

In such ways, Japan was undertaking its own religious projections onto an India it saw as a reflection of its own Buddhist culture. In the decades after the Calcutta visit of the art critic Okakura in 1901, Japanese Buddhist scholars became increasingly aware of the artistic heritage of Buddhism, which prompted a series of missions aimed at making photographic and painted copies of the statues and frescoes found in various Indian cave temples. Between 1902 and 1904, a major expedition was led by the Buddhist abbot Otani Kozui (1876–1948), who would later follow European explorers like Sven 'Hedin to the Buddhist caves of Chinese Central Asia as part of a more substantial venture in claiming—and exporting—Chinese Buddhist artifacts as part of Japan's cultural heritage.[139] Fifteen years later, the Bengali artist Mukul Chandra Dey encountered the art historian Sawamura Sentaro (1884–1930) and the artist Kanpa Asai (1897–1985) at the Ajanta Caves in southern India, where they had been sent on a commission by the publishers of *Kokka* (*Flower of the Nation*), the pioneering art-historical journal that sought to promote Japanese art in place of the vogue for Western aesthetics. Yet even this Buddhist-mediated encounter required the linguistic mediation of Europe, as Dey described how their only common language was English.[140]

As in the Bay of Bengal, Christian, Muslim, and Buddhist missionaries were followed to Japan by the other main evangelical players of the period: the Baha'is. Between 1916 and 1921, the Iranian Baha'i leader 'Abd al-Baha (1844–1921) wrote nineteen revelatory *Tablets* addressed to the Japanese people from his Palestinian exile at the other end of Asia, just as the militaristic interest in Japan was waning in Iran itself. In the *Tablets* he promoted his new religion of world peace as a replacement for Japan's ancestral Shinto and Buddhism.[141] Yet neither he nor any of his followers could either preach or write in Japanese. As a result, when the American Baha'i missionaries Agnes Alexander (1875–1971) and George Augur (1853–1927) sailed on his behalf to Yokohama, they resorted to the artificial language of Esperanto, which some of the Japanese intelligentsia were already learning as a means of communicating with the wider world.[142] After the first Baha'i meeting was held in Tokyo in 1914, the earliest Japanese conversions were all made through the proselytizing medium of Esperanto.[143] Such were the linguistic constraints of inter-Asian interaction that the spread to Japan of the Baha'i Arabic and Persian scriptures was achieved through an artificial language invented in Poland.

Japan's Many Indian Interpreters

Language was an obstacle that the promoters of Baha'ism shared with the Indians who took an interest in Japan from the nineteenth century onward. Like the first Persian printed works in Iran and Afghanistan, the earliest Indian-language books on Japan were derived from European accounts. Among them were the by-now familiar geography textbooks, which presented Japan alongside India as part of A'ishya and provided short outlines of its physical, human and—more problematically—cultural geography.[144] With the opening of Japan's treaty ports, from around 1860 the informational situation improved, in European as well as Indian languages. And once again Calcutta led the way in printing entire books on Japan, considerably earlier than either Iran or Afghanistan. As before, Christian missionaries acted as the crucial cultural intermediaries, in this case through their support of the Banga Bhashanubad Sabha (Calcutta Vernacular Literature Society), founded in 1851 in Calcutta.

Among the many English works whose translation the society oversaw was a pioneering Bengali book of 230 pages bearing the simple title *Jepan*, a name that itself signaled its Anglophone origins.[145] Published in 1863, *Jepan* was a translation of a celebratory American work bearing the far longer title *Narrative of the Expedition of an American Squadron to the Chinese Seas and Japan Performed in the Years 1852, 1853 and 1854, under the Command of Commodore M. C. Perry, United States Navy.*[146] The original author was Francis Lister Hawks (1798–1866), an American Episcopalian priest, who effectively acted as ghostwriter for the memoirs of Commodore Perry, who "opened" Japan with his gunboat diplomacy. Hawks's partially vicarious representations were translated by Bhudev Mukhopadhyay (1827–1894), a prominent educationalist and member of the Calcutta Vernacular Literature Society who served as the colonial government's director of public instruction in Bengal. If this foundational Indian printed account of Japan relied on similarly indirect sources to its subsequent Iranian counterparts, then it was far less outdated. As a result of Calcutta's closer connections to the Anglophone public sphere, Mukhopadhyay's translation appeared only seven years after the original version appeared in distant Washington, D.C. (An English summary appeared in the

Calcutta Review within two years of the original.)[147] Such were the initial informational stepping-stones for the modern Indian discovery of Japan.

Of similar provenance, the earliest Urdu printed book on Japan was an 1867 translation of Laurence Oliphant's report on the embassy of Lord Elgin, which appeared under the plain title of *Tarikh-i Chin u Japan* (*History of China and Japan*).[148] The purpose of Elgin's embassy of 1857 to 1859 had been to speed up the opening of China and then, in the wake of Perry's flotilla, Japan to foreign trade. It was a policy in which the Indian merchants of Bombay and Calcutta held a huge vested interest.[149] There is good reason, then, to suppose the translated *Tarikh-i Chin u Japan* owed its existence to this merchant interest in the Chinese and Japanese markets that, by the time the book was published nearly a decade after Elgin concluded his mission, were indeed opened to them by empire. Drawing on its already dated source, the short section of the Urdu text on Japan provided basic information on geography and dynastic history, along with ample evocative illustrations of the topknots and kimonos of Tokugawa officials who served a government that after the Meiji Restoration of 1868 no longer existed. Even so, it made rare use of the visual possibilities of lithography as a medium for inter-Asian understanding.

Like the similarly translated Persian *Mirat al-Zaman*, which was published in Bombay, these Bengali and Urdu translations were early outliers. It would be several decades before other books on Japan appeared in Indian languages. In the meantime, a year before the Iranian merchant Sahhafbashi visited Yokohama, an Urdu direct account of the country appeared in a chapter of the 1896 *Ma'sir-i Hamidi* (*Praiseworthy Passage*), which recounted the maritime grand tour taken by Nawab Hamid 'Ali Khan, the Muslim ruler of Rampur. In poetic purple prose, it celebrated what was effectively a princely pleasure trip to old temple and spa towns like Kyoto and Nikko. The nawab was aided by an English-speaking tour guide called Ito Sokusada, whose explanations of history and customs were noted down by the nawab's secretary for the book.[150] Far from sharing a common Asian language, the Indian nawab and his Muslim secretary communicated with their Japanese guide in English, though this did allow directly acquired information about Japan to find its way into Urdu. The result was still far from a substantial investigation, since the final book effectively comprised a touristic view of streets and shops, train stations and hotels, Samurai forts and celebrated temples. Even so, there were important pointers toward new intercultural knowledge, such as the recognition of two religions in Japan, including an unfamiliar one called Shinto, which made no use of idols.[151]

A more substantial work appeared in 1901, possibly as a result of the First Sino-Japanese War of 1894–1895, which marked the emergence of Japan as a new Asian power. The author was Ahmad Din, the headmaster of a school in the Punjabi city of Gujranwala, who compiled English sources into Urdu under the title *A'yina-i Japan* (*Mirror of Japan*).[152] Like his Iranian counterparts a couple of years later, he focused on Japan's "progress" (*taraqqi*), particularly in terms of military development. Two years later, the busy publishing houses of Lahore, where the *A'yina* was printed, also issued a history book. Bearing the simple title *Japan*—an English-derived name echoed in Bengali and Middle Eastern books alike—it was part of a "comprehensive series of world histories" intended for Punjab's flourishing Urdu schools.[153] Far more detailed than its few predecessors, its coverage ranged from geography, history, and "civilizational conditions" (*tamaduni halat*) to entire chapters on journalism, language, and literature.[154] But in a visual signal of its origins, the chapter on language illustrated Japanese writing through a copied image of a translated Christian prayer; the source book was one of the many Christian missionary studies of Japan.[155]

By 1905, however, the widening Indian bookshelf on Japan also included more practical language guides drawing on Calcutta and Bombay's links with Yokohama and Kobe. This was an important development, enabling more direct forms of communication. These pioneering guides to learning Japanese included Dinshaw Vaniya's *Japanis Sikshaka* (*Japanese Teacher*) and Ratanji Framji Sethna's *Japani Bhashano Bhomiyo* (*Japanese Language Guide*).[156] Published in Bombay in 1905 and 1906, respectively, both were based on Gujarati—a choice that reflected the dominant role of Gujarati Parsi, Muslim, and Hindu merchants in the India-Japan trade. A Bombay-based Parsi himself, Vaniya was a reporter for the moderate nationalist *Advocate of India* newspaper, and Sethna was the widely published author of *Jñanachakra* (*Circle of Wisdom*), the first Gujarati encyclopedia that compiled a vast miscellany of data from popular Victorian encyclopedias.

Both Vaniya's and Sethna's language guides contained alphabetical tables, transliterating the Japanese *hiragana* and *katakana* phonetic alphabets into Gujarati letters. Their main vocabulary and phrase sections, however, were based entirely on Japanese words transliterated into Gujarati, which in practice rendered them far less useful for learning to read or write Japanese, a task that in any case also required large numbers of *kanji* (Chinese-derived characters). But such learned tasks were not their primary purpose, for while both Vaniya and Sethna were sympathetic to the idea of modernizing Japan as a role model for India, the vocabularies they selected were intended primarily for fellow Gujarati traders. Vaniya included a lengthy section of commercial vocabulary, providing the Japanese terms for "commission," "buying on speculation," and "conditions of sale," as well as the various goods (cotton not least) that Hindu and Parsi merchants were exporting from Bombay to the factories and mills adjoining Kobe and Yokohama. This was good for intercultural commerce, but such trade lexicons offered little potential for understanding Japan's cultural traditions, particularly when no dictionaries or grammars emerged to supplement them.

Reflecting what we have seen across the Middle East, from 1904 the Russo-Japanese War inspired many more books in Urdu, Bengali, Gujarati, and other Indian languages, in genres that similarly ranged from sober reportage to epic verse. The earliest were plainly informational works drawn in large part on English newspapers, such as Muhammad Husayn Fazl's *Mukammil Mukhabarat-i Rus u Japan* (*Comprehensive Reports on Russia and Japan*) and Muhammad Ibrahim's *Jang-i Rus u Japan* (*The War of Russia and Japan*), which in a sign of the greater access to news in India were published while the fighting was still ongoing.[157] As news of the war—and of Japanese success—spread farther, literary works were composed that gave voice to a nascent Indian Japanophilia in synchrony with its Middle Eastern counterparts. Among them was an Urdu drama written within two months of the war's final volleys under the simple title *Jang-i Rus u Japan* (*The War of Russia and Japan*).[158]

The author of the play was Mawlwi Zafar 'Ali Khan (1873–1956), the editor of the *Dakan Rivyu* (*Deccan Review*), who would subsequently edit the influential anticolonial newspaper *Zamindar* (*Landlord*). A few years earlier, he published *Sayr-i Zulmat* (*Journey into Darkness*), a retitled translation of H. Rider Haggard's dubious African fantasy, *The People of the Mist*, and Khan's play made curious allusions to links between Japan and Africa.[159] The play's preface, penned by the celebrated literary scholar 'Abd al-Haqq (1870–1961), compared Japan's war with Russia with the wider history of European colonialism by making references to the German claim to Zanzibar and the Italian invasion of Ethiopia.[160] As for the play itself, its dramatis personae included not only the major Russian and Japanese generals and statesmen, but also several Muslim characters, created through Khan's attempt to tie the war to the Pan-Islamic causes he promoted throughout his career. In a key scene set in a Tokyo bazaar, a character called Muzaffar Khan reveals to his companion Iqbal Khan his plan to "propagate the religion of Muhammad" throughout Japan.[161] Echoing wider calls to convert Japan, Iqbal agrees, declaring that to spread

An Afghan imagines the Sea of Japan: Russia's defeat as lithographic drama. Muhammad Yusuf Riyazi, *'Ayn al-Waqayi'* (Mashhad: Daftar-i Bahr-i Naskha-yi Biguftagu, 1906). Courtesy of Afghanistan Digital Library, New York University.

Islam is every Muslim's highest duty. But then, in recognition of the barriers to inter-Asian communication, Iqbal bewails the fact that neither of them can speak Japanese sufficiently well to explain the spiritual beauties of their faith.[162] A decade later, the playwright tried to make life imitate art by sending a real-life Iqbal—the great philosopher-poet Muhammad Iqbal—on a mission to convert the Japanese; in 1914 he proposed the plan at the annual meeting of the Anjuman-i Himayat-i Islam (Society for the Support of Islam) in Lahore.[163]

A somewhat different expression of Urdu literary Japanophilia was Sharaf al-Din Ahmad Khan's *Saintalis Wafadar-i Japan* (*Forty-seven Loyal Japanese*), which recounted the famous tale of the forty-seven *ronin*.[164] Like the war reports, this was a translation from one of the several English versions by then available of the celebrated legend by Shunsho Tamenaga (1823–1886).[165] Since such Japanese terms as *ronin, shogun,* and *samurai* were wholly unfamiliar to Indian readers, Sharaf al-Din chose to render them in their approximate Indian equivalents, echoing the presentation of modern Japanese soldiers in the poetic guise of medieval Persian warriors in the Iranian *Mikadunama*. The result was a curious martial collage of Tokugawa Japan and Mughal India.

More military-themed works soon followed. In 1905 the Punjabi author Babu Khadim Husayn published an Urdu *Mikadunama* (*Book of the Mikado*) to celebrate the Japanese victory (it preceded its Persian counterpart by two years).[166] Here too, the country was of interest less for its cultural traditions than for its effective embrace of modernity. And so Husayn opened his panegyric with plentiful emphasis on Japan as a land of progress (*taraqqi*), a term that Indian Muslims shared with Ottoman modernizers who had translated it from the French.[167] (Developing the same theme, the Sikh author Kesar Singh Multani published a book in Punjabi entitled *Japan di Tarakki* [*Japan's Progress*], which, as itself a translation from Hindi, points to the further spread of such Japanophilic ideas.)[168] Unlike the subsequent Persian *Mikadunama*, however, Husayn's Urdu poem focused solely on the war, following each of its stages from the first exchange of gunfire in February 1904 to the destruction of Russia's Baltic Fleet in May the following year. Responding to the tale of the forty-seven *ronin* popularized by Sharaf al-Din's translation the previous year, Husayn divided his paean to Japanese heroism into forty-seven formal sections.[169] In a final flourish, to incorporate this newfound land into the older conventions of Urdu poetry, he closed his *Mikadunama* with a traditional *qita'-i tarikh*. This was an artful chronogrammatic couplet that encoded the date of the Japanese victory into the numerological value of the verse's Arabic letters.[170]

Hindu writers also took up these bellicose themes. In 1904 the Bengali political activist and educationist Sarala Devi Ghoshal (1872–1945) tried to establish a jujitsu training school in Calcutta.[171] Three years later, a Hindi book about the war was published by a former colonial soldier, Mahendulal Garg (1870–1942).[172] Echoing the informational role of Calcutta for Iranian accounts of the conflict, in 1907 a Bengali history of the defeat of Russia also appeared from the port's printers.[173] Like the Persian *Mikadunama*, it began with an overview of Japan's rapid rise to power. Another contributor to this martial Japanophilia was the Bengali Hindu nationalist Benoy Kumar Sarkar (1887–1949).[174] Rather than drawing implicit comparisons to the Indo-Muslim warriors of the Mughal Empire, as Sharaf al-Din had done in recounting the deeds of the forty-seven *ronin*, Sarkar made the extraordinary claim that Japan was indebted to the ancient Hindu traditions of the Sanskritic *kshatriya* (warrior caste). "Take militarism," he explained; "Hindustan [India] started the cult of Kshatriyaism, which in Japan is called *Bushido*."[175] As part of his sweeping historical vision that Japan (and China) owed its civilization to the Asian-wide impact of a "Greater India," Sarkar then went a step further, explaining that

Japan even owed its recent success against Russia to this Indian—or, rather, Hindu—influence: "Hindu thought is even now governing the Bushido morality of the Japanese soldiers," he declared.[176] This was not so much a recognition of Japan's military achievements, still less an understanding of Bushido's ties to Zen Buddhism. Instead, it was a projection onto Japan of a mythologized Hindu self.

Such ideas were by no means Sarkar's personal idiosyncrasy. When in 1907 Indian, Chinese, and Japanese students established the Asian Solidarity Society in Tokyo, its constitution celebrated the peaceful coexistence of Asia's Hindu, Buddhist, Confucianist, Daoist, and Zoroastrian faiths, but it made no mention of the continent's most widespread religion: Islam. Far from an oversight, this was part of the Hindu nationalist vision of its Indian members. Consequently, the constitution's preface blamed India's initial decline on the Muslim-ruled Mughal Empire, which it claimed crushed India's indigenous culture.[177]

As the counterpart to Muslim missionary endeavors, such Hindu projections continued over the following decades. By the 1930s, V. D. Savarkar (1883–1966), the most influential theorist of Hindu nationalism, was expanding Sarkar's ideas of Hindu-based solidarity with Japan. In a letter exchange between the Bengali anticolonial activist Rash Behari Bose, in Tokyo, and Savarkar, Bose declared to Savarkar—in a denial of more than two millennia of Buddhist assertions to the contrary—that "the Buddhists are also Hindus."[178] Bose then added that "every attempt should be made to create a Hindu bloc extending from the Indian Ocean up to the Pacific Ocean."[179] Savarkar and Bose even made plans to build a "Pan-Hindu" temple in Japan.[180] While this was certainly a declaration of Asian unity, it was an assertive projection of the Hindu self framed in boldly Indocentric terms. Yet against a background of decades of Christian, Muslim, and Baha'i outreach to Japan, as well as movements promoting inter-Buddhist solidarity, Sarkar's and Savarkar's approaches made paradoxical strategic sense. For rather than set about the colossal proselytizing task of actually converting Japan's population to Hinduism, it was far easier to simply claim that Buddhism was a Hindu sect. And so, through another form of self-discovery, Japan became a mirror of India.

The Campus as a Cultural Crossroads

By the 1920s, more accounts of Japan based on direct observations began to appear in other languages, such as the 1920 Punjabi book by Bhai Mohan

Singh Vaid (1881–1936). A social reformer and prolific author of popular works on hygiene and domestic technologies, Vaid described the activities of the Indian students who were by then enrolling in universities in both Japan and America.[181] In the wake of the war, the number of Indian students in Japan had risen from around fifty in 1906 to over one hundred in 1910, though in a presage of Japanese imperial attitudes many complained to the British authorities that they were treated "with contempt" by the citizens of Tokyo.[182] By the time of the Great Kanto Earthquake of 1923, which destroyed much of Yokohama, the port also housed a substantial Indian business community; in the fires that followed the quake, the properties of 170 Indian merchants were destroyed.[183] Such was the effect of the news that in faraway Lahore, an obscure author called Babu Hamdam published a long Punjabi poem about the tragedy.[184]

By this time, there were also a few Indian people teaching in Japan, such as Haraprasad Sastri (1882–1956), a Sanskrit scholar educated at the elite colonial Allahabad University. From 1916 to 1918, he lectured at Tokyo's Waseda University as part of the new Japanese interest in the early Indian history of their own Buddhist faith. Like the university students described by Vaid, Shastri learned to speak Japanese, becoming part of a new Indian cohort whose understanding of Japan was more linguistically informed.[185] But for the most part, this cohort did not write books, the result being that their subtler understanding of Japanese culture didn't enter the public sphere of print. Sastri's own memoir of Japan is a case in point, having been written in English and published posthumously, in the 1960s.[186]

This informational asymmetry between those who best understood Japan and those who published books about the country is seen most vividly in the case of the celebrated Bengali poet Tagore, who made five journeys to Japan (including two shorter transit visits). His travels show how Indian access to Japan emerged from Bengal's older imperial networks: the family fortune that funded his activities originated in the shipping company founded by his grandfather Dwarkanath Tagore (1794–1846), a prominent partner in empire who in 1839 helped build the crucial infrastructural corridor between Calcutta, Aden, and London.[187] Having studied in Brighton and London, his grandson first learned about Japanese poetry through translations in English, which also served as the linguistic basis for his exchanges with the circle of Okakura, whom he briefly met in Calcutta in 1902. But it was not until 1916 that Tagore made his first visit to Japan. His arrival in Yokohama three years after receiving the Nobel Prize for Literature was celebrated in major newspapers such as the *Asahi Shimbun* (*Morning Sun News*)—some 20,000 admirers awaited him at the Tokyo station, and large audiences attended his lectures (delivered in English).[188] But after he devoted several speeches to warning against the allure of nationalism and imperialism, his audiences dwindled. When he passed through Japan again the following year on his way home from lecturing in America, only two people waited to greet him at the dock.[189]

Having relied on English for his lectures in Tokyo, he used Asia's nascent European lingua franca to converse with the artist Yokoyama Taikan (1868–1958) in Calcutta and correspond with the Anglophone (and partly American-educated) literary critic Noguchi Yonejiro (1875–1947) in Tokyo.[190] He also wrote an elegiac and sensitive travelogue, *Japan-yatri* (*Journey to Japan*), as well as a series of haiku in Bengali, modeled on translations he read in English.[191] But in the absence of Japanese readers (or dictionaries) of Bengali, to translate his poetry into Japanese, enthusiasts such as Mashino Saburo (1889–1916) and Kora Tomi (1896–1993) had to rely on the English prose version of *Gitanjali* that Tagore had produced with the encouragement of W. B. Yeats, or else on the extempore English renditions he made during his five visits to Japan between 1916 and 1934.[192] But the more Tagore learned about Japan, and the more his audiences there learned of his criticism of Japanese plans to unite the Asian continent, the further apart these erstwhile friends drifted. By the time Japan's imperial Kwantung Army invaded Manchuria in September 1931, Tagore's Japanophilia had long faded.

In the meantime, other South Asian intellectuals had undertaken their own firsthand investigations, including the figure who wrote in greatest detail about Japan in the 1920s: Syed Ross Masood (1889–1937). Raised on the very top rung of India's colonial educational elite, the Oxford-educated Masood was the grandson of Sir Sayyid Ahmad Khan (1817–1898), the founder of the Mohammedan Anglo-Oriental College at Aligarh, who in 1869 sailed via the newly opened Suez Canal to escort his son—Masood's father—to study in Oxford, where Masood later followed in his footsteps. By 1922 Masood was director of public instruction in the princely state of Hyderabad, from where he was sent in his official capacity to Japan on a fact-finding journey about educational development.[193] As part of an Indian—or rather, Hyderabadi—venture in intellectual self-empowerment, the mission was meant to support curricular planning for Hyderabad's new Osmania University. Osmania was the first Indian university to teach entirely in Urdu.[194] Masood's institutional ties reflected the rising importance to inter-Asian exchange of such new universities.

With this educational agenda in mind, Masood hoped to learn how Japan had developed a system of modern scientific education in its own language rather than English. He was not the first Indian to take an interest in this question. Aided by the informational bridgehead of Calcutta, Bengali intellectuals were a generation ahead—at least in raising the question, if not necessarily in answering it as Masood now intended. More than thirty years earlier, Bhudev Mukhopadhyay, who served the colonial government as director of public instruction in Bengal, noticed that Japan was promoting a "Western" system of scientific education through its own language.[195] But having never been to Japan, Mukhopadhyay had apparently learned about this through his access to English reports, which in 1904 also fed into an article on Japanese "national education" in the *Calcutta Review*.[196] Writing in the wake of Japan's victory over Russia, the Bengali Asianist Benoy Kumar Sarkar had also highlighted the educational basis of Japan's ascent to power.[197] Amid the growing debate among Indian nationalists over vernacular education, Sarkar used Japan as a model for how India's languages might be similarly used to spread scientific learning more widely than such English-speaking institutions as the University of Calcutta, from which he had recently graduated. As he explained, "No philologist has yet ventured to assert the capabilities of the Japanese language as an instrument of modern expression are richer than those of . . . Dravidian or . . . Aryan languages of India."[198]

While there is no evidence that Masood ever read Sarkar's essay, reports about the quality of Japan's educational system reached other learned Indian circles. In response, Masood was dispatched by the government of the Nizam of Hyderabad on a fact-finding philological mission. The problem was that not only did he not speak—or read—Japanese; there was also no Urdu-Japanese dictionary to aid his investigations or, for that matter, any dictionary linking Japanese and another modern Indian language. The absence of such lexicographical tools now had higher stakes than the translation of poetry. It affected the possibility of educational exchange.

To understand how Masood navigated the various obstacles to his objectives, we can turn to the several writings that resulted from his mission, including the official report he wrote for the Nizam's government, which was published in English in 1923 as *Japan and Its Educational System,* then in Urdu two years later as *Japan aur uska Ta'limi Nazm u Nasq* (*Japan and Its Educational Order and Organization*).[199] He also wrote several shorter accounts, such as his 1926 *Ruh-i Japan* (*Spirit of Japan*), as well as a private diary, in which he recorded the social encounters that underlay his data collecting.[200]

Masood wrote in his diary that he was traveling "partly as a critic and partly as a student" in order to learn the "secret of Japan's wonderful progress."[201] It was the opposite task from that of his Japanese contemporaries who were sailing by steamship to India in search of the ancient sites of their Buddhist past, about which they wrote travelogues of their own voyages of self-discovery.[202] A year after Masood left Bombay aboard the *Wakasa Maru*, the Nippon Yusen Kaisha steamship line launched pilgrim package tours taking Japanese Buddhists to India.[203]

By contrast, Masood's self-empowering mission was to discover how Japan had successfully institutionalized modern technical education in its own language. But this presented several informational challenges, for his task required him not only to form social relations with Japanese professionals, but also to research their history and culture to identify the preconditions and subsequent stages of Japan's modernization. Fortunately, aboard ship Masood made friends with a fellow Indian passenger called Advani, who was to prove of practical help. As a merchant resident of Yokohama, Advani was sufficiently well known that when he and Masood reached Yokohama by train after disembarking at Kobe, a crowd of Indians was awaiting them.[204] From this point onward, for the practical aspects of his journey Masood was able to rely on this commercial network of Indian—in his case, mainly Muslim—émigrés. On landing at Kobe, he had immediately gone to the local branch of Messrs. Poohoomull Brothers, who had offices all across Asia. Not only did members of the Sindhi company's staff provide him with a room to stay in, but they also put at his disposal the services of their local Japanese translator.[205]

The same pattern unfolded in each of the cities Masood visited. In Yokohama he was helped by Bhagat, a Punjabi graduate of Waseda University who had settled down in Japan as an exporter of electrical goods to India.[206] Bhagat introduced Masood to other members of his merchant circle, so when Masood's hotel proved too expensive, Bhagat introduced him to another trader, Mirza 'Ali Raza from Bangalore, who found him an affordable house to rent.[207] But when it came to gathering information on Japan's intellectual and cultural life, Masood found his merchant hosts of limited help. After all, as an exporter of leather goods, Raza was hardly in a position to introduce him to Japanese professors and scientists. Instead, Raza introduced him to other Indian businessmen from Calcutta and Rangoon.[208] If this was not so much inter-Asian as intra-Indian interaction, a few of these traders, such as 'Abd al-Qadir of Madras and Jayyakar of Bombay, had at least lived in Japan for decades and taken Japanese wives and thence citizenship.[209] But while Masood noted that 'Abd al-Qadir "speaks Japanese like a Japanese," he was frustrated to find that even his network comprised only fellow businessmen from Yokohoma and Kobe, and no links to the university circles of Tokyo.[210] When Masood finally reached the capital, he was led to its Indian Club and introduced to a group of Indian commercial agents playing billiards. As he recorded in his diary, of the eighty Indians resident in Tokyo, all but two were Hindu silk exporters from Sindh.[211]

Fortunately, Masood carried a letter of introduction from Sir Mokshagun-dam Visvesvaraya (1860–1962), an engineer who served as a consultant to the Nizam's government in Hyderabad. Having himself inspected Japan's educational and industrial progress a few years beforehand, and written a report in English, Visvesvaraya had met Masood in Bombay on the eve of his departure to present him with a letter for a crucial contact: his former translator, Makino Toraji, who worked in Tokyo for the Bureau of Social Work.[212] It was Makino who finally introduced Masood to the minister of education and to a professor at the Imperial University.

At first Masood was delighted to discover that the professor in question, Takakusu Junjiro (1866–1945), was like himself a graduate of Oxford, where he too had acquired impeccable English.[213] This reflected Tagore's means of communication with his Japanese tour companion-cum-secretary, Kora Tomi, who had acquired excellent English at Columbia University.[214] But what Takakusu had mainly studied at Oxford with the German linguist Friedrich Max Müller was Sanskrit. Rather than an expert on science, he was Japan's leading scholar of Indian Buddhism. By the time he met Masood, Takakusu had become quite accustomed to hosting visiting Indians, having welcomed the Punjabi religious teacher Swami Rama Tirtha (1873–1906) in 1902.[215] Three years after his conversations with Masood, Takakusu wrote a five-part article, "What Japan Owes to India," for the Japanese Asianist journal *Young East*, which, for want of a shared Asian language, had to be issued in English.[216] Devoted to ancient spiritual teachings that had spread from Buddhist India to Japan, the subject of the article was hardly the technological ties Masood sought to establish. As Japanese and Indian intellectuals came in direct communicational contact, they looked to each other's lands for quite opposite purposes: the Japanese to recover their own religious past, and the Indians to find their own scientific future.

Nonetheless, during their meetings Takakusu was able to explain the basic methods of scientific education in Japan, such as the fact that, while Japanese words were used for most scientific concepts, English (i.e., Arabic) numerals were used for chemical formulae and mathematics.[217] By this time Bhagat, the graduate of Waseda University, had also presented Masood with letters of introduction to several other professors, whom Masood was increasingly eager to meet.[218] Through such connections, he began to find his way into more colleges and universities. He was given further introductions to a Japanese educational official called Ino, and to Ernest Speight, a British expatriate who, like Takakusu, lectured at the Imperial University, albeit teaching English rather than Sanskrit—or science.[219]

Masood now prepared written questionnaires in English that, after his newfound contacts translated them, he used to gather information on teaching methods at different colleges.[220] Gradually, he came to realize that the crucial intellectual step in Japan's progress (*taraqqi*)—that Turkish-transmitted French concept again—had been the creation of a new technical lexicon of scientific terms in Japanese. Without this, it would have been impossible to translate European scientific textbooks, to educate students with words and concepts that were familiar to them, and in turn to foster a cadre of scientifically educated citizens who could mold this domesticated science for their country's collective advancement.[221]

Through the intervention of the British ambassador, Sir Charles Eliot, a scholar of Buddhism and classical Chinese literature, Masood made headway in deciphering these linguistic puzzles by introducing him to another embassy employee, Harold Parlett, whose English-Japanese dictionary had already been through numerous editions.[222] Yet even here there remained obstacles to the transfer across Asia of what was in theory the universal knowledge of science. Though Masood noted in his diary that the meeting with Parlett was "most instructive . . . his knowledge of the Japanese language is very profound," unfortunately because Parlett was "not a science man, he could not answer my questions in detail."[223] Here the long-standing reliance on vicarious information about Japan revealed its consequences by way of the limitations it set on the ability of Indian investigators to pursue their own intellectual agendas.

Fortunately, Parlett did at least explain the crucial role that Chinese ideographs played in written Japanese; and this in turn gave Masood an idea for his own goal of translating scientific works into Urdu.[224] To better understand these linguistic developments, Masood hired a female Anglophone assistant called Ohgimi, who hailed from a respectable old Samurai family. With Parlett's and Ohgimi's assistance, Masood realized how Japan's modern scientific vocabulary had been coined by using classical Chinese root words. Consequently, the new lexicon of science resembled existing Chinese loanwords that were easier to remember and understand, as well as less alien, than

حروفات

ژاپونلرك من القديم استعمال ايتدكلرى حروفات (هيروغليف) چين حروفاتيدر .
بلكه حروفات دكلده هربرى برهجايه دلالت ايدراشكالدر . حروف تهجيدن هربرى ايچون
درت شكل وار :

قاتا قانه   هيرا غانه   ياماتو غانا   حونجى

A Siberian Tatar's language lesson: Japanese scripts in a Turkish travelogue. 'Abd al-Rashid Ibrahim, 'Alem-i Islam ve Japonya'da Intişar-ı Islamiyet, 2 vols. (Istanbul: Ahmed Saki Bey Matbaasi, 1910–1911). Photograph by Nile Green.

European loanwords. Using this model, he theorized that new Urdu scientific terms could be coined to similar effect on the basis of Arabic roots.[225] Over the following weeks, Ohgimi helped him compile a short dictionary of the Japanese counterparts for various English technical terms. The plan was that the ensuing English-Japanese technical dictionary would serve as the medium for a Japanese-Urdu counterpart he hoped would prove a valuable asset to Hyderabad's recently founded Dar al-Tarjuma translation bureau.[226]

With this ambition in mind, upon his return to India, Masood wrote up his report, *Japan and Its Educational System*, which was translated into Urdu by Muhammad 'Inayatullah, director of the translation bureau and son of the distinguished educational modernizer and mathematician Mawlwi Zaka'ullah (1832–1910).[227] Each version ran to almost four hundred pages, beginning with ten chapters tracing the history of Japan from antiquity to the arrival of Commodore Perry's gunships to its reemergence as a world power. The topics covered included a thorough account of the earliest contact with the Portuguese and the policies the shogun Hideyoshi developed in reaction, along with the controlled but limited ways in which Tokugawa Japan acquired "Western sciences" (*maghribi 'ulum*) through the so-called Dutch curriculum.[228] Masood also treated such key developments as the arrival of Commodore Perry's flotilla (the subject of that first Bengali printed book on Japan) and the subsequent political changes that culminated in the Meiji Restoration.[229] It was only after around 250 pages of historical background that he turned to his book's titular topic by analyzing Japan's educational system. Describing the early history of modern schooling, the opening of the first girls' college, the foundation of the first university, teacher training, and the advance of industrial schools, his coverage was quite thorough and drew more directly on his meetings with Japanese professors.[230] Over the course of these many chapters, although he devoted only nine of four hundred pages to religious traditions, Masood's search for scientific self-empowerment led to a deeper understanding of Japan's historical path to progress.

As for his Japanese-Urdu dictionary of technical terms, it was apparently never published.[231] Consequently, the university textbooks translated by Hyderabad's Translation Bureau were overwhelmingly English.[232] Undeterred, on a visit to Kabul to inaugurate its own university in 1933, Masood described the lessons of Japan to the Afghan prime minister and other officials.[233] He remained an enthusiastic booster of at least the idea of learning from Japan's educational example. In an unconscious echo of the title of Okakura's book from thirty years earlier, it was his own "ideal of the East."

Japan's rapid reinvention from bullied Asian archipelago to industrialized imperial power fostered new Japanophilic interests that reached from Istanbul to Calcutta. In the Ottoman Empire, Iran, and then Afghanistan, the Russo-Japanese War became the prime mover behind the first printed books on Japan as a newfound amity with Japan was born from an older enmity with Russia. In India at least, such political concerns inspired other interests in turn, as questions of Japan's economic transformation led to inquiries into its history and educational system, though the realms of culture and religion remained far less well charted by comparison. Japan was not so much of intrinsic interest, but it had potential as a model insofar as it could provide lessons for Arab,

Iranian, or Indian as well as Vietnamese and Malay intellectuals on how to develop their own societies. The encounter with the Japanese other, then, was primarily driven by concerns for the self that ranged from missions to convert its inhabitants to attempts to learn its self-empowering secrets.

So it was that, during the three decades after the Russo-Japanese War, officials and educators from the Middle East and India undertook their separate and often vicarious explorations of Japan. In differing degrees, they all drew on the imperial infrastructures connecting the ports of Japan to the rest of Asia and the better-developed studies of Japan in European languages that stretched back to the Jesuit inquiries of the seventeenth century. And so the most detailed books on Japan in Indian and Middle Eastern languages drew in large part on the mediation of European sources. There were reasons for this informational asymmetry: intercultural knowledge is a cumulative and collective enterprise, requiring tools like dictionaries and translations, and preferably institutions such as libraries and universities, where the findings of various researchers can be collected and transmitted to other investigators in turn. Despite the Japanophilia that swept across South and West Asia after the defeat of imperial Russia, whether in colonized or noncolonized regions, there were few attempts to institutionalize such investigations—to turn Japanophilia into Japanology. Consequently, publicly available knowledge about Japan drew on ad hoc, individual, and vicarious investigations.

Masood's state-funded mission was an exception, but this too was not sustained after his return, not least because of the deep ties that Hyderabadi officials had with the colonial Anglophone and Urdu educational system. "I dread to think what would have happened to Japan today," he wrote, "if they too like us had wasted their energies for a hundred years in trying to give to a foreign language the position which nature meant their mother tongue to have."[234] He was no doubt correct. But the fact remained that, whether through the Orientalist studies from which he compiled his history chapters, the dictionary supplied by Parlett, or the conversations he held with Japanese fellow Oxford graduates, Masood's intellectual engagement with Japan had been carried out wholly through the medium of the English language that was already emerging as Asia's main lingua franca.

By turning now to a remarkable two-volume Urdu study of Japan written by an Indian-language teacher in Tokyo, who was drawn into the shadowy circles of Japanese imperial intelligence, we will see how these dilemmas— and opportunities—of communication continued to shape Indo-Japanese interactions till the age of empire reached its cataclysmic conclusion with the outbreak of World War II.

4 • The Constraints of a Muslim Japanology

On November 19, 1930, an Indian called Muhammad Fazli embarked on the S.S. *Ranchi* to Japan. Seventy years after the forced opening of Japan to foreign trade, the two countries were by then close economic partners: the raw cotton supplied by Bombay's merchants proved indispensable to the Japanese mills that pushed their Manchester rivals out of Asian markets they had dominated for a century.[1] But unlike the merchants who pioneered the route he followed from Bombay to Yokohama, Fazli was traveling to take up a post as a teacher. A graduate of Aligarh Muslim University, his was to be a journey less between worlds than between schools. Japan was no longer the closed country of a century earlier, during the heady Meiji era of uncompromising reform, and its modernizers had scrupulously investigated the unknown societies of America and Europe. The school Fazli was heading to had been founded as part of this program: it was the Tokyo Gaikokugo Gakko, the School of Foreign Languages, designed to deepen understanding of the wider world. But as the Meiji spirit of Westernization gave way to nationalist and then imperialist calls for Japan to lead an Asian renaissance, the school also began teaching the languages of the Middle East and Asia. And so the young Muhammad Fazli was offered a post teaching Persian and Urdu.

Teaching two of the major languages of the Middle East and India, Fazli found himself at the intellectual apex of the West and South Asian interactions with Japan that had slowly begun seventy years earlier. In being positioned from his arrival in one of the universities that his compatriot—and fellow Aligarh alumnus—Masood struggled to enter, he had a rare opportunity to learn about the society, culture, and language of Japan. But even in a situation where language took the center stage, the exchange of knowledge was not necessarily equal in both directions. If informational asymmetry character-ized European and Indian knowledge of Asia, then it also characterized Japa-nese and Indian understanding of each other. As an independent state—and ascendant empire—Japan founded more formal, institutional mechanisms for studying the distant regions of Asia to which it was increasingly connected. The Tokyo School of Foreign Languages where Fazli taught was the most important of these new institutions, particularly for promoting knowledge of the Asian written languages that were the major obstacle to inter-Asian understanding.

Having surveyed the many Indian and Middle Eastern accounts of Japan published in the decades on either side of 1900, we will now look more closely at *Haqiqat-i Japan* (*The Truth about Japan*), in which Fazli described his re-markable experiences among professors and spies. The two lengthy volumes of his book comprised, first, a travelogue and, second, a survey, conveying ev-erything from history, literature, art, and religion to economic and political af-fairs. It was published in Delhi and Aurangabad in 1934, and again a few years later by the modernizing Barqi (Electric) Press; the initial print run totaled two thousand copies. This made Fazli not merely a significant contributor to pub-licly available knowledge about Japan; as the result of his fifteen-month resi-dence in Tokyo, his densely detailed *Haqiqat* also marked the informational high tide of the Indian, and Muslim, discovery of Japan before the outbreak of war with the British Empire.[2]

By placing Fazli's book in the contexts that shaped it, the following sections uncover the factors that both enabled and constrained what was perhaps the most thorough investigation of Japan that was published in the Middle East or India during the connecting Age of Empire.

Institutionalizing Inter-Asian Understanding

A graduate of India's elite Aligarh Muslim University, Fazli had earned the BA and BT degrees that qualified him for his position at the Tokyo language school that would employ him throughout his fifteen-month residence. At the time he arrived, much of the teaching was being conducted in wooden buildings erected after the Great Kanto Earthquake a decade earlier, build-ings that presented a stark contrast with the architecture of Aligarh, which had been carefully designed as an Islamic Oxford where Gothic quads were surmounted with tapering Mughal domes. Despite outward appearances, the Tokyo School of Foreign Languages was a remarkable educational enterprise whose intellectual—and imperial—goals diverged markedly from those of Fazli's alma mater. Whereas Aligarh had been founded to instill sufficient knowledge of the English language to allow Muslims to ascend through India's colonial administration, the Tokyo school was founded to deepen Japanese understanding of the Asian languages of not only the British but also the Russian, Dutch, and fading Qing empires, which still existed when the school was created.

If the Tokyo language school was designed to enable inter-Asian understanding, it was therefore on a no less imperial basis. Formally established in 1897, it was part of the new relationship with Asia marked by the founding of Japan's own colonial empire two years earlier. As Fazli himself explained, the school was a state institution that taught languages ranging from English, Dutch, Russian, and Portuguese to Chinese, Mongolian, Malay, Tamil, Persian, and Urdu.[3] Averaging twenty hours per week of instruction, each course was designed to provide practical proficiency in both reading and speaking.[4] Urdu had entered the syllabus in 1908 as part of the Intensive Course in Oriental Languages, which enrolled a dozen students that year. From that point onward, the school employed a series of Indian-language teachers, initially by hiring someone associated with the Indian trading community in nearby Yokohama.

When that initial arrangement proved unsuitable, a year later the school employed a better-educated replacement by the name of Muhammad Barakatullah—the same anticolonial activist who spent his evenings after work editing his English journal *Islamic Fraternity*.[5] But after renewing his contract in 1911, the school eventually expelled Barakatullah under political pressure from the British embassy. After all, under the terms of the Anglo-Japanese Treaty of Alliance, which were renewed in 1911, the two empires were formal allies, whatever anti-British activists like Barakatullah thought.

Over the following twenty years leading up to Fazli's arrival, the school hired a series of other Indian-language teachers. All of them were on two-year contracts: after the Barakatullah debacle, the school's administrators became more cautious in their vetting procedures. Rather than risk hiring another roaming revolutionary, they employed Indians with established professional ties to India's educational system. So Barakatullah was replaced by Davarilal Singh, a graduate of the prestigious University of Allahabad who had worked as a school inspector for the Allahabad municipality.[6] He was succeeded in turn by Hariharnath Tural Atal, who, like Fazli, was educated at Aligarh; he worked as a sub-deputy school inspector.

In the meantime, the school also appointed its first Japanese teachers of Urdu, who were graduates of the program. The most accomplished was Gamo Rei'ichi (1901–1977), who became Fazli's principal local interlocutor (and boss). The appointment of such local teachers was an important milestone in Japanese linguistic capacity building. And the institutionalization of language learning was taken further in 1921, when the Tokyo school was supplemented by the founding of the Osaka School of Foreign Affairs, where Urdu was also taught, albeit entirely by Japanese graduates of the Tokyo school.[7]

Such linguistic capacity took time to develop, particularly to the point that it produced translations of culturally significant texts rather than the conversational skills needed for more ad hoc communication. A case in point is Japanese knowledge of Iran, and the Persian language, which Fazli was also employed to teach. As late as the early 1900s, Persian still lingered on as a learned lingua franca across much of the Middle East, Central Asia, and India. But despite the arrival in Tehran in the 1880s and 1890s of a handful of Japanese diplomats and military officers, beyond travelogues these short-lived connections produced little by way of linguistic expertise, at least not of a sufficient level to translate Persian texts.

Understanding of linguistically embedded cultural and religious traditions developed more slowly—and vicariously, as seen with the first Japanese translations of Persian poetry by way of the *Ruba'iyat* of Omar Khayyam made by the Greek-Irish middleman Lafcadio Hearn (1850–1904). A keen Japanophile who during his years as a lecturer in English literature at Tokyo's Imperial University also became known as Koizumi Yakumo, in September 1896 Hearn delivered a public lecture on Khayyam. Among those in attendance was Kambara Ariake (1876–1952), an aspiring poet (and later a major novelist) who went on to publish his translations of Khayyam's *Ruba'iyat* twelve years later.[8] These, the first Japanese renditions of Persian poetry, were based on the famous Victorian version of Khayyam by Edward Fitzgerald. Then, in 1916, Kambara's lead was followed by Tsuchiya Bunmei (1891–1990), whose *Perushia shinwa* (*Legends of Persia*) offered Japanese readers their first glimpse of the medieval epic *Shahnama*, albeit a view likewise refracted through an abridged English version.

It was only in the early 1920s that the efforts to institutionalize Asian-language teaching in Japan made significant interpretive inroads through Iran with *Perusha bungaku shiko* (*A Study of Persian Literature*), a milestone 1922 survey by Araki Shigeru (1884–1932) of the Tokyo Imperial University.[9] Eight years later, an article appeared in an Iranian journal that made note of Araki Shigeru's book on Persian literature (which was also probably read by Fazli's students of Persian in Tokyo).[10] Accomplished linguist that he was, Araki—who had completed his studies at Columbia University under Abraham Williams Jackson (1862–1937), America's leading specialist on ancient Iran—nonetheless drew into his book a large amount of the European scholarship on Persian that had developed over the previous century or more. Twenty years earlier, Jackson had shipped to Columbia a collection of rare Persian manuscripts presented to him by the Parsis of Bombay, grateful for his promotion of their own cultural heritage. Through such circuitous routes, Japan's universities developed their own expertise on the unfamiliar regions of the continent they had learned to call "Ajia."[11] By comparison, the more direct method of bringing Indian teachers to Tokyo, paid at 250 yen per month, was far more efficient, not to say cost-effective, than sending every aspiring student to New York.[12] So it was that by the time Fazli arrived in Tokyo in 1930, he was expected to teach twenty-five students enrolled in both his Persian and Urdu classes.[13]

The timing of this rising interest in "Islamic" languages was no coincidence. Having long taken an interest in the Ottoman Empire, then in the Muslims of mainland China (Manchuria in particular), Japanese officials by the 1930s were developing a more deliberate system of intelligence concerning what they were by then conceiving—by way of another term taken from Europe—as the "Islamic world" (*isuramu sekai*).[14] This led to the ability to understand Muslim societies more directly than had previously been the case: in 1876 the first Japanese biography of the Prophet Muhammad was a translation of the antiquated and polemical *Life of Mahomet* that the English churchman Humphrey Prideaux had published in 1697.[15] As shown by the languages taught at the Tokyo school—including Malay, Persian, and Urdu—the Muslim-populated regions of South and Southeast Asia were of particular interest. These Islam-oriented investigations were further institutionalized through the funding of the *Isuramu Bunka Kyokai* (Islamic Culture Association) in 1937, followed by the *Kaikyoken Kenkyujo* (Institute of Islamic Studies) and the *Dai Nippon Kaikyo Kyokai* (Greater Japan Islam League) a year later.[16] The last sponsored a series of new translations, though even here the flow of inter-Asian understanding took European detours by drawing on various German studies of Islam and the *Short History of the Saracens* by the London-based Indian lawyer Syed Ameer Ali (1849–1928).[17] Japanese scholars also made three indirect translations of the Quran in the 1920s and 1930s.[18] While such translations were a major development in inter-Asian understanding, the exchange of intercultural knowledge was again asymmetrical, for there was no equivalent translation of any Buddhist book, Japanese or otherwise, into Arabic.

Institutional Underdevelopment in India

Before turning to Fazli's experiences as a direct participant in this uneven intercultural exchange, it is worth comparing Japan with India in terms of the institutional state of inter-Asian research. Despite the existence of such colonial institutions as the Asiatic Society of Bengal, in which Indians played important roles, there was no real Indian or Middle Eastern equivalent to the Tokyo School of Foreign Languages, particularly for teaching East Asian languages, and doing so in a way that would enable communication and translation directly rather than through English dictionaries. In the absence of such language-teaching institutions, Indians had to make do with commercially published beginners guides of Japanese phrases transliterated into Gujarati, such as Dinshaw Vaniya's *Japanis Sikshaka* (*Japanese Teacher*), published in Bombay in 1905.[19] But as we have seen, not only was this self-help book mainly in Gujarati script, but its vocabulary lists were aimed primarily at trade deals.

Outside Europe's imperial capitals, which each had its own language schools, the closest modern Asian counterpart to the state-funded schools in Tokyo and Osaka was found not in India but in the late Ottoman Empire. The first attempt to formalize Japanese language education had taken place there in 1891, when Noda Shotaro (1868–1904), a journalist for the prestigious newspaper *Jiji Shinpo* (*Current Events*), accepted the position of lecturer. His duties were to teach the Japanese language to selected Ottoman army and navy officers.[20] But this venture lasted for only two years, though as a consolation it did bring about Noda's conversion: as the first Japanese Muslim, he was feted in Ottoman journals such as *Musavver Cihan* (*Illustrated World*).[21] Even this state-funded Ottoman venture, however, had little lasting or public impact; the first basic printed language guide, *Japon Alfabesi* (*Japanese Alphabet*), did not appear till 1905 amid the enthusiasm surrounding the Japanese defeat of Russia.[22] In a reflection of wider patterns, albeit somewhat ironically in view of Ottoman sympathies, it was translated from Russian.

As victory raised interest in Japan all across Asia, in 1905 Rabindranath Tagore managed to recruit a Japanese language (and judo) teacher for his recently founded school at Shantiniketan, which in 1921 would become Visva-Bharati University. The teacher was Sano Jinnosuke (1882–1936), a graduate in political studies from Tokyo's Keio University.[23] But Tagore's early attempts at institutionalizing language study were short-lived. Though Sano would spend the next nine years in India, his career as a language teacher would last only a single year, and he subsequently became a military adviser to the princely state of Mysore. Moreover, his language class at Tagore's school had only eight students, all aged twelve and thirteen, though he did instruct them in the basics of the *katakana* syllabary, if not the more complex *kanji* characters.[24] Though Tagore and Sano had limited success in enabling a linguistically informed understanding of Japan, the experiment did result in a greater Japanese appreciation of India: after returning home, Sano used the Bengali he had learned to translate Tagore's 1909 novel, *Gora*, into Japanese and write a popular ethnography called *Indo oyobi Indojin* (*India and Its People*).[25]

As the infrastructure of empire afforded dozens of Japanese Buddhists the opportunity to sail to Calcutta and then travel by train to the Buddhist monuments being unearthed by colonial archaeologists, Sano was not the only Japanese to study Indian languages. Before the last quarter of the nineteenth century, traveling to India had been extremely hard and rare. The abstract status of India as the homeland of Buddhism had diminished through the rise of Sino- and Japanocentric models of the world during the early modern Tokugawa era, through which the importance of India dwindled even among learned Buddhists.[26] The promotion of a historicist approach to Buddhism that emphasized the contextual time and place of the religion's historical emergence was very much a product of Protestant European investigations of Buddhism, which subsequently had repercussions among Buddhists themselves, including those in Japan. Communications infrastructures made these changes more directly meaningful, as from the 1880s firsthand Japanese encounters with India were made possible by regular passenger steamship routes between Yokohama, Kobe, Calcutta, and Bombay.

What subsequently unfolded between the 1880s and 1930s was a Japanese discovery of India, along with Burma and Ceylon, which the infrastructures of empire rendered similarly accessible. Yet the Japanese scholars and pilgrims who sailed to the subcontinent were primarily involved in a journey of self-recovery in which India's archaeological monuments and manuscript libraries offered the potential to return Japanese Buddhism to its pure, original sources. Though language study played a central role in this process, it was not of the living languages of India, but of their ancient scriptural forebears. By far the most popular Indian language of study was Sanskrit, which a series of Japanese scholars went to India to learn in the decades on either side of

1900, while Masood's later Tokyo helper, Professor Takakusu, studied Sanskrit at Oxford.[27] Some even traveled to Tagore's Shantiniketan, but larger numbers opted for the Benares Sanskrit College, a more prestigious institution founded with the support of the East India Company in 1791.[28]

Among these seekers of the Buddhist self was Kawaguchi Ekai (1866–1945), who spent thirteen years studying in India and a further four tracing Buddhist manuscripts in Nepal and then Tibet (becoming the first Japanese to enter these mountain kingdoms), whose libraries British and Bengali scholars had been investigating together for several decades.[29] One of his mentors was Sarat Chandra Das, the bold exploratory pioneer of Anglo-Indian Tibetology.[30] With the help of Das—who had previously compiled a groundbreaking Tibetan-English dictionary—Kawaguchi worked on his own *Chibetto bunten* (*Tibetan Grammar*), before enrolling at Calcutta University to perfect his Sanskrit.[31] His residence in Calcutta also brought him into contact with members of the Maha-Bodhi Society, including the European Theosophists who issued an English translation of his 1904 travelogue, *Chibetto ryoko-ki* (*Three Years in Tibet*).[32] By the time he returned to Japan in 1915, Kawaguchi had assembled a large collection of Buddhist manuscripts in Sanskrit, Tibetan, and Nepali. He would spend the next three decades publishing translations of many of these texts into Japanese, as well as teaching Tibetan at a variety of Japanese universities.[33] Far from a unique figure, he was part of a larger cohort of Japanese who subsequently took up positions at Japanese universities or monasteries to teach the Sanskrit, Tibetan, and Pali they had studied, whether in colonial India, Burma, and Ceylon, or, more rarely, in independent Tibet and Nepal.[34] Yet like their European counterparts, some of these investigations were exercises in imperial outreach, whether presented in "Pan-Buddhist" or Asianist terms. A case in point is the 1901 journey to Lhasa by Narita Yasuteru (1864–1915), a foreign ministry affiliate who had previously worked on plans to develop the new Japanese colony of Taiwan.[35]

These exchanges ultimately produced far greater Japanese expertise in Indian (and Himalayan) languages than vice versa, but they were not entirely nonreciprocal. Another of these language students, Kimura Shozaburo, learned Sanskrit in Benares and Shantiniketan before taking up a lectureship at Calcutta University, where between 1918 and 1926 he taught Japanese as well as the history of Buddhism.[36] Two years after Masood was sent to Japan on behalf of Hyderabad's Osmania University, in 1924 Kimura was similarly sent by Calcutta University to establish ties with its Japanese counterparts.[37] Amid these increasingly institutionalized inter-Asian exchanges, at least two other

Japanese language students went on to teach at Calcutta University.[38] Though this pair may have taught Japanese informally, however, they were employed in Calcutta primarily to teach Sanskrit and Pali Buddhist texts as part of what had by the 1920s become the growing Indian interest in Buddhism.

So, if Japanese scholars were increasingly involved with their Indian counterparts, the latter were far more interested in recovering their own Buddhist heritage than in studying ancient texts in Japanese. Though dozens of Pali and Sanskrit texts were translated into Japanese, there appears to have been no corresponding translation into Indian languages of Japanese Buddhist texts.[39] The unevenness of this cultural exchange is perhaps even more striking when we consider that this period coincided with the successful projection of Zen in North America by Suzuki Daisetsu Teitaro, Zen's most important Anglophone popularizer.[40] Perhaps in India, by contrast, Japanese Buddhism seemed less authentic during the years when Buddhism was being reclaimed as part of India's own heritage.

Such asymmetry of intercultural understanding—particularly through formal language study and the translation of key texts—had inevitable consequences for Indian comprehension of Japanese culture. As we saw in the previous chapter, whether in Urdu or Bengali, Turkish or Persian, the books about Japan that multiplied in the decades after the defeat of Russia were written by authors who had no knowledge of written, or even spoken, Japanese. Yet by the 1930s, closer university-affiliated associations between learned Japanese and Indians held open the possibility of deeper and more direct forms of inter-Asian understanding. In being employed at the Tokyo School of Foreign Languages, Muhammad Fazli was the closest counterpart to the Japanese who taught at Calcutta University. By reconstructing his investigative journey, and comparing his Urdu book, *Haqiqat-i Japan*, with those of other Muslim travelers from elsewhere, we will see more clearly the constraints of both Indian and Middle Eastern attempts to turn Japanophilia into Japanology.

A Teacher's Interpretive Travels

Though Fazli's arrival in Tokyo in 1930 was a minor event in itself, it marked the start of a decade that witnessed the informational high-water mark of the intercultural knowledge that spread through the infrastructures of what were then not only European empires, but also an expanding Japanese one. By piecing together both the sources of information and strategies of interpretation that informed Fazli's *Haqiqat-i Japan*, we will see how this most determined

Indian investigator tried to live up to his book's titular promise of revealing the truth about a country that had been a fountain of misty fascination since the defeat of Russia some thirty years earlier.

Born in the small North Indian town of Pratabgarh, Fazli was thirty years old when he set off for Japan.[41] In a photograph he included in his subsequent book, he presented himself as a man of his time: wearing a three-piece Western suit and patterned silk tie (perhaps made in Japan), his waxed hair trimmed into a side parting above a toothbrush moustache. Traveling as an educated professional, he was part of the new cadre of intercultural investigators whose modern educations and institutional connections fed a far larger body of books on Japan than were produced by the much bigger cohort of merchants.[42]

This broader cadre among whom Fazli can be located included the Egyptian Muhammad Thabit, a secondary school teacher of language and literature from Cairo who wrote his *Jawla fi Rub' Asiya bayn Misr wa al-Yaban* (*A Tour through a Quarter of Asia between Egypt and Japan*), while Fazli was residing in Tokyo in 1931.[43] Traveling frugally aboard the steamers that crisscrossed maritime "Asia"—an English term by then also naturalized into Arabic—Thabit managed to make such an expedition every summer. Making full use of his steamship itinerary, he compared Cairo with Bombay and Colombo before moving on to inspect the port cities of Japan. He compared what he saw with customs back home, describing the clothes, foods, and manners of the local residents he observed. But he also continued to ride the weakening wave of Japanophilia, paying far more attention in his *Jawla fi Rub' Asiya* to the achievements of the Japanese than to those he saw as Asia's less "progressive" peoples. Looking at Japan through the prism of its prosperous ports, Thabit was particularly impressed by its commercial achievements. Nonetheless, his was inevitably a cursory inspection, leaving no time to learn languages. Nor were there any institutions in his home country capable of teaching him Japanese. Nonetheless, in the absence of more reliable information on the country in Arabic, his book provided Middle Eastern readers with at least an impression of the outward appearance of Japan's port cities and people.

In an extension of this method, Fazli's *Haqiqat* was built on observation and reading, as well as on the network of local informants he built up during his longer stay, albeit few of them Japanese. His travelogue volume—the first of the *Haqiqat*'s two parts—presented evocative descriptions of the modernizing Japanese cities of the early 1930s. By weaving his key concept words into accounts of the outward appearance of places and the people who lived there, these descriptions served as proof of both "progress" and the continued survival of "Eastern civilization." His admiration began as soon as he set ashore at Kobe, where he spent a day strolling around before reembarking. He wrote approvingly of Kobe's modern grid plan, its mostly concrete buildings, and wide public streets, which offered a contrast with many Indian cities of the period.[44] Walking through its markets, he was struck by the abundance of electricity, used not only for the practical purposes of lighting but also for decorating shop fronts. Even small shops were lit by neon signs, and the markets were packed with scarfless women and men in Western suits, much like his own.[45]

Such far-reaching modernization seemed to have reached every element of daily life, suggesting a society in which, whether through electricity or gas, machines appeared to do everything, including (in a contrast to India) powering rickshaws. Indeed, that form of transport was already largely outmoded in Japan, for the people of Kobe traveled instead mainly by trains, trams, taxis, buses, and every possible kind of motorcar. In Tokyo there was even an underground metro system. As was true of his Egyptian fellow teacher Muhammad Thabit, for Fazli Japanophilia could begin with the simple observation of technological and industrial progress. It need not require any interaction with the people or knowledge of their language. It required more basic observational methods, such as describing neon lights and underground trains that served as the symbolic evidence of progress that colonial Delhi (or Cairo) lacked.

Since Tokyo, "the largest city in Asia," was where Fazli subsequently spent most of his time, he provided detailed descriptions of not only its physical appearance and transport infrastructure, but also its many fine shops and hotels.[46] In a contrast to Delhi, he emphasized the centrality of Tokyo's royal quarter and imperial palace, pointing to a continuity that was lost in the empty Red Fort of the Mughals.

Adjacent to the royal quarter was Kojimachi, Tokyo's finest district and the location of its greatest houses, the old and new parliament buildings, government offices and foreign embassies, and the most important banking and commercial offices. The elegant Marunouchi district, meanwhile, was graced with eight-story department stores and parks filled with elegant cafés and restaurants.[47] In Ueno Park, there were also the impressive buildings of the Imperial Museum and Library and the Art School. Having provided a brief history of Tokyo's earlier development as the eastern capital of the Tokugawa shogunate, he was quite aware of the achievements of the city's builders after the devastating Great Kanto Earthquake of 1923. But as far as he was concerned, the earthquake and firestorms had been a boon in having made way for a more "enlightened design" based on wide public streets rather than narrow alleyways where house was piled upon house. In short, Tokyo was the architectonic expression of Asian *taraqqi*, or progress, the borrowed French key word of Fazli and his fellow modernists.

Though he seems not to have realized it, Fazli was actually responding to an Indian aesthetic that connected several Japanese cities to their counterparts in his homeland. Much of the Marunouchi district, as well as the Imperial Museum, were products of the earlier Meiji phase of Indo-Japanese exchange, having been built in the 1880s after designs the British architect Josiah Conder (1852–1920) adapted from the hybrid "Indo-Saracenic" style of colonial India.[48] Conder's own architectural teacher, Thomas Roger Smith (1830–1903), had designed several important buildings in Bombay. So, once again, the cities of Japan served as mirrors of their Indian counterparts. For as much as his admiration of Marunouchi was an appreciation of Japanese urbanism, it was also a recognition of the self in the other in which Europe played the role of architectural intermediary.

While this street-level empiricism was based on direct observation, it required minimal direct engagement with local people. Fazli could describe streets, hotels, and the outward appearance of Japanese people, for, like previous vernacular ethnographers, he made much of clothing, devoting attention to female attire that served as a symbolic moral register. But rather than criticize such clothing, he found that kimono-wearing women served to sartorially symbolize the continuity of Japanese culture amid the masculine march toward progress by men in Western suits. Such visual symbols served as the silent substitute for a shared language.

Empowering "Eastern Civilization"

Mere observation and description were not enough, though, to make meaning out of Japan for his Indian readers. To make sense of what he saw, Fazli drew on a series of basic concepts he carried with him from home. These were not the religious concepts deployed by the likes of 'Abd al-Khaliq in Burma, through which different cultures were measured against the moral yardstick of Islam. Instead, Fazli made use of the more recent and capacious concept of "Eastern culture" (*mashriqi tahzib*), which served as the counterpart to his broad category of "Eastern civilization" (*mashriqi tamaddun*), which was used by a whole generation of Indian and Middle Eastern modernists, who ranged from Asianists to secular nationalists.[49] A generation earlier, a similar adaptation of the term "civilization" into Japanese, by means of the neologism *bunmei,* had helped Okakura make his own claims of inter-Asian connection.[50] As we saw previously, as well as in translations of English textbooks on history, the concept of civilization had also been disseminated in Urdu through the translation of Gustave Le Bon's *Civilisations de l'Inde;* it was subsequently spread further by the popular historical novels of 'Abd al-Halim Sharar (1869–1926). But there was also an inter-Asian dimension to this process of conceptual transmission, since Indians also absorbed the Islamized language of civilization, or *tamaddun,* through their contacts with Muslim intellectuals in the Ottoman Empire, who had likewise absorbed it from French thinkers before passing it on to Indians in an Islamized terminology that disguised its European origin. As the concept was in turn expanded into hemispherical form—Western and Eastern, European and Asian—the terms "Eastern culture" and "Eastern civilization" served the likes of Fazli as higher-order categories than Islam (or, for that matter, Hinduism or Buddhism). This broader rubric of "cultures" and "civilizations" made it easier to find correspondences and connections between what the earlier conceptual schemes of specific religions had rendered separate.

In this way, modernists like Fazli were able to overcome the stumbling block seen in earlier Muslim accounts of Japan caused by its distinct Shinto and Buddhist religions, which, for some commentators at least, had worrying ethical implications. If the variations of religious specificity could be overlooked by placing them into the same conceptual basket of Eastern culture or civilization, then the Japanophiles' dilemma could be solved by brushing over the details of difference. In this way, Japan could be used to provide lessons on how to protect and empower any one of the particular religions that collectively made up "Eastern culture." This was important: Japan was so appealing to the new generation of nationalist intellectuals like Fazli precisely because it seemed to provide a model of how to become modern without becoming Western.[51] From the mid-1920s, when Ataturk and Reza Shah had set Turkey and Iran on the path of a secularizing and Westernizing modernity that was visibly expressed by banning fezzes and turbans in favor of European hats, this quest for a model of progress that remained anchored to Eastern traditions became all the more urgent. This was one of the major questions for both the Asian conservatives and progressives of the period, especially in the wake of the revulsion toward Western civilization that followed the First World War.

Fazli was in some ways comparable to Tagore, for both were interested in the maintenance of traditional culture. But, like other young men of his generation, Fazli was equally interested in the modernity and progress that Tagore viewed with greater skepticism. This demanded that he build a conceptual bridge that would help him interpret the visual evidence of what he saw in Japan and in turn described, and interpreted, for his readers back home. And so, in his *Haqiqat-i Japan,* Fazli presented Japan's political and economic achievements as being inseparable from the country's loyalty to its cultural traditions.

As a result of these at once progressive and conservative impulses, Fazli, like other Muslim admirers of Japan, made much of the apparent cultural continuity of Japanese life, even if it was not always easy to find evidence for it. It was clearly impossible for any visitor to Tokyo during the 1930s to ignore the visible results of Japan's encounter with America and Europe over the previous seventy years. One of the initial things that struck Fazli during his first hours on Japanese soil was the high proportion of Japanese wearing what he explicitly termed as Western (*maghribi*) clothing. This was all the more striking by comparison to India, for he estimated that around 25 to 30 percent of Japanese women were wearing Western clothes.[52] Then, as though to gloss over this inconvenient fact, he followed up this observation with a description of the traditional female kimono and included for emphasis an illustration taken from a tourist postcard. Perhaps there was a touch of nostalgia in Fazli's account of Japanese traditional clothing, for at least as he presented himself in the photograph at the front of his book, he himself dressed in a well-tailored Western suit.[53]

Similarly, although most of Tokyo's shops and buildings were designed in a Western style, the signs in front of them were all written in the "Chinese" (*chini*) script.[54] Even if the physical form was Western, then, Fazli was keen to emphasize that the motivating spirit remained Eastern. Though he did not mention it directly, this was after all the official policy known as *wakon yosai* (Japanese spirit, Western technology).

The importance given to upholding Eastern traditions meant that cultural institutions formed an important focus of Fazli's *Haqiqat,* whether libraries, publishers, museums, historical sites, learned societies, or traditional theaters.[55] Both in his travelogue and more particularly his second-volume survey, he paid much attention to the continued patronage of traditional arts and literature, not least through state investment in educational and cultural institutions. These were concerns he held in common with his predecessor Masood, concerns that in turn reflected their own background as graduates of the same

An Indian language teacher in
Japan. Shaykh Muhammad Badr
al-Islam Fazli, *Haqiqat-i Japan*,
2 vols. (New Delhi: Anjuman-i
Taraqqi-i Urdu, 1934). By permission of Anjuman Taraqqi Urdu
(Hind), New Delhi, India.

university (and in Masood's case, as Hyderabad's education minister). But in
addition to providing a summary of school and university systems as Masood
had done, Fazli paid greater attention to the development of the visual and
performance arts, as well as literature.[56]

If Masood had struggled to find a way into Japan's universities, then Fazli's
position as a salaried employee of the Tokyo School of Foreign Languages afforded him considerable access to and awareness of these aspects of Japanese
life. He was, for example, taken along with other overseas teachers from the
school to see several theater performances, including a traditional *No* drama.[57]
In what he took as pleasing evidence of the cultural affinities India and Japan
shared as fellow participants in "Eastern civilization," another theater performance was based on the ancient Hindu tale of Rama and Sita, in which the
Japanese actors all dressed in Indian clothes.[58] He was keen to unravel the
secret of balancing tradition and modernity, and his account of a third theater visit lent the opportunity to discuss both new drama and the *No* performance he conceived of as an example of national (*mulki*) drama, since both
types of play were performed in the same evening.[59] In his later discussion of

the visual arts—covering painting, sculpture, and architecture, in addition to music—his concerns for cultural integrity similarly led him to emphasize the Buddhist foundations of all Japanese art, in this way presenting institutionally supported arts as media of cultural continuity. Just a few decades earlier, such interpretations would have been far more challenging. But after the translation into Urdu of many Orientalist works on Buddhism, by the 1930s the Buddha was not merely a familiar figure. He had been reclaimed as an Indian. Writing in the wake of these developments, Fazli could now comfortably use the Buddha as further evidence of a common civilization that joined India with Japan, albeit by drawing on Lafcadio Hearn's *Gleanings in Buddha Field* for his account of Japanese Buddhism.[60]

This idea of the arts as a repository of both cultural integrity and connectivity—an idea shared with Tagore and his Japanese associates—was echoed elsewhere in Fazli's travelogue. On visiting the National Gallery of Art in Tokyo's Ueno Park, he noted critically how many Japanese painters copied European techniques (an indirect reference to the *Yoga* school of painting that flourished during the Meiji and Taisho eras before falling out of favor with the ascendant nationalists by the time of Fazli's visit).[61] He then remarked that he didn't like these paintings and much preferred the Japanese style (a reference to the newer nationalist *Nihonga* school). Here, too, he echoed Tagore, a painter as well as a poet who thirty years earlier had first promoted the notion of a Pan-Asian artistic heritage in conversation with the art theorist Okakura, though, as so often is the case, this heritage included Buddhist art but excluded its even more "Pan-Asian" Islamic counterparts. Since Tagore's meeting with Okakura in the early 1900s, this Asianist ideology of art had found subtler aesthetic expression with the neo-traditionalist painters who had emerged around Okakura at Tokyo's *Nihon Bijutsuin* (Japan Fine Arts Academy), including Kampo Arai (1878–1945) and Taikan Yokoyama (1868–1958), who also both spent time in Calcutta.[62] Inspired by the colonial archaeological recovery of Buddhist cave temples, particularly Ajanta, several of the Japanese and Indian artists in Tagore's circle paid visits to Ajanta to admire and even copy the gorgeous frescoes there. Though Fazli didn't name any Japanese artists directly, he viewed what he understood to be traditional Japanese paintings as conveniently direct and uncomplicated. Walking through the gallery, he could encounter Japanese culture without the linguistic complications of interacting with its living representatives.

Though Fazli had clearly moved on from his initial appreciation of Japan's urban infrastructure to an appreciation of its culture, his travelogue suggests that his underlying mode of engagement remained similar, more through visual observation than by verbal interaction. There is no evidence in his writings that he ever talked with authors, playwrights, artists, or curators about these artworks. While his approval of *Nihonga* painting was undoubtedly an appreciation of the culture of the Japanese, the latter played the role of silent partner to his interpretive reveries.

His subsequent account of literature dwelt in similarly appreciative detail on what he called "new literature," surveying the concerns of each of the major writers from the Meiji Restoration to 1930.[63] He also took an interest in the Japanese publishing scene, summarizing the history of the press and giving the titles and print runs of the country's leading newspapers, along with details of the specialist journals dealing with artistic and literary topics.[64] Ever in search of comparison with his homeland, he was providing parallels to the literary journals of the *Anjuman-i Taraqqi-i Urdu,* the Society for the Progress of Urdu, which would publish his own book. Yet he was nonetheless moving toward a deeper intellectual engagement, one that was based on reading rather than watching. Yet there is no evidence that he learned to read Japanese, or even speak it with any level of proficiency. For new concepts of commonality could not magically summon into existence a deeper comprehension of language and culture. Ideology and information were neither coeval nor coexistent. The abundant bibliography at the end of his *Haqiqat* shows that his survey of Japanese arts was derived from English works, such as Edward Dillon's *Arts of Japan* and Stewart Dick's *Arts and Crafts of Old Japan.*[65] Ironically, despite the attempts of Okakura to promote an Indo-Japanese artistic continuum, his *Ideals of the East* was not listed.

Fazli's knowledge of Japanese literature was similarly drawn from the English studies and translations he listed, particularly *A History of Japanese Literature* by William Aston (1841–1911), a longtime Tokyo resident and translator for the British legation there. That this mediated method was still fraught with potential misunderstandings may be gleaned by one of the books that appeared beneath the heading "literature" in his bibliography, under the short title *Japan Revealed* and with the author listed as John Paris. In fact, this was the pseudonym of the British diplomat Frank Ashton-Gwatkin (1889–1976), whose book comprised a series of burlesque English parodies of Japanese novels that caused considerable diplomatic scandal. Again, European informants were not necessarily reliable.

His concern for artistic connections to Japan's Eastern heritage also found expression in his account of ceremonies and religious sites. Fazli wrote impressive descriptions of the nationalist Shinto shrine of Yasukuni Jinja, which he termed a soldiers' memorial (*sipahiyun ki yadgar*), and of the temple (*mandir*) devoted to the Meiji emperor responsible for Japan's "greatness and progress."[66] He included photographs to render the effect of these national sites all the more imposing. Yet like Muslim Japanophiles everywhere, he faced the problem of how to square Japan's Buddhist and Shinto commitments with his own concerns. Others had previously overcome the problem through hopeful rumors of the mikado's imminent conversion to Islam or active attempts to convert the country to Islam. Still other émigré Muslims had become directly involved with pro-Muslim Asianist organizations, such as the *Ajia Gikai* (Asian Reawakening Society), which appropriated the European concept of Asia toward Japanese imperial ends.[67]

Writing twenty-five years after the rumors of the mikado's conversion had faded, Fazli was fully aware of the limited influence Islam had on the country. Yet he shared with other Indian and Middle Eastern writers on Japan the idea that cultural and religious traditions served as essential filters for harmful Western influences that could be avoided by modernizing the Japanese way. Thus, he focused his description of Japanese religion on Buddhism, making special excursions to the medieval towns of Kamakura and Nara to inspect the country's most important early temples. His sympathetic, even marveling accounts of the bronze statuary of Kamakura and the wooden temples of Nara were part of the formal Muslim appreciation of Buddhist art that was spreading in the 1920s and 1930s. His emphasis on the two gigantic statues of Buddha at Nara formed a strikingly admiring contrast to perplexed or negative Muslim accounts of Buddhist "idols" of a few decades earlier. Instead, just as British Christians had gradually learned to do in India, Ceylon, and Burma, he was then able to reconceptualize them as art rather than idolatry. This in turn prompted him to provide their art history in detail through a blend of direct observation and consulting Dillon's *Arts of Japan*.[68]

India's Muslims had a rich history of creating and admiring extraordinary works of art, but the discipline of art history was a more recent development, spreading into Asia through the writings of Okakura, Fazli's Ceylonese contemporary Ananda Coomaraswamy, and a series of forgotten pioneers who wrote in local languages. Although neither Okakura nor Coomaraswamy was cited in Fazli's bibliography, by the time he was writing the notion that statues belonged to the category of art rather than religion had spread widely among university-educated intellectuals in India and the Middle East. This aided the emergence of art-historical writings in such languages as Persian, Turkish,

Bengali, and Urdu where the loanword "art" was itself adopted to signify a new conceptualization of craft works that was subtly separate from such older Urdu and Persian terms as *hunar*.[69] Though Fazli is infinitely less famous than his Anglophone counterparts such as Coomaraswamy, his Urdu book reached a far larger Indian readership through its print run of several thousand copies.

Yet in a period in Japanese history when Buddhism was being repressed in favor of the "national" religion of Shinto, it is also revealing that, aside from the nationalist Yasukuni Jinja, Fazli chose not to describe Shinto sites in detail. In contrast to the religion of the Buddha, who by the time Fazli wrote had already been rehabilitated by India's most famous Urdu poet, Muhammad Iqbal, Shinto remained unfamiliar and wholly foreign. Buddhism, by contrast, provided a cultural link between India and Japan—evidence of a shared Eastern civilization—that for his own comparative purposes Fazli was no less keen to exploit than Japanese intellectuals traveling in the opposite direction to India.[70] For similar reasons, when the Indian anticolonial activist (and erstwhile Tokyo resident) Raja Mahendra Pratap published his futurist map of a postcolonial world a year after Fazli's book appeared, he gave his "Province of Pan-Asia" the alternative label of "Buddha."[71] However much Shinto was being promoted in Japan itself, this uniquely "national" religion possessed no such potential for Indian nationalists.

Muslims from elsewhere approached the matter differently. Coming from a country with no historical claims over Buddhism, the Egyptian nationalist Mustafa Kamil wrote approvingly of Shinto in his Arabic book *al-Shams al-Mushriqa* (*The Rising Sun*).[72] Faced with the dilemma of praising ancestor worship, which was only marginally less objectionable to a Muslim readership than idol worship, Kamil carefully defined Shinto not as a religion per se, but as a cultural tradition of respecting pious ancestors and elders. Shinto "does not go beyond the glorification of the forefathers of the mikado and the pious forebears and the emulation of their righteous deeds," he explained.[73] Like Fazli's presentation of Buddhism, here too the choice of key concept words was essential: Kamil chose the term "glorification" (*tamjid*) of ancestors rather than "worship" (*'ibada*), which would have made Shinto seem uncomfortably heretical to his Arab Muslim and Christian readers. He even went as far as claiming that the Japanese emperor didn't actually consider himself to be divine, but merely upheld Shinto rituals for the sake of national unity.[74] Moreover, for Kamil, this practice of glorifying the nation's ancestors offered a useful example to an Egypt in dire need of unity. In such ways, Japanese religiosity was interpreted for Asia's wider reading public in accordance with what interpreters like Fazli and Kamil considered the most useful lessons for empowering the self.

Yet using such broad categories as art, tradition, and Eastern civilization to make connections and comparisons could take intercultural understanding only so far. When it came to finer points of detail, the task of directly interpreting another society and culture was considerably more complicated.

Finding Sources on Japanese Society

If the casual empiricism of strolling through city streets was capable of revealing the visible evidence of Japanese progress, then to make sense of such observations, and link them to the invisible events of the historical past and the more cryptic operations of culture, commentators like Fazli had to resort to a larger corpus of knowledge by way of books in languages they could read.

In contrast to his first-volume travelogue, which was based on his own observations, this research enabled Fazli to write his second volume, which, along with the aforementioned sections on festivals, religion, and the arts, presented a detailed survey of Japanese society both past and present. Here he brought together over two hundred pages of data on history, geography, ethnography, sport, education, publishing, and politics, along with craft industries and international commerce (the latter including statistics on Japanese trade with India).[75] Despite the development of a fairly substantial Urdu bookshelf on Japan by the time Fazli was writing, for his second volume he opted for a method of informational outsourcing by drawing on the fifty or so English works cited in his bibliography. The only Urdu work among them was Masood's *Japan aur uska Ta'limi Nazm u Nasq* (*Japan and Its Educational Order and Organization*), which likewise drew substantially on English sources. As for other books by Indian authors, while he cited Tagore's *Spirit of Japan*, this was, strictly speaking, an English text based on lectures delivered to university students in Tokyo. The handful of Japanese works he cited were all in English translation.

As for the other works Fazli consulted, many were well known if, by the 1930s, in some cases rather dated works. This reliance on English sources informed even the section that provided prospective travelers with practical information on passport and visa regulations, local currency and exchanging rupees, and the purchasing of travel insurance, his source here being Basil Chamberlain's *Handbook for Travelers to Japan*, which belonged to the series of genteel travel guides issued by the London publisher John Murray.[76] The author he cited most extensively, however, was Lafcadio Hearn, who we have

previously seen acting as a cultural intermediary in another direction by introducing Omar Khayyam's *Ruba'iyat* to Japan. Alongside the romantic writings
of Hearn and the *Story of Old Japan* by Joseph Longford was John Ingram
Bryan's *The Civilisation of Japan*, which further aided Fazli in his civilizational
approach.[77] Even so, Longford's 1928 study was a relatively up-to-date source,
which suggests that Fazli had overcome the reliance by previous authors on
accounts that were often long out-of-date. Longford's study was also a broadly
respected if wholeheartedly imperial one: after retiring from the Japan Con-
sular Service, Longford had been appointed professor of Japanese at King's
College, London. As a university graduate himself, Fazli had a sense of the
importance of such institutional expertise. After his return home from Tokyo,
to access such expensive, imported books and so write the second volume of
his *Haqiqat*, Fazli may well have used the library of his and Masood's alma
mater, Aligarh Muslim University.

Yet even if much of the informational detail of Fazli's survey drew on the
larger bibliographic body of Anglophone studies, in bringing together so
much data into Urdu, his *Haqiqat* substantially raised Indian understanding
of the country. His work was more creative than mere compilation, though.
For as a venture in interpretation that combined observation, reading, and
reflection, his book acted as a conceptual and linguistic filter that tilted the
representations and information available in English toward what he regarded
as the most useful lessons for his Indian and Muslim readership.

Here the *Haqiqat* echoed Masood's book, which was issued by the same
publisher.[78] Likewise lacking knowledge of the Japanese language, Masood too
had been forced to draw on books in English, if not always works written by
Englishmen. In his travel diary, for example, Masood mentioned that aboard
his steamer from Bombay, he had "begun going through Prince Okuma's big
book on Japan," a reference to *Fifty Years of New Japan*, the English edition of
Kaikoku gojunen shi by the former prime minister Count Okuma Shigenobu
(1838–1922).[79] As Masood immediately recognized, it was "a most useful compilation."[80] For in Okuma's own words, the book sought to present "an authoritative account of the development of the Empire of Japan" by drawing lessons
from "the history of the past and . . . the characteristics of the people of Japan
and the unfolding of their national destinies."[81] And so knowledge of English
rather than of any Asian lingua franca afforded Masood indirect access to a
Japanese minister's perceptions of his country's history.

Fortunately, books were not Fazli's only informational augmentation to his
visual observations. Like Masood a decade earlier, Fazli was also able to use

the social networks created by seventy years of Japanese interactions with both Britain and British India. He described visits to Tokyo's Indo-Japanese Association (where Tagore had previously lectured) and meetings with the merchant members of Kobe's Hindustani Club (the partner to the club where Masood stayed in Tokyo).[82] Drawing on the infrastructure of empire, Fazli was invited to several social gatherings at the British embassy, where he was introduced to other visitors.[83] At one such diplomatic dinner, he met a Scotsman, Mr. Murray, who told him he had been friends at Cambridge with a Mr. Mukherjee, the principal of Mission College in Delhi.[84] Later in what appears to have been a congenial evening, Murray declared that Rabindranath Tagore was the world's finest writer in the English language. At the end of the dinner, the British ambassador provided Fazli with his car and chauffeur to drive him home.

While such encounters provide evidence of the social contexts from which, in addition to his observations and readings, Fazli gained his understanding of Japan, what is striking is that, in the two-hundred-odd pages of his travelogue volume, meetings with British and Indian expatriates appear far more frequently than encounters with Japanese people. His book gives the strong impression that his access to Japanese social networks was markedly limited in comparison to his easy entry to expatriate circles, perhaps because of his lack of proficiency in the Japanese language. In the absence of "native informants," Indian merchants and British diplomats provided their perspectives on Japan, but as must be the case with all expatriate communities, such information had a distinctly outsider profile. Even in Japan itself, inter-Asian—or, at least, Indo-Japanese—interactions were far from the easiest sources of understanding.

This indirect social profile of Fazli's knowledge of Japan is seen most clearly in his entry to the country's Muslim community, which centered on Tokyo's newly founded mosque.[85] By turning to his encounters with exiled fellow Muslims and the few local converts, we will see how his investigation of Japanese society became caught between two interwoven ventures in self-projection by way of Muslim attempts to promote Islam and Japanese attempts to deploy the religion in the service of imperial expansion. For as Fazli tried to move beyond the colonial confines of English books and Indian clubs, he was drawn ever deeper into an informational partnership with Japanese knowledge of Islam.

Finding Islam in Expatriate Japan

As recorded in his *Haqiqat* at least, Fazli's first encounter with a fellow Muslim in Japan was with one of his co-workers at the Tokyo School of Foreign

Languages. This was 'Abd al-Ghani, a Malay who for the previous eight years had been the Malay instructor at the school, where the language had been on the curriculum since 1908.[86] His predecessor, a Singaporean called Ibrahim bin Ahmad, who had taught at the school till his premature death in 1912, had been a close friend of the Indian political activist Barakatullah during his own years teaching there.[87] Judging by Fazli's account, 'Abd al-Ghani was to become his closest companion during his fifteen months in Tokyo.[88] Fazli gave few details of their discussions, but he probably learned much of what he reported about life in Japan from this long-term resident and Muslim fellow English speaker from another corner of Britain's Asian empire.

Through the connections he made with 'Abd al-Ghani and with Indian expatriates at the Hindustani Club, one day Fazli received a visit from a "Mister Ahmad," apparently an Indian Muslim merchant from Kobe.[89] Upon getting to know more about this visitor, however, Fazli learned he was in fact the son of an Indian Muslim father and a Chinese mother. Born and educated in Hong Kong, Ahmad had never actually visited India. Having lived for many years in Japan, he had married a Japanese wife and now worked in Kobe as an agent for the Sun Life Insurance Company, a line of work in which he was aided by his ability to speak English, Urdu, and Japanese. Ahmad was, then, the kind of multilingual commercial broker who resided all around maritime Asia, but who proved remarkably silent as authors, leaving the writing of books to the less linguistically adept.

Nonetheless, Ahmad did open several social and to some degree informational doors for Fazli by introducing him to the community of around sixty Indian Muslims who resided in Kobe. The most convenient time to meet them, it transpired, was when they gathered for Friday prayers at the city's Hindustani Club. This was an arrangement Ahmad had been trying to resolve for the past two years by gathering funds from Muslim traders in Kobe, Singapore, and India for the construction of a proper mosque. Fazli's meetings with Ahmad in turn brought him into contact with members of the larger Tatar Muslim community, made up of pro-czarist refugees who had fled the Soviet takeover of the Russian Empire.[90] By the early 1930s, there were as many as a thousand Tatars in Japan, mainly in Tokyo.[91] Mingling with these Tatar coreligionists, Fazli began to attend their makeshift Tokyo mosque, entering another social network of expatriate Muslims, albeit one different from the Indians based mainly in Kobe rather than the capital. A photograph he included in his *Haqiqat* showed the Tokyo mosque to be an ordinary if sizable Japanese house in external appearance. (In 1938 it was replaced by a purpose-built mosque, replete with

Building Islam in Japan: a match-box commemorating the completion of the Kobe Mosque. Collection of Nile Green.

dome and grand minaret.) During the time he was employed at the language school, Fazli made numerous visits to the mosque, describing one occasion in detail when he attended Friday prayers at which some fifty Tatars were present.[92] Having lived in Japan for almost fifteen years by the time he met them, they were potentially useful informants on Japanese life. But once again these informational sources were indirect. Even insofar as he could converse with them—there is no more evidence for his speaking Russian or Tatar Turkish than Japanese—the Tatar refugees were marginal to the mainstream Japanese society. Even their mosque was in a distant Tokyo suburb.

Nonetheless, through attending the mosque, Fazli was introduced to a man called Qurban 'Ali, whom he described as the mosque's imam.[93] In fact, he was rather more than that. The figure in question was Muhammad 'Abd al-Hayy Qurban 'Ali (1892–1972), the Tatar leader-in-exile and close cooperator with the Japanese against Soviet and Chinese interests.[94] Drawn into deploying his own expertise toward Japanese imperial ends, even before reaching Tokyo in 1924, Qurban 'Ali had used his fluency in Russian and Turkish to work for the Japanese in Manchuria as a translator. Such work was only a few steps removed from Fazli's perhaps unwitting imperial assistance in teaching Urdu to military and intelligence officer trainees at the School of Foreign Languages. Qurban 'Ali was quite familiar with the school, having previously written to the Japanese minister of education, urging him to add Turkish to its curriculum and providing a list of Russian dictionaries and grammars of Turkic languages that could be used.[95] If Fazli was a lone Indian language teacher in Japanese service, then he was clearly far from the only Muslim. As a supplier as much as a gatherer of intercultural knowledge, he was part of the larger enterprise of Japanese imperial intelligence in which by the 1930s knowledge of Asia's Muslims was playing an increasingly important part.[96]

Yet like Fazli, Qurban 'Ali was an intellectual for whom empire offered him the potential to expand his ties to other Asian regions, particularly to fellow Muslims he hoped to help through the high-level connections he forged with Japanese officials. Toward these ends, by the time Fazli met him in 1931, Qurban 'Ali was busy with the Tokyo'da Matbaa-i İslamiye (Tokyo Islamic Press) he had founded the previous year.[97] In a tangible example of the maritime interconnections of the Asian public sphere, the Tokyo Islamic Press used Arabic-script molds and fonts that had been shipped in crates across the whole length of the continent from Istanbul to Yokohama.[98] Its output was predominantly in Tatar Turkish, comprising thirty-eight books over the next seven years, which were shipped to Tatar exiles in Manchuria as well as to Turkey and Europe. The press also issued a journal, *Yeni Yapun Mukhbiri* (*New Japan Informer*), which provided news about Muslim communities across Asia, with a clear leaning toward Japanese policies, not least in Manchuria. In such ways, the press that Qurban 'Ali operated with Japanese support combined two overlapping agendas—self-protecting for the Tatar refugees and self-projecting for their empire-building hosts.

The results were a further entanglement of self-oriented ventures as copies of Qurban 'Ali's journal reached places such as Afghanistan, probably through the deliberate efforts of the Japanese embassy that opened in Kabul in 1934, at a time when Afghan officials were seeking new diplomatic allies of their own.[99] As both parties sought common ground through Islam, a year later an article appeared in the official journal *Kabol* that explored the changing status of Islam in Japan.[100] Its detailed overview focused on Qurban 'Ali's activities, describing his school, printing office, and journal, before moving on to the number of mosques, schools, and religious scholars that freely flourished in Japan and Manchuria. This happy state of affairs was bolstered by several photographs showing Qurban 'Ali in the company of Japanese officials, including one that depicted him reciting veres from the Quran to them.[101] The sources of this information were not in Japanese, but were articles in Qurban 'Ali's *Yeni Yapun Mukhbiri*, which Afghan officials could translate through their closer connections with Turkic Central Asia. (Many Afghans were themselves native speakers of Turkic languages.) Japanese officials were fully aware of this, which had led them to sponsor *Yeni Yapun Mukhbiri* as a linguistic intermediary to the Muslims of Asia, at least those with the ability to read its articles in simplified Turkic. Employing a native speaker like Qurban 'Ali to produce the journal also overcame the double Japanese difficulty of linguistic proficiency and propagandist legitimacy. And so, when Afghans came to read about religion in Japan in the pages of *Kabol*, their country's first cultural journal, the religion they read about was neither Shinto nor Buddhism, but an Eastern reflection of their own Muslim faith.

Through funding Qurban 'Ali's journal, Japan was able to deepen its ties with Turkic-reading communities of Muslims who resided from Manchuria through inland China to Central Asia and Turkey. But this wide linguistic arc still excluded many other Muslim communities, including those of India, which comprised the largest Muslim population of any region of the planet. And so, while Fazli certainly knew about the journal—he mentioned it in his book after presumably being shown around the printing house next door to the mosque—he was unable to read it. Once again, for lone individuals especially, inter-Asian interactions were constrained by linguistic barriers. Even when Qurban 'Ali himself communicated with Japanese officials, he wrote to them in the Russian that served as the lingua franca between the Tatar refugees and their fellow Asian hosts.[102]

Russian, Tatar, and Urdu, however, were not the only languages being negotiated through the Japanese policies toward Muslims into which Fazli was being drawn. There was also Arabic. In 1934 Qurban 'Ali's press issued a large Arabic edition of the Quran that was printed with Japanese government sponsorship, then shipped to dozens of Muslim communities from the Dutch East Indies to India and the Middle East.[103] But this proved easier than placing the Quran before Japan's own reading public. For although three translations of the Quran into Japanese were made in the 1920s and 1930s, the first complete and direct translation from the Arabic would not appear till 1950.[104] All the earlier Japanese versions drew on previous translations into European languages, not least through the input of the Christian convert Takahashi Goro (1856–1935), who had helped translate the New Testament into Japanese.[105] As they had around the Bay of Bengal, Christian missionaries took an early leading role in Japan's incorporation into Asia's maritime public sphere. Having been active in Calcutta since the early 1800s, the British and Foreign Bible Society had begun its Japanese operations in 1875, publishing the official "Meiji version" of the New Testament four years later in Tokyo.[106] As we saw in the previous chapter, Baha'is and Muslims then had followed them, albeit in the Baha'i case by using Esperanto to circumvent the challenge of language.

Comparatively belated as it may have been, the printing of the Quran in Tokyo raised hopes across Muslim regions of Asia that the thirty-year-old dream of the mikado's conversion might finally come true. Even in distant Kabul, the state-sponsored Tokyo Quran was celebrated by an article in Afghanistan's leading journal.[107] As two forms of self-projection overlapped, the article's Afghan author, Qasim Rishtiyya, expressed the hope that Japan might finally embrace Islam. In exploring the likelihood of this happy outcome, his article—published at the same time as Fazli's book—presented Afghan readers with an overview of Japan's recent history that framed its modernization in distinctly religious terms. In an echo of the earlier Egyptian Arabic take on Shinto, it explained that the reformist Meiji emperor rejected his divine status and saw himself merely as the leader of his people. Moreover, as part of his grand reform project, the emperor had sent representatives to all regions of the world to learn about "civilization," a key word of Fazli's contemporary study. As Rishtiyya explained, the emperor and his emissaries were fully aware that "the religions of Japan at the time, which were Buddhism [Buda'i], Shinto [Shintu], and so on, were based on mere superstition [khurafat]."[108] As a result, representatives of various world religions had arrived in Japan, though it took longer for Islamic missionaries to reach there. But now that situation had changed, Rishtiyya went on, for through combined Muslim and Japanese efforts, the Quran had finally been made available in Japan. It was hoped, the Afghan article concluded, that conversions would soon follow. Those aspirations spread further through the public sphere when Afghan articles on the Quran in Japan were republished in the Iranian magazine Payman (Promise).[109]

Such religious commitments also shaped Fazli's social encounters in Tokyo, with both Tatars and the few Japanese converts—encounters that in turn shaped his perception of the country. For among the other worshippers he encountered at the mosque was an unusual figure named Saburo, whom he later met again in private to take tea. Fazli referred to Saburo as the only Japanese convert in Tokyo. This was incorrect: another convert called Harun Kouzumi was helping train Qurban 'Ali's team of Tatar printers. But Fazli was right in adding that there were a few more Japanese Muslims in other regions of the country.[110] He also correctly mentioned that Saburo's conversion to Islam came out of his earlier scholarly work in Islamic studies; Saburo came from the Orientalist background of other Japanese converts.[111] Fazli learned that Saburo had converted after writing about Islam for the *Japanese Encyclopaedia*, during the research for which he came to realize that Islam "taught countless good things," particularly the doctrine of divine unity and the practice of religious tolerance.[112]

Yet Saburo's embrace of Islam was more than an act of appreciative sympathy with the faith of Asian others that, like Buddhism in Islamic languages, had even lacked a proper name in Japanese half a century earlier. There was also room for self-projection in Saburo's conversion. In a pointer to the complex dialectic of inter-Asian interaction, the account given of the mysterious "Mistar Suburu" in Fazli's *Haqiqat* makes it clear that this was Shimano Saburo (1893–1982). By the time Fazli met him, he was in fact an intelligence officer who had been working among the Tatars for the Japanese security services for over a decade.[113] A close associate of Kotaro Omar Yamaoka—another informant whom we saw becoming the first Japanese to reach Mecca—Saburo had been officially tasked with taking Qurban 'Ali to Tokyo in 1924. Since then, he had been a regular presence among the exiles at the Tokyo mosque, where Fazli first encountered him, quietly aiding Japan's imperial self-projection across Muslim Asia.

It is unclear whether Fazli was aware of the role played by a series of such converts in the service of Japanese espionage during the previous thirty years. But he did note the attendance of the prime minister's private secretary at one of the Tatar dinners he attended.[114] In any case, potentially at least, Saburo provided Fazli with more information on Japanese life even if he stood at some distance from the Shinto and Buddhist mainstreams of local society.[115]

Fazli's encounters with Saburo, Qurban 'Ali, and the other Tatar exiles show how engagements with the Asian other could take the form of a series of informational bargains as Tatar refugees and Indian-language teachers gained what they could for themselves or their people in return for what they taught to Japanese imperial officials. A generation earlier, both Indian and British knowledge of Tibet had been similarly expanded through colonial scholar-spies such as Sarat Chandra Das and scores of other courageous Indian investigators, the so-called *pandits,* who were loyal officers of empire. A generation later, as increasing numbers of Indians questioned their imperial loyalties, Indian understanding of Japan similarly developed through a set of imperial entanglements around Fazli's employment at the Tokyo School of Foreign Languages and even the people he met at the place he went to pray.

In Another Empire's Service

Such tangled knots of knowledge become all the more apparent when we return to Fazli's workplace and his reason for traveling to Tokyo. There he not only found himself in the service of another empire; he also found himself placed in an unequal informational exchange as Persian and Urdu instructor at the School of Foreign Languages, alongside similar teachers of Tamil, Malay, Chinese, and Mongolian.[116] By the time he commenced his duties at the school, these languages would soon play key roles in Japanese expertise over the regions that its armies either invaded or planned to invade in the Dutch East Indies, Malaya, Burma, and India, not to mention Manchuria. Even Mongolian became strategically significant through the Buryat peoples who inhabited the Siberian borderlands between Russia and China: in 1918 their "Pan-Mongol" bid for independence had attracted a Japanese investigative mission.[117] For while the initial impetus behind the language school had been to create a new diplomatic and commercial cadre as part of the liberal reforms of the Meiji era, by the time Fazli was employed there, the school was deeply embedded in the imperial expansion that Tagore had loudly denounced during his final lecture tours of Japan.

As for Fazli's fellow foreign teachers at the school, they appear to have been like himself: educated men from the far sides of Asia and Europe who, through a blend of ideology and want of better opportunities, found themselves working there. One such figure was his Malay friend, 'Abd al-Ghani. Another was a Belgian socialist who taught Dutch and French, which were useful intermediary languages given Japanese ambitions over French Indochina and the Dutch East Indies. The Belgian regaled Fazli with tales of adventure on the Trans-Siberian Railway, as well as extempore music performances, advice on exchanging Russian rubles for yen, and Marxist comparisons of the oppressed status of his native Flemish in Belgium with that of the vernacular languages of colonial India.[118]

Yet Fazli's account of the school vividly reflects the asymmetry of Indian and Japanese intercultural understanding. He was quite aware of the potential applications of the language skills he was teaching: he noted how students were expected to practice military drills along with their verb tables.[119] Yet even had he been able to speak Japanese, he was expressly forbidden to do so at the school by the terms of his employment, which restricted his ability to learn the language of his students and colleagues in exchange for teaching his own. As he explained in his book, foreign teachers at the school were not allowed to speak to their students in Japanese; they could speak only in the language of instruction, or else in English.[120]

This highly formalized system of language instruction offered a marked contrast with attempts to teach Japanese in colonial India, first at Shantiniketan and then at Calcutta University, which had begun when Tagore hired Sano Jinnosuke in 1905. But after Sano had quit his teaching post a year later to become a military adviser, the next quarter century witnessed by contrast a series of Indian teachers employed at the Tokyo School. The school not only was importing teaching staff from India, but, in an institutional response to the opportunities of the public sphere, also was busily acquiring books in Indian languages. As Fazli explained, the school housed an impressive library that held a hundred thousand books in fifteen different languages.[121] Browsing through its shelves, he estimated there were two thousand books in Urdu alone, including works by such leading literary figures as Shibli Nu'mani, Hali, Azad, Nazir Ahmad, Sarshar, Prem Chand, and Sharar, as well as a smaller collection of books in Bengali and Hindi.[122]

The collection had greatly expanded over the previous decade, before which the library had housed only a handful of Urdu books, which were massively supplemented through the efforts of Fazli's supervisor, Gamo Reïichi.[123] Part of the new generation of university-based scholars, Professor Gamo had made several extended visits to India. Besides being able to speak Urdu (which he used to communicate with Fazli), he was able to write the language sufficiently well to publish in Indian journals. As Japanese interest in India gathered pace—and with it, linguistic capacity building—two years after Fazli returned to Delhi, the first Japanese grammar of Urdu was published as Nomura Saichiro's *Shotoindogo Kenkyu* (*Elementary Guide to the Indian Language*).[124] Replacing the previous need to rely on an English dictionary of Urdu, Japan had linguistically liberated itself from vicarious dependance on European materials for interpreting Muslim India.[125]

This is amplified by Fazli's account of Tokyo's other libraries, especially what he called its Oriental Library, a reference to the Toyo Bunko founded in 1924. In addition to thousands of Western books, he explained that it contained thousands of Eastern manuscripts, particularly in its Chinese section, which he was unable to even begin to decipher.[126] It was only on a subsequent visit that he was relieved to find a hall on the fifth floor filled with Indian, Iranian, Egyptian, and Turkish books, the products of Asia's Indic and Islamic regions with which he clearly felt more comfortable.[127]

To what extent Fazli himself learned Japanese is difficult to ascertain, but the overall impression of his book is that he had limited social opportunities to do so. Aside from being expressly forbidden to speak Japanese with his students, who represented his most regular contact with Japanese people, Fazli's testimony presents his patching together information gleaned from Malay, Tatar, Indian, and British acquaintances rather than through conversations with Japanese themselves. Only very occasionally was a specific Japanese person mentioned, usually his supervisor, Professor Gamo, who recurs in Fazli's book as his principal Japanese interlocutor, with whom he in any case spoke Urdu. (Gamo also knew Persian and in 1941 published a book on the history and culture of Iran, followed in the decades after World War II by the first complete Japanese translation of Rumi's medieval poetic *Masnawi*.) Nor were there any lexicographical resources in Indian languages to help Fazli learn Japanese. Despite Masood's attempts a few years earlier, there did not even exist an Urdu-Japanese dictionary, so Fazli had to rely on English works to provide the seven-page Japanese word list at the end of his book.[128]

Comprising around 150 words, the list included the basic terms for numbers, time, transport, food, and greetings, along with miscellaneous words relating mainly to accommodation. This was certainly a more limited vocabulary than Dinshaw Vaniya's *Japanis Sikshaka* (*Japanese Teacher*), from 1905, but that was written in the Gujarati script that Fazli and countless other Indians were unable to read. Faced with India's internal language barriers, Fazli at least provided more linguistic data than had been transmitted in previous Urdu accounts of Japan, such as Farrukhi's 1896 *Ma'sir-i Hamidi*, which transcribed only a few basic words such as *kumbichwa* (i.e., *konnichiwa*, good day).[129] Nonetheless, Fazli's word list remained a limited traveler's lexicon, perhaps drawn from the *Handbook for Travelers to Japan* cited in his bibliography, whose author, Basil Chamberlain, was a professor of Japanese at Tokyo Imperial University and had previously published *A Handbook of Colloquial Japanese*.[130] Fazli certainly made no use of the Japanese script, instead presenting Japanese words in English transcriptions that were in turn transcribed and then translated into Arabic-script Urdu. As a tool for enabling readers to make further investigations, it was confined to such simple requests as directions to the port and the post office, a hotel room, and milk (an equally Indian and British request).

Despite his fifteen-month residence, when he came to write his second-volume survey of Japanese history, culture, and society, Fazli ultimately had to fall back on sources in English. The evidence lies again in his bibliography, in which he transcribed and translated into Urdu the names of the books he had consulted. As already noted, of around fifty works cited, all but two—Masood's Urdu educational study and the English version of Tagore's *Spirit of Japan*—were either European accounts of Japan or English translations of Japanese works.[131] Most frequently cited was the romanticizing Greek-Irish storyteller Lafcadio Hearn, while the handful of translated Japanese texts included the likes of Fujimoto Taize's *Nightside of Japan,* which provided tourist tips about theaters, geisha performances, and festivals.[132] Confined to expatriate circles, such were the limits of Fazli's exposure to local society that to move beyond street-level observations he was forced to rely on Inouye Jukichi's *Home Life in Tokyo*, written in English to give foreigners "a concise account of the life we lead."[133] If in terms of inter-Asian connection this was a step beyond European books, then as a means of entry to a domestic realm that remained closed to him, it remained mediation in another guise. Yet the final outcome was nonetheless that Fazli had written the most detailed depiction of Japan not only in Urdu, but perhaps in any Middle Eastern language too.

Patterns of Linguistic Succession

In March 1932, six months after the invasion of Manchuria and after fifteen months working for the Tokyo School of Foreign Languages, Fazli sailed to Calcutta aboard the Japanese steamer *Arizona Maru*.[134] The reasons behind his departure remain unclear: perhaps because of his dinners at the British embassy he was suspected of being a spy for the British, just as it seems British officials were keeping an eye on him themselves. Or perhaps his was a short-term contract like those of his immediate predecessors. Be that as it may, between India and Japan, Fazli had found himself caught between two empires as he tried to gather sufficient information to tell his countrymen the "truth about Japan" he promised in the title of his book.

The Tokyo School of Foreign Languages had little difficulty in finding a replacement. Within months of his departure, his post was taken up by a successor, Nur al-Hasan Barlas, who like Fazli was a graduate of Aligarh Muslim University and was similarly contracted to teach both Urdu and Persian.[135] Barlas stayed longer than Fazli, building ties that would see him remain through the Second World War, when the school and its teachers became key assets for the Japanese conquest of Asia. In the meantime, in 1936, Barlas compiled submissions from Tokyo for a special edition of the Delhi-based literary journal *Saqi* (*Wine Bearer*) devoted to Japan. The contributors he commissioned reflected the social circles in which Fazli had also moved. One set comprised Indian expatriate merchants and their wives, who wrote essays on matters either of commerce or of local color: Barlas called on his wife to write "Kasatusu ke Garm Chashme" ("The Hot Springs of Kusatsu"), about her visit to the famous spa town, and Hanifa Rashid Fatehali, the spouse of one of Kobe's leading Indian traders, penned a short biographical memoir, "Japan Tis Baras mein" ("Thirty Years in Japan").[136]

The other set of contributors were all Japanese. They wrote short, picturesque pieces on cherry blossoms and famous temples, along with a one-page summary of the tenth-century *Taketori Monogatari* (*Tale of the Bamboo Cutter*) and a report on contemporary student life.[137] All four contributors were from the School of Foreign Languages, two being Barlas's students, named only as Nakamura and Sato, and two his senior colleagues, Professor Sawa and Professor Gamo. Though Sawa Eizu would soon take up a position teaching Urdu at the Osaka University of Foreign Studies, Gamo Reïichi was the main Japanese informant mentioned in Fazli's book, who by the time his article appeared in *Saqi* had set off on a two-year learning tour of India and Iran funded by the Japanese Ministry of Education.[138] Barlas explained in his introduction that all four contributions had been written directly in Urdu since, as students and professors of the language, their authors could "write Urdu very correctly."[139] Supported by an expanding imperial state, Japanese Indology had clearly developed further than Indian Japanology.

This left one Japanese contributor, who wrote two short poems and an account of a journey to India.[140] This was Noguchi Yonejiro, the famous poet, journalist, and literary critic who had long corresponded with Tagore and had, a year earlier, been sent to India on an official mission to win support for Japan's invasion of China.[141] Since the California-educated Noguchi was a professor of English literature at Tokyo's Keio University, had written dozens of books and poetry anthologies in English, and used the language for his exchanges with Tagore and other Anglophone Indian intellectuals, he probably wrote his article and poem for *Saqi* in English, which were then translated by the Delhi-based literary critic Zafar Qureshi. Once again, the Indian understanding of Japan was mediated through shared knowledge of the English language, which was itself becoming an Asian lingua franca.

Writing from back home in India, Fazli also contributed an article to the *Saqi* special issue, in which he recounted how Europeans had come to dominate Japanese trade in the early Meiji period. If this was not quite trade leading to intercultural knowledge, then it was a sign of their critical entanglement.

But despite taking a job as a teacher (and then principal) at a Muslim high school, Fazli maintained his Japanese interests. In the same year that the special issue of *Saqi* appeared, he made use of a new imported communication technology to disseminate his understanding of Japan through a series of Urdu lectures on state-sponsored All India Radio.[142] Then he turned to literature, writing a collection of short stories called *Anokhe Afsane* (*Strange Tales*).[143] Meanwhile, in Tokyo, his successor, Barlas, compiled an Urdu anthology of Japanese children's songs for the same publisher that Masood and Fazli had used, echoing the recent fashion for Japan-themed children's stories in Bengali.[144] If the anthology was an inconsequential work by comparison to the nearly four hundred detailed pages of Fazli's *Haqiqat-i Japan*, then it was apparently an improvement in one major measure: in being translated directly from Japanese.

When the Empire of Japan declared war on the British Empire in December 1941, nearly four decades of Indian Japanophilia found a new outlet in the anticolonial Indian National Army to fight British and loyal Indian soldiers in Malaya and Burma. (Many other courageous Indian soldiers gave their lives fighting Japan before finally defeating the Imperial Japanese Army at Kohima and Imphal in 1944.) The Tokyo School of Foreign Languages also played its part in the war effort, not least because Urdu was the military lingua franca of the Indian soldiers being fought and captured, as well as in some cases recruited for the pro-Japanese Indian National Army (or *Azad Hind Fauj*, Free Indian Army, as it was known in Urdu). Thus, in 1942 Professor Sawa published an Urdu grammar printed with a specially acquired font; the following year, Professor Takahashi, also of the Tokyo School, published another; and shortly afterward Barlas and Fazli's shared supervisor, Professor Gamo, published a third guide to the language.[145] Finally, in 1944 Barlas published a manual of spoken Urdu, *Kani nichi-in kaiwa* (*Easy Japanese to Indian Conversation*).[146] Just as the defeat of Russia had inspired the earliest wave of Urdu studies of Japan, now in turn another war spurred Japan's peak engagement with Urdu as part of the plan to conquer India.[147] Ironically, those military engagements, and the nationalisms that drove them, would bring an end to the imperial connections that had enabled the Indian encounter with Japan.

Back in 1905, the Muslim discovery of Japan began as a scheme of protecting the self by learning empowering lessons from the defeat of Russia. Then, through gradually deepening engagements, Muslim missionaries made self-projecting bids to call the Japanese to Islam. But by the mid-1930s, as Fazli tried to discern what in the title of his book he dubbed "the truth about Japan," these developments had matured into a fuller appreciation of the East Asian other. And so, in contrast to many of the inter-Asian interactions we have seen around the Bay of Bengal, those between India and Japan were far more approving than polemical. Yet such positive dispositions were no guarantee of understanding, which required more than ideology to overcome barriers of language and culture fostered by geographical distance and the separation of centuries.

As the infrastructures of empire, both European and Japanese, placed Yokohama and Kobe in closer reach of their counterparts in the Middle East and India, Fazli's book constituted the informational high-water mark of the many studies of Japan written by Muslims in different languages. Yet for all its abundant detail, aside from the observation of the visible public life of cities and their inhabitants, his *Haqiqat-i Japan* substantially relied on indirect sources of information as Fazli was forced to fall back on third-party Indian, British, or even Tatar impressions of Japan rather than drawing on conversations or readings in Japanese. Even his experience of Japanese society occurred largely within the expatriate circles in which he socialized with other—often Muslim—foreigners. While admiring Japan's achievements, he remained socially distant from its people: his travelogue provides almost no record of encounters with specific Japanese other than his supervisor, Professor Gamo.

To interpret and contextualize his experiences, Fazli had to resort to the much larger body of English writings on Japan that far outweighed what was by the 1930s still only a shelf-full of Urdu books on the country, most written in the wake of the Russo-Japanese War. This was no less characteristic of other Indian and Middle Eastern depictions of Japan, many of whose compilers had never even set foot there and relied even more on secondhand sources. In 1934, the year that Fazli's book was published in Delhi, the elderly Rabindranath Tagore was reviving his attempts to have Japanese taught at his Visva-Bharati University through plans to establish a *Japani Bhavana* (Japanese Institute).[148] But his dream would not be realized for another twenty years, when the age of empires was all but over.[149]

The constraints faced by the likes of Fazli were in part the intellectual consequences of colonization, which prevented Indians from developing two of the four major means of intercultural learning. First, unlike students in London, with its School of Oriental Studies, and Tokyo, with its School of Foreign Languages, Indian students of other Asian cultures had fewer educational options than the ruling cadres of Britain, Japan, and other imperial powers. Calcutta certainly had the Asiatic Society of Bengal, in which Indians played an increasingly central role after the scholar of Sanskritic Buddhism Rajendralal Mitra became its first Indian president in 1885. Among the several subsequent Indian presidents was the other pioneering Bengali Buddhologist, Haraprasad Sastri. Nonetheless, the Asiatic Society remained primarily focused on India; its Indian presidents were generally scientists by the 1920s, and its publications in English. Despite the Japanological efforts of Tagore, his Visva-Bharati University had been unable to sustain its short-lived program of teaching Japanese, which left only Kimura Shozaburo's classes at Calcutta University.

Second, colonialism largely robbed Indians of the diplomatic careers that formed alternative outlets for the immersive knowledge of Japan and other regions that European diplomats subsequently distilled into many publications about the countries where they had served. This was not wholly the case, though, since India's princely states sponsored many missions to Japan that, while not being formal exchanges between fully sovereign states, did provide their Indian entourages with logistical and financial means to improve their understanding of Japan. Masood's educational mission on behalf of Hyderabad is an example. Nonetheless, this was not comparable to the earlier Ottoman engagement with Japan, which we saw in the previous chapter enabling Colonel Pertev Demırhan to accompany the Japanese forces as an observer during their war with Russia. In 1937 this bore further informational fruit when Demırhan (promoted to the rank of general) published *Japonlarin Asil Kuvveti: Japonlar Niçin ve Nasil Yükseldi? (The Sources of Japanese Strength: Why and How Did Japan Rise?)*, a shorter paperback counterpart to Fazli's investigation that turned to recent history to answer its titular question.[150]

The third major means for the development of European Japanology in this period, however, was open to Indians, namely, to serve as newspaper reporters or teachers in Japan's expanding college and university system. By the 1930s such careers had led to many formative publications on Japan in European languages, including the highly influential writings of the Greek-Irish author Lafcadio Hearn, who taught in Matsue, Tokyo, and Kumamoto. Fazli was one of a series of Indians who taught in Japan, but he was a rarity in writing a book about the country.

The fourth means of understanding Japan—through expatriate networks—was also open to Indians, for as early as the 1870s, Muslim, Hindu, and Parsi merchants were residents of port cities such as Kobe and Yokohama. Fazli and Masood both interacted with such merchants, even though merchants seem not to have written books about the country themselves. While colonialism certainly constrained the development of a direct, linguistically informed understanding of Japan, it didn't therefore render it impossible. Moreover, for all their shared fascination with the secrets of Japan's success, independent states such as Iran, Afghanistan, and the Ottoman Empire founded no counterparts to Tokyo's School of Foreign Languages to promote their comprehension of Asia at large.

In the absence of such institutional means of developing inter-Asian understanding, the Japanophilia that rippled across the continent after the sinking of the Russian fleet was not in itself a sufficient cause for the emergence of an independent Japanology. Asianist ideological commitment could not compensate for informational and linguistic shortfalls, because knowledge of Japan faced the same kinds of constraints that characterized other attempts to transfer intercultural understanding across such heterogenous regions of a notionally unitary continent. Even if Indian and Middle Eastern depictions of Japanese life were far more numerous (and positive) than studies of the Buddhist cultures of Southeast Asia, the Japanophiles faced similar informational obstacles—of language and script especially—that limited the scope for direct and deep engagements with the partners in Eastern civilization they so admired.

Lacking local language sources and indigenous informants, Fazli's *Haqiqat* exemplified a constrained mode of cross-cultural comprehension that depended on informational outsourcing, personal observations, and the abstract category of "civilization" to hold an Eastern mirror to his homeland. For as much as the *Haqiqat* emerged from an engagement with the Japanese other, it echoed the concerns with the self that shaped other Indian interactions with Japan as a source of lessons on self-empowerment.

Yet like its Middle Eastern counterpart, this Indo-Japanese dialogue—or "trialogue" that included Europe—did disseminate new knowledge to the wide readerships of the public sphere. For Fazli's reliance on European sources to leverage his own observations should perhaps not matter: the search for direct and discrete inter-Asian communication, "untainted" by European input, is after all a legacy of the Asianist and nationalist concerns of the period. Rather than indulge in a policy of interpretive nationalism by drawing solely on the limited data set of earlier Urdu sources, Fazli opted for a strategy of informational outsourcing and interpretive leverage that combined his own eyewitness evidence with data and explanation drawn from English works. In this sense, he used English as what linguists call a "pivot language," a widely used intermediary between languages (here Japanese and Urdu) for which there are few bilingual readers. A couple of his English sources were poorly chosen, but for the most part he selected books by authors with university affiliations like himself, then used his own critical judgment—and experience of the country—as a filtering check on grosser Orientalist misrepresentations. If this was far from a paragon of inter-Asian comprehension, then it was a practical response to the constraints he had to contend with.

In 1937, two years after Barlas and Fazli wrote essays for the literary journal *Saqi*, a series on Japanese poetry appeared in the Afghan journal *Ayina-yi 'Irfan (Mirror of Wisdom)*.[151] Like those in *Saqi*, the Afghan articles suited Japan's self-projecting policies that saw the arrival of their first ambassador to Kabul as part of an attempt to surround China.[152] Nonetheless, just as Afghan newspapers drew their reports on Japan from Russian sources, the essays on poetry were translated from English, leaving readers in Kabul to make what they could of comparisons of classical Japanese poets to Wordsworth and Keats rather than Rumi and Hafiz.[153]

However political the motivations, and however vicarious the sources, the essays still marked a significant step in intercultural understanding, lending Afghan poetry lovers their first glimpse of the great *Man'yoshu*, the *Collection of Ten Thousand Leaves*, compiled a thousand years earlier in Nara. A few months later, a similar article appeared in a Persian journal in Iran.[154] After a millennium of separate development, two of Asia's great literary traditions were finally aware of each other, albeit through European mediation. This was both the cost and benefit of the printed public sphere that Europe's empires first fostered for their own self-projections, but which in time provided the means for inter-Asian appreciations.

As for Fazli, he never lost his interest in Japan, or his belief that his own countrymen could learn from its "progress," at least in the arts if not in war. In 1946—the year between the disastrous collapse of the Japanese Empire and the calamitous conclusion to British rule in India—he published an Urdu translation of a book called *Nami-ko*, to which he added an explanatory subtitle: "Japan's most famous novel."[155] His preface made no mention of whether he had somehow mastered Japanese since leaving Tokyo, or instead made use of the successful English version by Shioya Sakae and Edwin Edgett.[156] Perhaps he thought the matter too pedantic to discuss; in either case, Indian readers could now access what he praised as the compelling prose and social criticism of Tokutomi Kenjiro (1868–1927). Aptly, it was a tale born of Tokutomi's own journey between cultures as a convert to Christianity. And so, as his heroine Nami lies dying as the novel approaches its climax, she is comforted by a kind old woman who recounts how a missionary once gave her a translated Gospel of Matthew. Then she hands Nami a Bible, which thereafter she kept by her bedside. Like the closing clue of a convoluted story, it points to the lingering role of the missionaries in linking Asia and Europe through books.

5 • Interpreting China across Maritime Asia

In 1806, within months of completing their Bengali version of the Bible, the committed little company of Baptist missionaries at Serampore, a few miles upriver from Calcutta, turned their attention toward China. By recruiting Johannes Lassar, an Armenian Christian who was raised in Macao, the missionary Joshua Marshman began his studies of literary Chinese that over the next two decades reaped several published harvests.[1] In 1809 he issued a flawed translation of the *Analects* of Confucius, followed five years later by a grammar of spoken and written Chinese, to which he appended a further rendition of the *Daxue* (*Great Learning*), one of the traditional Four Books of Confucianism.[2] Building on these investigations, a complete Chinese translation of the Christian scripture was published in 1823. For like the other missionary projects in Bengal, Bible translation was accompanied by endeavors to understand the religious systems the evangelicals were attempting to engage and overthrow, whether by identifying traditions of ethics on which to build or by discerning superstitions to critique.

Like Marshman's grammar and Confucian translations, the Chinese Bible was published by the Baptist Mission Press on the outskirts of Calcutta, fueling the invention of a rapidly improved series of fonts for printable Chinese characters. The first were cut from tamarind wood before early Chinese metal types were cast on the same foundry used to produce the many Arabic and Indic lettersets used for other translations.[3] And so, whether through the creation of language guides, the translation of essential texts, or the reinvention of Chinese printing in a manner suited to the European technologies that were spreading east from Bengal, Christian proselytizers made Calcutta a key site not only for producing knowledge about China, but for tying that distant land to the new maritime public sphere. When the famous missionary Robert Morrison (1782–1834) completed his *Grammar of the Chinese Language* in 1815, he shipped it from Macao to Calcutta for printing; and, when his monumental dictionary was published in three parts over the next eight years, the heavy financial burden of casting so many Chinese characters was funded by a £15,000 subvention from the East India Company.[4]

Calcutta had been increasingly trading with Qing imperial China since the middle of the eighteenth century, seeing a growing traffic of merchant vessels and handwritten reports by East India Company officials. But it was the missionaries who placed far more information on China into the public sphere in a manner that prompted responses from Chinese and Indian authors alike. For just as print technology was taken up by local actors in India, Ceylon, and Burma, in China a new generation of cultural entrepreneurs adopted the letterpress and then lithographic techniques the missionaries introduced through the treaty ports of Macao, Ningbo, Shanghai, and Guangzhou (formerly Canton).[5] As Shanghai, like Colombo and Rangoon beforehand, became the center of China's second print revolution, a new cohort of Buddhist publishers exported books and journals to coreligionists elsewhere.[6] It was also in Shanghai that in 1931 a pioneering Chinese translation of the Quran was published. Its sponsor was Silas Aaron Hardoon (1851–1931), an Iraqi Jew who grew up in Bombay before following many Indian merchants to make his fortune in Britain's coastal slice of China.[7] Through steam and print, commerce and conquest, the infrastructures of European empire conjoined the far reaches of Asia. Amid the competing self-projections that followed, both Asian and European intercultural understanding faced many a challenge.

Hardoon's Quran was embroiled in polemics that resounded from Istanbul to Shanghai, as ripples of response to the cycle of translations set in motion by the Christian missionaries washed up on the shores of China.[8] Yet during the century or so that separated Marshman's Chinese Bible from Hardoon's Chinese Quran and their attendant controversies, there also emerged an informational middle path. This consisted of Middle Eastern and Indian attempts to understand the history, culture, and religions of China. Five centuries after the Ming-sponsored sea journeys of Admiral Zheng He (1371–1433), empire, trade, and evangelicalism had reconnected the far regions of a continent whose inhabitants were just learning to think of as "Asia."

So from Marshman's and Hardoon's adopted homes of Calcutta and Bombay, a new corpus of knowledge was published in Bengali, Urdu, Gujarati, and Hindi, as well as Ottoman Turkish. Yet well into the twentieth century, the

Christian projections and Confucianist paradigms that shaped the foundation of European Sinology in colonial Calcutta continued to inform the way China was understood in the Middle East and India. But after numerous fraught attempts to interpret this Confucian history and culture, by the 1920s the discovery of Chinese Buddhism and Islam provided an East Asian mirror through which Indians and Arabs could project the self while appreciating the other.

A Maritime Sinological Geography

While the cultural encounter of the Middle East, India, and China is usually conceived through the model of the Silk Road, the geography that generated the modern Indian and Middle Eastern understanding of China was a distinctly maritime one, based in Calcutta, Bombay, and Istanbul, and from there branching out to inland cities such as Lucknow, Kabul, and Tehran. The Silk Road mirage of continuity with medieval interactions is woefully misleading. When books on China began to be published in Indian and Middle Eastern languages in the mid-nineteenth century, they constituted what was effectively a rediscovery of China in which the informational legacy of previous eras played little to no part. Even as traditional trade caravans continued to cross the Himalayan barriers between the Qing and British empires, they were no match for the scale of interaction—and information—between such port cities as Guangzhou and Calcutta.

Ironically, the alluring idea of a Silk Road was itself one of the intellectual products of the maritime opening of China by the European powers.[9] For as we saw earlier, the term was invented in 1877 by the German geologist Ferdinand von Richthofen, who was employed by the Qing imperial government to prospect potential routes, and coal deposits, for a railway inland from the coast. As the semantic offspring of the railroad, the Silk Road was itself a product of the infrastructures of empire. And so, to understand the ways in which China was both encountered and understood by the Indian and Middle Eastern authors who wrote in the decades on either side of Richthofen's railway mission, we will need to set aside the idea of the Silk Road, which was not taken up by Asian writers till much later.

Not only does the notion of the Silk Road divert attention from the maritime routes of Asia's modern self-discovery, but its idyll of easy connection also conceals the challenges of inter-Asian understanding. And China presented even greater intellectual obstacles than other regions of the continent. These obstacles were not only linguistic and orthographic, of language and script; they were also conceptual and theological: China's Confucian and Daoist traditions had no historical ties or conceptual commonalities with Indian or Middle Eastern cultures. This Confucian-Daoist impasse would encourage many interpreters of China from other regions of Asia to look at China through the more familiar lenses of Buddhism or Islam. In addition to the struggle to find terms to translate classical Chinese concepts—or even a recognizably standardized way to refer to religions or spell the names of such figures as Confucius—the sheer antiquity of China's past presented problems of a calendrical kind. With its different dating system, China forced numerous investigators to reckon with comparative chronologies to align the Chinese past with the histories of ancient India, the Muslim Middle East, and Christian Europe.

Turning to each of these challenges and the varied attempts to overcome them, in the following sections we will survey a wide range of works on China written in Indian and Middle Eastern languages between the 1840s and early 1900s. First, though, we will look at the imperial infrastructures and port city contacts through which this fraught new inter-Asian knowledge took shape—connections that also framed the first modern Chinese accounts of India.

Sino-Indian Imperial Connections

By the time the maritime public sphere began to emerge in the first half of the nineteenth century, the East India Company's involvement with China—and Indian merchant participation in it—was already over a century old. Drawn by the fashionable demand for tea in Europe, the company gained access to Guangzhou as early as 1713. By the early nineteenth century, it was financing the tea trade by exporting Indian opium to China, despite its sale, consumption, and then import being repeatedly banned by the Qing authorities.[10] Relentless attempts to maintain the illegal trade led to the two Opium Wars (1839–1842 and 1856–1860); China's defeats enabled the expansion of British and then other European trading privileges after the 1842 Treaty of Nanking and the 1858 Treaty of Tientsin legitimized the opium trade, ceded control of Hong Kong, and opened a series of "treaty ports" to foreign trade.

Although the East India Company generated enormous profits, it didn't engage directly in the China-India trade, instead gaining revenues by monopolizing the production of opium and imposing tariffs on private merchants.[11] These included not only British traders, but also India's Parsi, Armenian,

Jewish, and Bohra and Khoja Muslim merchants, who operated in varying degrees of competition and partnership with their European counterparts.[12] Although the British government ended the company's monopoly over the China trade in 1834, and the company was itself disbanded in 1858, Calcutta and Bombay remained central to the China trade, which enabled Indian as well as British merchants to make vast fortunes, not least through sending their own agents to Guangzhou and Hong Kong.[13]

Understandably, the opium wars prompted attempts by Chinese officials to learn about Britain and its Indian sources of opium (and soldiers). Two early Chinese accounts of British India were written in the wake of the Treaty of Nanking in *Haiguo tuzhi* (*Illustrated Records of Maritime Polities*) by Wei Yuan (1794–1857) and *Yinghuan zhilüe* (*Short Account of the Maritime Sphere*) by Xu Jiyu (1795–1873), which attempted to gather information in China itself about the East India Company's territories in India.[14] Building on and citing these works, official Qing missions were subsequently dispatched to Calcutta, particularly those of Huang Maocai in 1879 and Ma Jianzhong two years later, who both wrote eyewitness descriptions of British India.[15] Huang's mission was deliberately geared toward data gathering along a maritime itinerary that included Rangoon, Calcutta, and Bombay, in addition to the tea plantations of northeastern India he accessed via the railway that featured prominently in the several accounts of India he later wrote.[16] A member of the state literati educated in the Chinese classics, Huang was well aware of the account of India penned by the Buddhist pilgrim Xuanzang in the seventh century, which lent Huang's own books a certain nostalgia for an earlier era of Sino-Indian connections.[17] Meanwhile, Ma Jianzhong, a Chinese Catholic educated in Paris, sailed to Calcutta and Bombay as part of a delegation sent to negotiate the opium trade. Though Ma described the urban infrastructure of the ports in positive terms, he helped forge a negative perception of India as a "failed state" whose people had been unable to defend themselves against their British colonizers.[18] Thenceforth, if Indians would look to Japan for self-empowering lessons in success, Chinese intellectuals turned to India for self-protecting lessons in failure.

Nonetheless, when it came to moving beyond economic and political matters to fathoming India's more complex cultural fabric, the first generations of Chinese investigators faced far greater challenges that we will see echoed by their Indian contemporaries. Explaining the composition of the colonial Indian Army, for example, Huang claimed that half of its soldiers were Muslims and half were Buddhists (rather than the Hindus, for whose religion he lacked a name).[19] Similarly, when the subsequent diplomat Zhang Deyi (1847–1918) described the Parsi traders he encountered in Guangzhou in the 1870s, he explained that their religion was called "Zououlasitalan" (Zorastrianism) and was based—a plain error—on "the worship of the Sun, Moon, and the five planets."[20] Yet this was an understandable mistake because although Parsi merchants had been active in Guangzhou for over a century, such commercial connections had not yet evolved into an accessible written corpus of inter-cultural knowledge that curious locals like Zhang could read.

A similar state of affairs confronted the influential intellectual Kang Youwei (1858–1927) three decades later, during his two extended visits to India.[21] Having spent much of his adult life in Shanghai, in 1901 Kang boarded a steamship bound for Calcutta, before making a second visit to India eight years later via Madras and Bombay. Like the Japanese who also sailed there, Kang saw India in the mirror of his own Buddhist beliefs, visiting ancient sites such as the Maha-Bodhi temple at Bodhgaya, recently restored by the archaeologist Alexander Cunningham.[22] But the ability to visit India could not automatically overcome the lack of reliable information in Chinese. As Kang complained, "There is no Chinese account of Indian culture, religion, languages, architecture, and craftsmanship. Huang Maocai [the official who visited Calcutta in 1879] has made commendable efforts to examine the geography of Tibet and Yunnan, but has written nothing about Indian culture."[23]

Kang was consequently forced to rely on the politically oriented *Haiguo tuzhi* (*Illustrated Records of Maritime Polities*), compiled largely from European sources by the diplomat Wei Yuan in 1843.[24] But this was a general survey of Europe, Africa, and America, not only of India. Although *Haiguo tuzhi* was itself based on the geography textbooks that Christian missionaries had by then printed in China as well as India, Kang's search for more detailed knowledge led him to read other Christian accounts in turn, including a Chinese translation of a book on India by the Welsh Baptist missionary Timothy Richard (1845–1919).[25] Whether through his own direct experiences or the vicarious prejudices of Christian authors who elevated their Christ-like Buddha over the caste system of the Hindus that Kang likewise abhorred, in his own writings Kang similarly exalted a bygone Buddhism over India's living Hindu culture. Ultimately, the India that Kang admired was a substantially imagined place he conceived as the pure font of the Buddhism he placed with Confucianism and Taoism at the top of his hierarchy of Asian religions. If Kang's engagement with India was more a projection of the Chinese Buddhist self than an appreciation of the Indian Hindu and Muslim other, then the informational challenges he faced were not uniquely Chinese problems. For a corresponding series of interpretive obstacles confronted Indian investigators of China.

Lacking the educational and literary continuity that allowed a Chinese civil servant like Huang Maocai to have read the account of India written by Xuanzang some twelve centuries earlier, it was far more difficult for Indian (let alone Middle Eastern) authors to access, or even know of, ancient manuscripts in Chinese and Sanskrit that attested to that earlier period of Buddhist-based connections. The rediscovery of that distant era of Sino-Indian interactions took place only gradually, not gathering pace till the 1920s. Before then, China had to be effectively discovered anew in India through the tortuous, fortuitous, and sometimes misleading informational routes of the maritime public sphere.

China in Indian Ink

The earliest published accounts of China in Indian languages were inadvertent, appearing as sections of the geography textbooks translated by missionaries and their Indian colleagues and printed in Calcutta for the first colonial schools. From the 1830s, these included such primers as Clift's *First Geography*, which appeared in Bengali, Urdu, Tamil, and perhaps other languages, disseminating what was then still a starkly limited European understanding of China, along with the overarching category of "Asia."[26] Clift's textbook contained short sections devoted to each region of "Asia," which was presented as comprising China, Japan, Arabia, Armenia, and Bengal. (The remainder of India, *Hindustan,* was conceived as a separate entity and received its own chapter.) The translations of Clift also provided maps that showed the relative locations of India and China, along with a couple of pages of basic information on Chinese geography.[27] Though devoted mainly to physical geography, Clift's book offered a few cultural clues, claiming that "the Chinese are mostly Buddha-worshippers, and their prophet is Fu-Hi" (this a reference to the legendary first emperor, Fuxi).[28] If this was a most misleading statement, suggesting that Fuxi was the founder of Buddhism, then it reflected what, at the time Clift wrote his textbook, were then still confused European notions of both Buddhism and China. Still, even as they continued to promote such misunderstandings, translated geographies began to spread the recognition that the "religion of Bodh" was shared across Asia. As an Indian edition of George Duncan's *Jughrafiyya* explained, among the Chinese "the common religion is

Buddha-worship [*bodh-parasti*], just as it is among the Burmese and Siamese, though the Chinese worship Bodh under the name Fu."[29]

By the 1840s, Indian commercial connections with China were fostering demand for more detailed (and reliable) information on the region, particularly relating to trade opportunities. As British and Indian merchants increasingly competed over the lucrative opium trade, an employee of a Parsi firm with a branch in Guangzhou compiled a work in Gujarati to better inform his compatriots. Published in Bombay in 1844, Cowasjee Sorabjee Patell's book began with a preface that explained how European traders enjoyed various commercial advantages as a result of their greater understanding of China. "This book has been completed for the benefit of our countrymen [*deshis*], because our people are heavily involved with this country, and many of our compatriots also derive great profits from it. . . . Nevertheless our people remain largely ignorant of such an important place. . . . Because of their lack of awareness of so many things, they have to endure great obstacles in their profit-making business, while the European people, on account of their greater knowledge [of China], can carry out their own business affairs, while our people fall behind."[30] In seeking to remedy this, Patell's Gujarati survey of China was an intellectual enterprise in community self-interest. Nonetheless, as a result of those British advantages, he had to draw much of his data from Anglophone sources, signaling a three-way Eurasian "trialogue"—between China, India, and Europe—that would be reprised in various later books as well.

Patell was able to rely on his direct observations for the commercial chapters of his book, particularly the section dealing with different types of produce. But since his own experience was limited to port cities of the coast—principally Guangzhou—for information on the unknown interior, and especially on administrative and historical matters, he had to rely on what was already a more powerful imperial information system. For his chapters on geography, government, and other institutions of China, he thus turned to such English texts as Sir John Barrow's *Travels in China*. Based on Barrow's experience as a member of the first British embassy to Beijing in the 1790s, and his subsequent study of the Chinese language, it was a widely respected source, though in having appeared in 1804, it was already outdated by the time Patell drew on it.

So, for more up-to-date information, Patell referred to the *Chinese Repository*, published by Protestant missionaries in Guangzhou, which not only provided news but also explored historical and cultural topics, albeit from a markedly Christian perspective. Through the efforts of Chinese contributors and by way of the missionaries' language studies, the *Repository* was arguably the first Sinological journal, showing that Patell made judicious selections of his sources. For guidance on language, he similarly drew on the *Chinese Chrestomathy in the Canton Dialect* by the *Repository*'s founding editor, the American Elijah Coleman Bridgman (1801–1861). In this way, even ventures in intercultural understanding that derived directly from commercial ties, as Patell's plainly did, had to turn to the missionaries for linguistic, cultural, and historical questions that probed deeper than economic and political affairs.

The result of Patell's astute combination of his own inquiries and those of his more numerous Christian forebears was a massive expansion of the information available to Indian readers—or at least those from western India who read Gujarati. Other Indians would have to wait for books in their own languages, or turn to English texts themselves.

In the meantime, Patell's engagement with Chinese history forced him to confront the puzzle of multiple chronologies and dating systems that European scholars found equally perplexing. Because Patell was a member of Bombay's Parsi Zoroastrian community, which was embroiled in controversies about its own religious calendar, these questions hit closer to home. So it was that, after years of comparative investigations, in 1866 Patell published a groundbreaking book of tables identifying corresponding dates between the Christian, Jewish, Greek, Zoroastrian, Hindu, Muslim, Chinese, and even Japanese calendars.[31] But it was published in London, not in Bombay, and in English rather than Gujarati. Written in dialogue with the British and French Orientalists whose work he cited, it was his princely repaying of his earlier debt to European investigations of China. Patell opened his book with a line from the Latin poet Horace that voiced the practical ethos of this trader-turned-scholar: *Omne tulit punctum qui miscuit utile dulci* (He gains everyone's approval who mixes the pleasant with the useful).[32]

From Calcutta to China with Mr. Corcoran

Four years after Patell's book on China was printed in Bombay, in 1848 the Baptist Mission Press on the outskirts of Calcutta printed the first of two lengthy volumes of a pioneering Urdu work with the title *Tarikh-i Mamalik-i Chin* (*History of the Chinese Empire*).[33] Three decades previously, the same press had issued Marshman's Chinese grammar and the Chinese translation of the Bible he also oversaw. But the author of the *Tarikh* was neither a missionary like Marshman nor a merchant like Patell. He was an official translator for the East India Company's *Sadr Diwani 'Adalat*, the Supreme Court of Revenue established in Calcutta in 1772. He was Irish, which together with his official connections gave him extensive access to the libraries of both the Asiatic Society and the Baptists. His name was James Corcoran, and his history of China was written in an elegant literary Urdu that abounded with the learned phrases in Arabic and Persian he had acquired from his Indian teachers.

Together with Patel's Gujarati book from four years earlier, Corcoran's *Tarikh* marked an extraordinarily ambitious start to the appearance of printed accounts of China in Indian languages. Its two volumes comprised almost twelve hundred pages, albeit in large type. Corcoran's was an expensive book like its Gujarati predecessor (in his preface Patell had apologized to readers for its cost). But in 1864 the *Tarikh*'s wider circulation was assured when the great Hindu publishing impresario Nawwal Kishore issued a second edition, which in being both lithographed and compressed into half as many pages was far cheaper than the original version.[34]

Like Patell's, Corcoran's study was remarkably wide-ranging in its coverage for so early a work. The first volume effectively comprised a gazetteer of China's various provinces and a detailed account of its government, laws, language, religion, and other cultural practices. The second volume took up the history of China, from its quasi-mythological early emperors through to the First Opium War, with additional sections on its tributary states, such as Mongolia, Korea, and Tibet. Setting aside for a moment the issue of reliability, this scope raises the question about where Corcoran derived his information.

Of this Corcoran made no secret, explaining in his introduction that in the absence of detailed sources in Arabic and Persian, he had drawn on—and tried to critically compare—some twenty-five European works on China.[35] He accessed these books in Calcutta, but this was more than narrowly "colonial" knowledge. Ten of his sources were French, such as Jean-Baptiste Grosier's *Description générale de la Chine*, first published in 1788, along with works of medieval and even universal history such as Antoine Gaubil's *Histoire de Gentchiscan et de toute la dinastie Mongous*, published in 1739, and Voltaire's *Essai sur l'histoire générale* (1756).[36] Other sources were written by missionaries, such as the Italian Jesuit Martino Martini (1614–1661) and the German Lutheran Karl Friedrich Gützlaff (1803–1851), as well as representatives of the London Missionary Society, such as Walter Henry Medhurst (1796–1857), who had pioneered Malay printing in Malacca before turning toward China, and Calcutta's own Joshua Marshman, whose grammatical *Clavis Sinica* provided

Corcoran with his ideas about the Chinese language.[37] A particularly important source, especially for Corcoran's account of China's early dynasties, was the *Shujing* (*Classic of History*), which had recently been translated into English by Medhurst.[38] But other sources were of indubitably colonial provenance, such as the account of the Macartney embassy of 1793 written by the company grandee Sir George Leonard Staunton and the report on the First Opium War by Lieutenant John Ouchterlony of the Madras Army.[39] As for his information on Chinese religion, Corcoran relied in large part on the writings of Brian Houghton Hodgson, the East India Company's official investigating Buddhism while stationed in Kathmandu rather than China.

As these sources show, by the time Corcoran published his own work in 1848 and 1852, he was relying on investigations undertaken up to two centuries earlier. Aside from Lieutenant Ouchterlony's report on the war that ended in 1842, his most recent informants were the missionaries Gützlaff and Medhurst, who were based on the coast in Ningbo and Hong Kong. Since neither Europeans nor their Indian partners were allowed access to the interior of China until after the Second Opium War (which took place a decade after Corcoran's book was published), Corcoran's account of inland regions relied largely on the Macartney embassy, which had reached Beijing in 1793, and on Grosier's *Description générale*, which was based on an even earlier French embassy staffed largely by Jesuit priests.

From its foundational moment, then, the understanding of China that entered India's public sphere drew on a European engagement with China that already stretched back several centuries to the first Jesuit missions and that had since then produced a cumulative and published—if variously problematic—data set. European investigations were riddled with misapprehensions and presumptions, not least the "Confucian-centric" paradigm formed by early Jesuit writers such as Matteo Ricci and passed down to European academic Sinologists well into the twentieth century. More than a mere compilation of facts (and errors), Corcoran's Urdu text was a compilation of interpretations he attempted not only to render into some kind of intellectual coherence, but also to explain in terms and idioms that were comprehensible to his Indian readership. Even setting aside the problem of sources, the larger difficulty Corcoran (and, it is likely, his Indian assistant) faced was how to translate this information into Urdu. In the absence of an existing Sinological vocabulary in Urdu, or anything even approaching it, Cororan fell back on Mughal imperial terminology and Islamicate concepts that combined with his colonial sources to reflect China in a kind of Indo-European mirror.

China in the Indian public sphere: mass-market edition of Corcoran's history of China. [James Corcoran], *Tarikh-i Mamalik-i Chin* (Lucknow: Nawwal Kishore, 1864). Photograph by Nile Green.

By way of the emperor of China, the central personage of his text was thus called the *faghfur-i Khata,* "the Faghfur of Cathay," a label that stretched back to romantic depictions of the "fabulous east" in the tenth-century *Shahnama* of Firdawsi and other medieval Persian works. It was an enduring image that also passed into popular Urdu romances that flourished in the age of print when, a quarter century after Corcoran's work was published, a retelling of these old tales was printed in Bombay, recounting how the *faghfur* renounced his throne to become an ascetic.[40] Fanciful as it was, the *Qissa-i Faghfur-i Chin* (*Tale of the Chinese Emperor*) was still one of the earliest Indian-language books on China to enter the public sphere, showing how older conceptions of the region survived attempts by the likes of Patell and Corcoran to provide more accurate depictions. Around the same time, another Urdu literary text invoking these old poetic associations was published as Munshi Debi Prashad's *Arzhang-i Chin* (*Picture Book of China*).[41] A book of writing exercises in Urdu calligraphy, its title referenced the legendary depiction by medieval Persian poets of the prophet Mani as a great painter from China.

Nonetheless, terms like *faghfur* and the more general lexicon taken from India's Mughal Empire were Corcoran's linguistic wherewithal, making his depiction of a quite different imperial polity intelligible to an Indian readership. Though written by a middle-ranking Irish imperial administrator, the *Tarikh-i Mamalik-i Chin* was therefore an "Islamicate" text, in the sense of using language, idioms, and cultural references drawn from Islamic tradition to depict a non-Muslim society. Reinforcing this Islamicate character were the series of earlier Persian and to a lesser extent Arabic texts to which Corcoran also referred. These comprised the handful of medieval Arabic and Persian manuscript accounts of China from the relevant sections of the travelogue of Ibn Battuta (1304–1368 or 1377), the *Jami' al-Tawarikh* (*Compendium of Histories*) by the Persian vizier Rashid al-Din (1247–1318), and the similarly Mongol-era history by Fakhr al-Din al-Banakiti (d. 1330), itself derived from Rashid al-Din. In view of the age, brevity, and limitations of these medieval accounts (only Ibn Battuta had actually visited China—if indeed he did), Corcoran made far less use of them than of European sources. But he did make considerable use of Persian histories of Mughal India and Safavid Iran, such as *Habib al-Siyar* (*Friend of Biographies*) by Khwandamir (d. 1537) and *Tarikh-i Nigaristan* (*Picture Gallery of History*) by Ahmad Ghaffari (d. 1567).

Though these works weren't about China, they allowed Corcoran in his second volume to make various commensurable comparisons between Chinese and Indian history, as well as between biblical and Quranic history. A key part of this endeavor was his attempt to reconcile the antiquity of China's recorded past with the shared Christian and Muslim scriptural tradition of Noah's flood and the peopling of the planet by Noah's descendants.[42] To do so, however, required a degree of interpretive license and, indeed, criticism, which led Corcoran to explain that when the Chinese historians described a flood during the reign of the emperor Yao, their account was less accurate than that "proved" (*sabit*) in the Old Testament. Ironically, one of the words Corcoran correctly used in Urdu to refer to the flood was *tufan*. The source via Arabic of the English word "typhoon," *tufan* ultimately derived from the Chinese term *dai feng*, which Arab sailors had picked up in an earlier era of connection. But though Corcoran's overall framing conception of humanity as the children of Adam and Noah may have been common to Christians and Muslims, it was quite different from traditional Chinese (or for that matter Hindu) creation stories, which presented different clans and dynasties as the descendants of planets or deities.

Corcoran may have been helped by Indian scholars in accessing, reading, or compiling his book, or even learning of earlier Arabic and Persian accounts of China, though Banakiti's text had been translated and published in 1820 by the Reverend Stephen Weston (1747–1830), a churchman and romantic Orientalist whose dozens of short books included a concise dictionary of Chinese. A translation of Ibn Battuta had previously been published by the Cambridge Orientalist Samuel Lee (1783–1852), who was closely involved with the Calcutta missionaries in translating the Bible into Arabic and Persian.[43] By contrast, Ibn Battuta would not be printed in India, or translated into Urdu, till the end of the nineteenth century. In this respect, Corcoran may have been introducing the accounts of Ibn Battuta and Banakiti to an Indian reading public that had no access, or even awareness, of them, thus signaling the intertwined transmission routes of apparently "indigenous" knowledge as it traversed the distance of time as well as space. This was almost certainly the case with the Chinese historical source Shujing, which Corcoran summarized extensively, transliterating its title into Urdu as Shu King after the romanized version he took from the missionary Medhurst's English translation.[44] In this way, as the content of the Shujing passed into Urdu, inter-Asian understanding was mediated through the pivot language of English, which served as a missionary linguistic midwife.

In 1864 the shrewd commercial publisher Nawwal Kishore reprinted Corcoran's Tarikh as an affordable lithograph. This was probably a response to growing public interest in China as a result of the Second Opium War, in which many Indian soldiers participated. Such motivations presumably also lay behind Kishore's decision three years later to publish an Urdu translation of Laurence Oliphant's report on the 1857–1859 embassy of Lord Elgin, which appeared under the more marketable title of Tarikh-i Chin u Japan (History of China and Japan).[45] As interest in China grew, Kishore also issued a translation of the official report on the 1870 expedition to Yarqand, in Chinese Turkestan (now Xinjiang), led by Sir Thomas Forsyth, erstwhile commissioner of Punjab.[46] Forsyth's mission had been to gather information on the new state founded by Ya'qub Beg (1820–1877) after leading an anti-Qing rebellion among China's Muslim subjects.[47] A small number of Indian merchants involved in the trans-Karakorum trade with Yarqand had direct interests in the region, but this is not enough to explain the translation and its publication. The publisher Kishore rebranded the prosaic official report as a safarnama (travelogue), presumably in the hope of drumming up sales in line with those of other popular travel books. While there were many other colonial intelligence reports on the Qing Empire's Central Asian province of Xinjiang, this was a rare example of a printed account of China emerging from the older overland routes rather than through the new maritime geography of Europe's empires.

Unlike Forsyth's mission, Elgin's embassy had emerged from these ascendant port city connections, and it had great economic implications. Being expressly aimed at accelerating the opening of more Chinese ports to foreign trade, Elgin's was a policy in which many Indian merchants had large stakes.[48] During his extended stay in China, Elgin led the bombardment of Guangzhou during the Second Opium War, then negotiated the British sections of the Treaty of Tientsin. By the time the Urdu translation of his embassy report was published nearly a decade after the mission was concluded, Elgin had also served as viceroy of India, cementing the political and commercial ties between India and China, no less than the informational channels that ran between their ports. These imperial channels fed into Indian languages as the book written about Elgin's mission by his secretary, Laurence Oliphant, was translated into Urdu by an Indian Christian called Frederick Nundy and a Hindu by the name of Shiv Parshad. Yet for his insights into Chinese culture and society, Oliphant had relied especially on interviews conducted aboard ship with a Qing official brought back to Calcutta, which were carried out by a junior diplomatic interpreter, Chaloner Alabaster. The resulting picture of China was one—much like Corcoran's text—formed by several minds, and tongues, as it passed from Chinese into English and finally Urdu.

Similar informational routes shaped the early Bengali book on China, Krsnadhana Bandyopadhyaya's *Cinera Itihasa* (*History of China*), printed in Calcutta in 1865, a little more than a decade after Corcoran's counterpart.[49] It was similarly ambitious in scope, covering China's history from antiquity to the 1800s, along with its administrative system, religions, and way of life, with shorter accounts of its literature and philosophy. But as Bandyopadhyaya readily admitted in his introduction, he had drawn this information from the English works that were made available to him in Calcutta. But perhaps "advertised" is a more appropriate word than "admitted": before the rise of nationalist and Asianist sentiments, English sources of information may well have been regarded in India's print marketplace as the most reliable.

In terms of organization and content, Bandyopadhyaya's *Cinera Itihasa* began with physical geography, along with a description of Beijing, Nanjing, and Guangzhou (their names given in English), before moving on to animals and agricultural produce. The main part of the book, however, comprised eight short chapters of history from the early emperors onward, beginning with the "first man," Fuxi (Fo-hi), who it suggested was possibly the same person as Noah (a clear hint at Bandyopadhyaya's Christian sources). The historical summary continued through the much later Ming and Qing dynasties to the arrival of the British ambassador "Lord Mekartni" and the acquisition of Hong Kong in the First Opium War, and then concluding with the Treaty of Peking in 1860. Given that the book was published only five years later, it was remarkably up-to-date, a result of its author's location in the information hub of Calcutta. This also enabled Bandyopadhyaya to include a remarkably early and detailed Bengali biography of Confucius (*Konfuchi*), along with a summary of his teachings and an outline of China's language and literature (including its early invention of printing). Here Bandyopadhyaya drew on the Christian missionary investigations in which Calcutta had played so important a role, whether across the Bay of Bengal or as far as the East China Sea.

Reflections of a Gujarati Merchant

Not all early Indian-language accounts of China, however, passed through so many layers of transmission and translation. A case in point is the four-hundred-page *Cinani Musaphari* (*Chinese Journey*) of Damodar Ishwardas Library-wala, a Hindu clerk in the employment of a Khoja Muslim trading house who traveled to China in 1860 and published his book eight years later.[50] Emerging as it did from the trading circles of Bombay—the book's publication there was financed by a group of merchants acknowledged in the preface—*Cinani Musaphari* was written in Gujarati as an informational aid to the Sino-Indian trade that did so much to enrich the city.[51] This was not the first printed Gujarati work on China as such: we have already seen Patell's book and, as was the case with Urdu, there were also a few Gujarati translations of English accounts of the First Opium War and the Taiping Rebellion, as well as a tabulated guidebook for financial transactions among businesses in Bombay, Calcutta, and the treaty ports of China compiled by the Parsi merchant Horamji Pharamji, published in Bombay in 1851.[52] But like the similar merchant guides to weights and measures produced around the Bay of Bengal, Pharamji's book, in focusing on statistical data about currency conversions, bypassed the more difficult problems of accessing and translating cultural knowledge.

Ishwardas certainly shared Pharamji's commercial concerns, however, and these ultimately took center stage in his book, having enabled his journey from Bombay aboard a ship loaded with cotton and opium. Spending three years in Hong Kong, Ishwardas was able to gather a great deal of firsthand information, at least on economic life, presenting a markedly different picture from the dazzling ceremonial image of imperial China given by Corcoran, whose first volume focused on the vast inland possessions of the emperor, or *faghfur*. By contrast, Ishwardas focused on the coastal trading ports and on commercial data: his primary mission was one of gathering information on markets, goods, competitors, currency exchanges, and other commercial practices. But this also led him to incorporate ethnographic information on the Chinese people with whom Indians would necessarily need to trade directly if they were to avoid the European middlemen who were already better established there. Like other inter-Asian investigators operating elsewhere, Ishwardas relied on direct observations that had their interpretive limitations in turn. His strategy for making the varied populations of the treaty ports comprehensible to fellow Gujarati merchants who followed in his wake was to use such familiar terms and broad categories as *deśi* (fellow Gujarati), *pardeśi* (foreigner, European), and *Cinai* (Chinese).[53] This tripartite schema allowed him to map the social complexity of the bustling ports in a simplified manner that was manageable to what was after all an intended readership of traders.

Nonetheless, Ishwardas was also interested in Chinese culture. He devoted a short section to religions, which he enumerated as seven in number, namely, Daoism, Confucianism, Buddhism, Christianity, Roman Catholicism, Judaism, and Islam. Since several of these were already to some degree familiar to his readership—Bombay was home to Catholic and Jewish as well as Muslim communities—he focused on the first, unfamiliar three. Unlike other Indian authors, he presented Daoism as China's "original religion," adding a few brief notes on its founder, Lao Tzu (or Laozi), whose name he transcribed as "Liyoten" and also, with considerable phonetic accuracy, as "Layotszi." He explained that such was Lao Tzu's influence that, over time, even the emperor became a devotee. In contrast with European presentations of Daoism, which focused primarily on its philosophical character, Ishwardas outlined the rituals and austerities performed by its followers. Reflecting a remark in his preface that the ancient Chinese had followed a religion like that of the Hindus—he made repeated comparisons of Chinese and Hindu rituals—he described the key ceremony of Daoism. This consecrated the practitioner's entry to a state of renunciatory seclusion that led to a permanent state of enlightened bliss, for which Ishwardas used the Hindu term *samadhi*. This was perhaps the earliest printed Indian-language description of Daoism. But the interpretive cost of such primacy was having to present the religion of the Chinese other in the terminology of the Hindu self.

Turning to Confucianism, Ishwardas explained that it was followed by all ranks of society, from the humblest street beggars to the emperor himself. His insights were more than mere observation and hearsay and appear to have drawn on written sources of some kind, in this period probably meaning English accounts. He provided a brief outline of the biography of Confucius, explaining, for example, that the great sage lived 2,400 years earlier in a province called Lu and was raised by his mother after his father died when he was three years old. Ishwardas added that Confucius was also known by the title "Kiongzi," but he was unable to provide any specific information about his actual teachings. Other Indian authors would take up the challenge in later decades, albeit by drawing on summaries or translations written by European authors of varying trustworthiness.

Ishwardas also gave a brief account of Buddhism, which is worth quoting: "The third religion is that of 'Fo.' This religion is known in a variety of countries and languages by seven names: *buddh, buddhsi, gautam, soman, kodam, fu* [?], and *fo*. This religion entered China approximately 1,800 years ago during the time of the Mingti Shahanshah [Emperor Mingdi of the Han Dynasty]. After some years, three or four hundred religious teachers [*dharmguru*], who were practitioners [*chalavnar*] of the Buddhist religion, brought books to China from eastern India."[54]

In view of the early date of Ishwardas's book—more than three decades before the fraught attempts by Indian investigators to make sense of Buddhism in Burma—this description is remarkable for its broad historical accuracy. In an Urdu book about Ceylon from 1888, by contrast, another Indian merchant even declared that the Buddha had lived in China.[55] Other Indian writers used a variety of different names for the religion and its founder, so that readers would have difficulty realizing they were referring to the same religious tradition. Ishwardas astutely overcame this problem of nomenclature and taxonomy by listing together the various names by which the religion was known in different countries and languages, including *fo*, the Chinese vocalization of the written character used for the Buddha. These were important steps in interpretively linking China's religions with other regions of Asia.

Given that Ishwardas apparently couldn't read Chinese—his short section on language mentions only a few basic spoken greetings—his discussion of religion again raises the question of where he acquired his information. Unfortunately, he didn't list any of his sources, but in view of his sobriquet "*Librarywala*" (the librarian), which suggests employment at some point as a librarian, and the widespread English-speaking skills of Bombay's Gujarati traders, the most likely explanation for his detailed information on the history (particularly the dates) of China's religions is that he drew on English books available in Bombay, where he wrote his own book several years after returning there. One section of his book bears a close similarity to an account in the missionary Gützlaff's history of China, which was similarly drawn into Corcoran's Urdu text. But this makes perfect sense. Before he became a *Librarywala*, Ishwardas had been involved in trade, importing to Bombay things that were unavailable there, sometimes through partnerships with British brokers. In this case, the commodity was the information he sold in his book. Perhaps he considered its detail and accuracy more important than its directly inter-Asian provenance.

Over the next twenty years, Ishwardas's *Cinani Musaphari* was followed by several more Gujarati accounts of China, such as Keśavarama Govardhanadasa's *Jñananidhi* (*Treasure House of Knowledge*, 1871), which drew extensively on Ishwardas's book, and H. K. Dhabar's 1892 *Cin Desh* (*The Land of China*).[56] But none was on the scale of Ishwardas's book.

As Gujarati books on China tailed off toward the end of the 1800s, this sinking bibliographical trajectory reflected China's shrinking role in Bombay trade over the half century that followed the Second Opium War, particularly after the ports of Japan opened, starting in the 1860s. Trade had been unable to foster an enduring Indian discipline of Sinological investigation. Nor had the military defeats of China offered a source of Sinophilic inspiration comparable to the fascination with Japan that would follow the Russo-Japanese War.

Iranian Informational Outsourcing

Nonetheless, Bombay, like Calcutta, would remain a crucial hub for knowledge about China, not only in Gujarati but also in the Persian of the city's Iranian merchants and exiles. Around the same time that European sources were being drawn into the earliest books on China in Bengali, Gujarati, and Urdu, Iranians adopted the same stratagem as a way of rapidly redressing the dearth of recent information in their own language.

In Iran as in India, the earliest printed accounts of China apparently comprised sections of European geography textbooks. The most influential was the *Kitab-i Jam-i Jam* (*Book of the World-Revealing Goblet*).[57] Published in Tehran in 1855 and again in 1856 in Bombay, it was a survey of world geography; it was also one of the books we have seen disseminating the idea of "Asia" in

Persian. Its translator was Farhad Mirza Mu'tamad al-Dawla (1818–1888), an influential Iranian prince and official whose father, 'Abbas Mirza, had overseen the introduction of printing to Iran in 1817 following imports of the Persian New Testament, translated in Calcutta.[58] Farhad probably intended his translation as a textbook for Tehran's newly founded Dar al-Funun polytechnic, which educated several generations of officials and statesmen. But his translation found a wider readership when it was rapidly reissued by one of Bombay's Iranian commercial publishers, which brought it not only to a readership of trainee bureaucrats but also to Iran's merchant diaspora, to whom it lent information on regions not then described in Persian print.

Although Farhad gave the book the poetic title *The World-Revealing Goblet*, in reference to the magical chalice of the legendary Persian emperor Jamshid, it was actually, as we saw earlier, a translation of *A Comprehensive Grammar of Modern Geography and History*.[59] The original author, a bibliomaniac schoolmaster named William Pinnock, published several bookshelves of cheap educational texts that ranged from histories of England, America, and ancient Greece to works of natural history, such as his *Catechism of Ichthyology*. Among this abundant output were his sometimes ill-informed surveys of world geography, including the one that found its way to Tehran.

When translated into Persian, Pinnock's ten-page chapter on China represented less than 2 percent of the book as a whole.[60] Even so, it offered a glimpse of a mysterious empire that Farhad tried to render into familiar Persian categories, just as Corcoran was attempting at the same time in Calcutta with Urdu. Fortunately for Farhad, Pinnock's educational background in classical Greek and Bible studies afforded a degree of "Abrahamic" continuity that his Muslim translator could use in transmitting his English source text to Iranian readers. But while this made Pinnock's book more digestible in Persian, these shared Islamo-Christian categories had little in common with China's own self-representations.

This dilemma of whose terms and categories to deploy affected even basic depictions of space. Thus, Farhad titled one chapter "On the Clime of China [*iqlim-i chin*]" and opened it with the explanatory sentence that "the empire of China is in the central clime [*iqlim-i wasi*'] in the southeast of Asia [*asiya*]."[61] Innocuous as the title and sentence may seem, they point to Farhad's subtle conceptual translation of Pinnock's book not only into the Persian language but also into traditional Muslim geographical concepts based on the Greco-Arabic model of seven climes (*iqlim*). This was certainly not the Chinese notion of being the Middle Kingdom at the center of the world! Nor was it quite what Pinnock had meant; he had referred in English to the temperate zone of European geography (which elsewhere Farhad rendered accurately as *mantaqa-yi mu'tadila*). Although Farhad's *iqlim* and Pinnock's "zone" had shared origins in Greek geography, the concepts had long since diverged. But Farhad papered over these developments by linguistic legerdemain in order to bring his source text into congruence with the familiar "clime" paradigm of his readers. When Farhad did come across Pinnock's Anglicized version of the Chinese notion of the Middle Kingdom, he subtly upgraded this into the more impressive Middle Empire (*shahanshah-i wasat*). Fortunately, not only was this closer to the Chinese self-conception, but it also maintained congruence with older Persian conceptions of the grandeur of imperial China that lingered in popular literature. This impression was further upheld by Pinnock's description of China as being the "most populous country in the world," blessed with the most fertile soils on the planet.

This combination of the familiar and unfamiliar continued throughout the Persian translation, whether at the level of abstract concepts or names for specific places. Thus, while Pinnock's mention of China's dominion over "Tartary" was easily rendered as Farhad's "Tartaristan"—albeit with equivalent vagueness—this was not the case for "Peninsular Korea"; instead of finding an equivalent Persian term, Farhad transliterated it directly as "Pininshula-yi Kari."[62] Since Persian already possessed a widely used term for "peninsular" (*shaba-yi jazira* or simply *jazira*), it is unclear why Farhad adopted the English phrase, particularly when Iranian readers possessed no English-to-Persian dictionary to work out such unfamiliar loanwords as *pininshula*. Given this absence of lexicographical aids, Farhad himself might not have realized the meaning of the term, taking "Peninsular Korea" for a proper noun. This possibility suggests itself again when he subsequently described Guangzhou as the only *harbar* into which the emperor allowed foreign ships entry, transliterating the English word "harbor" rather than using its far more familiar Persian equivalent. These were not the only loanwords, for as was true of other Middle Eastern and Indian accounts of China (and Japan), place names were invariably given in their European forms, so that Farhad referred to Guangzhou as Canton and Beijing as Pekin.

The book's actual description of Guangzhou points to a more basic problem: Pinnock's amateurish unreliability as an informational source. This was compounded by the fact that even data that had been correct at the time Pinnock was writing in the 1830s had become outdated and incorrect by the time Farhad translated his book in 1855. Among the most crucial changes was the fact that, as a result of the First Opium War, Guangzhou was no longer the sole Chinese port that was open to foreign traffic, but had been joined by the first set of treaty ports. The same issues affected the various population numbers given, whether for Guangzhou, Beijing, China as a whole, or the footmen and cavalry of the imperial army.[63] Pinnock took much of this statistical data—a lot of it inevitably guesswork anyway—from the report of the Macartney embassy of 1793, which was also drawn into Corcoran's Urdu text.

In citing these statistics, Farhad adopted the English numerical of million (*milyun*) rather than the traditional Persian unit of 100,000, known as a *lak*.[64] And this issue of numerical translation in turn affected the calculation of historical time, a problem that faced all writers who confronted the deep antiquity of China's recorded past. The additional challenge for Farhad was that there was no Persian or Arabic equivalent to the BC dating system that European antiquarians had developed for their investigations of Greco-Roman and then broader world history. As a result, rather than Farhad inventing an Islamic alternative—a Before Hijra (i.e., before 622 CE) system that would involve both himself and his readers in making arithmetical calculation for every ancient date—he, like other Muslim translators of the period, simply adopted the Christian time line, which, because of the unfamiliarity of the title "Christ," he had to render as *qabl az 'Isa* (before Jesus). Nonetheless, this borrowed Christian calendrical system allowed Farhad and subsequent Muslim writers to domesticate Chinese history to their own scripture-based historical tradition by squaring the time line of China's early emperors with the biblical and Quranic story of the flood.

In this way, following Pinnock and echoing Corcoran's Urdu text, Farhad could explain that "the founder of the Chinese empire was Fuhi [Fuxi], who was also called Tin Si [Tianzi], that is, 'son of heaven.' One group among the historians say that he is identical with Nuh [Noah], peace be upon him, who after the storm [flood] settled down for a while with his descendants till they eventually built the tower of Babel. At that point, [Fuhi/Noah] set off for the east with a group of his offspring and traveled till he found the fertile land of China and founded an empire there."[65] (Elsewhere in the *Kitab-i Jam-i Jam*, Farhad followed Pinnock and used the same system to explain the peopling of Africa by descendants of Noah's son Ham.)[66]

Yet this convenient conjunction between traditional Muslim and Christian accounts of early human history had no place for China's own religious traditions. As Farhad plainly explained, "Their religion is idol worship [*but-parasti*]," going on to use his adopted Christian time line to explain that idolatry had spread there between 800 and 1,000 years "before Jesus."[67] Though the terminology of *but-parasti* offered no advancement over medieval Muslim characterizations of Buddhism—indeed, it was a retrogressive step from the Mongol-era account of Sakyamuni in Rashid al-Din's Persian *Jami' al-Tawarikh*—Farhad tempered it by adding a measure of doctrinal detail. "They believe that the divine light descended to earth several times and then departed again," he explained, "and that their idols reveal the divine glory and majesty. They also believe that spirits move from body to body and, since the creation, four buddhas [*budha*] have come down to earth, the fifth being due to appear in AD 4447."[68] Combined in these two sentences was a blend of Buddhist, Christian, and Muslim terminology. By selecting explanatory vocabulary in Persian, and by using Quranic terminology for idols (*asnam*), the divine spirit (*nur ilahi*), and its celestial descent (*nuzul*), Farhad tried to render these unfamiliar beliefs comprehensible (if clearly heretical) to his predominantly Muslim readership.

Yet what was most striking of all was the appearance of the word *budha*. Even though it was spelled in a form that echoed its European source rather than origins in a Chinese text, as a specifier for a particular religious personage the word represented an interpretive breakthrough compared to the use of *but*, the older Persian term for idol, just a page earlier. As we will see, Iranian conceptions of Buddhism—as well as the indigenous Chinese religions that Farhad didn't mention—would further develop in the 1900s. Before then, though, Iranian conceptions of China would take an even more tortuous interpretive route than Farhad Mirza's.

One such route was opened in 1893, when Bombay's Dutt Prasad Press issued the most detailed Persian account of China to be published before 1900. Bearing the title *Mirat al-Zaman dar Tarikh-i Chin u Machin u Japan* (*The Mirror of the Times through the History of China, Greater China, and Japan*), it was compiled by the prominent Bombay-based Iranian publisher Mirza Muhammad Malik al-Kuttab Shirazi, whose output included various contemporary works as well as many classical texts he put into affordable printed format for the first time.[69] Despite the book's title, Malik al-Kuttab explained in his short introduction, it was actually a compendium of two earlier sources. One of them was Lord Macartney's "book of travels" (*safarnama*), which Malik al-Kuttab partly translated into Persian and which Corcoran had earlier used for his Urdu text. But the other text that made up *Mirat al-Zaman* was altogether more mysterious. Malik al-Kuttab merely described it as a history of China written in 970 *hijri* (1562 CE) by a Christian priest called Iksus, which someone called Farangi Khan then translated into Persian from English.[70]

In fact, it was a translation not from English, but from Latin. The translator, nicknamed Farangi Khan, was actually Muhammad Zaman, a savant of the Safavid court of Shah 'Abbas of Persia. Such was Zaman's acumen in debating with Catholic missionaries that in the mid-1600s Shah 'Abbas II sent him to Rome to master the language of the Christians and dispute their doctrines more effectively.[71] As it happened, this polemical plan to project the Muslim self by learning Latin led to a new appreciation of the Christian—and then Confucian—other. This was so much the case that Muhammad Zaman grew to love the religion he studied and converted to Christianity, taking the Catholic name of Paulo. Fearful of being executed for apostasy if he returned to Iran, Muhammad-turned-Paulo Zaman instead traveled to Mughal India, where the Jesuits had an accepted place at the court of the emperor Shah Jahan. Moving between Isfahan, Rome, and Delhi, his composite identity won him the moniker Farangi Khan, "The Frankish Khan," or, in another version, Farangi Khwan, "The Reader of the Frankish Tongue."

It was at the Indian residence of one of his Jesuit hosts—a Dutchman called Hendrik Busi—that Zaman came across the Latin account of China that, around 1650, he translated into Persian, possibly at the request of a Mughal courtier. It circulated in a few manuscript copies under the generic title *Chinnama* (*The Book of China*) or *Tarikh-i Chin* (*History of China*), its source being none other than *De christiana expeditione apud sinas suscepta ab Societate Jesu* (*On the Christian Mission among the Chinese by the Society of Jesus*) by the great Jesuit missionary Matteo Ricci (1552–1610).[72]

This was the most influential, and accurate, account of China to emerge from the Catholic missions of the early modern period.

Over two hundred years later, the first printed edition of Zaman's Persian translation of Ricci's book (or, rather, part of it) was issued in Calcutta in 1864 on behalf of the Aligarh Scientific Society, the most prominent circle of Islamic modernists trying to adapt European learning for the greater good of Muslims.[73] In his preface, Zaman made plain its authorship by one of the "Christian fathers" (albeit without mentioning Ricci by name), who had sent the book from China to Europe, where it was published.[74] Building on this background (but adding to it an error), the front cover of the Calcutta edition stated that Zaman had translated the book from English (rather than Latin), a supposed source that echoed the other books that the Aligarh Scientific Society was translating. Since the town of Aligarh lies fewer than sixty miles from Agra, where Zaman and the Jesuits were partly based, a manuscript of Zaman's translation presumably found its way to one of the members of the Scientific Society, who were unaware of its more complex provenance in the Catholic Orientalism of the Counter-Reformation. Thirty years after that first belated printing in Calcutta, with the affordable cover price of twelve *annas,* one of these copies reached the émigré Iranian commercial publisher Malik al-Kuttab in Bombay, who in 1893 reissued it for a wider readership in Iran as well as India.

As for the actual content of the text, Zaman ignored Ricci's voluminous account of the Jesuit mission and focused on his descriptions of China's geography, political structure, and especially religions and systems of learning. As Farhad Mirza had when he translated English terms for his *Kitab-i Jam-i Jam,* Zaman had to find Persian conceptual equivalents for Chinese doctrines he encountered in Latin (the latter already a translation of Ricci's Italian notebooks). Moreover, this was not merely a Christian view of China, but a highly intellectualized Jesuit interpretation.[75]

From its first pages, the Persian text signaled its European provenance as the name China (*Chin*) was traced back to Ptolemy (*Bitaylmus*) and then Marco Polo, though in Zaman's Persian translation the Latin reference to a Venetian called Marcus Paulus was transformed into *Marqus Yunani,* Marcus the Greek.[76] Zaman also adopted the Christian BC dating system, albeit in explanatory longhand as "before the birth of Lord Jesus, peace be upon him."[77] What might seem to be the simpler transfer of statistical data presented an even greater challenge, particularly when compounded by the custom in both Latin and Persian of writing numbers in words rather than numerics. Thus, the statistic for the tax-paying adult population of China that appeared in Latin longform as "58 milliones, quingenta quinquaginta millia octingenta & unun" was rendered in the Persian version as "*yik sad u hasht milyun wa panch lak u pinja hazar u hasht sad u yik.*"[78] Thus, Ricci's original figure of 58,550,801 was inflated to 108,550,801, possibly by a copyist's error introduced during the process of printing. Although by the time the translation was published, that erroneous inflation was closer to (albeit still far from) what was by then the increased population of China of around 400 million, this statistical divergence demonstrates the kinds of informational slippages that were possible even when translating apparently straightforward statistical data.

Jesuitical investigations in Persian: Ricci's and Zaman's title pages. Matteo Ricci, *De christiana expeditione apud sinas suscepta ab Societate Iesu* (Augsburg: Apud Christoph. Mangium, 1615), and Mirza Muhammad Malik al-Kuttab Shirazi (comp.), *Mirat al-Zaman dar Tarikh-i Chin u Machin u Japan*, trans. Farangi Khan (Bombay: Dutt Prasad Press, 1893).

When it came to the extensive coverage of China's religions, the Persian translation further altered the meaning of the Latin—itself a distortion of the Italian translation of the original Chinese concepts—as Zaman sought equivalent terms that altered the meaning even more. As a Catholic missionary, Ricci was broadly critical of China's religions (if more positively disposed toward Confucianism). But Zaman went a step further by framing them through the generic category of "idol worship" (*but-parasti*), interposing the term into his translation of the first and last sentences of the opening paragraph of the religion chapter.[79] By contrast, the Latin text used the more abstract—if still heretical—concept of *atheismum* (atheism).

Ricci and Zaman then turned to each of the three religions of China, the first of which—what we now call Confucianism—Zaman labeled the *mazhab-i hukuma* (religion of the sages) for the Latin *litteratorum* (scholars). Here

Ricci's controversial approval of Confucianism was transferred into Persian. Following Ricci, Zaman explained that the religion of the sages was the most ancient of China's religions. Emphasizing its learned credentials, he pointed out the large number of books written by its followers. In approving terminology that would have resonated even more positively with Muslim than Christian readers, he declared that they worship only one God, who is unitary and single (*wahid mujarrad*).[80] Zaman admitted, however, that these sages did venerate "images" (*surat*) of their founder, which were kept in what he called monasteries (*dayr*), using a more Christian term than the Latin text did. As for the founder of the religion, his name was *Kunfyusyas*.[81] This Persian spelling offers further orthographic testimony to its Latin transmission route, since "Confucius" is a Latinization of "Kong Fuzi." Still, the mention of Confucius's name was important, as it gave Indian and Iranian readers a more specific identifier than the vaguer moniker of the "religion of the sages," which might well be applied to any religion.

By contrast, when Zaman wrote that "the second religion of the people of China is called Sikiyya and Imnuf," no reader of Persian would have recognized these names, whether around 1600 or 1900.[82] For want of an existing proper name for Buddhism in Persian, these were Zaman's transliterations of the utterly obscure Latin neologisms "Sciequia" and "Omitose." Through the similar lack of an even basic Buddhological vocabulary in Ricci's Europe of around 1600, these were Latinizations of the Chinese terms *Shijiamouni* and *Amituo Fo*, which were themselves taken from the Sanskrit names of the Buddhas Shakyamuni and Amitabha.[83] As a result, readers of the printed Persian edition would have found it very hard to link this mysterious cult with the religion that in other Persian and Urdu texts from around 1900 was beginning to be called *budh* or *buda'i*.

Undeterred by the absence of available labels, Zaman went on to summarize the key doctrines of the religion of *Sikiyya* and *Imnuf*, which included reincarnation (*tanasukh*) into many different worlds. Although followers maintained the admirable monastic virtues of asceticism (*riyazat*) and chastity (*parsa'i*) and lived in monasteries, they also built "idol houses" (*but-khana*), where they kept many "strange" images, made from bronze, marble, wood, and clay.[84] Through this choice of words, he reinforced centuries-old Persian stereotypes, emphasized in countless poems of the *but-khana-yi chin:* of China as the land of dangerously enchanting idols. Finally, he turned to the third religion of China, which he called *Lar Zu* after the name of its founder, Lao Tzu.[85] (This was the religion now known in English as Daoism.) Zaman declared that

Lar Zu himself "wrote no book about this religion."[86] Echoing Ricci's greater interest in Confucianism, here he overlooked the *Dao De Jing* (*Tao Te Ching*), the foundational text of Daoism. Finally, when it came to drawing conclusions about these religions, Ricci and Zaman viewed them through similar soteriological lenses: even China's otherwise admirable scholars "have fallen into error [*ghalat*] that leads to dangerous places [*mahlaka*], then hell [*hawiyya*], via heresy [*ilhad*] and infidelity [*zandaqa*]."[87]

Three centuries after these words were written and then translated, Malik al-Kuttab—the Bombay-based Iranian whose royally bestowed moniker meant "King of Books"—published Zaman's translation of Ricci's book. For want of alternative sources of information in Persian, the publisher resorted to a text that framed China through the missionary concerns of early modern Catholicism and an Arabic lexicon of heresy that emerged in the medieval Middle East. Although around 1900, readers of the printed Persian version may not have shared these older paradigms, the absence of available books on China in their language limited their ability to see Confucianism, Daoism, and Buddhism in more accurate and perhaps sympathetic terms. These constraints of intercultural knowledge were compounded further by the problem of labels, which made it difficult to compare and evaluate Zaman's evidence (especially about the religion of *Sikiyya* and *Imnuf*) when other accounts did become available. By 1900 the book's outdated information held considerable potential to mislead readers who overlooked the single reference to its original composition date in the Bombay printed version (its period or provenance was mentioned nowhere on the title page). Nonetheless, the publisher did try to make the book more up-to-date by adding his translated report from the Macartney mission, though even this extended coverage petered out in 1736.[88]

As a commercial publisher in Bombay, Malik al-Kuttab still made a shrewd choice in issuing Zaman's translation. Even if its depictions of legal, administrative, and economic conditions were woefully out-of-date by the time it was printed, and its reading of religions based on a blend of Christian and Muslim theology, the information contained in Zaman's translation of Matteo Ricci was still effectively nonpareil in the Persian channel of the public sphere. This was the result of Ricci's thirty years spent learning to read complex Confucian texts. Between a Beijing-based Jesuit, his Dutch editor, an Iranian convert, another Dutch Jesuit in Delhi, and an émigré publisher over two centuries later in colonial India, the transmission of a text written at the Ming court in Italian, published in Latin in Augsburg, rendered into Persian in Mughal Delhi, then reissued for Asian readers in Calcutta and then Bombay reveals the complex layers of translation involved in interpreting Chinese culture for other regions of the continent. Far from solely inter-Asian exchanges, these conduits of knowledge were truly Eurasian in scope.

Arabic and Turkish Alternatives

A similar mix of opportunities and obstacles shaped information available in Arabic. Several medieval accounts of China had been produced in Arabic in addition to Persian, including travelogues by Abu Zayd al-Sirafi, Sulayman al-Tajir, and Ibn Battuta. But these remained in manuscripts that were not published till the nineteenth century, and even then appeared far earlier in Paris and London than in the Middle East. When printed books on China did start to enter the Arabic channel of the public sphere, they followed similarly circuitous routes to their Persian counterparts. One such work comprised a summary of ancient history and survey of the world's religions, published in Istanbul in a combined edition in 1879.[89] The author was Siddiq Hasan Khan (1832–1890), an influential Indian religious scholar married to the female ruler of the princely state of Bhopal. In a reflection of his theological concerns (he also founded a Muslim reform movement), Siddiq Hasan outlined the ancient history of the world, from its creation to the development of various religions among different peoples, whom he conceived in Quranic terms as *umma* (religious communities). His ambit reached from the pharaohs and ancient Greece through Africa, Arabia, and Persia to India and then China. But like so many other authors of his time, Hasan suffered from an informational deficit that became particularly apparent in his sections on China, for which there were far fewer available sources in languages he could read.

Consequently, he presented China through generic prisms of idol worship and fire worship that drew on the older characterizations of Arabic heresiography works. Yet Hasan, like Zaman in his translation of Ricci, shared certain concerns with European Christian authors, particularly the problem of chronology that involved reconciling the deep history of the ancient world with the biblical and Quranic accounts of Creation. These concerns were similarly apparent in the summary of Chinese history included as an appendix to Zaman's Persian text. This, too, began by positioning Chinese antiquity in relation to the Islamo-Christian tradition of Nuh/Noah, going so far as to present a date— derived from comparative diluvial calculations by Christian antiquarians—of China's first emperor being "a descendent of Noah, peace be upon him, who was enthroned in the year 3203 before the messiah."[90]

Siddiq Hasan's inquiries used similar scriptural frameworks to fill the informational gap on China. Yet his books also point again to India's role in mediating ideas about China, however flawed or provisional such ideas may have been. Not only was Siddiq Hasan himself based in India, but both his works were first published there before being reissued in Istanbul five years later, in 1879.

This transmission route is also evident in one of the earliest printed Turkish books on China by way of *Çin ü Maçin* (*China and Greater China*), published in Istanbul in 1902.[91] Reflecting the role of Iranian exiles in Bombay, its author—or rather, compiler—was an Indian émigré by the name of Nusret 'Ali Han Dihlewi. Born in Delhi in 1848, Dihlewi launched himself into India's abundant public sphere by founding several newspapers with his father before eventually moving to Istanbul. There his language skills helped him find a position in the *Encümen-i Teftiş ve Muayene* (Council of Inspection and Examination), which reviewed and authorized books for publication (including translated works) on behalf of the Ottoman Ministry of Education.

A short description of Dihlewi survives in the Urdu travelogue of Shibli Nu'mani (1857–1914), who in the early 1890s made a journey of self-discovery through the Muslim Middle East in the company of his friend and colleague the Orientalist Thomas Arnold (1864–1930). After meeting Dihlewi in Istanbul, Shibli recorded that before joining the education ministry, his exiled compatriot had edited an anticolonial newspaper, which the British ambassador persuaded the Ottomans to ban.[92] But on a happier note, he added, Dihlewi now received a high salary from the ministry and had married a local Turkish woman.

Not that Dihlewi's was the first printed Turkish book on China. As in Bombay, the nineteenth century had seen a few geographical books published about China in Ottoman Istanbul. Echoing the printing of Mateo Ricci's translated seventeenth-century account, in 1854 a Turkish translation of the Persian *Khita'inama* (*Book of Cathay*) was printed in Istanbul.[93] Even older than Ricci's account, the *Khita'inama* was written in 1516 by Sayyid 'Ali Akbar, a Central Asian merchant who spent three months traveling through China on a mission to Beijing as part of the Ming imperial tribute system. Aside from the book's being four centuries old, however, 'Ali Akbar was unable to speak, let alone read, Chinese, with inevitable consequences for the information he transmitted.[94] Fortunately, in 1866 a more up-to-date geographical introduction to China was issued in Istanbul.[95]

Çin ü Maçin, the Turkish text subsequently compiled by the Indian émigré Dihlewi a generation later, shows the shared characteristics of such introductory works. A mere forty-five pages in length (around a quarter of which had illustrations), *Çin ü Maçin* was intended to provide an overview of a country about which little reliable information was available to the late Ottoman reading public. It opened with descriptions of physical geography and political borders (the Ottomans and China had a common neighbor in imperial Russia), along with details on rivers, lakes, mountains, climate, flora and fauna, as well as an outline of principal crops, trade goods, and mines.[96] The text then turned to political structure, including a list of foreign embassies in Beijing, before focusing in more detail on the imperial capital itself by way of its principal governmental, military, and religious buildings.[97] In an early signal of new interests among Muslim readers in colonial India as well as in the fading Ottoman Empire, the next section was devoted to the history of Islam in China. (Already the previous year, a short book on China's Muslims had been printed in Istanbul which tried to reconstruct how Islam had first spread in China.)[98] Dihlewi gave a historical overview, from the arrival of Islam in China during the lifetime of the Prophet down to that time, albeit with dates provided in the Christian calendar that hinted at its likely sources among the many Christian missionary reports on China's Muslims. As he noted, most Chinese Muslims were Hanafi Sunnis (implicitly like their co-religionists in the Ottoman Empire and India), though he provided the vastly inflated population figure of 50 million Muslims, which again echoed alarmist Christian miscalculations. After an outline of these same missionaries' promotion of Christianity in China, Dihlewi's *Çin ü Maçin* turned more briefly to other religions by way of Buddhism, Confucianism, and Daoism, describing their places of worship along with the primacy of venerating ancestors.[99] A final section described the customs, clothing, and appearance of the Chinese, a task aided by illustrations.[100]

Prefiguring the visual depictions of Japan published in the Persian *Mikadunama* a couple of years later, the illustrations were lithographic reproductions whose original engravings and artistic style suggest a European provenance. This was no less the case with the information presented in the book as a whole. For Dihlewi drew together data from several European works, chiefly a work by a certain "Mistar Midus," whom he acknowledged along with an unnamed Russian source.[101] The former appears to have been Thomas Taylor Meadows (1815–1868), who studied Chinese in Munich before entering the British colonial service and moving to Hong Kong, where he held the position of Chinese interpreter in Her Majesty's Civil Service and worked in intelligence in the run-up to the Second Opium War.[102] Meadows wrote two books on China, which were published in London and Bombay in the 1840s and 1850s.[103] Dihlewi's *Çin ü Maçin* was not only far shorter than either of Meadows's books, but also more selective about which topics were deemed to be of most value to its Ottoman audience. This was after all Dihlewi's job as an official government employee charged with translating useful educational works, reflecting Farhad's Persian translation of Pinnock's geography textbook for Iran's new state polytechnic. Yet both Dihlewi's *Çin ü Maçin* and Farhad's *Jam-i Jam* drew on source texts that were considerably outdated by the time they were translated, in the Ottoman case almost sixty years later. Dihlewi may also have drawn on other books he didn't mention, but his use of Meadows points to the issue of time delays in the transmission of information between languages, and to the highly contingent availability of specialized European books in cities such as Istanbul and Tehran.

Compilations of an Indian Newspaper Editor

This state of affairs was not static, though. In the years on either side of 1900, more books on China began to appear from the presses of the Ottoman Empire, Egypt, Iran, and especially India. While still only a handful in number, they were published more rapidly than before: the first decade of the century probably saw as many books on China issued in Arabic, Persian, and Ottoman Turkish as during the entire previous century. Not only were these books published at shorter intervals, but insofar as many of them were translations, most were also published soon after the initial appearance of their source books. This wasn't unique to works on China: increased transmission speed derived from the closer integration of global communications by this time. Nonetheless, the Boxer Rebellion of 1899–1901, which rattled through Indian as well as Ottoman newspapers, certainly raised interest in the region. The new accounts that ensued marked a new stage in attempts to comprehend Chinese society and culture across West and South Asia, though once again, India retained its earlier lead.

India maintained this advantage by having greater access to information on China, whether through the growing number of public libraries, bookshops, or newspapers that provided bilingual Indian authors with access to a larger array of sources in English, or whether through the far larger presence of Indian (rather than Middle Eastern) merchants, soldiers, and policemen working in China's treaty ports. Although in the next chapter we will see Chinese Muslims arriving in British-ruled Cairo, India's imperial infrastructure

further ensured the greater availability of English materials (including newspapers) that were harder to access in Middle Eastern cities, none of which
enjoyed anything comparable to Calcutta's and Bombay's close commercial
and political connections with Hong Kong and Shanghai.

One outcome of this imperial informational web was an unusually wide-
ranging Urdu account of China published in 1890, and again in 1904.[104]
Though a little over fifty pages long, *Halat-i Chin* (*Conditions in China*) provided a more sympathetic and dispassionate overview of customs and culture
than earlier publications. Its author, Ghulam Qadir Fasih (1860–1912), was in
a good position to compile such information as editor of the Urdu newspaper
Punjab Gazette. He was also helped by both his impeccable grasp of English
and his understanding of the tastes of his reading public. He had previously
translated an English edition of Alexandre Dumas's *Count of Monte Cristo*
under the more regionally evocative title of *Motiyan ka Jazira* (*The Island of
Pearls*). He had also translated many other popular novels, particularly *mistriz*
drawn from the penny-dreadful *Mysteries of London* series by George W. M.
Reynolds (1814–1879).[105] In an advertisement of his style, his nom de plume,
Fasih, meant "fluent." Combining rhetorical skills with commercial acumen,
Fasih founded his own publishing house, the Punjab Press, which issued his
newspaper as well as many of his books. Though the paper had an average
print run of just three hundred copies, his novels made him a well-known
figure across India's public sphere.[106] Still, his *Halat-i Chin* was more than
a mere entertainment: it was probably aimed at the growing reading market
of Punjabi migrant workers heading to Hong Kong and Shanghai, especially
soldiers and policemen, who were required to be literate in Urdu.

There was one important caveat, however: since Fasih hadn't himself visited China, he could offer no practical advice to these migrant workers. Instead, he gathered information from existing (largely English) sources. As
in his translations of fiction, he was helped by his Anglophone education at
the Scotch Mission High School in his hometown of Sialkot.[107] Adapting the
techniques of the missionaries who taught him, in 1899 Fasih published a trilingual Urdu-Persian-English translation of the Quran.[108] Six years earlier he
had chaired a major public debate between Henry Martyn-Clark (c. 1857–1916),
an Anglicized Afghan raised as a Christian, and Mirza Ghulam Ahmad, the
messianic leader of the Ahmadiyya sect of Muslims. After dragging on for two
weeks, the debate was published under the eye-catching title *Jang-i Muqaddas*
(*Holy War*) in the same year 'Abd al-Khaliq published his *Sayr-i Barhma* about
a parallel dialogue with the head of Burma's Buddhists.[109]

If Fasih was occasionally drawn into these polemical corners of the public sphere, he was far from a polemicist himself. While he was deeply interested in religion—the section of *Halat-i Chin* on China's religions represents nearly a third of the contents—the tone of his depiction was one of dispassionate curiosity.[110] Living by his printing press as much as his pen, he needed to ensure his books appealed not only to Muslims but to as broad an audience as possible among the Sikhs and Hindus who also read Urdu. This may have informed his decision to include twenty-five lithographic illustrations, which, though roughly drawn, brought his sprightly prose further to life.

In addition to religion, Fasih's *Halat-i Chin* covered a broad array of topics: geography, history, customs, key exports, forms of government, language, and literature. Like other early books on China, whether in Indian or Middle Eastern languages, it was intended as a comprehensive overview to make up for the lack of available information on the country. While not based on his direct experiences, it imitated Urdu travelogues through describing what China and the Chinese looked like, whether by way of the architecture of its cities ("very few ancient buildings except for Buddhist temples") or the appearance and clothing of its people.[111] Food habits were also noted, with the explanation that, owing to the widespread belief in reincarnation, the Chinese avoid eating meat for fear of ingesting the flesh of their relatives.[112] This focus on the lifestyles of ordinary people made up much of the text: compared to the two pages on history, Fasih devoted ten to customs surrounding marriage, child rearing, and death.[113]

He devoted even more space to surveying China's "three religions," noting that they all held ancestor worship (*buzurgan-parasti*) in common.[114] Transliterating English spellings, his depiction of Confucianism focused mainly on its founder's biography, a historicist approach drawn from the Protestant Christian sources that similarly shaped his account of Lao Tzu and the Buddha. He likewise shared the missionaries' views (and terms) that Confucianism was not truly a religion, but rather "a *politikal* and *soshial* doctrine that does not lead to knowledge of God, which is why people are not satisfied with it."[115]

Fasih's account of Daoism similarly demonstrated how "the grand and pure teachings of Lao Tzu have been completely forgotten," not least as a result of the rise of sorcerers to high positions at the imperial court.[116] Nonetheless, his sources did afford him a more accurate account of the "Buddha religion" (*budh-mazhab*) than many Indian books from before 1900. He thus outlined the Four Noble Truths and recounted how the religion first spread to China from India in 216 BC.[117] Later, he continued, around the fifth century AD, a

Picturing popular religion:
Indian lithograph of the Chinese
bodhisattva Guanyin. Ghulam
Qadir Fasih, *Halat-i Chin* (Lahore:
Munshi Fayz 'Ali Malik, 1904).
Photograph by Nile Green.

Chinese follower of *Budh* by the name of Fa Hin (i.e., Faxian, 337—c. 422) traveled to India and spent fourteen years collecting books before sailing home via the "Ceylon route."[118] It would not be till 1921 that the travelogue of China's other great pilgrim, Xuanzang (fl. 602–664), would be translated into Urdu from English as part of the rediscovery of ancient Indo-Chinese ties we will later see taking place during that decade.[119] But in 1890 Fasih's brief anecdote about Faxian marked an early moment in that inter-Asian historical recovery. In a notable recognition of the specificities of East Asian Buddhism, he also mentioned the popular veneration of the deity—or *bodhisattva*—Guanyin.

Still, his book wasn't all about religion and the past. With an eye to the labor migrants who formed part of his potential readership, Fasih also outlined the contemporary state of transport.[120] In part it was a word of warning: "In China, one cannot travel quickly: some parts of the country do not even have any roads."[121] But writing in the heyday of steam, he also described the rail system slowly expanding after "an English company had founded a small railway near a large port in 1876."[122] (This was a reference to the Shanghai line built by Jardine Matheson & Company, which enjoyed a profitable partnership with the Bombay Parsi entrepreneur Jamsetjee Jejeebhoy.) Fortunately, Fasih continued, a line was also being laid out to Beijing.

Whether as businessmen or policemen, the increasing Indian presence in China prompted other publications. In 1897, midway between the original edition and reprint of Fasih's *Halat-i Chin,* another fifty-page Urdu account was published with the simple title *Chin u Chini (China and the Chinese).*[123] Its nineteen short sections covered such topics as China's army, clothing, life-styles, and tea production, along with its "strange traditions and customs (*'ajib rasm u rawaj*)." But its longest sections by far were those dedicated to the Great Wall (and Grand Canal), and to the mysterious religious teacher called "Kong Fushi."[124] Responding to practical self-interest, the increasing Indian public demand for knowledge of China was enabling a deeper comprehension, and appreciation, of another Asian culture, albeit often with input from Europe. But language still remained a barrier to direct inter-Asian exchange. *Chin u Chini* provided no information on spoken or written Chinese; the only specific mention of language came when the word *cha* was explained as the source of the English word "tea."[125]

Cairo's Turn to China

Around the same time, parallel developments were afoot in the Middle East's main printing centers. Coinciding with the dramatic conclusion of the Boxer Rebellion, in 1901 a short Arabic book was published in Cairo: Abu al-'Izz Itribi and 'Abd al-'Aziz Hamad's *Nubdhah 'an al-Sin (Profile of China).*[126] The river port of Cairo is, of course, not technically part of Asia, but it supplied many texts to neighboring Arabophone regions of West Asia. *Nubdhah 'an al-Sin* was one such work. Printed on the press of the nationalist newspaper *al-Liwa (The Standard),* it built on the many shorter articles on China that over the previous decade or so had begun to appear in such newspapers as *al-Muqtataf (Selection), al-Mashriq (The East),* and *al-Manar (The Lighthouse).* In Arabic no less than Urdu, information was similarly collated by authors with access to newspapers that in turn often drew on European news reports.

Like its Ottoman near-contemporary work by the Indian émigré Dihlewi, the Arabic *Nubdhah* gave a basic informational overview of China's physical geography, provinces, geology, fauna, agricultural produce, famous cities, and trade, along with its political system, notable inventions, and traditions of learning.[127] It also provided an outline of China's history, from its ancient origins with the legendary emperor Yao to around 1900.[128] One of its coauthors, Itribi, had previously published a history of Egypt that incorporated European research into the pharaonic past, which deepened his interest in antiquity.[129] But despite this new Arabic attention to ancient China, the *Nubdhah* devoted greater attention to the more recent period, revealing European aggression by way of the Opium Wars, and then the Japanese invasion, which its authors argued resulted from the previous weakening of China by Europe. Though their use of dates in the Christian calendar suggests the authors had to rely on European sources for their historical outline, in the subsequent section on Islam in China, Itribi and Hamad emphasized medieval Arabic accounts, particularly that by the Moroccan traveler Ibn Battuta.[130] Pointing to the high status Islam had achieved under the Ming Dynasty, Itribi and Hamad described the high official positions that various Muslims reached, as well as their key roles in commerce before the rise of the oppressive Qing (or Manchu) rulers.[131]

Presaging the subsequent renewal of direct connections between Muslims from China, the Middle East, and India, Itribi and Hamad then mentioned a pilgrim called "Ma Te-Hsing" who had reached Mecca in 1839, and then visited Egypt and Istanbul, where he remained for two years before sailing home via Singapore.[132] The pilgrim in question was Ma Dexin (1794–1874), an influential Muslim leader from Yunnan who, upon returning home, taught his younger relatives and appointed them community leaders.[133] It was then that a great Muslim uprising—the so-called Dungan Revolt of 1862–1877—took place, in recounting which Itribi and Hamad outlined the hopeless attempts by Yunnan's Muslims to gain help from the perfidious British across the border in Burma.[134]

So it was that when China, and with it Burma, registered in the Arabic channel of the public sphere, it was either as a lesson in the dangers of colonization or as a plea for the plight of its Muslims. In this respect, Itribi and Hamad's *Nubdhah 'an al-Sin* echoed the Arabic history of Afghanistan written by the Iran-born impresario of Pan-Islamism, Jamal al-Din al-Afghani (1838–1897), and published in Alexandria, and then Cairo, around the same time, which likewise used Afghanistan to warn Arabs about British treachery.[135] Once again, learning about other regions of Asia provided lessons in protecting the self.

When the *Nubdhah* turned from China's Muslims toward other religions (*adyan*), it merely mentioned that three other religions existed there. Following European orthography, their founders were named in Arabic as *Konfusi-*

yus, La'o Tsu, and *Buddha,* whose teachings had "entered China with some Indian traders, early in the third century before Christ."[136] Brief as it was, the outline of the teachings of Confucius and Lao Tsu was highly positive, presenting them primarily as moralists and philosophers. The use of the Arabic term *falsafa* (philosophy) was a strategic one, aimed at universalizing their teachings rather than tying them to alien religious systems. Even so, Confucius's doctrines appeared remarkably similar to those of the Prophet Muhammad, for Confucius "used to say in all his teachings that there is One God, who manages the universe with his wisdom, and that this God is the One who should be worshiped and not others."[137] So even if Confucians were not Muslims, their great teacher had promoted doctrines fundamentally similar to Islam's. And so things went well until the emperor Shi Wong Te (Shi Huang) "ordered the burning of books" and "persecuted scientists and philosophers, as four hundred of them were buried in a single day while they were still alive, which was the reason for delaying the development of philosophical sciences in China for more than a thousand years."[138] In Itribi and Hamad's Arabic book, then, as in Zaman's Persian version of Ricci, which appeared a year earlier in Bombay, early Chinese monotheism was shown to have declined from its primordial purity. If this early Arabic printed study of China was largely appreciative, then it refracted the biases of its European sources through the prism of Muslim monotheism.[139]

The problem of vicarious sources was even greater in Iran than in Egypt. There the early twentieth century also saw the appearance of books on China, though unlike Itribi and Hamad's selective redirecting of European information, they were wholesale translations of European works. The first of these appeared in 1906, the *Tarikh-i Chin* (*History of China*), a translation of a French general survey by Jean-Pierre Guillaume Pauthier (1801–1873).[140] Reflecting the position of the Indian Dihlewi, officially tasked with compiling his *Çin ü Maçin* in Istanbul, the Persian translator Muhammad Nadim al-Sultan was Iran's minister of publications.[141] Pointing again to India's importance as informational intermediary, Nadim al-Sultan had previously made an extensive tour of India rather than China; around 1900, other officials in Tehran had corresponded with an Iranian publisher in Calcutta about founding a society there to translate many more European texts into Persian.[142] Completing this circle of connections, Pauthier—the original French author of the *Tarikh-i Chin*— was a scholar of India as well as of China, who also translated one of the earliest Persian texts printed in Calcutta.[143] Unfortunately, Pauthier's combined interests led him to inter-Asian interpretive dead ends by way of speculations about the shaping influence of the ancient Hindu Upanisads on the Daoist teachings of Lao Tzu.[144] Not only was Pauthier a rather unreliable informant, but, by the time his book was translated in Tehran, it was also outdated, having been published nearly seventy years earlier. In 1906, when his book was translated, the ancient imperial order he described was on the verge of collapse. China was a very different place from what it had been in the 1830s, when his book was originally published in Paris.

If the problem of time delays continued to affect book translations, newspapers offered alternative options. Around the same time Pauthier's book was translated, a serialized history of China appeared in the newspaper *Adab* (*Conduct*), which, in the run-up to the Iranian Constitutional Revolution of 1905–1911, also featured articles on the Japanese defeat of Russia. As Iran then entered its short-lived constitutionalist period, interest was reciprocated as Chinese journals such as *Dongfang zazhi* (*Eastern Miscellany*) began reporting on political developments in Iran, albeit largely by way of the British Chinese-language newspaper, *Lundun taiwushi bao* (*Times of London*).[145] However vicarious the data, this sense of shared Sino-Iranian developments prompted the Persian translation of a more recent account of the Boxer Rebellion, which appeared under the title *Tarikh-i Jang-i Chin ba Duwwal-i Muttahida-i Urup* (*The History of the War of China with the United Countries of Europe*).[146] Its source text was written by Arnold Henry Savage Landor (1865–1924), a British painter and travel writer who also wrote extensively about India and Tibet. Hardly a disinterested observer, Landor had, upon the fall of Beijing, joined the Japanese and European forces in their victory parade. But at least the book was only a decade old when it reached readers in Tehran.

The Interpretive Dilemmas of Direct Observation

Breaking with this reliance on European works, the first years of the twentieth century saw the publication of a series of travelogues and other firsthand accounts of China. This was particularly the case in Indian languages, though shorter, direct accounts of China increasingly featured in Middle Eastern texts, too. In part, this was a result of the presence of increasing numbers of Indian soldiers who, from the First Opium War through the 1940s, served in China in the regiments of the East India Company and then the colonial Indian Army.[147] Other Indians—particularly Sikhs from Punjab—worked as policemen or private watchmen in Hong Kong and Shanghai.

By 1860 around seven thousand Indian soldiers served alongside the larger contingent of British troops who helped the Qing government suppress the Taiping Rebellion, whose leader, Hong Xiuquan (1814–1864), had declared himself the younger brother—and successor—of Jesus Christ after reading missionary pamphlets.[148] The increasing participation of Indian soldiers in Chinese conflicts prompted interest back home. The large proportion of Punjabi Sikhs and Muslims who served in the colonial Indian Army meant that books of vernacular militaria were an important part of the publishing landscape of the province; so, Punjabi participation in various colonial conflicts fed back into the book market to lend a martial twist to intercultural knowledge. Drawing on what was still a vibrant Punjabi tradition of heroic war ballads, in 1899 a versified Urdu account of the war was published from the inland print emporium and Punjabi capital of Lahore.[149]

A few years later, the role of Indian regiments in suppressing the Boxer Rebellion yielded a larger bibliographical harvest in the appearance of several accounts of the campaign, and of China more generally, in a number of other Indian languages. A detailed direct account appeared in Hindi: the Indian officer Thakur Gadadhar Singh's *Chin Me Terah Mas* (*Thirteen Months in China*), which had a print run of a thousand copies.[150] Its three hundred detailed pages were the combined result of Singh's dual sources of information, and dual purposes, combining as he did vicarious and eyewitness testimony by embedding an overview of Chinese history into a personal campaign memoir. At one level, the book presents a vividly dramatic account of various military encounters that draw on older oral traditions of Indian martial narratives that were passed down to the colonial barracks.[151] But Singh went further and deeper than these old hero ballads by trying to analyze the political and cultural motivations that led to the Boxer uprising. If his discussions of the rise of European power in the region and Chinese imperial policies in response relied on the fuller English sources on these topics, like Itribi and Hamad in Arabic, he nonetheless tried to circumvent colonial interpretations of the conflict to come to his own conclusions, which were often considerably more sympathetic than those of European reporters. Hence, his anecdotes of Indian individual and regimental bravery in suppressing the rebellion were tempered by dismayed discussions of looting and atrocities against innocent Chinese victims.[152]

Like other soldiers of empire, Indian or British, Singh still lived in a world in which religion played an important role in military life, and this led him to

recount the Boxers' belief in their supernatural powers with credible serious-
ness.[153] He also reported on the activities of the Christian missionaries who
were so familiar a feature of his homeland.[154] As his book moved on from
the details of the war to history and culture more broadly, he paid particular
attention to religions.[155] Here, as throughout *Chin Me Terah Mas,* Singh lev-
eraged his direct observations by drawing more detailed explanations from
the several English works he consulted and cited. In this way, he was able to
combine his firsthand and often poetic depictions of Beijing's main temples
with doctrinal summaries acquired through his subsequent reading, echoing
the methods of Indian investigators of Burma and especially Japan. This was
an effective strategy, overcoming the problem of outdated information in so
many previous works by combining his own contemporary eyewitness evidence with data on the historical and cultural background taken from earlier
European texts. In making sense of all this for his readers, Singh repeatedly
compared Chinese practices to what he regarded as commensurable customs
among different communities in India and Burma.[156] Viewing China through
this Indian interpretive lens allowed him to find sympathetic common
ground between the sage Shri Sukdev and Lao Tzu, between Hindu hermit-
ages and Buddhist lamaseries, albeit at the distorting cost of translating them
into Indic conceptual terms such as *akhara* and *gurukul.*[157] Although this was
a semantic projection of the Indian self, it enabled a greater appreciation of
the Chinese other.

A similar approach was taken in another Hindi book, *Chin Durpan (Mirror
of China),* written by Mahendulal Garg, a contemporary of Singh who served
in the 7th Rajput Regiment. Knowing Buddhism originated in India, Garg
declared China "a neighbor, coreligionist, and brother of Aryavarta," using
the ancient Sanskrit term for northern India meaning "abode of the noble
ones."[158] But he also speculated beyond his direct knowledge by claiming that
consequently Chinese people often call themselves "Hindus."[159]

The search for equivalent or comprehensible terms meant that, far from
being able to simply "say what they saw," even eyewitness authors like Garg
and Singh were drawn into the challenging work of cultural interpretation,
particularly when writing what were often the first detailed books on China
in their languages.[160] This was even the case when information was translated
from European sources. In the case of Zaman's version of Matteo Ricci, this
had led him to render into Persian the unintelligible Latin term *Sciequia* as a
name for Buddhism. Singh similarly incorporated English terms or spellings
for Chinese cultural traditions, though these were thankfully more intelligible

Subaltern Sinographers: Indian guards keep watch over the treaty ports of China.
Postcard, c. 1900. Collection of Nile Green.

to many of his readers. Singh's Anglophone sources included the writings of
Robert Hart of the Chinese Imperial Maritime Customs Service and the popular author Neville P. Edwards, as well as Landor's book on the Boxer Rebellion,
which was also translated wholesale into Persian.[161] Consequently, Landor
shaped Iranian perceptions of the conflict to a greater degree than Singh's
multiperspective account, which combined his own participant observations
with the larger number of sources available in India.

In being structured through military conflict, Singh's experiences provided
him with little direct engagement with educated Chinese people, who might
have acted as alternative informants to his British book list. But for such Indian newcomers to China, there in any case remained the obstacle of language:
even had Singh had time to learn it, the pidgin of the treaty ports was of far less
use in Beijing, particularly for the complex cultural investigations he tried to
undertake. While he did include in his Hindi book a short section on language,
it was only a brief outline of little more than a page that drew on the closer missionary engagement with Chinese.[162] As he modestly concluded, "What more
can an unknown soldier write in relation to words and language?"[163]

Yet, as it happened, the Boxer Rebellion did lead to an exceedingly rare
Indian-language guide to spoken Chinese. Published in the same year as

Singh's *Chin Me Terah Mas*, it was written by a military hospital assistant called Narayanaprasada Sukula.[164] Bearing the simple title *Chini Ziban* (*The Chinese Language*), it comprised a little over forty pages of words and short phrases translated into Hindi and Urdu and then transliterated into their respective scripts. It opened with a short preface in which Sukula explained that he had compiled his introduction to the Chinese language because no other such book existed in either Hindi or Urdu, and "because, without language, a man is like a dumb mute [*gongi*] and because, without language, no activity is possible."[165] He added that he had therefore produced his book for his Indian brothers in China. Although it was printed in the Indian town of Aligarh, its cover price was accordingly given in cents, the Calcutta-minted currency used in Hong Kong and Shanghai, where China's largest Indian communities were located.

As for its linguistic content, the first half of Sukula's booklet comprised word lists on a considerably broad range of topics, which, after the fundamental matters of the physical world and numbers, moved through the family, the body, and religion to schooling, games, city and household, shopping, clothing, travel, trade, wildlife, the army, and politics. Though Sukula gave no explanation of grammar or the Chinese writing system, the second half of his booklet enabled more complex communication by way of complete phrases relating to the practical issues of travel, sickness, talking to local servants, and (the longest section) shopping in local markets.

Sukula's *Chini Ziban* was the Sino-Indian companion to the handful of other Indian-language guides to Burmese and Japanese. Despite the violent context of its compilation amid the work of Indian soldiers in suppressing the Boxer Rebellion, this forgotten pamphlet marked a small linguistic milestone in modern intercultural interaction between South and East Asia. In a sign of the sheer novelty of such a text that surely distressed its author, the first page was of errata that corrected the many subsequent misprints of Chinese words.

Direct Encounters on the Way to Japan

In the years after the Boxer Rebellion, the aforementioned Indian soldier, Gadadhar Singh, found himself attracted by Japan as its own empire rose from the ashes of China's. This may have begun from his encounters with Japanese soldiers while serving in Beijing after Chinese troops murdered the

Japanese diplomat Sugiyama Akira. Whatever the font of this new interest, the last section of Singh's *Chin Me Terah Mas* contained an admiring account of Japan.[166] He was subsequently among the many people inspired by the latter's victory over Russia, which roused him to write a Hindi work on the traditional way of the Samurai warrior, titled simply *Bushido*.[167] The Russo-Japanese war also inadvertently led to accounts of China's ports being included as en route appendages to travelogues concerned primarily with Japan, which we have seen garnering growing interest across Asia in the early 1900s.

One such travel writer was Indumadhav Mullick (1869–1917), a former philosophy lecturer at Calcutta's Bangabasi College who recounted his experiences in his Bengali book, *Chin Bhramana* (*Travels in China*).[168] In 1904 he sailed via Rangoon to Hong Kong, where he spent several months. Mullick appears by his own account to have mainly spent his time among what was by then Hong Kong's extensive Indian community, his account of the Chinese being based largely on the eyewitness empiricism of watching people in the streets and encountering them in shops. Communication was difficult, he explained, because "very few people know English. Those who know a little speak in Pidgin English."[169] As for the Chinese language itself, it was "extremely difficult."[170] Fortunately, after Mullick moved on to the treaty port of Amoy (now Xiamen), he was befriended by a young shipping agent called Sui Jun who worked with foreign traders. Not only did Sui speak English, but he had also visited Calcutta. Evidently pleased to renew his acquaintance with Bengalis, Sui guided Mullick around the sights of Amoy and explained to him the meaning of various customs. As Mullick candidly confessed to his readers, "Without his help it would not have been possible for me to see anything in a distant place like Amoy."[171] On another occasion, it was a "yellow-robed English-knowing priest" who informed him about basic religious beliefs.[172] Like Masood's grasp of Japan, Mullick's understanding of China was haphazardly shaped by local people who happened to speak English.

This was no less the case for grander visitors such as Jagatjit Singh, the maharaja of the Punjabi princely state of Kapurthala, who visited China (and Japan) in 1903. Three years later, responding to interest caused by the Russo-Japanese war, he published a book (in Urdu and English editions) recounting his comfortably first-class itinerary.[173] In a vivid contrast to Gadadhar Singh, the maharaja was feted by European officials, whether British, Russian, or German, at every one of the ports he called at, as well as by Sir Ernest Satow, the British minister to Beijing. Like those of other travelers, his journey was structured by the imperial infrastructures of steam; he sailed to Hong Kong, then Shanghai, Yantai, and Tianjin, whence he traveled by the new French train line to Beijing before returning to Tianjin to take another train north to Shanhaiguan, then a train on the Russian Trans-Siberian railroad via Dalian to Russian-occupied Lüshun (then Port Arthur), whence he finally sailed on to Japan.[174] The specific sites he visited formed what was already becoming an established sightseeing route: he took in Beijing's celebrated Temple of Heaven, lamasery, and Temple of Confucius (which "contained nothing of striking interest") and then a portion of the Great Wall.[175]

The maharaja mixed mainly with European officials, and his understanding was molded by their perceptions: he was guided around Beijing by "Mr. Jones, an excellent Chinese scholar of the British legation."[176] When it came to making his own interpretations, the maharaja drew comparisons with Indian customs, describing a traditional theater performance in Shanghai as being like an enactment of the Ram-Lila legends that similarly appeared in Fazli's description of a traditional No drama in Tokyo.[177] Nonetheless, the maharaja was far less sympathetic to the Chinese people he observed from a social distance, remarking with disapproval that "patriotism and public spirit had no existence," while labeling Beijing "the City of Chaos and Evil Odors" and criticizing local cuisine as "positively revolting."[178] This last remark was somewhat ironic given that, as noted earlier, when the maharaja served Indian food to a party of elite Iranian travelers he subsequently encountered in Kyoto, in their Persian account of the meeting they said the dinner was too spicy.[179]

That same Iranian party also traveled through China on their way to Japan, leaving an account of their experiences written by the senior official Mahdi Quli Hidayat, whose description of Japan we encountered in chapter 3. Using the same ports and railroads, they visited exactly the same places as Maharaja Jagatjit Singh (albeit in reverse order), even staying in the same grand hotels, such as the Astor House Hotel in Tianjin.[180] Having previously been employed as director of the Post, Customs, and Telegraph Office in Tabriz, the forty-year-old Hidayat was a keen observer of China's communications infrastructure, commenting regularly on steamships, railways, newspaper publishing, and postal services.[181] (He later used postcards as illustrations for his book.) Nonetheless, in meeting mainly with European officials—having studied in Berlin, Hidayat socialized extensively in the German-administered port of Qingdao—and Iranian merchants (mostly tea exporters) who hosted his party in Shanghai, his direct interactions with Chinese people were limited, so he too observed them as an outsider.[182] And like the maharaja, the Iranians followed a nascent tourist route, likewise visiting a traditional Chinese theater, Beijing's Temple of Confucius, and an accessible section of the Great Wall during their ten days in the capital of the crumbling Qing Empire.[183]

Nonetheless, like other Middle Eastern and Indian interpreters of East Asia, in the 120 pages of his travelogue devoted to China, Hidayat did his best to interpretively leverage his observations by drawing on European studies, especially the writings of Austrian diplomat Ernst von Hesse-Wartegg.[184] This was particularly the case regarding religions, enabling him to append discrete sections of doctrinal summary to the visually descriptive reports of his visits to places of worship. In discussing Lao Tzu, the founder of Daoism, he thus mentioned several "German books" and "translations into French, English, and German" of the *Dao De Jing*.[185] Hidayat also did his best to draw on the few medieval Persian accounts of China. Discussing the birth of the Buddha, he briefly mentioned the fourteenth-century history of Banakiti previously cited in James Corcoran's pioneering Urdu text, and he referred to Rashid al-Din's *Jami' al-Tawarikh* regarding the Mongol Empire that briefly united Iran and China.[186]

Turning a Persian mirror to the east, Hidayat also tried to interpret Chinese religions through apparently commensurable concepts drawn from his own tradition. Highly educated and cultured as he was, far from being solely reliant on French and German books, he was able to draw on the rich vocabulary of Persian Sufi poetry and Arabic metaphysical thought. In this way, he presented the teachings of Confucius and Lao Tzu as being complementary by means of the Islamic binary of the exoteric (*zahiri*) and esoteric (*batini*) aspects of cosmic Truth, one stressing compliance with external moral laws, the other emphasizing the pursuit of the inner spiritual path.[187] He then gave Muslim meaning to Chinese legends of creation, which, despite his having learned of them through European sources, he reinterpreted in terms of Sufi metaphysical doctrines of the changing manifestations of primordial pure Being.[188]

Here, there sounded a pleasing echo of prior intercultural interpretations in China itself. Though there is no evidence that Hidayat knew this, his reading of the Confucian tradition through Islamic philosophical concepts reflected the earlier methods of Chinese Muslim authors of the Chinese-language *Han Kitab* texts that similarly tried to draw parallels between Confucianism and Islam.[189] Hence, in a rare Persian account of nirvana (the word itself transliterated), Hidayat defined this state as being "like a lantern which is burned out such that nothing of it remains [*baqi*]." Here he deployed a key Sufi concept that he subsequently amplified by comparing nirvana to a verse by the medieval mystical poet Sana'i of Ghazna:

> *Bimir ay dust pish az marg,*
> *Agar 'umr-i abad khwahi.*

> Die, o friend, before death,
> If you desire eternal life.[190]

Yet like his Arab and Ottoman contemporaries, the Iranian Hidayat was deeply interested in China's Muslims. Moreover, he and his travel companions made direct contact with local coreligionists in Beijing by visiting two mosques there.[191] For one of the mosques, he transcribed what he took to be its Chinese name into Arabic script as "*Chin men waytu layasheh.*" This appears to have been more of an address than a name, referring to the mosque's location in the region of Beijing "outside [*waytu*] the Qianmen gate."[192] He also mentioned that the mosque's imam was of Central Asian Bukharan descent, noting his name as Nur al-Din. (This was presumably in addition to his Chinese name, which Hidayat didn't record.) What enabled their interactions was that this imam knew a little Arabic.[193] In a tantalizing glance of the renewal of medieval connections between Iran and China, he showed the Iranian party a Quran, several Arabic works on jurisprudence, and a manuscript of a law book in Persian.[194]

Hidayat's description of these manuscripts—and the mosque where they were kept—suggests the latter may have been the Tiaozhou Hutong mosque, which treasured a hand-copied Quran attributed to "Hua Baba, the *fanren* (barbarian-Westerner)"—a reference to a Muslim from somewhere west of China.[195] Alternatively, the Iranians might have visited Beijing's more famous Niujie mosque, which housed a fourteenth-century Quran with interlinear Persian translation and a similarly Yuan/Mongol-era copy of the *Kitab al-Hidaya* (*Book of Guidance*) by al-Marghinani (d. 1197).[196] Such was the *Hidaya*'s continued importance across Muslim Asia as a legal handbook that it had been one of the earliest works translated by the East India Company in Calcutta, whereas just a few years before Hidayat inspected its manuscript in Beijing, an Urdu translation was issued in Lucknow by the Hindu commercial publisher Nawwal Kishore, who had also published Corcoran's early Urdu book on China.[197] Yet sitting in the mosque that Beijing morning in 1903, Hidayat could only marvel at how such Persian texts had reached there. Baron von

Richthofen's newly coined notion of a Silk Road that long linked Iran with China had not yet been translated into Persian.

Nonetheless, the Iranian visit to the mosque coincided with the onset of a new era of Muslim interactions across the Middle East, China, and India. Convinced of the need to ameliorate the conditions of his coreligionists, Hidayat's senior companion, the former prime minister Mirza 'Ali Asghar Khan Atabek, donated funds to restore the Niujie mosque.[198] Then, within a year of the Iranians' visit, the Ottoman government began a self-projecting outreach to China's Muslims by sending orthodox Hanafi religious instructors from Istanbul to Beijing.[199] Just as Hidayat was adding a potted history of Islam in China to his memoir of the mosque encounter, in the early 1900s the Ottoman authors Abdülaziz Efendi and Hasan Tahsin published two books devoted to the subject of Islam in China.[200] Articles on the subject were also increasingly appearing in popular Istanbul newspapers such as İkdam (Effort). Consequently, within a couple of years, these connections saw a new Muslim school opened beside the Niujie mosque. It was directed by two Ottoman instructors, Hafiz Ali Rıza and Hafiz Hasan Efendi.

In 1906 the Muslims of Beijing received another Ottoman visitor, Süleyman Şükrü (1865–1922?).[201] The scion of a wealthy landowning family, having sailed first to Bombay, Şükrü reached Shanghai by a steamship via Rangoon before heading inland to Beijing, where he stayed in a lodge run by ethnic Chinese Muslims known as Hui.[202] Like Hidayat, Şükrü penned a brief account of Confucianism and Buddhism based on his visits to a few famous temples. He was guided by a local Hui called Muhammad Sa'id, who translated between Chinese and Arabic for Şükrü.[203] As a result of one such mediated interview, Şükrü transcribed into his diary the Chinese names for Confucianism (rujia) and Buddhism (fojiao).[204] But unlike his Iranian contemporary, when it came to describing the temples he saw, Şükrü, for want of a more accurate Turkish vocabulary, fell back on the old terminology of the "house of idols" (put-hane) and its "idol worshippers" (abade-i asnam).[205] This was nonetheless understandable: for as we saw in chapter 2, what appears to have been the first Turkish book on Buddhism would not be published for another quarter century.

When the Siberian Tatar 'Abd al-Rashid Ibrahim (1857–1944) reached Beijing in 1909 after a long journey on the Trans-Siberian Railroad, his interests remained focused more on the religion of the self than on the Confucian or Buddhist other. We have already encountered Ibrahim promoting Islam in Japan, though he also spent three months in China, apparently on behalf of Japanese Asianists hoping to form an alliance with China's Muslim minority.[206] Ibrahim tried to gather information on the state of Islam across the ailing Qing Empire, data he fed into the book on his evangelizing travels he published the following year in Istanbul.[207] He was helped in his inquiries by Wang Kuan (also known as 'Abd al-Rahman), a scholar affiliated with the same Niujie mosque associated with the previous Ottoman visitors to Beijing. Having made the pilgrimage to Mecca in 1906, Wang Kuan knew some Arabic. But if this helped Ibrahim surmount China's formidable language barriers, then it further polished the looking glass through which he saw China as a reflection of the Muslim self.

Ibrahim's evaluation of Chinese Islam thus became a critique of both self and other as the concerns of a member of imperial Russia's Muslim minority were projected onto their similarly outnumbered Chinese brethren. And so Chinese Islam was seen as having declined from an earlier period of purity, particularly through the inability to read or access what, like other Muslim reformists, Ibrahim regarded as Arabic core texts. Unable to read the rich corpus of Chinese-language texts on Islam written during previous centuries, Ibrahim saw Chinese Islam as inferior to its Middle Eastern counterpart. More alarming still, having lost touch with Arabic made China's Muslims easy prey for the Christian missionaries who had lately turned their attention to them: like the Iranian Hidayat, Ibrahim described the arrival of missionaries.[208]

But when it came to giving a figure for the number of Muslims in China, both authors gave overestimates that ironically derived from Christian missionary fantasies: Hidayat gave a figure of 20 million, and Ibrahim massively overestimated up to 80 million.[209] Both suffered from the same lack of information that led them to resort to German or Russian sources. Now that ties with China's Muslims had been reestablished, however, that would begin to change, as we will see in the next chapter.

As was the case among other regions of Asia, political and economic connections did not automatically produce intercultural knowledge between India, the Middle East, and China. From the appearance of early printed texts in the 1840s well into the 1900s, authors writing in Arabic, Persian, Turkish, Hindi, Urdu, Gujarati, and Bengali found it difficult to access direct, reliable, or recent information on China. In the absence of indigenous informants, and lacking the ability to read Chinese sources, most of these writers turned to the far more abundant studies of China in European languages, whether English, French, German, Russian, or even Latin. Nor were Indian or Middle

Eastern authors necessarily able to assess or access the most reliable of these informants. This allowed not only long-outdated data to pass into the Asian public sphere, but also problematic conceptions of China that derived from Europe, such as the enduring Confucianist paradigm that the Jesuit Matteo Ricci transmitted to his European as well as his Asian readers.

Yet these obstacles and limitations should not detract from the achievements of the authors examined here, who often read their European sources comparatively and critically. For after the early direct accounts by the Bombay merchants Patell and Ishwardas, in the 1900s the appearance of other travelogues helped mitigate this long-standing reliance on European informants. But here too were constraints, because the places, persons, and experiences these travelers described were limited to the coastal geography of steamship ports and the few and fixed routes of China's rail network. The imperial infrastructures that enabled these interactions also thereby confined them. The most astute travelers, such as Hidayat and Singh, learned to leverage their observations by combining them with European sources to make maximum interpretive mileage from their restricted journeys. But limitations remained in this method, not least the many flaws in European understanding. That none of the Indian or Middle Eastern travelogue authors apparently spoke or read Chinese further constrained their accuracy as inter-Asian informants, prompting dependence on pidgin, English, or occasionally Arabic to communicate verbally.

This brings us to the biggest challenge of all: interpreting China's cultural, religious, and intellectual traditions, which were inevitably expressed in writing. Different interpreters of China developed different approaches to this problem, from Zaman's decision to adopt Ricci's intellectualized Latin elevation of the Confucian "religion of the scholars" to Hidayat's resort to Persian Sufi poetry to explain the doctrines of Daoism, and the similarities Ishwardas drew between Chinese temples and popular Hindu worship. Yet right down to adopting the Latin rendition of Confucius's name, Confucianism—and Daoism—was presented in terms derived from the Orientalists, and especially missionaries, of Europe. This dependence was not only because Confucian and Daoist texts were written in classical Chinese, for which there were no grammars or dictionaries in Middle Eastern and Indian languages. It was perhaps also because, as late as 1900, learned Indians, Arabs, Ottomans, and Iranians had so little sense of affinity or ownership toward these unfamiliar religions that they sometimes lacked even names in their languages.

Whether as a consequence or cause of this, by the 1900s no direct translations of major Confucian or Daoist texts had apparently been published in

Indian or Middle Eastern languages. Nor were there any "Pan-Confucian" or "global Daoist" movements comparable to the Pan-Islamist and Pan-Buddhist networks that encouraged other Asian coreligionists to learn common languages to communicate and reinvigorate what they perceived as their common tradition. Even Chinese Buddhism remained largely aloof after the Ceylonese Buddhist missionary Dharmapala's short visit to Shanghai in 1893 failed to attract local Buddhists to his projection of his own Theravada tradition. Busy with their own print-based projections, Shanghai's new Buddhist organizations meanwhile developed alternative visions of Buddhist unity.[210]

By the early 1900s, even the spread of the grand idea of "Asia" had lent little motivation for Indian and Middle Eastern scholars to chart the linguistic and philosophical depths of China's distinct cultural traditions. But over the following decades, projections of the self paved the way for appreciations of the other as Muslims made pioneering translations of Confucius and Hindus pored over block-printed texts of Chinese Buddhism.

6 • China in the Mirrors of Buddhism and Islam

Around 1923 a brilliant young Chinese scholar from rural Hunan province took a steamship to Calcutta to pursue his education.[1] Unable to speak any Indian languages, he carried a Mandarin-English phrasebook published by Shanghai's Commercial Press.[2] With this basic linguistic equipment, he managed to communicate with local coreligionists in Calcutta, who sent him by train to Lucknow. There he was enrolled in a local seminary before being dispatched in turn to the newly founded Jamia Millia university. Mastering both English and Urdu, he completed a bachelor's degree before returning to the seminary, where he wrote a book in Urdu to explain the history of his people to an Indian readership. Simply and definitively, the book was titled *Chini Musulman* (*The Chinese Muslims*). This was not an account of a Buddhist or Confucian China, but an ethnography and history of its Islamic minority. Based on Chinese sources that bypassed the earlier reliance on European informants, it was the result of Muslim educational networks that reached further and deeper than the various other Indian attempts to interact with and understand China that evolved in the 1920s and 1930s.

The author, Hai Weiliang, was a member of the community of Chinese-speaking Hui, who are also referred to here as Sino-Muslims to distinguish them from the Uyghur and other Turkic Muslims of China. Long separated from their coreligionists elsewhere, these Sino-Muslims had developed their own intellectual tradition, based on Chinese-language interpretations of medieval Persian Sufi works that correlated their religion to the larger Confucian mainstream of their surroundings. But as the Asian communications revolution connected his community to other regions, and the books being published there, Hai became one of a small but influential cohort of Sino-Muslims who left their homeland to rediscover their religion through the Arabic language of the Quranic scripture. Equipped with the firm grasp of the language he acquired in Lucknow's modern Nadwat al-ʿUlama seminary, Hai left India after writing his book in the Urdu he also learned there. He completed his religious studies in Cairo, where he joined a small group of fellow Hui who were just then publishing accounts of China in Arabic.

By placing Hai Weiliang's learned and lengthy book into this wider context, we will see it as part of larger attempts to engage with China across India and the Middle East alike. These attempts differed from previous ventures in intercultural knowledge by emerging from formal educational institutions, whether new secular universities or religious seminaries. From China, Japan, and India to Iran, Afghanistan, and Egypt, this more institutionalized approach to inter-Asian understanding found expression in a corresponding range of languages, from Urdu and Bengali to Persian and Arabic. It also took several different forms: Muslim and Buddhist, religious and secular, Pan-Buddhist, Pan-Islamist, and Asianist. Yet the knowledge that emerged from each of these projects was shaped by the familiar dialectic of self and other.

Despite their different agendas, new studies of China—and Chinese studies of the Middle East and India—were made possible by the same imperial infrastructure of port cities and printing centers. This maritime informational geography also overlapped with educational institutions, and Calcutta continued to play an oversized role. Beyond this infrastructure context, there were also commonalities in content between the deeper engagements with China that developed from the 1920s, particularly by tracing evidence of older inter-Asian ties through more documentary forms of historical inquiry, albeit at times by incorporating European sources or methods. Even Hai Weiliang—who tried to channel Chinese knowledge directly to Indian readers—drew on methods that his Indian Muslim teachers had for their own intellectual purposes previously adopted from the British. Once again, in modern times at least, the search for a purely indigenous form of inter-Asian understanding proves to be as elusive as it is illusory.

After looking at the new Indian investigations of China that developed in the 1920s and 1930s, and then the deeper interest in Chinese culture seen in Middle Eastern works of the period, we will turn to Hai Weiliang and his fellow Sino-Muslim students, who not only wrote in Urdu about their own community history but also translated Confucius into Arabic. As Bengalis claimed China as part of a Buddhist- or Hindu-based "Greater India," and Chinese intellectuals developed their own ideas of what different parts of the continent held in common, Asia's self-discovery continued to unfold through projections of the self that fostered partial appreciations of the other.

Bengali Sinology between Spirituality and Ideology

Expanding through the 1920s, by the 1930s the Indian émigré population in the ports of China peaked at about 10,000, most of them soldiers, policemen, and traders.[3] Correspondingly, Calcutta and Bombay, along with Rangoon and to a lesser extent Colombo, became home to Chinese diaspora communities. The first Chinese settler in India was purportedly a tea merchant called Yang Dazhao, who had settled in Calcutta as early as the 1770s.[4] By 1857 he had been followed to Calcutta by around five hundred Cantonese and Hakka, who worked as shoemakers, carpenters, and small-scale opium dealers, as well as several Qing officials and reformists forced into exile by their opposition to either British or Chinese policies.[5] Reflecting the expanding trade connections in the wake of the Opium Wars, a parallel Chinese community of around the same size emerged in Bombay.[6] Just as the Indian presence in China saw the founding of religious institutions, such as the several Indian mosques established in Hong Kong from the 1880s, the Chinese presence in India's ports saw the founding of temples to Guandi and Guanyin, as well as several *huiguan* (native-place associations) of the kind found throughout the Chinese diaspora in maritime Asia.[7] By around 1940, the Chinese population in India had grown to over 25,000.[8]

It was also in Bombay, and especially Calcutta, that a concentration of Indian expertise on China began to emerge. But while gifted ordinary residents of the two ports may well have learned to speak Cantonese or Hakka dialect with their immigrant neighbors, the university-educated Bengali Sinologists moved in different spatial and social circles from the Cantonese cobblers and the Hakkas who worked in the tanning of animal hides that respectable Hindus considered ritually polluting.[9] Rather than learning spoken dialects and drawing on living oral informants, Calcutta's bilingual Indian intelligentsia, fluent in English and Bengali, amplified Calcutta's previous role as an informational hub on China by translating or summarizing books and articles from English. In many cases, these English works had been compiled with substantial Chinese assistance, pointing again to the role of Europeans as inter-Asian intermediaries.

From the 1920s, however, the expansion of Indian universities gave rise to a new generation of scholars who learned to read classical Chinese texts directly, hoping to bypass the long-standing mediation of European (and often missionary) informants. As Indian educational networks reached from Calcutta to Shanghai by way of London and Paris, a pioneering circle of Bengali scholars developed a more linguistically robust Indian Sinology. After drawing on three centuries of European investigations of China fostered by empire and evangelicalism, this new generation of Indian investigators took their inquiries in new directions that placed India itself in the central position. In the meantime, after the visit to Calcutta in 1902 by Okakura Kakuzo, the pioneering Japanese Asianist, Bengal had also become India's main outpost of Asianism. This added an ideological impetus to the study of China that promoted not so much the study of Chinese traditions in and of themselves as the history of Indo-Chinese connections in which China was cast as the recipient of Indian culture.

This conceptual emphasis on connection was an integral feature of the Asianist paradigm. By resurrecting an earlier age of Asian interactions, scholarship was tasked with providing a proof-tested past template for present-day anticolonial alliances. Yet whether in writing of the past or in planning the future, this search for solidarity always raised the unstated question: Unity on whose terms? In this way, Asianist visions of Sino-Indian connections served as another outlet for projections of the self, especially via connections in ancient and early medieval times, when India could be positioned as the dominant cultural partner.

By the early 1900s, Chinese and Indian revolutionaries were already learning of their common political conditions and conceiving a shared meta-identity through the borrowed idea of "Asia." Insofar as there was direct contact between Chinese and Indian proponents of Asianism, it came in large part through Japan, where such influential theorists as Zhang Taiyan (1869–1936) met Bengali counterparts like the Stanford-educated Surendra Mohan Bose.[10] In 1907 in Tokyo they established the Association of Asian Affinity, which promoted a selective vision of Asian unity that excluded the continent's most widespread culture: Islam. Although Zhang translated articles from Anglophone Indian journals such as the *Indian Sociologist* and *Free Hindustan* for his exile newspaper *Min Bao* (*People's Tribune*), published in Tokyo from 1905 to 1910, these newfound Asianist affinities did not automatically foster detailed intercultural knowledge, not least because many of these radicals were scornful of Asia's cultural heritage.[11] While colonial censorship restricted the association's reach into the public sphere—British and Japanese officials clamped down on its publications—the continued existence of linguistic and other interpretive barriers between India and China further restrained their appreciation of each other's cultures, unless they resorted to the easier mediation of European studies.

Over the following decades, Indian and Chinese nationalists continued to seek common cause as the universalized language of nationalism allowed political ideas to travel comparatively easily.[12]

But translating and sharing vague (and ultimately third-party) political slogans like "independence" and "unity"—or "Asia" and "nation"—proved easier than transferring knowledge of Indian and Chinese cultural traditions, which through millennia of development contained manifold subtleties of existential and moral meaning. The interwoven ideologies of nationalism and Asianism could distort as much as enable this search for deeper understanding.

This dilemma is seen most vividly in the writings of the Bengali intellectual Benoy Kumar Sarkar. In 1916 he published *The Chinese Religion through Hindu Eyes,* which echoed the even more grandiose claims of his other book from the same year, *The Beginning of Hindu Culture as World-Power.*[13] Sarkar was closely associated with India's elite Anglophone educational institutions, holding bachelor's and master's degrees from Calcutta University, where he was later appointed professor of economics.[14] And like other anticolonial activists of the period, he made effective use of the transport networks that converged on Calcutta, sailing not only to Europe but also to Egypt, China, and Japan (twice), as well as Japan's colony of Korea.[15] This maritime intellectual geography would shape his contribution to Chinese studies when he researched, wrote, and published his *Chinese Religion through Hindu Eyes* during a stay in Shanghai in 1915. Its port city publisher, the Commercial Press, was an appropriate one for an author who had recently disembarked from Calcutta, for it would later supply the Sino-Muslim student Hai Weiliang with the English dictionary he used to communicate with other Calcutta Indians.

Yet though Sarkar was a committed Asianist, and a talented linguist who learned French, Italian, and German, he was not in any substantive sense a Sinologist. As he explained in his preface, he researched his book by making use of the library of the Christian Literature Society in Shanghai, where he was helped by the Welsh Baptist missionary (and scholar of Buddhism), the Reverend Dr. Timothy Richard (1845–1919).[16] Continuing the use of European scholarship seen in previous decades, along with Okakura's English *Ideals of the East* (itself completed in Calcutta), Sarkar's extensive bibliography drew mainly on missionary and Orientalist studies of China and Japan, albeit read in relation to studies of Hindu religiosity by Bengali scholars.[17]

But the resulting book—*Chinese Religion through Hindu Eyes*—was no passive compilation of previous works. It was instead a determined attempt to combine European Sinology with Hindu theology in pursuit of his own ideological agenda. As both an Asianist and Hindu nationalist, this meant reconciling several potentially competing frameworks into an upright overall posture of Hindu self-projection.

While Japanese Asianists positioned their own nation (and empire) as the leader of Asian unity, most forcefully through their euphemistically colonial Greater East Asia Co-Prosperity Sphere, for Sarkar the solution was to present China and Japan as part of a "Greater India" whose deep historical roots lay in the South Asian origins of East Asia's borrowed Buddhist culture. As Sarkar presented the long history of Asian civilization, India was therefore the teacher, Japan and China its pupils.[18]

Yet this unifying solution produced its own problems in turn. Not only did it demote the indigenous Confucian, Daoist, and Shinto dimensions of Chinese and Japanese culture in its search for an Indian and therefore Buddhist-based model of unity; it also challenged Sarkar's Hindu nationalist commitments by likewise requiring India to squeeze into this Buddhist mold. His solution was to present Buddhism as itself a form of Hinduism. Ultimately, this allowed him to conclude that, across India, Japan, and China, "the eight hundred millions of human beings in the Far East should be considered as professing the same faith," namely, the Buddhism that was itself merely a form of Hinduism.[19] It is with good reason that his fellow Bengali scholar Satadru Sen has recently described Sarkar as a "notoriously contrarian thinker."[20]

In making such casuistical arguments, Sarkar drew evidentiary data from dozens of European books about the religions and history of China and Japan he accessed through the Shanghai library of the Christian Literature Society. But at the same time, he rejected the larger interpretations of these source texts, particularly when it came to recognizing the distinct origins and philosophical differences between Asia's religions, which he had to overlook to make his case for overall unity. To frame Buddhism, Confucianism, Daoism, and Shinto as all versions of Hinduism, he also rejected the long-standing claims of various Christian missionaries that the religions of Asia were originally forms of monotheism that were slowly debased over time.[21] This was an idea that also appealed to various Muslim commentators on China's religions, as well as Calcutta's monotheist Hindu reformists. But Sarkar's solution was to downplay Islam as little more than a crude medieval political force preventing an Asian unity that was properly based on the true creed of polytheism.[22]

For "not only in Asia, but all over the world, man has ever been a polytheist."[23] This was not so much an engagement with difference as a denial of its existence, which led Sarkar to ask rhetorically in his concluding chapter, "Are the Chinese and the Japanese, then, Hindus? The answer is 'yes.'"[24]

Although his *Chinese Religion* was written in English, Sarkar's Indocentric conception of China also fed into his various Bengali writings, whether his many articles for Calcutta-based journals or his 1922 book, *China Sabhyatar A, Aa, Ka, Kha (ABCD of Chinese Civilization)*.[25] By the time *Chinese Religion* was published, the notion of Buddhism as a form of Hinduism was also being promoted by V. D. Savarkar, the most influential theorist of Hindu nationalism, whom we have already seen planning to build a "Pan-Hindu" temple in Japan. In Savarkar's similarly self-projecting formula, Buddhism "was only a reformation movement among the Hindus. Hence Buddhists are as much Hindus as Protestants are Christians."[26]

It would, however, prove to be the efforts of the great Bengali poet Tagore that enabled a deeper and more direct Indian comprehension of Chinese traditions, albeit as a result of his disillusioned turn against nationalism after his visits to China and Japan. Despite the criticisms of Chinese socialists and nationalists alike, his rejection of nationalist politics paved the way for his promotion of a fuller appreciation of China's traditional Confucian as well as Buddhist culture, which in his transcendental version of Asianism he presented as expressions of an overarching "Eastern spirituality."

In April 1924 Tagore sailed to Shanghai aboard the Japanese steamship *Atsatu Maru* at the start of a six-week lecture tour.[27] Following the infrastructural and ideological connections that linked the ascendant Indian engagement with China to the Japanophilia of previous decades, Tagore's visit was part of an itinerary that also took in Japan. Taking the train inland from the coast, he was hosted by the *Jiangxueshe* (Beijing Lecture Association), which had previously arranged a lecture tour by the British philosopher Bertrand Russell.[28] But unlike the latter, Tagore was no atheist materialist; nor for that matter was he a modernist or nationalist like his hosts. Instead, he had come to preach to the Chinese the virtues of their ancestral Confucian traditions. In his lectures—which were delivered in English and translated verbatim by Xu Zhimo (1897–1931), an innovative American-educated poet—Tagore tried to persuade his Chinese audiences to avoid the spiritually blind alleys of materialism and nationalism that Japan had chosen to follow.[29]

It was less than two decades since Chinese reformers had abolished the more-than-a-millennium-old Confucianist civil service exams, and Tagore's lectures were met with open hostility. As Qu Qubai (1899–1935), a leading communist intellectual and admirer of Russell, wrote in an article in caustic response, "Mr. Tagore, thank you! There is already plenty of Kongmeng [Confucius and Mencius] in our country."[30] Even Chen Duxiu (1879–1942), the leftist poet who in 1915 had first translated Tagore into Chinese from the English version of his *Gitanjali,* now penned articles denouncing the lectures.[31] It was not only in Shanghai that Tagore was facing criticism. When the roving Iraqi journalist Younis Bahri (c. 1903–1979) founded an Arabic journal in Java, he denounced Tagore for exacerbating the colonial repression of Muslims by presenting Islam as a religion that was foreign to Asia.[32]

Despite being cast as a reactionary in China itself, upon his return to Calcutta, Tagore published his lectures and then set about building the institutional wherewithal for Indians at least to learn from the traditions the Chinese radicals and reformers were themselves rejecting.[33] A superbly sensitive man of letters, Tagore knew the importance of understanding a culture through its own language. Reflecting on the youthful attempts to appreciate Goethe and Heine in English translation that had prompted him to take German lessons from a Protestant missionary, in one of his lectures he had declared that "languages are jealous: They do not give up their best treasures to those who try to deal with them through an intermediary belonging to an alien rival."[34] Couched in characteristic metaphor, it was a perceptive précis of the dilemma of reliance on European translations.

We have already seen how, in 1905, Tagore had recruited a Japanese language teacher for his school at Shantiniketan, northwest of Calcutta, which amid the rapid expansion of Indian universities became Visva-Bharati University in 1921. Consolidating his turn from Japan toward China, he then tried to build on his language experiment by recruiting a Chinese teacher instead.[35]

The first language instructor he employed emerged from the maritime geography of the Asian public sphere. Dr. Lim Ngo-Chiang was the principal of a Chinese school in Rangoon, who invited Tagore to give a lecture there and acted as his interpreter after his steamship called at the Burmese port en route to Shanghai.[36] Rangoon was a sensible place to recruit a teacher of Chinese, since it hosted not only a substantial Chinese population, but also a multilingual one: it was there that in 1902 a unique phrasebook had been published for English, Tamil, Urdu, and Chinese, albeit all in Burmese characters.[37] (In 1918 the similar Chinese presence in British Malaya prompted the publication in the port of Penang of a short dictionary of English, Malay, and spoken Hokkien dialect, albeit in romanized script, which was similarly impractical for reading Chinese.)[38] But Tagore's aims went beyond bolstering trade through teaching basic oral commercial phrases. Such was his abhorrence of Asia's sprawling business networks that in his travelogue *Japan-yatri* (*Journey to Japan*) he pronounced "from the wharves at Calcutta to these in Hong Kong, I have seen the ugly face of commerce in every port," adding, "I cannot help but think of commerce as an animal, as a pre-historic monster."[39] Instead of promoting trade, he aimed to inculcate a deeper appreciation of Chinese poetry he had himself read in English translation.[40]

In 1925 Lim accepted Tagore's invitation and made his own journey across the Bay of Bengal to become the first Chinese-language teacher at Visva-Bharati University.[41] But although he contributed a short article on early Chinese literature to the university journal, Lim left after little more than a year, like his Japanese predecessor, which led Tagore to seek a replacement among China's maritime diaspora. He selected Tan Yunshan (1898–1983), a lay Buddhist scholar whom he met in Singapore in 1927, where Tan already worked as a language teacher after a failed career as a newspaper editor.[42]

Tagore and Tan's joint venture was by no means an immediate success, not least for lack of funding and the broader interest that could provide it. Consequently, Tan also left Visva-Bharati and found more regular work on a Chinese newspaper in Rangoon.[43] But over the course of the next decade, as China's ascendant nationalists also recognized the soft power potential of Asianism, Tan succeeded in winning the support of the Nanjing-based Sino-Indian Cultural Society, established by the Kuomintang, the ruling nationalist party, in 1933.[44] That same year, the society funded the publication of Tan's *Yindu zhouyou ji* (*Travelogue to India*), which combined descriptions of coastal cities such as Calcutta with an evocative account of an inland journey in the footsteps of Xuanzang, the Chinese Buddhist pilgrim who would serve as the patron saint of this new phase in Sino-Indian relations.[45] The timing was effective insofar as a decade earlier a Hindu scholar had translated Xuanzang's travelogue into Urdu, albeit from an English version.[46] The Urdu Xuanzang was published by the Punjab Religious Book Society, which missionaries had founded in 1866.

Through Tan's efforts, in 1937 the Kuomintang's financial support finally led to the foundation of the Cheena Bhavana (Chinese Institute) at Visva-Bharati University, along with a large library of Chinese-language books, all overseen by Tan as academic inter-Asian impresario. In the meantime, Tagore hosted two influential European scholars as visiting professors: the Frenchman Sylvain Lévi, who arrived in 1921 to lecture on Sanskrit and Tibetan, and the Italian Giuseppe Tucci (1894–1984), who spent 1923–1924 introducing

Indian students to Chinese and Tibetan Buddhist texts.[47] Tan initiated a re-ciprocal research program aimed at translating into Indian languages "lost" works of Sanskrit Buddhism that survived in Chinese and Tibetan transla-tions from a thousand years earlier.[48] One of their first students was Vasudev Gokhale (1900–1991), who went on to translate several such Tibetan and Chi-nese Buddhist texts and to teach Chinese at the Bhandarkar Oriental Research Institute in Poona, inland by train from Bombay.[49]

Founded in 1917, by the following year the Bhandarkar institute was issu-ing its own research journal in English. Its goal was to promote the research of Indian scholars of Sanskrit and Pali, albeit with European input. In the journal's first issue, its founder, Sir Ramakrishna Bhandarkar (1837–1925), counseled his learned compatriots that "our critical studies must be conducted conjointly with European scholars."[50] Even so, the studies of ancient manu-scripts that appeared in the institute's *Annals* were geared more toward an In-dian self-discovery than the investigation of other Asians; Gokhale's studies of China did not appear in its pages till the late 1930s.[51] Though Gokhale did not share Sarkar's self-projecting notion of China as part of a Hindu civilization, his was still a view of China through the lens of Indian Buddhism.

Meanwhile, at the Cheena Bhavana in Bengal, China's non-Buddhist heri-tage was of similarly limited interest, since neither Confucianism nor Daoism could be traced back to India.[52] As the title of a 1923 book by Visva-Bharati's professor of history Phanindra Nath Bose (1896–1932) put it, the purpose of the Cheena Bhavana was primarily to highlight the influence of "the Indian teachers in China."[53] Though this may have seemed appealing from the In-dian side, Chinese intellectuals were starting to see the matter quite differ-ently. Hu Shih (1891–1962), a highly influential philosopher, historian, and diplomat, began presenting Buddhism as responsible for undermining the rational, humane, and protoscientific dimensions of China's indigenous cul-ture, which led him to decry the "dead weight of over a thousand years of In-dianization."[54] Far from sharing the self-projecting vision of the Bengali boost-ers of Buddhism, Hu proclaimed that "with the new aids of modern science and technology, and of the new social and historical sciences, we are confident that we may yet achieve a rapid liberation from the two thousand years' cul-tural domination by India."[55]

The new Indian interest in a Buddhist-framed China carried on regardless. During the same years that Tagore and Tan began to institutionalize Indian Sinology, two other Bengalis set out on their own interpretive journeys across Asia by heading to Paris. Kalidas Nag (1892–1966) and Prabodh Chandra Bag-chi (1898–1956) were both graduates of Calcutta University (though Nag had

first studied at the city's Scottish Church College). They were both also associated with the Greater India Society, which Nag had cofounded in 1924 while
still a student. Two years later, he published a short English book titled *Greater
India*, which in 1929 was translated into Hindi.[56] In the meantime, he had
proceeded to Paris, writing a doctoral dissertation on ancient Indian international diplomacy.[57] Learning French enabled him to channel Francophone
research on Buddhism back to Calcutta, as he did with his translation of Joseph Hackin's report on archaeological excavations in Afghanistan that further demonstrated the cultural reach of India far beyond its borders.[58] Aptly,
the translation appeared in the *Journal of the Greater India Society* that Nag had
helped establish.

Nag's and Bagchi's interests in a *Maha-Bharat*, or "Greater India," whose
influence stretched far across Asia, would not lead to the kinds of distortions
seen in Sarkar's *Chinese Religion through Hindu Eyes*. Even so, they still viewed
China in terms of its ancient links with—and debt to—India. But unlike
Sarkar (who was content to rely on the mediation of earlier English studies of
China) and Nag (whose quest for an ever-greater Greater India soon saw him
turn his projections to the Pacific), Bagchi was so much committed to China
that he learned to read its classical writings, which he saw as a conduit for
ideas first formed in Sanskrit.[59] For even Baghchi was concerned with Indian-
derived Buddhism rather than Confucianism or Daoism.

Building on the work of the Bengali rediscoverers of Buddhism a generation earlier, Bagchi had set out by learning Sanskrit at Calcutta University
before being drawn to further studies at Visva-Bharati University by the arrival of Sylvain Lévi in 1921.[60] Though Lévi was a Sanskritist by training, his
research in French colonial Southeast Asia—or *Indochine*, in its suggestive
French formulation—had drawn him toward the fusion of Indian and Chinese traditions, particularly through the prism of Buddhism, which formed
the mainstay of his publications. Through the confluence in Calcutta of these
distinct but corresponding Bengali and French conceptions of a "Greater India," Bagchi set out with Lévi on the next stages of his Sinological journey.
Far from taking him directly to China, this took him first to the Royal Durbar Library of Nepal, which we have seen as the bibliographical front line for
India's earlier rediscovery of Buddhism; then through Indochina, where the
river port of Hanoi had emerged as a Francophone Asian research center to
parallel Calcutta; and finally to Japan, whose old monastic libraries Lévi had
made known to European researchers of Chinese Buddhism.[61] After spending
time at the École Française d'Extrême-Orient in Hanoi, in 1923 Bagchi sailed
to France for doctoral studies with Lévi and Henri Maspero (1883–1945), who

Enter the academics: Professor Prabodh Chandra Bagchi at Visva-Bharati University. Photograph by Ratna Sinha (Bagchi) and Sudhir Khastogir, 1956. Wikimedia Commons.

was then completing his monumental *La Chine antique* and whose expertise also came partly through investigations in French colonial *Indochine*.[62] Bagchi finally reached China after these circuitous itineraries in 1924, when he traveled with Nag and Tagore on the latter's disastrous lecture tour.[63]

Returning home two years later, Bagchi went on to teach at both Calcutta University and, from the mid-1940s, Visva-Bharati University. But like other members of this new generation of university-educated scholars, he wrote most of his learned output in English or French, whether his historical survey of Indo-Chinese cultural relations or his recondite philological studies of Chinese translations of the Sanskrit Buddhist canon.[64] Though he did publish some shorter general articles in Bengali, his books were not translated till the 1950s and later.[65] But even if Bagchi did not place his findings primarily in the Indian-language channels of the public sphere, he did make use of its maritime informational geography by publishing most of his writings in India's port cities, whether through Calcutta's *Bulletin of the Greater India Society*, the

Calcutta Review, the *Sino-Indian Studies* journal he founded in the 1940s, or the Calcutta and Bombay editions of *India and China: A Thousand Years of Cultural Relations.*[66] If present-day unity with China was harder to find, the past offered Bagchi easier terms—especially when the terms were set by Indian Buddhism.

Meanwhile, between the 1920s and 1940s, China was making its own redis-covery of Buddhism. This was neither its own traditional Han Buddhism (*han-chuan fojiao*) nor the ancient Sanskrit texts being edited in Bengal. Instead, it was a new encounter with Tibetan teachings. For while the rise of nationalism saw secularists and neo-Confucianists denounce the deleterious influence of Indian Buddhism on China, small circles of Tibetan lamas and their Chinese disciples translated scores of esoteric Tibetan texts into modern Chinese. Among the key figures were the master Geshé Dorjé Chöpa (1874–19?) and the Chinese monk Guankong (1902–1989), who launched new organizations such as Beijing's Bodhi Study Association (*Puti Xuehui*) to publish their out-put.[67] Emphasizing reincarnated lamas and complex tantric rituals, these texts differed markedly from China's familiar Mahayana canon. But in emerging from China's longtime Tibetan vassal state, this was nonetheless a Buddhism that seemed to belong to China more than the Ceylonese and Indian traditions being projected by the missionary Dharmapala and the Greater India Society.

Even so, this was not a pristine inter-Asian encounter. Various Tibetan texts were filtered through the English versions of Walter Evans-Wentz (1878–1965), a Stanford-educated Theosophist who moved to British-ruled Darjeeling to help the Sikkimese scholar Kazi Dawa Samdup (1868–1922) translate the *Ti-betan Book of the Dead* into English.[68] After Samdup began teaching Tibetan at the University of Calcutta (where the Baptist Mission Press published his groundbreaking dictionary), Evans-Wentz spent the 1920s promoting Tibetan Buddhism far beyond its Himalayan homeland.[69] This not only saw English translations retranslated into Chinese, but also prompted Chinese translators to use Latin-script transliterations as phonetic aids for the pronunciation of unfamiliar Tibetan terms crucial to Tantric practice.[70] In such ways, between Beijing, Palo Alto, Calcutta, and Paris, the Chinese and Indian rediscoveries of Buddhism were more than narrowly inter-Asian developments.

Glimpses of China (and Buddha) from Afghanistan, Iran, and Turkey

Though Bengal became the South Asian intellectual bridgehead for mul-tiple flows of information on China, whether from London or Saigon, by the

1920s new developments were also under way in Afghanistan and Iran that led to a somewhat improved understanding of China. Despite the shared orientation toward antiquity and ties to India's larger public sphere, there were fewer publications on China in Persian compared to India, partly through the relative underdevelopment of universities in Iran and Afghanistan, and partly through the absence of a motivating counterpart to the search for a Greater India. Nonetheless, between the 1920s and 1940s several more accurate short accounts of China were published in Iran and Afghanistan alike. Given that neither country had formal diplomatic relations with modern China before the 1940s, these interests were more scholarly than political, except insofar as they related to domestic cultural politics.[71]

While neither Afghanistan nor Iran reared professional Sinologists like Bagchi, these more accurate accounts of China were, as in India, connected to the emergence of new educational institutions. In Afghanistan, this development was closely tied with India, which supplied modernist Muslim teachers for the Lisa-i Habibiyya (Habibia Lycée), founded in 1903 as the country's first modern high school. When the first Afghan university was being founded in the early 1930s, advice was similarly sought from a delegation of distinguished Indian Muslims that included Ross Masood, whom we have previously seen studying the universities of Japan, and Sulayman Nadwi, whom we will encounter as the educational patron of the Chinese student Hai Weiliang. Meanwhile, as primary public education expanded during the secularizing reign of King Amanullah Khan (r. 1919–1929), the same Indian connections were used to commission Afghan textbooks, including a *History of Nations* series that included a volume on China (as well as another on Japan). Around fifty pages long, it was published in 1926 in India on commission from the Afghan government.[72] Spreading among young Afghans conceptions of geography that ultimately derived from Europe, the textbook located China within East Asia (*Asiya-yi sharqi*).

Described on its cover as a translation (apparently from Turkish), the textbook gave outlines of China's geography, flora and fauna, agricultural produce (particularly tea), and trade (especially silk), as well as the customs and appearance of its people. (The "limitless" authority of parents was mentioned approvingly.) Religion also received brief coverage.[73] But beyond the vague mention that China had "several different religions," the focus was primarily on its tiny Muslim minority, who, in an inflated statistic, were said to number some sixty million.[74] There was, however, a nominal mention of the religion of *Bod,* the Buddha, which at least now had a proper name in place of the *but-parasti,* or idol worship, that still persisted in Afghan publications into the twentieth century.

Then, in the 1930s, Buddhism suddenly became a subject of tremendous interest to a new circle of Afghan scholars associated with the *Anjuman-i Tarikh-i Afghanistan* (Historical Society of Afghanistan), especially its director, Ahmad 'Ali Kuhzad.[75] Countering the self-projections of the Greater India Society in Calcutta, Kuhzad set about recovering the competing history of a "Greater Afghanistan" that was based on the Kushan Empire, which, from its summer capital at Begram, near Kabul, held sway far across Central Asia and India. Like Bagchi and Nag, Kuhzad studied with French savants at the Délégation Archéologique Française en Afghanistan, particularly Alfred Foucher and Joseph Hackin, and spent a formative year in Rome. A year after Nag published his translation of one of Hackin's Afghan excavation reports in the *Journal of the Greater India Society*, Kuhzad made his name by publishing a Dari translation of Hackin's report on the Bamiyan Buddhas.[76] Like his Bengali contemporaries, in subsequent works Kuhzad drew the corpus of European scholarship into his own interpretation of Afghanistan's far-reaching Buddhist past. He would not learn Chinese like Bagchi, but Kuhzad nonetheless made a pioneering Dari translation from French of sections of Sima Qian's famous *Shiji* (*Records of the Grand Historian*).[77] Yet this was not an account of China so much as an account by China of an ancient "greater Afghanistan." The selected section of the *Shiji* was an admiring report by the emissary Zhang Qian, who around 130 BCE was sent to the kingdom of Dayuan, which bordered on modern Afghanistan. Kuhzad's translation thus echoed Bagchi's search for ancient Sino-Indian relations. But it offered a glimpse of China through the magnifying glass of the Afghan self.

While nationalist Iranian intellectuals of the period were also promoting their own civilizational antiquity, there was little role in it for either Buddhism or China. Nonetheless, several short studies of China did emerge amid the opening of the Universisty of Tehran and the Parisian educations of the privileged few. They appeared in the new scholarly journals that were also developing in Iran, such as *Farhang* (*Culture*) and *Taqaddum* (*Progress*), in which a pair of articles on Confucius was published in 1928 and 1929.[78] (These were the same journals we previously saw featuring translated European articles on Buddhism.) Here the Chinese sage was presented as part of two parallel series on "great men of the world" and "great men of the East." Both articles took a historicizing approach to Confucius, placing him into his social and political context. Both also seem to have drawn on European scholarship, to which Iranian intellectuals were increasingly exposed through their studies in Germany and France. (Both articles used Christian dates, and the *Farhang* piece maintained the French transliterations of Chinese names.) In this way, in contrast to the Buddhist prism of Bengali scholars, the two anonymous Persian articles presented China to the Iranian reading public through the Confucianist paradigm first formulated by Matteo Ricci's Renaissance Jesuits and still dominant in European accounts of China till the 1940s. As the piece in *Taqaddum* concluded, "From the time of the Han dynasty [202 BCE–220 CE] till today, over and again the laws and philosophy of Confucius have stood up against all internal and external foes, because it is the laws and philosophy of Confucius that make the nation of China a single unified body."[79] By the time the Iranian articles appeared, several decades after the old order was overturned in the 1912 revolution, this picture of Confucian continuity was far from still the case. Nonetheless, the authors tried to render Confucius relevant to the contemporary secularizing concerns of the Iranian self by presenting him as a philosopher (*filasuf*) rather than a religious teacher and by conceiving China not in the old Persianate imperial terms seen in previous texts but as a modern *millat,* or nation-state.

The problem of vicarious and outdated information was exacerbated by the lack of direct diplomatic relations with China. While a Sino-Iranian treaty had been signed in 1920, it was not until 1934 that the first Iranian consul, Husayn Kai-Ustuvan, was sent to Shanghai after serving in Karachi. Even then, his concerns were more commercial than cultural, his focus being on securing tea and silk exports in return for Iranian opium.[80] Consequently, Iran developed nothing comparable to the late Ottoman strategic outreach to China's Muslims, despite the fact that Persian Sufi texts had been central to Sino-Muslim learning for centuries. As late as 1923, even a Muslim reformist bookseller in Beijing carried "a stock of Persian and Arabic works, numbering one hundred and twenty-eight."[81] But these older Persian-based ties among Muslims in Iran, Afghanistan, and China were not renewed on anything like a comparable scale to the intellectual connections we will now see being forged through Arabic or even Urdu.[82] Unlike their Muslim contemporaries in India and elsewhere in the Middle East who developed a growing interest in Islam in China, the secularizing Iranian intelligentsia saw China either as a modern nationalist republic or as the ancient land of Confucius.

At the same time that Iranian intellectuals were taking an interest in China, parallel—if ultimately linguistically deeper—developments were under way in the neighboring new Republic of Turkey, founded on the ruins of the Ottoman Empire by Mustafa Kemal Atatürk in 1923. Twelve years later, Atatürk established a Faculty of Language, History, and Geography—including a chair in Sinology—at the nascent university in his new capital of Ankara. To build on the late Ottoman alliance with Germany, German scholars were recruited to train Turkey's first cadre of professional Sinologists, beginning with the Berlin-educated Annemarie von Gabain (1901–1993), who spent two years in Ankara as a visiting professor between 1935 and 1937.[83] Gabain was as much a Turkologist as a Sinologist, however, having specialized in the early medieval Uyghur manuscripts that the German imperial explorer Albert von le Coq had taken to Berlin between 1902 and 1914 from Turfan in the Chinese Central Asian province of Xinjiang. Gabain's focus on these Old Turkic texts perfectly suited her sponsors' agenda. She was invited to Ankara at the recommendation of Ayşe Afet İnan (1908–1985), a historian, anthropologist, and adopted daughter of Atatürk who promoted the ascendant "Turkish history thesis" (*Türk Tarih Tezi*), which sought to prove a primordial Turkish migration from a Central Asian homeland posited as a civilizational cradle to rival European claims of Greece and Mesopotamia as the first fonts of civilization.[84]

After İnan helped found the Turkish Historical Society (*Türk Tarih Kurumu*) in 1931, the Chinese past was increasingly viewed through the lenses of Turkish nationalism in ways that paralleled developments associated with the Historical Society of Afghanistan. So it was that when Gabain returned to Germany, she was replaced in Ankara by Wolfram Eberhard (1909–1989), another German Sinologist who together with the Berlin-based Tatar linguist Reşid Rahmeti Arat (1900–1964) had just published another volume of the Old Turkish texts from Turfan.[85] After Arat moved to the newly founded Istanbul University in 1933—and was later elected to the Turkish Historical Society—Eberhard settled in Ankara, where for the next eleven years he held the chair in Chinese studies. Through conversations with local colleagues and investigations of ancient sources, Eberhard developed a grand theory about the shaping influence of Central Asia's early Turkic peoples on subsequent Chinese civilization. His theory found fullest expression in a book he wrote in Turkish that, through its affinity with the official "Turkish history thesis," was published by the Turkish Historical Society.[86]

Both reflecting and rivaling the Indocentric vision of the Chinese past being developed in the universities of India by scholars linked with the Greater India Society, this Turkocentric approach was also—perhaps ironically—applied to Indian history. Consequently, when Indian studies were introduced to Ankara's Faculty of Language, History, and Geography in 1936, India's past was framed primarily through a focus on the "Turkish" medieval sultans of Delhi and the similarly "Turkish" Mughal emperors who followed them.[87] (For Bengali and other Hindu nationalists, meanwhile, this era of "Muslim domination" was presented not only as the nadir of Indian history but as causing the rupture of Asia's Buddhist-built unity.) Thus, the leading Turkish nationalist historian, Mehmet Fuat Köprülü (1890–1966), published a study of Turkish poems patronized by the Ghaznavid sultans who ruled medieval North India, whereas other historians investigated the "Turkish empire" of the Mughals or translated the Persian court memoir of the Mughal princess Gulbadan Begum, as a window into an era of Turkish greatness that was devoid of the stigmas of the recently discarded Ottomans.[88]

In such ways, the nationalist intellectual heyday of the 1930s witnessed a Turkish self-discovery in India and China as both regions were conceived as repositories of a grand Turkish past. Nonetheless, the founding of Ankara's Faculty of Language, History, and Geography, along with its accompanying journal and monograph series, paved the interpretive way for a deeper engagement with Asian difference by way of India's—and China's—own distinctive traditions.

Just as in Bengal, where Tagore and his collaborator Tan Yunshan drew on the financial support of China's ruling nationalist Kuomintang party to build a library of Chinese-language books at Visva-Bharati University, so in Ankara did funds from Turkey's ruling nationalists help establish a parallel collection of specialist works on India.[89] Yet such inter-Asian investigations again involved European partners, including Wolfram Eberhard, who began his task of training local scholars by devising a system for transcribing Chinese words into Turkish.[90]

China's Quest for Asia's Islamic Learning

In the meantime, Chinese scholars—Muslims especially—were making their own inquiries about the Middle East and India. Far from doing so in intellectual isolation, they were drawing on Arabic books and journals printed in Istanbul, Cairo, and Singapore that were exported to China.[91] Moreover, the vast Arabic and Persian output of India's commercial presses, which were imported through Shanghai and Guangzhou by Gujarati merchant middlemen, made India appear to many Sino-Muslims as a major center of Islamic learning—as indeed it was.[92] In response, in the 1920s and 1930s, a series of Chinese students set off for the Middle East and India alike, where they would not only deepen their own understanding of Islam, but also teach their hosts about a China seen through the prism of the Muslim self, as Islam became the mutually comprehensible means for each region to understand the other.[93]

When Hai Weiliang, the Chinese student with whom this chapter began, disembarked in Calcutta, he was neither the first nor last Sino-Muslim to travel to British India (which technically included Burma). The colonial conquest of Burma had brought the Chinese province of Yunnan, home to many Muslim merchants who had long traded with the Burmese highlands, within easier reach of the railway that led to Rangoon, from where steamships departed daily for Calcutta. This in turn led to an increase in the number of Chinese pilgrims to Mecca, initiated by the Yunnanese leader Ma Dexin, who traveled via Rangoon and on his return in 1848 wrote his *Chaojin Tuji* (*Record of Pilgrimage*) to show others how to follow his journey.[94] Many did so, including Ma Lianyuan (1841–1903), who used Ma Dexin's guidebook to similarly make the hajj by way of Burma from Yunnan.[95]

In Mecca, Ma Lianyuan studied with one of the many learned Indians who had made the Holy City their home, before moving to India, where he spent several years teaching in Kanpur. One of his teachers was Rahmatullah Kairanawi (1818–1893), whose *Izhar ul-Haqq* (*Demonstration of Truth*) voiced the fullest Indian Muslim response to Christian missionary critiques. (It also aptly made brief mention of Confucius.) These were not uniquely Indian concerns, for the missionaries had also reached interior regions of China, including Yunnan. As early as 1865, Ma Dexin wrote his *Juli Zhizheng* (*Confrontation on Truth*) after being given a Bible and a Catholic catechism by Bishop Jean-Joseph Fenouil (1821–1907) of the Société des Missions Étrangères.[96] By the end of the century, it was Ma Lianyuan's turn, after the Reverend Herbert Rhodes (1867–1941) of the China Inland Mission presented him with several Christian tracts and an Arabic translation of the Bible. After reading them, and discerning thereby the differences with Muslim doctrine, Ma Lianyuan wrote a critique in response titled *Bian li mingzheng yulu* (*Quotations on Clear Explanation and Evidence*).[97] Amid the dialectic between knowledge of self and other, the Asian communications revolution gave Sino-Muslims access to Christian teachings just as it allowed them to make the pilgrimage to Mecca.

Following the examples set by Ma Dexin and Ma Lianyuan, some stayed on in Mecca as students, but others studied in India. In 1897 one such student wrote a short account in Urdu of his Indian education, published under his Arabic name, Murtaza Husayn Sinawi, in the Punjabi town of Firozpur.[98] Other Sino-Muslims studied in the Middle East, one of the earliest being Wang Jingzhai (1879–1949), a cleric from the port city of Tianjin, who in 1921 began his studies in Cairo.[99]

The infrastructures of empire—especially along Britain's crucial Indo-Egyptian route—carried an increasing number of student and pilgrim passengers from China. Between 1923 and 1936, some 834 Sino-Muslims sailed to Mecca, culminating in 1937, when 170 were counted aboard a single steamer from Shanghai.[100] Drawn by the reputation of Egypt's great medieval seminary al-Azhar, in 1931 a group of four Sino-Muslim students disembarked in Port Said, having taken a French mail steamer that docked en route at Singapore, Colombo, and Aden.[101] All four were from Yunnan, which reflected the region's empire-enabled connections with Muslim Asia. A few months later, they described their sea journey in an article sent back to the recently founded journal *Yuehua* (*Crescent China*), the leading forum of China's Muslim reformists, who were sponsoring the quartet's studies in a quest for the pure Arabic roots of their faith.[102] Over the following years up to 1947, annual cohorts were sent to Cairo, totaling thirty-five students in all.[103] Though limited in number, their influence was magnified by the translations they made for *Yuehua* from articles in Arabic journals such as *al-Fath* (*Victory*).[104] Translating between Chinese and Arabic—and Urdu—these young Sino-Muslims were developing the deepest and most direct intellectual engagements across China, the Middle East, and India.

In 1933 an Arabic letter font was shipped to China from Cairo, and then used as a model for casting further fonts that allowed Sino-Muslims to print far more Arabic texts that deepened these Arabizing developments in turn.[105] A few years later, Egypt's King Farouq donated over four hundred Arabic books to the Chengda Shifan Xuexiao (Chengda Normal School) in Beijing.[106] Founded in 1925 as the counterpart to other new educational institutions for Muslims emerging elsewhere in Asia, the school was intended to rear modern Sino-Muslim patriots, using a syllabus that combined Arabic-oriented Islamic studies with science, math, history, and English. Graduates deployed the latter as a lingua franca to forge contacts with fellow Muslims in India, Malaya, and even the Dutch East Indies (now Indonesia).[107] In 1931 the school also began sending graduates for higher studies overseas, whether in Egypt, India, or sometimes Turkey. There they immersed themselves in the languages of an Islamic Asia.

Between Appreciation and Polemic, Again

Yet these inter-Asian Muslim connections also came with the polemical cost incurred elsewhere through links to the printed public sphere. Like those in Egypt, students in India translated articles for *Yuehua* from the flourishing Urdu periodical press. Hai Weiliang, the student who arrived in Calcutta with an English phrasebook, made several translations from Urdu, including an article describing the ideas of the influential Indian philosopher-poet Sir Muhammad Iqbal, who served as a Muslim counterpart to Tagore.[108] The larger Indian outreach to China, however, came through the missionary enterprises of the Muslim Ahmadiyya sect, which by 1921 had at least one representative there, by the name of Ghulam Mujtaba.[109] The Ahmadiyya soon established a more formal missionary outpost in Hong Kong under Yunus Ahmad Mohideen, who in 1926 published a Chinese translation of the Quran based on the English version of his fellow Ahmadi Muslim—and respected member of London's Liberal Club—Muhammad 'Ali (1874–1951).[110] Following methods adopted from Christian missionaries, Mohideen distributed various other Ahmadiyya publications, using the same techniques of giving away free copies.[111] Chinese translations of entire Ahmadiyya books also began to appear, such as Muhammad Manzur Ilahi's *Muslim Catechism* (rendered as *Da wen*).[112] Ahmadiyya writings also found their way into Chinese-run journals, such as *Yuehua, Zhengdao* (*Justice*), and the China Muslim Literary Society's *Zhongguo Huijiao Xuehui Yuekan* (*China Muslim*), whose editors translated articles from the Ahmadiyya's London-based *Islamic Review*.[113] By the 1930s, as Sino-Indian connections flowed increasingly through London, the *Islamic Review* was in turn including articles mailed from China.[114]

In the meantime, Ha Decheng, the influential leader of Shanghai's Sino-Muslims, had visited India and been impressed by the Ahmadis' efforts to promote Islam, not least through Muhammad 'Ali's Quran translation.[115] These self-projecting efforts were associated mostly with the Lahore branch of the Ahmadiyya, who considered their Punjabi founder, Mirza Ghulam Ahmad, as a "renewer" rather than a "prophet" or "messiah." This subtlety was not always apparent, though. In the Arabic *al-Manar* journal, read by China's Muslim reformists, the pioneering Syrian Salafi Rashid Rida issued a fatwa condemning Muhammad 'Ali's Quran translation on the mistaken grounds that he was a follower of the messianic Qadiani branch of the Ahmadiyya.[116]

Sending an article from Lucknow to the leading Sino-Muslim journal *Yuehua* in 1932, Hai Weiliang also waded into these debates by warning his compatriots against reading works by the "heterodox" Ahmadiyya and encouraging them to focus on the study of reformist Arabic texts being printed in Cairo.[117] Criticizing the followers of Mirza Ghulam Ahmad for undermining Muslim unity by spreading sectarianism, Hai also referred readers to anti-Ahmadiyya articles in Middle Eastern journals.[118] With Sino-Muslim reformists already in dispute with their traditionalist Sufi coreligionists at home, the importing of the Ahmadiyya controversy drew Muslim China into the polemical public sphere. It was the unexpected price of their discovery of Asia's wider—and sometimes bewildering—forms of Islam.

The controversy surrounding the Ahmadiyya Quran translation belonged to a growing set of debates about how best to render the scripture in Chinese. The disagreements drew on over a century of missionary translations of the Bible into Chinese. For China's Muslims, these Christian efforts became particularly acute in the early twentieth century, when the China Inland Mission began distributing Christian tracts and Bible portions in Arabic. In the wake of the 1910 World Missionary Conference, several new organizations had been founded that focused on China's Muslims, reaching inland from the treaty ports by making use of the expanding railway system.[119] Texts originally printed for the Middle East were now handed out in the towns of the Chinese interior, pointing to the ever-widening reach of the Asian public sphere, and the Christian missionaries' role therein.

Echoing earlier developments around the Bay of Bengal, Sino-Muslim religious leaders entered public debates with the missionaries, who deployed techniques of vernacular preaching and scripture printing first developed in India, which prompted China's Muslims to respond with scriptural counter-evidence from the Quran.[120]

By January 1916 the spread of these debates had led three hundred Muslim leaders from across northern China to assemble in Beijing at a conference (itself a borrowing of missionary methods) to decide on a collective response.[121] Two years later, Xu Yuyi, a Sino-Muslim from Hunan, printed a pamphlet intended as a rejoinder to the missionaries. In combining a Muslim catechism with a detailed response to the Christian critiques that concluded by recounting the Quranic version of the life of Jesus, the pamphlet resembled the early Muslim imprints from Calcutta.[122] Xu Yuyi's polemic rapidly went through three reprints, only to provoke a larger response from the more organized Christian missions.

Sino-Muslim leaders' larger response to the missionaries, however, was to provide more public access to the Quran as an alternative to the deluge of Chinese and Arabic Bibles. Short, handwritten Chinese primers on the Quran had existed for centuries, but they covered only around 3 percent of its content.[123] Amid the increased evangelical urgency of the 1920s and the heightened national consciousness that followed the anti-imperialist May Fourth

Movement from 1919, a rapid and competing sequence of Chinese-language Qurans was put into print.

Yet these ventures in inter-Asian scriptural translation prompted further disagreements in turn. The first complete Chinese Quran, published in December 1927, was quickly rejected as doubly lacking authenticity. Not only was its translator, Li Tiezheng, not a Muslim, but he was also unable to read Arabic, which forced him to rely on a Japanese translation by Sakamoto Ken-ichi, itself based on a Victorian English rendering by the Reverend John Medows Rodwell.[124] First published in 1861, Rodwell's translation was intended to aid Christian self-projection, albeit by improving understanding of Islam: as he stated in his preface, "A line of argument to be adopted by a Christian missionary in dealing with a Muhammadan should be, not to attack Islam as a mass of error, but to show that it contains fragments of disjointed truth—that it is based upon Christianity and Judaism partially understood."[125] Ironically, the first complete Chinese Quran translation was therefore an indirect consequence of the Christian campaigns that Sino-Muslims were trying to circumvent. The gradual outcome for both parties was an entangled but deeper understanding of the religion of the self and other.

Four years later, the next Chinese Quran appeared, the Shanghai edition we saw sponsored in the previous chapter by the Iraqi Jewish émigré from Bombay, Silas Aaron Hardoon (and his Chinese Buddhist wife).[126] Although Hardoon's translation team included a Muslim, it was headed by a Buddhist— and hence was similarly viewed with suspicion by China's Muslims at large. Moreover, like its predecessor, it rendered the Quran into archaic literary Chinese that was far less intelligible to a mass public readership than the written vernacular Chinese (or *Baihua*) being promoted in the modernizing wake of the May Fourth Movement.[127] The solution was for local Muslim scholars to prepare their own version directly from Arabic. And here the students sent to the Middle East proved crucial, as the encounter between East and West Asia enabled the Sino-Muslims' own journey of self-discovery.

In 1932 Wang Jingzhai, a Cairo-educated imam, published the first complete Quran translation from the original Arabic. Aptly, Wang was from the port city of Tianjin, which had long served as one of the key outposts of the Christian missionaries.[128] Unfortunately, he too adopted archaic literary Chinese, which elevated the Quran's divine message but restricted its public comprehension. Despite the influence of the British and American missionaries, the Chinese were not yet "Muslim Protestants" who were happy to render holy writ in the language of everyday speech. It would not be till 1946 that the first partially vernacular Chinese Quran appeared, appropriately in Shang-hai, where European publishing methods had most fully transformed China's classical culture of print.

Yet the encounter with Christians did not merely produce polemics and translations; as in the other regions of Asia, it also generated understanding of others, whether by spreading greater Chinese familiarity with Christian ideas or by disseminating corresponding Christian familiarity with Muslim—or Confucian—texts. In the Calcutta of 1809, the Protestant outreach to China had begun with a translation of Confucius's *Analects*. This dialogue of self and other also generated more accurate Christian understanding of Islam in China, culminating in the influential 1910 monograph by Marshall Broomhall (1866–1937) of the China Inland Mission, which we will see feeding back into Indian Muslim attempts to apprehend China's Islamic traditions.[129] In the meantime, Middle Eastern Muslims were also learning about their Chinese coreligionists in what would amount to a degree of intellectual interaction between the two regions perhaps without precedent in all history.

From the Chinese Quran to the Arabic Confucius

The crescendo of Christian outreach to China's Muslims in the 1920s strongly contributed to the decision to send students to study the Arabic sources of their religion overseas. There they informed their hosts about the "neglected problem" of Islam in China (to borrow the subtitle of Broomhall's book), prompting increased Middle Eastern interest in this imperiled minor-ity. A series of Arabic publications ensued, providing more accurate informa-tion not only about the Sino-Muslims themselves, but also about the cultural traditions of China at large as projections of the Muslim self led to new ap-preciations of the Confucian other.

One of these students was Ma Jian (1906–1978), a precocious youth from Yunnan who arrived in Cairo in 1931 after earlier studies at the Chengda Nor-mal School in Beijing.[130] Like other Sino-Muslims abroad, Ma Jian took on a more familiar Arabic name and so became known as Muhammad Makin.[131] After three years of intense Arabic studies, he made a major contribution to the Middle Eastern comprehension of China by writing an Arabic book with the bilingual Arabic-Chinese title *Nazra Jami'a ila Tarikh al-Islam fi al-Sin wa Ahwal al-Muslimin fiha: Zhongguo Huijiao Gaiguan* (*A General View of the His-tory of Islam in China and the Conditions of Its Muslims*).[132] In 1935 he published an even more striking work in Cairo: the first direct Arabic translation of the

Analects of Confucius, to which he appended a short biography of Confucius himself.[133]

Both books were published by Muhibb al-Din al-Khatib (1886–1969), the founder of Cairo's influential Salafi Press, which exported books and magazines to readers of Arabic throughout maritime Asia, including China.[134] As far as al-Khatib was concerned, the goal was to increase awareness of the plight of the Sino-Muslims among their Middle Eastern coreligionists, which also meant understanding the dominant Confucian culture among which China's Muslims had long had to live.[135] But even if this was the publisher's intention, many Arab readers—Christian as well as Muslim—used the translation of the *Analects* as a means of understanding Confucianism as such. Ma Jian made Confucius more acceptable to such readers by presenting him not as a religious rival to Muhammad or Jesus, but instead as an ancient Chinese philosopher (*faylasuf*). The use of this more neutral term was deliberate, since it avoided positioning Confucius (his name rendered into Arabic from the Latin rather than the Chinese pronunciation) as a rival religious prophet.

It was not only Confucius who was finding his translated way to the Middle East at this time. In 1937 Lao Tzu made his Levantine debut through a Hebrew version of the *Dao De Jing* (*Tao Te Ching*) made by a Zionist Orientalist and a retired mandarin, and published in the Old City of Jerusalem.[136]

As for the ninety-page edition of Ma Jian's Arabic history of Chinese Islam, it was far more polished and professional than previous Middle Eastern or Indian books on China. In addition to the Chinese characters used for its bilingual title—perhaps the first time Chinese was printed in West Asia— and critical apparatus (footnotes and corrections), Ma Jian's book included photographs of mosques, reproductions of Chinese Qurans (in Arabic and in translation), and a photograph of its author as the frontispiece, dressed in a broad-lapeled European suit and tie—the sartorial symbols of Islamic modernism.[137] The other photographs served to make China seem familiar; the views of mosques were chosen specially to emphasize Middle Eastern elements, whether Arabic script across a prayer niche, the "Arabic minaret" of a mosque in Guangzhou, an Arabic Quran page, or the grave of the purported early Arab transmitter of Islam to China, Sa'd ibn Abi Waqqas (c. 596–c. 674). Through the imported technology of photography, China was presented as a Muslim mirror of the Middle East.

Across its ten chapters, Ma Jian's book recounted the arrival of Islam in the time of the Prophet; the encounter with indigenous religions (leading to outlines of Confucianism, Daoism, and Buddhism); and a survey of the intellectual, political, economic, and social conditions of China's Muslims, with a particular focus on educational institutions. Its final section was devoted to the students who had come to Cairo, as though to emphasize the importance of education as the mechanism of Muslim unity that ultimately proved stronger than the culturally hollow calls of Asianism.

Explaining Sino-Muslim History in Urdu

At the same time that Ma Jian was writing his account on China's Muslims in Arabic, in India his fellow student Hai Weiliang was writing a far longer book in Urdu. Since disembarking a decade earlier in Calcutta, Hai had made such progress with the language of his teachers that his book carried the seal of approval of Muhammad 'Inayatullah, the former head of the Translation Department at Hyderabad's Osmania University who had previously rendered Masood's book on Japan into Urdu.[138] But now the languages of South and East Asia were directly connected.

This was a remarkable achievement for a young man raised in a village in the rural Shaoyang region of Hunan province, where he received his early education at a local mosque. But Hai's intelligence had been quickly recognized. He was sent in his youth to the provincial capital of Changsha, then to the Xiaotaoyuan (Peach Orchard) mosque in Shanghai, the port-city center of Sino-Muslim reform.[139] Before he sailed to India, his studies probably comprised the older *Han Kitab* syllabus of Islamic texts in Chinese, supplemented by learning Arabic letters, prayers, and perhaps reading a short Quranic primer in Arabic.[140] Like other students in his cohort, to improve his Arabic he was then sent overseas, in his case to Calcutta, from where he was put on a train to Lucknow at the recommendation of 'Abd al-Razzaq Malihabadi (1895–1959), who had hosted him upon his arrival in Calcutta.[141] An Indian scholar and journalist who had spent three years studying in Egypt, Malihabadi had previously published articles in Arabic journals such as Cairo's *al-Manar* and Istanbul's Urdu-Arabic *Jihan-i Islam* (*Islamic World*), which were probably known to Hai's mentors in Shanghai. In this way, print paved the way for more direct inter-Asian interactions along this communicational geography of port cities.

Originating in the Lucknow region, Malihabadi had written to Sulayman Nadwi (1884–1953), a celebrated scholar with close ties to the city's famous Nadwat al-'Ulama seminary, where Malihabadi had himself studied. As Nadwi later recalled, Hai was sent to Lucknow to begin his studies, before being dispatched to the newly opened Jamia Millia Islamia university, where he audited classes before being formally enrolled.[142] Having begun learning English with the phrasebook he brought from Shanghai, he then learned Urdu and managed to complete a bachelor's degree at Jamia Millia, writing a thesis on the nationalism of Sun Yat-sen.[143] Though both Chinese and Indian Muslims were exploring the new nationalist politics, Hai's primary goal on leaving China had been to pursue religious studies. So he then returned to Lucknow's Nadwat al-'Ulama seminary and focused on the Arabic at the core of its curriculum, learning to read, write, and speak the language.[144] Toward the end of his time there, he wrote his Urdu work, *Chini Musulman,* completing it on October 20, 1933, while his mentor, Nadwi, was visiting Kabul with Ross Masood to offer advice on Afghanistan's first university.[145] By the time the book was actually published eighteen months later, Hai had moved on to Cairo, joining Ma Jian at the medieval al-Azhar seminary. But through his *Chini Musulman,* Hai had left his mark with a major contribution to Indian understanding of China, albeit a partial understanding shaped by the self-projections of two minority communities.

Like Ma Jian's Arabic counterpart, Hai's *Chini Musulman* appeared at a time of growing Indian Muslim interest in a China they now viewed through the lens of Islam. The Urdu journal *Ma'arif,* edited by Hai's patron, Sulayman Nadwi, had featured occasional articles on China since 1920, the earliest of which were short but laudatory overviews of Chinese civilization (*tamaddun*) drawn from English sources.[146] But by the 1930s, specific articles on China's Muslims began to appear in *Ma'arif,* including an account of the propagation (*isha'at*) of Islam in China.[147] The April 1936 issue included an Urdu translation of an Arabic article on China's Muslims mailed from British-ruled Cairo by Ma Jian, who two years earlier had published his Arabic book on the topic, while the outreach efforts of other members of Hai's circle back home saw similar articles appear in the Singapore-based Arabic journal *al-Huda* (*Guidance*).[148]

Still, not all Urdu texts then drew on reliably direct data, as older fantasies continued to be peddled in print. Published in 1930, one such work was *Chin aur Bengal ka Jadu* (*Bengali and Chinese Magic*), which gave simple instructions for over a hundred different spells whose purposes ranged from curing the sick to predicting the future, mostly by copying numerological squares to make talismans.[149] As its title suggested, China remained part of a mystically nebulous orient that, viewed from Lahore, where the chapbook was printed, began a thousand miles east, in Bengal.

Nonetheless, nascent, direct links between Indian and Sino-Muslims were providing a more dependable, if still problematic, data stream. Consequently,

a generation after Indian missionaries like 'Azmi Dihlawi dreamed of converting Japan, attention was now diverted by the discovery of a vast community
of Muslims in China. Even so, their population was reckoned to be far larger
than it actually was. Through a blend of inflated estimations by Christian missionaries and data from an inaccurate census, in the mid-1930s the number
of Muslims in China was reckoned to be as high as 50 million, then around
one-eighth of China's total population.[150] For Indian Muslims, increasingly
confronted with their own minority status amid the competing Indian nationalisms of Britain's imperial twilight, this vast overestimate made the Sino-
Muslims seem natural allies as Asia's only Islamic minority of comparable
size.[151] Faced with the limited, outdated, and vicarious information on China
available in Urdu, local Muslim intellectuals found Hai's arrival in India an
extraordinary opportunity to gain a direct understanding of their Chinese
alter egos.

Consequently, assuming the roles of geographer, historian, and ethnographer, Hai faced demands to explain his country and community in a language
and terminology his hosts could understand. As his mentor, Nadwi, explained
in his foreword to Hai's book:

> The Muslims of India are largely unacquainted with the conditions of
> the Chinese Muslims; indeed, they don't even know whether or not the
> Chinese Muslims are currently thriving. In India, the earliest informa-
> tion on [Sino-Muslim] relations came from the former Aligarh College
> professor, Mr. Arnold, whose book *The Preaching of Islam*—which ap-
> peared in 1896—described in twenty pages, from pages 115 to 334 [*sic*],
> the history of the propagation of Islam, along with some details on the
> religious conditions of the Chinese Muslims based on European sources.
> Since then, Indian Muslims have been longing to hear about the current
> state of their Muslim brothers who settled so far away.[152]

Nadwi's opening statement points to the silent partner in this inter-Asian
conversation. For Nadwi had adopted a Christian missionary–derived concep-
tion of seeing religious history in terms of deliberate programs of propaga-
tion. Here he used the term *isha'at*, which was similarly adopted by the new
Muslim missionary organizations, such as the *Ahmadiyya Anjuman-i Isha'at-i
Islam* (Ahmadiyya Society for the Propagation of Islam), which were reaching
China by this time. As for the English book he cited, it was *The Preaching of
Islam*, by Sir Thomas Walker Arnold (1864–1930), written as a liberal, late-
Victorian counterblast to earlier Christian claims that Islam had been spread

violently by the sword. Drawing on what was by the 1890s a vast library of Orientalist and missionary studies of Islam, Arnold presented a counternarrative of peaceful propagation that reached right across Asia as far as China.

Arnold's positive picture had a considerable effect on the college-educated Muslims of the next generation, partly through his teaching position (as Nadwi mentioned) at Aligarh's Muhammadan Anglo-Oriental College, where he introduced Nadwi's own mentor, Shibli Nu'mani, to European methods of historical research, and later at Government College, Lahore.[153] Piecemeal from 1904 and then fully in 1913, *The Preaching of Islam* was translated into Urdu, particularly its section on China, and by the 1920s its influence had reached even further through a Turkish translation issued in Istanbul, where we previously heard Nu'mani describing the Indian translator of a book on China into Turkish.[154] It was even cited in an article written by a Sino-Muslim for the Ahmadiyya's missionary journal.[155] But when Nadwi wrote his foreword to Hai's Urdu book, his purpose in citing Arnold on the first page was to demonstrate the importance of Hai's *Chini Musulman* as an informational turning point that rendered the old reliance on Europeans obsolete.

Yet if Hai was seen as an improvement on vicarious European informants on China, then he was also in some ways the Muslim equivalent of the earlier Asian protégés of the Christian missionaries. For he was likewise given a religious education by his Muslim mentors, who opened institutional doors and international networks to him in pursuit of their own self-projecting—or self-protecting—agendas. But like Asia's many Christian converts, Hai had his own aims as well. These found expression in his book as he strove to balance the interests of his patrons with the needs of his compatriots to forge empowering alliances with overseas Muslim allies.

Hai's introduction, which followed Nadwi's foreword, tried to join these two agendas. "Outside countries are very little acquainted with the conditions of Chinese Muslims," he began by echoing Nadwi.

> Till now, many respectable people have not even known whether or not there are any Muslims in China. One reason for this is that for a long time the Chinese Muslims have remained without relations [*be ta'luq*] with their outside brothers, so that they became a forgotten people. And the other reason is that no book has been written about them to properly explain their way of life. Undoubtedly, Christian missionaries have written books about the Chinese Muslims, but they are written from their particular viewpoint and also have their shortcomings. Feeling this

deficiency, over the past few years I investigated the Chinese Muslims through Chinese sources. . . . I know well that the complaint of my Muslim brothers is that the Chinese Muslims sit in their remote corner of the Far East [aqsa-i sharq], completely without connections, so that people from outside cannot meet them and so that they cannot see their outside brothers. So, I wrote this book to try to settle that complaint. . . . As this introduction shows, the Chinese Muslims do not wish to sit alone in their corner any longer: their hearts and souls are longing to meet you, and are calling to you with great love and sincerity.[156]

This emotive closing call notwithstanding, Hai, like Nadwi, used the new vocabulary of professionalized investigation that was the calling card of the generation of scholars emerging from universities and modern seminaries. Nadwi set the tone by citing specific pages from Arnold, but both he and and his protégé referred to sources (makhazun, zariyun) in the new critical language of modern Muslim historians. As Hai made clear, no longer would Indian Muslims have to rely on vicarious translations and secondhand information from Christian missionaries: they could now turn instead to a Sino-Muslim who would draw without bias on the Chinese sources. But in having to write his book in Lucknow, far from the libraries of his homeland, this was not as straightforward a proposition as it sounded, for intercultural understanding is rarely a solo endeavor.

An Inter-Asian Self-Historian

The first chapters of Hai's Chini Musulman presented a history of China's Muslims from the initial introduction of Islam to the revolution of 1911.[157] Yet this was no simple matter of rendering into Urdu a sequence of events and developments that were clearly established and agreed on. For history is not just a narrative of facts, either known or unknown, preserved or forgotten, shared or shielded from view. It is constantly reshaped and reenvisioned, through new evidence and categories, narratives and imperatives, in response to the changing demands of different periods, each with its new authors and audiences. In the first decades of the twentieth century, this was especially true of the two Asian regions and communities between which Hai was trying to transfer historical knowledge.

In India, new conceptions of history had gradually been disseminated through the missionary schools that spread from Calcutta over the nineteenth century, beginning with Indian-language editions of Indian history by John Clark Marshman, whose missionary father had initiated Chinese studies in Calcutta. With the development of colonial higher educational institutions, particularly the Muhammadan Anglo-Oriental College founded at Aligarh in 1875, Indian Muslim intellectuals adapted data, narratives, and research methods from European models.[158] The most influential of the new historians was Shibli Nu'mani, the protégé of Thomas Arnold, whose Urdu biographies of medieval Muslim luminaries used the sources and critical methods of the Orientalists to revitalize the study of his own tradition.[159] Nu'mani also gained influence through sixteen years of teaching at Aligarh before in 1905 being appointed principal of the recently founded Nadwat al-'Ulama seminary, where Hai studied two decades later. Having traveled to the Middle East with Arnold, Nu'mani not only absorbed ideas from the author of *The Preaching of Islam* (cited on the first page of Hai's book), but also emphasized the importance of renewing India's intellectual ties with the Middle East, particularly by mastering modern and classical Arabic.[160]

More directly, Nu'mani's chief disciple, Sulayman Nadwi, passed these developments to Hai in turn as his mentor in Lucknow. By the time Hai came to write his book, Nadwi was writing a parallel study titled *'Arabon ki Jahazrani (The Arab Navigations)*, based on lectures he delivered in Bombay.[161] But whereas Hai's book connected South Asia with East Asia, Nadwi's sibling study connected South and West Asia. To do so, they both turned to early Arab intermediaries whose seaborne navigations had connected the far sides of the continent through Islam. For Nadwi, looking back from his lecture podium in Bombay to an age before Europe's empires took control of the oceans, the seas that stretched from the Middle East to China were originally a space of Muslim history. Like Bengali scholars in Calcutta rediscovering ancient Buddhist ties to China, Nadwi was trying to recover a self-history of inter-Asian interactions that long predated the arrival of Europeans. But just as Bagchi and Nag had realized in Paris, to recover that past Nadwi often had to turn to Orientalist printed editions of old Arabic geographies and travelogues. Nonetheless, Nadwi's notion of a connecting ocean conjoined by pious Arab sailors proved central to his protégé Hai's depiction of the Chinese past.

Similar transformations of history writing were already under way in China itself, where the incremental effect of missionary schools in the nineteenth century, the republican revolution in 1911, and the May Fourth Movement in the 1920s brought radical changes in the way history was conceived, and not only by Muslims.[162] Europeans such as Johan Gunnar Andersson (1874–1960) helped local scholars like Li Chi (1896–1979) develop a nationalist archaeology of self-discovery by unearthing an early Chinese civilization at Yangshao in 1921 and evidence for early dynasties, such as the Han-era tomb of General Huo Qubing.[163] (Forty years earlier, the American Edward Morse had inadvertently inaugurated Japanese nationalist archaeology by spotting ancient Jomon vessels—the world's earliest pottery—turned up during the construction of the Yokohama-Tokyo railroad.)[164] Reflecting developments elsewhere in Asia, new educational and research institutions were founded. The Academia Sinica was inaugurated in the republican capital of Nanjing in 1928 with the goal of recovering the ancient Chinese past at the recently discovered site of Anyang, where it was hoped scientific excavations would prove the existence of what European scholars dismissed as the "mythological" first dynasties described in classical Chinese histories.[165] As the adoption of typography fostered a larger public sphere, as in India, history played an important role in shaping the "new public opinion" (xin yulunjie) through the launch of scores of journals.[166] Muslims were active participants in these developments, whether through the Chengda Normal School, or through the twenty or so journals in which they debated the new ideas reaching them from the Middle East, India, Japan, and Europe alike.[167]

Lacking the autochthonous roots of Confucianists and Daoists, China's Muslims discovered their past not by digging in the soil of Yangshao and Anyang, but by reconnecting with other regions of Asia. They were helped by a maritime recovery: the Ming Dynasty Muslim navigator Zheng He, who led seven exploratory voyages as far as India, Arabia, and East Africa and became a flagship figure in recounting their inter-Asian past. Long forgotten, the memory of Zheng He had been reawakened in 1905 when, from exile in Tokyo, the journalist Liang Qichao (1873–1929) published an essay celebrating "The Great Navigator of Our Mother Country."[168] Liang had previously translated European texts, and written biographies of Bismarck and Nelson espousing the Great Man theory of history, which he adapted for Zheng He. Then in 1933 the leading French Sinologist, Paul Pelliot, published a study of Zheng He's travels that was quickly translated into Chinese by the historian Feng Chengjun (1887–1946), who had studied in Paris.[169] In 1924, the Arabic travelogue of Ibn Battuta had been partly translated into Chinese by another historian, Zhang Xinglang (1888–1951). So, by the time Hai was writing his book, both Ibn Battuta and Zheng He, as a homegrown "Chinese Navigator," offered further evidence for Sino-Muslim relations with distant regions that echoed the maritime history being written by his Indian mentor.

In India as in China, these changes in history writing likewise influenced
Muslims, particularly in the wake of the 1911 Chinese republican revolution
that presented Sino-Muslim scholars with the political imperative of demonstrating how their community was related to the larger Han-dominated
nation.[170] The key issue here was to demonstrate the difference between the
Sino-Muslim Hui community and the Turkic Uyghur Muslims of the Chinese
Central Asian province of Xinjiang by presenting the Hui as an ethnically Chinese kinfolk of the majority Han who had converted to Islam at some point
in the past. Determining that point, and the process by which it happened,
became the key historiographical burden of the new Sino-Muslim intellectuals. In 1935 two books were published that represented major responses to
this dilemma. One was *Zhongguo Huijiaoshi yanjiu* (*Studies in the History of
Chinese Islam*) by the Sino-Muslim nationalist Jin Jitang (1908–1978), which
was published in Beijing for a Chinese audience.[171] The other was Hai's *Chini
Musulman*, which in being written in Urdu for an Indian audience afforded its
author a degree of interpretive liberty. For though Hai was similarly concerned
with demonstrating "Hui-Han" harmony—national unity between Muslim
and non-Muslim Chinese—across the long span of China's past, he also deployed history toward the transnational cause of Muslim unity.

It was against this background that Hai began his Urdu book by posing
the pressing historical questions of how Islam initially came to China, who its
first Muslims were, and by which route they had arrived.[172] He commenced on
his extended answer by turning to the pre-Islamic past to demonstrate "how
China had relations [ta'luqat] with other countries of Asia in ancient times."[173]
In a nod to the modern research methods he had acquired at the Jamia Millia
university, he admitted that there was little evidence in terms of buildings,
documentation, or even coins, but in outline at least it still seemed clear that
the cause of these early connections was commerce.[174] As to when these trade
links began, he pointed to the Cha'o (Zhou) era, for which he gave the Christian timeline of 1122 to 246 BC, noting that more evidence survived from the
subsequent Han Dynasty, especially under Emperor Wu (r. 140 to 86 BC),
who sent his ambassador Jang Jiyan (Zhang Qian) to Central Asia to promote
friendship and unity (*dusti aur ittihad*) between the Chinese and other peoples
of Asia.[175] This was the same mission that attracted the attention of the Afghan
historian Kuhzad and led him to translate the relevant section of Sima Qian's
history into Dari from the French. Hai likewise turned next to Sima Qian,
referencing his *Shiji* as providing evidence for the thousands of Arab and Iranian merchants who circulated in and out of China in the Han era.[176] What all

this showed, Hai concluded, was that China's trade with the lands of the Arabs began "in the first centuries of the Christian era" and gradually expanded thereafter.[177] Whether through the unitary idea of "Asia," the Christian dating system, or more subtle historical methods, Hai turned European concepts to his own inter-Asian purposes.

It was under the Tang Dynasty, he continued, that Islam made its first appearance on Chinese soil. Normalizing its arrival, he pointed out first that this was a period when the other major religions of West Asia (*maghribi Asiya*)—Buddhism, Christianity, and Judaism—were likewise brought to China.[178] After sketching the rise of Islam through the early Arab conquests of Iran, Central Asia, and the Xinjiang region of China, which he insisted on calling "Eastern Turkistan," he recounted a conversion narrative that proved central to his task of demonstrating the origins of the Sino-Muslims. For it was amid these Arab conquests in the time of Qutayba ibn Muslim, who governed Central Asia in the early eighth century, that a tribe (*qabila*) known as the Hu'i Chhi was converted to Islam. Afterward, they migrated to the western regions of China. It was the name of this tribe, he explained, that provided the subsequent name for Muslims in the Chinese language as *Hui-hui*.[179]

After peace was subsequently agreed on between the Tang and Arab armies fighting for control of Central Asia, Muslims were allowed to settle in the Tang imperial capital of Chang'an (now Xian) and marry Chinese women.[180] Many other Muslim migrants followed them in subsequent centuries, finding refuge in Chang'an, where they too took local wives and became loyal subjects of the emperor. As a result of these centuries of intermarriage and accommodation to local customs, Hai continued, their descendants became like Chinese people in all their customs except for their religion. While the height and facial features of Muslims in northern China still show their partially Turk and Tatar ancestry, he explained, the Muslims of western and southern China are physically indistinguishable from the "ordinary Chinese," that is, the Han. Through this inter-Asian picture of conversion, migration, and assimilation, Hai sought to reconcile the partly foreign origins of China's Muslims with the pressing political demand for national unity.

Yet he also had his other agenda of using history to demonstrate the unity of China's Muslims with their coreligionists in other regions of Asia. To do so, he turned away from what he called the overland "dry route" (*khushki ke rasta*) through Central Asia toward the sea route (*bahri rasta*) to eastern China. "Arabs packed their goods and commodities into boats and ships," he wrote, "and sailed through the Indian Ocean to Java and the islands of the East Indies, passing Nanhai to arrive at the southern Chinese port of Canton."[181] If here Hai echoed the history of Arab navigations around the Indian Ocean that his Indian mentor was just then completing, it was also a narrative shaped partly by Arnold's *Preaching of Islam* and the Muslim proselytizing that emerged in response to the Christian missionaries. For while Hai described the maritime arrival of Islam as being enabled by earlier trade connections, he presented its key actors as preachers (*mubalighin*) who came with the deliberate aim of the propagation of Islam (*isha'at-i Islam*).[182] It was the same Urdu phrase used earlier to translate the title of Arnold's book.

Mentioning unspecified Tang Dynasty chronicles along with traditions handed down at the old mosque in Guangzhou, Hai described four such preachers being sent to propagate Islam during the reign of the "Rightly Guided" caliphs who succeeded the Prophet Muhammad, a period he equated with the reign of the Tang emperor Taizong (r. 626–649). One of these preachers was the Prophet's companion and kinsman Sa'd ibn Abi Waqqas, who was said to have built the famous Huaisheng Mosque in order to "make Canton [Guangzhou] the center of his proselytization [*tabligh*], from where he undertook the propagation [*isha'at*] of Islam in various regions of southern China."[183] When Sa'd eventually returned home, he was sent back to China by the third caliph, 'Uthman (r. 644–656), who appointed him as ambassador to the Tang Empire, after which Sa'd died and was buried in Guangzhou. (Here Hai added a scholarly footnote questioning the authenticity of the grave.)[184] As for the three other pioneering Arab preachers, one was sent to the port of Changzhou on the Yangtze, which because of the Arab merchants who sailed upriver became a "center of propagation" into inland China, while the third and fourth evangelists settled in the southern port of Quanzhou and similarly propagated their faith from there. Hai maintained this missionary framework when he turned to the activities of Sa'd ibn Abi Waqqas at the Tang court, where he was presented as continuing his earlier dedication to the propagation of Islam.[185]

Though Sa'd was long revered among Sino-Muslims (often under the name Wan Kesi), the textual record of his ties with China by no means dated back to the time of the Tang emperor Taizong or the caliph 'Uthman. Instead, the story of Sa'd's embassy mainly took shape in the eighteenth century, particularly in the *Huihui yuanlai* (*Origins of the Sino-Muslims*), written in 1712 by Liu Sanjie, a prominent scholar from Nanjing.[186] As evidence for the story, Hai cited the *Tianfang Zhisheng Shilu* (*True Record of the Perfected Sage of Islam*) by Liu Sanjie's celebrated son, Liu Zhi (c. 1660–1730), which for his Indian readers he gave the Arabic title *Sirat al-Nabi* (*Biography of the Prophet*).[187] More normative in Indian and Middle Eastern terms, this title lent the tale legitimacy. But there was no evidence in early Arabic or Chinese sources for Sa'd ever having traveled anywhere near China—something various European scholars had pointed out by the time Hai was writing.

Mediating among the European, Indian, and Chinese models of history writing that were converging in his lifetime, Hai frankly recognized this problem, which prompted his admission at the start of his section on Sa'd that "the exact date of the arrival of Islam is a difficult question, and some Westerners say there is no guiding source or conclusive proof."[188] But by tying the origins of Islam in China to the very links with the Arabs of West Asia that Hai and his cohort claimed to be renewing rather than forging afresh made Sa'd too important a historical linchpin to surrender so easily. For not only had Hai expressly set out to correct the Christian missionary depiction of Islam in China, but he was also trying to demonstrate the primordial ties of the Sino-Muslims to the pure Arabian fount of Islam.

Hai's solution echoed the methods of both his modernist contemporaries at home and his Indian teachers at the Nadwat al-'Ulama seminary, who similarly sought to bolster the formal historical evidence for key figures of early Muslim tradition without sacrificing the core of traditional narratives. So, on the one hand, Hai discarded the more supernatural elements of the story of Sa'd's embassy. The most prominent such element was the story of the predictive dream of the Tang emperor: as recounted by Liu Sanjie in the eighteenth century and others thereafter, the emperor dreamed of his palace roof being upheld by a green-robed and white-turbaned figure and upon waking sent envoys to the "Western regions," who brought Sa'd's Arab entourage to the Tang court, whence they saved the empire from collapse.[189] Hai, by contrast, offered a disenchanted if modernized version, presenting Sa'd as a diplomat and missionary. It was a narrative framed less by faith in the supernatural than by the more technical problems of determining exact dates. If Hai had set out to challenge Christian missionary accounts, then as part of the subtle process of dialogue, he had finished by adopting elements of the Protestant approach to religious history by way of methodological source criticism, skepticism toward miracles, and a paradigm of evangelical propagation. It was this version of Sino-Muslim history that he transmitted to India in Urdu. Having recently rewritten their own past in similarly Protestant mode, the Indian Muslims who hosted Hai accepted his narrative as commensurable with their own revised history.

In the subsequent chapters of his book, Hai worked his way through the status of Muslims during the successive Chinese dynastic eras.[190] Right through to the Manchu era, which began in 1644, this was a story of positive relations between China's rulers and their Muslim subjects. But under the iron hand of the Manchus, the Muslims were forced into a series of rebellions. Fortunately, in the wake of the 1911 revolution, Muslims were granted "religious and intellectual freedom" by the new nationalist government, which allowed them to work together with their "compatriots" (hamwatanun) to build the unity of the Chinese nation.[191] Repeating the nationalist credo of various Sino-Muslim contemporaries, Hai concluded his history by declaring that progress for one's country and one's religious community is the same thing.[192]

While his main focus was on China's Muslims, his book also provided Indian Muslim readers with what was for many of them their first detailed overview of Chinese history more generally (not least through his decision to structure the Islamic past through China's dynastic periods). Once again, projections of the Muslim self fostered appreciation of the Confucian other. By pointing occasionally toward sources in Chinese, he also introduced his Indian readers to authors who were undoubtedly less familiar than Confucius and Lao Tzu, whose vague shadows had dominated earlier Urdu accounts of Chinese civilization. When introducing the early Confucian historian Sima Qian, Hai glossed him as being "the Chinese Ibn Khaldun," in reference to the celebrated fourteenth-century Arab historian.[193] Yet in referring to Ibn Khaldun, he inadvertently pointed toward the complex modern entanglements of European and Muslim intellectual life. Like various other medieval manuscript works, Ibn Khaldun's Muqaddima had been mostly forgotten for centuries, only to be resurrected through the combined efforts of French Orientalists and Cairo-based reformists, including Hai's hero in the cause of Muslim unity, Jamal al-Din al-Afghani.[194] It was through this twofold rediscovery that Ibn Khaldun reached India in a 1904 Urdu translation by Muhammad Insha'allah, the owner of the newspaper Watan who had close contacts with Cairo's reformists and who also translated the Egyptian journalist Jirjawi's Rihla al-Yabaniyya (Japanese Journey).[195] If Hai was seeking in Ibn Khaldun a common Arab intellectual reference point to unite India and China, then once again Europe crept into the process of inter-Asian connection.

This was also the case with several of the key concepts on which Hai relied to render the Chinese past intelligible, particularly the notions of progress (taraqqi) and civilization (tamaddun) appropriated from Europe by earlier Muslim scholars. This was not only a consequence of Hai's writing in Urdu in colonial India. By the early 1930s the translated concept of civilization was also appearing in the writings of other Sino-Muslims, such as Li Tingbi, whose historical articles in the journal *Yuehua* drew extensively on the British historian Arnold Toynbee (1889–1975), who had just published a travel account of China and whose civilizational model of world history was taking influential shape.[196] Yet no less striking is the absence of the romantic terminology of the Silk Road, which had yet to have its effect in Urdu, or for that matter in Chinese or English. It would not be until five years after Hai finished his *Chini Musulman* that the term was popularized in English through the 1938 translation of Sven Hedin's book *Sidenvägen* (*The Silk Road*), and another twenty years until it was adopted in China as the neologism *sichou zhi lu*, after the translation of the American geographer Owen Lattimore's *The Pivot of Asia*.[197] Back in 1933 Hai had to rely on a far less evocative Urdu label: "the dry route." As for the challenge of reconciling the Chinese and Islamic dating systems, Hai resolved this by a mediating recourse to the Christian time line used in the previous generation of Middle Eastern and Indian accounts of China.

This may in turn suggest that some of his dates were derived from, or at least checked against, English texts to which he had readier access in the libraries of the Jamia Millia university and the Nadwat al-'Ulama seminary. At one point he specifically cited the missionary Marshall Broomhall's *Islam in China* (though, true to his goals, he corrected one of Broomhall's dates).[198] Here lay the informational dilemma of *Chini Musulman*: in being written by a highly educated insider informant who was fully literate in Chinese and Urdu, the book was a breakthrough in the development of a robust Indian-language Sinology. But at the same time, it was restrained by the source materials Hai had available to him in Lucknow, could afford to have posted by publishers from back home, or could remember having read in his youth. Even had he been willing to make a bibliographical expedition to Bengal, the substantial library of Chinese books at Tagore's Visva-Bharati University would not open till three years after he completed his book. As Hai plaintively remarked when referring to a set of five Chinese sources, "The aforementioned books are not in my possession, so I cannot say what is written in them."[199] In a footnote elsewhere, he recounted how he had sent a letter to a Beijing-based publisher to learn more details about the biography of the savant Liu Zhi, only to be told in a reply that nothing was written about his life.[200]

That Hai was in some measure able to overcome these informational barriers was an inadvertent outcome of the infrastructure of empire. The books he did cite directly were recently printed editions sent to him on the mail steamers that connected Calcutta to the treaty ports of China.

Translating Tradition, Reforming Religion

Yet even when Hai was able to access—or remember—particular Chinese books, he still faced the problem of making China's Islamic traditions both linguistically intelligible and theologically respectable to Indian Muslim readers. For over a millennium, Islamic teachings had been adapted to the Chinese environment, culminating in three centuries of Chinese-language texts (the so-called *Han Kitab*) that calibrated Islam to Confucianist norms. Consequently, it was no small task for Hai to make Chinese Islamic doctrines recognizably "Islamic" to Muslims in India. But Hai was determined to do so, devoting a great deal of detail to discussions of creeds, texts, and sects.

His chapter on the formal creeds (*'aqa'id*) followed by Sino-Muslims seemed designed to reassure Indian readers of the conformity of their distant coreligionists with what was regarded as approved doctrine in Indian seminaries.[201] He based his summary on a printed nineteenth-century Chinese primer, which he translated into Urdu in its ten-page entirety.[202] Whether he had a copy in his possession in Lucknow is unclear: he didn't cite a particular edition, as he did for texts he managed to have sent to him. He explained, however, that most Sino-Muslims memorized the text by heart and could recite it from memory, which suggests that this was also his means of transmitting the text into Urdu.[203] The old skills of memorization could still be of use in the age of print, helping fill the vast bibliographical gap caused by the lack of Chinese books in India.

Explaining the creation of the universe from the "hidden treasury" of undifferentiated pre-eternal divine Being, the primer explained how, from his ineffable essence, Allah had first created reason (*'aql*) and selfhood (*nafs*), before further manifesting his infinite attributes in the various levels of creation down to the world of nature. After creating the "father of humankind" (i.e., Adam), Allah made the peoples and tribes, each human uniting selfhood (*nafs*) and the heart (*qalb*). As the organ of spiritual perception, the heart is capable of guiding every person back through the chain of creation to his or her divine origins through the threefold route of submission (*islam*), faith (*iman*), and thence truth (*haqq*). But at the pinnacle of creation stands Muhammad, the "seal of the prophets," who "has incorporated all religions into Islam and gathered all of Allah's commandments into the noble Quran, so that Islam is the world's best religion and the holy Quran the best scripture, and as such is a guide to the peace of the world."[204]

Underlying this summary of Sino-Muslim beliefs was a complex intellectual history involving Hai's itinerant forerunners. As he explained, the Chinese text from which he was translating had been written by Hajji Muhammad Yusuf Yunnani, then published by his learned friend Ma Lianyuan, who, Hai added in a linking nod to his readership, died in the Indian town of Kanpur.[205] Albeit under his Arabic name, the first person Hai mentioned here was Ma Dexin, whom we have seen making a pioneering journey to Mecca from his home region of Yunnan in the 1840s. The second person mentioned—Ma Lianyuan—was his follower, who pursued the same itinerary via Burma a few decades later. In referencing these figures, Hai was emphasizing what he regarded as the orthodox lineage of Sino-Muslim teachers, for both men had not only made the pilgrimage to Mecca but also studied at al-Azhar in Cairo. Their names probably meant nothing to Hai's Indian readers, but, during his time in Kanpur in 1902, Ma Lianyuan had published an Arabic commentary on the *Tianfang Xingli* (*Metaphysics of Islam*) written by the eighteenth-century "Muslim Confucianist" Liu Zhi.[206] But in its appearing under Ma Lianyuan's Arabic name, there was even less likelihood that this earlier bibliographical link with India would have been spotted by Hai's readers.[207]

Be that as it may, the doctrines Hai described would have been familiar to a learned Indian readership, for they ultimately derived from a source that was shared by Indian and Chinese Muslims. This was the Sufi teachings of the medieval Andalusian mystic Ibn 'Arabi (1165–1240), albeit as transmitted to India and China through the Sufi classics of Persian poetry. During the centuries in which they were digested and domesticated in China, these teachings were subsequently harmonized with Confucian teachings, most fully in Liu Zhi's *Metaphysics*.[208] Then, as those teachings were in turn passed on and revised in the 1800s by Ma Dexin in the wake of his hajj, and finally translated into Urdu by Hai, their Confucian costume was cast aside to leave no trace of being distinctly Chinese. For in his eagerness to show Sino-Muslims as sharing a common creed with coreligionists elsewhere, Hai wrote in a highly Arabicized Urdu whose metaphysical terminology showed no trace of the former centuries of collusion with Confucianism.

In presenting Sino-Muslim tradition to his Indian coreligionists, Hai found himself involved in a project of Arabic-based reformation as much as Chinese-to-Urdu translation. And so, shown through the mirror of Islam, the

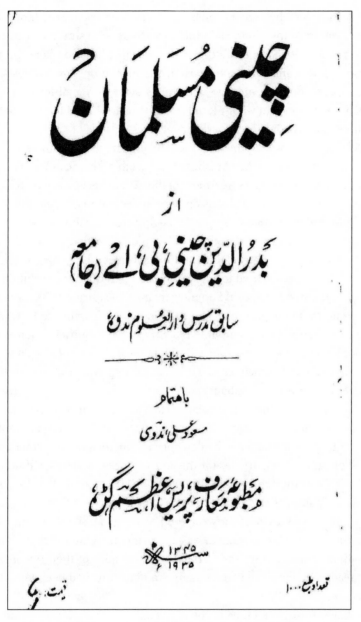

A Chinese self-history in Urdu: front cover of Hai Weiliang's book.
Badr al-Din Chini [Hai Weiliang], *Chini Musalman* (Azamgarh: Ma'arif
Pris, 1935). By permission of Darul Musannefin Shibli Academy,
Azamgarh, India.

Sino-Muslims lost their chief Chinese characteristics and looked more like the Middle Eastern Arabs whom Hai's Indian teachers were similarly resurrecting as role models. Walking an interpretive tightrope, he faced here a problem common to all translators: the decision whether to opt for "domestication" or "foreignization"—to preserve a culture's alterity by maintaining foreign words or to present it in wholly familiar terms instead.[209] In the cause of inter-Muslim solidarity, Hai opted for the latter.

This tension between providing accurate information on Sino-Muslim tradition and rendering China's Muslims recognizably Islamic in Urdu (and Arabic) terms also shaped Hai's treatment of the various sects into which his Muslim compatriots were divided. His opening statement made clear his negative attitude toward such divisions: "In the beginning, the Chinese Muslims had no sects."[210] This happy state of unity (Islamic rather than Asian) continued for a thousand years, he explained, till the seventeenth century, when small doctrinal differences started to appear. He then described the evolution of the Jahriyya and Kufiyya, two rival Sufi movements that spread across Gansu province through what he presented as a deliberate proselytizing strategy.[211]

Yet in presenting what amounted to almost two centuries of tense sectarian conflict, Hai repeatedly emphasized that these disputes (*ikhtilaf*) were not about fundamental principles of faith, concerning which all the sects were in agreement, but merely about matters of custom.[212] Recounting these developments through the public sphere, Hai was not so much participating in the polemical debates that spread more widely through print as attempting to defuse inter-Muslim disputes by downplaying the degree of former conflict. He had already written articles for the journal *Yuehua* warning Chinese readers about following the Indian Ahmadiyya on the grounds that they spread sectarian division. If this in itself was a step toward printing polemic, then it was one he saw as necessary for the greater good of promoting Muslim unity. The solution, he explained, was a return to the Quran—though not the Ahmadiyya translation we saw earlier. It was because of their inability to directly read their scripture that so many Sino-Muslims had been led astray by divisive sectarians.[213]

We have already seen how in the 1920s and 1930s the Chinese translation of the Quran preoccupied so many of Hai's contemporaries. Amid this Sino-Muslim scriptural self-discovery, the chapter Hai devoted to China's Islamic textual tradition was similarly directed to the centrality of the Quran.[214] In line with the historicizing trends of his Indian teachers, his approach was a chronological and contextual one, tracing the development of Sino-Muslim teachings over time, albeit time structured through the Chinese imperial dynasties and dated through the Christian calendar.[215] Between the seventh and thirteenth centuries, he explained, despite the fact that there were already many Muslims in China, they did not write any books in Chinese, nor did they make any contribution to Arabic learning.[216] This state of affairs continued under both the Tang and Yuan dynasties, when many powerful Muslims were courtiers of the great Kublai Khan and when various Chinese historians wrote admiringly of Muslim scientific learning. But then, Hai went on, during the Ming era many Arabic books were collected for the imperial library, albeit mainly relating to astrology, and some were translated into Chinese.

Trying to recover with learned precision this earlier period of inter-Asian exchange, Hai provided several detailed examples. He was highlighting the Arab contribution to Chinese culture at exactly the same time that in Calcutta Prabodh Chandra Bagchi and the Greater India Society were promoting the influence of Indian Buddhism on China.[217] But there was as yet no Muslim counterpart to the publication and study of Sanskrit Buddhist manuscripts and their Chinese translations gathering pace around Bagchi. As Hai lamented, it was unclear whether there survived any extant manuscripts of the Ming translations from Arabic mentioned in the Chinese chronicles of the period. To try to find out, he had turned to the port-based publisher that had provided him with an English phrasebook at the start of his travels. But having consulted the "Oriental" catalogue of Shanghai's Commercial Press, he could find no mention of those works of Arabic astrology. "My interpretation of this," he concluded, "is that those manuscripts have disappeared. But the matter is worth further research."[218]

That last word—research (*tahqiq*)—nonetheless placed Hai among his university-educated contemporaries like Bagchi in Bengal, who were likewise making their investigations with new levels of professionalism.

Turning from astrological to religious texts, Hai went on to survey the development of the Sino-Muslim textual tradition that emerged under the late Ming Dynasty and flourished under the Qing Dynasty, despite his negative depiction of the latter elsewhere in his book as "foreign Manchus." Here he focused on Liu Zhi, the aforementioned Muslim Confucianist who was probably the most celebrated representative of the *Han Kitab*, or Chinese Book, tradition.[219] Pronouncing Liu Zhi "universally respected," Hai gave a short outline of his education that mentioned youthful studies of Confucius and a year spent scrutinizing Buddhist texts, along with the fuller commitment to learning Arabic that led Liu to convert to Islam. After this turning point, Hai explained, Liu went on to write over a hundred books. Mindful of his larger goal of making Sino-Muslims seem recognizably Islamic to his Indian readers, to emphasize Liu's commitment to both Islamic orthodoxy and Arabic, Hai declared his most famous book to be his biography of the Prophet Muhammad.[220] Hai provided only the Arabic title, ignoring the Chinese title *Tianfang Zhisheng Shilu* (*True Record of the Perfected Sage of Islam*), which would appear far less normative to his Indian readers. He adopted the same linguistic mirroring strategy when listing Liu's other works, presenting them with more prestigious (and intelligible) Arabic titles.

As he had the medieval Arabic astrological manuscripts, here too Hai lamented the loss of most of Liu Zhi's works. By way of explanation, he turned to the new sphere of print that had become so important to the Muslim public intellectuals projecting their ideas through the connected ports of China, Singapore, the Middle East, and India. The reason most of Liu's hundred-odd works were now unknown, Hai reasoned, was "probably because there was no typography or lithography during his time, only wood-block printing, so only some of his books were printed."[221] Fortunately, he continued, in 1925 a new edition of Liu's life of the Prophet Muhammad had been published. It was this version Hai had drawn on for his discussion, pointing again at the enabling role of the public sphere in Asia's self-discovery. The printing of Liu's biography of the Prophet allowed Hai to link his own people to the Middle East, where he himself traveled next to study.

After listing the names of half a dozen other Qing Dynasty scholars, and giving the titles of their books in Arabic, Hai finally turned his attention to translations of the Quran. As we have seen, in China as in India half a century earlier, Muslim reformists had tried to give ordinary believers access to the Quran through printed translations, although they thereby prompted disputes in both regions alike. So here Hai had to tread a careful explanatory path: to overstate the problem of access to the Quran would make Sino-Muslims appear to have grossly strayed from the clear commands of scripture. But to understate their efforts at translating the scripture would make light of the great efforts of Hai's reformist generation. So he opened the section with a compromise: "No one can deny the reality that the Holy Quran arrived in the land of China on the very first day that the Muslims opened the gate to China and entered. But it is a pity that for thirteen centuries no one then tried to translate it."[222]

Hai went on to describe the rapid sequence of Quran translations we have seen from the 1920s, beginning with the version the non-Muslim scholar Li

Tiezheng made from a previous Japanese translation, which "caused uproar," only to be followed by another version distributed by the Iraqi Jewish magnate Silas Aaron Hardoon, who was "Shanghai's biggest banker and landlord."[223] Fortunately, Hai concluded, there was a happy ending to these scriptural misadventures, for both versions had been lately superseded by the direct translation from the Arabic made by Wang Jingzhai.[224] Wang had studied at Cairo's al-Azhar, he added, but had also been in contact with Hai's Indian mentor, Sulayman Nadwi. And so the dissemination of Islam across Asia that began with the proselytizing travels of Sa'd ibn Abi Waqqas thirteen centuries earlier completed its full historical cycle as this little circle of coreligionists from the Middle East, India, and China came together in a common quest for knowledge.

Here Hai's history reached what he saw as an appropriate conclusion: through renewed connections that were less inter-Asian than inter-Islamic, the Sino-Muslims had discovered the scriptural source of true knowledge. The Chinese self and its Arab and Indian others were united not by the terrestrial language of Asianism, but by the shared cosmic map and moral commands of the Quran.

Between a Muslim and a Confucian Past

Yet as both a Muslim and a patriot, Hai felt his concerns were for all his fellow citizens of the new Republic of China. He had already noted how many non-Muslims profitably read the Chinese-language primer on Islamic doctrine he had summarized.[225] And this brings us finally to the question of how he presented China's other religious communities to his Indian readers. Inevitably, projecting China through the mirror of Islam turned the gaze of his readers away from China's majority population, whom he referred to in the generic negative as simply non-Muslims (ghayr-muslim). While he noted approvingly that Sino-Muslims refused to marry their daughters to these non-Muslims, he no less admiringly pointed out that the latter "possess a great culture and civilization."[226] But Hai's patriotism by no means led him to religious relativism: he firmly maintained that Islam was the only true religion. Even China's non-Muslims seemed to admit this, he claimed, because their name for Islam was qing zhen jiao, which meant either the "pure and true religion" or the "sacred and special religion."[227]

This moniker provided him with the opportunity to reconcile traditional Muslim and Confucian visions of history through a narrative that drew together their two founder figures, the first human, Adam, and the first emperor, Yao:

> When Adam's descendants spread across the earth to the east and the west, his lineage flourished and different lifestyles emerged. Nonetheless, misleading religious deviations [*bid'at*] and superstitions [*khurafat*] did not develop. It seems that the era of Yao was not long after the time of Adam (peace be upon him), and the tradition and narration of Adam's religion was preserved by Yao's laws. That seems to be why, in Yao's time, there was no outlet for superstition. But after the era of the Chin and Han dynasties, superstitions began to spread and various vain fantasies became prevalent. That seems to be why in this era various texts and sayings were passed around that polluted Chinese minds. The knowledge of Truth was hidden from their eyes of mental perception, and in the place of spiritual certainty [*yaqin*] and faith [*iman*] there appeared doubt [*shak*] and misleading religious deviations. From this time on, the lives of China's people fell into darkness. So, it was an assistance [to China] that the Arab people were not denied the blessing we call prophethood. Because the Arabs are exalted through the fact that the Prophet appeared among them and gave them rightful guidance when, near the end of the sixth century, there came the greatest prophet of all, whose name is Muhammad, peace be upon him. He brought a book that gives guidance on every aspect of life and raises the rules of living to the level of perfection. For this reason, this religion is regarded [in China] as the most "sacred" [*muqaddas*] and "special" [*khas*] of all religions. And "sacred" translated into the Chinese language is *tsang* [*qing*] and the translation of "special" is *chiang* [*zhen*]. So that is why the religion of Islam is called *tsang chiang* [*qing zhen*] in Chinese.²²⁸

Echoing the earlier attempts of Christian missionaries, and the Indian texts that drew on them, to harmonize the biblical story of Noah with the Chinese creation story, Hai was trying here to make a corresponding place in that past for Muhammad and the Quran. Now that the Muslim scripture had finally been translated into Chinese, he hoped the Quran might finally fulfill its divinely ordained role by replacing the superstitions that had misled the Chinese people for millennia. Like 'Abd al-Khaliq preaching to the Buddhists of Burma, Hai believed the Quran held the unique potential to guide to salvation his Confucian and Buddhist compatriots, whom he cared for greatly.

Two years after Hai's book was published, a translation of a Chinese classic was published by the Jamia Millia Islamia university in Delhi, where he had taken his BA. The book was an Urdu rendition of the *Shujing* (*Classic of History*), traditionally—if incorrectly—attributed to Confucius. As we saw earlier, the *Shujing* had previously passed into Urdu in summarized and sometimes bowdlerized form in James Corcoran's 1848 history of China. Now, nearly ninety years later, the Indian literary critic Asad 'Ali Anwari made a complete translation, to which he appended almost two hundred pages of commentary, detailing not only the life of Confucius, but also China's history, religions, and literature more generally.[229] In this way, India's Urdu-reading public was provided with an alternative Confucianist depiction of China's past that averted Hai's determinedly Islamic picture.

Since Anwari was primarily a modernist literary scholar, his book also offered a secular nationalist rather than a religious reformist reading of China. And so his was not an Islamic interpretation of China: the first emperor, Yao, appeared in Anwari's book with no reference to Adam or Noah (though by holding up a South and West Asian mythological mirror, he did compare China's first human, Pangu, with the Hindu Brahma and the Iranian Yima).[230] To find such inter-Asian links between Indian selves and Chinese others, Anwari derived most of his evidence from European authors such as Lionel Giles (1875–1958), Keeper of the Department of Oriental Manuscripts at the British Museum, who had read widely in classical Chinese literature, and Émile Hovelaque (1865–1936), a French commentator on international relations who, lacking Giles's knowledge of written Chinese, drew merely on a brief tour of the country.[231] Bringing Confucianism to India through the entangled routes that defined so much of Asia's self-discovery, Anwari turned to European informants who were far from uniformly reliable.

Fortunately, Anwari by no means took their statements at face value and did his best to critically compare these secondary sources. Nonetheless, his interpretation of China's past was still based on European frameworks, right down to borrowing the English term "classics" (*klasik*) that Orientalists brought up on Latin and Greek had used to conceptualize the Confucian curriculum. (This also influenced the common English translation of *Shujing* as the *Classic of History* rather than *Book of Documents*.) As for Anwari's translation of the *Shujing* itself, his source was an English version made by the obscure Walter Gorn Old (1864–1929).[232]

Born in Victorian West Bromwich amid the soot of the industrial English Midlands, Old had been seduced by the dazzling vision of an Eastern spiritual reawakening propagated by the Theosophical Society. After joining the Theosophists, he took up the amateur study of Asian languages and ancient astrology, writing on the latter under the celestial pen name Sepharial. These interests overlapped in ancient China, leading him to the *Shujing* as a record of both religion and astrology. But for linguistic guidance, he had to turn to the translation by the Scottish missionary James Legge (1815–1897). In 1904 Old's version of the *Shujing* was published by the Theosophical Publishing Society in the Hindu holy city of Benares, where thirty years later Anwari rendered it into Urdu. Anwari's secular nationalism thus inadvertently drew on the occult undercurrents of the public sphere that also contributed to the Indian and Middle Eastern rediscovery of Buddhism.[233]

A few years earlier, Anwari's fellow literary scholar 'Abd al-Qadir Sarwari had published an Urdu translation of Chinese and Japanese short stories by apparently drawing on a previous English adaptation.[234] Fazli had similarly resorted to the same mediated methods in recounting Japan's ancient history from William Aston's English version of the *Nihongi (Japanese Chronicles)*.[235] So, in the final analysis, neither Sarwari's translated modernist tales nor Anwari's version of the *Shujing* was a comparable achievement to either Hai's book on China's Muslims or the Arabic translation of the *Analects* of Confucius made by his fellow student Ma Jian in 1935, because the latter were both based on direct readings and renditions of Chinese sources. Like the investigations of the Christian missionaries, and the Japanese Buddhist monks who studied Sanskrit and Pali sutras in Tibet and Ceylon, the inquiries of their committed Muslim counterparts were more linguistically robust than those of secularizing Asianists or nationalists. Thus it was that after a Chinese translation of the *Arabian Nights* that was based on an English version appeared from Shanghai's Commercial Press in 1930, it was Na Xun (1911–1999), another Sino-Muslim student at Cairo's al-Azhar, who then made the first direct translation from Arabic.[236] Completing this bibliographical circle between China, India, and Egypt was Muhammad Hasan A'zami. An Indian professor who taught in Cairo, A'zami wrote an Urdu study of Egypt's intellectual scene before compiling a five-volume Arabic-Urdu dictionary and writing an Arabic book on the Indian thinker Muhammad Iqbal, which introduced Middle Eastern readers to Iqbal's synthesis of the mysticism of Rumi and the philosophy of Henri Bergson.[237]

Though inter-Asian interpreters like A'zami and Hai took ideas from Europe, their concerns were for the protection and projection of the Muslim self. And so in Hai Weiliang's *Chini Musulman*, the Indian Muslim discovery of China made its most direct intellectual inroads through seeing China in the mirror of Islam, just as A'zami presented India to Arabs in the terms of a common "Islamic culture" (*thaqafa al-Islamiyya*). This was more than the casual

talk of connection and unity favored by the era's many Asianists. For although
Bengali nationalists like Sarkar, Nag, and Bagchi tried to renew India's Buddhist bonds with China, the Sanskrit-based ties they dreamed of restoring had
dwindled a thousand years earlier. By contrast, the Arabic educations that allowed Chinese, Indian, and Middle Eastern scholars to communicate ideas
both directly and deeply had not merely survived the centuries, but had been
revived through infrastructures of steam and print built to bolster Europe's
empires.

With the outbreak of the Second Sino-Japanese War, economic ties between
India and China quickly evaporated: the Japanese assault on Shanghai in September 1937 caused an Indian exodus, as around nine hundred sailed that
month aboard the S.S. *Elephanta* alone.[238] In the ports of mainland China and
Hong Kong, the occupying forces seized control of larger Indian companies
and froze private bank assets.[239] After the final mass repatriations of Indians
from China in the mid-1940s, the Indian presence in China, except for Hong
Kong, all but disappeared.[240] A century of close economic connections had
been less successful in placing intercultural knowledge of China into the Indian public sphere than the religious and educational networks that reached
not only India but beyond the foreign-drawn frontiers of Asia as far as Egypt.
  Seeing this clearly, the Kuomintang, China's ruling nationalist party, did
its best to instrumentalize these religious networks, both old and new, Buddhist and Muslim. In January 1940 this led to the arrival in Calcutta of the
Buddhist reformist teacher Taixu (1890–1947), on a Kuomintang-sponsored
mission to win support against Japan from Indian nationalist politicians on
the basis of their ancient Buddhist ties.[241] For over a decade, Taixu had been a
member of the Calcutta-based Maha-Bodhi Society, founded by Dharmapala,
the Ceylonese protégé of the Theosophists. Completing this circle of Eurasian
connections, Taixu traveled on a steamer from Rangoon in the company of the
Paris-trained Bengali Sinologist Professor Bagchi.[242] Meanwhile, several official delegations comprising the Sino-Muslim former students in the Middle
East and India were dispatched by the Kuomintang to different regions of
Asia. Led by the polyglot Ma Tianying (1900–1982), one party sailed to British Malaya and the Dutch East Indies. There they invoked a shared history
of Arab connections to remind Southeast Asia's Muslims of their common
ties to China in the same way that Hai had in the book he wrote for India's
Muslims.[243] Another student party sailed on pilgrimage to Mecca, calling at

Calcutta, Cairo, and Istanbul, where their language skills were put to political use in public meetings that painted Japan as the imperialist heir to Europe.[244]

Japan was quick to follow suit. With its own Muslim connections that we have seen developing over previous decades, Tokyo dispatched a competing delegation to Mecca consisting of Sino-Muslims from its colony in Manchuria.[245] A key part of the surrounding Japanese propaganda was the conversion to Islam of a cousin of Puyi, Manchuria's puppet-emperor.[246] From Port Arthur to Calcutta, Kabul, and Cairo, the news echoed through the public sphere.[247] After decades of self-projection, the dream of the Islamic Japanophiles of converting the mikado had almost come true. But by 1940, Japan was no longer the idealized potential partner it had once appeared. The Sino-Muslim students played an important part in that shift by setting their own terms—both Chinese and Muslim—for the rubric of Asian unity. A handful of members of a tiny religious minority had become China's most skilled cultural middlemen with other regions of Asia.

These largely forgotten multilingual students were perhaps more effective than their celebrated counterparts for whom Asian unity was more a means to a political end than a vision that reckoned with complexities and contradictions of moral and cultural substance. Although the heady writings of Gandhi, inspired by Indian and Christian ethics alike, were translated into Chinese (and Arabic), culminating in a close relationship between the fellow nationalists Jawaharlal Nehru and Chiang Kai-shek, aspirations of Asianist unity were quickly dashed.[248] In the wake of India's independence in 1947 and the communist victory in China two years later, hopes of a postcolonial resurrection of ancient ties collapsed amid sharp disagreements over the invasion of Tibet in 1950, which led to the Sino-Indian War of 1962.[249] The destruction of Tibetan culture ended Indian hopes of reviving the Buddhist-based connections of ancient times.

For his part, Hai Weiliang spent World War II as a Kuomintang diplomat in Iran, where he put his superb linguistic talents to good service by learning Persian.[250] When India won independence, he was transferred to Delhi, where he again made use of his flawless Urdu, though when China's Communist Party came to power, his position was promptly terminated.[251] Rather than return home, Hai went into exile in Taiwan, serving its anticommunist diplomacy for several more decades.[252] But he did not give up his learned contributions to the Sino-Muslim version of Asia's self-discovery. Drawing on five different languages, he published a follow-up to his Urdu book, this one written in Arabic. It was not that he had forgotten what he had learned in India, for in recovering the long history of Sino-Arab relations, in many ways his Arabic book was the counterpart to the history of Indo-Arab relations that his mentor, Sulayman Nadwi, had written in Urdu during Hai's time in Lucknow.[253] In their titles, both books used the same Arabic-derived term for "relations," which carries a stronger, more emotional, and more familial meaning than the recent Anglophone historical concept of cold "connection."

Nor, even amid these more direct and deeper ties, did the European input into inter-Asian exchange disappear. In 1945 another Chinese student, Muhammad Tawadu' (1902–1958), wrote an Arabic history of China's Muslims that was published by the foreign propagation section of the Muslim Brotherhood, itself founded in response to Swedish missionary activity.[254] Binding more tightly these knotted self-projections between Muslims in India, the Middle East, and China, two years later an Arabic translation of Thomas Arnold's *Preaching of Islam* was published in Cairo.[255] This was the same text cited on the first page of Hai Weiliang's *Chini Musulman*, which Arnold wrote in rejoinder to the anti-Muslim denigrations of earlier Christian critics. For whether as allies or adversaries, Europeans were part of a colloquy of learning that no single continent could confine.

Conclusions • "Asia Finds Herself"

Soon to become India's first prime minister, in March 1947 Jawaharlal Nehru welcomed delegates from the Middle East, China, and Southeast Asia to the Asian Relations Conference in New Delhi.[1] As he explained in his opening speech, the gathering aimed to inaugurate a postcolonial era of peaceful cooperation, and heightened comprehension, between the peoples and nations of a liberated continent. Looking back over the previous century, Nehru theorized that "one of the consequences of the European domination of Asia has been the isolation of the countries of Asia from one another," though this might now end through "an interchange of visits and exchanges of students and professors so that we might get to know one another better."[2] Happily, he pledged, in that optimistic twilight of empire, "a change is coming over the scene now and Asia is again finding herself."[3]

With his brilliant command of English, burnished through studies at Harrow and Cambridge, Nehru conjured an evocative image of a continent on the verge of *re*discovering itself after centuries of colonial separation. Yet like other Anglophone elites, he was less aware of the investigations made over the previous century by authors writing in the languages of Asia itself. Far from emerging from colonially enforced "isolation," Asia had already "found herself" through the heightened interactions enabled by the infrastructures of empire and a communications revolution inadvertently triggered by Christian missionaries. As much as Nehru's conference marked the dawn of a new epoch of postcolonial unity among an Asian constellation of independent nations, it also marked the zenith of the age of Europe's empires that spread the idea on which the whole enterprise was premised: "Asia."

We began by discussing the allure of Asianism—the ideology "claiming that Asia can be defined and understood as a homogenous space with shared and clearly defined characteristics"—that inspired so many assertions of continental unity.[4] Saaler and Szpilman, two leading specialists on Asianism, have argued that during the decades on either side of 1900 the term "Asia" "came to represent a specific geopolitical space bound together by such commonalities as a shared history, close cultural links, a long record of diplomatic relations, trade exchanges, and the notion of a 'common destiny.'"[5] Yet even amid the unprecedented integration of different regions through the political and economic mechanisms of colonization, we have seen that "commonalities" were not always apparent to Asian observers themselves. For when we turned to Asian-language texts to see how the characteristics of different regions and cultures actually were "defined and understood" in practice, the seductive specter of unity quickly faded away. In case after case, attempts to comprehend the diverse cultural realities of that vast continent were confronted with challenges that ideologues chose to ignore more often than engage. When it came to the more challenging work of truly investigating different cultures, relatively few of the figures involved in the heavy linguistic and interpretive labor were committed to the dogma of Asian unity.

Nonetheless, as Saaler and Szpilman correctly point out, "calls for Asian solidarity, integration, and unity were accompanied by endeavors to create an Asian identity by postulating commonalities and identifying traditions of interaction and interrelationship."[6] By looking at several such "postulating" endeavors, we have seen they were highly selective to the point of becoming exclusive. In searching for terms of unity, different Asianists emphasized the unifying role of one culture or region over another, whether by promoting templates of Buddhist, Baha'i, Hindu, or Muslim religious unity; by developing a civilizational model of a Greater India that absorbed Japan and China while disregarding their indigenous traditions; or by the more violent creation of Japan's own colonial Greater East Asia Co-Prosperity Sphere. All these were projections of the self over the silenced culture of the other.

This in turn helps explain the relatively minor contributions that Asianists made to intercultural knowledge: investigating the variant and plainly different cultural traditions of other "Asian" peoples threatened to undermine the claims of unity. Even the most scholarly Asianists, such as Calcutta's Professor Bagchi, focused on the unifying thread of "Indian-derived" Buddhism rather than China's indigenous Confucianist and Daoist traditions, not to mention the rival unifying claims of Islam. From the 1920s, for some political thinkers, a convenient solution to the problem of Asia's cultural diversity was found in communism: if religious and other traditions were mere false consciousness, then they could be ignored, or even eradicated, in the higher cause of socialist collectivism. For communists, the cost of unifying Asia (or at least such large sections of it as Soviet Central Asia and the former Qing Empire) was therefore the destruction of its traditional cultures, a policy that later reached its symbolic yet logical pinnacle in the destruction of the tomb of Confucius during the Cultural Revolution.[7] For nationalists, by contrast, Asian unity served as a means of promoting the culture of one Asian people to the point of denying or diminishing the contributions of others. In an irony that is nonetheless in tune with the European origins of the idea of "Asia," these unifying ideologies of communism and nationalism were likewise imported from Europe.

Yet for all the efforts of Asianist activists and European geographers, relatively few people across the continent came to think of themselves as being "Asian," particularly as a primary category of identity. In his perceptive study of Okakura and Tagore, the canonical Asianists with whose meeting we began, the Indian critic Rustom Bharucha has stated that "belongingness to a larger imagined community called Asia does not exist [in India]. . . . The fact is that Asia does not have the same discursive weight or political valency in all parts of the continent designated as Asia."[8] Bharucha reminds us that even today, four hundred years after Europeans first introduced "Asia" to Qing and Ottoman mapmakers, and more than a century after Indian and Japanese anticolonialists appropriated the term for political purposes, a sense of "belonging" to Asia has a patchy appeal across the continent itself, let alone a project of unity predicated on Japanese, Indian, or Chinese dominance.[9]

By treating the term "Asia" with skepticism, the previous chapters have sketched a more complex pattern of intercultural understanding than the smooth but vague lines inscribed by lofty pledges of unity. This responds to the warning by the historian of China Rebecca Karl about "the historical erasures on which reifications of ahistorical 'Asian-ness' rely."[10] Building on this point, the Chinese critic Wang Hui has argued that "modern Asian imaginaries are based mainly on interstate relations and seldom deal with Asia's complex ethnicities, regional communications and forms of interaction that are conventionally grouped under the category of empire."[11] The previous chapters have tried to build on these critiques by looking beyond superficial continental or national categories to see how empire brought together various ethnic and ethical communities through new mechanisms of communication and new conceptual categories.

Rather than take Asian unity, or even "Asianness," for granted as a starting position, we have instead examined how specific people from different corners of the space marked "Asia" on modern maps came into direct or vicarious contact and then tried to understand one another. By ranging between basic language guides to demanding translations of the Quran and Confucius, our survey has taken a broad view of what such intercultural understanding might mean. Through this evidence-based, bottom-up approach, the story of Asia's self-discovery has moved away from celebrated Anglophones like Okakura and Nehru, who have served merely as prominent bookends for our shelves of little-known works written in Asian languages by missionaries, journalists, bureaucrats, students, and even the occasional soldier. Undertaking their investigations for a variety of reasons, these unsung interpreters have shown that the development of inter-Asian understanding was a difficult, contested, and constrained process. Their achievements have long been concealed by the easy claims of Asianism.

The challenges of intercultural knowledge have been overlooked or underplayed by even the most astute scholarly commentators. In a thought-provoking essay, the anthropologist Engseng Ho has argued that the notion of a static Asian continent should be replaced with a "networked" model he calls Inter-Asia, which should be "thought of not as a unitary continent but an old world crisscrossed by interactions between parts that have *known and recognized one another for centuries.*"[12] Yet even as we have pursued the mobility, connection, and circulation that Ho considers crucial for rethinking Asia's past, we have seen they didn't lead seamlessly to knowledge and recognition in the ways he and many others have assumed. Caught up in the fashionable search for a "world crisscrossed by interactions," few researchers have paused to examine what, how, and how much was actually "known and recognized" across the languages and religions of Asia's different regions.

Like the recent proliferation of the Silk Road paradigm of history, which has amplified particular periods of interaction as permanent norms, the alacrity of this search for connection has fostered tacit assumptions about the degree, accuracy, and ease of intercultural comprehension, not least by collapsing transfers of knowledge into the easier flow of trade goods.[13] But even as we have seen intercultural understanding emerge from the maritime geography of colonial commerce, the content of such knowledge was shaped by more complex currents than the straighter shipment of commodities—because acquiring cultural competence is a quite different enterprise from learning how to use trade goods, such as silk, or even how to adopt imported technologies, such as gunpowder (or printing presses).

In contrast to the simpler task of integrating an imported tool or object into one's existing worldview, intercultural understanding demands the ability to mentally assemble and then imaginatively enter another worldview, from the basic axioms of foundational texts through their myriad implications. (Nonliterate cultures present even greater obstacles, causing them to be all but overlooked in Asia's public sphere.) And to understand how any specific community in practice applied, modified, or rejected their traditions requires the further ability to access and interpret historical and ethnographic evidence. Whether linguistic and orthographic or moral and conceptual, the barriers are formidable. As the historian Sanjay Subrahmanyam has written about European attempts to comprehend India: "The process of learning was anything but simple. This was for a number of reasons, some quite practical and others more conceptual or intellectual in nature."[14] The same was true of inter-Asian understanding because across any section of the planet—whether between Europe and India or India and China—intercultural knowledge is necessarily a historical development, shaped over time by the kinds of opportunities and vicissitudes we have traced.

To map these challenging transfers of knowledge, we have had to grapple repeatedly with the issue of language. Complex cultural knowledge is always embedded in language (as well as in different writing systems among highly developed literary cultures), creating interpretive barriers that are especially challenging across regions of great linguistic and religious variety. And so the comprehension of other cultures has always confronted high linguistic and orthographic barriers across Asia. This was much more so than in Europe, with its far fewer language groups and scripts. As we have seen, as late as 1940 (and in many cases much later), there existed very few printed dictionaries or grammars linking Asian languages. Other than a small number of basic phrasebooks (usually focused on practicalities of travel and trade), the main exceptions were language guides intended to deepen understanding *within* religious traditions, such as Malay Muslim dictionaries of Arabic and Ceylonese Buddhist dictionaries of Sanskrit. Though rightly celebrated in recent scholarship, the interreligious translations between Persian and Sanskrit that were sponsored at the Mughal imperial court in the seventeenth century, or the Mandarin renderings of Muslim teachings in Confucian terms around the same time in the Qing Empire, did not typify the more tenuous forms of cross-cultural knowledge across Asia at large. When Qing or Mughal savants found equivalences between different mythological and theological systems, this came as the slowly evolving consequence of centuries of sustained contact among learned Confucians, Muslims, and Hindus in the chanceries and courts of cohesive imperial states. It was not some natural state of intellectual communion based on the illusory grounds that European geographers had decided they were all part of "Asia."

Though it is easy to speculate about the degree to which knowledge of other cultures was transmitted through informal oral channels—as undoubtedly to some degree it was—the surest evidence of the historian is the written record. Moreover, despite what specific individuals might have learned and passed on through spoken conversations, it was only through the public sphere of print that such knowledge could move beyond the restricted confines of particular places to reach higher numbers of people. And it was only through texts printed in languages understood by ordinary people that knowledge could reach larger populations beyond the narrower confines of the privileged few who read English, Russian, or French. Yet even then Asia's many different languages divided knowledge into the separate linguistic channels of the public sphere, so that Asia's communications revolution was no purveyor of unity, not least because print also became an amplifier of many kinds of polemic.

All this suggests we should adopt a position of epistemological skepticism and recognize, as cognitive scientists have established through formal experiments, that people often know less about the world than they (or we) assume.[15] Such assumptions of knowledge are just as often made about the past, as we anachronistically project later knowledge onto earlier times, or project what was known by one social group, or in one region, onto other people and places. This is especially the case when we place too much trust in faulty large-scale paradigms, such as "Asia," Asianism, and the "Silk Road" (or, for that matter, "East and West," or "the Orient"). As we have seen, close attention to the evidence—evidence of not only *who* individually knew *what,* but also *how* their knowledge was disseminated to particular linguistic communities of readers—suggests that inter-Asian understanding had to be patched together from sources of variable reliability, ranging from direct reports by eyewitness travelers who knew no local languages to vicarious European accounts with many shortcomings of their own. In sum, people from the different parts of the map marked "Asia" often knew less about each other's cultures than has long been assumed.

There are good, even ethical, reasons to accept this state of affairs, or at least to engage with the evidence. As the world historian Jeremy Adelman has recently argued, "If we are going to make good on any hope for a globally oriented history to inform a fragile, interdependent world, it will help to be more modest, to admit limits and disruptions, to be more uncomfortable, and to consider the sources of human detachments, ambivalences, and resistances to integration."[16] With this in mind, I have tried in the previous chapters to recognize the multiple ways—critical, admiring, ambivalent—in which different societies, religions, and cultures were conceived and presented through the new public sphere that emerged from the continent's empire-driven interconnections.

The resulting knowledge was hard-won, provisional, and partial in both senses of the term. Learning in detail about another culture and its living people is far more difficult than invoking an abstract alliance with it, especially when such knowledge is not already available but must be gathered from scratch. This is immediately apparent in the book by Okakura that opened with the famous declaration: "Asia is one." As hinted by his text's full title—*The Ideals of the East, with Special Reference to the Art of Japan*—after making various generalizations about Asia at large, when Okakura turned to proving his theory of unity, he quickly retreated to his cultural home ground in what we have seen was a familiar interplay of self and other.

Nonetheless, as other attempts to promote the religion or culture of the self led to investigating those of the other, even polemical exchanges could generate understanding, just as they had previously for Christian missionaries. In some cases, then, self-projecting investigations incrementally led to new appreciations of the complexity and value of Asia's other religions and cultures. In other cases, such positive outcomes were outweighed by the destabilizing effect of disputes that widened existing social boundaries, particularly around the Bay of Bengal, where such conflicts have regrettably long outlived the age of empires. Inter-Asian investigations did not always work for the wider social good, then, any more than Europe's Orientalism always led to such appreciative paeans to the Buddha as Edwin Arnold's *Light of Asia*. But whether polemical or approving, they were part of the timeless dialectic of self and other.

For all their imperfections, the texts we have examined were far more detailed and accurate than the trickle of Indian and Middle Eastern accounts of Buddhist Southeast Asia, China, and Japan that were produced over the previous centuries. To give just a few obvious examples, there was simply no earlier counterpart to the translation of the Quran into Japanese; of Japanese poetry into Persian; of Confucius into Arabic; or of the Buddhist *Dhammapada* into such Indian languages as Urdu and Telugu. Given that some of the investigators we have followed had to begin their research from scratch, their achievements were very considerable. What 'Abd al-Khaliq, for example, came to learn about the "religion of Burma"—including an ability to read its core scriptures and perhaps even debate with its learned preceptors—was truly remarkable considering that he sailed from India without any concept (or even name) for Buddhism.

Fraught, flawed, or vicarious as they sometimes were, the achievements of such forgotten pioneers become still more apparent when we fully recognize the interpretive challenges they faced. On first principles no less than in practice, there is no reason why Buddhism, Confucianism, or Shinto should be more intelligible to a "fellow Asian" from the Middle East or India than to a European. The interpretive barriers were in fact similar: Bengali and Arabic are no closer to Chinese and Japanese than English and French. But as we have seen in practice, European researchers had by the nineteenth century acquired a series of interpretive and informational advantages over their Asian counterparts. One set of advantages came from the intellectual legacy of what by 1850 was already nearly three centuries of Christian missionary investigations into the languages, religions, and cultures of Asia. Having been committed to print from the outset, and stored in accessible libraries in Europe's universities and seminaries, these earlier findings (which included such key tools as dictionaries, grammars, and core translations) could be cumulatively built on by succeeding generations of colonial Orientalists.

A second set of advantages accrued from the informational and communicational apparatus of European empire building, which, as decades of research on Orientalism have shown, directly and indirectly funded all manner of investigations, the results of which were in turn relayed back to Europe. By contrast, one of the consequences of colonization was to undermine the institutionalization of inter-Asian understanding, leaving colonized societies like India with no equivalent to London's School of Oriental and African Studies (or Tokyo's School of Foreign Languages), at least until the 1920s, when Indian-directed institutions, such as Tagore's Visva-Bharati University, began yielding interpretive fruit. Since the accurate understanding of other cultures requires collaborative and cumulative investigations over multiple generations, this bequeathed postcolonial nations such as India and Pakistan with an institutional underdevelopment that Nehru hoped to begin remedying by proposing "exchanges of students and professors." In subsequent decades, several such inter-Asian institutes were established, although they largely used English as their lingua franca.

A final set of interpretive and informational advantages that European researchers had over their Asian counterparts derived from Europe's physical and linguistic geography. This allowed scholars to circulate more easily among the main Orientalist hubs of London, Paris, Berlin, and Saint Petersburg and to communicate with one another, in person, by posted letter, or in print, in the key scholarly languages of English, French, and German that Orientalists shared from Budapest to Edinburgh and then beyond to the United States. Just in India, the sheer variety of languages and scripts presented far more formidable barriers to the flow of information in comparison to those of the closely knit cadre of European Orientalists, with their shared networks that linked the universities of Europe with the Asiatic Society in Calcutta and the École Française d'Extrême-Orient in Hanoi. Even when we have seen Indian scholars taking leading positions in the Asiatic Society and at Calcutta University, their writings in English and to some extent Bengali had little reach into the multiple languages of the Asian public sphere. In practice, for many Asian researchers these barriers were most easily circumvented by reliance on a colonial lingua franca, whether English, Russian, or French. Even in noncolonized regions—such as Iran and Afghanistan— French, Russian, and German served a similar function by lending access to the larger informational resources of Orientalists and Christian missionaries, whose writings we have also seen translated in Japan to kickstart its own colonial data-gathering on regions that were reconceived as *Tōyō* (the Orient) or *Ajia* (Asia).[17]

The purpose of pointing to the varied ways in which many (though by no means all) of Asia's intercultural investigators opted for such informational outsourcing is not to set up some kind of posthumous competition between European Orientalists and their Asian counterparts. Far from it. As a series of careful studies has shown, countless forgotten Asian scholars made crucial contributions to European knowledge of Asia. The dichotomy of Orientalism and its Asian alternative is ultimately just as illusory as the notion of an Asia that is wholly separate from and opposite to Europe. As an Indian historian of China, Tansen Sen, has argued, to escape such false binaries "intra-Asian interactions . . . must be conceived within the larger context of Afro-Eurasian networks."[18] What we have traced here, then, is the lesser-known Asian side of that larger knowledge exchange by which people from South and West Asia learned about East and Southeast Asia through communicational infrastructures or informational resources inadvertently provided by Europeans, as well as by North Africans with regard to the important role of Egypt as Cairo became the most important intellectual hub for Muslims from India, China, and Southeast Asia alike. Rather than emerging from some natural or timeless framework of inter-Asian interaction in which Europe was a sudden late-coming interloper, when Indian and Iranian scholars learned about Confucius through European translations, and when a Chinese student translated the *Analects* into Arabic, these were all ultimately parts of a larger and longer world historical process of Eurasian and even Afro-Eurasian interaction in which intercultural knowledge was always challenging for everyone.

In the modern period the economic and political dimensions of this process are well known—this is the history of colonization—but what we have traced are some of its intellectual dimensions. And so, while on the one hand, Europe's empires constrained the development of independent polities that might have sponsored such knowledge through their own diplomatic cadres and universities, on the other hand, they created an inter-Asian communications infrastructure that made available the ripe and rotten fruits of Orientalist research through a public sphere that ultimately reached from London to Tokyo, with Calcutta as the informational middle point. Far from finding that inter-Asian understanding flourished best when farthest from European influence, we have seen that far more, and earlier, books about East and Southeast Asia seem to have been published in the languages and ports of colonial India. As Calcutta and Bombay became major informational sorting houses, multiple sources of data—whether vernacular or European sources mailed from Shanghai or London—were transferred into other languages in turn, including the Persian, Arabic, and Turkish read in the Middle East. By contrast, noncolonized regions, such as Iran and Afghanistan, had to rely on fewer informational sources, whether direct or vicarious, as well as slower transmission speeds. The authors whose works we have examined were therefore not merely contemporaneous with empire. They also in different degrees made use of the technologies, concepts, and data it made available. Yet our authors were not simply reducible to empire. Far from being trapped in the discursive prison of "Orientalism," Asia's self-discovers deployed the resources of empire toward their own divergent ends. Instead of adding to old ideological dichotomies, this points to the more complex interdependency of Asia and Europe—or, rather, of Eurasia as a whole.[19]

This process of Eurasian intellectual entanglement and interdependency has continued through the colonial into the postcolonial period, particularly through the adoption of English not merely as an Asian language, but as *the* main language of inter-Asian communication.[20] Insofar as the question of a unifying Asian language has ever practically been raised, it has always been a question of linguistic unity on whose terms. Though a century ago some Japanese and Chinese intellectuals sought a neutral solution in Esperanto, which was itself invented in Mitteleuropa and then promoted afar by prosely-tizing Baha'is, in practice it is English that has become the primary language of inter-Asian interaction.[21] This was no less the case for the official state-level interactions that began with Nehru's 1947 conference, as seen at the Bandung Conference of 1955, which adopted English as its working language, and with subsequent regional organizations, such as the Association of Southeast Asian Nations (ASEAN), which, despite its motto of "One Vision, One Identity, One Community," similarly selected English as its working language.[22] Just as the cultural legacy of earlier imperial conquests saw written Persian and Chinese become learned lingua francas across large regions of Asia during the medi-eval and early modern periods, so in the modern era has English assumed that function—and increasingly so as the age of Europe's empires has faded into the past and English has become an Asian language itself.

Thus it was that, since the nineteenth century, people from the different regions of Asia came to learn of one another in considerable part through languages such as English and French, and occasionally the Latin used by Jesuits and the Esperanto invented by a Polish ophthalmologist. We can eas-ily condemn this as the familiarly ugly story of Orientalism, of "asymmetrical power relations," of the colonial warping of an otherwise perfect pattern of inter-Asian understanding that flourished over previous centuries. But while neighboring communities within specific regions and states had learned much about each other—particularly through such cultural intermediaries as the Persianate Hindus and Confucianized Muslims of the early modern period—no such pattern of perfect, or even detailed, intercultural comprehen-sion had ever previously existed across Asia as a whole.

Nor is it ever likely to. Human knowledge, especially of other people, is al-ways imperfect and flawed, and more often than not vicarious and mediated. Asia's self-discovery was neither a unique nor a self-contained process, but part of a larger sequence of dialogues—both cooperative and confrontational—between people from various corners of Eurasia who contributed to the differ-ent linguistic channels of a growing public sphere. It is a final irony that the most direct, geographically widespread, and linguistically robust inter-Asian networks were probably those developed by Muslims between China, the Middle East, Southeast Asia, and India: followers of the very religion that many Asianists from Okakura onward excluded from their models of Asian unity.

A thousand years earlier, paper had spread westward from Chang'an to Samarqand, then Baghdad, and through the Umayyad caliphate to Xàtiva (in Arabic, al-Shatiba) in Spain. From there, paper reached Christian Europe, enabling a medieval communications revolution that laid the material basis for Europe's own self-discovery in the Renaissance, for the birth of printing, and eventually for the Orientalists' investigations of the different lands their maps labeled "Asia." Then, with the rise of Europe's empires, amid the many unintended consequences of conquests planned to fill the coffers of distant colonial capitals, Europe inadvertently repaid the favor and helped Asia find herself.

The resulting inter-Asian understanding was not some mystical state of awareness that existed outside language, still less outside the time and space of history. Instead, it comprised a finite corpus of "things that were known," of representations and information of varying accuracy. In trying to reassemble that corpus of knowledge—or at least its Middle Eastern and Indian limbs— we have pored over publications whose parameters of comprehension were shaped by barriers and breakthroughs that defined what investigators could learn and then communicate to their readers. Over and again, we have seen how these Asian engagements with difference involved projections of the self as much as appreciations of the other. Buddhists, Baha'is, and Muslims sought either to connect with existing coreligionists or to convert followers of other religions, often at the cost of suppressing distinct versions of their own faiths that had developed over centuries of relative isolation. Meanwhile, Hindu, Shinto, Confucian, and secular nationalists sought to unify different regions of Asia in the terms of their own "civilizational" heritage, promoting a Greater India that had shaped the cultures of East and Southeast Asia, or an imperial Japan pitched as the natural leader of its lesser Asian siblings. Other investigators—the Japanophiles especially—turned to distant regions in search of self-protecting lessons that would uplift their own people.

Yet such projections of the self also led to greater involvement, understanding, and sometimes sympathy with the other. In some cases, this came through seeing one's own dilemma in the conditions of another, as happened when colonized Indians contemplated China's defeated Boxer Rebellion. In other cases, translations of stories, poems, and scriptures allowed the other to speak as directly as possible across the barriers of belief and language. Here sympathy grew from greater knowledge that allowed the other to be seen as being valuable in itself. And in yet other cases, sympathy developed through the merging of self and other, whether through claiming Buddhism for India (or Afghanistan), converting Burma and Japan to Baha'ism or Islam, or collapsing different faiths into an ecumenical spiritual "East" in the vision of Tagore. Then the whirligig of human understanding rotated again as appreciations of the other turned into projections of the self.

The knowledge that emerged from these varied ventures was molded by individual motivations and shared ideologies, along with guiding ideas—of progress, civilization, even "Asia" itself—that first emerged in Europe before rippling through a new public sphere. Yet for all that, the result was a substantial and still-growing body of intercultural awareness that otherwise might never have developed. Ever since inter-Asian understanding assumed its modern forms in the age of empires, it has been shaped by the perpetual tension between self and other that defines every attempt to comprehend difference. That at least is a common dilemma shared by every continent, language, and culture.

In 1947, as Nehru prepared his speech in New Delhi, two landmark Turkish books were published in Ankara that detailed the history of Buddhism and of China by drawing directly on sources in Sanskrit, Pali, and classical Chinese.[23] The previous year, the first Turkish translation of Lao Tzu's *Dao De Jing*, the founding text of Daoism, had also been printed in Turkey's capital.[24] All three works came from the "exchanges of students and professors" for which Nehru was calling. But they didn't arise from the closed inter-Asian interactions he hoped to promote. For the authors of the two histories were Walter Ruben (1899–1982) and Wolfram Eberhard, a Jewish Indologist and an anti-Nazi Sinologist who fled Hitler's Germany and took refuge in Turkey, where Nehru's nationalist counterpart, Kemal Atatürk, found them positions at Ankara's nascent university.[25] As for the translation of the *Dao De Jing*, it was made by Eberhard's brilliant Turkish protégé, Muhaddere Nabi Özerdim (1916–1991).

Here was not so much an intellectual competition between Asia and Europe, a contest between Orientalism and its rivals, as a picture of individual cooperation in the shared pursuit of knowledge that was bolstered by new national institutions. For though Eberhard wrote in the Turkish he learned from his students, he taught them to read Chinese in turn, preparing Muhaddere Özerdim, the young woman who translated Lao Tzu, to further her studies in China.[26] As Nehru greeted the political delegates at his conference, Özerdim was immersing herself in classical and spoken Chinese after sailing to Shanghai on a British cargo ship and taking lessons with local teachers at a Beijing school founded by American missionaries. She would later become Turkey's most distinguished Sinologist, just as Ruben's former students became the first Turkish professional Indologists.[27]

From Nazi Germany and Kemalist Turkey to late colonial India and Republican China, these tangled knots of knowledge point to a history of intercultural understanding that was larger than the confines of Asia itself. For what unfolded in miniature in Ankara was not a narrowly Asian self-discovery, but a larger Eurasian one. By the 1940s, it was increasingly a global one that involved not only American missionaries but universities too, such as Berkeley, where Eberhard taught for the rest of his career after leaving Turkish Sinology in Özerdim's capable hands. Perhaps Nehru knew none of this—nor Chairman Mao, whose advancing army forced Özerdim to flee Beijing, curtailing her studies; she sailed home via Calcutta, through which so much knowledge had been shipped over the previous century.

Like the poet Du Fu's stranger who thinks of home by the Yangtze and Han rivers, Özerdim took a journey between the places of self and other. Then she returned, changed, to where she began. Perhaps that is an apt place for us to end.

Notes

Introduction

1. Okakura Kakuzo, *The Ideals of the East, with Special Reference to the Art of Japan* (London: John Murray, 1903), 1. For the context of this celebrated statement, see Brij Tankha, "Okakura Tenshin: 'Asia Is One,' 1903," and Jing He, "Okakura Tenshin and Pan-Asianism, 1903–06," in Sven Saaler and Christopher W. A. Szpilman (eds.), *Pan-Asianism: A Documentary History,* 2 vols. (Lanham, Md.: Rowman & Littlefield, 2011), vol. 1. For fuller consideration, see Rustom Bharucha, *Another Asia: Rabindranath Tagore and Okakura Tenshin* (New Delhi: Oxford University Press, 2006). In the interests of keeping this book to a reasonable length, the bibliography lists only primary sources.

2. Inaga Shigemi, "Okakura Kakuzô's Nostalgic Journey to India and the Invention of Asia," in Susan Fisher (ed.), *Nostalgic Journeys: Literary Pilgrimages between Japan and the West* (Vancouver: Institute of Asian Research, University of British Columbia, 2001). For a broader overview, see Sven Saaler and Christopher W. A. Szpilman, "Introduction: The Emergence of Pan-Asianism as an Ideal of Asian Identity and Solidarity, 1850–2008," in Saaler and Szpilman, *Pan-Asianism,* vol. 1.

3. Shigemi, "Okakura Kakuzô's Nostalgic Journey," 120.

4. Inaga Shigemi, "Okakura Kakuzō and India: The Trajectory of Modern National Consciousness and Pan-Asian Ideology across Borders," trans. Kevin Singleton, *Review of Japanese Culture and Society* 24 (2012): 39. On the spread of the idea of "Asia" in Japan, see Matsuda Kōichirō, "The Concept of 'Asia' before Pan-Asianism," in Saaler and Szpilman, *Pan-Asianism,* vol. 1. On the related emergence of the concept of an Asian "Orient" developed in Meiji Japan through the neologism *Toyo,* see Stefan Tanaka, *Japan's Orient: Rendering Pasts into History* (Berkeley: University of California Press, 1993), 3–14.

5. Claude Markovits, "L'Asie: Une invention européenne?" *Monde(s): Histoire, Espaces, Relations* 3 (2013): 53–66. On parallel issues with regard to Africa, see V. Y. Mudimbe, *The Idea of Africa* (Bloomington: Indiana University Press, 1994), chap. 3.

6. Carolien Stolte and Harald Fischer-Tiné, "Imagining Asia in India: Nationalism and Internationalism (ca. 1905–1940)," *Comparative Studies in Society and History* 54, 1 (2012): 65.

7. On these issues for the early modern period, see Sanjay Subrahmanyam, "One Asia, or Many? Reflections from Connected History," *Modern Asian Studies* 50, 1 (2016): 5–43.

8. Among a vast literature, the most comprehensive and eloquent accounts of the period's anticolonial activists are Tim Harper, *Underground Asia: Global Revolutionaries and the Assault on Empire* (Cambridge: Harvard University Press, 2020), and Pankaj Mishra, *From the Ruins of Empire: The Revolt against the West and the Remaking of Asia* (London: Penguin, 2012).

9. Stephen N. Hay, *Asian Ideas of East and West: Tagore and His Critics in Japan, China, and India* (Cambridge: Harvard University Press, 1970), and more recently, Pratyay Banerjee and Anindya Kundu (eds.), *Tagore and Japan: Dialogue, Exchange and Encounter* (New Delhi: Synergy Books, 2016), and Bangwei Wang, Tan Chung, Amiya Dev, and Wei Liming (eds.), *Tagore and China* (Beijing: Central Compilation and Translation Press, 2011).

10. On various regional versions of Asianism, see Cemil Aydin, *The Politics of Anti-Westernism in Asia: Visions of World Order in Pan-Islamic and Pan-Asian Thought* (New York: Columbia University Press, 2007); Maria Moritz, "'The Empire of Righteousness': Anagarika Dharmapala and His Vision of Buddhist Asianism (c. 1900)," in Marc Frey and Nicola Spakowski (eds.), *Asianisms: Regionalist Interactions and Asian Integration* (Singapore: National University of Singapore, 2016); Kamal Sheel, "Hu Shih and 'The Indianisation of China': Some Comments on Modern Chinese Discourses on India," *China Report* 50, 3 (2014): 177–188; Christopher W. A. Szpilman, "The Dream of One Asia: Ōkawa Shūmei and Japanese Pan-Asianism," in Harald Fuess (ed.), *The Japanese Empire in East Asia and Its Postwar Legacy* (Munich: Iudicium, 1998); Brian Tsui, "The Plea for Asia: Tan Yunshan, Pan-Asianism and Sino-Indian Relations," *China Report* 46, 4 (2010): 353–370; and Renée Worringer, "Pan-Asianism in the Late Ottoman Empire, 1905–1912," in Camron Michael Amin, Benjamin C. Fortna, and Elizabeth B. Frierson (eds.), *The Modern Middle East: A Sourcebook for History* (Oxford: Oxford University Press, 2006).

11. Saaler and Szpilman, "Introduction," 2.

12. Rebecca E. Karl, "Creating Asia: China in the World at the Beginning of the Twentieth Century," *American Historical Review* 103, 4 (1998): 1096–1118; Pekka Korhonen, "Leaving Asia? The Meaning of *Datsu-A* and Japan's Modern History," *Asia-Pacific Journal* 11, 50, 1 (2013): 1–18; and Carolien Stolte, "Compass Points: Four Indian Cartographies of Asia, c. 1930–55," in Frey and Spakowski, *Asianisms*.

13. For notable exceptions, see Cemil Aydin, "Orientalism by the Orientals? The Japanese Empire and Islamic Studies (1931–1945)," *İslam Araştırmaları Dergisi (Journal of Islamic Studies, ISAM, Istanbul)* 14 (2005): 1–36; Wurlig Borchigud, "Between Chi-

nese Nationalism and Soviet Colonisation: A Chinese Orientalist's Narration of Inner and Outer Mongolia (1926–1927)," *Inner Asia* 4, 1 (2002): 27–46; Arif Dirlik, "Chinese History and the Question of Orientalism," *History and Theory* 35 (1996): 96–118; Laura Hostetler, *The Qing Colonial Enterprise: Ethnography and Cartography in Early Modern China* (Chicago: University of Chicago Press, 2001); Kenji Kuroda, "Pioneering Iranian Studies in Meiji Japan: Between Modern Academia and International Strategy," *Iranian Studies* 50, 5 (2017): 651–670; Ussama Makdisi, "Ottoman Orientalism," *American Historical Review* 107, 3 (2002): 768–796; Matthew W. Mosca, "Empire and the Circulation of Frontier Intelligence: Qing Conceptions of the Ottomans," *Harvard Journal of Asiatic Studies* 70, 1 (2010): 147–207; Fabio Rambelli, "The Idea of India (*Tenjiku*) in Premodern Japan: Issues of Signification and Representation in the Buddhist Translation of Cultures," in Tansen Sen (ed.), *Buddhism across Asia*, vol. 1 (Singapore: Institute of South East Asian Studies, 2014); Umar Ryad, "'An Oriental Orientalist': Aḥmad Zakī Pasha (1868–1934), Egyptian Statesman and Philologist in the Colonial Age," *Philological Encounters* 3 (2018): 129–166; and Tanaka, *Japan's Orient*. For an important reconceptualization of Orientalism writ large, see Jürgen Osterhammel, *Unfabling the East: The Enlightenment's Encounter with Asia* (Princeton: Princeton University Press, 2018).

14. Stolte, "Compass Points," 68.

15. Anna Aslanyan, *Dancing on Ropes: Translators and the Balance of History* (London: Profile, 2021), 3.

16. Andrea Acri, Kashshaf Ghani, Murari K. Jha, and Sraman Mukherjee (eds.), *Imagining Asia(s): Networks, Actors, Sites* (Singapore: ISEAS-Yusof Ishak Institute, 2019), especially chaps. 1–3. More broadly, and influentially, see Martin W. Lewis and Kären E. Wigen, *The Myth of Continents: A Critique of Metageography* (Berkeley: University of California Press, 1997). From a more literary perspective, see John M. Steadman, *The Myth of Asia: A Refutation of Western Stereotypes of Asian Religion, Philosophy, Art and Politics* (New York: Simon & Schuster, 1969), and Stefan Tanaka, "Asia: A Fallacy of Misplaced Concreteness," *boundary 2* 46, 3 (2019): 23–45.

17. Markovits, "L'Asie." See also Prasenjit Duara, "Asia Redux: Conceptualizing a Region for Our Times," *Journal of Asian Studies* 69, 4 (2010): 963–983; Nile Green, "Re-Thinking the 'Middle East' after the Oceanic Turn," *Comparative Studies of South Asia, Africa and the Middle East* 34, 3 (2014): 556–564; and Magnus Marsden and Till Mostowlansky, "Whither West Asia? Exploring North-South Perspectives on Eurasia," *Journal of Eurasian Studies* 10, 1 (2019): 3–10.

18. Markovits, "L'Asie," whose arguments are expanded in Subrahmanyam, "One Asia, or Many?"

19. Hostetler, *Qing Colonial Enterprise*, 56, and Sayoko Sakakibara, "Localizing Asia: Mapping Japan, Asia, and Europe in the Early Modern World," in Martijn Storms et al. (eds.), *Mapping Asia: Cartographic Encounters between East and West* (Cham: Springer, 2019).

20. On these new Chinese geographical works based on missionary input, see Jessie Gregory Lutz, *Opening China: Karl F. A. Gützlaff and Sino-Western Relations, 1827–1852* (Grand Rapids: William B. Eerdmans, 2008), chap. 7.

21. Fred W. Drake, *China Charts the World: Hsu Chi-Yü and His Geography of 1848* (Cambridge: East Asian Research Center of Harvard University, 1975); Karl, "Creating Asia," 1100–1101; and Jane Kate Leonard, *Wei Yuan and China's Rediscovery of the Maritime World* (Cambridge: Council on East Asian Studies, Harvard University, 1984).

22. Korhonen, "Leaving Asia?"

23. John J. Curry, "An Ottoman Geographer Engages the Early Modern World: Katip Çelebi's Vision of East Asia and the Pacific Rim in the *Cihânnümâ*," *Osmanlı Araştırmaları/Journal of Ottoman Studies* 40 (2012): 221–257.

24. I have directly consulted the first printed edition: Mustafa ibn 'Abdullah Haci Halife [Katib Çelebi], *Cihan-nüma* (Istanbul: Ibrahim Müteferrika, 1732).

25. Conrad Malte-Brun, *al-Jughrafiyya al-'Umumiyya*, trans. Rifa'at Rifa' al-Tahtawi, vols. 1, 3 (Cairo: Matba'at Bulaq, 1834). Tahtawi's volume 3 was devoted mainly to Asia (*Asiya*). Volume 2 was apparently never published.

26. Geoffrey Roper, "The Arabic Educational Books Printed in Malta in the Nineteenth Century: Who Read Them and Where?" in Philip Sadgrove (ed.), *From Ancient Arabia to Modern Cairo* (Oxford: Oxford University Press, 2012), esp. 113, 118–119 on the Arabic atlas and geographies.

27. Geoffrey Roper, "Arabic Printing in Malta, 1825–1845: Its History and Its Place in the Development of Print Culture in the Arab Middle East" (PhD diss., University of Durham, 1988), 248.

28. For *Asiya* and its component parts, see Rifa'at Rifa' al-Tahtawi, *Kitab al-Kanz al-Mukhtar fi Kashf al-Aradi wa al-Bahar* (Cairo: Matba'at Maktab al-Tubjiyya, 1834), 58–64.

29. Charles Frederick de Brocktorff, *Atlas, ay Majmu'a Kharitat Rasm al-Ard* (Malta: Church Missionary Society, 1835); its fourth part is on Asia (*Asiya*).

30. Mir 'Abd al-Latif Khan Shushtari, *Tuhfat al-'Alam wa Zayl al-Tuhfah: Safarnama wa Khatirat*, ed. Samad Muwahid (Tehran: Kitabkhana-yi Tahuri, 1363/1984), 243–244.

31. Firaydun Adamiyyat, *Amir Kabir va Iran* (Tehran: Intisharat-i Kharazmi, 2007), 380–381.

32. Ibid., 381; and Mirza Rafa'il, *Jahan-numa* (Tabriz: n.p., 1851).

33. William Pinnock, *A Comprehensive System of Modern Geography and History*, 2nd ed. (London: Holdsworth & Ball, 1834), trans. Farhad Mirza Mu'tamad al-Dawla as *Kitab-i Jam-i Jam* (Tehran: Chapkhana-yi Allah Quli Khan Qajar, 1856). Later textbooks include the anonymously authored *Jughrafi* (Tehran: Karkhana-yi 'Ali Quli Khan, 188?); Husayn Quli Mirza 'Imad al-Saltana, *Kitab-i Mir'at al-'Alam dar 'Ilm-i Hayat va Jughrafiyya* (Tehran, 1897); Mirza Aqa Khan Muhandis Muhasib al-Dawla, *Usul-i 'Ilm-i Jughrafiyya* (Tehran: n.p., 1900).

34. *Mir'at al-Arz: Ya'ni Mukhtasar-i Jughrafiyya-i 'Alam* (Lahore: Matba'-i Islamiyya, 1905), 9–10.

35. Markovits, "L'Asie," 57–63, and Subrahmanyam, "One Asia, or Many?" 15–18.

36. *Mir'at al-Aqalim*, 3rd ed. (Calcutta: Calcutta School Book Society, 1839); Horace William Clift, *First Geography for Natives; or, Guide to the Map of the World* (Calcutta: Calcutta School Book Society, 1836), was translated into several languages, including an Urdu version by Mir Ghulam 'Ali, *'Ilm-i Jughrafiyya* (Calcutta: n.p. [Calcutta School Book Society?], 1851).

37. William Edwards, *Jam-i Jahan-numa*, translated into Urdu by Babu Shiv Parshad (Lucknow: Munshi Nawwal Kishore, 1860). The cover states that this second edition had a print run of 5,000 copies.

38. From around 1860, George Duncan's *Introduction to the Geography of the World*, in three parts (one on Asia), was issued in Hindi, Urdu, Tamil, and Telugu. The Sindhi textbook, based on Henry Morris, *Geography* (Madras: Madras School Book Society, 1857), was translated as Hinri Maris, *Jughrafiyya Jadid* (Karachi: School Book Society, 1861).

39. *Asiya-vistaraya* (Colombo: Christian Vernacular Education Society, 1891), described in Don Martino de Zilva Wickremasinghe, *Catalogue of the Sinhalese Printed Books in the Library of the British Museum* (London: British Museum, 1901), 15.

40. For example, George Duncan, *Jughrafiyya: Hissa Awwal: A'ishya*, translated into Urdu by 'Abd al-Razzaq (Madras: Foster Press, 1877), featured different transliterations of "Asia" on the cover and in the text.

41. Wang Hui, "The Idea of Asia and Its Ambiguities," *Journal of Asian Studies* 69, 4 (2010): 988. More fully, see Wang Hui, *The Politics of Imagining Asia*, ed. Theodore Huters (Cambridge: Harvard University Press, 2011).

42. Subrahmanyam, "One Asia, or Many?" 41.

43. Ibid.

44. Amid a large literature on these developments, see Sushil Mittal (ed.), *Surprising Bedfellows: Hindus and Muslims in Medieval and Early Modern India* (Lanham, Md.: Lexington Books, 2003), and Audrey Truschke, "Defining the Other: An Intellectual History of Sanskrit Lexicons and Grammars of Persian," *Journal of Indian Philosophy* 40, 6 (2012): 635–668.

45. Amid another large literature, see James D. Frankel, *Rectifying God's Name: Liu Zhi's Confucian Translation of Monotheism and Islamic Law* (Honolulu: University of Hawai'i Press, 2011), and Zvi Ben-Dor Benite, *The Dao of Muhammad: A Cultural History of Muslims in Late Imperial China* (Cambridge: Harvard University Press, 2005).

46. Edward A. Alpers, *East Africa and the Indian Ocean* (Princeton: Markus Wiener, 2009); Julia Clancy-Smith, *Mediterraneans: North Africa and Europe in an Age of Migration, c. 1800–1900* (Berkeley: University of California Press, 2011); Molly Greene, *A Shared World: Christians and Muslims in the Early Modern Mediterranean* (Princeton:

Princeton University Press, 2000); and Thomas R. Metcalf, *Imperial Connections: India in the Indian Ocean Arena, 1860–1920* (Berkeley: University of California Press, 2007).

47. Sven Hedin, *Sekishoku ruto tohaki*, trans. into Japanese by Yokichi Takayama (Tokyo: Ikuseisha, 1939).

48. Tamara Chin, "The Invention of the Silk Road, 1877," *Critical Inquiry* 40, 1 (2013): 194–219; Nile Green, "From the Silk Road to the Railroad (and Back): The Means and Meanings of the Iranian Encounter with China," *Iranian Studies* 48, 2 (2015): 165–192; and Daniel C. Waugh, "Richthofen's 'Silk Roads': Towards the Archaeology of a Concept," *Silk Road* 5, 1 (2007): 1–10.

49. For recent critical approaches with regard to antiquity, see Warwick Ball, "'Band Wagon and Gravy Train': Uses and Abuses along the Silk Road," *Afghanistan* 2, 2 (2019): 171–194; and Khodadad Rezakhani, "The Road That Never Was: The Silk Road and Trans-Eurasian Exchange," *Comparative Studies of South Asia, Africa and the Middle East* 30, 3 (2010): 420–433.

50. On the analytical limits of "connectedness," see Jeremy Adelman, "Words from Jeremy Adelman," in "Discussion: The Futures of Global History," *Journal of Global History* 13, 1 (2018): 18–21.

51. On such early modern travel and ethnographic writings, see Muzaffar Alam and Sanjay Subrahmanyam, *Indo-Persian Travels in the Age of Discoveries, 1400–1800* (Cambridge: Cambridge University Press, 2007); Giancarlo Casale, *The Ottoman Age of Exploration* (Oxford: Oxford University Press, 2010); Simon Digby, "Beyond the Ocean: Perceptions of Overseas in Indo-Persian Sources of the Mughal Period," *Studies in History* 15, 2 (1999): 247–259; Hostetler, *Qing Colonial Enterprise;* Muhammad Ismail Marcinkowksi, *From Isfahan to Ayutthaya: Contacts between Iran and Siam in the 17th Century* (Kuala Lumpur: Pustaka Nasional, 2005); Matthew W. Mosca, "Cišii's Description of Xinjiang: Its Context and Circulation," in Takahiro Onuma, David Brophy, and Yasushi Shinmen (eds.), *Xinjiang in the Context of Central Eurasian Transformations* (Tokyo: Toyo Bunko, 2018); and Hashem Rajabzadeh, "Japan as Described in *Safina-ye-Solaimani*, a Seventeenth Century Travel-Book in Persian," *Journal of Osaka University of Foreign Studies* 5 (1991): 189–205.

52. On these developments in Europe, see Jürgen Osterhammel, *Unfabling the East: The Enlightenment's Encounter with Asia* (Princeton: Princeton University Press, 2018).

53. James L. Gelvin and Nile Green (eds.), *Global Muslims in the Age of Steam and Print, 1850–1930* (Berkeley: University of California Press, 2014), and Roland Wenzlhuemer, "The Role of Infrastructure in Transregional Ventures," in Matthias Middell (ed.), *The Routledge Handbook of Transregional Studies* (Abingdon, U.K.: Routledge, 2018).

54. Duara, "Asia Redux," 964.

55. On the effect of the Suez Canal on linking West and South/Southeast Asia, see Valeska Huber, "Multiple Mobilities, Multiple Sovereignties, Multiple Speeds: Exploring Maritime Connections in the Age of Empire," *International Journal of Middle East-*

ern Studies 48, 4 (2016): 763–766. Cairo's Bulaq district was where Arabic printing developed after its introduction to Egypt by Napoleon in the early 1800s.

56. Cf. Philip D. Curtin, *Cross-Cultural Trade in World History* (Cambridge: Cambridge University Press, 1984).

57. For rare investigations of these orthographic issues in the region, see Matthew W. Mosca, "Comprehending the Qing Empire: Building Multilingual Competence in an Age of Imperial Rivalry, 1792–1820," *International History Review* 41, 5 (2019): 1057–1075, and Ronit Ricci, "Reading a History of Writing: Heritage, Religion and Script Change in Java," *Itinerario* 39 (2015): 419–435. On Japanese attempts to circumvent these problems through the adoption of Esperanto, see Sho Konishi, "Translingual World Order: Language without Culture in Post-Russo-Japanese War Japan," *Journal of Asian Studies* 72, 1 (2013): 91–114.

58. Albert Welter and Jeffrey Newmark (eds.), *Religion, Culture, and the Public Sphere in China and Japan* (New York: Palgrave Macmillan, 2017). Cf. the previous patterns of Judeo-Christian-Muslim encounters as analyzed in Brian A. Catlos and Alex J. Novikoff (eds.), "Interfaith Dialogue and Disputation in the Medieval Mediterranean," special issue of *Medieval Encounters* 24, 5–6 (2018).

59. Philip C. Almond, *The British Discovery of Buddhism* (Cambridge: Cambridge University Press, 1988), and Lionel Obadia, *Bouddhisme et Occident: La diffusion du bouddhisme tibétain en France* (Paris: L'Harmattan, 1999), chaps. 1–2.

60. Susannah Heschel and Umar Ryad (eds.), *The Muslim Reception of European Orientalism: Reversing the Gaze* (London: Routledge, 2018); and François Pouillon and Jean-Claude Vatin (eds.), *After Orientalism: Critical Perspectives on Western Agency and Eastern Re-appropriations* (Leiden: Brill, 2014).

61. Amid an enormous literature, see Carol A. Breckenridge and Peter van der Veer (eds.), *Orientalism and the Postcolonial Predicament: Perspectives on South Asia* (Philadelphia: University of Pennsylvania Press, 1993); James Clifford and George E. Marcus (eds.), *Writing Culture: The Poetics and Politics of Ethnography* (Berkeley: University of California Press, 1986); Robert Irwin, *For Lust of Knowing: The Orientalists and Their Enemies* (London: Allen Lane, 2006); Osterhammel, *Unfabling the East;* Edward Said, *Orientalism* (New York: Pantheon, 1978); Steadman, *Myth of Asia;* and Sanjay Subrahmanyam, *Europe's India: Words, People, Empires, 1500–1800* (Cambridge: Harvard University Press, 2017).

62. C. A. Bayly, *Empire and Information: Intelligence Gathering and Social Communication in India, 1780–1870* (Cambridge: Cambridge University Press, 1996); Mark Ravinder Frost, "Pandora's Post Box: Empire and Information in India, 1854–1914," *English Historical Review* 131, 552 (2016): 1043–1073; and Martin Thomas, *Empires of Intelligence: Security Services and Colonial Disorder after 1914* (Berkeley: University of California Press, 2008). See also the more recent comparative work on economic information by Bishnupriya Gupta, "Discrimination or Social Networks? Industrial Investment in Colonial India," *Journal of Economic History* 74, 1 (2014): 141–168, and Michael

O'Sullivan, "Vernacular Capitalism and Intellectual History in a Gujarati Account of China, 1860–68," *Journal of Asian Studies* 80, 2 (2021): 267–292.

63. Sandria B. Freitag (ed.), "Aspects of the 'Public' in Colonial South Asia," special issue of *South Asia* 14, 1 (1991); Arvind Rajagopal (ed.), *The Indian Public Sphere: Readings in Media History* (New Delhi: Oxford University Press, 2009); John-Paul Ghobrial, *The Whispers of Cities: Information Flows in Istanbul, London, and Paris in the Age of William Trumbull* (Oxford: Oxford University Press, 2013); Tatsuro Hanada, "The Japanese 'Public Sphere': The Kugai," *Theory, Culture & Society* 23, 2–3 (2006): 612–614; William T. Rowe, "The Public Sphere in Modern China," *Modern China* 16, 3 (1990): 309–329; J. Barton Scott and Brannon D. Ingram, "What Is a Public? Notes from South Asia," *South Asia* 38, 3 (2015): 357–370; Jun Uchida, "The Public Sphere in Colonial Life: Residents' Movements in Korea under Japanese Rule," *Past & Present* 220 (2013): 217–248; Rudolf G. Wagner, "The Role of the Foreign Community in the Chinese Public Sphere," *China Quarterly* 142 (1995): 423–443; Welter and Newmark, *Religion, Culture, and the Public Sphere.* For broader comparative considerations, see Valeska Huber and Jürgen Osterhammel, "Introduction: Global Publics," in Huber and Osterhammel (eds.), *Global Publics: Their Power and Their Limits, 1870–1990* (Oxford: Oxford University Press, 2020), and Ralph Schroeder, "Historicizing Media, Globalizing Media Research: Infrastructures, Publics, and Everyday Life," *Journal of Global History* 14, 3 (2019): 437–453.

64. Hartmut Wessler and Rainer Freudenthaler, "Public Sphere," *Oxford Bibliographies in Communication,* https://www.oxfordbibliographies.com/view/document/obo-9780199756841/obo-9780199756841-0030.xml.

65. On parallel developments in the Mediterranean in this period, albeit mainly regarding Arabic political debates, see Dyala Hamzah, "Introduction: The Making of the Arab Intellectual: Empire, Public Sphere and the Colonial Coordinates of Selfhood," in Hamzah (ed.), *The Making of the Arab Intellectual: Empire, Public Sphere and the Colonial Coordinates of Selfhood* (New York: Routledge, 2012).

66. Graham Shaw, "Calcutta: Birthplace of the Indian Lithographed Book," *Journal of the Printing Historical Society* 27 (1998): 89–111.

67. Nile Green, "Stones from Bavaria: Iranian Lithography in Its Global Contexts," *Iranian Studies* 43, 3 (2010): 305–331, and Christopher A. Reed, *Gutenberg in Shanghai: Chinese Print Capitalism, 1876–1937* (Vancouver: University of British Columbia Press, 2007).

68. On such censorship, see, for example, Gu'il Kuhan, *Tarikh-i Sansur dar Matbu'at-i Iran* (Tehran: Agah, 1981–1983), and Ipek K. Yosmaoğlu, "Chasing the Printed Word: Press Censorship in the Ottoman Empire, 1876–1913," *Turkish Studies Association Journal* 27, 1–2 (2003): 15–49.

69. Nile Green (ed.), *The Persianate World: The Frontiers of a Eurasian Lingua Franca* (Oakland: University of California Press, 2019), and Francis Robinson, "Ottomans—Safavids—Mughals: Shared Knowledge and Connective Systems," *Journal of Islamic Studies* 8, 2 (1997): 151–184.

70. Joshua A. Fogel, *Articulating the Sinosphere: Sino-Japanese Relations in Space and Time* (Cambridge: Harvard University Press, 2009).

71. On such precolonial South Asian travel accounts of Burma, and the joint "Anglo-Persian" investigations sponsored by the Asiatic Society of Bengal, see Arash Khazeni, *The City and the Wilderness: Indo-Persian Encounters in Southeast Asia* (Oakland: University of California Press, 2020), chaps. 3–7.

72. Sanjay Subrahmanyam, "Par-delà l'incommensurabilité: pour une histoire connectée des empires aux temps modernes," *Revue d'histoire moderne et contemporaine* 54, 4 (2007): 34–53.

73. On the history of Urdu printing in Calcutta and Madras, see Sayyid Muqit al-Hasan, *Kalkatta ke Qadim Urdu Mataba' aur unki Matbu'at: Ek Tazkira* (Calcutta: 'Usmaniyya Buk Dipu, 1982), and 'Alim Saba Nawidi, *Tamil Nadu mein Urdu: 1824 ta 1986* (Madras: Tamil Nadu Urdu Pablikeshanz, 1998).

74. Nile Green, "The Trans-Border Traffic of Afghan Modernism: Afghanistan and the Indian 'Urdusphere,'" *Comparative Studies in Society and History* 53, 3 (2011): 479–508.

75. Roland Wenzlhuemer, "London in the Global Telecommunication Network of the Nineteenth Century," *New Global Studies* 3, 1 (2009): 1–32. There were also the dozens of English-language newspapers based in the ports of East Asia. See Peter O'Connor, *The English-Language Press Networks of East Asia, 1918–1945* (Folkestone, U.K.: Global Oriental, 2010).

76. Gupta, "Discrimination or Social Networks?" For political implications, see Daniel Headrick, "A Double-Edged Sword: Communications and Imperial Control in British India," *Historical Social Research* 35, 1 (2010): 51–65.

77. Tim Winter, *Geocultural Power: China's Quest to Revive the Silk Roads for the Twenty-first Century* (Chicago: University of Chicago Press, 2019).

78. Okakura, *Ideals of the East*, 1–3, cited in Subrahmanyam, "One Asia, or Many?" 42–43.

Chapter 1. Learning through Polemics in the Bay of Bengal

1. On the precolonial period, see Jos J. L. Gommans and Jacques Leider (eds.), *The Maritime Frontiers of Burma: Exploring Political, Cultural, and Commercial Interaction in the Indian Ocean World, 1200–1800* (Leiden: KITLV Press, 2002), and Rila Mukherjee (ed.), *Pelagic Passageways: The Northern Bay of Bengal before Colonialism* (Delhi: Primus Books, 2011). On the modern history of economic migration across the region, and its cultural ramifications, see Sunil Amrith, *Crossing the Bay of Bengal: The Furies of Nature and the Fortunes of Migrants* (Cambridge: Harvard University Press, 2015).

2. Mofakhkhar Khan, "History of Printing in Bengali Characters Up to 1866" (PhD thesis, University of London, 1976), esp. chaps. 4–5, on the East India Company and missionary printing of Bengali, respectively; M. Siddiq Khan, "The Early History of

Bengali Printing," *Library Quarterly* 32, 1 (1962): 51–61; and C. A. Storey, "The Beginnings of Persian Printing in India," in J. D. Cursetji Pavry (ed.), *Oriental Studies in Honour of Cursetji Erachji Pavry* (London: Oxford University Press, 1933). On Persian texts produced in Bengal during the East India Company era, see P. T. Nair, "Decline of Persian Studies in Calcutta," *Indo-Iranica* 52 (1999): 1–42.

3. Sayyid Muqit al-Hasan, *Kalkatta ke Qadim Urdu Mataba' aur unki Matbu'at: Ek Tazkira* (Calcutta: 'Usmaniyya Buk Dipu, 1982).

4. Anindita Ghosh, "An Uncertain 'Coming of the Book': Early Print Cultures in Colonial India," *Book History* 6 (2003): 23–55.

5. On the Chinese and Japanese adoption of European lithography and typography, see Christopher A. Reed, *Gutenberg in Shanghai: Chinese Print Capitalism, 1876–1937* (Vancouver: University of British Columbia Press, 2007), and Nathan Shockey, *The Typographic Imagination: Reading and Writing in Japan's Age of Modern Print Media* (New York: Columbia University Press, 2019).

6. J. Barton Scott and Brannon D. Ingram, "What Is a Public? Notes from South Asia," *South Asia* 38, 3 (2015): 357–370.

7. Marcelo Dascal, "On the Uses of Argumentative Reason in Religious Polemics," in Theo L. Hettema and Arie Van der Kooij (eds.), *Religious Polemics in Context* (Assen: Royal Van Gorcum, 2004).

8. Ibid., 6.

9. Ibid., 3, 4.

10. On the intellectual background, see Nile Green, "Parnassus of the Evangelical Empire: Orientalism and the English Universities, 1800–50," *Journal of Imperial and Commonwealth History* 40, 3 (2012): 337–355.

11. Ram Ram Basu, *Dharma Pustakera Duta* (Serampore: Mission Press, 1804).

12. Joshua Marshman, *Bhedabheda* (Serampore: Mission Press, 1807).

13. Brian Hatcher, *Bourgeois Hinduism, or The Faith of the Modern Vedantists* (New York: Oxford University Press, 2008), chap. 5.

14. *Sacha 'Isa'i: Ramhari aur ek Shakhs Sadhu Apas mein in Baton ki Guftagu Karti [sic] Hain* (Calcutta: Calcutta Christian Tract and Book Society, 1829). The title translation is not literal, but given as provided on the bilingual title page. To allow future researchers to make fuller inquiries than I am able to, subsequent notes and the bibliography provide full citations to all primary sources mentioned, however fleetingly.

15. Ibid., 20.

16. *Muhammadi u 'Isawi Din ka Muqabala* (Calcutta: Calcutta Christian Tract and Book Society, n.d. [c. 1835]) and *Tahqiq al-Iman* (Calcutta: Calcutta Christian Tract and Book Society, n.d. [c. 1835]). The latter bears the English title *On Various Ceremonies Practised by Muhummedans* rather than a translation of its Urdu title, *Tahqiq al-Iman*. Although these two works and those cited in notes 20 and 21 lack publication dates, my inspection and comparison of the copies held in the Angus Library at Regent's Park

College, Oxford, suggest that they date from the same period as the Christian Tract and Book Society's c. 1835 *Sacha 'Isa'i*.

17. On the print run and cost, see *Tahqiq al-Iman*, 20.

18. Ibid., 13.

19. On "proof" (*sabit*), see ibid., 16–19.

20. *Is Mursala mein Nabi Allah Hone ki Dalilen Hain* (Calcutta: Calcutta Christian Tract and Book Society, n.d. [c. 1835]).

21. *Musalmani Mazhab ko Chor Dene ka Sabab* (Calcutta: Calcutta Christian Tract and Book Society, n.d. [c. 1835]).

22. On Sura Yunus, see ibid., 19.

23. On the Hindustani press and its early imprints, see al-Hasan, *Kalkatta ke Qadim Urdu Mataba'*, 29–58.

24. G. A. Grierson, "The Early Publications of the Serampore Missionaries," *Indian Antiquary* (June 1903): 241–254.

25. Nile Green, *Bombay Islam: The Religious Economy of the West Indian Ocean, 1840–1915* (New York: Cambridge University Press, 201), chap. 1.

26. Nile Green, *Terrains of Exchange: Religious Economies of Global Islam* (New York: Oxford University Press, 2015), 67–68, 113–115.

27. By the 1880s, Calcutta was home to a series of Urdu newspapers, such as *Akhbar Dar al-Sultanat* (*Capital City News*) and *Amir al-Akhbar* (*Commander of News*). Even as late as the 1970s, Urdu speakers made up 70 percent of Calcutta's Muslim population. See Moulana Abdul Khallaque Nadvi, *Catalogue of Urdu Books in Possession of the Library of the Asiatic Society*, 2 vols. (Calcutta: Asiatic Society, 1992–1995), 2:986–996, and M. K. A. Siddiqui, *Muslims of Calcutta: A Study in Aspects of Their Social Organisation* (Calcutta: Anthropological Survey of India, Government of India, 1974), 25.

28. Nile Green, "Jawād (Sometime Nathaniel) Sābāṭ b. Ibr. Sābāṭal-Ḥasanī and the Text *al-Barāhīn as-Sābāṭīya*," in John Chesworth (ed.), *Christian-Muslim Relations: A Bibliographical History, 1500–1900* (Leiden: Brill, 2021), vol. 18.

29. Marc Gaborieau, *Le Mahdi incompris: Sayyid Ahmad Barelvi (1786–1831) et le millénarisme en Inde* (Paris: CNRS Éditions, 2010), 137–149 (the 1822 and 1824 imprints of *Sirat al-Mustaqim* and *Taqwiyyat al-Iman* are discussed on 155–156 and 288). On the widening circles of polemics triggered by the *Taqwiyyat al-Iman*, see SherAli Tareen, *Defending Muhammad in Modernity* (Notre Dame: University of Notre Dame Press, 2020).

30. J. R. C. [James Russell Colvin], "Notice on the Peculiar Tenets Held by the Followers of Syed Ahmed, Taken Chiefly from the 'Sirat ul Mustaqim,'" *Journal of the Asiatic Society of Bengal* 1, 11 (1832): 479–498; the additional publications are named on 494. Unfortunately, I have been unable to trace these original imprints. The earliest Calcutta publication for any of Sayyid Isma'il's books given in Muqit al-Hasan's year-by-year bibliography of early Calcutta printed books is for an 1848 printing of his *Mansab-i Imamat*. See al-Hasan, *Kalkatta ke Qadim Urdu Mataba'*, 167.

31. Mawlwi 'Abdullah Nizam al-Din, *Haqiqat al-Salat* (Calcutta: n.p., 1837).

32. Mawlwi 'Abd al-Jabbar of Calcutta, *Jawab Fawt al-Iman ka* (Calcutta: n.p., 1843).

33. See, for example, Abdul Jaleel, "Religious Rivalries in Eighteenth-Century Malabar: The Diasporic Writings of a Hadrami Scholar," in Mahmood Koria and Michael N. Pearson (eds.), *Malabar in the Indian Ocean: Cosmopolitanism in a Maritime Historical Region* (New Delhi: Oxford University Press, 2018).

34. On jurisprudential attempts to minimize the social impact of such "disagreements" (*ikhtilaf*), see Mohammad Hashim Kamali, "The Scope of Diversity and '*Ikhtilāf*' (Juristic Disagreement) in the Sharī'a," *Islamic Studies* 37, 3 (1998): 315–337, and John Walbridge, "The Islamic Art of Asking Questions: '*Ilm al-Ikhtilāf* and the Institutionalization of Disagreement," *Islamic Studies* 41, 1 (2002): 69–86.

35. J. B. P. More, *Muslim Identity, Print Culture and the Dravidian Factor in Tamil Nadu* (New Delhi: Orient Longman, 2004), 80–81.

36. Syed Safiullah, "Urdu Journalism in Tamilnadu from 1840 to 1850," *Annals of Oriental Research* 27, 1–2 (1977): 2–3, and E. M. Wherry, *The Muslim Controversy: Being a Review of Christian Literature Written in the Urdu Language for the Propagation of the Christian Religion and the Refutation of Islam* (Madras: Christian Literature Society, 1905).

37. Wherry, *The Muslim Controversy*, 117–118.

38. More, *Muslim Identity*, 35–36, 53–55; a bibliography of printed Tamil Muslim polemical texts in Arwi is on 282–288.

39. Ibid., 130–135.

40. Nile Green, "Persian Print and the Stanhope Revolution: Industrialization, Evangelicalism and the Birth of Printing in Early Qajar Iran," *Comparative Studies of South Asia, Africa and the Middle East* 30, 3 (2010): 473–490.

41. Abbas Amanat, "Mujtahids and Missionaries: Shi'i Responses to Christian Polemics in the Early Qajar Period," in Robert Gleave (ed.), *Religion and Society in Qajar Iran* (London: Routledge, 2004), 128, 147.

42. Samuel Lee (ed. and trans.), *Controversial Tracts on Christianity and Mohammedanism by the Late Rev. Henry Martyn and Some of the Most Eminent Writers of Persia* (Cambridge, U.K.: J. Smith, 1824).

43. Green, *Terrains of Exchange*, 136–138, and Christine Schirrmacher, *Mit den Waffen des Gegners: Christlich-muslimische Kontroversen im 19. und 20. Jahrhundert* (Berlin: Klaus Schwarz, 1992), 144–151.

44. Schirrmacher, *Mit den Waffen des Gegners*, 155–163.

45. Ibid., 275.

46. Leirvik Oddbjørn, "History as a Literary Weapon: The Gospel of Barnabas in Muslim-Christian Polemics," *Studia Theologica* 56, 1 (2002): 4–26.

47. Rashid Rida (ed.), *Injil Barnaba* (Cairo: Matba'at al-Manar, 1907), and Mawlwi Muhammad Halim Sahib Ansari (trans.), *Injil-i Barnabas* (Lahore: Hamidiyya Stim Pres, 1916). For detailed discussion of the Arabic translation, see Umar Ryad, *Islamic Reformism and Christianity: A Critical Reading of the Works of Muḥammad Rashīd Riḍā*

and His Associates (1898–1935) (Leiden: Brill, 2009), chap. 5. As Ryad clarifies on 214n8, the Arabic version actually appeared in 1908.

48. On the debates about its authorship, see Oddbjørn, "History as a Literary Weapon," 13–20.

49. Michael Winship, "Early Thai Printing: The Beginning to 1851," *Crossroads: An Interdisciplinary Journal of Southeast Asian Studies* 3, 1 (1986): 48.

50. E. D. T. Kularatne, "The Wesleyan Methodist Mission in the Printing and Publishing Industry in the 19th Century Ceylon," *Journal of the Royal Asiatic Society of Sri Lanka*, n.s., 42 (1997): 213–242.

51. Winship, "Early Thai Printing," 46.

52. Helen James, "Adoniram Judson and the Creation of a Missionary Discourse in Pre-Colonial Burma," *Journal of Burma Studies* 7 (2002): 1–28. On the 1817 Gospel of Matthew and the many subsequent Baptist publications in Burmese, see F. D. Pinney, *The American Baptist Mission Press: Historical, Descriptive, 1816–1916* (Rangoon: American Baptist Mission Press, 1917).

53. Rev. J. Wade, *Dictionary of Boodhism and Burman Literature* (Moulmain: American Mission Press, 1852).

54. Aurore Candier, "De la collaboration coloniale: Fortune des missions catholiques françaises en Birmanie, 1856–1918," *Revue Française d'Histoire d'Outre-Mer* (2000): 177–203.

55. Michael W. Charney, *Powerful Learning: Buddhist Literati and the Throne in Burma's Last Dynasty, 1752–1885* (Ann Arbor: Center for Southeast Asian Studies, 2006), 190.

56. Jörg Schendel, "Christian Missionaries in Upper Burma, 1853–85," *South East Asia Research* 7, 1 (1999): 61–91.

57. Andrew Jenson, *Encyclopedic History of the Church of Jesus Christ of Latter-Day Saints* (Salt Lake City: Deseret News, 1941), 207.

58. "Hindu Priests Coming Over to Burma," National Archives of Myanmar, accession no. 3096 (file 249P, box 194).

59. Juliane Schober, "Colonial Knowledge and Buddhist Education in Burma," in Ian Harris (ed.), *Buddhism, Power and Political Order* (Abingdon, U.K.: Routledge, 2007), 58. On the Tehran Quran, see Nile Green, *The Love of Strangers: What Six Muslim Students Learned in Jane Austen's London* (Princeton: Princeton University Press, 2016), 310.

60. On Taw Sein Ko's activities, see Penny Edwards, "Relocating the Interlocutor: Taw Sein Ko (1864–1930) and the Itinerancy of Knowledge in British Burma," *South East Asia Research* 12, 3 (2004): 277–335.

61. David Geary, *The Rebirth of Bodh Gaya: Buddhism and the Making of a World Heritage Site* (Seattle: University of Washington Press, 2017), and Steven E. Kemper, *Rescued from the Nation: Anagarika Dharmapala and the Buddhist World* (Chicago: University of Chicago Press, 2015).

62. Geary, *Rebirth of Bodh Gaya*, 30–31.

63. Juliane Schober, *Modern Buddhist Conjunctures in Myanmar: Cultural Narratives, Colonial Legacies, and Civil Society* (Honolulu: University of Hawai'i Press, 2011), 41, 65–66.

64. On this generative interaction, see Alexey Kirichenko, "From Thathanadaw to Theravada Buddhism: Constructions of Religion and Religious Identity in Nineteenth- and Early Twentieth-Century Myanmar," in Thomas David DuBois (ed.), *Casting Faiths: Imperialism and the Transformation of Religion in East and Southeast Asia* (London: Palgrave Macmillan, 2009), 23–45.

65. For the Burmese translation, see Schober, *Modern Buddhist Conjunctures*, 63. The Japanese version appeared as Henry Steel Olcott, *Bukkyo mondo* (Tokyo: Bussho Shuppankai, 1886).

66. Martin Baumann, "Modernist Interpretations of Buddhism in Europe," in David L. McMahan (ed.), *Buddhism in the Modern World* (London: Routledge, 2012), 89–113.

67. See Gueth's autobiography, published as Bhikkhu Nyanatiloka, *Der erste deutsche Bhikkhu: Das bewegte Leben des ehrwürdigen Nyānatiloka (1878–1957) und seine Schüler,* ed. Hellmuth Hecker (Konstanz: Universität Konstanz, 1995).

68. Alicia Turner, "The Irish Pongyi in Colonial Burma: The Confrontations and Challenges of U Dhammaloka," *Contemporary Buddhism* 11, 2 (2010): 129–172.

69. Lionel Obadia, *Bouddhisme et Occident: La diffusion du bouddhisme tibétain en France* (Paris: L'Harmattan, 1999), chaps. 5, 6.

70. Schober, *Modern Buddhist Conjunctures,* 64.

71. Daniel Jeyaraj, "Tamil Missionaries in East Africa and Burma in the 19th Century," in George Sam and Andrew F. Walls (eds.), *Diaspora Christianities: Global Scattering and Gathering of South Asian Christians* (Minneapolis: Augsburg Fortress, 2018), 44–56.

72. Brent D. Singleton, "Introduction: Mohammed Alexander Russell Webb," in Singleton (ed.), *Yankee Muslim: The Asian Travels of Mohammed Alexander Russell Webb* (Rockville, Md.: Wildside Press, 2006), 9–54.

73. Mohammed Alexander Russell Webb, *Isha'at-i Islam,* translated into Urdu by Mawlwi Hasan 'Ali (Lahore: n.p., 1893).

74. Yehya-en-Nasr Parkinson, *Muslim Chivalry* (Rangoon: British Burma Press, 1909), and Parkinson, *Essays on Islamic Philosophy* (Rangoon: British Burma Press, 1909).

75. Eusuf Sahle Poo, *Proof of Prophet Muhammad from the Holy Bible and Way to Paradise for Eternal Life* (Rangoon: Propagation Dept. of the Jamiat-ul-Ulema of Burma, 1934).

76. Richard Fox Young and G. P. V. Somaratna, *Vain Debates: The Buddhist-Christian Controversies of Nineteenth-Century Ceylon* (Vienna: Indological Institute of the University of Vienna, 1996).

77. Tilak Kularatne, *History of Printing and Publishing in Ceylon, 1736–1912* (Dehiwala: Tilak Kularatne, 2006), 125.

78. Statistic cited from John Murdoch and James Nicholson, *Classified Catalogue of Printed Tracts and Books in Singhalese* (Madras: C. Foster, 1868), in Mark Frost, "'Wider Opportunities': Religious Revival, Nationalist Awakening and the Global Dimension in Colombo, 1870–1920," *Modern Asian Studies* 36, 4 (2002): 943.

79. Elizabeth J. Harris, "A Case of Distortion: The Evangelical Missionary Interpretation of Buddhism in Nineteenth Century Sri Lanka," *Dialogue* 21 (1994): 19–42.

80. Elizabeth Harris, *Theravāda Buddhism and the British Encounter: Religious, Missionary and Colonial Experience in Nineteenth Century Sri Lanka* (Abingdon, U.K.: Routledge, 2006), 202.

81. Henry Morris, *The Life of John Murdoch: The Literary Evangelist of India* (London: Christian Literature Society for India, 1906), 222.

82. Young and Somaratna, *Vain Debates*, chap. 3.

83. Don Martino de Zilva Wickremasinghe, *Catalogue of the Sinhalese Printed Books in the Library of the British Museum* (London: British Museum, 1901), 102, 129. Since I cannot read and therefore have not consulted these Sinhala books directly, in the following notes I provide only references to Wickremasinghe's *Catalogue*, rather than full bibliographical citations.

84. Ibid., 26.

85. Young and Somaratna, *Vain Debates*, 66. The analytical category of "Protestant Buddhism" was first developed and defined by Richard Gombrich and Gananath Obeyesekere, *Buddhism Transformed: Religious Change in Sri Lanka* (Princeton: Princeton University Press, 1988), 215–216.

86. Tilak Kularatne, *History of Printing and Publishing in Ceylon, 1736–1912* (Dehiwala: Tilak Kularatne, 2006), 172, which cites the society's own 1890 report.

87. Wickremasinghe, *Catalogue*, 138.

88. Ibid., 154–156.

89. Richard M. Jaffe, *Seeking Śākyamuni: South Asia in the Formation of Modern Japanese Buddhism* (Chicago: University of Chicago Press, 2019), chap. 1.

90. This statement is based on the bibliographical entries in Wickremasinghe, *Catalogue*.

91. Ibid., 13–14, 125, 210.

92. The earliest Sinhala translation I have been able to locate is much later: *al-Quran* (Colombo: Colombo Moors' Islamic Cultural Home, 1961).

93. This statement is based on consulted catalogues of Sinhala printed books.

94. Philip C. Almond, *The British Discovery of Buddhism* (Cambridge: Cambridge University Press, 1988), 7–32, and Obadia, *Bouddhisme et Occident*, chaps. 1, 2.

95. Almond, *British Discovery*, 22.

96. Ibid., 54–68, and Ananda Wickremeratne, *The Genesis of an Orientalist: Thomas William Rhys Davids and Buddhism in Sri Lanka* (Delhi: Motilal Banarsidass, 1984), 143–174.

97. Sudeshna Guha, *Artefacts of History: Archaeology, Historiography and Indian Pasts* (Delhi: Sage, 2015), chap. 1.

98. For example, *'Ilm-i Jughrafiyya* (Calcutta: n.p., 1851), was an Urdu translation by Mir Ghulam 'Ali of Clift, *Clift's First Geography*, 50–51.

99. John Clark Marshman, *The History of India from Remote Antiquity to the Accession of the Mogul Dynasty* (Serampore: Baptist Mission Press, 1837).

100. For example, John Clark Marshman, *Bharatabarsera Itihasa*, translated into Bengali by Gopal Lal Mitra (Serampore: Baptist Mission Press, 1840), and John Clark Marshman, *Tarikh-i Hindustan*, translated into Urdu by Mawlwi 'Abd al-Rahman (Serampore: Baptist Mission Press, 1859).

101. D. H. Emmott, "Alexander Duff and the Foundation of Modern Education in India," *British Journal of Education Studies* 13, 2 (1965): 160–169.

102. Advertisement, *Calcutta Review* 1, 1 (1844): i.

103. For example, "Literature and Origins of Buddhism," *Calcutta Review* 49, 98 (1869): 83–124; "Buddhism and the Sankhya Philosophy," *Calcutta Review* 53, 106 (1871): 191–203; "Buddha as a Philosopher," *Calcutta Review* 84, 167 (1887): 16–35; and 84, 168 (1887): 362–380; Ramchandra Basu, "Buddha as a Man," *Calcutta Review* 82, 163 (1886): 65–84; T. W. L. Rhys Davids, "Buddhist India: Story of the Nations," *Calcutta Review* 118, 236 (1904): 258–259; Arthuloti, "Buddha and Early Buddhism," *Calcutta Review* 75, 149 (1882): xix; J. Long, "Indian Buddhism: Its Origin and Diffusion," *Calcutta Review* 4, 8 (1845): 241–281; E. Storrow, "Rise, Principles and Tendencies of Buddhism," *Calcutta Review* 19, 38 (1853): 256–297; and Sir Monier Monier-Williams, "Buddhism in Its Connexion with Brahmanism and Hinduism, and in Its Contrast with Christianity," *Calcutta Review* 91, 181 (1890): ii–ix.

104. For example, "Buddha as a Moralist," *Calcutta Review* 83, 165 (1886): 36–56; "Buddha and Christus," *Calcutta Review* 118, 236 (1904): 256–257; and K. S. MacDonald (ed.), "Story of Barlaam and Joasaph, Buddhism and Christianity," *Calcutta Review* 102, 203 (1896): x–xi.

105. For example, Emil Schlagentweit, "Buddhism in Tibet, Illustrated by Literary Documents and Objects of Religious Worship, with an Account of the Buddhist Systems Preceding It in India," *Calcutta Review* 39, 78 (1864): 446–448. Even the journal's articles on China and Japan didn't focus on the versions of Buddhism still practiced there.

106. David M. Waterhouse (ed.), *The Origins of Himalayan Studies: Brian Houghton Hodgson in Nepal and Darjeeling, 1820–1858* (London: RoutledgeCurzon, 2004).

107. Raja Rajendralal Mitra, *Buddhism and Odinism: Their Similitude* (Calcutta: Baptist Mission Press, 1858).

108. Raja Rajendralal Mitra, *The Sanskrit Buddhist Literature of Nepal* (Calcutta: Asiatic Society of Bengal, 1882).

109. Rama Kundu, "'In Thine Immeasurable Mercy and Goodness': Buddha in Tagore's Imagination," in Mohit K. Ray (ed.), *Studies on Rabindranath Tagore* (New Delhi: Atlantic, 2004), 216.

110. Nobin Chandra Das, *The Miracles of Buddha: Being a Translation in English Verse from Kshemendra's Kalpalata* (Calcutta: Hare Press, 1895); the Tibetan source is discussed on vii.

111. Nobin Chandra Das, *A Note on the Ancient Geography of Asia, Compiled from Válmíki-Rámáyana* (Calcutta: Buddhist Text Society of India, 1896).

112. Hariprasad Sastri, *Catalogue of Palm-Leaf and Selected Paper Manuscripts Belonging to the Durbar Library, Nepal*, 2 vols. (Calcutta: Baptist Mission Press, 1905).

113. His research travels were described in his own words in Sarat Chandra Das, *Indian Pandits in the Land of Snow*, ed. Nobin Chandra Das (Calcutta: Baptist Mission Press, 1893).

114. Sarat Chandra Das, *Bodhisattvabadana Kalpalata: Akhaṇḍa* (Calcutta: Baptist Mission Press, 1912–1916).

115. Krishnakumar Mitra, *Bhuddhadeva-charitra*, trans. Narayana Hemachandra (Bombay: n.p., 1889). On other Bengali accounts of Buddhism, see Sudhansu B. Barua, *Studies in Tagore and Buddhist Culture* (Calcutta: Sahitya Samsad, 1991), and Kemper, *Rescued from the Nation*, chap. 4.

116. Review of *Asoka-Charita* in *Calcutta Review* 96 (1893): 75–77.

117. Kundu, "'In Thine Immeasurable Mercy,'" 215.

118. Douglas Ober, "Translating the Buddha: Edwin Arnold's *Light of Asia* and Its Indian Publics," *Humanities* 10, 3 (2021): 1–18.

119. Ibid., 3.

120. Almond, *British Discovery*, 1. The Japanese translation of Arnold's poem was made by Taro Nakagawa and published as *Ajia no koki* (Tokyo: Kyokyo shoin, 1890). The Thai version appeared in 1927.

121. For example, Paul Carus, *Kalyanadharma*, Urdu translation of *The Gospel of Buddha* by Sheobart Lal Varman (Jalandhar: Matba'-i Shahim-i Hind, 1902). Although Carus became a naturalized U.S. citizen, he had completed his PhD in Theology at Tübingen in his native Germany.

122. Fortunately, the key terms *samsara* and *nirvana* were shared by Hindus and Buddhists, and Carus's definitions were translated ibid., 2–5.

123. Paul Carus, *Injil Budha*, translated into Arabic by 'Isa Mikha'il Saba (Beirut: Maktabat Sadir, 1953).

124. Ananda Kentish Coomaraswamy, *Buddha and the Gospel of Buddhism* (London: Harrap, 1916).

125. See ibid., bibliography, 348. Aside from Okakura's *Ideals of the East*, the only cited texts by non-European authors are P. L. Narasu's *The Essence of Buddhism* (1907) and K. Nukariya's *The Religion of the Samurai* (1913).

126. Hariprasad Sastri, *Discovery of Living Buddhism in Bengal* (Calcutta: Sanskrit Press Depository, 1897).

127. Ibid., 3–4.

128. Kemper, *Rescued from the Nation*, 287.

129. On the completion-cum-editing of Okakura's *Ideals of the East* in Calcutta, see Inaga Shigemi, "Okakura Kakuzô's Nostalgic Journey to India and the Invention of Asia," in Susan Fisher (ed.), *Nostalgic Journeys: Literary Pilgrimages between Japan*

and the West (Vancouver: Institute of Asian Research, University of British Columbia, 2001), 124–126.

130. Sastri, *Discovery,* 22–23; comparisons are on 26–27.

131. Hariprasad Sastri (ed.), *Hajar Bacharer Purano Bangala Bhasaya Bauddhagan-o-Doha* (Calcutta: Bangiya Sahitya Parisad, 1916).

132. Gregory Schopen, "Archaeology and Protestant Presuppositions in the Study of Indian Buddhism," *History of Religions* 31, 1 (1991): 1–23.

133. Xuanzang, *Ek Chini Sayyah ka Safarnama jo Angrezi se Tarjuma Kiya Gaya* (translator unnamed) (Lahore: Punjab Religious Book Society, 1921).

134. Hiuen Tsiang (Xuanzang), *Si-Yu-Ki: Buddhist Records of the Western World,* trans. Samuel Beal, 2 vols. (London: Paul, Trench, & Trubner, 1884).

135. G. K. Nariman, *Literary History of Sanskrit Buddhism* (Bombay: Indian Book Depot, 1923), chap. 2.

136. G. K. Nariman, "Afghanistan To-day," *Islamic Culture* 1 (1927): 252–258.

137. Nile Green, "The Afghan Discovery of Buddha: Civilizational History and the Nationalizing of Afghan Antiquity," *International Journal of Middle East Studies* 48, 4 (2016): 47–70.

138. Nariman, *Literary History,* 133.

139. Susan Bayly, "Imagining 'Greater India': French and Indian Visions of Colonialism in the Indic Mode," *Modern Asian Studies* 38, 3 (2004): 703–744.

140. Kemper, *Rescued from the Nation,* chap. 4.

141. Geary, *Rebirth of Bodh Gaya,* chaps. 1, 2.

142. Ibid., 282.

143. Victor van Bijlert, "Buddhism as the Pinnacle of Ancient Indian Morality: Tagore and Vivekananda Interpreting the Figure of Buddha," in Madhu Bhalla (ed.), *Culture as Power: Buddhist Heritage and the Indo-Japanese Dialogue* (New Delhi: Routledge India, 2021).

144. Kemper, *Rescued from the Nation,* 289–291; quotation on 289.

145. Torkel Brekke, *Makers of Modern Indian Religion in the Late Nineteenth Century* (Oxford: Oxford University Press, 2002), 59–60.

146. This statement is based on articles published in the early years of *Journal of the Buddhist Text Society of India.*

147. P. V. Bapat, *The Sutta Nipāta/Sutanipāto: One of the Oldest Canonical Books of the Buddhism for the First Time Edited in Devanagari Characters* (Poona: Arya Bushana, 1924).

148. Rev. David Gilmore, *A Brief Vocabulary to the Pali Text of Jatakas I–XL for the Use of Students Preparing for the First Examination in Arts in Calcutta University* (Rangoon: American Baptist Mission Press, 1895).

149. Benimadhab Barua and Sailendranath Mitra (eds. and trans.), *Prakrit Dhammapada* (Calcutta: University Press, 1921).

150. Ghulam Husayn Mirza Salih, *Tarikh-i Sifarat-i Hajji Khalil Khan wa Muhammad Nabi Khan bih Hindustan* (Tehran: Kawir, 2000).

151. The text has been published as Fazlullah Husayni, "Safarnama-yi Hind, Kashmir u Barma (Guzarish-i Safar-i Nawisanda bih Hind u Barma ta'i Salha-yi 1290–1294 Q.)," ed. Firishta Kushki, *Payam-i Baharistan* (Fall 2011): 709–781. I am most grateful to Mana Kia for providing access to this text.

152. Ibid., 746.

153. Ibid., 748–754.

154. Ibid., 757.

155. Ibid.

156. Ibid.

157. Ibid., 760–763, 766–767.

158. Ibid., 764–765.

159. Arash Khazeni, *The City and the Wilderness: Indo-Persian Encounters in Southeast Asia* (Oakland: University of California Press, 2020), chap. 2.

160. Ibid., 55.

161. Akhlaq Ahmad Ahan, *Hindustan mein Farsi Sahafat ki Tarikh* (Delhi: Afif Off-set Printers, 2008), and Abdus Subhan, *Early Persian Newspapers of Calcutta* (Kolkata: Maulana Abul Kalam Azad Institute of Asian Studies, 2002).

162. Together with his brother, Jalal al-Din also founded several other Persian journals in Calcutta, such as *Azad* (*Free*) and *Tamaddun* (*Civilization*), as well as the Urdu newspaper *Kulkatta* (*Calcutta*) and an Urdu edition of *Habl al-Matin*. See E. G. Browne, *The Press and Poetry of Modern Persia* (Cambridge: University Press, 1914), 28–29, 143.

163. Mirza Sayyid Hasan Kashani, *Mukalima-yi Sayyah-i Irani ba Shakhs-i Hindi*, ed. Ghulam Husayn Mirza-Salih (Tehran: Kawir, 2001). For a discussion of this text, see Mana Kia, "Indian Friends, Iranian Selves, Persianate Modern," *Comparative Studies of South Asia, Africa and the Middle East* 36, 3 (2016): 398–417.

164. Zayn al-'Abidin Maragha'i, *Siyahatnama-yi Ibrahim Beg*, 2 vols. (Calcutta: Matba'a-yi Habl al-Matin, 1906–1909).

165. On the journal, see Browne, *Press and Poetry*, 41. For context, see Vanessa Martin, "Aqa Najafi, Haj Aqa Nurullah, and the Emergence of Islamism in Isfahan, 1889–1908," *Iranian Studies* 41, 2 (2008): 162.

166. I. Hamed, "Un journal persan de l'Inde," *Révue du Monde Musulman* 2, 5 (1907): 246, and Niku Himmat, "Da'i al-Islam," *Danish* 218 (1951): 437–439.

167. Browne, *Press and Poetry*, 86.

168. Monica Ringer, *Pious Citizens: Reforming Zoroastrianism in India and Iran* (Syracuse, N.Y.: Syracuse University Press, 2011). See also B. K. Karanjia, "Parsi Pioneers of the Press (1822–1915)," in Pheroza J. Godrej and Firoza P. Mistree (eds.), *A Zoroastrian Tapestry: Art, Religion & Culture* (Ahmedabad: Mapin, 2002), and C. J. Madan, "The Parsis of Calcutta," in Sukanta Chaudhuri (ed.), *Calcutta: The Living City*, 2 vols. (Calcutta: Oxford University Press, 1990), 2:62–63.

169. Afshin Marashi, *Exile and the Nation: The Parsi Community of India and the Making of Modern Iran* (Austin: University of Texas Press, 2020), chaps. 1, 4.

170. Mitra J. Sharafi, "Bella's Case: Parsi Identity and the Law in Colonial Rangoon, Bombay and London, 1887–1925" (PhD diss., Princeton University, 2006).

171. Ibid., chap. 4.

172. Ibid., chaps. 6, 7.

173. Green, *Bombay Islam*, 122–124, and *Terrains of Exchange*, 135–136.

174. Christopher Buck, "The Kitab-i Iqan: An Introduction to Baha'u'llah's Book of Certitude with Two Digital Reprints of Early Lithographs," *Occasional Papers in Shaykhi, Babi and Baha'i Studies* 2, 5 (1998): 1–27.

175. On these networks, see Juan R. I. Cole, "Religious Dissidence and Urban Leadership: Baha'is in Qajar Shiraz and Tehran," *Iran* 37 (1999): 123–142.

176. Moojan Momen, "Jamál Effendi and the Early History of the Bahá'í Faith in South Asia," *Bahá'í Studies Review* 9 (1999), https://bahai-library.com/momen_jamal_effendi.

177. Ibid.

178. Ibid.

179. Ibid. Unfortunately, I have been unable to trace a copy of this text.

180. Ibid.

181. Sydney Sprague, *A Year with the Baha'is of India and Burma* (London: Priory Press, 1908).

182. Ibid., 24.

183. Fazil Mazandarani, *Tarikh-i Zuhur al-Haqq*, 9 vols. (Tehran: Mu'asasa-yi Milli-yi Matbu'at-i Amri, 1975), vol. 7, pt. 2, 851–852.

184. Sayyah ['Abbas Effendi], *Bab al-Hayat,* trans. into Urdu by Sayyid Mustafa Rumi (Lahore: Nawwal Kishore, 1908). For the original Persian text, with an English translation, see Sayyah ['Abbas Effendi], *Maqala-yi Shakhsi Sayyah kih dar Qaziyyih-i Bab Nivishta Ast,* ed. and trans. E. G. Browne, 2 vols. (Cambridge: Cambridge University Press, 1891).

185. Denis MacEoin, *Sources for Early Babi Doctrine and History: A Survey* (Leiden: Brill, 1992), 169–170.

186. Sayyid Mustafa Rumi, "*Dibacha,*" in Sayyah, *Bab al-Hayat,* 1.

187. Ibid.

188. Ibid.

189. Ibid., 2.

190. Sayyah, *Bab al-Hayat,* 5–48.

191. Ibid., 9–10.

192. Ibid., 29.

193. Ibid., 49–199.

194. Objectives outlined in *The Burma Moslem Society* (Rangoon: Burma Moslem Press, 1910), 1–2. All Muslims could join the society, but its constitution ordained that

its executive committee could comprise only Burmese Muslims (which it defined as Muslims of "Burmese race").

195. Mawlwi 'Abd al-Hayy, *'Aqd al-Fara'iz fi Nazm al-'Aqa'id* (Rangoon: Burma Muslim Press, 1910).

196. Mawlwi 'Abd al-Hayy, *al-Mudafa' al-Illahiyya fi al-Radd 'ila al-Babiyya* (Delhi: Matba'-i Ansari, 1910). The author's position at Rangoon's Jam'a Masjid is given on the title page and the colophon on page 44.

197. Ibid., 15, referring to Rumi's *da'wat* (proselytizing). 'Abd al-Hayy referred to the organization as the *Anjuman-i Isha'at-i Baha'iyan* (Baha'i Propagation Society) rather than its correct name, *Anjuman-i Baha'iyan-i Rangun* (Baha'i Society of Rangoon). His mention of its being directed by Mustafa Rumi and Mirza Mahmud makes it clear, however, that he was referring to the same entity.

198. Prices are given on the covers of both books.

199. 'Abd al-Hayy, *al-Mudafa' al-Illahiyya*, 15. *'Uruj u Nuzul* was issued in Rangoon in 1903, and *Jawab-i Likchar-i Qadiyani* appeared in 1908. See the bibliographical list of Urdu works in "Bahá'í Publications in Oriental Languages," *Bahá'í World* 7 (1936–1938): 737–738.

200. 'Abd al-Hayy, *al-Mudafa' al-Illahiyya*, 15, where he used the term *mansukh*.

201. Ibid.

202. Ibid.

203. Ibid.

204. Ibid., 1–15.

205. Ibid., 1–2.

206. Ibid., 7.

207. Ibid., 14–15.

208. Though the term *mazhab* has a long and complex history in Arabic and other Islamic languages, by the early twentieth century its Urdu usage can be taken as equivalent to "religion."

209. Ibid., 22.

210. Ibid.

211. Ibid., 23–28.

212. Ibid., 44.

213. Juan R. I. Cole, "Rashid Rida on the Baha'i Faith: A Utilitarian Theory of the Spread of Religions," *Arab Studies Quarterly* 5, 3 (1983): 276–291.

214. Umar Ryad, *Islamic Reformism and Christianity: A Critical Reading of the Works of Muhammad Rashid Rida and His Associates (1898–1935)* (Leiden: Brill, 2009), 153–154.

215. *Al-Ashraq/The Dawn* (Rangoon: Syed Mustafa Roumie, 1923–). On Mustafa Rumi's literary activities in Urdu, see also Sabir Afaqi, *Barma mein Urdu* (Islamabad: Muqtadara-i Qawmi Zaban, 1989), 8.

216. *Al-Ashraq/The Dawn* 1, 1 (1923), English front cover.

217. Ibid., Persian front cover.

218. Mawlwi Fazl al-Din, *Baha'i Mazhab ki Haqiqat* (Qadian: Manijar Buk Dipo, 1925). My thanks to Michael O'Sullivan for providing me with a copy of this text.

219. The edition's one thousand copies are mentioned in Fazl al-Din, *Baha'i Mazhab*, cover; for the history, see pp. *alif* and *ba*.

220. Ibid., 1.

221. Ibid., 2–4, 40–45.

222. Ibid., 22–31.

223. Ibid., 6–19; dowry (*mahr*) is on 13, and divorce (*talaq*) is on 18–19.

224. Ibid., 84–96; the quotation is on 84.

225. Ibid., 97–104.

226. Ibid., 105–107, using the powerful term *munkir* (denier of God).

227. John H. Hanson, "Jihad and the Ahmadiyya Muslim Community: Nonviolent Efforts to Promote Islam in the Contemporary World," *Nova Religio: The Journal of Alternative and Emergent Religions* 11, 2 (2007): 77–93.

228. The text of one of Kamal al-Din's 1920 Rangoon lectures is given in Khwaja Kamal-ud-Din, *Islam to East and West: A Collection of Lectures Given in Different Countries* (Lahore: Woking Muslim Mission and Literary Trust, 1935), 73–98. On the Ahmadi controversy in Arwi books and journals, see More, *Muslim Identity*, 114–117, 132.

229. Ahmad Buzurg Samalki, *Ma'raka-i Rangun* (Karachi: Khatm-i Nabuwwat Akidimi, 2010). Thanks to Michael O'Sullivan for bringing this text to my attention.

230. Ahmad Najib Burhani, "Conversion to Ahmadiyya in Indonesia: Winning Hearts through Ethical and Spiritual Appeals," *Sojourn: Journal of Social Issues in Southeast Asia* 29, 3 (2014): 657–690, and Iqbal Singh Sevea, "The Ahmadiyya Print Jihad in South and Southeast Asia," in R. Michael Feener and Terenjit Sevea (eds.), *Islamic Connections: Muslim Societies in South and Southeast Asia* (Singapore: Institute of Southeast Asian Studies, 2009).

231. Burhani, "Conversion to Ahmadiyya," 663–669.

232. This statement is based on the listings in Graham Shaw and Mary Lloyd (eds.), *Publications Proscribed by the Government of India: A Catalogue of the Collections in the India Office Library and Records and the Department of Oriental Manuscripts and Printed Books, British Library Reference Division* (London: British Library, 1985). There are far too many relevant entries in multiple languages to cite, and the numbers rapidly increase through the 1920s and 1930s. Aside from religious polemics, the other major categories of prohibited books were German World War I–era then Bolshevik propaganda and anticolonial political activism.

233. Muhammad Shams al-Din, "History of Hatim Ta'i" (Rangoon, 1889), described without a transcription of the title in L. D. Barnett, *A Catalogue of the Burmese Books in the British Museum* (London: British Museum, 1913), 62.

234. Maung Myit and Maung Mya, "The History of the Turkey Empire" (Mandalay, 1907), described without a transcription of the title in Barnett, *Catalogue*, 146.

Chapter 2. The Muslim Discovery of Buddhism

1. Michael W. Charney, *Powerful Learning: Buddhist Literati and the Throne in Burma's Last Dynasty, 1752–1885* (Ann Arbor: Center for Southeast Asian Studies, 2006).

2. Thant Myint-U, *The Making of Modern Burma* (Cambridge: Cambridge University Press, 2001), 152.

3. Juliane Schober, "To Be Burmese Is to Be Buddhist: Formations of Buddhist Modernity in Colonial Burma," in Thomas Borchert (ed.), *Theravada Buddhism in Colonial Contexts* (New York: Routledge, 2018), 21–41, and Mark R. Woodward, "When One Wheel Stops: Theravada Buddhism and the British Raj in Upper Burma," *Crossroads: An Interdisciplinary Journal of Southeast Asian Studies* 4, 1 (1989): 57–90.

4. Amid a vast literature on Indian migration to Burma and its complex social contours, see Sunil Amrith, *Crossing the Bay of Bengal: The Furies of Nature and the Fortunes of Migrants* (Cambridge: Harvard University Press, 2015), 119–122, 146–152, and Nalini Ranjan Chakravarti, *The Indian Minority in Burma: The Rise and Decline of an Immigrant Community* (Oxford: Oxford University Press, 1971). Most earlier research on Indian accounts of their Burmese experiences draws only on Indian Anglophone sources, however. See, for example, Aung San Suu Kyi, *Burma and India: Some Aspects of Intellectual Life under Colonialism* (Shimla: Indian Institute of Advanced Study, 1990). What little work exists on non-Anglophone Indian responses to Burma still deals with such elites as the Nehrus and Tagores. See Thaw Kaung, "Tagore in Myanmar: Travels, Translation and Impact," *Myanmar Studies Journal* 1, 1 (2013): 61–82; and Shobna Nijhawan, "At the Margins of Empire: Feminist-Nationalist Configurations of Burmese Society in the Hindi Public (1917–1920)," *Journal of Asian Studies* 71, 4 (2012): 1013–1033. On Bengali cultural interactions, see Swapna Bhattacharya, *India-Myanmar Relations, 1886–1948* (Kolkata: K. Bagchi, 2007), chap. 4.

5. Mawlwi 'Abd al-Khaliq Khan Muwahid, *Sayr-i Barhma* (Lucknow: Matba' Mina-i Lakhnaw, 1893).

6. William Stevenson Meyer (ed.), *The Imperial Gazetteer of India*, 26 vols. (Oxford: Clarendon Press, 1908–1931), 21:28.

7. B. H. Badley, "Oudh," *Indian Evangelical Review* 6 (1879): 50.

8. Hunter et al., *Imperial Gazetteer*, 21:28.

9. Muwahid, *Sayr-i Barhma*, 1.

10. Ibid.

11. Ibid., 33.

12. Muhammad 'Abd al-Hayy, *Musulmanan-i Barhma aur Ta'lim* (Rangoon: Matba'-i Muhammad Ibrahim, 1918).

13. Muwahid, *Sayr-i Barhma*, 1.

14. Muhammad Ghouse, *Intustani-Tamizh Vokabileri* (1882; repr., Rangoon: n.p., 1885), listed in the bibliography of Arabo-Tamil imprints in J. B. P. More, *Muslim Identity, Print Culture and the Dravidian Factor in Tamil Nadu* (New Delhi: Orient Longman, 2004), appendix 1, 288.

15. George Orwell, *Burmese Days* (1934; repr., London: Penguin, 1986), 121.

16. Sabir Afaqi, *Barma mein Urdu* (Islamabad: Muqtadara-i Qawmi Zaban, 1989), 8.

17. Mu'in al-Din 'Aqil (ed.), "Tazkira-i '*Gulshan-i Sukhan*': Barma mein Urdu Sha'iri ka Sunahra Dawr," *Khuda Bakhsh Librari Jarnal* 162 (2010): 27–48. Most of the poets featured in *Gulshan-i Sukhan* were born in the 1900s, the oldest being Sayyid Husayn Sayyid; see ibid., 38. Ahmar's biography and selections from his poetry are also given in Afaqi, *Barma mein Urdu*, 9–12.

18. Mohammed Mohiyuddin and Mohammed Sulaiman, "Islamic Education in Myanmar: A Case Study," in Monique Skidmore and Trevor Wilson (eds.), *Dictatorship, Disorder and Decline in Myanmar* (Canberra: Australian National University, 2008), 182.

19. Aftab Ahmad Khan, *Ripurt Mut'alliq Ijlas Bist u Siwwum-i Al Indiya Muhammadan Anglu Ariyintal Ijukeshnal Kanfarans ba-muqam-i Rangun Mun'aqidah 29, 30, 31 Disambar 1909* (Aligarh: Matba'-i Ahmadi, 1910). This contains summaries of the various speeches made by delegates, including Chishti's sermon on 132–142.

20. Muhammad Ibrahim, *Hukm al-Salat: Chivalkar* (Bombay: n.p., 1890).

21. These texts are, respectively, Maung Hko [Mirza 'Abbas], *Nuri Taw Kyan* (Moulmein: n.p., 1889); Hazrat Ali, *Sakhawetnama*, trans. Ismail Hajjo Arif Nana, Ibrahim Ali Naki, and Muhammad Yusuf (Rangoon: n.p., 1898); Muhyi al-Din ibn 'Abd al-'Aziz, *Shajarat al-Iman* (Rangoon: n.p., 1896); and Muhyi al-Din ibn 'Abd al-'Aziz, *Faza'il al-Shuhur* (Rangoon: n.p., 1896). Statements are based on content summaries in L. D. Barnett, *A Catalogue of the Burmese Books in the British Museum* (London: British Museum, 1913). I have also inspected these books (some of them partly bilingual) at the British Library, however, having traced them through Barnett's *Catalogue*.

22. As outlined in Barnett, *A Catalogue:* Muhammad Ibrahim, *Añña-vada-niggaha-ovada kyan* (Rangoon: n.p., 1891); and Ibrahim, *Añña-vada-niggaha-vijja-htoy kyan* (Rangoon: n.p., 1892).

23. Kaung, "Tagore in Myanmar."

24. This was the case even in regions such as Kashmir, where the presence of Islam and Buddhism chronologically overlapped. See Walter Slaje, "Buddhism and Islam in Kashmir as Represented by Rājataraṅgiṇī," in Blain Auer and Ingo Strauch (eds.), *Encountering Buddhism and Islam in Premodern Central and South Asia* (Berlin: de Gruyter, 2019). As Slaje plainly states (155), "I have not found any trace of a direct intellectual encounter between Islam and Buddhism in Kashmir."

25. Anna Akasoy, "The Buddha and the Straight Path: Rashīd al-Dīn's Life of the Buddha: Islamic Perspectives," in Anna Akasoy, Charles Burnett, and Ronit Yoeli-Tlalim (eds.), *Rashid al-Din: Agent and Mediator of Cultural Exchange* (London: Warburg Institute Colloquia, 2012), 173–196, and Francesco Calzolaio and Francesca Fiaschetti, "Prophets of the East: The Ilkhanid Historian Rashīd al-Dīn on the Buddha, Laozi and Confucius and the Question of His Chinese Sources (Part 1)," *Iran and the Caucasus* 23, 1 (2019): 17–34.

26. On other medieval accounts, see Daniel Gimaret, "Bouddha et les bouddhistes dans la tradition musulmane," *Journal Asiatique* 257 (1969): 273–316.

27. On the selective and patchy process of publishing only some of the manuscript works of previous centuries, see Ahmed El Shamsy, *Rediscovering the Islamic Classics: How Editors and Print Culture Transformed an Intellectual Tradition* (Princeton: Princeton University Press, 2020).

28. The statement regarding the unavailability in print of *Jami' al-Tawarikh* is based on online and printed catalogues of South Asian imprints.

29. Thibaut d'Hubert, "A Persian Account of the Religious Customs of the Magh (Arakanese) from Early Colonial Bengal," *Iranian Studies* 51, 6 (2018): 947–959, and d'Hubert "'India Beyond the Ganges': Defining Arakanese Buddhism in Persianate Colonial Bengal," *Indian Economic & Social History Review* 56, 1 (2019): 1–31.

30. Arash Khazeni, *The City and the Wilderness: Indo-Persian Encounters in Southeast Asia* (Oakland: University of California Press, 2020), chap. 5.

31. Farhad Mirza, *Kitab-i Jam-i Jam* (Tehran: Chapkhana-yi Allah Quli Khan Qajar, 1856).

32. Pinnock, *Comprehensive System of Modern Geography*.

33. Mirza, *Kitab-i Jam-i Jam*, 498.

34. Ibid., 500.

35. "Mujasima-ha'i Kulkula dar Afghanistan," *Sharaf* 34 (September 1885): 138–140. The name Kulkula (or, in local Hazara pronunciation, Ghulghula) was the ethnohistorical name for the ruins of the "City of Screams" (Shahr-i Ghulghula).

36. Minoru Inaba, "The Narratives on the Bāmiyān Buddhist Remains in the Islamic Period," in Auer and Strauch, *Encountering Buddhism and Islam*, and Asadullah Melikian-Chirvani, "L'évocation littéraire du bouddhisme dans l'Iran musulman," in Jean Aubin (ed.), *Le monde iranien et l'Islam*, 13 vols. (Geneva: Droz, 1974), vol. 2.

37. "Mujasima-ha'i Kulkula," 138.

38. The informational source of the 1879 visit of the Russian ambassador Monsieur Zharuski is clearly stated ibid., 138. For the source text that the *Sharaf* article summarized, see Ivan Lavrovich Yavorski, *Journey of the Russian Embassy through (Account of the Journey of the Russian Mission to) Afghánistán and the Khanate of Bukhára in 1878–1879*, trans. E. R. Elles and W. E. Gowan, 2 vols. (Calcutta: Government of India, Indian Army Intelligence Branch, 1885), 130–152. Thanks to Llewelyn Morgan for identifying the source from the unique copy of Yavorski in the British Library.

39. This statement is based on my inability to locate a printed Russian edition of Yavorski's diary.

40. Alexander Burnes, *Travels into Bokhara*, 3 vols. (London: John Murray, 1835), vol. 2, image facing 157. My thanks again to Llewelyn Morgan for pointing me toward this.

41. Ibid., 2:159, 161.

42. This statement is based on extensive searches of Persian printed book catalogues and online library databases (including the National Library of Iran). Naturally, subsequent research may to some degree modify this conclusion.

43. Siddiq Hasan Khan, *Luqtat al-'Ajlan mimma Tamassu ila Ma'rifatihi Hajat al-Insan wa fi Akhiriha Khabi'at al-Akwan fi Iftiraq al-Umam 'ala al-Madhahib wa al-Adyan* (Istanbul: Matba'at al-Jawa'ib, 1879). Thanks to Sohaib Baig for bringing this source to my attention.

44. Butrus al-Bustani, "Buddha," in al-Bustani (ed.), *Da'irat al-Ma'arif* (Beirut: n.p, 1876–), vol. 5. Thanks to Ilham Khuri-Makdisi for this lead. On the *Da'irat,* see Albert Hourani, "Bustani's Encyclopaedia," *Journal of Islamic Studies* 1 (1990): 111–119. Pointing to Bustani's inspiration, the Arabic title was a literal translation of the Greek-derived term *encyclopedia.*

45. On the American Transcendentalists' approach to Buddhism, see Lionel Obadia, *Bouddhisme et Occident: La diffusion du bouddhisme tibétain en France* (Paris: L'Harmattan, 1999), 60–61.

46. "al-Diyana al-Budhiyya," *al-Hilal* 8, 10 (February 1900): 290–295.

47. Edwards, *Jam-i Jahan-numa,* 4.

48. Ibid., 3.

49. Mirza Muhammad Kazim Barlas, *Sayr-i Darya* (Moradabad: Matba'-i Ahsan al-Mataba', 1867 [printing error for 1898]).

50. Ibid., 68.

51. Lala Śrirama (trans.), *Dharma Buddha* (Moradabad: n.p., 1889), and Urdu translation of T. W. Rhys Davids, *Buddhism: Being a Sketch of the Life and Teachings of Gautama, the Buddha* (London: Society for Promoting Christian Knowledge, 1877).

52. On Rhys Davids's interpretation of Buddhist history, see Charles Hallisey, "Roads Taken and Not Taken in the Study of Buddhism," in Donald S. Lopez (ed.), *Curators of the Buddha: The Study of Buddhism under Colonialism* (Chicago: University of Chicago Press, 1995), and Ananda Wickremeratne, *The Genesis of an Orientalist: Thomas William Rhys Davids and Buddhism in Sri Lanka* (Delhi: Motilal Banarsidass, 1984), 143–174.

53. Pandit Ramnath Kushal, *Mahatma Bodh ke Mukhtasar Sawanih 'Umri* (Lahore: Khadim al-Ta'lim, 1892).

54. For the rendering of Arnold, see ibid., 12–13.

55. Ibid., 2.

56. Ibid., 19, 20–21.

57. Ibid., 21.

58. Ibid., 1.

59. On the nascent revival of Buddhism in North India at this time, see Geary, *Rebirth of Bodh Gaya,* chap. 1.

60. Ramadasa Chabildasa, *Padmini-Čampuh,* ed. Syed Ali Bilgrami (Bombay: n.p., 1888).

61. Sydney Sprague, *A Year with the Baha'is of India and Burma* (London: Priory Press, 1908), 31.

62. On medieval Arabic and Persian accounts of Buddhism, see Gimaret, "Bouddha et les bouddhistes dans la tradition musulmane."

63. Khazeni, *City and the Wilderness*, 155.

64. Muwahid, *Sayr-i Barhma*, 2.

65. Ibid., 9.

66. Khazeni, *City and the Wilderness*, chap. 5.

67. Muwahid, *Sayr-i Barhma*, 17.

68. Ibid., 9.

69. Ibid., 9–12, 18–20, 26–27.

70. Ibid., 1, 3–4, 6, 9, 13, 17–18, 28, 33–35.

71. Thanks to Robert Buswell and Patrick Pranke for advice on these matters. Any errors remain my own.

72. Note that *pahya* is often romanized as *paya* or *hpaya*. The epithet is also given to monks, pagodas, and kings. I am deeply grateful to Patrick Pranke for identifying the Burmese terms and text names in this section of the chapter.

73. Muwahid, *Sayr-i Barhma*, 2.

74. Ibid., 4.

75. Ibid. The Burmese referents for the names 'Abd al-Khaliq rendered as 'Dajalla' and 'Ma Daniga' remain unclear.

76. Ibid., 5.

77. Sanjukta Das Gupta, "Writing Travel across the Bay of Bengal: Bengali Accounts of Burma in the Early 20th Century," *IIAS Newsletter* 85 (2020): 39. On similar Indocentric attitudes of later Bengali writers on Burma, see Devleena Ghosh, "Burma-Bengal Crossings: Intercolonial Connections in Pre-Independence India," *Asian Studies Review* 40, 2 (2016): 158. The word "Burma" derives from the unrelated Burmese autonym *ba.ma*, the colloquial form of *mranma*.

78. Muwahid, *Sayr-i Barhma*, 5, 6–7, 9.

79. Ibid., 7, 9.

80. Ibid., 9.

81. John Perry, "The Waning of Indo-Persian Lexicography: Examples from Some Rare Books and Manuscripts of the Subcontinent," in Kambiz Eslami (ed.), *Iran and Iranian Studies: Essays in Honor of Iraj Afshar* (Princeton: Zagros, 1998), 329–340.

82. This statement is based on my own investigations and the surveys in John Considine (ed.), *The Cambridge World History of Lexicography* (Cambridge: Cambridge University Press, 2019).

83. Audrey Truschke, "Defining the Other: An Intellectual History of Sanskrit Lexicons and Grammars of Persian," *Journal of Indian Philosophy* 40, 6 (2012): 635–668.

84. Myint-U, *Making of Modern Burma*, 252.

85. Muwahid, *Sayr-i Barhma*, 33.

86. Ibid.

87. Adoniram Judson, *Judson's English and Burmese Dictionary* (Rangoon: W. H. Sloan for the American Baptist Mission Press, 1877).

88. Muwahid, *Sayr-i Barhma*, 34.

89. William Henry Begbie and Abraham Joseph, *A Vocabulary: English, Burmese, Hindustani & Tamil* (Rangoon: Albion Press, 1877).

90. Jamal Abu, *Myamya Saga Arthawali* (Surat: n.p., 1892), as summarized in Barnett, *Catalogue.*

91. Ghouse, *Intustani-Tamizh Vokabileri*, included Burmese vocabulary. I draw here on the summary in the catalogue appendix to More, *Muslim Identity*, 288–289.

92. Muhammad Kazim Barlas, *Lisan al-Jaza'ir* (Moradabad: Matba' Ahsan al-Mataba', 1897). Thanks to Torsten Tschacher for providing access to this text.

93. San Hia Hbaw, *Hindi bhisa saga* (Rangoon: n.p., 1882), and Hba Kyu, *Hku-hnit-bhasa-saka* (Rangoon: n.p., 1902). See also the two later manuals of Hindustani-Burmese conversation: *Hindii-vachanalankara kyans* (Rangoon: n.p., 1906) and Moung Po Tha, *Hhot Thas* (Rangoon: n.p., 1910), as summarized in Barnett, *Catalogue.*

94. Yussuf Rautar, *Ready Reckoner*, ed. Broker M. Essoof Rawuther (Rangoon: Yussuf Rautar, 1901).

95. Ahmad 'Ali [U Aung Hmat], *The Burmese Hindustani Conversation Manual* (Mandalay: Ratana Theiddi Press, 1905), and Ahmad 'Ali [U Aung Hmat], *The English, Hindustani and Burmese Manual, in English and Burmese* (Mandalay: India Press, 1905).

96. John Barr, *Taqdis al-Lughat* (Lucknow: n.p., 1873), translated from Barr's *Bible Index* (1852). As a scripture-based aid to dating ancient history, the Urdu text also contained a chronological table.

97. Muwahid, *Sayr-i Barhma*, 34n.

98. Ibid.

99. Ibid., 36–37.

100. Ibid., 6, 9, 28, 33–39.

101. Ibid., 36–39.

102. Ibid., 34–35.

103. Ibid., 28.

104. Ibid.

105. Ibrahim, *Hukm al-Salat: Chivalkar.* The Burma-printed texts were, respectively, Maung Hko [Mirza 'Abbas], *Nuri Taw Kyan* (Moulmein: n.p., 1889); Hazrat Ali, *Sakhawetnama*, trans. Ismail Hajjo Arif Nana, Ibrahim Ali Naki, and Muhammad Yusuf (Rangoon: n.p., 1898); Muhyi al-Din ibn 'Abd al-'Aziz, *Shajarat al-Iman* (Rangoon: n.p., 1896); *Faza'il al-Shuhur* (Rangoon: n.p., 1896); Ibrahim, *Añña-vada-niggaha-ovada kyant.* I have inspected these partly bilingual books at the British Library, having traced them via Barnett, *Catalogue*, on whose content summaries I draw.

106. Siraj, *Bibi Khadija Tha-hkin ma Vatthu*, trans. into Burmese by Maung Hia Tin (Mandalay: n.p., 1911), and Maung Hia Tin, *Hujjat al-Islam* (Mandalay: n.p., 1911) as summarized in Barnett, *Catalogue.*

107. U Kran (trans.), *Yacan' chura 'a cum 'a lan 'nhan'dui'a Ratac' Kyam'* (Mandalay: Khyaniya Ca pum nhip' Tuik', 1909), identified through British Library records. On the 1910 "Indian Muslim" translation, which I have been unable to trace, see Jean A. Berlie, *The Burmanization of Myanmar's Muslims* (Bangkok: White Lotus, 2008), 80.

108. Muwahid, *Sayr-i Barhma*, 23–24.

109. Woodward, "When One Wheel Stops," 65–66.

110. Statistics and sources are cited in Myint-U, *Making of Modern Burma*, 208.

111. Woodward, "When One Wheel Stops," 68.

112. Myint-U, *Making of Modern Burma*, 221.

113. Muwahid, *Sayr-i Barhma*, 13.

114. Khin Htwe Yi, "The Methodist Mission in Upper Myanmar Proper (1886–1914)," in Ohn Kyi (ed.), *Studies in Myanma History*, 2 vols. (Yangon: Than Tun Diamond Jubilee Publication Committee, 1998), 1:157–158.

115. "Bahá'í Publications in Oriental Languages," *Bahá'í World* 7 (1936–1938): 738.

116. For the primary colonial account of the office of thathanabaing, see J. George Scott, *Gazetteer of Upper Burma and the Shan States*, 5 vols. (Rangoon: Superintendent of Government Printing, 1900), pt. 1, vol. 2, 3–5. For a more favorable depiction, see Charles Henry Allan Bennett, "The Thathanabaing," *Buddhism: A Quarterly Illustrated Review* 1, 4 (1904): 177–208. In preference to the more accurate but obscure translation of *thathanabaing* as "Keeper of the *Sasana*," I have adopted "primate," as given in Myint-U, *Making of Modern Burma*, 73.

117. Muwahid, *Sayr-i Barhma*, 12.

118. Ibid., 13.

119. Ibid., 12.

120. Ibid., 13.

121. Ibid.

122. Ibid., 13–17.

123. *Tanasukh ki Asliyat* (Lahore: n.p., 1893).

124. Muwahid, *Sayr-i Barhma*, 15.

125. Ibid., 14–15.

126. Ibid., 14; "reason" is expressed as *'aql*.

127. Ibid., 16.

128. Ibid., 17.

129. Ibid.

130. Ibid.

131. Marcelo Dascal, "On the Uses of Argumentative Reason in Religious Polemics," in Theo L. Hettema and Arie Van der Kooij (eds.), *Religious Polemics in Context* (Assen: Royal Van Gorcum, 2004), 8.

132. Ibid., 7–8.

133. Juliane Schober, "Colonial Knowledge and Buddhist Education in Burma," in Ian Harris (ed.), *Buddhism, Power and Political Order* (London: Routledge, 2007), 60–61.

134. Juliane Schober, *Modern Buddhist Conjunctures in Myanmar: Cultural Narratives, Colonial Legacies, and Civil Society* (Honolulu: University of Hawai'i Press, 2011), 64.

135. Erik Braun, *The Birth of Insight: Meditation, Modern Buddhism, and the Burmese Monk Ledi Sayadaw* (Chicago: University of Chicago Press, 2013).

136. Ledi Sayadaw, *Thathanawithodani (Sasanavisodhani)*, vol. 1 (1919; repr., Yangon: Hanthawaddi Pitakat Pon-hneik Taik, 1954), 118–190; the section on Islam is on 126–127. Thanks to Patrick Pranke for providing this reference and explaining the contents of the text, which I have not consulted directly.

137. Thanks to Michael O'Sullivan for first bringing this source to my attention and to Sohaib Baig for helping me decipher its minuscule print.

138. Mawlwi Muhammad Husayn, editorial, *Ittihad-i Mazahib-i 'Alam* 10 (March 1915): 5. Though edited from Rangoon, like 'Abd al-Khaliq's book, the journal was actually printed in Lahore.

139. Husayn, editorial, *Ittihad-i Mazahib* 1–2 (February 1908): 37–38.

140. Ibid., 39.

141. Sena Nayaka, *Masihi Mazhab ka Makhraj Bodh Dharma Hai* (Jalandhar: n.p., 1902).

142. Nicolas Notovitch [sic], *La vie inconnue de Jésus-Christ* (Paris: Paul Ollendorff, 1894).

143. Mirza Ghulam Ahmad, *Masih Hindustan Mein* (Qadian: Mission Press, 1908). Ahmad cited various European authors, including Notovich. Apparently, Ahmad's text was originally written in 1899.

144. Leirvik Oddbjørn, "History as a Literary Weapon: The Gospel of Barnabas in Muslim-Christian Polemics," *Studia Theologica* 56, 1 (2002): 10.

145. For detailed analysis of the sources for Ahmad's claims, see Günter Grönbold, *Jesus in Indien: Das Ende einer Legende* (Munich: Kösel, 1985). On Christian missionary responses to Ahmad's teachings about Jesus, see Spencer Lavan, "Polemics and Conflict in Ahmadiyya History: The 'Ulamā,' the Missionaries, and the British (1898)," *Muslim World* 62, 4 (1972): 283–303.

146. Ahmad Shah, *Four Years in Tibet* (Benares: Lazarus Press, 1906), 10, 18–19.

147. Ibid., 15.

148. Ibid., 22.

149. Ibid., 33.

150. Ahmad Shah, *Sayr-i Tibbat,* trans. into Urdu by Anis Ahmad (Delhi: Matba'-i Makhzan, 1909).

151. On the dates of the journey and subsequent account, see Marc Gaborieau, introduction to Khwaja Ghulam Muhammad, *Récit d'un voyageur musulman au Tibet,* ed. and trans. Marc Gaborieau (Paris: C. Klincksieck, 1973), 7–8.

152. Ibid., 94 (Urdu), 95 (translation).

153. Ibid., 74, 75.

154. Ibid., 74: *budhist mazhab* (Buddhist religion).

155. Charuchandra Basu (trans.), *Dhammapad* (Calcutta: Wilkins Press, 1904). Another Bengali version soon followed from the pen of the Calcutta-educated teacher and librarian Satish Chandra Mitra (1872–1931), as *"Dhammapada" Namaka Pali Granthera Banganubada* (Calcutta: Keshab, 1905).

156. F. Max Müller (trans. into English), *Dhampad,* translated into Urdu by Bishan Nara'in (Moradabad: Babu Banwarsi La'l, 1909).

157. Ibid., i–ii.

158. Chandu Lal Chawwalwala (trans.), *Dhampad* (Delhi: Lala Bhansi, 1927); Nara-indas Rattanmal Malkani (trans.), *Dhampadu* (Hyderabad, Sindh: Bundhu Ashramu, 1926).

159. Annie Besant (trans. Khubcandu Mevaramu Makhijani), *Maut Hiku Bhano* (Hyderabad, Sindh: Bundhu Ashramu, 1926).

160. Alaka Atreya Chudal, *A Freethinking Cultural Nationalist: A Life History of Rahul Sankrityayan* (New Delhi: Oxford University Press, 2016).

161. Ibid., 151.

162. Ibid., 153, 160–161.

163. Dharmanand Kosambi, *Dharmanand Kosambi: The Essential Writings,* trans. and ed. Meera Kosambi (Ranikhet: Permanent Black, 2010).

164. Dharmanand Kosambi, "A Narrative (*Nivedan*)," ibid., 78.

165. The Marathi text of *Buddha, Dharma ani Sangha* is translated in Kosambi, *The Essential Writings,* 243–311. See also the helpful chronological bibliography of Kosambi's Marathi, Gujarati, and Hindi writings in ibid., 414–417.

166. Kosambi, *The Essential Writings,* 416.

167. Velcheru Narayana Rao, *Text and Tradition in South India* (Albany: State University of New York Press, 2016), chap. 11.

168. Ibid., 363–375.

169. Ibid., 375.

170. Dasu Narayanaravu (trans.-adapter), *Sangitarasatarangini yanu Buddha Nataka-muby* (Kakinada: Suryanarayanaravu, 1907), cited in Rao, *Text and Tradition,* chap. 11.

171. Kilambi Rangacaryudu (trans.), *Dhammapadamu: Vacanamu* (Cennapuri [Madras]: Nargeshvararu, 1927), discussed in Rao, *Text and Tradition,* chap. 11.

172. On the Telugu translation of Aśvaghosa's Sanskrit *Saundarananda,* see Rao, *Text and Tradition,* 375–379.

173. Douglas Ober, "Translating the Buddha: Edwin Arnold's *Light of Asia* and Its Indian Publics," *Humanities* 10, 3 (2021): 3, 12–14.

174. Edwin Arnold, *Asia da Chanan,* trans. Gurbakhsh Singh Preetlari (Lahore: n.p., 1938).

175. Ober, "Translating the Buddha," 3. On Sindhi, see Asudomalu Tekchandu Gidvani, *Budhisatva* (Hyderabad, Sindh: Jethmal Parsram Gulraj, 1927). If my identification is correct, Gidvani may have been educated at Oxford and then at the bar in London.

176. In Urdu alone, biographies and translations included Munshi Amir Ahmad 'Alawi, *Gautam* (Lucknow: Dar al-Nazir Press, 1923); Prakash Devji, *Budh Devji ki Sawanih 'Umri* (Lahore: Mercantile Press, 1922); Mim Hafiz Sayyid, *Gautam-i Budh: Sawanih-i Hayat wa Ta'limat* (Delhi: Anjuman-i Taraqqi-i Urdu, 1942), as well as poetic

representations, such as Pandit Brij Narayan Chakbast Lakhnawi, *Muraqqa'-i 'Ibrat u Khak-i Hind* (Lucknow: Matba'-i Fakhr al-Mataba', 1909), 18. As *Gautam*, the Buddha was also poetically celebrated in Persian in 1932 by Muhammad Iqbal in his *Jawid-nama*. See Muhammad Iqbal, *Kulliyat-i Ash'ar-i Farsi-yi Mawlana Iqbal Lahawri* (Tehran: Kitabkhana-yi Sana'i, 1964), 296.

177. Mohandas Karamchand Gandhi, *An Autobiography: The Story of My Experiments with Truth*, trans. Mahadev Desai (1949; repr., Boston: Beacon Press, 1993), 67–68, 160. Gandhi also directly met with the vegetarian Arnold in London; ibid., 58. I have not discussed here Nehru's *Glimpses of World History* (written in 1934–1935) since it was not translated into Indian languages until after the period in question.

178. Vinayak Damodar Savarkar, *Hindutva: Who Is a Hindu?* 5th ed. (Bombay: Veer Savarkar Prakashan, 1969), 19; there is further discussion of Buddhism on 16–26. Written in English, the original edition was issued, also in Bombay, in 1923, before being translated into Marathi, Hindi, and other regional languages.

179. Vinayak Chaturvedi, "Violence as Civility: V. D. Savarkar and the Mahatma's Assassination," *South Asian History and Culture* 11, 3 (2020): 239–253.

180. Munshi Nazir Ahmad Sahib Barilwi, *Waqa'at-i Barhma* (Lahore: Matba'-i Khadim al-Ta'lim Panjab, 1901).

181. Ibid., 8–15.

182. Ibid., 8–9.

183. The text was simply titled *The History of India*. See ibid., 8.

184. Muwahid, *Sayr-i Barhma*.

185. Muhammad Sultan, *Mukhtasar Tarikh-i Dakan* (Hyderabad: Matba'-i Nazir-i Dakan, 1916), 4. On the date of the Buddha's birth as 596 BC, see also *Imperial Gazetteer of India* 1: 407, and index, 562. The date differed from that given twenty years earlier by another Hyderabadi official, Syed Ali Bilgrami, who gave the Buddha's death date as 481 BC in his *Short Guide to the Cave Temples of Elura* [*Ellora*] (Madras: Asylum Press, 1898), 6.

186. Sultan, *Mukhtasar Tarikh*, 4. He also added that "this religion no longer exists in India."

187. Sayyid Abu Zafar Nadwi, *Safarnama-i Brahma* [*sic*] (Delhi: Mahbub al-Matabi', 1921), 33.

188. Ibid., 37.

189. Ibid., 38. The work is also cited in the bibliography on prefatory page *waw*, along with Corcoran's pioneering Urdu history of China, which was evidently still being read sixty years later.

190. Gustave Le Bon [Monsieur Liban], *Tamaddun-i Hind*, trans. Sayyid 'Ali Bilgrami (Agra: Matba'-i Shamsi, 1913).

191. Ibid., read in comparison with the original French edition. It is worth noting that during this period both Indian and Ottoman Muslims were absorbing into their vocabulary Le Bon's key term, *civilisation*, through the calque translation, *tamaddun*.

192. Émile Guimet and Gustave Le Bon, *Mirages indiens: De Ceylan au Népal, 1876–1886* (Paris: Phébus, 1992); Le Bon's travelogue is on 179–262 and the discussion of Mitra on 252.

193. Bilgrami, *Short Guide*, 5–8; the quotation is on 6. Bilgrami's emphasis on Buddhism rather than Hinduism at Ellora was probably because, at the time he wrote, colonial archaeologists regarded the earliest of its rock-cut monastery-temples as Buddhist.

194. Translation of a relevant section of Shirazi's text and discussion of other precolonial accounts of the caves in Carl W. Ernst, "Admiring the Works of the Ancients: The Ellora Temples as Viewed by Indo-Muslim Authors," in David Gilmartin and Bruce B. Lawrence (eds.), *Beyond Turk and Hindu: Rethinking Religious Identities in Islamicate South Asia* (Gainesville: University Press of Florida, 2000).

195. Tamkin Sahib Kazimi, "Maghar Illura," *Ma'arif* 18, 4 (October 1926): 261–274.

196. "Mistar Burgis" is mentioned several times, for example ibid., 267, 270, presumably in reference to James Burgess, *The Rock Temples of Elurâ or Verul* (Bombay: Education Society's Press, 1877). Between 1886 and 1889, Burgess served as director general of the Archaeological Survey of India.

197. T. W. Rhys Davids, *Buddhist India* (1903), translated into Urdu by Mawlwi Sayyid Sajjad Sahib as *Buddhisti Hind* (Hyderabad: Dar al-Tab'-i Jami'a-i 'Usmaniyya, 1922).

198. Kazimi, "Maghar Illura," 261, and Bilgrami, *Short Guide*, 6.

199. "Bodh-Mazhab ki ek Qadim Yadgar Pishawar mein," *Ma'arif* 30, 2 (August 1932): 130–135.

200. Ibid., 131. Beal's translation of Xuanzang is the same one discussed earlier.

201. Nihar-ranjan Ray, *Brahmanical Gods in Burma: A Chapter of Indian Art and Iconography* (Calcutta: University of Calcutta, 1932).

202. Nihar-ranjan Ray, *Sanskrit Buddhism in Burma* (Calcutta: University of Calcutta, 1936), 5.

203. Mukul Chandra Dey, *My Pilgrimages to Ajanta and Bagh* (New York: George H. Doran, 1925). Dey made his two extended visits in 1917 and 1919.

204. Ibid., 240.

205. Ibid. Collotype was a process for printing high-quality photographic images in books and journals.

206. Ghulam Yazdani, *Guide to Ajanta Frescoes* (Hyderabad: Archaeological Department, 1927); Yazdani, *Ajanta ki Naqqashi ma' Tasawir.* (Munich: Bruchmann, 1935); and Yazdani, *Ajanta: The Colour and Monochrome Reproductions of the Ajanta Frescoes Based on Photography,* 4 vols. (London: Oxford University Press, 1930–1955).

207. "Shama-a'i az Mazhab-i Buda," *Taqaddum* 5 (December 1927): unpaginated.

208. The Persian transliteration of the Pali title is inevitably ambiguous, but I am reasonably confident that this is the text in question.

209. "Shama," unpaginated. On the critical theme of the "age of speed" (*'asr-i sur'at*) in other Iranian publications of the period, see Cyrus Schayegh, *Who Is Knowledgeable*

Is Strong: Science, Class, and the Formation of Modern Iranian Society, 1900–1950 (Berkeley: University of California Press, 2009), 101–103.

210. Nile Green, "New Histories for the Age of Speed: The Archaeological-Architectural Past in Interwar Afghanistan and Iran," *Iranian Studies* 54, 3–4 (2021): 349–397.

211. ʿA.N.G., "Buda," *Farhang* 4, 4–5 (1929): 122–132. This semi-anonymous publication was part 2 of a three-part article, of which I have had access only to two parts, this being the longer.

212. No specific sources are mentioned in ibid., but the romanized transliterations of various Buddhist terms clearly point to a European (most likely French) source text.

213. Ibid., 128.

214. Xuanzang, *Ek Chini Sayyah.*

215. *Mir'at al-Arz: yaʿni Mukhtasar Jughrafiyya-yi ʿAlam* (Kabul: n.p. [Government Press?], 1906), 9–10. Its purpose as a textbook for all Afghan schoolchildren is stated on the cover. The term *A'ishiya* was still being used in a subsequent 1923 Afghan geography textbook. See *Jughrafiyya-yi Kuchak* (Lahore: Mufid-i ʿAm Press, 1923), printed in India in an edition of 10,000 copies; see the cover, 16–18, and 25. Thanks to Marjan Wardaki for pointing me toward these textbooks.

216. *Mir'at al-Arz*, 8. I have "transcalculated" the numbers, which are provided in units of *kurur* and *lak* [*sic*].

217. Ibid., 24.

218. Annick Fenet, *Documents d'archéologie militante: La mission Foucher en Afghanistan (1922–1925)* (Paris: Académie des Inscriptions et Belles-Lettres, 2010).

219. "Mujasima-ha'i Kulkula." More broadly, see Annick Fenet (trans. Nile Green), "Archaeology in the Reign of Amanullah: The Difficult Birth of a National Heritage," in Nile Green (ed.), *Afghan History through Afghan Eyes* (New York: Oxford University Press, 2015).

220. Nile Green, "The Afghan Discovery of Buddha: Civilizational History and the Nationalizing of Afghan Antiquity," *International Journal of Middle East Studies* 48, 4 (2016): 47–70, and Green, "From Persianate Pasts to Aryan Antiquity: Transnationalism and Transformation in Afghan Intellectual History, c. 1880–1940," *Afghanistan* 1, 1 (2018): 1–42.

221. André Godard, Madame [Yedda] Godard, and Joseph Hackin, *Asar-i Atiqa-yi Buda'i-yi Bamiyan*, trans. Ahmad ʿAli Khan [Kuhzad], 2 vols. (Kabul: Anjuman-i Adabi-yi Kabul, 1936); this was a translation of *Les antiquités bouddhiques de Bamiyan* (Paris: G. van Oest, 1928).

222. Llewelyn Morgan, *The Buddhas of Bamiyan* (Cambridge: Harvard University Press, 2012), 32. On a 1932 Afghan postage stamp of the Buddhas, see Green, "Afghan Discovery," 62.

223. Eduar Şure [Édouard Schuré], *Budda,* trans. Haydar Rifat (Istanbul: Genç Türk Kitaphanesi, 1933).

224. This is based on my perusal of Ian Proudfoot, *Early Malay Printed Books* (Kuala Lumpur: Academy of Malay Studies and University of Malaya, 1993), and online databases.

225. Quran, Sura 95 (*al-Tin*): 1–3.

226. Roy Srirupa, "A Symbol of Freedom: The Indian Flag and the Transformations of Nationalism, 1906–2002," *Journal of Asian Studies* 65, 3 (2006): 495–527. On subsequent attempts to claim Buddha as part of a Pakistani national narrative, see Andrew Amstutz, "A Pakistani Homeland for Buddhism: Displaying a National History for Pakistan beyond Islam, 1950–1969," *South Asia: Journal of South Asian Studies* 42, 2 (2019): 237–255.

227. On such later exegetes, see Reza Shah Kazemi, *Common Ground between Islam and Buddhism* (Louisville: Fons Vitae, 2010).

228. Quran, Sura 49 (*al-Hujurat*): 13.

Chapter 3. Lessons from Japan between India and Iran

1. Heinrich Schliemann, *La Chine et le Japan au temps présent* (Paris: Librairie Centrale, 1867), 81.

2. Claude Markovits, *The Global World of Indian Merchants: Traders of Sind from Bukhara to Panama* (Cambridge: Cambridge University Press, 2000), and Hiroshi Shimizu, "The Indian Merchants of Kobe and Japan's Trade Expansion into Southeast Asia before the Asian-Pacific War," *Japan Forum* 17, 1 (2005): 25–48.

3. Whereas the sailing distance between Kobe and San Francisco, its main port of contact across the Pacific, stands at 4,831 nautical miles, the shipping route from Kobe to Bombay is only slightly longer at 5,140 nautical miles. Distances are based on actual shipping routes as calculated using https://www.searoutes.com/routing/. The Kobe-Bombay distance is based on the standard shipping route via the Straits of Malacca and Colombo.

4. Takashi Oishi, "Indo-Japan Cooperative Ventures in Match Manufacturing in India: Muslim Merchant Networks in and beyond the Bengal Bay Region, 1900–1930," *International Journal of Asian Studies* 1, 1 (2004): 49–85.

5. Nile Green, "Making the First Mosque in Japan," in Green, *Terrains of Exchange: Religious Economies of Global Islam* (New York: Oxford University Press, 2015); Markovits, *Global World*, chap. 4.

6. "Sassoon, J. David," and "Tata, Jamshetji N.," in *The Cyclopedia of India: Biographical, Historical, Administrative, Commercial,* 3 vols. (Calcutta: Cyclopedia Publishing Co., 1907), 1:280, 392–394.

7. "Yokohama Specie Bank," ibid., 399.

8. Muhammad Rabi' Ibn-Muhammad Ibrahim, *Safina-yi Sulaymani: Safarnama-yi Safir-i Iran bih Siyam,* ed. 'Abbas Faruqi (Tehran: Danishgah-i Tihran, 1999). See also Hashem Rajabzadeh, "Japan as Described in *Safina-ye-Solaimani,* a Seventeenth

Century Travel-Book in Persian," *Journal of Osaka University of Foreign Studies* 5 (1991): 189–205.

9. On the wider effects of the war across Asia, see Ramparkash Dua, *The Impact of the Russo-Japanese (1905) War on Indian Politics* (Delhi: S. Chand & Co., 1966); Klaus Kreiser, "Der japanische Sieg über Russland (1905) und sein Echo unter den Muslimen," *Die Welt des Islams* 21, 1 (1981): 209–239; and Renée Worringer, "Rising Sun over Bear: The Impact of the Russo-Japanese War upon the Young Turks," in François Georgeon (ed.), *L'ivresse de la liberté: La révolution de 1908 dans l'empire ottoman* (Paris: Peeters, 2012).

10. Barbara Watson Andaya, "From Rūm to Tokyo: The Search for Anticolonial Allies by the Rulers of Riau, 1899–1914," *Indonesia* 24 (1977): 123–156; Selçuk Esenbel, *Japan, Turkey and the World of Islam* (Leiden: Brill, 2011); Alain Roussillon, *Identité et modernité: Les voyageurs égyptiens au Japon* (Paris: Actes Sud, 2005); and Renée Worringer (ed.), *The Islamic Middle East and Japan: Perceptions, Aspirations, and the Birth of Intra-Asian Modernity* (Princeton: Markus Wiener, 2007).

11. François Georgeon, "Un voyageur tatar en Extrême-Orient au début du XXe siècle," *Cahiers du Monde Russe et Soviétique* 32, 1 (1991): 47–59; Stephen N. Hay, *Asian Ideas of East and West: Tagore and His Critics in Japan, China, and India* (Cambridge: Harvard University Press, 1970); Michael F. Laffan, "Making Meiji Muslims: The Travelogue of 'Ali Ahmad al-Jarjawi," *East Asian History* 22 (2001): 145–170; and My-Van Tran, "Japan through Vietnamese Eyes (1905–1945)," *Journal of Southeast Asian Studies* 30, 1 (1999): 126–146.

12. Mustafa Kamil Pasha, *Matahari Memancar: Tarikh Kerajaan Jepun* (Singapore: Matbaah al-Imam, 1906), briefly described in Ian Proudfoot, *Early Malay Printed Books* (Kuala Lumpur: Academy of Malay Studies and University of Malaya, 1993), 340.

13. Cemil Aydin, *The Politics of Anti-Westernism in Asia: Visions of World Order in Pan-Islamic and Pan-Asian Thought* (New York: Columbia University Press, 2007), and Carolien Stolte and Harald Fischer-Tiné, "Imagining Asia in India: Nationalism and Internationalism (ca. 1905–1940)," *Comparative Studies in Society and History* 54, 1 (2012): 65–92.

14. The 1905 Hindi article is quoted in Luzia Savary, *Evolution, Race and Public Spheres in India: Vernacular Concepts and Sciences (1860–1930)* (London: Routledge, 2019), 76.

15. Rustom Bharucha, *Another Asia: Rabindranath Tagore and Okakura Tenshin* (New Delhi: Oxford University Press, 2006).

16. Mirza, *Kitab-i Jam-i Jam*, 507–508.

17. Pinnock, *Comprehensive System of Modern Geography*.

18. Ibid., 453, and Mirza, *Kitab-i Jam-i Jam*, 507.

19. Pinnock, *Comprehensive System of Modern Geography*, 453.

20. This is the year the book is mentioned in this way in Fayz Muhammad Katib Hazarah, *The History of Afghanistan: Fayz Muhammad Katib Hazarah's* Siraj al-

Tawarikh, trans. Robert McChesney and Mohammad Mehdi Khorrami, 6 vols. (Leiden: Brill, 2013–2016), 3:1138.

21. Selçuk Esenbel, "Shoes and Modern Civilization between Racism and Imperialism: The 1880 Yoshida Masaharu Mission of Meiji Japan to Qajar Iran as Global History," *Global Perspectives on Japan* 2 (2020): 12–47, and Tadahiko Ohtsu and Hashem Rajabzadeh, "Japan iii: Japanese Travelers to Persia," *Encyclopædia Iranica*, http://www.iranicaonline.org/articles/japan-iii-japanese-travelers-to-persia.

22. Kenji Kuroda, "Pioneering Iranian Studies in Meiji Japan: Between Modern Academia and International Strategy," *Iranian Studies* 50, 5 (2017): 651–670, and Hisae Nakanishi, "Iranian Studies in Japan," *Iranian Studies* 20, 2–4 (1987): 131–159.

23. Esenbel, "Shoes," 32.

24. The word *Persia* derives from the Greek name for the ancient region of Pars. Although modern Iranians refer to that region as Fars, they refer to their country itself as Iran.

25. Anja Pistor-Hatam, "Progress and Civilization in Nineteenth-Century Japan: The Far Eastern State as a Model for Modernization," *Iranian Studies* 29, 1–2 (1996): 111–126.

26. Mirza Muhammad Malik al-Kuttab Shirazi, comp., *Mirat al-Zaman dar Tarikh-i Chin u Machin u Japan* (Bombay: Dutt Prasad Press, 1893).

27. Ibid., 107–109.

28. See the discussion in chapter 5.

29. Ibrahim Sahhafbashi Tihrani, *Safarnama-yi Ibrahim Sahhafbashi*, ed. Muhammad Mushiri (Tehran: Shirkat-i Mu'allifan, 1985), 85.

30. Ibid., 87–88, 86.

31. Ibid., 88.

32. Ibid., 86.

33. Ibid., 87.

34. Ibid., 90.

35. Ibid., 86.

36. The text is also known as the *Nippo Jisho* (*Japanese-Portuguese Dictionary*). On its compilation and reproduction, see Michael Cooper, "The Nippo Jisho," *Monumenta Nipponica* 31, 4 (1976): 417–430. Other European dictionaries were produced in the interim centuries, such as Philipp Franz von Siebold, *Epitome linguae Japonicae* (Batavia: Lands Drukkerij, n.d. [1826]), which Siebold (1796–1866) compiled during his six years on the island of Dejima off Nagasaki.

37. I am grateful to Professor So Yamane for showing me Gozaemon's lexicon and explaining its contents.

38. Sahhafbashi, *Safarnama*, 85.

39. Ibid., 91.

40. Ibid., 76.

41. Ibid., 88.

42. Muwahid, *Sayr-i Barhma*, 30.

43. Ohtsu and Rajabzadeh, "Japan iii. Japanese Travelers."

44. Ibid.

45. For Hidayat's biography, see Mahdi Bamdad, *Sharh-i Hal-i Rijal-i Iran*, 6 vols. (Tehran: Zavvar, 1984), 2:455–459, 4:184–187, and 6:196–198. Hidayat later wrote a three-volume world geography.

46. Mahdi Quli Hidayat, *Safarnama-yi Tasharruf bih Makka-yi Mu'azzama* (Tehran: Chapkhana-yi Majlis, n.d. [c. 1945]), 93.

47. Ibid., 94.

48. Ibid., 100.

49. Ibid., 103–104.

50. Ibid., 94, 96, 97, 99, 113.

51. Ibid., 125.

52. Max Put, *Plunder and Pleasure: Japanese Art in the West, 1860–1930* (Leiden: Hotei, 2000).

53. Philippe Sichel, *Notes d'un bibeloteur au Japon* (Paris: E. Dentu, 1883).

54. Hidayat, *Safarnama*, 95–96.

55. Ibid., 97, 105.

56. Ibid., 116–140.

57. Ervand Abrahamian, *Iran between Two Revolutions* (Princeton: Princeton University Press, 1982), 89.

58. Hidayat, *Safarnama*, 107.

59. Ibid., 98.

60. Jagatjit Singh, *Safar-i Chin u Japan u Jawa* (Lahore: Matba'-i Guru Gobind Singh Press, 1906); and His Highness the Raja-i-Rajgan Jagatjit Singh of Kapurthala, *My Travels in China, Japan and Java* (London: Hutchinson, 1905).

61. Singh, *My Travels in China, Japan and Java*, 152.

62. Hidayat, *Safarnama*, 98.

63. Pistor-Hatam, "Progress and Civilization."

64. Several journalists republished their reports in book form—e.g., Frederick Palmer, *With Kuroki in Manchuria* (New York: Scribner's, 1904). For the poem in *Nasim-i Shamal* (April 14, 1908), by Ashraf al-Din of Gilan, see E. G. Browne, *The Press and Poetry of Modern Persia* (Cambridge: University Press, 1914), 191–193.

65. Mata'us Khan Malikiyans, *Mamlikat-i Shams-i Tali' ya Dawlat-i Zhapun* (Tehran: Dar al-Taba'a-i Farus, 1904).

66. Ibid., *muqadima* (introduction), no pagination.

67. Ibid., 45–50.

68. Ibid., 45–46.

69. Ibid., 47.

70. Cited in Farzin Vahdat, *God and Juggernaut: Iran's Intellectual Encounter with Modernity* (Syracuse, N.Y.: Syracuse University Press, 2002), 136–151.

71. Malikiyans, *Mamlikat*, 44.

72. Ibid., 83.

73. Ibid.

74. Ibid.

75. Ibid.

76. Ibid.

77. Philip C. Almond, *The British Discovery of Buddhism* (Cambridge: Cambridge University Press, 1988), chap. 3.

78. Malikiyans, *Mamlikat*, 86.

79. Ibid., 87.

80. Ibid., 88.

81. Husayn 'Ali Shirazi, *Mikadunama* (Calcutta: Matba'-yi Habl al-Matin, 1907). The date of publication is given on the cover as Jumada al-Sani 1325 (July 1907).

82. Roxane Haag-Higuchi, "A Topos and Its Dissolution: Japan in Some 20th-Century Iranian Texts," *Iranian Studies* 29, 1–2 (1996): 74, and Kreiser, "Der japanische Sieg," 222.

83. Sayyid Jalal al-Din Mu'ayyid al-Islam, *Tafriz* (preface), in Shirazi, *Mikadunama*, n.p.

84. Shirazi, *Mikadunama*, 8–11, 16–17.

85. On the peace treaty, see ibid., 99.

86. Mu'ayyid al-Islam, *Tafriz*, n.p.

87. Both illustrators' signatures are on the same images; see, for example, the portrait of Admiral Kamimura in Shirazi, *Mikadunama*, facing 23.

88. American Library Association, *A.L.A. Portrait Index: Index to Portraits Contained in Printed Books and Periodicals*, 3 vols (New York: Franklin, 1906), 2:785, 816.

89. A. Merthan Dündar, "The Effects of the Russo-Japanese War on Turkic Nations: Japan and Japanese in Folk Songs, Elegies, and Poems," in Selçuk Esenbel (ed.), *Japan on the Silk Road: Encounters and Perspectives of Politics and Culture in Eurasia* (Leiden: Brill, 2017). Dündar also discusses the many Turkic poems and songs composed in the Russian Empire that celebrated the heroism of Turkic Muslims who fought *for* Russia, albeit often as conscripts.

90. Baqir Khan Tabrizi, *Tarikh-i Aqsa-yi Sharq ya Muharaba-yi Rus u Zhapan* (Tehran: Hajji Shaykh Ahmad Kitabfurush-i Shirazi, 1913).

91. Ibid., 2–3.

92. I have tried without success to identify this informant through numerous re-romanizations of the name.

93. Osman Sena'i and 'Ali Fu'ad, *Rus-Zhapun Seferi*, 5 vols. (Istanbul: Ketabkhana Islam ve Askari, 1905).

94. Pierre Loti [Piyer Loti], *Japonya Seyahatnamesi*, translated into Ottoman Turkish by M. Saffet (Kostantiniye [Istanbul]: Matbaa-i Ebüzziya, 1893).

95. This statistic is cited in Dündar, "Effects of the Russo-Japanese War," 200.

96. Pertev Demırhan, *Rus-Japon Harbinden Alınan Maddi ve Manevi Dersler ve Japonların Esbab-ı Muzafferiyyeti* (Istanbul: Kanaat Matbaası, 1913). On the military

missions, see Michael Penn, "East Meets East: An Ottoman Mission in Meiji Japan," in Worringer, *Islamic Middle East.*

97. Tabrizi, *Tarikh-i Aqsa,* 2.

98. Ibid.

99. Ibid., 12.

100. On the lack of further Persian books on Japan after the end of the Constitutional Period in 1911, see Hashem Rajabzadeh, "Japan xiii: Translations of Japanese Works into Persian," *Encyclopædia Iranica,* https://www.iranicaonline.org/articles/japan-xiii -translations-of-japanese-works-into-persian, which dates the first actual translations from Japanese to the 1950s.

101. Isma'il Kushan, *Impiraturi-yi Zhapun: az Badw-i Tashkil ta Kunun* (Tehran: Kitabfirushi-yi Danish, 1938). Rajabzadeh does not mention this work.

102. Muhammad Yusuf Riyazi, *'Ayn al-Waqayi'* (Mashhad: Daftar-i Bahr-i Naskha-yi Biguftagu, 1906).

103. Ibid., 526–527. Cf. the illustration of sinking Russian ships during the Battle of Port Arthur in Shirazi, *Mikadunama,* 40.

104. Walter Saise, "A Visit to Afghanistan," *Proceedings of the Central Asian Society* (April 1911): 11.

105. *Siraj al-Akhbar* 2, 14 (1912): 13.

106. Mahmud Tarzi (trans.), *Tarikh-i Muharaba-yi Rus u Zhapun.* 5 vols. (Kabul: Kutubkhana-yi Matba'-yi 'Inayat, 1915).

107. Ibid., 1:70–71.

108. Ibid., 72.

109. Ibid.

110. Siamak Adhami, "The Conversion of the Japanese Emperor to Islam: A Study of Central Asian Eschatology," *Central Asiatic Journal* 43, 1 (1999): 1–9.

111. Rashid Rida, "Da'wat al-Yaban ila al-Islam," *al-Manar* 8, 18 (November 13, 1905), and Rida, "Da'wat al-Islam fi al-Yaban," *al-Manar* 9, 1 (February 1906): 75–78.

112. "Mubashhiru al-Budhiyya fi Inkiltira," *al-Hilal* 14, 1 (October 1905): 50–51.

113. "Hadji Mohammed 'Ali," *Révue du Monde Musulman* 3 (August–December 1907): 118–128. Thanks to Michael O'Sullivan for directing me to this source.

114. Muhammad Sarfaraz Khan 'Azmi Dihlawi, *Muballigh-i Islam ki Mumalik-i Japan, Inglistan u Barma wa Ghaira mein: Tablighi Sargarmiyon ka Tazkira* (Delhi: Qari Buk Dipu, n.d. [c. 1925]), 13.

115. "Au Japon," *Révue du Monde Musulman* 2, 5 (1907): 240.

116. "Japan aur Islam: Japaniyun ki 'Aql u Firasat ka Subt," *Ittihad-i Mazahib-i 'Alam* 1–2 (February 1908): 1. Thanks to Sohaib Baig for bringing this article to my attention.

117. Ulrich Brandenburg, "Imagining an Islamic Japan: Pan-Asianism's Encounter with Muslim Mission," *Japan Forum* (2018): 12–13.

118. Ulrich Brandenburg, "The Multiple Publics of a Transnational Activist: Abdürreşid İbrahim, Pan-Asianism, and the Creation of Islam in Japan," *Die Welt des*

Islams 58, 2 (2018): 143–172; and Nobuo Misawa and Göknur Akçadağ, "The First Japanese Muslim: Shôtarô Noda (1868–1904)," *Annals of Japan Association for Middle East Studies* 23, 1 (2007): 85–109.

119. See, for example, the front page of of *Musavver Cihan*, June 24, 1891.

120. 'Abd al-Rashid Ibrahim, *'Alem-i Islam ve Japonya'da Intişar-ı Islamiyet*, 2 vols. (Istanbul: Ahmed Saki Bey Matbaasi, 1910–1911).

121. Ibid., 1:220.

122. Aydin, *Politics of Anti-Westernism*, 113–114. I have taken the dates of Barakatullah's employment from Suzuki Takeshi, "Tokyo gaikokugo gakko no indojin kyoshi" (Indian Teachers of the Tokyo School of Foreign Studies), in Memorial Publishing Committee of the Ten-Year Death Anniversary of Professor Gamo Reïichi (ed.), *Gamo Reïichi sensei kinen ronsho* (Tokyo: Gamo Reïichi sensei jukkaiki kinen kankokai, 1987), 91. I am most grateful to Eric Tojimbara for translating this chapter for me.

123. "Christian Combination against Islam," *Islamic Fraternity* 3, 3 (1912): 1. Thanks to Cemil Aydin for sharing copies of this long-elusive journal.

124. Muhammad Barakatullah writing in *Islamic Fraternity* 1, 5 (1910): 1.

125. Ibid.

126. *Missions: A Baptist Monthly Magazine* 4 (1913): 596.

127. Steven E. Kemper, *Rescued from the Nation: Anagarika Dharmapala and the Buddhist World* (Chicago: University of Chicago Press, 2015), chap. 2.

128. Ibid., 20, and "Islam in Japan," *Journal of the Maha-Bodhi Society* 19 (1911): 29.

129. Kemper, *Rescued from the Nation*, 118, 149–185.

130. On commercial plans, see ibid., 155, 224.

131. The debate is translated ibid., 163–184. For context, see Edwin Lee, "Nichiren and Nationalism: The Religious Patriotism of Tanaka Chigaku," *Monumenta Nipponica* 30, 1 (1975): 19–35.

132. Richard M. Jaffe, *Seeking Śākyamuni: South Asia in the Formation of Modern Japanese Buddhism* (Chicago: University of Chicago Press, 2019), 37–39, 54–58.

133. Ibid., 13.

134. Translated and quoted ibid., 46.

135. Ibid., 47.

136. Ibid., 55.

137. Ibid., 57.

138. David Geary, *The Rebirth of Bodh Gaya: Buddhism and the Making of a World Heritage Site* (Seattle: University of Washington Press, 2017), chap. 1. On the later Japanese Buddhist students who went to Ceylon, see Jaffe, *Seeking Śākyamuni*, 69.

139. Yasuko Fukuyama, "Japanese Encounters with Ajanta," in Madhu Bhalla (ed.), *Culture as Power: Buddhist Heritage and the Indo-Japanese Dialogue* (New Delhi: Routledge, 2020), and Imre Galambos, "Buddhist Relics from the Western Regions: Japanese Archaeological Exploration of Central Asia," in Nile Green (ed.), *Writing Travel in Central Asian History* (Bloomington: Indiana University Press, 2013). On the cultural

politics of other Japanese ventures in Central Asia during this period, see the essays in Esenbel, *Japan on the Silk Road.*

140. Dey, *My Pilgrimages to Ajanta*, 42–43, 52–55; the discussion of communicating in English is on 43.

141. 'Abdu'l-Bahá and Shoghi Effendi, *Japan Will Turn Ablaze! Tablets of 'Abdu'l-Bahá, Letters of Shoghi Effendi and Historical Notes about Japan* (Tokyo: Bahá'í Publishing Trust, 1974), 21–32.

142. Agnes Baldwin Alexander, *History of the Baha'i Faith in Japan, 1914–1938* (Osaka: Baha'i Publishing Trust Japan, 1977), 14, 20–23.

143. Ibid., 12–14.

144. Such early Indian-language geographical accounts of Japan included Duncan, *Jughrafiyya*, 65–70, and Edwards, *Jam-i Jahan-numa*, 44–51.

145. Sushila Narsimhan, "In Search of a Non-Western Education Model: Syed Ross Masood of Hyderabad Turns to Japan," paper presented at the conference "India and Japan: Unearthing Lesser-Known Linkages," New Delhi, June 2018, https://mosai.org .in/wp-content/uploads/2019/09/Narsimhan_Sushila_Full-Paper.pdf. Aside from the preamble on Mukhopadhyay's *Jepan*, which I gratefully acknowledge, this paper appears—somewhat ironically—to derive in large part from Nile Green, "Forgotten Futures: Indian Muslims in the Trans-Islamic Turn to Japan," *Journal of Asian Studies* 72, 3 (2013): 611–631.

146. Francis Lister Hawks, *Narrative of the Expedition of an American Squadron to the China Seas and Japan Performed in the Years 1852, 1853 and 1854, under the Command of Commodore M. C. Perry, United States Navy* (Washington, D.C.: A. O. P. Nicholson by order of Congress, 1856).

147. "Japan Opened: Compiled from the *Narrative of the American Expedition to Japan in the Year 1852–53–54*," *Calcutta Review* 31, 62 (1858): xlix–l.

148. Laurence Oliphant, *Tarikh-i Chin u Japan*, translated into Urdu by Frederick Nundy and Munshi Shiv Parshad (Lucknow: Munshi Nawwal Kishore, 1867).

149. Amar Farooqui, *Opium City: The Making of Early Victorian Bombay* (New Delhi: Three Essays Collective, 2006).

150. Mawlana Farrukhi, *Ma'sir-i Hamidi* (Agra: Matba'-i Mufid-i 'Am, 1896), 63–167. For a fuller study, see Moinuddin Aqeel, "A Culture Shock: A Narrative of the Late 19th Century Japan in Urdu," *Area and Culture Studies* 53 (1996): 135–151.

151. Farrukhi, *Ma'sir-i Hamidi*, 74, and Aqeel, "Culture Shock," 139.

152. Ahmad Din, *A'yina-i Japan* (Lahore: Khadim al-Ta'lim Pres, 1901).

153. Sayyid Muhammad Ibrahim 'Ajami (trans.), *Japan* (Lahore: Hamidiyya Pres, 1903).

154. Ibid., 42–50.

155. Ibid., 43.

156. Dinshaw Vaniya, *Japanis Sikshaka* (Bombay: Gujarati, 1905), and Ratanji Framji Sethna, *Japani Bhashano Bhomiyo* (Bombay: n.p., 1906).

157. Muhammad Husayn Fazl, *Mukammil Mukhabarat-i Rus u Japan* (Moradabad: n.p., 1904), and Muhammad Ibrahim, *Jang-i Rus u Japan* (Moradabad: n.p., 1904).

158. Mawlwi Zafar 'Ali Khan, *Jang-i Rus u Japan* (Hyderabad: Matba' Akhtar-i Dakan, 1905).

159. H. Rider Haggard [Ra'idar Hagird], *Sayr-i Zulmat ba Taswir*, translated into Urdu by Mawlwi Zafar 'Ali Khan (Hyderabad: Matba'-i Shams, 1900).

160. 'Abd al-Haqq, "Tamhid," in Khan, *Jang-i Rus u Japan*, 4.

161. Khan, *Jang-i Rus u Japan*, 186.

162. Ibid., 186–187.

163. 'Abd al-Majid Salik, *Zikr-i Iqbal: Hazrat 'Allama Iqbal ke Savanih-i Hayat* (Lahore: Bazm-i Iqbal, 1955), 82. Thanks to So Yamane for directing me to this source.

164. Sharaf al-Din Ahmad Khan, *Saintalis Wafadar-i Japan* (Rampur: n.p., 1904).

165. The likely source text is the abbreviated version of Shunsho's classic by Algernon Bertram Freeman-Mitford Redesdale, *The Tale of Forty-Seven Ronins* (Tokyo: Jiujiya, 1892).

166. Babu Khadim Husayn, *Jang-i Rus u Japan: al-Ma'ruf bih Mikadunama Manzum* (Ambala: Impiriyal Printing Works, 1905).

167. Ibid., *bab* 1, 6–7.

168. Kesar Singh Multani, *Japan di Tarakki* (Multan: Kesar Singh, 1908).

169. Husayn structured these sections as *bab* in traditional generic form.

170. Husayn, *Jang-i Rus u Japan*, 176.

171. Rajat Kanta Ray, "Moderates, Extremists, and Revolutionaries: Bengal, 1900–1908," in Richard Sisson and Stanley A. Wolpert (eds.), *Congress and Indian Nationalism: The Pre-Independence Phase* (Berkeley: University of California Press, 1988), 66–67.

172. Mahendulal Garg, *Japandarpan* (Prayag: Indian Press, 1907), cited in Savary, *Evolution, Race and Public Spheres*, 81.

173. Umakanta Hajari, *Nabya Japana o Rusha Japana Yuddhera Itihasa* (Calcutta: Divine Press, 1907).

174. For an outline of his career, see Vineeta Sinha, "Benoy Kumar Sarkar (1887–1949)," in Syed Farid Alatas and Vineeta Sinha (eds.), *Sociological Theory beyond the Canon* (London: Palgrave Macmillan, 2017).

175. Quoted in Satadru Sen, "Benoy Kumar Sarkar and Japan," *Economic and Political Weekly* 48, 45–46 (2013): 68.

176. Ibid. See also the essay by Saratchandra Das, "The Sword of Japan," *Calcutta Review* 74, 288 (1917): 113–117.

177. Rebecca E. Karl, "Creating Asia: China in the World at the Beginning of the Twentieth Century," *American Historical Review* 103, 4 (1998): 1113–1115.

178. Rash Behari Bose to Savarkar, July 11, 1938, Nehru Memorial Museum and Library, Savarkar Private Papers, R6450/23, quoted in Stolte and Fischer-Tiné, "Imagining Asia," 86 and n. 109.

179. Ibid.

180. Carolien Stolte, "Compass Points: Four Indian Cartographies of Asia, c. 1930–55," in Marc Frey and Nicola Spakowski (eds.), *Asianisms: Regionalist Interactions and Asian Integration* (Singapore: National University of Singapore, 2016), 67. As it happened, by this time there was already a small Hindu temple in Kobe constructed by the city's Indian—albeit neither Bengali nor Hindu nationalist—merchants. But by 1935 it was dwarfed by the nearby mosque built with donations from Indian Muslim merchants based as far away as Singapore, Rangoon, and Calcutta. On the temple, see *New East* 2 (1918): 94. On the founding of the mosque, see Green, *Terrains of Exchange,* chap. 7.

181. Mohan Singh Vaid, *America te Japan de Vidyarthi* (Tarn Taran: Mohan Singh Vaid, 1920).

182. Statistics and official statement by thirty-five students in Tokyo are cited in Stolte and Fischer-Tiné, "Imagining Asia," 70nn21, 23.

183. Shimizu, "Indian Merchants," 28.

184. Babu Hamdam, *Japan da Bhuñcha* (Lahore: Ram Das Bhatia, 1923).

185. Hari Prasad Shastri, *Echoes of Japan: 1916–1918* (London: Shanti Sadan, 1961), 47.

186. Ibid.

187. Blair B. Kling, *Partner in Empire: Dwarkanath Tagore and the Age of Enterprise in Eastern India* (Berkeley: University of California Press, 1976), 90–91.

188. Bharucha, *Another Asia*, 7.

189. Ibid., and Stolte and Fischer-Tiné, "Imagining Asia," 78.

190. On the English letters they exchanged, see Zeljko Cipris, "Seduced by Nationalism: Yone Noguchi's 'Terrible Mistake': Debating the China-Japan War with Tagore," *Asia-Pacific Journal* 5, 11 (2007): 1–14.

191. Rabindranath Tagore, *Japan-yatri* (Calcutta: Indian Publishing House, 1920), translated by Shakuntala Rao Sastri as *A Visit to Japan* (New York: East West Institute, 1961).

192. Debanjan Ghosh, "Tagore's Literature in Japanese Language," and Probir Bikash Sarker, "Kora Tomi and Rabindranath," in Pratay Banerjee and Anindya Kundu (eds.), *Tagore and Japan: Dialogue, Exchange and Encounter* (New Delhi: Synergy Books, 2016), 134 and 145–147, respectively.

193. Rather than use a technically standard transliteration, I have maintained Masood's own preferred English spelling of his name.

194. On the university's formation, see Kavita Datla, "A Worldly Vernacular: Urdu at Osmania University," *Modern Asian Studies* 43, 5 (2009): 1117–1148.

195. Narsimhan, "In Search of a Non-Western Education."

196. K. W. Rama Rau, "National Education in Japan," *Calcutta Review* 119, 238 (1904): 446–456.

197. Sen, "Benoy Kumar Sarkar and Japan."

198. Quoted ibid., 65–66, from an essay by Sarkar focusing mainly on France.

199. Syed Ross Masood, *Japan and Its Educational System: Being a Report Compiled for the Government of His Exalted Highness the Nizam* (Hyderabad: Government Central Press, 1923); and Syed Ross Masood [Sayyid Ras Mas'ud], *Japan aur uska Ta'limi Nazm u Nasq* (Aligarh: Anjuman-i Taraqqi-i Urdu, 1925).

200. Syed Ross Masood [Sayyid Ras Mas'ud], *Ruh-i Japan* (Hyderabad: Matbu'a-i Dar al-Matba'-i Sarkar-i 'Ali, 1926); and Syed Ross Masood, *Travels in Japan: Diary of an Exploring Mission*, ed. Jalil Ahmad Kidwai (1922; repr., Karachi: Ross Masood Education and Culture Society of Pakistan, 1968).

201. Masood, *Travels in Japan*, 5.

202. Jaffe, *Seeking Śākyamuni*, 116–118. More broadly, see D. Max Moerman, "Buddhist Japan and the Global Ocean," in Fabio Rambelli (ed.), *The Sea and the Sacred in Japan: Aspects of Maritime Religion* (London: Bloomsbury Academic, 2018).

203. Ibid., and Masood, *Travels in Japan*, 5.

204. Masood, *Travels in Japan*, 20.

205. Ibid., 17, 19.

206. Ibid., 28.

207. Ibid., 28–31.

208. Ibid., 31, 62–63.

209. Ibid., 46–47.

210. Ibid., 47.

211. Ibid., 31.

212. Ibid., 4, 34, and Mokshyagundam Visvesvaraya, *Reconstructing India* (London: P. S. King & Son, 1920).

213. Masood, *Travels in Japan*, 35–36.

214. Sarker, "Kora Tomi and Rabindranath," 146–147.

215. Puran Singh, *The Story of Swami Rama: The Poet Monk of the Punjab* (Madras: Ganesh, 1924), 120–138; the meeting with "Professor Takakutsu" is on 127.

216. Jaffe, *Seeking Śākyamuni*, 122–123.

217. Masood, *Travels in Japan*, 41.

218. Ibid., 8.

219. Ibid., 43, 57. See also David Lelyveld, "*Jutē Hain Japani Kaprē Inglistani*: Sayyid Ross Masood's Passage to Japan," in Alireza Korangy (ed.), *Urdu and Indo-Persian Thought, Poetics, and Belles Lettres* (Leiden: Brill, 2017).

220. Lelyveld, "*Jutē Hain*."

221. On the issues surrounding a scientific lexicon during a previous Hyderabadi fact-finding tour of Britain, see Nile Green, "The Antipodes of 'Progress': A Journey to the End of Indo-Persian," in Abbas Amanat and Assef Ashraf (eds.), *The Persianate World: Rethinking a Shared Sphere* (Leiden: Brill, 2018), 216–251.

222. Masood, *Travels in Japan*, 47. The dictionary was Ernest Miles Hobart-Hampden and Sir Harold George Parlett, *An English-Japanese Dictionary of the Spoken Language* (Yokohama: Kelly & Walsh, 1904).

223. Masood, *Travels in Japan*, 47–48.

224. Ibid.

225. Effectively, this was what was done by various Muslim modernists, including educational reformers in Egypt.

226. Masood, *Travels in Japan*, 49. On the Translation Department, see Majid Bidar, "Dar al-Tarjuma 'Usmaniyya," in *Armaghan-i Jashn-i Almas Jami'a 'Usmaniya* (Hyderabad: Jami'a 'Usmaniyya, 1979), 221–228.

227. Thanks to David Lelyveld for advice on the role of 'Inayatullah.

228. Masood [Mas'ud], *Japan aur uska Ta'limi*, 35–78, 93–103. Masood listed his English source materials for this survey in his bibliography.

229. Ibid., 119–129, 141–200.

230. Ibid., 262–481.

231. This conclusion is based on my own negative findings, as well as the parallel statements in Lelyveld, "*Jutē Hain*," and the editorial note in Masood, *Travels in Japan*, 49.

232. This statement is based on my perusal of the Dar al-Tarjuma book collection at Columbia University's Butler Library.

233. The conversation was described at the time by Masood's travel companion Sayyid Sulayman Nadwi in *Sayr-i Afghanistan* (Lahore: Sang-i Mil, 2008), 22.

234. Masood, *Japan and Its Educational System*, 349.

Chapter 4. The Constraints of a Muslim Japanology

1. Hiroshi Shimizu, *Anglo-Japanese Trade Rivalry in the Middle East in the Inter-War Period* (London: Ithaca Press, 1986) and Shimizu, "The Indian Merchants of Kobe and Japan's Trade Expansion into Southeast Asia before the Asian-Pacific War," *Japan Forum* 17, 1 (2005): 25–48.

2. Shaykh Muhammad Badr al-Islam Fazli, *Haqiqat-i Japan*, 2 vols. (Delhi: Anjuman-i Taraqqi-i Urdu, 1934).

3. Ibid., 1:26–27.

4. Suzuki Takeshi, "Tokyo gaikokugo gakko no indojin kyoshi," in Memorial Publishing Committee of the Ten-Year Death Anniversary of Professor Gamo Rei'ichi (ed.), *Gamo Rei'ichi Sensei Kinen Ronsho* (Tokyo: Gamo Rei'ichi Sensei Jukkaiki Kinen Kankokai, 1987), 87–107. My thanks again to Eric Tojimbara for translating this article for me. On the subsequent history of Urdu teaching at the school, see Mujtuba Husayn, *Japan Chalo* (Hyderabad: Hassami Buk Dipu, 1983), 60–64.

5. Takeshi, "Tokyo gaikokugo gakko," 91–92.

6. Ibid., 93.

7. Ibid., 90. The School of Foreign Affairs was subsequently renamed the Osaka University of Foreign Studies. On Persian and "Hindustani" Urdu teaching there, see Hisae Nakanishi, "Iranian Studies in Japan," *Iranian Studies* 20, 2–4 (1987): 133.

8. Hashem Rajabzadeh, "Japan xii: Translations of Persian Works into Japanese," *Encyclopædia Iranica,* http://www.iranicaonline.org/articles/japan-xii-translations-of -persian-works-into-japanese.

9. Takeshi Aoki, "Japan vi. Iranian Studies in Japan, Pre-Islamic Period," *Encyclopæ- dia Iranica,* http://www.iranicaonline.org/articles/japan-vi-iranian-studies-in-japan -pre-islamic-period.

10. 'Abd al-Wahhab al-Husayni Qa'im-i Maqami, "Adabiyat-i Farsi dar Zhapun," *Ar- maghan* 11, 4 (July 1930): 306–310.

11. On similar Japanese-European interactions with regard to Buddhist Asia, see Imre Galambos, "Buddhist Relics from the Western Regions: Japanese Archaeologi- cal Exploration of Central Asia," in Nile Green (ed.), *Writing Travel in Central Asian History* (Bloomington: Indiana University Press, 2013), and Sven Saaler, "Fukushima Yasumasa's Travels in Central Asia and Siberia: Silk Road Romanticism, Military Re- connaissance, or Modern Exploration?" in Selçuk Esenbel (ed.), *Japan on the Silk Road: Encounters and Perspectives of Politics and Culture in Eurasia* (Leiden: Brill, 2017).

12. The salary grades are given in Takeshi, "Tokyo gaikokugo gakko," 95–104.

13. Ibid., 102.

14. Cemil Aydin, "Orientalism by the Orientals? The Japanese Empire and Islamic Studies (1931–1945)," *Islâm Araştırmaları Dergisi* 14 (2005): 1–36, and Haneda Masashi, "La découverte du 'monde musulman' dans le Japon des années 1930," in Denise Aigle, Isabelle Charleux, Vincent Goossaert, and Roberte Hamayon (eds.), *Miscella- nea Asiatica: Mélanges en l'honneur de Françoise Aubin* (Sankt Augustin: Steyler Verlag, 2010). On the earliest Japanese accounts of Islam, see Fabio Rambelli, "Muhammad Learning the Dao and Writing Sutras: Early Japanese Representations of Muhammad," in Christiane J. Gruber and Avinoam Shalem (eds.), *The Image of the Prophet between Ideal and Ideology* (Leiden: de Gruyter, 2014).

15. Hans Martin Krämer, "Pan-Asianism's Religious Undercurrents: The Reception of Islam and Translation of the Qur'an in Twentieth-Century Japan," *Journal of Asian Studies* 73, 3 (2014): 619–640; the translation of Prideaux is mentioned on 621.

16. Aydin, "Orientalism by the Orientals?" 16–17.

17. Ibid.

18. Krämer, "Pan-Asianism's Religious Undercurrents."

19. Dinshaw Vaniya, *Japanis Sikshaka* (Bombay: Gujarati Printing Press, 1905).

20. Nobuo Misawa, "The Beginning of the Japanese Language Education in the Ottoman Empire," *Journal of Ottoman Studies* 41 (2013): 253–278.

21. *Musavver Cihan,* June 24, 1891, 1. On the reception of such publications in Japan, see Nobuo Misawa, "The Influence of the Ottoman Print Media in Japan: The Link- age of Intellectuals in the Eurasian World," *Kyoto Bulletin of Islamic Area Studies* 2, 2 (2009): 36–42.

22. 'Ali Rıza, *Japon Alfabesi* (Istanbul: Matbaa-i Kütüphane-i Cihan, 1905). Cf. the more rapid development of Turkic language studies in Japan discussed in Klaus

Röhrborn, "The Beginning of Turkish Philology and Linguistics in Japan," in Esenbel, *Japan on the Silk Road*.

23. Gita A. Keeni, "Study of Japanese Language at Visva-Bharati, Santiniketan: Its Past, Present and Future Prospects," in P. A. George (ed.), *Japanese Studies: Changing Global Profile* (New Delhi: Northern Book Centre, 2010), and Nabin Panda, "Tagore and Japanese Language: From the Writings of Sano Jinnosuke," in Pratyay Banerjee and Anindya Kundu (eds.), *Tagore and Japan: Dialogue, Exchange and Encounter* (New Delhi: Synergy Books, 2016), 19–21.

24. Panda, "Tagore and Japanese Language," 23.

25. Debanjan Ghosh, "Tagore's Literature in Japanese Language," in Banerjee and Kundu, *Tagore and Japan*, 134.

26. Fabio Rambelli, "The Idea of India (*Tenjiku*) in Premodern Japan: Issues of Signification and Representation in the Buddhist Translation of Cultures," in Tansen Sen (ed.), *Buddhism across Asia: Networks of Material, Intellectual and Cultural Exchange* (Singapore: Institute of South East Asian Studies, 2014), chap. 12.

27. Richard M. Jaffe, *Seeking Śākyamuni: South Asia in the Formation of Modern Japanese Buddhism* (Chicago: University of Chicago Press, 2019), chaps. 1–2.

28. Ibid., 83–88. On the earlier history of the Sanskrit College and its intellectual exchanges with British scholars, see Michael S. Dodson, *Orientalism, Empire, and National Culture: India, 1770–1880* (New York: Palgrave Macmillan, 2007).

29. Paul Hyer, "Narita Yasuteru: First Japanese to Enter Tibet," *Tibet Journal* 4, 3 (1979): 12–19; Jaffe, *Seeking Śākyamuni*, chap. 2; Naoji Okuyama, "The Tibet Fever among Japanese Buddhists of the Meiji Era," in Monica Esposito (ed.), *Images of Tibet in the 19th and 20th Centuries* (Paris: École Française d'Extrême-Orient, 2008). Hyer notes (13) that Kawaguchi reached Lhasa in March 1901, followed by Narita Yasuteru in December of the same year.

30. Jaffe, *Seeking Śākyamuni*, 78–81.

31. Ibid., 82–83.

32. I have given the English title as it appeared in translation. See Ekai Kawaguchi, *Three Years in Tibet, with the Original Japanese Illustrations* (Benares: Theosophical Publishing Society, 1909).

33. Jaffe, *Seeking Śākyamuni*, 89–90.

34. Ibid., 5, chaps. 1, 2.

35. Hyer, "Narita Yasuteru." Like Kawaguchi, whose veracity he questioned, Narita also published an account, *Shin-zo nishi (Journal of a Journey into Tibet)*.

36. Jaffe, *Seeking Śākyamuni*, 223–235, and Keeni, "Study of Japanese Language," 260. Kimura later changed his name to Ryukan, then in 1931 to Nichiki or Nikki.

37. Jaffe, *Seeking Śākyamuni*, 225–226.

38. These were Yamakami Tensen (1878–1957) and Masuda Jiryo (1887–1930). Both later taught at Japanese universities. See ibid., 250–251.

39. I have based this statement on my perusal of various catalogues of Indian-language printed books of the period and searches on WorldCat and other electronic library databases.

40. Among a vast secondary literature, see James William Coleman, *The New Buddhism: The Western Transformation of an Ancient Tradition* (New York: Oxford University Press, 2002), chap. 3. My searches suggest that Middle Eastern– and Indian-language books on Zen spread only in the 1980s and 1990s, probably drawing from American English works rather than directly from Japanese.

41. Biographical details taken from "Fazli, Badrul Islam," in A. M. Barque (ed.), *All-India Trade Directory and Who's Who for 1942* (Lahore: Barque, 1943), 544.

42. Alain Roussillon, *Identité et modernité: Les voyageurs égyptiens au Japon* (Paris: Actes Sud, 2005).

43. Muhammad Thabit, *Jawla fi Rub' Asiya bayn Misr wa al-Yaban* (Cairo: al-Matba'at al-Rahmaniyya, 1932). On Thabit's travels in general, see Jacob M. Landau, "Muhammad Thabit: A Modern Arab Traveller," *Journal of Arabic Literature* 1, 1 (1970): 70–74; and Roussillon, *Identité et modernité*, 55–63.

44. Fazli, *Haqiqat*, 1:10–13.

45. Ibid., 10–11.

46. Ibid., 15–24.

47. Ibid., 17–19, 22–23.

48. Richard M. Jaffe, "Buddhist Material Culture, 'Indianism,' and the Construction of Pan-Asianism in Prewar Japan," *Material Religion* 2, 3 (2006): 274. On these complex circulations of architectural forms and interpretations, see also Sebastian Conrad, "Greek in Their Own Way: Writing India and Japan into the World History of Architecture at the Turn of the Twentieth Century," *American Historical Review* 125, 1 (2020): 19–53.

49. On the wider use of the concept of civilization in Hindi and Urdu texts of the period, see Luzia Savary, *Evolution, Race and Public Spheres in India: Vernacular Concepts and Sciences (1860–1930)* (London: Routledge, 2019), chap. 1. On civilization in Vietnamese and Thai texts of the period, see Yufen Chang, "Spatializing Enlightened Civilization in the Era of Translating Vernacular Modernity: Colonial Vietnamese Intellectuals' Adventure Tales and Travelogues, 1910s–1920s," *Journal of Asian Studies* 76, 3 (2017): 627–654, and Thongchai Winichakul, "The Quest for 'Siwilai': A Geographical Discourse of Civilizational Thinking in the Late Nineteenth and Early Twentieth-Century Siam," *Journal of Asian Studies* 59, 3 (2000): 528–549. On Japan specifically as a "civilizational" model for Middle Eastern intellectuals, see Anja Pistor-Hatam, "Progress and Civilization in Nineteenth-Century Japan: The Far Eastern State as a Model for Modernization," *Iranian Studies* 29, 1–2 (1996): 111–126.

50. On the new Meiji "language of ideology" more generally, see Carol Gluck, *Japan's Modern Myths: Ideology in the Late Meiji Period* (Princeton: Princeton University Press, 1985), chap. 8.

51. As the Turkish historian Selçuk Esenbel has pointed out, "Both Japanese Pan-Asianists and Muslim intellectuals were concerned with the existential issue of how to be part of the modern world and benefit from its assets while preserving native cultures." See Esenbel, "Japan's Global Claim to Asia and the World of Islam: Transnational Nationalism and World Power, 1900–1945," *American Historical Review* 109, 4 (2004): 1145–1146.

52. Fazli, *Haqiqat*, 1:11.

53. On such nostalgia for a bygone past as a theme of European travelogues to the Middle East around this time, see Ali Behdad, *Belated Travelers: Orientalism in the Age of Colonial Dissolution* (Durham, N.C.: Duke University Press, 1994).

54. Fazli, *Haqiqat*, 1:24.

55. Ibid., 19–21, 26–27, 52–53, 63–66, 78–80, 115–122, 143–146.

56. Ibid., 2:86–91, 102–122, 172–182.

57. Ibid., 1:63–66.

58. Ibid. On the likely sources of the play Fazli saw, see Fabio Rambelli, "The Story of Prince Rama in Japan: Sources and Transformations," in Gauri Parimoo Krishnan (ed.), *Ramayana in Focus: Visual and Performing Arts of Asia* (Singapore: Asian Civilisation Museum, 2010).

59. Fazli, *Haqiqat*, 1:63–66.

60. Hearn's 1897 book is the only specific work on Buddhism cited in Fazli's bibliography. Ibid., 2:226.

61. Ibid., 1:52–53.

62. Rustom Bharucha, *Another Asia: Rabindranath Tagore and Okakura Tenshin* (New Delhi: Oxford University Press, 2006), 76–83, and Shigemi Inaga, "The Interaction of Bengali and Japanese Artistic Milieus in the First Half of the Twentieth Century (1901–1945): Rabindranath Tagore, Arai Kanpō, and Nandalal Bose," *Japan Review* 21 (2009): 149–181.

63. Fazli, *Haqiqat*, 2:107–122.

64. Ibid., 123–134.

65. Ibid., 224.

66. Ibid., 1:20–21

67. Barbara Watson Andaya, "From Rūm to Tokyo: The Search for Anticolonial Allies by the Rulers of Riau, 1899–1914," *Indonesia* 24 (1977): 139; Esenbel, "Japan's Global Claim," 1148–1169; François Georgeon, "Un voyageur tatar en Extrême-Orient au début du XXe siècle," *Cahiers du Monde Russe et Soviétique* 32, 1 (1991): 54–57; and Renée Worringer, "'Sick Man of Europe' or 'Japan of the Near East'? Constructing Ottoman Modernity in the Hamidian and Young Turk Eras," *International Journal of Middle East Studies* 36, 2 (2004): 217–218.

68. Fazli, *Haqiqat*, 1:115–122, 143–146.

69. On the emergence of Middle Eastern and South Asian discourses of art history, see Nile Green, "New Histories for the Age of Speed: The Archaeological-Architectural

Past in Interwar Afghanistan and Iran," *Iranian Studies* 54, 3–4 (2021): 349–397; Partha Mitter, *Art and Nationalism in Colonial India, 1850–1922: Occidental Orientations* (Cambridge: Cambridge University Press, 1995); and Deniz Türker, "Hakky-Bey and His Journal *Le Miroir de l'Art Musulman*, or, *Mir'āt-ı ṣanāyi'-ı islāmiye* (1898)," *Muqarnas* 31 (2014): 277–306.

70. On Japanese travelers to "Buddhist India" in this period, see Jaffe, *Seeking Śākyamuni*, chap. 3.

71. Carolien Stolte, "Compass Points: Four Indian Cartographies of Asia, c. 1930–55," in Marc Frey and Nicola Spakowski (eds.), *Asianisms: Regionalist Interactions and Asian Integration* (Singapore: National University of Singapore, 2016), 54. Cartographically removing Islam from Asia, Pratap instead gave Africa the sobriquet "Mohemmod."

72. Michael F. Laffan, "Mustafa and the Mikado: A Francophile Egyptian's Turn to Meiji Japan," *Japanese Studies* 19, 3 (1999): 280–281.

73. Translated ibid., 280.

74. Ibid.

75. On trade statistics, see Fazli, *Haqiqat*, 2:194–195.

76. Ibid., 1:209–223, 2:227.

77. The bibliography is ibid., 2:224–227.

78. Ibid., 2:226.

79. Masood, *Travels in Japan*, 5, and Shigénobu Okuma, *Fifty Years of New Japan: Kaikoku gojunen shi*, trans. and ed. Marcus B. Huish, 2 vols. (London: Smith & Elder, 1909).

80. Masood, *Travels in Japan*, 5.

81. Okuma, *Fifty Years of New Japan*, 1:vii.

82. Fazli, *Haqiqat*, 1:51–52, 111–112.

83. Ibid., 28, 89–90.

84. Ibid., 90.

85. Ibid., 111–114. For fuller discussion of this Muslim circle, see Nile Green, "Forgotten Futures: Indian Muslims in the Trans-Islamic Turn to Japan," *Journal of Asian Studies* 72, 3 (2013): 611–631.

86. Andaya, "From Rūm to Tokyo," 146.

87. "A Sad Event," *Islamic Fraternity* 3, 3 (1912): 4.

88. Fazli, *Haqiqat*, 1:30.

89. Ibid., 111–113.

90. Larisa Usmanova, *The Türk-Tatar Diaspora in Northeast Asia: Transformation of Consciousness: A Historical and Sociological Account between 1898 and the 1950s* (Tokyo: Rakudasha, 2007).

91. Esenbel, "Japan's Global Claim," 1156–1157.

92. Fazli, *Haqiqat*, 1:113–114.

93. Ibid., 112.

94. Selçuk Esenbel, "Kurban Ali and the Tatar Community in Japan," in Sven Saaler and Christopher W. A. Szpilman (eds.), *Pan-Asianism: A Documentary History*, 2 vols. (Lanham, Md.: Rowman & Littlefield, 2011), vol. 1. Qurban ʿAli was also known in Russianized form as Kurbanaliev.

95. Ibid., 226–227.

96. Kelly A. Hammond, *China's Muslims and Japan's Empire: Centering Islam in World War II* (Chapel Hill: University of North Carolina Press, 2020), esp. chap. 3, on the role of Muslim exiles in Tokyo.

97. Ali Merthan Dündar, "The Turco-Tatar Diaspora in Japan and *Tokyo'da Matbaa-i İslamiye*," in Ali Merthan Dündar and Nobuo Misawa (eds.), *Books in Tatar-Turkish Printed by Tokyo'da Matbaa-i İslamiye (1930–38)* (Tokyo: Toyo University Asian Cultures Research Institute, 2010).

98. Ibid., 18.

99. On the beginning of Afghan-Japanese diplomatic relations, see Hammond, *China's Muslims and Japan's Empire*, 209–210.

100. Sayyid Mushir Khan Tarzi, "Islam dar Japan," *Kabul* 10 (1936?): 71–83. The author was a relative of the first Afghan ambassador to Japan, Habibullah Khan Tarzi, who served in Tokyo from 1933 to 1939.

101. Ibid., facing 77 and 83. The second photograph also featured ʿAbd al-Rashid Ibrahim, whose activities were discussed in chap. 3.

102. See the Russian letter to officials translated in Esenbel, "Kurban Ali," 228–230.

103. Dündar, "Turco-Tatar Diaspora," 19.

104. Krämer, "Pan-Asianism's Religious Undercurrents," 620, 630–631.

105. Ibid., 625.

106. Nile Green, *Terrains of Exchange: Religious Economies of Global Islam* (New York: Oxford University Press, 2015), 256.

107. Qasim Khan Rishtiyya, "Aya Japan bih Islam Musharraf Khwahad Shud?" *Kabul* 4, 3 (1934): 82–83. The Tokyo Quran, and its "explanation" (*tawzi*) in Japanese by the Tokyo Islamic Society, is also discussed in Tarzi, "Islam dar Japan," 78.

108. Rishtiyya, "Aya Japan," 79–80.

109. *Payman* 2, 7 and 2, 8 (1935), cited in Haag-Higuchi, "A Topos and Its Dissolution," 81.

110. Nakamura Kojiro, "Early Japanese Pilgrims to Mecca," *Orient: Report of the Society for Near Eastern Studies in Japan* 12 (1986): 47–57. On Harun Kouzumi, see Dündar, "The Turco-Tatar Diaspora," 18–19.

111. On the nexus between Japanese converts, Islamic studies, and intelligence work, see Cemil Aydin, "Overcoming Eurocentrism? Japan's Islamic Studies during the Era of the Greater East Asia War (1937–45)," in Renée Worringer (ed.), *The Islamic Middle East and Japan: Perceptions, Aspirations, and the Birth of Intra-Asian Modernity* (Princeton: Markus Wiener, 2007), 153–156; and Esenbel, "Japan's Global Claim," 1165–1169.

112. Fazli, *Haqiqat*, 1:114.

113. Yukiko Hama, "Russia from a Pan-Asianist View: Saburo Shimano and His Activities," *Ab Imperio* 3 (2010): 227–243.

114. Fazli, *Haqiqat*, 1:113.

115. It is unclear in which language Saburo and Fazli could have communicated, since Saburo was principally a Russian speaker. But having graduated from the Philology Department of Petrograd University, he may also have spoken English.

116. Fazli, *Haqiqat*, 1:26–27.

117. Tatiana Linkhoeva, "The Buryat-Mongol National Movement and Japanese Interests in Siberia, 1917–1919," in Evan Dawley and Tosh Minohara (eds.), *Beyond Versailles: The 1919 Moment and a New Order in East Asia* (Lanham, Md.: Lexington Books, 2020). Thanks to an anonymous reader for this suggestion.

118. Fazli, *Haqiqat*, 1:29–30.

119. Ibid., 26–27, and Takeshi, "Tokyo gaikokugo gakko," 102.

120. Fazli, *Haqiqat*, 1:27.

121. Ibid., 28–29.

122. Ibid.

123. I have identified Gamo more fully from mentions of him in various issues of the *Memoirs of the Research Department of the Toyo Bunko* from the 1930s. Gamo is also briefly discussed in Takeshi, "Tokyo gaikokugo gakko," 99.

124. Saichiro Nomura, *Shotoindogo kenkyu* (Tokyo: Subundo Shuppanbu, 1934). I am grateful to So Yamane for directing me to this work, which fortunately includes romanized transcriptions as well as katakana.

125. On the use of the English-Urdu dictionary at the school, see Takeshi, "Tokyo gaikokugo gakko," 99.

126. Fazli, *Haqiqat*, 1:20.

127. Ibid., 78–80.

128. Ibid., 2:216–223.

129. Mawlana Farrukhi, *Ma'sir-i Hamidi* (Agra: Matba'-i Mufid-i 'Am, 1896), 75.

130. Fazli, *Haqiqat*, 2:227. Chamberlain had permanently left Japan in 1911, so his other works cited by Fazli were somewhat dated.

131. Ibid., 224–227.

132. The earliest English translation was Taize Fujimoto, *The Nightside of Japan* (London: T. W. Laurie, 1914). However, Fazli drew on the 1927 reprint, also issued by Laurie, which I have consulted in turn.

133. Jukichi Inouye, *Home Life in Tokyo* (Tokyo: Tokyo Printing Co., 1910), 3.

134. Fazli, *Haqiqat*, 1:135–137, 147–149.

135. Takeshi, "Tokyo gaikokugo gakko," 103–104. Barlas's assumption of Fazli's position at the school is discussed in the introduction to Nur al-Hasan Barlas and Shahid Ahmad Dihlawi (eds.), *Salnama-i Saqi-i Dihli: Japan Nambar* 13, 1 (January 1936): 5. On Urdu teaching at the Tokyo school after Barlas left in 1949, see Husayn, *Japan Chalo*, 60–64.

136. Missiz [Mrs.] Barlas, "Kasatusu ke Garm Chashme," and Hanifa Rashid Fate-hali, "Japan Tis Baras mein," both in Barlas and Dihlawi, *Salnama-i Saqi,* 52–57 and 42–46, respectively.

137. Rei'ichi Gamo [Prafisar R. Gamu], "Sakura ka Phul," in Barlas and Dihlawi, *Salnama-i Saqi,* 47–52; Prafisar Yizu Sawa, "Tudaji ka Mandir," ibid., 81–83; Prafisar Yizu Sawa, "Huriyuji Budh Mandir," ibid., 99–101; Mistar K. Nakamura, "Takituri ki Ka-hani," ibid., 101–102; and Mistar U. K. Satu, "Japani Talib 'Ilm ki Zindagi," ibid., 102–105.

138. Takeshi, "Tokyo gaikokugo gakko," 104.

139. These Japanese contributors' connection to the language school and thereby to Barlas are discussed in his introduction to the *Saqi* special issue. See Nur al-Hasan Barlas, "Guzarish," in Barlas and Dihlawi, *Salnama-i Saqi,* 7.

140. Noguchi Yonejiro [Prafisar Yun Naguchi], "Meri Sha'iri aur Shahr-i 'Ajib ko," and "Mein ne Hindustan ko kiya Pa'id," in Barlas and Dihlawi, *Salnama-i Saqi,* 162–163 and 166–168, respectively.

141. On Noguchi's trip, see Zeljko Cipris, "Seduced by Nationalism: Yone Noguchi's 'Terrible Mistake': Debating the China-Japan War with Tagore," *Asia-Pacific Journal* 5, 11 (2007): 2.

142. Program details are listed in *Indian Listener* 1, 9 (April 1936): 456, and 1, 17 (August 1936): 856.

143. Muhammad Badr al-Islam Fazli, "Tasirat ki Ek Jhalk," in Barlas and Dihlawi, *Salnama-i Saqi,* 16–23, and Shaykh Muhammad Badr al-Islam Fazli, *Anokhe Afsane* (Panipat: Hali Akaidmi, 1938).

144. Nur al-Hasan Barlas, *Japani Bachchun ke Git,* 2 vols. (Delhi: Anjuman-i Taraqqi-i Urdu, 1940). On Bengali children's stories that "praised the modernity of Japan's cities but simultaneously resorted to orientalist exoticization," see Satadru Sen, "Benoy Ku-mar Sarkar and Japan," *Economic and Political Weekly* 48, 45–46 (2013): 67. On poems and songs celebrating Japan that spread through oral and printed means in Turkic languages, see A. Merthan Dündar, "The Effects of the Russo-Japanese War on Turkic Nations: Japan and Japanese in Folk Songs, Elegies, and Poems," in Esenbel, *Japan on the Silk Road.*

145. I am grateful to Professor So Yamane for sharing with me his Urdu PowerPoint presentation about these language books. By 1942 Sawa Eizu was employed by the Osaka University of Foreign Studies.

146. Takeshi, "Tokyo gaikokugo gakko," 104.

147. By comparison, at the outbreak of war, few British military officers had been trained in Japanese; only sixteen of the thirty-four British and Indian army officers who had studied the language were still in active service, of whom a mere three had attended staff colleges in India. See Azharudin Mohamed Dali and Zaffar Iqbal Junejo, "A Contextual Review of the Selected English Writings on Japan's Secret War Theatre, 1941–1945," *Asia Pacific* [Pakistan] 37 (2019): 74.

148. Keeni, "Study of Japanese Language," 260.

149. On these postcolonial developments, based at Visva-Bharati and then at Delhi University, see Sushila Narsimhan, "Japanese Studies in India: Major Trends and Challenges," in George, *Japanese Studies*.

150. General Pertev Demırhan, *Japonlarin Asil Kuvveti: Japonlar Niçin ve Nasil Yükseldi?* (Istanbul: Cumhuriyet Matbaasi, 1937).

151. ʿAli Asghar Khan (trans.), "Shaʿiri dar Japan," *Ayina-yi ʿIrfan* 85 (1937) to 91 (1938).

152. On Japanese-Afghan relations during the 1930s, see Hammond, *China's Muslims and Japan's Empire*, 203–219.

153. For such Afghan news reports, see, e.g., "Chin u Japan," *Anis* 5, 46–47 (April 1932): 19.

154. "Shiʿr u Shaʿiri-yi Zhapun," *Mihr* 5, 3 (1938).

155. Badr al-Islam Fazli (trans.), *Namiku: Japan ka Sab se Mashhur Nawal* (Delhi: ʿIlmi Pris, 1946). He had briefly discussed the novel in *Haqiqat*, 2:119.

156. Ibid., preface, 3–4. Kenjiro Tokutomi, *Nami-ko: A Realistic Novel*, trans. Edwin Edgett and Sakae Shioya (London: G. P. Putnam's Sons, 1904). Born in Japan, Shioya (1873–1961) learned English at a Methodist missionary school before studying at the University of Chicago. On the international influence of his and Edgett's translation, see Isabelle Lavelle, "Tokutomi Kenjirō's *Hototogisu*: A Worldwide Japanese Best-Seller in the Early Twentieth Century?" *Transcommunication* 3, 1 (2016): 97–121. *Hototogisu* (The Cuckoo) was the novel's original title.

Chapter 5. Interpreting China across Maritime Asia

1. Elmer H. Cutts, "Chinese Studies in Bengal," *Journal of the American Oriental Society* 62, 3 (1942): 171–174, and Daniel Kam-To Choi, "The Baptist Endeavours in Biblical Translation in China before the Chinese Union Version," *Journal of the Royal Asiatic Society* 30, 2 (2020): 341–364. Lassar (1781–1835?) was also known as Hovhannes Ghazarian.

2. Joshua Marshman (trans.), *The Works of Confucius: Containing the Original Text, with a Translation* (Serampore: Mission Press, 1809), and Marshman (trans.), *Clavis Sinica: Elements of Chinese Grammar; With a Preliminary Dissertation on the Characters, and the Colloquial Medium of the Chinese, and an Appendix Containing the Ta-Hyoh of Confucius with a Translation* (Serampore: Mission Press, 1814). For a contextual evaluation, see Chris Murray, "'Wonderful Nonsense': Confucianism in the British Romantic Period," *Interdisciplinary Literary Studies* 17, 4 (2015): 593–616.

3. Cutts, "Chinese Studies," 172.

4. Yang Huiling, "The Making of the First Chinese-English Dictionary: Robert Morrison's Dictionary of the Chinese Language in Three Parts (1815–1823)," *Historiographia Linguistica* 41 (2014): 299–322.

5. Christopher A. Reed, *Gutenberg in Shanghai: Chinese Print Capitalism, 1876–1937* (Vancouver: University of British Columbia Press, 2007).

6. Francesca Tarocco, *The Cultural Practices of Modern Chinese Buddhism: Attuning the Dharma* (London: Routledge, 2007), 46–80.

7. Chiara Betta, "Silas Aaron Hardoon and Cross-Cultural Adaptation in Shanghai," in Jonathan Goldstein (ed.), *The Jews of China*, vol. 1, *Historical and Comparative Perspectives* (Armonk, N.Y.: Sharpe, 1999), 216–229.

8. Stefan Henning, "God's Translator: Qu'ran Translation and the Struggle over a Written National Language in 1930s China," *Modern China* 41, 6 (2015): 631–655.

9. Tamara Chin, "The Invention of the Silk Road, 1877," *Critical Inquiry* 40, 1 (2013): 194–219, and Daniel C. Waugh, "Richthofen's 'Silk Roads': Towards the Archaeology of a Concept," *Silk Road* 5, 1 (2007): 1–10.

10. Janardan Kumar, *Indo-Chinese Trade, 1793–1833* (Bombay: Orient Longman, 1974), and J. F. Richards, "The Opium Industry in British India," *Indian Economic & Social History Review* 39, 2–3 (2002): 149–180. See also Madhavi Thampi, *Indians in China, 1800–1949* (New Delhi: Manohar, 2005).

11. Tansen Sen, *India, China, and the World: A Connected History* (Lanham, Md.: Rowman & Littlefield, 2017), 253.

12. John Hinnells, "The Parsis in Hong Kong and the China Seas," in Hinnells, *The Zoroastrian Diaspora: Religion and Migration* (Oxford: Oxford University Press, 2005), and Thampi, *Indians in China*, 77–80.

13. Farooqui, *Opium City*; Tansen Sen, "Kolkata and China: Some Unexplored Links," *China Report* 43, 4 (2007): 393–396; and Madhavi Thampi and Shalini Saksena, "China in the Making of Bombay," in Sushila Narsimhan and G. Balatchandirane (eds.), *India and East Asia: Learning from Each Other* (New Delhi: Manak, 2004).

14. Jane Kate Leonard, *Wei Yuan and China's Rediscovery of the Maritime World* (Cambridge: Council on East Asian Studies, Harvard University, 1984), and Fred W. Drake, *China Charts the World: Hsu Chi-Yü and His Geography of 1848* (Cambridge: East Asian Research Center of Harvard University, 1975). For a broader overview, see Tansen Sen, "Chinese Sources on South Asia," in Rila Mukherjee (ed.), *Beyond National Frames: India, South Asia and the World* (Delhi: Primus, 2015).

15. Chengjie Lin, "Ma Jianzhong and Wu Guangpei's Visit to India and Their Diaries," *Asia-Pacific Studies* (1991): 55–72, and Sen, *India, China, and the World*, 262–270.

16. Sen, *India, China, and the World*, 265–269.

17. Ibid., 267.

18. Ibid., 263.

19. Ibid., 291.

20. Quoted ibid., 278.

21. Nicolas Idier, "Kang Youwei 康有爲 (1858–1927) and India: The Indian Travels of a Cosmopolitan Utopian," in Anne Cheng and Sanchit Kumar (eds.), *India-China: Intersecting Universalities* (Paris: Collège de France, 2020), and Liu Xi, "Kang Youwei's Journey to India: Chinese Discourse on India during the Late Qing and Republican Periods," *China Report* 48, 1–2 (2012): 171–185.

22. Idier, "Kang Youwei," 113.

23. Quoted ibid., 115.

24. Leonard, *Wei Yuan.*

25. Idier, "Kang Youwei," 115.

26. Horace William Clift, *First Geography for Natives; or, Guide to the Map of the World* (Calcutta: n.p., 1836), translated into Urdu by Mir Ghulam 'Ali as *'Ilm-i Jughrafiyya* (Calcutta: Calcutta School-Book Society Press [?], 1851); on "Asia," albeit in English pronunciation as *Aysha,* see 23–52.

27. On China, see Clift, *'Ilm-i Jughrafiyya,* 38–40, 51.

28. Ibid., 51, where the terms *bodh-parast* and *paighambar* both appear.

29. Duncan, *Jughrafiyya,* 51.

30. Kavasji Sorabji Patel [Cowasjee Sorabjee Patell], *Account of China: Comprising a View of the Topography, History, Manners, Customs, Languages, Literature, Arts, Manufactures, Commerce, Religion, Jurisprudence, etc. of the Chinese Empire,* 2 vols. (Bombay: Courier Press, 1844), 1: chaps. 1, 2, 4. My thanks to Michael O'Sullivan for providing this translation.

31. Cowasjee Sorabjee Patell, *Cowasjee Patell's Chronology, Containing Corresponding Dates of the Different Eras Used by Christians, Jews, Greeks, Hindus, Mohamedans, Parsees, Chinese, Japanese, etc.* (London: Trübner, 1866).

32. Ibid., viii.

33. James Corcoran [Jaymz Karkuran], *Tarikh-i Mamalik-i Chin aur Dusre Mulkon aur Qawmon ki jo Farman Bardar ya Bajguzar Faghfur-i Khata ke Hain: Ibtida-yi Nawabadi-yi Dunya ba'd Tufan-i Nuh se,* 2 vols. (Calcutta: Baptist Missionary Society, 1848–1852). Corcoran's book is also discussed in Javed Ali Khan, *Early Urdu Historiography* (Patna: Khuda Bakhsh Oriental Library, 2005), 419–432.

34. [James Corcoran], *Tarikh-i Mamalik-i Chin* (Lucknow: Nawwal Kishore, 1864).

35. Corcoran [Karkuran], *Tarikh-i Mamalik-i Chin,* 1:3–4.

36. The list of sources is given ibid., 1:4.

37. Ibid. The works in question were Martino Martini, *Description géographique de la Chine* (Paris: S. Mabre-Cramoisy, 1666); Karl Friedrich Gützlaff, *China Opened; or, A Display of the Topography, History . . . etc of the Chinese Empire* (London: Smith, Elder, 1838); and W. H. Medhurst, *China: Its State and Prospects, with Special Reference to the Spread of the Gospel* (Boston: Crocker & Brewster, 1838). On the context and intellectual influence of Gützlaff and his fellow Protestant missionaries, see Jessie Gregory Lutz, *Opening China: Karl F. A. Gützlaff and Sino-Western Relations, 1827–1852* (Grand Rapids: William B. Eerdmans, 2008).

38. W. H. Medhurst, trans., *Ancient China: The Shoo King, or the Historical Classic* (Shanghai: Mission Press, 1846).

39. The works referred to were George Staunton, *An Authentic Account of an Embassy from the King of Great Britain to the Emperor of China,* 2 vols. (London: W. Bulmer, 1797), and John Ouchterlony, *The Chinese War: An Account of All the Operations of the*

British Forces from the Commencement to the Treaty of Nanking (London: Saunders & Ottey, 1844).

40. *Qissa-i Faghfur-i Chin* (Bombay: n.p., 1874).

41. Munshi Debi Prashad, *Arzhang-i Chin* (Kanpur: Matba'-i Nizam, 1871).

42. Corcoran [Karkuran], *Tarikh-i Mamalik-i Chin,* 2:19–20.

43. Abu Sulayman Dawud Banakiti, *A Chinese Chronicle,* trans. Stephen Weston (London: William Clarke, 1820), and Ibn Battutah, *The Travels of Ibn Battutah,* trans. Samuel Lee (London: Oriental Translation Committee, 1829).

44. Corcoran [Karkuran], *Tarikh-i Mamalik-i Chin;* the title is transliterated as *Shu King* on 2:19 and the summary of its contents is given in 2: chaps. 2–5.

45. Oliphant, *Tarikh-i Chin u Japan.* On the mission and its original English report, see Q. S. Tong, "Traveling Imperialism: Lord Elgin's Missions to China and the Limits of Victorian Liberalism," in Douglas Kerr and Julia Kuehn (eds.), *A Century of Travels in China: Critical Essays on Travel Writing from the 1840s to the 1940s* (Hong Kong: Hong Kong University Press, 2007).

46. Sir Thomas Douglas Forsyth [Ti Di Forsayath], *Safarnama-i Ti Di Forsayath Kamishnar sabaq Jalandhar babat-i Safar-i Yarqand* (Lucknow: Munshi Nawwal Kishore, 1872).

47. Kim Hodong, *Holy War in China: The Muslim Rebellion and State in Chinese Central Asia, 1864–1877* (Stanford: Stanford University Press, 2004).

48. Farooqui, *Opium City.*

49. Krsnadhana Bandyopadhyaya, *Cinera Itihasa* (Calcutta: Stanhope Press, 1865). I am most grateful to Dr. Nandini Bhattacharya for providing me with notes on this text.

50. Damodar Ishwardas, *Cinani Musaphari* (Bombay: Nowrojee Framjee, 1868), examined in Michael O'Sullivan, "Vernacular Capitalism and Intellectual History in a Gujarati Account of China, 1860–68," *Journal of Asian Studies* 80, 2 (2021): 267–292. I am most grateful to Mike for sharing his notes on Ishwardas's text.

51. Farooqui, *Opium City.*

52. O'Sullivan, "Vernacular Capitalism and Intellectual History."

53. Ibid., 277–280.

54. Ishwardas, *Cinani Musaphari,* 214. Translation by Michael O'Sullivan.

55. Barlas, *Sayr-i Darya,* 68.

56. O'Sullivan, "Vernacular Capitalism and Intellectual History," 288.

57. Mirza, *Kitab-i Jam-i Jam.*

58. Nile Green, "Persian Print and the Stanhope Revolution: Industrialization, Evangelicalism, and the Birth of Printing in Early Qajar Iran," *Comparative Studies of South Asia, Africa and the Middle East* 30, 3 (2010): 473–490.

59. Pinnock, *Comprehensive System of Modern Geography.*

60. Mirza, *Kitab-i Jam-i Jam,* 498–508.

61. Ibid., 498.

62. Ibid.

63. Ibid., 499–500.

64. Spelling and definition of Persian *lak* from Francis Joseph Steingass, *A Comprehensive Persian-English Dictionary* (London: Routledge & K. Paul, 1892), 1126.

65. Mirza, *Kitab-i Jam-i Jam*, 500–501.

66. Ibid., 511.

67. Ibid., 500.

68. Ibid., 501.

69. Mirza Muhammad Malik al-Kuttab Shirazi, comp., *Mirat al-Zaman dar Tarikh-i Chin u Machin u Japan* (Bombay: Dutt Prasad Press, 1893).

70. Ibid., 1–2, with only Zaman's nickname, Farangi Khan. Malik al-Kuttab cut Zaman's preface, explaining how he found the Latin text.

71. Biographical information from Nabil Hadi, *Dictionary of Indo-Persian Literature* (Delhi: Abhinav, 1995), 172–173.

72. Matteo Ricci, *De christiana expeditione apud sinas suscepta ab Societate Iesu*, ed. Nicholas Trigault (Augsburg: Apud Christoph. Mangium, 1615). I have checked my schoolboy Latin reading of the sections discussed below against Louis J. Gallagher, *China in the Sixteenth Century: The Journals of Matteo Ricci* (New York: Random House, 1953).

73. Muhammad Zaman Khan, *Tarikh-i Chin* (Calcutta: Mission Press for Aligarh Scientific Society, 1864).

74. Ibid., 1.

75. Amid a vast secondary literature, see David E. Mungello, *Curious Land: Jesuit Accommodation and the Origins of Sinology* (Honolulu: University of Hawaii Press, 1989).

76. Zaman in Shirazi, *Mirat al-Zaman*, 2.

77. Ibid., 3.

78. Ricci, *De christiana expeditione*, 7, and Zaman in Shirazi, *Mirat al-Zaman*, 4.

79. Zaman in Shirazi, *Mirat al-Zaman*, 64–65. Cf. Ricci, *De christiana expeditione*, 104–105.

80. Zaman in Shirazi, *Mirat al-Zaman*, 65–66.

81. Ibid., 65, 68.

82. Ibid., 68.

83. Ricci, *De christiana expeditione*, 109.

84. Zaman in Shirazi, *Mirat al-Zaman*, 69.

85. Ibid., 71.

86. Ibid., 70.

87. Ibid., 73.

88. Ibid., 106–107. The last dates actually mentioned are 1859 and 1882, but the historical coverage effectively ends in 1736. For further discussion of Farangi Khan's translation, see Nile Green, "Matteo Ricci as an Islamicate Informant: Two Moments of Connection in the Persian Afterlives of a Latin Account of China," *Journal of the Royal Asiatic Society* 32 (2022).

89. Siddiq Hasan Khan, *Luqtat al-'Ajlan mimma Tamassu ila Ma'rifatihi Hajat al-Insan wa fi Akhiriha Khabi'at al-Akwan fi Iftiraq al-Umam 'ala al-Madhahib wa al-Adyan* (Istanbul: Matba'at al-Jawa'ib, 1878–1879). Thanks to Sohaib Baig for bringing the contents of this text to my attention.

90. Zaman in Shirazi, *Mirat al-Zaman*, 73.

91. Nusret 'Ali Han Dihlewi, *Çin ü Maçin* (Istanbul: Hurshid Matba'asï, 1902). Thanks again to Sohaib Baig for this information.

92. Shibli Nu'mani, *Safarnama-i Rum u Misr u Sham* (1914; repr., Azamgarh: Dar al-Musanifin, 2010), 107.

93. 'Ali Ekber, *Tercüme-i Tarih-i Nevadir-i Çin Maçin* (Istanbul: Tophane-i Amire İstihkam Alayları Litografya Destgahı, 1854).

94. On 'Ali Akbar's inability to speak Chinese, see Kaveh Hemmat, "Children of Cain in the Land of Error: A Central Asian Merchant's Treatise on Government and Society in Ming China," *Comparative Studies of South Asia, Africa and the Middle East* 30, 3 (2010): 436, 438.

95. *Çin Devleti* (Istanbul: Erzincanlı Matba'asï, 1866).

96. Dihlewi *Çin ü Maçin*, 1–7.

97. Ibid., 29–31.

98. 'Abd al-'Aziz Kulcalı, *Çîn'de Dîn-i Mübîn-i İslâm ve Çîn Müslümânları* (Istanbul: Mahmud Beg, 1901).

99. Dihlewi, *Çin ü Maçin*, 32–35.

100. Ibid., 36–40.

101. Ibid., 7, 29.

102. John K. Fairbank, "Meadows on China: A Centennial Review," *Far Eastern Quarterly* 14, 3 (1955): 365–371.

103. Thomas Taylor Meadows, *Desultory Notes on the Government and People of China, and on the Chinese Language* (London: Allen, 1847), and Meadows, *The Chinese and Their Rebellions, Viewed in Connection with Their National Philosophy, Ethics, Legislation, and Administration* (London: Smith, Taylor, 1856). From an initial comparison, the latter work seems the more likely source.

104. Munshi Ghulam Qadir Fasih, *Halat-i Chin* (Sialkot: Panjab Pres, 1890; repr., Lahore: Munshi Fayz 'Ali Malik, 1904).

105. C. M. Naim, "Homage to a 'Magic-Writer': The *Mistrīz* and *Asrār* Novels of Urdu," in Bodhisattva Chattopadhyay, Aakriti Mandhwani, and Anwesha Maity (eds.), *Indian Genre Fiction: Pasts and Future Histories* (London: Routledge, 2019).

106. On the print run of Fasih's newspaper, see Government of India, *Report on the Administration of the Punjab and Its Dependencies, 1896–97* (Lahore: Government Press, 1897), appendix 1, 321.

107. Naim, "Homage."

108. *Qur'an Majid ma' Tarjuma Ingrizi, Urdu, Farsi* (Sialkot: Punjab Press, 1899).

109. Mirza Ghulam Ahmad, *Jang-i Muqaddas* (Amritsar: Riyaz Hind Pres, n.d. [c. 1894]).

110. Fasih, *Halat-i Chin,* 36–51.

111. Ibid., 5–7, 9–10.

112. Ibid., 8.

113. Ibid., 10–16, 51–54.

114. Ibid., 36. Unfortunately, Fasih did not name any of his sources specifically.

115. Ibid., 40.

116. Ibid., 41.

117. Ibid.

118. Ibid., 43.

119. Xuanzang, *Ek Chini Sayyah.* As far as I can determine, Faxian's travelogue was not translated into South Asian languages till the 1960s, when versions appeared in Hindi, Bengali, and Tamil, as well as Burmese.

120. Fasih, *Halat-i Chin,* 26–27.

121. Ibid., 26.

122. Ibid.

123. Muhammad Shafi' al-Din Khan, *Chin u Chini* (Moradabad: Shams al-Mataba', 1897).

124. Ibid., 13–27, 42–50.

125. Ibid., 31–32.

126. Abu al-'Izz Itribi and 'Abd al-'Aziz Hamad, *Nubdhah 'an al-Sin* (1901; repr., Cairo: Mu'assasah Hindawi, 2015). Thanks to Sohaib Baig for tracking down a copy for me.

127. Ibid., 9–11, 29–36.

128. Ibid., 12–26.

129. Abu al-'Izz Itribi, *al-Durr al-Muntakhab fi Tarikh al-Misriyyin wa al-'Arab,* 2 vols. (Cairo: n.p., 1894).

130. Itribi and Hamad, *Nubdhah,* 26–29.

131. Ibid., 27–28.

132. Ibid., 28. The Arabic transliteration of the romanized version of the Chinese name still presents considerable challenges. So I am most grateful to Jonathan Lipman for identifying this "Ma Te-Hsing" (aka Ma Fuchu) as Ma Dexin.

133. "Ma Te-Hsing" (i.e., Ma Dexin) was also discussed in Gabriel Devéria, *Origine de l'Islamisme en Chine: Deux légendes musulmanes chinoises, pèlerinages de Ma Fou-tch'ou* (Paris: Imprimerie Nationale, 1895). Devéria included a facsimile of the Chinese-Arabic history of Chinese pilgrimages to Mecca that Ma had written. For a more recent study of the text, see Kristian Petersen, "The Multiple Meanings of Pilgrimage in Sino-Islamic Thought," in Jonathan Lipman (ed.), *Islamic Thought in China: Sino-Muslim Intellectual Evolution from the 17th to the 21st Century* (Edinburgh: Edinburgh University Press, 2016), 93–98.

134. Itribi and Hamad, *Nubdhah,* 28–29.

135. Jamal al-Din al-Afghani, *Kitab Tatimmat al-Bayan fi Tarikh al-Afghan* (Cairo: Matba'at al-Mawsu'at, 1901).

136. Itribi and Hamad, *Nubdhah*, 37.

137. Ibid., 33.

138. Ibid.

139. So far as I can tell, there appear to have been no published book-length Arabic direct travel accounts of China from this period.

140. Muhammad Nadim al-Sultan, *Tarikh-i Chin* (Tehran: Matba'-i Khurshid, 1906), and Jean-Pierre Guillaume Pauthier, *Chine; ou description historique, géographique et littéraire de ce vaste empire* (Paris: F. Didot, 1839).

141. Thanks to Farzin Vejdani for this information on Nadim al-Sultan.

142. Mohamad Tavakoli-Targhi, "Historiography and Crafting Iranian National Identity," in *Iran in the 20th Century: Historiography and Political Culture*, ed. Touraj Atabaki (London: I. B. Tauris, 2009), 20–21.

143. Ramkrishna Bhattacharya, "G. Pauthier: French Orientalist and the First Translator of Rammohun," *Journal of the Asiatic Society of Bengal*, n.s., 39 (1997): 1–10.

144. Jean-Pierre Guillaume Pauthier, *Mémoire sur l'origine et la propagation de la doctrine du Tao* (Paris: Librarie Orientale de Dondey-Dupré, 1831), 53–79.

145. Yidan Wang, "Chinese-Iranian Relations, xvi. Impact of the Constitutional Revolution in Iran," *Encyclopaedia Iranica*, https://www.iranicaonline.org/articles/chinese-iranian-xvi.

146. Arnold Henry Savage Landor, *Tarikh-i Jang-i Chin ba Duwwal-i Muttahida-i Urup dar Sal-i Yikhazar u Sisad u Hizhdah* (Tehran: Karkhana-yi Janab Aqa Mirza 'Ali Asghar, 1911). On the challenges faced by other translators of Landor's book, and that of his Russian counterpart Dmitry Yanchevetsky (1873–1934), see Anna Aslanyan, *Dancing on Ropes: Translators and the Balance of History* (London: Profile, 2021), chap. 16.

147. Thampi, *Indians in China*, chap. 6.

148. John S. Gregory, "British Intervention against the Taiping Rebellion," *Journal of Asian Studies* 19, 1 (1959): 11–24, and Madhavi Thampi, "Indian Soldiers, Policemen and Watchmen in China in the Nineteenth and Early Twentieth Centuries," *China Report* 35, 4 (1999): 403–437. Gregory (16) gives the figure of around 7,000 Indian troops present in 1860.

149. 'Abd al-Shakkur Khan, *Jangnama-i Taipuhu* (Lahore: Matba'-i Ghaniri, 1899).

150. I have relied on Anand A. Yang, Kamal Sheel, and Ranjana Sheel's superb translation in Gadadhar Singh, *Thirteen Months in China: A Subaltern Indian and the Colonial World*, ed. Anand A. Yang (New Delhi: Oxford University Press, 2017). On the print run, see Yang, introduction, 5.

151. On other vernacular Indian military writings from this period, see Nile Green, *Islam and the Army in Colonial India: Sepoy Religion in the Service of Empire* (Cambridge: Cambridge University Press, 2009).

152. Singh, *Thirteen Months*, 292–299.

153. Ibid., 115–117.

154. Ibid., 76–77.

155. Ibid., 195–219.

156. See, for example, ibid., 209, 213, 214, 240, 241, 244, 247, 251, 275.

157. Ibid., 209, 214.

158. Quoted in Kamal Sheel, "India-China 'Connectedness': China and Pan-Asianism in the Late Nineteenth- to Mid-Twentieth-Century Writings in Hindi," in Tansen Sen and Brian Tsui (eds.), *Beyond Pan-Asianism: Connecting China and India, 1840s–1960s* (New York: Oxford University Press, 2020), 160.

159. Ibid., 161.

160. Hindi journal articles on China also began to appear from the 1900s, picking up in the 1930s. See ibid., 156, 164, 168–177.

161. On Singh's sources, see Yang's introduction to Singh, *Thirteen Months*, 8, 173–174n2, 180nn103–106, 181nn116–127.

162. Ibid., 222–223.

163. Ibid., 223.

164. Narayanaprasada Sukula, *Chini Ziban* (Aligarh: Wadiya Sagar Pris, 1902), issued in a first edition of five hundred copies.

165. Ibid., 1.

166. Singh, *Thirteen Months*, 283–287.

167. Yang, introduction, to Singh, *Thirteen Months*, 4. On other accounts of China in Hindi journals from the 1920s and 1930s, see Luzia Savary, *Evolution, Race and Public Spheres in India: Vernacular Concepts and Sciences (1860–1930)* (London: Routledge, 2019), 76–77.

168. Narayan Sen, "China as Viewed by Two Early Bengali Travellers: The Travel Accounts of Indumadhav Mullick and Benoy Kumar Sarkar," *China Report* 43, 4 (2007): 465–484. The Bengali text was published in 1911.

169. Ibid., 472.

170. Ibid.

171. Ibid.

172. Ibid., 471.

173. Raja-i-Rajgan Jagatjit Singh, *Safar-i Chin u Japan u Java* (Lahore: n.p., 1906), and His Highness the Raja-i-Rajgan Jagatjit Singh of Kapurthala, *My Travels in China, Japan and Java, 1903* (London: Hutchinson, 1905); his motivation for writing because of the war is stated explicitly on page v of the latter.

174. Singh, *My Travels in China*, 11–56.

175. Ibid., 35.

176. Ibid.

177. Ibid., 21.

178. Ibid., vi, 19, 30. To avoid misrepresenting Jagatjit Singh's words, I have quoted here from his own English text.

179. Hidayat, *Safarnama*, 98.

180. Ibid., 23–92; the hotel is mentioned on 30–31.

181. Ibid., 23–24, 29–30, 60–61, 64–65, 85, 92.

182. Ibid., 65.

183. Ibid., 27–28, 42, 59–60.

184. Barbara Stöcker-Parnian, "An Unusually Long Way to the Kaaba: Reflexions in the Safarnāma-ye Makka of Mehdiqoli Hedayat," in Ralf Elger and Yavuz Köse (eds.), *Many Ways of Speaking about the Self: Middle Eastern Ego-Documents in Arabic, Persian, and Turkish* (Wiesbaden: Harrassowitz, 2010), 110.

185. Hidayat, *Safarnama,* 44.

186. Ibid., 44, 73.

187. Ibid.

188. Ibid., 44–45.

189. Even so, the *Han Kitab* writers differed from Hidayat in regarding Daoism as heterodox and destructive despite its profundity. Thanks to Jonathan Lipman for this point.

190. Quoted in Hidayat, *Safarnama,* 45. He also subsequently quoted two couplets by Rumi.

191. Ibid., 47–51.

192. Thanks to Jonathan Lipman, and Xi Yang, for interpreting this onomastic riddle. Any errors remain my own.

193. Hidayat, *Safarnama,* 47.

194. Ibid.

195. Thanks again to Jonathan Lipman, who derived this information from a catalogue of Chinese mosques by Wu Jianwei, a Hui scholar from Ningxia. The Tiaozhou Hutong mosque was founded under the late Ming, but entirely reconstructed during the Kangxi period (1661–1722) of the Qing.

196. I have been aided in identifying these works by H. T. Norris, "The *Muṣḥaf* in Beijing's (Bikīn's) Oldest Mosque," *Journal of Qur'anic Studies* 3, 1 (2001): 123–134.

197. Al-Marghinani, *'Ayn al-Hidaya,* trans. Sayyid Amir 'Ali (Lucknow: Munshi Nawwal Kishore, 1896).

198. Mozafar Bakhtiyar, "China," in Geoffrey Roper (ed.), *World Survey of Islamic Manuscripts,* 4 vols. (London: al-Furqan, 1994), 4:86.

199. Ali Merthan Dündar, "An Analysis on the Documents Related to China: Materials in the Ottoman and Republic Archives of Turkey," *Eurasian Studies* (2009): 332, 343.

200. Hidayat, *Safarnama,* 48–51; Abdülaziz Efendi, *Çin'de Dîn-i Mübîn-i İslam* (Istanbul: Mahmut Bey Matbaası, 1901); and Hasan Tahsin, *Çîn'de İslâmiyet* (Istanbul: Tercüman-ı Hakikat Matbaası, 1904).

201. Alexandre Papas, "Voyageurs ottomans et tatars en Extrême-Orient: Un dialogue entre islam, confucianisme et lamaïsme," in Nathalie Clayer and Erdal Kaynar (eds.), *Penser, agir et vivre dans l'empire Ottoman et en Turquie: Études réunies pour François Georgeon* (Louvain: Peeters, 2013).

202. Ibid., 218, 221.

203. Ibid., 221–224.

204. Ibid., 223–224.

205. Ibid. For *abade-i asnam*, Papas gives the more tactful French translation *adorateurs*.

206. Noriko Yamazaki, "Abdürreşid İbrahim's Journey to China: Muslim Communities in the Late Qing as Seen by a Russian-Tatar Intellectual," *Central Asian Survey* 33, 3 (2014): 405–420, esp. 406.

207. 'Abd al-Rashid Ibrahim, *'Alem-i Islam ve Japonya'da Intişar-ı Islamiyet*, 2 vols. (Istanbul: Ahmed Saki Bey Matbaasi, 1910–1911), 1:509–603 on China.

208. Ibid., 552–553, 567–571, and Hidayat, *Safarnama*, 47–51.

209. Hidayat, *Safarnama*, 48, and Yamazaki, "Abdürreşid İbrahim," 407. I have based this translation on Hidayat's statistic of "forty *kurur*"; a Persian (as distinct from an Indian) crore was 50,000, according to Steingass, *Comprehensive Persian-English Dictionary*, 1025.

210. Tarocco, *Cultural Practices*, 25–95.

Chapter 6. China in the Mirrors of Buddhism and Islam

1. Circumstances reconstructed from John Chen, "Islam's Loneliest Cosmopolitan: Badr al-Din Hai Weiliang, the Lucknow-Cairo Connection, and the Circumscription of Islamic Transnationalism," *ReOrient* 3, 2 (2018): 120–139, and Sulayman Nadwi, introduction to Badr al-Din Chini [Hai Weiliang], *Chini Musalman* (Azamgarh: Ma'arif Pris, 1935), i–ii. Thanks to Chen, "Islam's Loneliest Cosmopolitan," 121–122, for making the identification of Badr al-Din as Hai Weiliang, which enabled me in turn to recognize him as the author of *Chini Musalman*.

2. On the phrasebook, see Chen, "Islam's Loneliest Cosmopolitan," 123. On the Commercial Press, see Christopher A. Reed, *Gutenberg in Shanghai: Chinese Print Capitalism, 1876–1937* (Vancouver: University of British Columbia Press, 2007), 212–225. The work that Hai used was the latest in a series of spoken-language guides that were published in the treaty ports as a result of the spread of modern printing, most notably the six-volume guide to Cantonese and English compiled by T'ong Ting-Ku (1832–1892), who worked as the local agent for the Calcutta- and Guangzhou-based Jardine Matheson & Co. See T'ong Ting-Ku, *Ying u Tsap Ts'un; or, The Chinese and English Instructor*, 6 vols. (Canton: n.p., 1862).

3. Madhavi Thampi, *Indians in China, 1800–1949* (New Delhi: Manohar, 2005), 17.

4. Zhang Xing and Tansen Sen, "The Chinese in South Asia," in Tan Chee-Beng (ed.), *The Routledge Handbook of the Chinese Diaspora* (New York: Routledge, 2013), 206.

5. Ibid., 207–213, and Tansen Sen, "Kolkata and China: Some Unexplored Links," *China Report* 43, 4 (2007): 395.

6. Xing and Sen, "Chinese in South Asia."

7. Ibid., 214–218.

8. Ibid., 207.

9. On the large-scale Hakka involvement in Calcutta's tanning industry from the 1910s onward, see Ellen Oxfield, "Still 'Guest People': The Reproduction of Hakka Identity in Calcutta, India," in Nicole Constable (ed.), *Guest People: Hakka Identity in China and Abroad* (Seattle: University of Washington Press, 1996).

10. B. R. Deepak, "The Colonial Connections: Indian and Chinese Nationalists in Japan and China," *China Report* 48, 1–2 (2012): 147–170.

11. Ibid., 150.

12. Roy Bar Sadeh, "Debating Gandhi in *al-Manar* during the 1920s and 1930s," *Comparative Studies of South Asia, Africa and the Middle East* 38, 3 (2018): 491–507, and Brian Tsui, "Decolonization and Revolution: Debating Gandhism in Republican China," *Modern China* 41, 1 (2014): 59–89. More broadly, see Brian Tsui, "The Plea for Asia: Tan Yunshan, Pan-Asianism and Sino-Indian Relations," *China Report* 46, 4 (2010): 353–370.

13. Benoy Kumar Sarkar, *The Chinese Religion through Hindu Eyes: A Study in the Tendencies of Asiatic Mentality* (Shanghai: Commercial Press, 1916). See also Sarkar, *The Beginning of Hindu Culture as World-Power (A.D. 300–600)* (Shanghai: Commercial Press, 1916).

14. Vineeta Sinha, "Benoy Kumar Sarkar (1887–1949)," in Syed Farid Alatas and Vineeta Sinha (eds.), *Sociological Theory beyond the Canon* (London: Palgrave Macmillan, 2017), 303–304.

15. Ibid., 304.

16. Sarkar, *Chinese Religion*, xv–xvi.

17. Ibid., bibliography, xxix–xxxii.

18. Satadru Sen, "Benoy Kumar Sarkar and Japan," *Economic & Political Weekly* 48, 45–46 (2013): 61–70.

19. Sarkar, *Chinese Religion*, 303.

20. Satadru Sen, *Benoy Kumar Sarkar: Restoring the Nation to the World* (London: Routledge, 2015), 1.

21. Sarkar, *Chinese Religion*, 276–280.

22. Ibid., 233–236

23. Ibid., 277.

24. Ibid., 301.

25. Sen, "Kolkata and China," 393–396, and Sinha, "Benoy Kumar Sarkar," 304n2, 306.

26. Carolien Stolte, "Compass Points: Four Indian Cartographies of Asia, c. 1930–55," in Marc Frey and Nicola Spakowski (eds.), *Asianisms: Regionalist Interactions and Asian Integration* (Singapore: National University of Singapore, 2016), 65. Stolte dates Savarkar's initial definition of Hindu-Buddhist unity to 1923.

27. Sisir Kumar Das, "The Controversial Guest: Tagore in China," *China Report* 29, 3 (1993): 237–273, and Chao Ren, "Revisiting Tagore's Visit to China: Nation, Tradition,

and Modernity in China and India in the Early Twentieth Century," *ASIANetwork Exchange* 18, 2 (2011): 112–133.

28. Ren, "Revisiting Tagore's Visit," 114.

29. On the lectures, see Wei Liming, "Historical Significance of Tagore's 1924 China Visit," in Wang Bangwei, Tan Chung, Amiya Dev, and Wei Liming (eds.), *Tagore and China* (Beijing: Central Compilation and Translation Press, 2011); a critical assessment of Xu Zhimo's translations is on 27–29.

30. Quoted ibid., 119.

31. Liming, "Historical Significance," 22–23.

32. Younis Bahri, *Majalat al-Kuwayt wa'l-'Iraq* 2 (1931): 38–43, cited in Gabriel Lavin, "The Airwaves in Arabia, c. 1933–1940," in *Culture Made in Arabia* (Abu Dhabi: Sorbonne University Press, forthcoming). Since 1916, Tagore had been much translated into Arabic, albeit via English.

33. Rabindranath Tagore, *Talks in China: Lectures Delivered in April and May, 1924* (Calcutta, 1925; repr., New Delhi: Rupa, 2002).

34. Ibid., 21–22.

35. Uma Das Gupta, "Sino-Indian Studies at Visva-Bharati University: Story of Cheena-Bhavana, 1921–1937," in Bangwei et al., *Tagore and China*.

36. Tansen Sen, *India, China and the World: A Connected History* (Lanham, Md.: Rowman & Littlefield, 2017), 307–308. Das Gupta notes the school's specific location was Kemendine (now Kyimyindaing), on the outskirts of Rangoon. See Das Gupta, "Sino-Indian Studies," 64.

37. Maung Hba Kyu, *Hku-Hnit-Bhasa-Saka* (Rangoon, 1902).

38. Chia Boon Teat, *Dictionary of Malay, English and Romanized Hokkien Chinese* (Penang: printed by author, 1918), described in Ian Proudfoot, *Early Malay Printed Books* (Kuala Lumpur: Academy of Malay Studies and University of Malaya, 1993), 212–213.

39. Tagore, *Visit to Japan*, 51.

40. On Tagore's reading of Arthur Waley's translations, see Amiya Dev, "Tagore and Classical Chinese Poetry," in Bangwei et al., *Tagore and China*, 296–297.

41. Sen, *India, China and the World*, 307, 373n7.

42. Ibid.

43. Ibid., 308.

44. Tsui, "Plea for Asia."

45. On the travelogue, see Tsui, "Decolonization and Revolution," 74–75.

46. Xuanzang, *Ek Chini Sayyah*.

47. Das Gupta, "Sino-Indian Studies," 65.

48. Tsui, "Plea for Asia," 361.

49. Aryadeva, *Aksara-çatakam: The Hundred Letters: A Madhyamaka Text after Chinese and Tibetan Materials*, ed. and trans. Vasudev Gokhale (Heidelberg: Otto Harrassowitz, 1930). See also Gokhale's short memoir: Vasudev Gokhale, "Early Sinological

Studies at Santiniketan," in Sahitya Akademi (ed.), *Rabindranath Tagore: A Centenary Volume, 1861–1961* (New Delhi: Sahitya Akademi, 1961).

50. R. G. Bhandarkar, "Text of the Inaugural Address," *Annals of the Bhandarkar Oriental Research Institute* 1, 1 (1918): 6.

51. V. V. Gokhale, "The Pañcaskandhaka by Vasubandhu and Its Commentary by Sthiramati," *Annals of the Bhandarkar Oriental Research Institute* 18, 3 (1937): 276–286.

52. Gokhale, "Early Sinological Studies."

53. Sen, *India, China and the World*, 302. As Sen notes, the book drew largely on nineteenth-century (European) scholarship.

54. Hu Shih, "The Indianization of China: A Case Study in Cultural Borrowing," in Shih Hu (ed.), *English Writings of Hu Shih*, 2 vols. (New York: Springer, 2013), 2: 163.

55. Ibid. For an analysis, see Kamal Sheel, "Hu Shih and 'The Indianisation of China': Some Comments on Modern Chinese Discourses on India," *China Report* 50, 3 (2014): 177–188.

56. Kalidas Nag, *Greater India* (Calcutta: Prabasi Press, 1926). The Hindi translation was published as a textbook for the Dayanand Anglo-Vedic College under the title *Visal Bharat ka Itihas* (Lahore: Anusandhana Vibhaga, 1929). On the wider intellectual context, see Susan Bayly, "Imagining 'Greater India': French and Indian Visions of Colonialism in the Indic Mode," *Modern Asian Studies* 38, 3 (2004): 703–744.

57. The dissertation was published as Kalidas Nag, *Les théories diplomatiques de l'Inde ancienne et l'Arthaçâstra* (Paris: Maisonneuve, 1923).

58. Joseph Hackin, "Archaeological Explorations of the Neck of the Khair Khaneh (Near Kabul)," trans. Kalidas Nag, *Journal of the Greater India Society* 3, 1 (1936): 23–35.

59. Kalidas Nag, *India and the Pacific World* (Calcutta: Greater India Society, 1941).

60. On Bagchi's career, I have relied on Suniti Kumar Chatterji, "In Memoriam: Prabodh Chandra Bagchi," in Prabodh Chandra Bagchi, *India and China: Interactions through Buddhism and Diplomacy: A Collection of Essays by Professor Prabodh Chandra Bagchi*, ed. Bangwei Wang and Tansen Sen (London: Anthem Press, 2011), and Akira Yuyama, "Prabodh Chandra Bagchi (1898–1956): A Model in the Beginnings of Indo-sinic Philology," *Annual Report of the International Research Institute for Advanced Buddhology at Soka University* 5 (2002): 137–146.

61. Sylvain Lévi, "Rapport sur une mission dans l'Inde et au Japon," *Comptes Rendus de l'Académie des Inscriptions et Belles-Lettres* (1899): 71–92, and Lévi, "Matériaux japonais pour l'étude du bouddhisme," *Bulletin de la Maison Franco-Japonaise*, série française, 1 (1927): 1–63.

62. Jeannine Auboyer, "Henri Maspero (1883–1945)," *Artibus Asiae* 10, 1 (1947): 61–64. Bagchi's European training in this respect mirrors that of his younger Chinese contemporary, and later colleague, Ji Xianlin (1911–2009), who during the 1930s studied Sanskrit and Pali in Germany. See Tansen Sen, "Introduction: Ji Xianlin and Sino-Indology," *China Report* 48, 1–2 (2012): 1–10.

63. Sen, *India and the World*, 316.

64. Prabodh Chandra Bagchi, "India and China: A Thousand Years of Cultural Re-lations," *Bulletin of the Greater India Society* 2 (1927): 1–42; Bagchi, *Le canon bouddhique en Chine: Les traducteurs et les traductions,* 2 vols. (Paris: Librarie Orientaliste Paul Geuthner, 1927); and Bagchi, *Deux lexiques sanskrit-chinois: Fan Yu Tsa Ming De Li Yen et Fan Yu Ts'ien Tsen Wen De Yi-Tsing,* 2 vols. (Paris: Librarie Orientaliste Paul Geuthner, 1929–1937).

65. This interim conclusion is based on my own bibliographical findings. Three of Bagchi's Bengali essays are translated in his *India and China: Interactions,* 203–216.

66. Prabodh Chandra Bagchi, *India and China: A Thousand Years of Cultural Relations* (Bombay: Hind Kitab, 1944).

67. Gray Tuttle, "Translating Buddhism from Tibetan to Chinese in Early-Twentieth-Century China (1931–1951)," in Matthew T. Kapstein (ed.), *Buddhism between Tibet and China* (Boston: Wisdom, 2009), 241–279. On the larger role of "pan-Buddhism" in Republican China's attempts to reclaim older Qing imperial control over Tibet and surrounding regions, see Gray Tuttle, *Tibetan Buddhists in the Making of Modern China* (New York: Columbia University Press, 2005). Thanks to John Chen for directing me to these readings.

68. On Evans-Wentz, see Donald S. Lopez Jr., *The Tibetan Book of the Dead: A Biography* (Princeton: Princeton University Press, 2011), chaps. 1, 2. For his influence on Chinese translations, see Tuttle, "Translating Buddhism," 242, 246, 255, 261–262.

69. Lama Dawasamdup Kazi, *An English-Tibetan Dictionary: Containing a Vocabulary of Approximately Twenty Thousand Words with Their Tibetan Equivalents* (Calcutta: Baptist Mission Press, 1919).

70. Tuttle, "Translating Buddhism," 242, 261–262, 265, 267, and the romanized phonetic scheme adopted to transcribe Tibetan into Chinese in fig. 4 on 261.

71. Nader Entessar, "The People's Republic of China and Iran: An Overview of Their Relationship," *Asia Quarterly* 1 (1978): 79–88, and Gerald Segal, "China and Afghanistan," *Asian Survey* 21, 11 (1981): 1158–1174.

72. Sayyid Riza 'Ali Zadah (trans.), *Tarikh-i Millal: Chiniyan* (Lahore: Matba'-i Mufid-i 'Am, 1926). The print run of 1,000 copies is stated on the front cover.

73. Ibid., 26.

74. Ibid.

75. Nile Green, "The Afghan Discovery of Buddha: Civilizational History and the Nationalizing of Afghan Antiquity," *International Journal of Middle East Studies* 48, 4 (2016): 47–70.

76. André Godard et al., *Asar-i Atiqah-i Buda'i-yi Bamiyan,* translated into Dari by Ahmad 'Ali Khan [Kuhzad], 2 vols. (Kabul: Anjuman-i Adabiyat-i Kabul, 1937), and Hackin, "Archaeological Explorations."

77. Sima Qian, *Tayan,* translated into Dari by Ahmad 'Ali Kuhzad (Kabul: Anjuman-i Tarikh-i Afghanistan, 1948). This was the section from Sima Qian's famous *Shiji* describing the Han Dynasty embassies sent to the Central Asian kingdom of the Dayuan

(literally, "Great Ionians") in present-day Uzbekistan. Since the Francophone Kuhzad could not read Chinese, he necessarily relied on a previous translation, possibly Édouard Chavannes, *Les mémoires historiques de Se-ma Ts'ien,* 5 vols. (Paris: Ernest Leroux, 1895–1905).

78. "Buzurgan-i Jahan: Kunfusiyus," *Farhang* 4, 1 (1928): 18–25, and "Buzurgan-i Mashriq: Kunfusiyus: Filasuf u Muqanan-i Chin," *Taqaddum* 11 (April 1929): 659–672.

79. "Buzurgan-i Mashriq, 672.

80. Thanks to William Figueroa for this information.

81. Mark E. Botham, "Modern Movements among Chinese Mohammedans," *Muslim World* 13, 3 (1923): 296. Unfortunately, Botham did not specify how many were Persian and how many Arabic, though the latter presumably formed the majority.

82. Shortly after the period covered here, Iran's first ambassador to China (albeit to the Republican capital of Nanjing) wrote a firsthand account based on his year in residence. See Sayyid Mahdi Farrukh, *Yik Sal dar Kishvar-i Asmani-yi Chin* (Tehran: Sharikat-i Sihami, 1952).

83. Hasan Eren, "Annemarie von Gabain (1901–1993)," *Türk Dili* 495 (1993): 213–215, and Seriye Sezen, "Bir Türk Sinologun Gözünden Devrim Öncesinin Çin'i: 'Eski Çin'den Notlar,'" *Ankara Üniversitesi Dil ve Tarih-Coğrafya Fakültesi Dergisi* 51, 2 (2011): 155–167.

84. On the ideological context of the Turkish history thesis, see Umut Uzer, *An Intellectual History of Turkish Nationalism: Between Turkish Ethnicity and Islamic Identity* (Salt Lake City: University of Utah Press, 2016), chaps. 3, 4.

85. Gerd Wädow, "Ein Sinologe in der Türkei: Wolfram Eberhard (1909–1989) und seine Zeit in Ankara (1937–1948)," in Christopher Kubaseck and Günter Seufert (eds.), *Deutsche Wissenschaftler im türkischen Exil: Die Wissenschaftsmigration in die Türkei, 1933–1945* (Würzburg: Ergon Verlag in Kommission, 2016). See also Reşid Rahmeti Arat and Wolfram Eberhard, *Türkische Turfan-Texte,* vol. 7 (Berlin: Verlag der Preußischen Akademie der Wissenschaften, 1936).

86. Wolfram Eberhard, *Çin Tarihi* (Ankara: Türk Tarih Kurumu Basimevi, 1947). On the circumstances in Ankara surrounding the development of Eberhard's Turkic-influence theory, see Wädow, "Ein Sinologe in der Türkei," 247–249.

87. For an overview of these developments, see H. Hilal Sahin, "General Review of Scientific Studies Carried Out in Turkey Relating to History of India," *Türkiyat Mecmuası/Journal of Turkology* 30, 1 (2020): 231–268.

88. Mehmet Fuat Köprülü, "Gazneliler Devrinde Türk Şiiri," *Türk Dili ve Edebiyatı Hakkında Araştırmalar* (1934): 2–32. Subsequent works in this vein include Halis Bıyıktay, *Timurlular Zamanında Hindistan Türk İmparatorluğu* (Ankara: TTK Yayınları, 1941), and Gülbeden, *Hümâyûnnâme,* translated into Turkish by Abdürrab Yelgar (Ankara: TTK Yayınları, 1944).

89. For the Ankara library's contents at that time, see the pioneering Turkish Indological catalogue completed in 1942: Walter Ruben and Meliha Torkak (eds.), *Hint Iptidaîlerinin ve Hinduların Eski ve Yeni Eşya Katalogu* (Ankara: Uzluk, 1942).

90. Wolfram Eberhard, *Türk Alfabesiyle Cince Heceleri Transkripsionu* (Ankara: Sinoloji Enstitütü Nesryati, 1938). For a critical evaluation of Turkish Sinology in the decades after his departure, however, see Eyüp Saritaş, "On the General Characteristics of Sinology Researches in Turkey," *Humanities and Social Sciences* 3, 6 (2015): 293–298.

91. On the journals being subscribed to by Sino-Muslims, see John Chen, "'Just Like Old Friends': The Significance of Southeast Asia to Modern Chinese Islam," *Sojourn* 31, 3 (2016): table 1.

92. Masumi Matsumoto, "Rationalizing Patriotism among Muslim Chinese: The Impact of the Middle East on the *Yuehua* Journal," in Stéphane Dudoignon, Komatsu Hisao, and Kosugi Yasushi (eds.), *Intellectuals in the Modern Islamic World: Transmission, Transformation, Communication* (London: Routledge, 2006).

93. For earlier periods, see Jonathan Lipman, *Familiar Strangers: A History of Muslims in Northwest China* (Seattle: University of Washington Press, 1997).

94. Yuan-lin Tsai, "Pilgrimage and Hui Muslim Identity in the Republican Era," in Kuo Cheng-tian (ed.), *Religion and Nationalism in Chinese Societies* (Amsterdam: Amsterdam University Press, 2017), 185. On the *Chaojin Tuji* itself, see Kristian Petersen, "The Multiple Meanings of Pilgrimage in Sino-Islamic Thought," in Jonathan Lipman (ed.), *Islamic Thought in China: Sino-Muslim Intellectual Evolution from the 17th to the 21st Century* (Edinburgh: Edinburgh University Press, 2016), 93–98.

95. Kristian Petersen, "Shifts in Sino-Islamic Discourse: Modelling Religious Authority through Language and Travel," *Modern Asian Studies* 48, 2 (2014): 366.

96. Wai Yip Ho, "Juli Zhizheng," in David Thomas (ed.), *Christian-Muslim Relations, 1500–1900* (Leiden: Brill), http://dx.doi.org/10.1163/2451-9537_cmrii_COM_32468.

97. Wai Yip Ho, "Bian li mingzheng yulu," in Thomas, *Christian-Muslim Relations*.

98. Murtaza Husayn Sinawi, *Majmu'a-i Ijazat* (Ferozpur: n.p., 1897) which I could not trace.

99. Matsumoto, "Rationalizing Patriotism," 123.

100. Zvi Ben-Dor Benite, "'Nine Years in Egypt': Al-Azhar University and the Arabization of Chinese Islam," *Hagar: Studies in Culture, Polity and Identities* 8, 1 (2008): 123n16.

101. George K. Harris, "Al-Azhar through Chinese Spectacles," *Moslem World* 24, 2 (1934): 178.

102. Ibid. *Yuehua* was founded in 1929 and ran until 1948, issuing 4,000 copies at its height.

103. Benite, "'Nine Years in Egypt,'" 108.

104. For a discussion of the influence of these journals, see Chen, "'Just Like Old Friends,'" whose table 1 contains a complete list of foreign journals received by *Yuehua*. More broadly, see Zvi Ben-Dor Benite, "Taking 'Abduh to China: Chinese-Egyptian Intellectual Contact in the Early Twentieth Century," in James L. Gelvin and Nile Green (eds.), *Global Muslims in the Age of Steam and Print, 1850–1930* (Berkeley: University of California Press, 2014); and especially John Tseh-han Chen, "Islamic Modernism in China: Chinese Muslim Elites, Guomindang Nation-Building, and the Limits of the Global Umma, 1900–1960" (PhD diss., Columbia University, 2018).

105. Chen, "Islamic Modernism," 76.

106. Benite, "'Nine Years in Egypt,'" 112, and Matsumoto, "Rationalizing Patriotism," 133, which gives the date of the library's opening as September 1936.

107. Chen, "'Just Like Old Friends,'" 692, and Matsumoto, "Rationalizing Patriotism," 124.

108. Hai Weiliang, "Indu zhuming Huijiao shiren Ikeba boshi zhi lunzheng [The Famous Indian Poet Iqbal's Political Discussions]," Yuehua 5, 29 (October 25, 1933), cited in Matsumoto, "Rationalizing Patriotism," 141n32.

109. Ghulam Mujtaba is mentioned in numerous Ahmadiyya publications from the 1910s and 1920s. See the list of missionaries in Moslem Sunrise 1, 1 (1921): unpaginated front matter.

110. This section on the Ahmadiyya draws on Zeyneb Hale Eroglu Sager, "Islam in Translation: Muslim Reform and Transnational Networks in Modern China, 1908–1957" (PhD diss., Harvard University, 2016), chap. 5, esp. 178–179.

111. Ibid.

112. Ibid., 179.

113. Ibid.

114. Muhammad Sulaiman Ying Kwang Yu, "Islam in China," Islamic Review 23, 6 (June 1935): 229–238; 23, 7 (July 1935): 242–248; and 23, 8 (August 1935): 281–285.

115. Masumi Matsumoto, "Protestant Christian Missions to Muslims in China and the Islamic Reformist Movement," Annual Reports of the Japanese Association of Middle Eastern Studies 21, 1 (2005): 162.

116. Sager, "Islam in Translation," 193.

117. Hai Weiliang, "Jinggao guonei rexin jiaowu zhi tongbao [A Word of Caution to My Coreligionists at Home Who Eagerly Seek News of Islam outside China]," Yuehua 4, 6 (1932): 11–14, cited and discussed in Chen, "Islamic Modernism," 84.

118. Chen, "Islamic Modernism," 85.

119. Matsumoto, "Protestant Christian Missions," 150, 155–160.

120. Raphael Israeli, "The Cross Battles the Crescent: One Century of Missionary Work among Chinese Muslims (1850–1950)," in Israeli, Islam in China: Religion, Ethnicity, Culture, and Politics (Lanham, Md.: Lexington Books, 2002), 231–233.

121. Ibid., 234.

122. Ibid. Israeli refers to this figure as "Xu Yu-i," which is not a standard romanization. The correct pinyin may be either Xu Yuyi or Xu Youyi. Thanks to Jonathan Lipman for advice.

123. Stefan Henning, "God's Translator: Qu'ran Translation and the Struggle over a Written National Language in 1930s China," Modern China 41, 6 (2015): 636, gives the figure as "about a thirtieth."

124. Ibid., 635–636; and Jin Yijiu, "The Quran in China," Contributions to Asian Studies 17 (1982): 96–101.

125. John Medows Rodwell, preface to El-Kor'an; or, The Koran: Translated from the Arabic, 2nd ed. (London: Bernard Quaritch, 1876), xxiin1.

126. Chiara Betta, "Silas Aaron Hardoon and Cross-Cultural Adaptation in Shanghai," in Jonathan Goldstein (ed.), *The Jews of China*, vol. 1, *Historical and Comparative Perspectives* (Armonk, N.Y.: Sharpe, 1999), 216–229, and Henning, "God's Translator," 636.

127. Henning, "God's Translator," 644–651.

128. Ibid., 636. Wang later translated the medieval Persian *Gulistan* of Sa'di as *Zhen-jing hua-yuan* (*Ethereal Garden*), published by the Beijing Muslim Press in 1947.

129. Marshall Broomhall, *Islam in China: A Neglected Problem* (London: China Inland Mission, 1910).

130. Ma Haiyun, "Patriotic and Pious Muslim Intellectuals in Modern China: The Case of Ma Jian," *American Journal of Islamic Social Sciences* 23, 3 (2006): 54–70.

131. "Makin" was an attempt to Arabize his Chinese name, Ma Jian, rather than an Arabic name as such, hence his appearance in Urdu publications as Machin.

132. Muhammad Makin al-Sini [Ma Jian], *Nazra Jami'a ila Tarikh al-Islam fi al-Sin wa Ahwal al-Muslimin fiha* (Cairo: Matba 'at al-Salafiyya, 1934). Thanks to John Chen for directing me to this source and to Sohaib Baig for supplying scans of Makin.

133. Muhammad Makin [Ma Jian], *Kitab al-Hawar li-Kunfusiyus Faylasuf al-Sin al-Akbar* (Cairo: al-Jami'a al-Islamiyya wa Maktabatuha, 1935). Still, the introduction used Confucius's Latin name; Christian dates; and "Far East" (*Sharq al-Aqsa*), not 'Asia.' Ibid., 5–14. Also Benite, "Taking 'Abduh."

134. Al-Khatib also worked with the Jami'a al-Islamiyya press. On Hai Weiliang's subsequent links with him, see Chen, "Islam's Loneliest Cosmopolitan," 131.

135. Benite, "Taking 'Abduh," 259.

136. Lao Tzu, *Sefer ha-derekh ve-'Orah Mesharim*, translated into Hebrew by Aaron Zeev Aescoly (Jerusalem: R. Mas, 1937). Thanks to an anonymous reader for pointing me to this work.

137. Makin al-Sini [Ma Jian], *Nazra Jami'a*, 2, 5, facing 7, facing 8, facing 9, 40, 66.

138. 'Inayatullah's assessment is summarized in Nadwi, untitled foreword to Chini [Hai Weiliang], *Chini Musalman*, ii.

139. Chen, "Islam's Loneliest Cosmopolitan," 123.

140. Thanks to Jonathan Lipman for advice. Any errors remain my own.

141. Nadwi, untitled foreword to Chini [Hai Weiliang], *Chini Musalman*, i–ii.

142. Ibid., and Chen, "Islam's Loneliest Cosmopolitan," 123.

143. Chen, "Islam's Loneliest Cosmopolitan," 123. Chen rightly notes that Hai "enrolled at Aligarh," though it is worth noting this was not Aligarh Muslim University but Jamia Millia, which was located in the town of Aligarh before it relocated to Delhi in 1925. That Hai's BA was from Jamia is stated on the cover of his Urdu book.

144. Nadwi, untitled foreword to Chini [Hai Weiliang], *Chini Musalman*, ii.

145. The date and place of book's completion are given in Chini [Hai Weiliang], *Chini Musalman*, 2.

146. For example, "Chin ki Tamadduni 'Azmat," *Ma'arif* 5, 6 (June 1920): 452–454; "Tamaddun-i Chin ki Qadamat," *Ma'arif* 9, 1 (January 1922): 67–69; and "Diwar-i Chin," *Ma'arif* 11, 5 (May 1923): 380–381.

147. Mawlwi 'Abd al-Quddus, "Chin mein Isha'at-i Islam," *Ma'arif* 27, 6 (June 1931): 442–451; and 28, 1 (July 1931): 46–57.

148. Muhammad Machin [*sic*], "Chin mein Musulmanon ki Mawjuda Halat," *Ma'arif* 37, 4 (April 1936): 295–302, and Chen, "'Just Like Old Friends,'" 696.

149. Hakim Azhar Dihlawi, *Chin aur Bengal ka Jadu* (Lahore: Sanat Singh & Sons, 1930?). I have had access only to a later reprint: New Delhi: Jasim Buk Dipu, n.d.

150. Masumi Matsumoto, "Sino-Muslims' Identity and Thoughts during the Anti-Japanese War: Impact of the Middle East on Islamic Revival and Reform in China," in *Annals of Japan Association for Middle East Studies* 18, 2 (2003), 42, citing a Chinese report from 1936.

151. Barbara K. Pillsbury, "The Muslim Population of China: Clarifying the Questions of Size and Ethnicity," *Journal of Muslim Minority Affairs* 3, 2 (1981): 35–58. Even in 2020, China's combined Muslim population was probably no higher than 20 or 25 million.

152. Nadwi, untitled foreword to Chini [Hai Weiliang], *Chini Musalman*, i.

153. Katherine Watt, "Thomas Walker Arnold and the Re-Evaluation of Islam, 1864–1930," *Modern Asian Studies* 36, 1 (2002): 55–56.

154. For the China sections in Urdu, see Thomas Walker Arnold, "Isha'at-i Islam Chin aur Majma' al-Jaza'ir Mala'i Mein," in Arnold, *Mazmun* (Aligarh: Matba' Fayz-i 'Am, 1906), 5–16. The Turkish version appeared as Arnold, *İntişar-ı İslam Tarihi* (Istanbul: Yeni Matbaa, 1927).

155. Muhammad Sulaiman Ying Kwang Yu, "Islam in China," *Islamic Review* 23, 6 (1935): 231.

156. Chini [Hai Weiliang], *Chini Musalman*, 1–2.

157. Ibid., 3–38.

158. Muhammad Qasim Zaman, "A Venture in Critical Islamic Historiography and the Significance of Its Failure," *Numen* 41, 1 (1994): 26–50.

159. On parallel developments among Arab historians at this time, see Ahmed El Shamsy, *Rediscovering the Islamic Classics: How Editors and Print Culture Transformed an Intellectual Tradition* (Princeton: Princeton University Press, 2020), chaps. 5 and 8.

161. Sayyid Sulayman Nadwi, *'Arabon ki Jahazrani* (Bombay: Islamik Risarch Asusi'ashun, 1935).

162. Q. Edward Wang, *Inventing China through History: The May Fourth Approach to Historiography* (Albany: State University of New York Press, 2001).

163. Corinne Debaine-Francfort, *The Search for Ancient China* (London: Thames & Hudson, 1999), 13–34.

164. Simon Kaner, "Archaeology in Tokyo," *World Archaeology* 10, 1 (2021): 23. Recently, however, Chinese archaeologists have dislodged Japan's title of ceramic primacy by claiming discoveries of pottery much earlier than Jomon ware.

165. Debaine-Francfort, *The Search for Ancient China*, 30.

166. Wang, *Inventing China*, 160–170.

167. Rudolf Loewenthal, *The Mohammedan Press in China* (Peking: Synodal Commission in China, 1938).

168. Thanks to an anonymous reader for this point.

169. Chen, "'Just Like Old Friends,'" 727.

170. Zvi Ben-Dor Benite, "From 'Literati' to 'Ulama': The Origins of Chinese Muslim Nationalist Historiography," *Nationalism and Ethnic Politics* 9, 4 (2003): 83–109.

171. Benite, "From 'Literati to 'Ulama,'" 99–100.

172. Chini [Hai Weiliang], *Chini Musalman*, 3.

173. Ibid.

174. Ibid., 4.

175. Ibid., 5–6. Hai provided the dates in Christian form.

176. Ibid., 6.

177. Ibid., 7.

178. Ibid., 8.

179. Ibid., 8–9, 92–94.

180. Ibid., 9–10.

181. Ibid., 13.

182. Ibid., 13–14.

183. Ibid., 14.

184. Ibid., 14–15.

185. Ibid., 20–22.

186. Zvi Aziz Ben-Dor [Benite], "'Even unto China': Displacement and Chinese Muslim Myths of Origin," *Bulletin of the Royal Institute for Inter-Faith Studies* (2002–2003): 106–107.

187. Chini [Hai Weiliang], *Chini Musalman*, 14–15.

188. Ibid., 20.

189. See the version by Liu Sanjie translated in Ben-Dor [Benite], "'Even unto China,'" 106–107.

190. Chini [Hai Weiliang], *Chini Musalman*, 22–37.

191. Ibid., 38.

192. Ibid.

193. Ibid., 6.

194. Robert Irwin, *Ibn Khaldun: An Intellectual Biography* (Princeton: Princeton University Press, 2018), chap. 10, esp. 190.

195. 'Abd al-Rahman Ibn Khaldun, *Muqaddima-i Tarikh Ibn Khaldun ka Urdu Tarjuma*, translated into Urdu by Muhammad Insha'allah (Lahore: Matba'-i Hamidiyya, 1904).

196. Chen, "Islamic Modernism," 114, and Arnold Toynbee, *A Journey to China; or, Things Which Are Seen* (London: Constable, 1931).

197. Tamara Chin, "The Invention of the Silk Road, 1877," *Critical Inquiry* 40, 1 (2013): 195n6. The calque neologism *sichou zhi lu* is sometimes abbreviated to *si lu*.

198. Chini [Hai Weiliang], *Chini Musalman*, 111.

199. Ibid., 29.

200. Ibid., 101n.

201. Ibid., 65–76.

202. Ibid. Hai did not specifically name the text, but he noted that it had 1,536 characters (*huruf*). This suggests that it might have been Liu Zhi's *Benjing* (*Root Scripture*), the first section of his *Tianfang Xingli*, of which Ma Lianyuan made an Arabic translation in 1898, giving it the Arabic title *al-Lata'if* (*The Subtleties*). The Chinese and Arabic texts are presented together in Sachiko Murata, William C. Chittick, and Wei-ming Tu, *The Sage Learning of Liu Zhi: Islamic Thought in Confucian Terms* (Cambridge: Harvard University Press, 2009), 15, who remark on "how little [the Arabic translation] reflects the thoroughly Chinese character of Liu's text."

203. Chini [Hai Weiliang], *Chini Musalman*, 65.

204. Ibid., 76.

205. Ibid., 65.

206. As noted earlier, Ma Lianyuan also made an Arabic translation of Liu Zhi's *Benjing*, with the Arabic title *al-Lata'if*.

207. 'Abd al-Hakim Muhammad Nur al-Haqq ibn al-Sayyid Luqman al-Sini, *Sharh al-Lata'if* (1902; repr., Kanpur: Mahmud al-Matabi', 1924), cited in Murata et al., *Sage Learning of Liu Zhi*, 637.

208. The text is edited and translated, with extensive commentary, in Murata et al., *Sage Learning of Liu Zhi*.

209. On "domestication" versus "foreignization," see Anna Aslanyan, *Dancing on Ropes: Translators and the Balance of History* (London: Profile, 2021), 135–144.

210. Chini [Hai Weiliang], *Chini Musalman*, 77.

211. Ibid., 77–87. On these rival movements, see Lipman, *Familiar Strangers*.

212. Chini [Hai Weiliang], *Chini Musalman*, 80, 85.

213. Ibid., 86.

214. Ibid., 94–109.

215. Benite, "From 'Literati' to 'Ulama.'"

216. Chini [Hai Weiliang], *Chini Musalman*, 94.

217. Ibid., 95–97.

218. Ibid., 100.

219. Ibid., 101–104.

220. Ibid., 191; also 14–15.

221. Ibid., 103. Further pointing to the importance of print, Hai gave a list of twenty-one Muslim journals, along with an outline of their development since the 1911 revolution. See ibid., 108–109.

222. Ibid., 104–105.

223. Ibid., 106.

224. On Wang Jingzhai, see Henning, "God's Translator."

225. Chini [Hai Weiliang], *Chini Musalman,* 65.

226. Ibid., 40, 42.

227. Ibid., 88, where the Arabic-script transliteration is given as *tsang ching chi'u.*

228. Ibid., 89–90. In the final two sentences, I have given Hai's Urdu transliterations of Chinese words in the main text, followed by the standard pinyin equivalents in square brackets.

229. Sayyid Asad 'Ali Anwari [Faridabadi], *Sahifa-i Chin, ma' Mukhtasar Tarikh-i Chin wa Halat-i Kanfiyushas* (Delhi: Maktaba-i Jami'a, 1937).

230. Ibid., 148–149. On Arabic translations of Sanskrit classics via English in the 1940s, see Esmat Elhalaby, "Empire and Arab Indology," *Modern Intellectual History* (2021): 1–25.

231. Albeit in complicated transliteration, the names of Giles and Hovelaque appear repeatedly. See, for example, Anwari, *Sahifa,* 26–29, 34, 98–99, 129.

232. Confucius [misattributed], *The Shu King; or, The Chinese Historical Classic, Being an Authentic Record of the Religion, Philosophy, Customs and Government of the Chinese from the Earliest Times,* trans. Walter Gorn Old (Benares: Theosophical Publishing Society, 1904).

233. For other such cases, see Nile Green (ed.), "The Global Occult," special issue of *History of Religions* 54, 4 (2015).

234. 'Abd al-Qadir Sarwari, *Chini aur Japani Afsane* (Hyderabad: Anjuman-i Taraqqi-i Urdu, 1930).

235. W. G. Aston, *Nihongi: Chronicles of Japan from the Earliest Times to A.D. 697* (London: Trübner, 1896), cited in Fazli, *Haqiqat,* 2:224 and drawn on throughout 2: chap. 4.

236. Rui Zhang, "A Look at Chinese Translations of *The Arabian Nights,*" *Clarion* 18 (2015), https://www.bu.edu/clarion/18/rui-zhang.htm.

237. Muhammad Hasan A'zami, *Aj ka Misr* (Lahore: Urdu Akidimi, 1941); A'zami, *al-Mu'jam al-A'zam: 'Arabi Urdu Lughat,* 5 vols. (Hyderabad, Sindh: Idarat Ma'arif Islamiyya, 1946–1953); and A'zami, *Falsafat Iqbal wa al-Thaqafa al-Islamiyya fi al-Hind wa Bakistan* (Cairo: Dar Ihya' al-Kutub al-'Arabiyya, 1950). Shortly afterward, an anthology of Iqbal's poetry was translated into Arabic by Amira Nur al-Din Dawud as *Durar min Shi'r Iqbal: Sha'ir al-Islam wa-Faylasufihi* (Baghdad: Maba'at al-Ma'arif, 1951). Also see Souleymane Diagne, "Achieving Humanity: Convergence between Henri Bergson and Muhammad Iqbal," in Chad Hillier and Basit Koshul (eds.), *Muhammad Iqbal: Essays on the Reconstruction of Modern Muslim Thought* (Edinburgh: Edinburgh University Press, 2015). The Cairo professorship is attested in A'zami, *Aj ka Misr,* 3.

238. Thampi, *Indians in China,* 216.

239. Ibid.

240. Ibid., 17, 215–219.

241. Tansen Sen, "Taixu's Goodwill Mission to India: Reviving the Buddhist Links between China and India," in Nayanjot Lahiri and Upinder Singh (eds.), *Buddhism in Asia: Revival and Reinvention* (New Delhi: Manohar, 2016).

242. Ibid., 308–310.

243. Chen, "'Just Like Old Friends.'"

244. John T. Chen, "Re-Orientation: The Chinese Azharites between Umma and Third World, 1938–55," *Comparative Studies of South Asia, Africa and the Middle East* 34, 1 (2014): 24–51, and Yufeng Mao, "A Muslim Vision for the Chinese Nation: Chinese Pilgrimage Missions to Mecca during World War II," *Journal of Asian Studies* 70, 2 (2011): 373–395.

245. Selçuk Esenbel, "Japan's Global Claim to Asia and the World of Islam: Transnational Nationalism and World Power, 1900–1945," *American Historical Review* 109, 4 (2004): 1145–1146; Kelly A. Hammond, *China's Muslims and Japan's Empire: Centering Islam in World War II* (Chapel Hill: University of North Carolina Press, 2020), chap. 3; and Mikiya Koyagi, "The Hajj by Japanese Muslims in the Interwar Period: Japan's Pan-Asianism and Economic Interests in the Islamic World," *Journal of World History* 24, 4 (2013): 849–876.

246. Derk Bodde, "Japan and the Muslims of China," *Far Eastern Survey* 15, 20 (1946): 311–313.

247. The news appeared in *Kabul* (March 22, 1935), the same journal where the historian Kuhzad translated French archaeological reports on the rediscovery of Afghanistan's Buddhist past. Reports also appeared in Cairo's *al-Fath*, and probably elsewhere. See Bodde, "Japan," 313.

248. On the Arabic and Chinese Gandhi translations, see, respectively, Sadeh, "Debating Gandhi," and Tsui, "Decolonization and Revolution." On the effect of the conflict, see Ramachandra Guha, "An Asian Clash of Civilisations? Revisiting the Sino-Indian Conflict of 1962," *Economic and Political Weekly* 46, 44–45 (2011): 51–61, and, closer to the time, G. Eric Hansen, "The Impact of the Border War on Indian Perceptions of China," *Pacific Affairs* 40, 3–4 (1967): 235–249.

249. Amid a growing secondary literature, see Sen, *India and the World*, chap. 4, and Chung Tan and Ravni Thakur, "Enchantment and Disenchantment: A Sino-Indian Introspection," in Tan Chung (ed.), *Across the Himalayan Gap: An Indian Quest for Understanding China* (New Delhi: Indira Gandhi National Centre for the Arts, 1998).

250. Chen, "Re-Orientation," 24.

251. Ibid.

252. Hai died in Taipei on May 7, 2006, where his funeral was held at the Taipei Grand Mosque. Thanks to John Chen for this information.

253. Badr al-Din Hayy al-Sini [Hai Weiliang], *al-'Alaqat bayn al-'Arab wa al-Sin* (Cairo: Maktabat al-Nahda al-Misriya, 1950), discussed in Chen, "Islam's Loneliest Cosmopolitan," 135–136, and its Urdu predecessor, Sayyid Sulayman Nadwi, *'Arab u Hind ke Ta'luqat* (Allahabad: Hindustan Press, 1930).

254. Muhammad Tawadu' [Pang Shiqian], *al-Sin wa al-Islam* (Cairo: Dar al-Tiba'a wa-al-Nashr al-Islamiyya li-al-Ikhwan al-Muslimin, 1945). The first section (1–35) surveys ancient Chinese history, including the writings of Confucius, Mencius, and Lao

Tzu, before turning to the origins (61–73) and current condition (84–176) of Islam in China. Tawadu' also referenced (62) the writings on Islam in China by the Quaker missionary Isaac Mason (1870–1939). Note that Tawadu''s Chinese name was Pang Shiqian. See Chen, "Re-Orientation," 39–46, which first directed me to Tawadu''s text.

255. Thomas Walker Arnold [Sir Tumas W. Arnuld], *al-Da'wa ila al-Islam: Bahth fi Tarikh Nashr al-'Aqida al-Islamiyya* (Cairo: Maktabat al-Nahda al-Misriyya, 1947).

Conclusions

1. On the conference, its context, and its outcomes, see Michele L. Louro, *Comrades against Imperialism: Nehru, India, and Interwar Internationalism* (Cambridge: Cambridge University Press, 2018); Gopa Sabharwal, "In Search of an Asian Vision: The Asian Relations Conference of 1947," in Andrea Acri, Kashshaf Ghani, Murari K. Jha, and Sraman Mukherjee (eds.), *Imagining Asia(s): Networks, Actors, Sites* (Singapore: ISEAS–Yusof Ishak Institute, 2019); and Tansen Sen, *India, China, and the World: A Connected History* (Lanham, Md.: Rowman & Littlefield, 2017), 338–347.

2. Jawaharlal Nehru, "Asia Finds Herself," in Nehru, "Selected Speeches," *India Quarterly* 45, 4 (1989): 398, 400.

3. Ibid., 396.

4. Definition quoted from Carolien Stolte and Harald Fischer-Tiné, "Imagining Asia in India: Nationalism and Internationalism (ca. 1905–1940)," *Comparative Studies in Society and History* 54, 1 (2012): 65.

5. Sven Saaler and Christopher W. A. Szpilman, introduction to Saaler and Szpilman (eds.), *Pan-Asianism: A Documentary History,* 2 vols. (Lanham, Md.: Rowman & Littlefield, 2011), 1:2.

6. Ibid.

7. Sang Ye and Geremie R. Barmé, "Commemorating Confucius in 1966–67: The Fate of the Confucius Temple, the Kong Mansion and Kong Cemetery," *China Heritage Quarterly* 20 (2009), https://web.archive.org/web/20180414215458/http://www.chinaheritagequarterly.org/scholarship.php?searchterm=020_confucius.inc&issue=020.

8. Rustom Bharucha, *Another Asia: Rabindranath Tagore and Okakura Tenshin* (New Delhi: Oxford University Press, 2006), xvi; Bharucha goes on to note that "Singapore needs 'Asia' in a way that India does not."

9. Ibid. Ironically, but ultimately quite logically, the country where the category "Asian" carries most "discursive weight or political valency" is probably the United States, where "Asian" expanded from a category in Anglophone terminology to state censuses, foreign affairs, academia, and wider society, eventually being absorbed as a primary self-ascription in a way it is not in many regions of Asia itself.

10. Rebecca E. Karl, "Creating Asia: China in the World at the Beginning of the Twentieth Century," *American Historical Review* 103, 4 (1998): 1118.

11. Wang Hui, "The Idea of Asia and Its Ambiguities," *Journal of Asian Studies* 69, 4 (2010): 988.

12. Engseng Ho, "Inter-Asian Concepts for Mobile Societies," *Journal of Asian Studies* 76, 4 (2017): 907; emphasis added.

13. For critical assessments of the increasingly hegemonic Silk Road paradigm, see Tamara Chin, "The Invention of the Silk Road, 1877," *Critical Inquiry* 40, 1 (2013): 194–219; Nile Green, "From the Silk Road to the Railroad (and Back): The Means and Meanings of the Iranian Encounter with China," *Iranian Studies* 48, 2 (2015): 165–192; and Tim Winter, *Geocultural Power: China's Quest to Revive the Silk Roads for the Twenty-first Century* (Chicago: University of Chicago Press, 2019).

14. Sanjay Subrahmanyam, *Europe's India: Words, People, Empires, 1500–1800* (Cambridge: Harvard University Press, 2017), 17.

15. See the summaries of recent cognitive science research in Steven A. Sloman, *The Knowledge Illusion: Why We Never Think Alone* (New York: Riverhead, 2017).

16. Jeremy Adelman, "Words from Jeremy Adelman," in "Discussion: The Futures of Global History," *Journal of Global History* 13, 1 (2018): 20–21.

17. Stefan Tanaka, *Japan's Orient: Rendering Pasts into History* (Berkeley: University of California Press, 1993).

18. Tansen Sen, "The Intricacies of Premodern Asian Connections," *Journal of Asian Studies* 69, 4 (2010): 991. See also Sen, "China-India Studies: Emergence, Development, and State of the Field," *Journal of Asian Studies* 80, 2 (2021): 363–387.

19. On Eurasia as a more effective unit of analysis than a dichotomized Asia and Europe, see Chris Hann, "A Concept of Eurasia," *Current Anthropology* 57, 1 (2016): 1–27, and a critical evaluation by Jeremy Smith and Paul Richardson, "The Myth of Eurasia: A Mess of Regions," *Journal of Borderlands Studies* 32, 1 (2017): 1–6. As Jürgen Renn has recently argued on an even larger scale, "The colonial empires further hastened globalization processes by laying the groundwork for a knowledge economy that enabled the collection of global data." See Renn, *The Evolution of Knowledge: Rethinking Science for the Anthropocene* (Princeton: Princeton University Press, 2020), 279.

20. Gerhard Leitner, Azirah Hashim, and Hans-Georg Wolf (eds.), *Communicating with Asia: The Future of English as a Global Language* (Cambridge: Cambridge University Press, 2019); and Azirah Hashim and Gerhard Leitner (eds.), *English in Southeast Asia and ASEAN: Transformation of Language Habitats* (New York: Routledge, 2020).

21. See Chih-p'ing Chou, "Utopian Language: From Esperanto to the Abolishment of Chinese Characters," in Carlos Yu-Kai Lin and Victor H. Mair (eds.), *Remembering May Fourth: The Movement and Its Centennial Legacy* (Leiden: Brill, 2020); and Ian Rapley, "Sekaigo: Esperanto, International Language, and the Transnational Dimension to Japan's Linguistic Modernity," *Japan Forum* 32, 4 (2020): 511–530.

22. ASEAN Charter, article 34: "The working language of ASEAN shall be English." See https://web.archive.org/web/20151109180154/http://www.asean.org/archive/publications/ASEAN-Charter.pdf. More broadly, see Andy Kirkpatrick, *English as a Lingua*

Franca in ASEAN: A Multilingual Model (Hong Kong: Hong Kong University Press, 2010).

23. Eberhard, *Çin Tarihi*, and Walter Ruben, *Buddhizm Tarihi* (Ankara: Ankara Üniversitesi Dil ve Tarih Coğrafya, 1947). Three years earlier, Ruben had also published with Cemil Ziya Şanbey a Turkish study of ancient Indian history: *Eski Hind Tarihi* (Ankara: İdeal Matbaa, 1944).

24. Laozi, *Taoizm: Dao De Jing*, translated into Turkish by Muhaddere Nabi Özerdim (Ankara: Milli Eğitim Basımevi, 1946).

25. Gerd Wädow, "Ein Sinologe in der Türkei: Wolfram Eberhard (1909–1989) und seine Zeit in Ankara (1937–1948)," in Christopher Kubaseck and Günter Seufert (eds.), *Deutsche Wissenschaftler im türkischen Exil: Die Wissenschaftsmigration in die Türkei, 1933–1945* (Würzburg: Ergon Verlag in Kommission, 2016).

26. Seriye Sezen, "Bir Türk Sinologun Gözünden Devrim Öncesinin Çin'i: 'Eski Çin'den Notlar,'" *Ankara Üniversitesi Dil ve Tarih-Coğrafya Fakültesi Dergisi* 51, 2 (2011): 155–167.

27. H. Hilal Sahin, "General Review of Scientific Studies Carried Out in Turkey Relating to History of India," *Türkiyat Mecmuası/Journal of Turkology* 30, 1 (2020): 231–268, and Sezen, "Bir Türk Sinologun." In 1963, for example, Abidin Itil—one of Ruben's former students—would publish his pioneering Turkish *Sanskrit Klavuzu* (*Guide to Sanskrit*).

BIBLIOGRAPHY
OF PRIMARY SOURCES

Being too numerous to list separately, secondary sources are cited only as notes.

Books and Articles

'Abd al-Quddus, Mawlwi. "Chin mein Isha'at-i Islam." *Ma'arif* 27, 6 (June 1931): 442–451; and 28, 1 (July 1931): 46–57.

'Abdu'l-Bahá and Shoghi Effendi. *Japan Will Turn Ablaze! Tablets of 'Abdu'l-Bahá, Letters of Shoghi Effendi and Historical Notes about Japan.* Tokyo: Bahá'í Publishing Trust, 1974.

Abu, Jamal. *Myama Saga Arthawali.* Surat: n.p., 1892.

Afaqi, Sabir. *Barma mein Urdu.* Islamabad: Muqtadara-i Qawmi Zaban, 1989.

al-Afghani, Jamal al-Din. *Kitab Tatimmat al-Bayan fi Tarikh al-Afghan.* Cairo: Matba'at al-Mawsu'at, 1901.

Ahmad, Ashraf al-Din. *Tabaqa-i Muhsiniyya.* Calcutta: Matba'-i Urdu Ga'id, 1889.

Ahmad, Mirza Ghulam. *Jang-i Muqaddas.* Amritsar: Riyaz Hind Pres, n.d. [c. 1894].

———. *Masih Hindustan mein.* Qadian: Mission Press, 1908.

Ahmad, Sayyid [Khan, Sayyid Ahmad]. *Ahkam-i Ta'am-i Ahl-i Kitab.* Lucknow: Munshi Nawwal Kishore, 1868.

'Ajami, Sayyid Muhammad Ibrahim (trans.). *Japan.* Lahore: Hamidiyya Pres, 1903.

Akbar, Sayyid 'Ali [Khita'i]. *A History of Cathay: A Translation and Linguistic Analysis of a Fifteenth-Century Turkic Manuscript.* Edited and translated by Ildiko Beller-Hann. Bloomington: Indiana University Research Institute for Inner Asian Studies, 1995.

———. *Khita'inama: Sharh-i Mushahidat-i Sayyid 'Ali Akbar Khita'i, Mu'asir-i Shah Isma'il Safawi dar Chin.* Edited by Iraj Afshar. Tehran: Markaz-i Asnad-i Farhangi-yi Asiya, 1979.

Akif, Syed Abu Ahmad. *Reflections of Japan in Pakistani Eyes: An Anthology of Impressionistic Travel Writing about Japan by Pakistani Authors.* Karachi: Na'ay Ufaq, 1992.

'Alam, Mahbub. *Tazkira-i 'Urabi Pasha Mashhur Misri Muhib al-Watan.* Lahore: Paisa Akhbar Press, 1904.

'Alawi, Munshi Amir Ahmad. *Gautam.* Lucknow: Dar al-Nazir Press, 1923.

'Ali, Ahmad [Hmat, U Aung]. *The Burmese Hindustani Conversation Manual.* Mandalay: Ratana Theiddi Press, 1905.

———. *The English, Hindustani and Burmese Manual, in English and Burmese.* Mandalay: India Press, 1905.

'Ali, Hazrat. *Sakhawetnama.* Translated into Burmese by Ismail Hajjo Arif Nana, Ibrahim Ali Naki, and Muhammad Yusuf. Rangoon: n.p., 1898.

'Ali, Mir Ghulam. *'Ilm-i Jughrafiyya.* Calcutta: Calcutta School Book Society Press [?], 1851.

Amritsari, Hafiz 'Abd al-Rahman Sahib. *Safarnama-i Bilad-i Islamiyya.* 2 vols. Lahore: n.d. [c. 1900].

'A.N.G. "Buda." *Farhang* 4, 4–5 (1929): 122–132.

Anonymous. "Budh-Mazhab ki ek Qadim Yadgar Pishawar mein." *Ma'arif* 30, 2 (August 1932): 130–135.

———. "Buddha and Christus." *Calcutta Review* 118, 236 (1904): 256–257.

———. "Buddha as a Moralist." *Calcutta Review* 83, 165 (1886): 36–56.

———. "Buddha as a Philosopher." *Calcutta Review* 84, 167 (1887): 16–35; and 84, 168 (1887): 362–380.

———. "Buddhism and the Sankhya Philosophy." *Calcutta Review* 53, 106 (1871): 191–203.

———. *The Burma Moslem Society.* Rangoon: Burma Moslem Press, 1910.

———. "Buzurgan-i Jahan: Kunfusiyus." *Farhang* 4, 1 (1928): 18–25.

———. "Buzurgan-i Mashriq: Kunfusiyus: Filasuf u Muqanan-i Chin." *Taqaddum* 11 (April 1929): 659–672.

———. "Chin ki Tamadduni 'Azmat." *Ma'arif* 5, 6 (June 1920): 452–454.

———. *Çin Devleti.* Istanbul: Erzincanlı Matba'asï, 1866.

———. "Diwar-i Chin." *Ma'arif* 11, 5 (May 1923): 380–381.

———. "al-Diyana al-Budhiyya." *al-Hilal* 8, 10 (February 1900): 290–295.

———. *Hindii-vachanalankara kyans.* Rangoon: n.p., 1906.

———. "Hindu Priests Coming Over to Burma." National Archives of Myanmar, accession no. 3096 (file 249P, box 194).

———. *Is Mursala mein Nabi Allah Hone ki Dalilen Hain.* Calcutta: Calcutta Christian Tract and Book Society, n.d. [c. 1835].

———. "Japan Opened: Compiled from the *Narrative of the American Expedition to Japan in the Year 1852–53–54.*" *Calcutta Review* 31, 62 (1858): xlix–l.

———. *Jughrafi.* Tehran: Karkhana-yi 'Ali Quli Khan, 188?

———. *Jughrafiyya-yi Kuchak.* Lahore: Mufid-i 'Am Press, 1923.

———. "Literature and Origins of Buddhism." *Calcutta Review* 49, 98 (1869): 83–124.

———. *Mir'at al-Aqalim.* 3rd edition. Calcutta: Calcutta School Book Society, 1839.

————. *Mir'at al-Arz: ya'ni Mukhtasar Jughrafiyya-yi 'Alam*. Kabul: n.p. [Government Press?], 1906.

————. "Mubashhiru al-Budhiyya fi Inkiltira." *al-Hilal* 14, 1 (October 1905): 50–51.

————. *Muhammadi u 'Isawi Din ka Muqabala*. Calcutta: Calcutta Christian Tract and Book Society, n.d. [c. 1835].

————. "Mujasima-ha'i Kulkula dar Afghanistan." *Sharaf* 34 (September 1885): 138–140.

————. *Musalmani Mazhab ko Chor Dene ka Sabab*. Calcutta: Calcutta Christian Tract and Book Society, n.d. [c. 1835].

————. *The Nagoya Muslim Mosque: A Souvenir Booklet Issued in Commemoration of the Opening Ceremony*. Nagoya: Nagoya Turkish Tatar Islamic Association, 1937.

————. "Presses Worked and Newspapers Published." National Archives of Myanmar, accession no. 1223 (file 5P-2, box 35), 2–5.

————. *Qissah-i Faghfur-i Chin*. Bombay: n.p., 1874.

————. *Sacha 'Isa'i: Ramhari aur ek Shakhs Sadhu Apas mein in Baton ki Guftagu Karti [sic] Hain*. Urdu translation from Bengali. Calcutta: Calcutta Christian Tract and Book Society, 1835.

————. "Shama-a'i az Mazhab-i Buda." *Taqaddum* 5 (December 1927): unpaginated.

————. "Sh'ir u Sha'iri-yi Zhapun." *Mihr* 5, 3 (1938).

————. *Tahqiq al-Iman*. Calcutta: Calcutta Christian Tract and Book Society, n.d. [c. 1835].

————. "Tamaddun-i Chin ki Qadamat." *Ma'arif* 9, 1 (January 1922): 67–69.

————. *Tanasukh ki Asliyat*. Lahore: n.p., 1893.

———— [Corcoran, James]. *Tarikh-i Mamalik-i Chin*. Lucknow: Nawwal Kishore, 1864.

————. "Visit by Moslem Missionary." *Straits Times* [Singapore], October 7, 1936.

Anwari, Sayyid Asad 'Ali [Faridabadi], *Sahifa-i Chin, ma' Mukhtasar Tarikh-i Chin wa Halat-i Kanfiyushas*. Delhi: Maktaba-i Jami'a, 1937.

'Aqil, Mu'in al-Din (ed.). "Tazkira-i 'Gulshan-i Sukhan': Barma mein Urdu Sha'iri ka Sunahra Dawr." *Khuda Bakhsh Librari Jarnal* 162 (2010): 27–48.

Araki, Shigeru. *Perusha bungakoshi-ko*. Tokyo: Iwanami Shoten, 1922.

Arat, Reşid Rahmeti, and Wolfram Eberhard. *Türkische Turfan-Texte*, vol. 7. Berlin: Verlag der Preußischen Akademie der Wissenschaften, 1936.

Armstrong, Rev. W. F. "Missions to the Muslims of Burma." *Baptist Missionary Magazine* 89 (1909): 60–62.

Arnold, Edwin. *The Light of Asia, or The Great Renunciation (Mahâbhinishkramana); Being the Life and Teachings of Gautama, as Told in Verse by an Indian Buddhist*. London: Trübner & Co., 1880. Translated into Punjabi by Gurbakhsh Singh Preetlari as *Asia da Chanan*. Lahore: n.p., 1938.

Arnold, Sir Thomas Walker [Arnuld, Sir Tumas W.]. *The Preaching of Islam: A History of the Propagation of the Muslim Faith*. London: A. Constable & Co., 1896; translated into Arabic as *al-Da'wa ila al-Islam: Bahth fi Tarikh Nashr al-'Aqida al-Islamiyya*. Cairo: Maktabat al-Nahda al-Misriyya, 1947.

————. *İntişar-ı İslam Tarihi*. Istanbul: Yeni Matbaa, 1927.

———. "Isha'at-i Islam Chin aur Majma' al-Jaza'ir Mala'i mein." In Arnold, *Mazmun*, 5–16. Aligarh: Matba' Fayz-i 'Am, 1906.

Aryadeva, *Aksara-çatakam: The Hundred Letters: A Madhyamaka Text after Chinese and Tibetan Materials.* Edited and translated by Vasudev Gokhale. Heidelberg: Otto Harrassowitz, 1930.

Ashraf, Khalid. *Qari Sarfaraz Husayn 'Azmi Dihlawi: Shakhsiyat wa Nawul-Nigari.* Delhi: Ejukeshnal, 1990.

Azad, Asrar Ahmad. *Surkh Chin ka Rahnuma.* Delhi: Progresyu, 1944.

Azad, Muhammad Husayn. *Sayr-i Azad.* Lahore: n.p., n.d.

A'zami, Muhammad Hasan. *Aj ka Misr.* Lahore: Urdu Akidimi, 1941.

———. *Falsafat Iqbal wa al-Thaqafa al-Islamiyya fi al-Hind wa Bakistan.* Cairo: Dar Ihya' al-Kutub al-'Arabiyya, 1950.

———. *al-Mu'jam al-A'zam: 'Arabi Urdu Lughat,* 5 vols. Hyderabad, Sindh: Idarat Ma'arif Islamiyya, 1946–1953.

Azhar Dihlawi, Hakim. *Chin aur Bengal ka Jadu.* 1930? Reprint, New Delhi: Jasim Buk Dipu, n.d.

Aziz, M. Abdul. *The Crescent in the Land of the Rising Sun.* London: Blades, East & Blades, 1941.

Badi', Mirza Hasan Khan. *Tarikh-i Basra.* Calcutta: Matba'-yi Habl al-Matin (?), 1914.

Bagchi, Prabodh Chandra. *Le canon bouddhique en Chine: Les traducteurs et les traductions,* 2 vols. Paris: Librarie Orientaliste Paul Geuthner, 1927–1938.

———. *Deux lexiques sanskrit-chinois: Fan Yu Tsa Ming De Li Yen et Fan Yu Ts'ien Tsen Wen De Yi-Tsing,* 2 vols. Paris: Librarie Orientaliste Paul Geuthner, 1929–1937.

———. "India and China: A Thousand Years of Cultural Relations." *Bulletin of the Greater India Society* 2 (1927): 1–42.

———. *India and China: A Thousand Years of Cultural Relations.* Bombay: Hind Kitabs, 1944.

Banakiti, Abu Sulayman Dawud. *A Chinese Chronicle.* Translated by Stephen Weston. London: William Clarke, 1820.

Bandyopadhyaya, Kedaranatha. *Cina yatri.* Allahabad: Indiyana Presa, 1925.

Bandyopadhyaya, Krsnadhana. *Cinera Itihasa.* Calcutta: Stanhope Press, 1865.

Bapat, P. V. *The Sutta Nipāta/Sutanipāto: One of the Oldest Canonical Books of the Buddhism for the First Time Edited in Devanagari Characters.* Poona: Arya Bushana, 1924.

Barilwi, Munshi Nazir Ahmad Sahib. *Waqa'at-i Barhma.* Lahore: Matba'-i Khadim al-Ta'lim Panjab, 1901.

Barlas, Mirza Muhammad Kazim. *Lisan al-Jaza'ir.* Moradabad: Matba'-i Ahsan al-Mataba', 1897.

———. *Sayr-i Darya.* Moradabad: Matba'-i Ahsan al-Mataba', 1867 [printing error for 1898].

Barlas, Missiz [Mrs.]. "Kasatusu ke Garm Chashme." *Salnama-i Saqi-i Dihli: Japan Nambar* 13, 1 (1936): 52–57.

Barlas, Nur al-Hasan. "Guzarish." *Salnama-i Saqi-i Dihli: Japan Nambar* 13, 1 (1936): 6–9.

———. *Japani Bachchun ke Git*, 2 vols. Delhi: Anjuman-i Taraqqi-i Urdu, 1940.

Barlas, Nur al-Hasan, and Shahid Ahmad Dihlawi (eds.). *Salnama-i Saqi-i Dihli: Japan Nambar* 13, 1 (January 1936).

Barr, John. *Taqdis al-Lughat*. Lucknow: n.p., 1873.

Barretto, Joseph. *Kitab-i Shams al-Lughat*. Calcutta: Chapkhana-i Hindustani, 1801.

Basu, Charuchandra (trans.). *Dhammapad*. Calcutta: Wilkins Press, 1904.

Basu, Ramchandra. "Buddha as a Man." *Calcutta Review* 82, 163 (1886): 65–84.

Basu, Ram Ram. *Dharma Pustakera Duta*. Serampore: Mission Press, 1804.

Begbie, William Henry, and Abraham Joseph. *A Vocabulary: English, Burmese, Hindustani & Tamil*. Rangoon: Albion Press, 1877.

Besant, Annie. *Maut Hiku Bhano*. Translated into Sindhi by Khubcandu Mevaramu Makhijani. Hyderabad, Sindh: Bundhu Ashramu, 1926.

Bhathena, B. N. *Kisse-Sanjan: A Palpable Falsehood*. Bombay: Balsara & Co., 1943.

Bhiksu, Santi, and Prabodh Chandra Bagchi (eds.). *Jnanaprasthana-sastra of Katyayainputra Retranslated into Sanskrit from Chinese Version of Hiuan Tsang Sastri*. Santiniketan: Visvabharati, 1955.

Bhuri, Ratanshah Rustomji. *Silonni Tavarikh*. Bombay: Vartaman Chapakhana, 1908.

Bilgrami, Syed Ali. *A Short Guide to the Cave Temples of Elura*. Madras: Asylum Press, 1898.

Bird, George W. *Wanderings in Burma*. Bournemouth: F. J. Bright & Son, 1897.

Biśvasa, Ramanatha. *Lal Chin*. Calcutta: Paryatakaprakaśanabhavana, 1943.

———. *Maranavijayi Chin*. Calcutta: Bhattacharya Sons, 1941.

Bıyıktay, Halis. *Timurlular Zamanında Hindistan Türk İmparatorluğu*. Ankara: TTK Yayınları, 1941.

Brocktorff, Charles Frederick de. *Atlas, ay Majmu'a Kharitat Rasm al-Ard*. Malta: Church Missionary Society, 1835.

Broomhall, Marshall. *Islam in China: A Neglected Problem*. London: China Inland Mission, 1910.

Burgess, James. *The Rock Temples of Elurâ or Verul*. Bombay: Education Society's Press, 1877.

Burnes, Alexander. *Travels into Bokhara*, 3 vols. London: John Murray, 1835.

al-Bustani, Butrus (ed.). *Da'irat al-Ma'arif*. Beirut: n.p., 1876–.

Carus, Paul. *The Gospel of Buddha*. Chicago: Open Court, 1894.

———. *Injil Budha*. Translated into Arabic by 'Isa Mikha'il Saba. Beirut: Maktabat Sadir, 1953.

———. *Kalyanadharma*. Translated into Urdu by Sheobart Lal Varman. Jalandhar: Matba'-i Shahim-i Hind, 1902.

Chabildasa, Ramadasa. *Padmini-Ćampuh*. Edited by Syed Ali Bilgrami. Bombay: n.p., 1888.

Chawwalwala, Chandu Lal (trans.). *Dhampad*. Delhi: Lala Bhansi, 1927.

Chini [al-Sini], Badr al-Din Hayy [Hai Weiliang]. *al-'Alaqat bayn al-'Arab wa al-Sin*. Cairo: Maktabat al-Nahda al-Misriyya, 1950.

Chini, Badr al-Din [Hai Weiliang]. *Chini Musalman*. Azamgarh: Ma'arif Pris, 1935.

———. *Chin wa 'Arab ke Ta'lluqat aur unke Nata'ij: Chin ke 'Arab aur Digar Mamalik-i Islamiyya ke Sath . . . Ta'lluqat*. Karachi: Anjuman-i Taraqqi-i Urdu, 1949.

Cinai, Horamajaji Pharammaji. *Cina ane Ingalanda Khatena Veparanum Ganita Pusataka*. Bombay: Daphtara Aśakara Chapakhannammam Chapaiuñche, 1860.

———. *The Commercial Calculator; or, Tables of Exchange between England and China, China and Calcutta & China and Bombay*. Bombay: Samachar Press, 1851.

Clift, Horace William. *First Geography for Natives; or, Guide to the Map of the World*. Calcutta: Calcutta School Book Society, 1836.

Confucius [misattributed]. *The Shu King; or, The Chinese Historical Classic, Being an Authentic Record of the Religion, Philosophy, Customs and Government of the Chinese from the Earliest Times*. Translated by Walter Gorn Old. Benares: Theosophical Publishing Society, 1904.

Coomaraswamy, Ananda Kentish. *Buddha and the Gospel of Buddhism*. London: Harrap, 1916.

Corcoran, James [Karkuran, Jaymz]. *Tarikh-i Mamalik-i Chin aur Dusre Mulkon aur Qawmon ki jo Farman Bardar ya Bajguzar Faghfur-i Khata ke Hain: Ibtida-yi Nawabadi-yi Dunya ba'd Tufan-i Nuh se*, 2 vols. Calcutta: Baptist Missionary Society, 1848–1852.

Das, Nobin Chandra. *The Miracles of Buddha: Being a Translation in English Verse from Kshemendra's Kalpalata*. Calcutta: Hare Press, 1895.

———. *A Note on the Ancient Geography of Asia, Compiled from Válmiki-Rámáyana*. Calcutta: Buddhist Text Society of India, 1896.

Das, Sarat Chandra (trans.). *Bodhisattvabadana Kalpalata: Akhanda*. Calcutta: n.p., 1912–1916.

———. *Indian Pandits in the Land of Snow*. Edited by Nobin Chandra Das. Calcutta: Baptist Mission Press, 1893.

Davids, T. W. Rhys. *Buddhism: Being a Sketch of the Life and Teachings of Gautama, the Buddha*. London: Society for Promoting Christian Knowledge, 1877.

———. *Buddhist India* (1903). Translated into Urdu by Mawlwi Sayyid Sajjad as *Buddhisti Hind*. Hyderabad: Dar al-Tab'-i Jami'a-i 'Usmaniyya, 1922.

———. "Buddhist India: Story of the Nations." *Calcutta Review* 118, 236 (1904): 258–259.

———. *Dharma Buddha*. Translated into Urdu by Lala Śrirama. Moradabad: n.p., 1889.

Demırhan, General Pertev. *Japonlarin Asil Kuvveti: Japonlar Niçin ve Nasil Yükseldi?* Istanbul: Cumhuriyet Matbaasi, 1937.

Devji, Prakash. *Budh Devji ki Sawanih 'Umri*. Lahore: Mercantile Press, 1922.

Dey, Mukul Chandra. *My Pilgrimages to Ajanta and Bagh*. New York: George H. Doran, 1925.

Dhabar, H. K. *Chin Desh: Containing a Succinct View of the Moral and Social Character, Manners, Customs, Language and Religion of Its Inhabitants*. Bombay: Union Press, 1892.

Dihlawi, Muhammad Sarfaraz Khan 'Azmi. *Muballigh-i Islam ki Mumalik-i Japan, Inglistan u Barma wa Ghaira mein: Tablighi Sargarmiyon ka Tazkira*. Delhi: Qari Buk Dipu, n.d. [c. 1925].

Dihlewi, Nusret 'Ali Han. *Çin ü Maçin*. Istanbul: Hurshid Matba'asï, 1902.

Din, Ahmad. *A'yina-i Japan*. Lahore: Khadim al-Ta'lim Pres, 1901.

al-Din, Mawlwi Fazl. *Baha'i Mazhab ki Haqiqat*. Qadian: Manijar Buk Dipo, 1925.

Duncan, George. *Jughrafiyya: Hissa Awwal: A'ishya*. Translated into Urdu by 'Abd al-Razzaq. Madras: Foster Press, 1877.

Dündar, Ali Merthan, and Nobuo Misawa (eds.). *Books in Tatar-Turkish Printed by Tokyo'da Matbaa-i İslamiye (1930–38)*. Tokyo: Toyo University, Asian Cultures Research Institute, 2010 (digitized texts on CD-ROM).

Eberhard, Wolfram. *Çin Tarihi*. Ankara: Türk Tarih Kurumu Basimevi, 1947.

———. *Türk Alfabesiyle Cince Heceleri Transkripsionu*. Ankara: Sinoloji Enstitütü Nesryati, 1938.

Edwards, William. *Jam-i Jahan-numa*. Translated into Urdu by Babu Shiv Parshad. Lucknow: Nawwal Kishore, 1860.

Efendi, Abdülaziz. *Çin'de Dîn-i Mübîn-i İslam*. Istanbul: Mahmut Bey Matbaası, 1901.

Ekber, Ali. *Tercüme-i Tarih-i Nevadir-i Çin Maçin*. Istanbul: Tophane-i Amire İstihkam Alayları Litografya Destgahı, 1854.

Farrukh, Sayyid Mahdi. *Yik Sal dar Kishwar-i Asmani-yi Chin*. Tehran: Sharikat-i Sihami, 1952.

Farrukhi, Mawlana. *Ma'sir-i Hamidi*. Agra: Matba'-i Mufid-i 'Am, 1896.

Fasih, Ghulam Qadir. *Halat-i Chin*. 1890. Reprint, Lahore: Munshi Fayz 'Ali Malik, 1904.

——— (trans.). *Ka'unt af Manti Kristu ya Motiyan ka Jazira*. Sialkot: Punjab Gazette Press, n.d.

Fatehali, Hanifa Rashid. "Japan Tis Baras mein." *Salnama-i Saqi-i Dihli, Japan Nambar* 13, 1 (1936): 42–46.

Fazl, Muhammad Husayn. *Mukammil Mukhabarat-i Rus u Japan*. Moradabad: n.p., 1904.

Fazli, Shaykh Muhammad Badr al-Islam. *Anokhe Afsane*. Panipat: Hali Akaidmi, 1938.

———. *Haqiqat-i Japan*, 2 vols. Delhi: Anjuman-i Taraqqi-i Urdu, 1934.

——— (trans.). *Namiku: Japan ka Sab se Mashhur Nawal*. Delhi: 'Ilmi Pris, 1946.

———. "Tasirat ki Ek Jhalk." *Salnama-i Saqi-i Dihli: Japan Nambar* 13, 1 (1936): 16–23.

Forsyth, Sir Thomas Douglas [Forsayath, Ti Di]. *Safarnama-i Ti Di Forsayath Kamishnar sabaq Jalandhar babat-i Safar-i Yarqand*. Lucknow: Munshi Nawwal Kishore, 1872.

Fujimoto, Taize. *The Nightside of Japan*. London: T. W. Laurie, 1914.

Furukawa, Nobuyoshi. *Perushia-kiko*. Tokyo: n.p., 1890. Translated into Farsi by Kinji Eura and Hashim Rajabzada as *Safarnama-yi Furukawa*. Tehran: n.p., 2005.

Gamo, Reï'ichi [Gamu, Prafisar R.]. "Sakura ka Phul." *Salnama-i Saqi-i Dihli: Japan Nambar* 13, 1 (1936): 47–52.

Gandhi, Mohandas Karamchand. *An Autobiography: The Story of My Experiments with Truth*. Translated by Mahadev Desai. 1949. Reprint, Boston: Beacon Press, 1993.

Ghouse, Muhammad. *Intustani-Tamizh Vokabileri*. 1882. Reprint, Rangoon: n.p., 1885.

Gidwani, Asudomalu Tekchandu. *Budhisatva*. Hyderabad, Sindh: Jethmal Parsram Gulraj, 1927.

Godard, André, Madame [Yedda] Godard, and Joseph Hackin. *Asar-i Atiqa-yi Buda'i-yi Bamiyan*, 2 vols. Translated into Dari by Ahmad 'Ali Khan [Kuhzad]. Kabul: Anjuman-i Adabi-yi Kabul, 1936.

Gondvi, Asghar. *Tuhfa-i Cin*. Allahabad: Indiyan Pres, 1934.

Guimet, Émile, and Gustave Le Bon. *Mirages indiens: De Ceylan au Népal, 1876–1886*. Paris: Phébus, 1992.

Gülbeden [Gulbadan Begum]. *Hümâyûnnâme*. Translated into Turkish by Abdürrab Yelgar. Ankara: TTK Yayınları, 1944.

Haci Halife, Mustafa ibn 'Abdullah [Katib Çelebi]. *Cihan-nüma*. Istanbul: Ibrahim Müteferrika, 1732.

Hackin, Joseph. "Archaeological Explorations of the Neck of the Khair Khaneh (Near Kabul)." Translated by Kalidas Nag. *Journal of the Greater India Society* 3, 1 (1936): 23–35.

Haggard, H. Rider [Hagird, Ra'idar]. *Sayr-i Zulmat ba Taswir*. Translated into Urdu by Mawlwi Zafar 'Ali Khan. Hyderabad: Matba'-i Shams, 1900.

Hajari, Umakanta. *Nabya Japana o Rusha Japana Yuddhera Itihasa*. Calcutta: Divine Press, 1907.

Hamdam, Babu. *Japan da Bhuñcha*. Lahore: Ram Das Bhatia, 1923.

Hasan Tahsin. *Çîn'de İslâmiyet*. Istanbul: Tercüman-ı Hakikat Matbaası, 1904.

al-Hayy, Mawlwi 'Abd. *'Aqd al-Fara'iz fi Nazm al-'Aqa'id*. Rangoon: Burma Muslim Press, 1910.

———. *al-Mudafa' al-Illahiyya fi al-Radd 'ila al-Babiyya*. Delhi: Matba'-i Ansari, 1910.

———. *Musulmanan-i Barhma aur Ta'lim*. Rangoon: Matba'-i Muhammad Ibrahim, 1918.

Hazarah, Fayz Muhammad Katib. *The History of Afghanistan: Fayz Muhammad Katib Hazarah's Siraj al-Tawarikh*. Translated by Robert McChesney and Mohammad Mehdi Khorrami, 6 vols. Leiden: Brill, 2013–2016.

Hedin, Sven. *The Silk Road*. London: George Routledge & Sons, 1938. Translated into Japanese by Yokichi Takayama as *Sekishoku ruto tohaki*. Tokyo: Ikuseisha, 1939.

Hidayat, Mahdi Quli. *Safarnama-yi Tasharruf bih Makka-yi Mu'azzama*. Tehran: Chapkhana-yi Majlis, n.d. [c. 1945].

Hko, Maung ['Abbas, Mirza]. *Nuri Taw Kyan*. Moulmein: n.p., 1889.

Hobart-Hampden, Ernest Miles, and Sir Harold George Parlett. *An English-Japanese Dictionary of the Spoken Language*. Yokohama: Kelly & Walsh, 1904.

Honjuku, Ienori. "A Sea Voyage to the Persian Gulf (1880)." Translated by Yukie Suehiro and Michael Penn. *Shingetsu Electronic Journal of Japanese-Islamic Relations* 2 (2007): 40–54.

Husayn, Babu Khadim. *Jang-i Rus u Japan: al-Ma'ruf bih Mikadunama Manzum*. Ambala: Impiriyal Printing Warks, 1905.

Husayni, Fazlullah. "Safarnama-yi Hind, Kashmir u Barma (Guzarish-i Safar-i Navisanda bih Hind u Barma ta'i Salha-yi 1290–1294 Q.)." Edited by Firishta Kushki. *Payam-i Baharistan* (Fall 2011): 709–781.

Ibn 'Abd al-'Aziz, Muhyi al-Din. *Faza'il al-Shuhur*. Rangoon: n.p., 1896.

———. *Shajarat al-Iman*. Rangoon: n.p., 1896.

Ibn Battuta. *'Aja'ib al-Asfar Shaykh Ibn Batuta ka Safarnama*. Translated into Urdu by Khan Sahib Mawlwi Muhammad Husayn. Ferozpur: Rafa-i 'Am Lahawr, 1898.

———. *The Travels of Ibn Battutah*. Translated by Samuel Lee. London: Oriental Translation Committee, 1829.

Ibn Khaldun, 'Abd al-Rahman. *Muqaddima-i Tarikh Ibn Khaldun ka Urdu Tarjuma*. Translated into Urdu by Muhammad Insha'allah. Lahore: Matba'-i Hamidiyya, 1904.

Ibrahim, 'Abd al-Rashid. *'Alem-i Islam ve Japonya'da Intişar-ı Islamiyet*, 2 vols. Istanbul: Ahmed Saki Bey Matbaasi, 1910–1911. Partially translated as François Georgeon with Işık Tamdoğan-Abel, *Abdürrechid Ibrahim: Un tatar au Japon: Voyage en Asie (1908–1910)*. Paris: Sindbad-Actes Sud, 2004.

Ibrahim, Muhammad. *al-Hukm al-Salat: Chivalkar*. Bombay: n.p., 1890.

———. *Jang-i Rus u Japan*. Moradabad: n.p, 1904.

Ibrahim, Muhammad Rabi' Ibn-Muhammad. *Safina-yi Sulaymani: Safarnama-yi Safir-i Iran bih Siyam*. Edited by 'Abbas Faruqi. Tehran: Danishgah-i Tihran, 1999.

'Imad al-Saltanah, Husayn Quli Mirza. *Kitab-i Mir'at al-'Alam dar 'Ilm-i Hayat wa Jughrafiyya*. Tehran: n.p., 1897.

Inouye, Jukichi. *Home Life in Tokyo*. Tokyo: Tokyo Printing Co., 1910.

Iqbal, Muhammad. *Durar min Shi'r Iqbal: Sha'ir al-Islam wa Faylasufihi*. Translated into Arabic by Amira Nur al-Din Dasud. Baghdad: Maba'at al-Ma'arif, 1951.

———. *Kulliyat-i Ash'ar-i Farsi-yi Mawlana Iqbal Lahawri*. Tehran: Kitabkhana-yi Sana'i, 1964.

Ishwardas, Damodar. *Cinani Musaphari*. Bombay: Nowrojee Framjee, 1868.

Itribi, Abu al-'Izz, and 'Abd al-'Aziz Hamad. *Nubdhah 'an al-Sin*. 1901. Reprint, Cairo: Mu'assasah Hindawi, 2015.

al-Jabbar, Mawlwi 'Abd. *Jawab Fawt al-Iman ka*. Calcutta: n.p., 1843.

Jagatjit Singh, Raja-i-Rajgan. *My Travels in China, Japan and Java*. London: Hutchinson, 1905.

———. *Safar-i Chin u Japan u Jawa*. Lahore: Matba'-i Guru Gobind Singh Pres, 1906.

Jang, Bahadur Yar. *Siyahat-i Mamalik-i Islamiyya: Bahadur Yar Jang ka Ruznamcha*. Karachi: Bahadur Yar Jang Akadmi, 1988.

Jarjawi, 'Ali Ahmad. *al-Rihla al-Yabaniyya*. Cairo: Matba' al-Irshad, 1910.

———. *Safarnama-i Japan: Ek Musalman Sayyah 'Ali Ahmad Jarjawi Aiditar Akhbar al-Irshad Qahirah (Misr) ke Safar-i Japan ke Halat*. Translated into Urdu by Hasan Miyan Phulwari and Muhammad Insha'allah. Lahore: Hamidiyya Stim Pres, 1908.

al-Jawhari, Isma'il ibn Hammad, et al. *Kitab al-Surah min al-Sihah dar Lughat-i 'Arabi Mubayyina bih Farsi*. Calcutta: Matba'-i Mawlwi Shukr Allah, 1812–1815.

Jawnpuri, Mawlana Karamat 'Ali. *Bay'at-i Tawba*. Calcutta: n.p., 1838.

Judson, Adoniram. *Judson's English and Burmese Dictionary*. Rangoon: W. H. Sloan for the American Baptist Mission Press, 1877.

Kaccayana. *Kachchayano's Pali Grammar: Translated and Arranged on European Models; with Chrestomathy and Vocabulary*. Translated by Francis Mason. Toungoo: Institute Press, 1868.

Kamal-ud-Din, Khwaja. *Islam to East and West: A Collection of Lectures Given in Different Countries*. Lahore: Woking Muslim Mission and Literary Trust, 1935.

Karl, Jahn, ed. *Die Chinageschichte des Rašid ad-Din (Persische Version, aus der Bibliothek des Topkapi Sarayi, Hazine, Nr. 1653. Arabische Version "Fragment," aus der Bibliothek der Royal Asiatic Society, A. 27)*. Vienna: Böhlau, 1971.

Kasama, Akio. *Sabaku no kuni: Perushiya, Toruko, Arabiya*. Tokyo: n.p., 1935. Translated into Farsi by Hashim Rajabzada as *Safarnama wa Khatirat-i Aki'u Kazama: Nakhustin Wazir-Mukhtar-i Zhapun dar Iran*. Tehran: Anjuman-i Asar wa Mafakhir-i Farhangi, 2001.

Kashani, Mirza Sayyid Hasan. *Mukalima-yi Sayyah-i Irani ba Shakhs-i Hindi*. Edited by Ghulam Husayn Mirza-Salih. Tehran: Kawir, 2001.

Kazi, Lama Dawasamdup. *An English-Tibetan Dictionary: Containing a Vocabulary of Approximately Twenty Thousand Words with Their Tibetan Equivalents*. Calcutta: Baptist Mission Press, 1919.

Kazimi, Tamkin Sahib. "Maghar Illura." *Ma'arif* 18, 4 (October 1926): 261–274.

Khan, 'Abd al-Shakkur. *Jangnama-i Taipuhu*. Lahore: Matba'-i Ghaniri, 1899.

Khan, Aftab Ahmad. *Ripurt Mut'alliq Ijlas Bist u Siwwum-i Al Indiya Muhammadan Anglu Ariyintal Ijukeshnal Kanfarans ba-muqam-i Rangun Mun'aqidah 29, 30, 31 Disambar 1909*. Aligarh: Matba'-i Ahmadi, 1910.

Khan, 'Ali Asghar (trans.). "Sha'iri dar Japan." *'Ayina-yi 'Irfan* 85 (1937) to 91 (1938).

Khan, Farangi [aka Zaman, Paulo/Muhammad]. *Tarikh-i Chin*. In *Mirat al-Zaman dar Tarikh-i Chin u Machin u Japan*. Compiled by Mirza Muhammad Malik al-Kuttab Shirazi. Bombay: Dutt Prasad Press, 1893. (See also Khan, Muhammad Zaman.)

Khan, Mawlwi Zafar 'Ali. *Jang-i Rus u Japan*. Hyderabad: Matba'-i Akhtar-i Dakan, 1905.

Khan, Muhammad Shafi' al-Din. *Chin u Chini*. Moradabad: Shams al-Mataba', 1897.

Khan, Muhammad Zaman [Khan, Farangi]. *Tarikh-i Chin.* Calcutta: Baptist Mission Press for Aligarh Scientific Society, 1864.

Khan, Sharaf al-Din Ahmad. *Saintalis Wafadar-i Japan.* Rampur: n.p., 1904.

Khan, Siddiq Hasan. *Luqtat al-'Ajlan mimma Tamassu ila Ma'rifatihi Hajat al-Insan wa fi Akhiriha Khabi'at al-Akwan fi Iftiraq al-Umam 'ala al-Madhahib wa al-Adyan.* Istanbul: Matba'at al-Jawa'ib, 1879.

Köprülü, Mehmet Fuat. "Gazneliler Devrinde Türk Şiiri." *Türk Dili ve Edebiyatı Hakkında Araştırmalar* (1934): 2–32.

Kosambi, Dharmanand. *Dharmanand Kosambi: The Essential Writings.* Translated and edited by Meera Kosambi. Ranikhet: Permanent Black, 2010.

Kuhzad, Ahmad 'Ali. "Kashf-i Mutun-i Qadima-yi Sanskrit dar Bamiyan." *Aryana* 2, 7 (July 1944): 1–7.

Kulcalı, 'Abd al-'Aziz. *Çîn'de Dîn-i Mübîn-i İslâm ve Çîn Müslümânları.* Istanbul: Mahmud Beg, 1901.

Kushal, Pandit Ramnath. *Mahatma Bodh ke Mukhtasar Sawanih 'Umri.* Lahore: Khadim al-Ta'lim, 1892.

Kushan, Isma'il. *Impiraturi-yi Zhapun: az Badw-i Tashkil ta Kunun.* Tehran: Kitabfirushi-yi Danish, 1938.

Lakhnawi, Pandit Brij Narayan Chakbast. *Muraqqa'-i 'Ibrat u Khak-i Hind.* Lucknow: Matba'-i Fakhr al-Mataba', 1909.

Landor, Arnold Henry Savage. *China and the Allies.* London: Heinemann, 1901. Translated into Farsi as *Tarikh-i Jang-i Chin ba Duwwal-i Muttahida-i Urup dar Sal-i Yikhazar u Sisad u Hizhdah.* Tehran: Karkhana-yi Janab Aqa Mirza 'Ali Asghar, 1911.

Lane-Poole, Stanley. *The Moors in Spain.* London: T. Fisher Unwin, 1887. Translated into Urdu by Muhammad Hamid 'Ali as *Karnama-i Mur, ya Musulmanun ki Hazar Sala Hukumat-i Yurap mein, ya'ni Tarikh-i Andulus Urdu.* Lahore: Rahmani Press, 1894.

Laozi. *Taoizm: Dao De Jing.* Translated into Turkish by Muhaddere Nabi Özerdim. Ankara: Milli Eğitim Basımevi, 1946.

Le Bon, Gustav. *Les Civilisations de l'Inde.* Paris: Firmin-Didot, 1887. Translated into Urdu by Sayyid 'Ali Bilgrami as *Tamaddun-i Hind.* Agra: Matba'-i Shamsi, 1913.

Lee, Samuel, ed. and trans. *Controversial Tracts on Christianity and Mohammedanism by the Late Rev. Henry Martyn and Some of the Most Eminent Writers of Persia.* Cambridge, U.K.: J. Smith, 1824.

Lévi, Sylvain. "Matériaux japonais pour l'étude du bouddhisme." *Bulletin de la Maison Franco-Japonaise,* série française, 1 (1927): 1–63.

———. "Notes sur des manuscrits sanscrits provenant de Bamiyan (Afghanistan) et de Gilgit (Cachemire)." *Journal Asiatique* 220 (1932): 1–45.

———. "Rapport sur une mission dans l'Inde et au Japon." *Comptes Rendus de l'Académie des Inscriptions et Belles-Lettres* (1899): 71–92.

Lillie, Arthur. "Buddha and Early Buddhism." *Calcutta Review* 75, 149 (1882): xix.

Liu Zhi. *Benjing*. Translated into English by Sachiko Murata, William C. Chittick, and Wei-ming Tu as *The Sage Learning of Liu Zhi: Islamic Thought in Confucian Terms*. Cambridge: Harvard University Press, 2009.

Long, J. "Indian Buddhism: Its Origin and Diffusion." *Calcutta Review* 4, 8 (1845): 241–281.

Loti, Pierre *Japoneries d'automne*. Paris: Calmann Lévy, 1893. Translated into Ottoman Turkish by M. Saffet as *Japonya Seyahatnamesi*. Kostantiniye [Istanbul]: Matbaa-i Ebüzziya, 1893.

MacDonald, K. S. (ed.). "Story of Barlaam and Joasaph, Buddhism and Christianity." *Calcutta Review* 102, 203 (1896): x–xi.

Machin, Muhammad [Muhammad Makin/Ma Jian]. "Chin mein Musulmanon ki Mawjuda Halat." *Ma'arif* 37, 4 (April 1936): 295–302.

Makin, Muhammad [Ma Jian]. *Kitab al-Hawar li-Kunfusiyus Faylasuf al-Sin al-Akbar*. Cairo: al-Jami'a al-Islamiyya wa Maktabatuha, 1935.

———. *Nazra Jami'a ila Tarikh al-Islam fi al-Sin wa Ahwal al-Muslimin fiha*. Cairo: al-Matba'at al-Salafiyya, 1934.

Malikiyans, Mata'us Khan. *Mamlikat-i Shams-i Tali' ya Dawlat-i Zhapun*. Tehran: Dar al-Taba'a-i Farus, 1904.

Malkani, Naraindas Rattanmal (trans.). *Dhampadu*. Hyderabad, Sindh: Bundhu Ashramu, 1926.

Mallik, Indumadhav. *Cin Bhraman*. Calcutta: S. C. Mazumdar, 1911.

Malte-Brun, Conrad. *al-Jughrafiyya al-'Umumiyya*. Translated into Arabic by Rifa'at Rifa' al-Tahtawi, vols. 1, 3. Cairo: Matba'at Bulaq, 1834.

Maragha'i, Zayn al-'Abidin. *Siyahatnama-yi Ibrahim Beg*, 2 vols. Calcutta: Matba'-yi Habl al-Matin, 1906–1909.

Marsden, Edmund, and Thomas Alford Smith. *Geography for Junior and Senior Classes*. London: Macmillan, 1921. Translated into Urdu by Mawlwi Sayyid Hashimi Sahib Faridabadi as *Jughrafiyya-i 'Alam*, 2 vols. Hyderabad: Dar al-Taba'-i 'Usmaniyya, 1924.

Marshman, John Clark. *The History of India from Remote Antiquity to the Accession of the Mogul Dynasty*. Serampore: Baptist Mission Press, 1837. Translated into Bengali by Gopal Lal Mitra as *Bharatabarsera Itihasa*. Serampore: Baptist Mission Press, 1840. Translated into Urdu by Mawlwi 'Abd al-Rahman as *Tarikh-i Hindustan*. Serampore: Baptist Mission Press, 1859.

Marshman, Joshua. *Bhedabheda*. Serampore: Mission Press, 1807.

——— (trans.). *Clavis Sinica: Elements of Chinese Grammar; With a Preliminary Dissertation on the Characters, and the Colloquial Medium of the Chinese, and an Appendix Containing the Ta-Hyoh of Confucius with a Translation*. Serampore: Mission Press, 1814.

———. *The Works of Confucius: Containing the Original Text, with a Translation*. Serampore: Mission Press, 1809.

Masood, Syed Ross. *Japan and Its Educational System: Being a Report Compiled for the Government of His Exalted Highness the Nizam.* Hyderabad: Government Central Press, 1923.

———— [Mas'ud, Sayyid Ras]. *Japan aur uska Ta'limi Nazm u Nasq.* Aligarh: Anjuman-i Taraqqi-i Urdu, 1925.

————. *Ruh-i Japan.* Hyderabad: Matb'a-i Dar al-Matba'-i Sarkar-i 'Ali, 1926.

————. *Travels in Japan: Diary of an Exploring Mission.* Edited by Jalil Ahmad Kidwai. 1922. Reprint, Karachi: Ross Masood Education and Culture Society of Pakistan, 1968.

Mazandarani, Fazil. *Kitab Zuhur al-Haqq.* 9 vols. Tehran: Mu'asasa-yi Milli-yi Matbu'at-i Amri, 1975.

Mirza, Farhad. *Kitab-i Jam-i Jam.* Tehran: Chapkhana-yi Allah Quli Khan Qajar, 1856.

Mitra, Krishnakumar. *Bhuddhadeva-charitra.* Translated by Narayana Hemachandra. Bombay: n.p., 1889.

Mitra, Raja Rajendralal. *Buddhism and Odinism: Their Similitude.* Calcutta: Baptist Mission Press, 1858.

Mitra, Satish Chandra. *"Dhammapada" Namaka Pali Granthera Banganubada.* Calcutta: Keshab, 1905.

————. *The Sanskrit Buddhist Literature of Nepal.* Calcutta: Asiatic Society of Bengal, 1882.

Monier-Williams, Monier. "Buddhism in Its Connexion with Brahmanism and Hinduism, and in Its Contrast with Christianity." *Calcutta Review* 91, 181 (1890): ii–ix.

Morris, Henry. *Geography.* Madras: Madras School Book Society, 1857. Translated into Sindhi as Hinri Maris, *Jughrafiyya Jadid.* Karachi: School Book Society, 1861.

Muhammad, Khwaja Ghulam. *Récit d'un voyageur musulman au Tibet* [*Safarnama Lasa*]. Facsimile manuscript and French translation by Marc Gaborieau. Paris: C. Klincksieck, 1973.

Muhasib al-Dawla, Mirza Aqa Khan Muhandis. *Usul-i 'Ilm-i Jughrafiyya.* Tehran: n.p., 1900.

Müller, F. Max (trans. into English). *Dhampad* [*Dhammapada*]. Translated into Urdu by Bishan Nara'in. Moradabad: Babu Banwarsi La'l, 1909.

Multani, Kesar Singh. *Japan di Tarakki.* Multan: Kesar Singh, 1908.

Muwahid, Mawlwi 'Abd al-Khaliq Khan. *Sayr-i Barhma.* Lucknow: Matba' Mina Lakhnaw, 1893.

Nadim al-Sultan, Muhammad. *Tarikh-i Chin.* Tehran: Matba'-i Khurshid, 1906.

Nadwi, 'Abd al-Quddus Hashimi. *Safarnama-i Chin: Ishtiraqi Chin ki Waqi'ati Taswir.* Karachi: Maktaba Mihr-i Nimruz, 1957.

Nadwi, Sayyid Abu Zafar, *Safarnama-i Brahma* [*sic*]. Delhi: Mahbub al-Matabi', 1921.

Nadwi, Sayyid Sulayman. *'Arabon ki Jahazrani.* Bombay: Islamik Risarch Asusi'ashun, 1935.

———. *'Arab u Hind ke Ta'luqat*. Allahabad: Hindustan Press, 1930.

———. *Sayr-i Afghanistan*. Lahore: Sang-i Mil, 2008.

Nag, Kalidas. *Greater India*. Calcutta: Prabasi Press, 1926

———. *India and the Pacific World*. Calcutta: Greater India Society, 1941.

———. *Les théories diplomatiques de l'Inde ancienne et l'Arthaçâstra*. Paris: Maisonneuve, 1923.

———. *Visal Bharat ka Itihas*. Lahore: Anusandhana Vibhaga, 1929.

Nakamura, K. "Takituri ki Kahani." *Salnama-i Saqi-i Dihli: Japan Nambar* 13, 1 (1936): 101–102.

Nariman, G. K. [Gushtaspshah Kaikhushro]. "Afghanistan To-day." *Islamic Culture* 1 (1927): 252–258.

———. *Literary History of Sanskrit Buddhism*. Bombay: Indian Book Depot, 1923.

Nayak, Jatindra Kumar, and Parthasarathi Bhaumik (eds.). *Memories, Images, Imagination: An Anthology of Bangla and Oriya Writings on Colonial Burma*. Calcutta: Department of Comparative Literature, Jadavpur University, 2010.

Nayaka, Sena. *Masihi Mazhab ka Makhraj Bodh Dharma Hai*. Jalandhar: n.p., 1902.

Nehru, Jawaharlal. "Selected Speeches." *India Quarterly* 45, 4 (1989): 367–401.

Nizam al-Din, Mawlwi 'Abdullah. *Haqiqat al-Salat*. Calcutta: n.p., 1837.

Noguchi Yonejiro [Naguchi, Prafisar Yun]. "Meri Sha'iri aur Shahr-i 'Ajib ko." *Salnama-i Saqi-i Dihli: Japan Nambar* 13, 1 (1936): 162–163.

———. "Mein ne Hindustan ko kiya Pa'id." *Salnama-i Saqi-i Dihli: Japan Nambar* 13, 1 (1936): 166–168.

Nomura, Saichiro. *Shotoindogo kenkyu*. Tokyo: Subundo Shuppanbu, 1934.

Notovitch [*sic*], Nicolas. *La vie inconnue de Jésus-Christ*. Paris: Paul Ollendorff, 1894.

Nu'mani, Shibli. *Safarnama-i Rum u Misr u Sham*. 1914. Reprint, Azamgarh: Dar al-Musanifin, 2010.

Okakura, Kakuzo. *The Ideals of the East, with Special Reference to the Art of Japan*. London: John Murray, 1903.

Okuma, Shigénobu. *Fifty Years of New Japan: Kaikoku gojunen shi*, 2 vols. Translated and edited by Marcus B. Huish. London: Smith & Elder, 1909.

Oliphant, Laurence. *Narrative of the Earl of Elgin's mission to China and Japan in the years 1857, '58, '59*. London: W. Blackwood and Sons, 1859. Translated into Urdu by Frederick Nundy and Munshi Shiv Parshad as *Tarikh-i Chin u Japan*. Lucknow: Munshi Nawwal Kishore, 1867.

Palmer, Frederick. *With Kuroki in Manchuria*. New York: Scribner's, 1904.

Parkinson, Yehya-en-Nasr. *Essays on Islamic Philosophy*. Rangoon: British Burma Press, 1909.

———. *Muslim Chivalry*. Rangoon: British Burma Press, 1909.

Patell, Cowasjee Sorabjee. *Account of China: Comprising a View of the Topography, History, Manners, Customs, Languages, Literature, Arts, Manufactures, Commerce, Reli-*

gion, Jurisprudence, etc., of the Chinese Empire, Together with a General Sketch of the Late British Expedition in China, 2 vols. Bombay: Courier Press, 1844.

———. *Cowasjee Patell's Chronology, Containing Corresponding Dates of the Different Eras Used by Christians, Jews, Greeks, Hindus, Mohamedans, Parsees, Chinese, Japanese, etc.* London: Trübner, 1866.

Pauthier, Jean-Pierre Guillaume. *Chine; ou description historique, géographique et littéraire de ce vaste empire.* Paris: F. Didot, 1839.

———. *Mémoire sur l'origine et la propagation de la doctrine du Tao.* Paris: Librarie Orientale de Dondey-Dupré, 1831.

Pinnock, William. *A Comprehensive System of Modern Geography and History.* 2nd edition. London: Holdsworth & Ball, 1834.

Pirzada, Hajji Muhammad Ali. *Safarnama-yi Hajji Pirzada,* ed. Hafiz Farmanfarma'iyan, 2 vols. Tehran: Danishgah-i Tihran, 1963–1964.

Poo, Eusuf Sahle. *Proof of Prophet Muhammad from the Holy Bible and Way to Paradise for Eternal Life.* Rangoon: Propagation Dept. of the Jamiat-ul-Ulema of Burma, 1934.

Prashad, Munshi Debi. *Arzhang-i Chin.* Kanpur: Matba'-i Nizam, 1871.

Qa'im-i Maqami, 'Abd al-Wahhab al-Husayni. "Adabiyat-i Farsi dar Zhapun." *Armaghan* 11, 4 (July 1930): 306–310.

Qian, Sima. *Tayan.* Translated into Dari by Ahmad 'Ali Kuhzad. Kabul: Anjuman-i Tarikh-i Afghanistan, 1948.

al-Quran [with Sinhala translation]. Colombo: Colombo Moors' Islamic Cultural Home, 1961.

Qur'an Majid ma' Tarjuma Ingrizi, Urdu, Farsi. Sialkot: Punjab Press, 1899.

Rangacaryudu, Kilambi (trans.). *Dhammapadamu: Vacanamu.* Chennai: Nargeshvararu, 1927.

Rautar, Yussuf. *Ready Reckoner.* Edited by Broker M. Essoof Rawuther. Rangoon: Yussuf Rautar, 1901.

Redesdale, Algernon Bertram Freeman-Mitford. *The Tale of Forty-Seven Ronins.* Tokyo: Jiujiya, 1892.

Ricci, Matteo. *De christiana expeditione apud sinas suscepta ab Societate Iesu.* Translated into Latin and edited by Nicholas Trigault. Augsburg: Apud Christoph. Mangium, 1615.

Rida, Rashid. "Da'wat al-Islam fi al-Yaban." *al-Manar* 9, 1 (February 1906): 75–78.

———. "Da'wat al-Yaban ila al-Islam." *al-Manar* 8, 18 (November 13, 1905): 705–712.

Rishtiyya, Qasim Khan. "Aya Japan bih Islam Musharraf Khwahad Shud?" *Kabul* 4, 3 (1934): 78–84.

Riyazi, Muhammad Yusuf. *'Ayn al-Waqayi'.* Mashhad: Daftar-i Bahr-i Naskha-yi Biguftagu, 1906.

Rıza, 'Ali. *Japon Alfabesi.* Istanbul: Matbaa-i Kütüphane-i Cihan, 1905.

Ruben, Walter. *Buddhizm Tarihi*. Ankara: Ankara Üniversitesi Dil ve Tarih Coğrafya, 1947.

Ruben, Walter, with Cemil Ziya Şanbey. *Eski Hind Tarihi*. Ankara: İdeal Matbaa, 1944.

Ruben, Walter, and Meliha Torkak (eds.). *Hint Iptidaîlerinin ve Hinduların Eski ve Yeni Eşya Katalogu*. Ankara: Uzluk, 1942.

Sahhafbashi Tihrani, Ibrahim. *Safarnama-yi Ibrahim Sahhafbashi*. Edited by Muhammad Mushiri. Tehran: Shirkat-i Mu'allifan, 1985.

Saise, Walter. "A Visit to Afghanistan." *Proceedings of the Central Asian Society* (April 1911): 3–22.

Samalki, Ahmad Buzurg. *Ma'raka-i Rangun*. Karachi: Khatm-i Nabuwwat Akidimi, 2010.

Sarkar, Benoy Kumar. *The Beginning of Hindu Culture as World-Power (A.D. 300–600)*. Shanghai: Commercial Press, 1916.

———. *The Chinese Religion through Hindu Eyes: A Study in the Tendencies of Asiatic Mentality*. Shanghai: Commercial Press, 1916.

———. *Lectures on China, Japan and India*. New York: n.p., 1917.

Sarwari, 'Abd al-Qadir. *Chini aur Japani Afsane*. Hyderabad: Anjuman-i Taraqqi-i Urdu, 1930.

Sastri [Shastri], Haraprasad. *Catalogue of Palm-Leaf and Selected Paper Manuscripts Belonging to the Durbar Library, Nepal*, 2 vols. Calcutta: Baptist Mission Press, 1905.

——— [Hariprasad]. *Discovery of Living Buddhism in Bengal*. Calcutta: Sanskrit Press Depository, 1897.

——— (ed.). *Hajar Bacharer Purano Bangala Bhasaya Bauddhagan-o-Doha*. Calcutta: Bangiya Sahitya Parisad, 1916.

Satu, U. K. "Japani Talib 'Ilm ki Zindagi." *Salnama-i Saqi-i Dihli: Japan Nambar* 13, 1 (1936): 102–105.

Savarkar, Vinayak Damodar. *Hindutva: Who Is a Hindu?* 5th ed. Bombay: Veer Savarkar Prakashan, 1969.

Sawa, Eizu [Sawa, Prafisar Yizu]. "Huriyuji Budh Mandir." *Salnama-i Saqi-i Dihli: Japan Nambar* 13, 1 (1936): 99–101.

———. "Tudaji ka Mandir." *Salnama-i Saqi-i Dihli: Japan Nambar* 13, no. 1 (1936): 81–83.

Sayadaw, Ledi. *Thathanawithodani (Sāsanavisodhanī)*, vol. 1. 1919. Reprint, Yangon: Hanthawaddi Pitakat Pon-hneik Taik, 1954.

Sayyah ['Abbas Effendi]. *Bab al-Hayat*. Translated into Urdu by Sayyid Mustafa Rumi. Lahore: Nawwal Kishore, 1908.

———. *Maqala-yi Shakhsi Sayyah kih dar Qaziyyih-i Bab Nivishta Ast*. Edited and translated by E. G. Browne, 2 vols. Cambridge: Cambridge University Press, 1891.

Sayyid, Mim Hafiz. *Gautam-i Budh: Sawanih-i Hayat wa Ta'limat*. Delhi: Anjuman-i Taraqqi-i Urdu, 1942.

Schlagentweit, Emil. "Buddhism in Tibet, Illustrated by Literary Documents and Objects of Religious Worship, with an Account of the Buddhist Systems Preceding It in India." *Calcutta Review* 39, 78 (1864): 446–448.

Schliemann, Heinrich. *La Chine et le Japan au temps présent*. Paris: Librairie Centrale, 1867.

Sena'i, Osman, and 'Ali Fu'ad. *Rus-Zhapun Seferi*, 5 vols. Istanbul: Ketabkhana Islam ve Askari, 1905.

Sethna, Ratanji Framji. *Japani Bhashano Bhomiyo*. Bombay: n.p., 1906.

Shah, Ahmad. *Four Years in Tibet* (Benares: Lazarus, 1906). Translated into Urdu by Anis Ahmad as *Sayr-i Tibbat*. Delhi: Matba'-i Makhzan, 1909.

Shastri, Hari Prasad. *Echoes of Japan, 1916–1918*. London: Shanti Sadan, 1961.

Shirazi, Husayn 'Ali. *Mikadunama*. Calcutta: Matba'-yi Habl al-Matin, 1907.

Shirazi, Mirza Muhammad Malik al-Kuttab, comp. *Mirat al-Zaman dar Tarikh-i Chin u Machin u Japan*. Bombay: Dutt Prasad Press, 1893.

Shushtari, Mir 'Abd al-Latif Khan. *Tuhfat al-'Alam wa Zayl al-Tuhfah: Safarnama wa Khatirat*, ed. Samad Muwahid. Tehran: Kitabkhana-yi Tahuri, 1363/1984.

Sichel, Philippe. *Notes d'un bibeloteur au Japon*. Paris: E. Dentu, 1883.

Siebold, Philipp Franz von. *Epitome linguae Japonicae*. Batavia: Lands Drukkerij, n.d. [1826].

Sinawi, Murtaza Husayn. *Majmu'a-i Ijazat*. Ferozpur: n.p., 1897.

Singh, Gadadhar Thakur. *Chin Me Terah Mas*, translated by Anand A. Yang, Kamal Sheel, and Ranjana Sheel as *Thirteen Months in China: A Subaltern Indian and the Colonial World*. New Delhi: Oxford University Press, 2017.

Singh Vaid, Mohan. *America te Japan de Vidyarthi*. Tarn Taran: Mohan Singh Vaid, 1920.

al-Sini, 'Abd al-Hakim Muhammad Nur al-Haqq ibn al-Sayyid Luqman [Ma Lianyuan]. *Sharh al-Lata'if*. 1902. Reprint, Kanpur: Mahmud al-Matabi', 1924.

al-Sini, Badr al-Din Hayy [Hai Weiliang; see also Chini, Badr al-Din]. *al-'Alaqat bayn al-'Arab wa al-Sin*. Cairo: Maktabat al-Nahda al-Misriyya, 1950.

al-Sirafi, Abu Zayd Hasan ibn Yazid, and Sulayman al-Tajir. *Relation des voyages faits par les arabes et les persans dans l'Inde et à la Chine dans le IXe siècle de l'ère chrétienne: Texte arabe imprimé en 1811 par les soins de feu Langlés*, ed. Joseph Toussaint Reinaud (Paris: Imprimerie Royale, 1845).

Siraj. *Bibi Khadija Tha-hkin ma Vatthu*. Translated into Burmese by Maung Hia Tin. Mandalay: n.p., 1911.

Sprague, Sydney. *A Year with the Baha'is of India and Burma*. London: Priory Press, 1908.

Sprenger, Alois. *Report of the Researches into the Muhammadan Libraries of Lucknow*. Calcutta: Office of the Superintendent of Government Printing, 1896.

Storrow, E. "Rise, Principles and Tendencies of Buddhism." *Calcutta Review* 19, 38 (1853): 256–297.

Strauss, C. T. *The Buddha and His Doctrine*. London: W. Rider & Son, 1923. ['Stras, Mistar']. Translated by Shiv Narayan Shamim as *Bodh aur uska Mat*. Lahore: Kashi Ram Press, 1926.

Sukula, Narayanaprasada. *Chini Ziban*. Aligarh: Wadiya Sagar Pris, 1902.

Sultan, Muhammad. *Mukhtasar Tarikh-i Dakan*. Hyderabad: Matba'-i Nazir-i Dakan, 1916.

Tabrizi, Baqir Khan. *Tarikh-i Aqsa-yi Sharq ya Muharaba-yi Rus u Zhapan*. 2 vols. Tehran: Hajji Shaykh Ahmad Kitabfurush-i Shirazi, 1913.

Tagore, Rabindranath. *Japan-yatri*. Calcutta: Indian Publishing House, 1920.

———. *Talks in China: Lectures Delivered in April and May, 1924*. 1925. Reprint, New Delhi: Rupa, 2002.

———. *A Visit to Japan*. Translated by Shakuntala Rao Sastri. New York: East West Institute, 1961.

Tahsin, Hasan. *Çîn'de İslâmiyet*. Istanbul: Tercüman-ı Hakikat Matbaası, 1904.

al-Tahtawi, Rifa'at Rifa'. *Kitab al-Kanz al-Mukhtar fi Kashf al-Aradi wa al-Bahar*. Cairo: Matba'at Maktab al-Tubjiyya, 1834.

Tarzi, Mahmud (trans.). *Tarikh-i Muharaba-yi Rus u Zhapun*, 5 vols. Kabul: Kutubkhana-yi Matba'-yi 'Inayat, 1915.

Tarzi, Sayyid Mushir Khan. "Islam dar Japan." *Kabul* 10 (1936?): 71–83.

Tawadu', Muhammad [Pang Shiqian]. *al-Sin wa al-Islam*. Cairo: Dar al-Tiba'a wa al-Nashr al-Islamiyya li-al-Ikhwan al-Muslimin, 1945.

Thabit, Muhammad. *Jawla fi Rub' Asiya bayn Misr wa al-Yaban*. Cairo: al-Matba'at al-Rahmaniyya, 1932.

Thanisari, Muhammad Ja'far. *Kala Pani: Tawarikh-i 'Ajib*. 1880. Reprint, Lahore: Sang-i Mil, 2012.

Tin, Maung Hia. *Hujjat al-Islam*. Mandalay: n.p., 1911.

T'ong, Ting-Ku. *Ying u Tsap Ts'un; or, The Chinese and English Instructor*, 6 vols. Canton: n.p., 1862.

Vaniya, Dinshaw. *Japanis Sikshaka*. Bombay: Gujarati, 1905.

Varman, Shiv Brit Lal. *Parsiyun ki Muqaddas wa Asmani Kitab*. Jullunder: Satya Dharam Pracharak, 1905.

Visvesvaraya, Mokshyagundam. *Reconstructing India*. London: P. S. King and Son, 1920.

Wade, Rev. J. *Dictionary of Boodhism and Burman Literature*. Moulmain: American Mission Press, 1852.

Webb, Mohammed Alexander Russell. *Isha'at-i Islam*. Translated into Urdu by Mawlwi Hasan 'Ali. Lahore: n.p., 1893.

Wherry, E. M. The *Muslim Controversy: Being a Review of Christian Literature Written in the Urdu Language for the Propagation of the Christian Religion and the Refutation of Islam*. Madras: Christian Literature Society, 1905.

Xuanzang. *Ek Chini Sayyah ka Safarnama jo Angrezi se Tarjuma Kiya Gaya*. (Translator unnamed.) Lahore: Punjab Religious Book Society, 1921.

Yavorski, Ivan Lavrovich. *Journey of the Russian Embassy through (Account of the Journey of the Russian Mission to) Afghánistán and the Khanate of Bukhára in 1878–1879,*

2 vols. Translated by E. R. Elles and W. E. Gowan. Calcutta: Government of India, Indian Army Intelligence Branch, 1885.

Yazdani, Ghulam. *Ajanta: The Colour and Monochrome Reproductions of the Ajanta Frescoes Based on Photography*, 4 vols. London: Oxford University Press, 1930–1955.

———. *Ajanta ki Naqqashi ma' Tasawir*. Munich: Bruchmann, 1935.

———. *Guide to Ajanta Frescoes*. Hyderabad: Archaeological Department, 1927.

Yoshida, Masaharu. *Kaikyo tanken Perushia no tabi*. Tokyo: n.p., 1894. Translated into Farsi by Hashim Rajabzada as *Safarnama-yi Masaharu Yushida: Nakhustin Firistada-yi Zhapun bih Iran dar Dawra-yi Qajar*. Mashhad: Mu'assasah-i Chap u Intisharat-i Astan-i Quds-i Razawi, 1994.

Yu, Muhammad Sulaiman Ying Kwang. "Islam in China." *Islamic Review* 23, 6 (June 1935): 229–238; 23, 7 (July 1935): 242–248; and 23, 8 (August 1935): 281–285.

Zada, Sayyid Riza 'Ali (trans.). *Tarikh-i Millal: Chiniyan*. Lahore: Matba'-i Mufid-i 'Am, 1926.

Periodicals Consulted

Anis. Kabul: Muhiy al-Din Anis/Government Press, 1927– (newspaper).

al-Ashraq/The Dawn. Rangoon: Syed Mustafa Roumie, 1923– (journal).

Calcutta Review. Calcutta: Sanders & Cones, 1844– (journal).

Farhang. Rasht: Matba'a-i 'Urwat al-Wusqa, 1919–? (journal).

Genuine Islam. Singapore: All Malaya Muslim Missionary Society, 1936–1941 (journal).

Islamic Fraternity. Tokyo: Mohammad Barakatullah, 1909–1914? (journal).

Ittihad-i Mazahib-i 'Alam. Rangoon: Mawlwi Muhammad Husayn, c. 1907–? (journal).

Journal of the Buddhist Text Society of India. Calcutta: Buddhist Text Society of India, 1893– (journal).

Journal of the Maha-Bodhi Society. Calcutta: Maha-Bodhi Society, 1892–1901 (journal).

Kabul: 'Ilmi, Adabi, Ijtima'i, Tarikhi. Kabul: Anjuman-i Adabi-yi Kabul, 1931–1978 (journal).

Ma'arif. Azamgarh: Dar al-Musanifin, 1916– (journal).

al-Manar. Cairo: Matba'at al-Manar, 1898–1935 (journal).

Musavver Cihan. Istanbul: Musavver Cihan, 1891– (journal).

Singapore Free Press and Mercantile Advertiser. Singapore: J. H. Moor, 1835– (newspaper).

Siraj al-Akhbar. Kabul: Matba'a-yi Mashin Khana-yi Dar al-Saltana-yi Kabul, 1911–1919 (newspaper).

Taqaddum. Tehran: Taqqadum, 1927–1929 (journal).

INDEX

Italic page numbers refer to figures

'Abbas Mirza, 233
'Abd al-Baha 'Abbas Effendi, 72, 73, 158
'Abd al-Ghani, 197
'Abd al-Haqq, 162
'Abd al-Hayy, Mawlwi, 74, 75–77, 80, 87
'Abd al-Jabbar, Mawlwi, 43
'Abd al-Khaliq Muwahid: background
   and life in Burma, 86–87, 88; conversion of population to Islam, 97,
   101, 111; debate with thathanabaing,
   111–113; disputation of Buddhism,
   84–85, 86; investigation of the "religion of Burma," 96–103; knowledge
   of Buddhism and research on it, 84–
   86, 130–131; knowledge of Buddhism
   in "religion of Burma," 85, 86–87,
   89–91, 95–96; language studies,
   skills, and tools, 98, 99, 103, 104,
   105–106, 107, *108*; polemical aspects
   of research, 98, 101, 109, 112–113;
   printed books in Burma, 109; on
   reincarnation, 111–112; texts consulted
   in Burma, 99–100, 101–102, 105. See
   also *Sayr-i Barhma*
'Abd al-Latif Khan, Mir, 66–67

'Abd al-Shakur Lakhnawi, 81
Adab (Tehran journal), 252
Adam (first human), in China and
   Islam, 310, 311
Adelman, Jeremy, 322
al-Afghani, Jamal al-Din, 250, 301
Afghanistan: "Asia" as term (*A'ishiya*),
   13, 128; and Buddhism, 62, 126, 128–
   129, 153, 279; and China, 278–279;
   education and universities, 173, 278;
   and Japan, 152–154, *163*, 199–200,
   201, 212; printed books, 128; printing
   and presses, 152, 153
Afnan, prominent Baha'i family, 70
Ahmad, Mirza Ghulam, 115, 246, 285
Ahmadiyya branch/sect of Islam,
   79–81, 285–286
Ahmad Khan, Sayyid, 167
A'ishiya, Dari term for "Asia," 13, 128
A'ishya, Urdu term for "Asia," 13, 58
Ajanta, Buddhist caves/frescoes, 126,
   158, 190
Ajia, Japanese term for "Asia," 11
Alabaster, Chaloner, 228
Aleni, Giulio, 11

Buddha Gautama (*continued*)
India, 63; and Islam, 100, 102, 114,
128; and Persia, 127–128; in Quran,
131, 132, 1154. *See also* Shingutama
Buddhism: and annexation of Burma
and Ceylon, 83; art in, 124, *125*,
126, 158, 190, 192; in China, 61–62,
219–221, 231, 236, 240, 247–248,
264, 277; errors of facts and dates,
102–103; and Europeans, 50, 54, 59–
60, 122–123, 126, 130, 148; fraudulent
manuscripts, 115–116; as Hinduism,
270, 271; iconography, *125*; informational channels, 62–64; and
inter-Asian understanding, 129–132;
intra-Buddhist encounters, 156–158;
investigations of texts published in
India, 53–62, 84, 89, 181–183; and
Islam, 121–129, 131, 132; in Japan, 60,
140, 147–148, 153, 156–158, 169, 170,
181–182, 183, 192, 193; knowledge by
Muslims, 84, 89–96, 131; missionary
organizations and activities, 49–51,
52–53, 157–158; origin, 54, 122, 123;
Protestant form, 52, 53; rediscovery
in India, 54, 58, 84, 85, 118, 122,
132, 183, 275–277; reliable information about, 129–130; religious texts
and polemics, 46, 49–50, 51–53, 55,
84–85, 111–114; translations of, 75,
116–120; and Urdu language, 60,
61–62, 94–96, 116–118, 121–122, *125*,
131
Buddhism in Burma: beliefs of
"natives," 97–98; debate of 'Abd
al-Khaliq with thathanabaing, 111–113;
disputation, 84–85, 86; divine
incarnations in, 100–102; end of
state sponsorship and demise of,
83–84, 109–110; investigation by
'Abd al-Khaliq Muwahid, 84–86,

96–103; Islam as model, 99–101,
102; knowledge by outsiders, 66, 75;
knowledge of, and 'Abd al-Khaliq
Muwahid, 85, 86–87, 89–91, 95–96;
missionary activity, 49–50, 84, 113;
and reincarnation, 111–112; thathanabaing in, 83, 110–113
Buddhist Catechism (Olcott), 52, 53
Buddhist Text Society of India, Calcutta,
63–64
Buddhist Theosophical Society, Colombo, 52, 53
Buddhist Tract Society, Colombo and
Rangoon, 51
Burma: annexation by British, 83,
109–110; and Baha'ism, 70, 71–72,
74, 75–76, 77–79, 96–97, 110; life after annexation, 96–97, 110; missionary organizations and missionaries,
49–50, 110; Muslim publications,
88–89, 109; Muslims and Islam, 87;
printed books, 46, 47, 109, 113; print
technology, 49; religious noninterference policies, 83–84; religious
polemics, 46, 50, 113; religious
printing/texts, 46–51, *48*, 113; travelogue of Iranians, 66; use of Urdu
and books in Urdu, 87–88, 105, 121.
See also Buddhism in Burma
Burmese language, 96, 98, 105–107,
108, 109
Burnes, Alexander, 92, *93*
Buryat peoples of Mongolia, 202
but (idol): and Buddhism, 236; origin,
97; statues as, 92; as term and notion, 66, 123–124, 140
but-khana ("idol houses"), 240
but-parasti (idol worship): and Buddhism, 92, 126, 278; in Burma,
66, 97; in China, 235–236, 239; as
religion, 128

Calcutta (Kolkata): and Buddhism, 54, 56–58, 60–61, 62–64; Buddhist missionaries, 49; and China, 214–215, 267–277; as hub for inter-Asian understanding, 30–31, 34, 149–150; information and texts on Japan, 148, 149, 159; inter-Asian dictionaries and language tools, 104; and ports of Japan, 134; printers in, 36, 43, 66–68, 233; printing of texts and scripts, 36–37, 38; religious polemics, 39–43, 42, 81; travelogue of Iranians, 65–66; and unity of Asia, 34–35; Urdu as language, 41, 43

Calcutta Review, 56, 168

Calcutta University, 64, 182–183

Carus, Paul, 59–60

Çelebi, Katib, 11–12

Ceylon (Sri Lanka): "Asia" as term and idea, 13; Bible and Christian texts, 46, 51; books on, 157; British policies, 83; and Buddhism, 62–63, 83, 157–158; religious polemics, 46, 50, 51; religious printing and texts, 51–52, 53

"channels" of information, 26

Cheena Bhavana (Chinese Institute), at Visva-Bharati University, 273–274

Chen Duxiu, 272

Chengda Shifan Xuexiao (Chengda Normal School), 284

China: "Asia" as term (*Yaxiya* and *Yazhou*), 11; and Buddhism, 61–62, 219–221, 231, 236, 240, 247–248, 264, 277; challenges to interpretation of, 216–217, 262–264; and Christian missionaries, 214–216, 219, 221–222, 224, 237–239, 283, 286, 288; and conceptions of history, 295–297; connections with India, 217–220; dating system, 217,

222, 235–236; Europe as source, 219, 220, 221–222, 223–224, 228, 233, 236–237, 246, 251, 254–255, 262–263, 269–270; firsthand accounts, 252–256; illustrations in books on, 244; Indians in, 252–258, 313; and intercultural knowledge, 241–242, 313; knowledge of China by Indians, 220–224, 245–246, 267–268, 269–275; knowledge of India by Chinese, 218–220, 265–266, 267, 273–274; and maritime public sphere, 214–215, 216–217, 218, 269; and Muslims (*see* China and Islam); presence in India, 267; print technology, 214–215; religion (in general), 230–232, 235–236, 238–241, 247–248, 248, 254, 269–271, 274–275, 277, 298; trade with Europe and colonies, 217–218, 221, 228, 229–230; trade with Muslims, 297–298; travelogues on, 257–259, 263

China and Islam: and Calcutta, 267–277; Chinese Muslims in India, 265–266, 282–285, 290–291, 292; differences and unity, 297, 306, 313–314; Europe as source, 289, 292–293, 295, 296, 301–302, 311–312; institutionalization of inter-Asian understanding, 266; interpretation of history and rediscovery of past, 296–297, 300, 306, 307, 309–311; Islamic sources on, 226; Islam in China, 244, 259–262; knowledge of and books on China, 139, 215–217, 258–264, 265, 288–290, 291; Muslims in, 154, 244, 250–251, 259–262, 289, 290, 291–292, 293–294, 297, 309; origin, history and propagation, 297–302; and polemics, 284–288; and Quran, 215,